The Rock and the Tower

The Rock and the Tower

How Mary created Christianity

By S.P. Laurie

Hypostasis

Published by Hypostasis Ltd.
71-75 Shelton Street, Covent Garden
London WC2H 9JQ
www.hypostasis.co

Email: info@hypostasis.co

ISBN: 978-1-912029-00-6

To Angela, Isabella, Rose & James. For all the years it took to write.

Contents

Preface

This book has been over ten years in the writing. It is a large book and only the first of three planned volumes. Yet if anything the book is too short for its scope. It attempts nothing less than a complete rewriting of the history of early Christianity. The word "paradigm" has become devalued by overuse. Its modern meaning comes from *The Structure of Scientific Revolutions* by Thomas S. Kuhn. A paradigm was more than just an idea or concept; it was a theory that led to a whole new way of perceiving a subject. In this book, I offer a new paradigm for the origins of Christianity.

I have tried to make things easy for the reader. The book is organised into chapters, each taking one bite-sized chunk out of the whole. Each chapter has a brief introduction to tell you the subject of that chapter. Most importantly, at the end of the chapter is a list of the key points. This means that you do not have to read every single chapter first time through. You can skip to the key points without losing the flow of the overall argument.

The idea behind the shaman paradigm is intuitively simple. Jesus was not a physical person but a spiritual entity who was believed to have appeared through a shaman who is the true founder of the religion. The shaman grew up in a Jewish sect who were looking for the return of the Christ. This sect thought of the Christ as a great angelic being, the one and only true son of the ultimate God, created before time and before all the other angels. The Christ had taken human form and come to earth more than once. In his last incarnation he had been crucified both on earth by men and, simultaneously, in heaven by seventy fallen angels. The sect believed that these seventy angels each represented a Gentile nation and that the Christ, the King of the Jews, represented Israel. The death of the Christ meant the destruction of Israel/Judea which was defeated and taken into captivity by the Assyrians and the Babylonians, and which was now ruled by their spiritual successors, the Romans.

For hundreds of years the sect waited for the apocalypse and the re-birth/resurrection of the Christ. They believed he would soon appear in the skies at the head of an angelic army to defeat the Gentile oppressors and establish the Kingdom of God on earth. They developed a calendar for the whole history of the earth, past, present, and future, which predicted that the time of the coming was at hand. It was the dawning of the third "day" since the Christ's death; not a literal day but a great day, a week of generations. But Christ never came in the way they expected.

The shaman was born into a leading family within the sect and could claim descent from King David. When the shaman was about thirty, they made an announcement that must have shocked their family and the other members of the sect. The shaman said that the Christ had returned, but he had come in spiritual and not physical form. He had been reborn and res-urrected through the medium of the shaman. He was in the world spiritu-ally and would establish a spiritual kingdom, but most men and women were blind and could not see him. The first reaction to this was predictable. The shaman was thought to be mentally ill, to be possessed by demons. But the shaman was able to get some others to see the Christ also, starting with twelve who became the shaman's first followers. The shaman's faction grew until it took control of the sect, although some never did accept the shaman's revelations. And even most of the shaman's followers clung to the hope that the Christ would soon appear in the skies, visible to every-one.

It has taken a long time to piece together this picture. I started with the simple idea that the first Christians had only known the spiritual resurrect-ed Jesus and that he must have appeared first through a shaman. Of course, this is not really a new paradigm at all. The idea that Jesus was not a historical person goes back to the nineteenth century. It was revived in modern times by G.A. Wells who pointed out that Paul in his letters seems to show no knowledge of Jesus as a person. Like many others, I first came across the idea not through Wells, but through the best-selling book *The Jesus Mysteries* by Freke and Gandy. When I first read this book, it had a major impact on me. But when I started my own researches several years later, I became disillusioned. The standard of scholarship was poor; it mixed up evidence from different periods and places. Most of the book's arguments and conclusions had to be rejected, including the idea that Jesus was originally a pagan God. Yet despite these failings, it remained, at a high level, a tremendous inspiration. The idea that Jesus had always been spiritual and not a physical man made a great deal of intuitive sense. It could explain why Jesus was worshipped from the start as a divine being almost on the same level as God.

The devil though was in the detail. Most professional scholars rejected the myth theory, and their reasons could not be ignored. There was one person though who had already addressed many of the issues and that was Earl Doherty. At the time, I read him through his *Jesus Puzzle* website, although he has since published a book of the same name. Doherty's conception was that Jesus was spiritual, existing in the lower heaven immediately above the physical world where he was crucified by demons (the Jews thought heaven had either three or seven levels). He gave a lot of attention to Paul's letters, following Wells in arguing that Paul knew Jesus in the spiritual sense only and showed no knowledge of Jesus as a man who had lived in the recent past. The standard reply to these arguments was that absence of evidence was not evidence of absence; Paul did not mention the details of Jesus' life because he was only interested in the theological Jesus. Doherty showed how absurd this argument was. If Paul were preaching that God had come to earth in human form through Jesus, then his listeners would have demanded to know all about Jesus' life on earth, what he did and what he said. They would not have allowed Paul to remain silent. Most damaging of all, with one or two minor exceptions, Paul does not tell us what Jesus taught. He never gives us Jesus' own words and does not repeat or paraphrase a single parable.

Doherty also did a good job at dealing with the scant external evidence for the historical Jesus such as in the writings of Josephus, pointing out how this was all in reality quite late and dependent upon Christian sources. He trumped the argument that Paul says that Jesus was "born of woman" by showing how this depends upon a poor translation of the Greek. Ironically, the word Paul actually used for "born" was regarded by early Christians as dangerous evidence for a spiritual and not physical Jesus. However, his attempts to explain Paul's references to the brethren of the Lord, including James who is specifically called "brother of the Lord" were less convincing.

The Jesus myth school was not the only strand that led to the shaman paradigm. Even more important was my growing acquaintance with the early Christian writings excluded from the New Testament. Two works, in particular, had a profound influence upon me: the Gospels of Thomas and Philip. I was fascinated with Thomas from the first time I read it, and that fascination has only grown over the years. A fierce scholarly debate has raged over the dating of Thomas with some scholars thinking it is very early. There is much less debate over the Gospel of Philip which everyone agrees is second-century, although it probably incorporates earlier sources and traditions. However, Philip had one advantage over the enigmatic Thomas; it was easier to understand. A key concept in Philip was the "bridal chamber", the union of a person and their spirit. The bridal chamber was also found in Thomas which developed the idea that every man and woman was a twin with both a visible and invisible component. The physical person was in the world whereas their spirit was in a middle realm between heaven and earth. The spirit was in great danger for it was in a place of death, a place ruled by demons. Jesus came to redeem the spirit and bring it into the kingdom of God.

If Jesus was in the spiritual realm, then the shaman must be his earthly twin. However, the person-spirit pairing was represented as a marriage, a male-female combination. The implication was clear but remarkable. If Jesus were the male spirit, then the shaman must be female. Christianity had been founded by a woman.

I had all the pieces of the puzzle, yet they did not fit together! The idea that the shaman was female was supported by some of the resurrection accounts, where Christ appears first to Mary the Magdalene. But there was an alternative tradition from Paul that it was Cephas who first saw the risen Christ. And then there was the troubling information also from Paul about the family of Jesus. What did it all mean? The problems went round and round in my head as I struggled to understand what the evidence was telling me. Then, in the course of one sleepless night, everything became clear. The Jesus movement was persecuted from the start and in the early years it had been necessary to protect the shaman's identity through a pseudonym. Identical traditions were coming down under both the shaman's real name and this pseudonym. As a result, the identity of the shaman had fragmented into multiple characters in the gospels. At first I was sceptical, but the more I looked, the more evidence I found to support this conclusion.

This was the beginning not the end of my quest. Immediately, I wrote a short piece called the Book of Mary that explored the idea both analytically and imaginatively. Then I started on the task of developing the theory in full. I thought this would take a few years, but ten years later the task is still incomplete.

This book is concerned with the search for the shaman's identity and with telling the shaman's story. Although intended as the first volume of the series, it has been written as a coherent whole. The second book will focus on the beliefs of the apocalyptic sect into which the shaman was born, the beliefs which underlay Christianity. It will include a full treatment of some elements mentioned in this volume but which, because of space, have had to be deferred to the next volume: most significantly the Deep Source and the authorship of Luke-Acts, which is a fascinating story in its own right.

This is my chance to thank my wife Angela for the support she has shown me over many years; never once has she complained about the time I was spending on this project. On a practical level, she has proofread the text and corrected my lamentable lack of commas. Her comments on the initial draft caused me to rethink the book's structure and to break it down into smaller, more focused chapters with the key points at the end of each. I think the reader will also thank her for this.

Chapter 1

The shaman paradigm

Christianity alone among the major religions of the world has a man as both founder and subject. Jesus is supposed to have been a Jewish carpenter from Galilee, a teacher of wisdom who died on the cross deserted by his followers. Yet he is also worshiped as the Son of God who redeems from death all those who believe in him, and who will return at the end of time to rule heaven and earth. This dichotomy is the central mystery of Christian origins. How is it possible for a man, an artisan teacher, to be worshipped as God?

We will consider the three approaches that have been used to resolve this mystery; the Jesus of belief, the historical Jesus of scholarship and the Jesus of myth, and we will show why none of these can be correct. Instead, we will look to how religions actually start and evolve a new, radical, solution; the "shaman paradigm".

The three views of Jesus

In the Gospel of Thomas when Jesus asks his disciples to describe what he is like they give him three different answers; one says "*You are a righteous angel*", a second "*You are a philosopher of wisdom*", and the third, Thomas, "*My mouth cannot utter what you are like*".[1] People have been trying to answer the same question for the last two thousand years. The answers that may be given today can be placed into three types like the three answers of the disciples.

The Traditional Jesus: Jesus was the righteous son of God who took human form to redeem mankind by giving himself as an offering for man's sin. He was born through the virgin Mary and was the supposed son of the carpenter, Joseph. He started his ministry aged about thirty and formed an inner group of twelve disciples. He amazed his followers both by his teachings and by his many miracles. His downfall came one Passover when he was crucified by the Romans as the result of a conspiracy by the Jews. Although his followers were initially downcast, they were amazed when he rose from the dead after three days. The resurrected Jesus gave his followers the gift of the Holy Spirit and founded his church by commanding his former disciples to spread the word to both Jew and Gentile. Because of his perfect sacrifice all who believe in him will be saved to eternal life.

The Traditional, centred as it is in the death and resurrection of Jesus, works as a religion. It has thrived for millennia, and many millions of people have experienced the mystery of the resurrection and found Jesus within. Their lives have changed. They may be poor, but they have become spiritually rich, less self-centred, caring, more giving, more loving. Although the traditional form of Christianity is fading to the point of near extinction in much of Europe and beginning to fade in North America, it is still winning vast numbers of adherents and growing strongly in many developing countries.

The problem with the Traditional though is that we know it cannot be true. The sickness of the church in those countries that are most educated and advanced is a symptom of a deadly disease; the gospel account is contradicted by science. We cannot today believe that Jesus was resurrected from the dead, that he was able to walk on water or that he performed the miracles he is supposed to have done in the gospels. We cannot believe that he was born of a virgin or that he was the son of God. Indeed with our scientific knowledge of the workings of the human body and brain it is difficult to conceive even what could be meant by a man being the son of God.

And so we must turn to the second view of Jesus. This is the view that has been developed as the Christian texts began to be studied as historical documents by sceptical minds rather than sacred writings.

The Traditional Secular Jesus: Jesus was a wandering philosopher of wisdom, a Galilean carpenter who became a religious charismatic. In this new view Jesus was a man; a great man, but just a man. Revolutionary in his moral teachings, he preached the boundless love of God and the coming kingdom of God. He operated within apocalyptic Judaism and believed that the world would shortly come to an end. In the new Kingdom of Heaven the poor, the humble and the good would get their reward and the rich and powerful would be condemned. Although Jesus was not teaching rebellion against the Romans, some of his followers began to look upon him as the Messiah, the Christ. This was a dangerous situation, and his downfall came when he entered into Jerusalem and made a disturbance in the temple. The Romans were seriously alarmed and the prefect Pontius Pilate resolved to have him crucified with the tacit agreement of the Jewish priestly establishment. He died on the cross, deserted by his supporters. After his death some of his followers had hallucinations that he had come back to them from the dead. His cult developed until it became a separate religion from Judaism which Jesus himself had never intended.

The Traditional Secular is the territory of historical Jesus scholarship. It is related to the Traditional because it takes the same starting point but eliminates the supernatural elements. The assumption is that if you deduct all the supernatural and theologising elements of the gospel story then you will get to what must have actually happened. This assumption is false.

The first sign that it is false is that the Traditional Secular does not work as a religion. Most students who are believing Christians are repelled by the "historical Jesus" when it is taught to them. This is because it erases all the religious elements that make Christianity what it is. Jesus is no longer the son of God, he is not resurrected and does not rule in his kingdom. He saves no one. The failure of the Traditional Secular as a religion indicates its failure as history. How is it possible for a religion that does not work to give rise by a series of accidents to one which works so powerfully?

The essential problem with the Traditional Secular is that it fails to account for the most remarkable feature of Christianity, a feature that it shares with no other religion; Jesus is both the prophet/founder and the subject of the religion. This works in the Traditional Supernatural but does not make sense in the Traditional Secular. Jesus the man, unlike a divine Jesus, cannot teach of himself as redeemer and Son of God.

To address this problem, all the Traditional Secular theories are based on the idea that the religion that Jesus taught as prophet (let us call it "J") did not have himself as its subject, but that after he died his followers changed it into a completely different religion (let us call it "X") in which Jesus as Christ became the subject. The religion X is effectively the Christianity that has come down to us today, and we know it works as a religion but what about J? If Jesus did not teach himself as the son of God then what was J about? The answer is basically nothing; for when you take out all the things that Jesus could not have taught about if he were just a man then nothing remains other than a few vague moral teachings.

If the Traditional Secular view is true then Jesus could not have been a Christian. He could not have taught the crucifixion as the perfect sacrifice for sin because he would not have been aware of his own approaching death and would have not have looked upon himself as perfect. He could not have taught or predicted the resurrection. He could not have promised that he would come in the sky at the time of the apocalypse and as the son of God rule the heavenly kingdom that would be established at the end of time. He could not have taught that the bread was his flesh, and the wine his blood. He could certainly have no understanding of the inner spiritual experience of Jesus, an experience that Paul talks about and which Christians still feel today.

In fact, there is not a shred of evidence that the religion J ever existed. It might be possible for a peasant preacher to be considered the son of God given enough time for mythologising; say a few hundred years or several generations. But what we find is that the religion X is fully formed in the very earliest sources, such as the Gospel of Thomas, or the letters of Paul written no more than two decades after the supposed date of the crucifixion. The religion X does not arise at the end of a period of development but is there at the beginning. Jesus is always the subject of the religion and there exists not a single Christian document in which he is not the subject of the religion.

If the religion J that could have been taught by a real flesh and blood Jesus never existed then did Jesus ever exist? And so we come to the radical third view.

The Mythical Jesus: Jesus was myth not a man. He was always "the son of God" and developed from one or more of the many dying and resurrected gods of the eastern Mediterranean world. His cult probably emerged from the collision of Greek and Jewish culture that was occurring at the time, both through the large Jewish Diaspora scattered throughout the Greek world and by the Hellenisation of Palestine itself. Some Jews began adopting the Greek mystery religions to their own culture by recasting the role of the dying god-man as the Jewish Messiah. These groups developed into the early gnostic Christian sects who combined worship of Jesus with a hybrid Jewish-Greek religious setting. The new religion combined secret inner "gnostic" mysteries with outer rituals and instruction for followers who had yet to progress to the inner level. Some of these outer followers founded their own churches and taking a literal interpretation of the myths thought that Jesus had been a man who had lived in the recent past. From these beginnings orthodox Christianity began to develop, greatly encouraged by the writing of the fictional Gospel of Mark from which all the other canonical gospels are derived. From the start the proto-orthodox church was antagonistic to the gnostic groups, who were declared to be heretical culminating in the banning and destruction of the gnostics following the conversion of the Roman Emperor Constantine.

The great virtue of the Mythical is that Jesus is always the subject of the religion and has always been divine. There is no need for the hypothetical religion J because the religion is X from the very start. Under the Mythical view, the spiritual experiences of Christians do not appear out of nowhere fully formed but are the result of a long process of evolution stretching back thousands of years. Christianity is the end result of a series of steps each of which is a fully functioning spiritual religion in its own right. This contrasts with the Traditional Secular where the religion X involving the resurrection and Jesus as the son of God appears as an unlikely accidental product from the most unpromising of beginnings. However, the advantages of the Mythical come at a cost; there is the difficulty of explaining how the gospel accounts emerged from mythical material.

The biggest problem though is the complete lack of early evidence for the Mythical in its standard form. All the earliest materials indicate that Christianity emerged from a Jewish context. Although some forms of gnosticism did involve paganism, there is no evidence that they were in existence before the second century. It is clear from the earliest texts such as the letters of Paul, the Gospel of Thomas and the New Testament gospels that Christianity did not descend from pagan religion.

The Traditional Supernatural, the Traditional Secular, and the Mythical must all be rejected. None of the three is an accurate representation of reality. Each leads to a dead end. To move forward, we must seek a new paradigm.

The paradigm shift

To make progress we must reduce the problem to its simplest essentials. There are three principles that we would expect from any explanation:

1. The explanation should be consistent with science as regards observable phenomenon in the universe of space and time - there should be no "walking on water". This does not preclude a spiritual dimension but means that the facts as they can be observed objectively should not conflict with natural science.

2. The explanation should show a pattern that is typical of the origins and development of a new religion - Christianity should not be a special case.

3. The explanation should show a continuity of religious beliefs and experience between the foundation of the religion and its subsequent development - there can be a gradual evolution, but no massive U-turn as the religion develops.

Each of the three views we have considered conflicts with one or more of these principles. The Traditional Supernatural conflicts with both 1 and 2; the Traditional Secular with both 2 and 3; and the Mythical conflicts with 2.

The key to a new paradigm is the second principle that Christianity can be expected to have developed in much the same way as any other religion. When we look at the origins of new religions we can see that one form predominates; a mystic or shaman receives revelations from a divine authority, a "visitor from heaven", through spiritual possession, visions or dreams. The founder passes on these teachings to his or her followers and the authority of the "visitor from heaven" is used as the basis for new religious practices and beliefs. Religions are inherently conservative and individuals will not change their beliefs and practices without believing that a divine authority is commanding them to make such a change.

If we apply this to Christianity then is Jesus the mystic/shaman? The problem with this is that it would get us back again to the Traditional Secular. We have seen that this cannot account for Jesus as the subject of the religion without introducing the hypothetical religion J, that is nothing like the Christ centred religion X that we observe from the earliest times. Moreover, if Jesus were the shaman then who is the "visitor from heaven" who gives divine authority for the new beliefs of the movement? Jesus never refers to such a "visitor from heaven" in the gospels. The only authority that Jesus gives for his teachings is himself.

No, Jesus is not the shaman founder. The only solution that fits is that Jesus is the "visitor from heaven". Only as the "visitor from heaven" can Jesus both be the mechanism by which the message comes to earth and at the same time be the subject of the religion. This means that Jesus was not a physical man but the Son of God, the resurrected Messiah, from the very start. Under this view, the crucifixion cannot have happened at the hands of the Romans but was an essentially mythic event that lay deep in the past of the first Christians. The resurrected Jesus has appeared in first century Palestine through the medium of the founder. He was then seen by many others including Paul, who is an eyewitness of this spiritual experience of

Jesus. It is only on the authority of a divine Jesus that the human founder could have dispensed with the Jewish Law. The Law was believed by the early Jesus movement to have been given down by angelic authority through Moses, and only a greater heavenly authority than Moses and the angels could abrogate it. Jesus is this greater authority.

The sayings of Jesus would have been spoken by the shaman founder in a state of spiritual possession by Jesus. They were attributed to Jesus and not the founder because the founder was believed to be a conduit, a bridge between the worlds, with the sayings originating with Jesus. Such sayings would be treasured and preserved, and we are likely to have many of them today in such sources as the Gospel of Thomas and the New Testament gospels.

The shaman theory ties in with evidence of the earliest so-called "heresy" of Docetism, which was prevalent among Christians in the first century. Docetism is the name given to the belief that Jesus had a spiritual rather than a physical nature. Later Docetists seem to have believed that Jesus had a spiritual body and drifted like a hologram over the earth. But we can see Docetism as preserving a distorted memory of the true origins of the movement. The belief that Jesus had a "spiritual body" did not originally mean that he was like a hologram but that he could only be seen spiritually by the few, the ones who Paul calls the "perfect". The early Jesus movement believed that Jesus was in a sense physically present on the earth but that most people could not see or hear him because they had been blinded and deafened by the great angel who ruled the world. Only when they had been reborn spiritually through the medium of the shaman founder could they regain the senses that had been lost. Many "miracles" recorded in the gospels are about Jesus giving sight and hearing to the blind and deaf; originally this would be spiritual sight and hearing, but when Jesus came to be seen a physical man then his miracles become physical also.

So who was the shaman? One thing is certain; we are not looking for anyone obscure. The shaman/founder must have been the most esteemed person in the movement and the third principle, continuity of belief, means that this feeling of reverence and holiness must have been passed down to succeeding generations. However, the role of the founder has been obscured by the rise of the literalistic gospels starting with Mark. To find the identity of the founder we will need to go through all the early materials including the literalistic gospels, and piece together the evidence. In this search we will be led by three criteria to help us identify the founder; they must be highly esteemed, they must be the first human leader, and they must be the first witness of the resurrection.

At the risk of jumping ahead, we will set out some of the findings of this investigation. We will see that there is only one person who could be the shaman, that this person is a woman, and that her name was Mary. We shall see that the identity of this prophetess has fragmented with the growth of literalism. She used several titles and more than one name, and these have split into separate characters in the gospels. In everyday life she was known under the names Mary of Joses (Joseph) and Mary of James, it being normal in first century Judea to identify a woman in relation to the male. Among the titles she used the most prominent are Mary the virgin, and Mary the Magdalene. This last did not mean that she came from Magdala in Galilee, but that she was "the tower" which meant the temple.

The Jewish religious culture of the time was extremely patriarchal, and the role of women was minimised. It would have been completely unthinkable for a woman to be a religious leader, much less hold the exalted spiritual position that Mary did in the movement. As a matter of survival, it was necessary for Mary, while in Judea, to disguise her role which she did using a male pseudonym. This was not a name, but another title meaning the rock, Cephas, which when translated into Greek becomes Peter. The rock is complementary to the tower. The two can be traced back to the same source, the Animal Apocalypse, written hundreds of years before the Jesus movement and surviving as part of the Book of Enoch. In the Animal Apocalypse, the tower stands for the temple, and the rock stands for the holy mountain; the tower and the rock are the two paths by which the presence of God enters into the world.

The titles that Mary used were not necessarily unique to her. She gave the rock title as a mark of honour to one of her "sons", Simon called Peter, and she may also have given the tower title to another "son" James. From the start this caused confusion. In his letters, Paul refers to Simon using the Greek form Peter and to Mary under the Aramaic form Cephas. Others did not understand the distinction and the two were soon hopelessly confused so that in the gospels we can find many stories relating to the founder being attributed to Simon Peter.

The fragmentation of the shaman's identity into the separate characters of Mary the Magdalene, Mary the mother of Jesus and Cephas/Peter explains why the identity of the shaman has remained obscured. If this fragmentation had not taken place, the role of the shaman would be obvious from the gospel materials.

Beyond the gospels

To understand the origins of Christianity we must take apart the sacred scriptures of Christianity. This is not intended to be a destruction, but a restoration. The Christian reader, though, may not see it this way. To the traditional Christian, the texts are precious and sacred. By saying the gospel accounts are "untrue" we are potentially violating their faith. This conflict arises because we can look at the New Testament scriptures in two quite different ways.

The New Testament texts are both sacred scriptures and historical evidence. In some cases, they were written within a few decades of the time of the founder with the letters of Paul written while the founder was still alive. As such they are vital evidence to enable the historical reconstruction of the origins of Christianity. But if they are to function as evidence we cannot treat them uncritically. We cannot accept the gospels unconditionally as historical accounts but must continually ask how the stories have been put together, what sources they have used, and how the gospel writers have distorted these sources with their own interpretations.

The purpose of this book is this historical reconstruction. We want to understand what people did, what they said, what they wrote, and most of all, what they believed. The Jesus movement developed in a real universe of space and time, and the events that took place are objective facts even though obscured by two thousand years of history. The past exists and, in principle, it can be recovered, even though in practice this recovery is problematic. Nor does the past depend on an individual's belief systems or culture; whether a person is a Christian, a follower of another religion or an atheist, they should all agree on the past provided they have sufficient information. In reality, we do not have enough information, and it is here that room for subjectivity enters into the reconstruction.

What is important to our quest is not the gospels but what came before the gospels. What are the sources that the gospel writers used? What did the very first Christians believe about Jesus and how are those beliefs reflected in the disparate collection of texts that we call the New Testament? The Gospels were all written after 70, and we need to take our search back in time to the very origins of the movement.

The basic picture that emerges is that the gospels are fictions. In the first century, the Jesus movement expanded very rapidly throughout the Roman Empire. This expansion was chaotic with little central control. The problem the movement faced was that it was expanding in a hostile environment. To the Romans, the movement was illegal and potentially troublesome. The Jewish authorities regarded it as deeply blasphemous and were actively persecuting it from the very start. We have an eyewitness to this early Jewish persecution; before Paul joined the movement in the mid-30s AD, he was one of its persecutors. To safeguard against the Jewish establishment the movement encoded its beliefs in sayings that would seem obscure to the uninitiated, sayings that have been preserved in the Gospel of Thomas. It was also vitally important to hide the identity of the leaders, particularly while those leaders were living under the reach of the authorities in Jerusalem. So they operated using titles like "Cephas" (the rock) and "the Magdalene" (the tower). Only those in the inner circle would know the true meaning of these titles which indicated the unique spiritual and scriptural role assigned to the shaman. Only later, in the wider Roman world, did this disguise become less necessary so that real names could be used.

So towards the end of the first century, we have many thousands of Christians scattered around the Roman Empire, most having no contact with anyone who had known the founder. They inherited mystic sayings that were utterly obscure and traditions of the founder that were circulating in different forms and under a number of different names. What these believers needed was a simple story of the origins of the movement and a simple exposition of the teachings of Jesus. And this was what the first gospel writer, the author of Mark, gave them. Although he was to have a huge influence on the development of world culture, we know nothing about him, not even his name. He was probably a Gentile and lived far from the centre of the movement. His gospel was a brilliant attempt at placing the story of Jesus into a coherent whole, although it was wrong in all essential aspects. A rapid succession of other authors developed the story further and within a few decades the Gospels of Matthew, Luke and John were all written. Ironically, these derivative works were so successful that they replaced the Gospel of Mark, which almost disappeared.

The gospel story of Jesus was not the result of conspiracy but bewilderment. The gospel writers simply could not understand the mystic sayings, so they literalised them into a form that they, and their readers, could relate to. This bewilderment is evident from the Gospel of Mark. When Jesus is asked about the meaning of the parables, he tells his disciples that they are meant to be impenetrable to all except those in the inner circle.[2] It is ironic that the parables, as presented in the gospels, are in fact very easy to understand. This is a clue that the gospels have got it wrong. They have attached their own explanations to the parables, and we must recover their true meaning from a relatively uncorrupted source, the Gospel of Thomas.

The Easter Egg

To the believer, the gospels are far more than historical documents. They act as a catalyst that transforms a person, like water into wine. Software engineers have a term for a secret code written in a piece of software; they call it an "Easter Egg". When a certain sequence of keystrokes is entered, the program will suddenly reveal a function that until then has been hidden. We can think of the human mind as also having, buried deep within it, an Easter Egg. The brain, in its normal operation, is a biological survival machine optimised to pass on the individual's genes to future generations. But when the Egg is triggered, it activates a quite different function, access to a different, spiritually experienced world.

We can regard the Easter Egg in two ways. To the atheist, it is a bug in the code, an irrational deviation from the proper purpose of the brain. To them, religion is like a computer virus to which the human mind is susceptible, and the spiritual is a type of delusion to which their own intellect is impervious. But another explanation is possible, although it requires a belief in a more complex reality than the normal scientific viewpoint would admit. Perhaps the purpose of humanity is to carry the virus, and the survival coding of the brain is the vehicle that transmits, preserves, and propagates the Easter Egg.

If this were the case, then the Easter Egg would be buried beneath biological survival code because we have to live in the real world, the universe of space and time. We have to eat, survive, find mates, protect the next generation. And so for most people, most of the time, the Easter Egg must be inoperative. In the physical world, we are subject to the iron laws of evolution. Only those who can compete in the brutal game of survival will pass on their genes, and the hidden code, to the next generation. We may have to fight and kill, to safeguard our own resources and take those of others. And if our generation does not have to do these things it is only because our ancestors did the dirty work for us. The modern Western world seems to offer a comfortable reprieve from the forces of evolution but, alas, our reprieve is only temporary. The law of Malthus has not been repealed but is operating today in most of the world. Evolution selects for a high birth rate and eliminates those who limit their breeding. The world's resources are finite so, with an expanding population, conflict between nations and individuals is inevitable.

The spiritual is not just a distraction from the evolutionary struggle, but it operates perversely in the opposite direction. Instead of competition, we have love, instead of taking, giving, instead of war, pacifism. In the spiritual there is no "us" and "them"; all people are equal, each potentially the receptacle of God's spirit. The spiritual can never win, can never control the world because evolution will inevitably force people against one another. It was a truth understood by the Jesus movement that the world is under the control of evil forces. But neither can the spiritual ever be eliminated.

The Christian Easter Egg is triggered by the central mystery of the crucifixion and resurrection. For the Easter Egg to work, Jesus must not be just man, but man and God. The crucifixion of a mere man would have no meaning beyond pity. This myth of the God-man dying to be reborn into a new spiritual life recurs again and again across human civilisations. We shall see that it was prevalent in the cultures around the Jews and present among the Jews. The spiritual machinery of the Jesus movement was not created from scratch but evolved from earlier forms. It is effective because these previous forms of the myth were effective, and because the shaman improved further upon them.

Those who are not Christians will give many reasons why Christian belief is irrational. It makes no sense that God should demand a sacrifice, that he should kill an innocent and perfect man. If God is all powerful why does he not just forgive people? Also, how is it possible that Jesus can be both man and God? The Jew or Muslim will point out that this very notion is blasphemous, a deviation from the pure monotheism of their own faith. This is all true, yet misses the point. Rationality is a superficial accretion to the human mind. Computer software will only work if it is written in the operating language of the machine on which it is run. The human brain has its own "operating language" which is buried deep within us and which developed from our animal life. It is not the language of abstractions and rational thoughts. It is emotional and sensory, involving concepts such as male and female, fire and water, heaven and earth. In this operating language the crucifixion and resurrection are valid, powerful, operators.

It should be emphasised that Easter Egg can be understood in atheistic terms as purely a psychological change applying to the individual. The existence of religious transformation does not imply the existence of God. But if we were to take a religious perspective, we would see the Easter Egg as upgrading the connection to God to higher bandwidth. The first Christians called this high bandwidth state "life" as opposed to the natural low bandwidth state which they called "death".

For a computer code to operate it must be run. We may download a program, but while it just sits on the storage disk of a computer, it is inactive. To "run" the Easter Egg, an individual must experience the crucifixion and resurrection. For most of Christian history, this has been achieved through the gospels. The gospels took the myth and turned it into a story presented as history. It is not sufficient to just read this gospel story; you must believe that it is true. If we read or hear the story, and believe in it, we run the code in our minds, and if we are capable we will unlock the Egg. It is not for nothing that the Christian religion attaches so much importance to belief.

If we interpret and question the gospels, we destroy their potency. In much of the developed world, people have stopped believing in the gospels and so the Easter Egg lies dormant and un-triggered. Christianity becomes nothing more than a tradition, at which point its further decline is inevitable. The result of the loss of the spiritual is that people live lives of unrelenting triviality (what atheists call "enjoying themselves"). This process has already happened in Europe and is now happening in America.

So we have a dilemma. It is possible that the transformation of the Easter Egg is perfectly valid, yet to trigger it we have to believe in something, the gospel account, that is clearly untrue. There is nothing inconsistent in this; the trigger is just a code, and there is no reason that a code should correspond to anything real in the universe of space and time. Yet we have to believe in the code to run it.

The dilemma is not insoluble. The shaman did not have the gospels, nor did Paul, nor did any other Christian in the first decades of the movement. Neither did these first Christians lack anything spiritually compared to those inducted through the gospel story. In the beginning, the transmission of the experience of Jesus was spiritual and personal. We shall see how the first transformations were effected by the shaman, who acted as "mother" in the rebirth of the individual from death into life. Later this role was delegated to others, starting with the apostles, who were many in number and not just twelve. The process was powerful yet cumbersome. At each step away from the founder something was lost. What the gospels did was to encode the mystery in a literalistic story and make it available for mass consumption. A written document did not lose its effectiveness through transmission and enabled Christianity to expand on an industrial scale.

Although much was gained, much also was lost. The original spiritual beliefs were buried among the literalisations of the gospels. The original transcendent Jesus became a physical man who lived and died in the recent past. There was no central authority to contradict this belief; by the time the gospels were written the shaman and most of the apostles were dead at the hands of the Roman and Jewish persecutors of the movement.

Key points

1. The Traditional Jesus of belief works as a religion but conflicts with science.

2. The Traditional Secular Jesus starts with the Jesus of belief and removes the supernatural elements. However, it cannot explain how the Christ-centred religion we observe in all the earliest texts could have emerged from anything that a physical Jesus could have taught. It requires a massive U-turn from Jesus' followers who would have to reject all of Jesus' teachings in favour of a completely different set of beliefs.

3. The Mythical assumes that Jesus started as a Jewish version of the god-man found in several mystery religions in the ancient world. As Christianity expanded some churches came to believe that Jesus had really been a man, and it was from these communities that the gospels developed.

4. The great advantage of the Mythical Jesus is that it explains how Christianity could function as a religion. It has evolved from mystery religions which gave their followers a deep spiritual experience. However, there is no evidence that Christianity did have pagan origins and all the earliest sources are Jewish in nature.

5. Any valid explanation should satisfy three conditions; it must be consistent with science as concerns observable phenomenon, it should follow a pattern typical of the origins of other religions, and it must not involve a sudden U-turn by the founder's followers. Neither the Traditional Jesus nor the Traditional Secular nor the Mythical satisfies these criteria.

6. A new religion normally develops from a shaman-founder who has visionary or spiritual experiences of a "visitor from heaven". The visitor from heaven is the authority for the new beliefs which are communicated by the shaman to his or her followers. Sometimes a literary path is followed in which teachings are presented as having come from a prophet or other authoritative figure who lived in the ancient past.

7. Under the Shaman Paradigm, Christianity emerged from a shaman-founder with Jesus as the "visitor from heaven". This explains why Jesus is both the subject of the religion and also the source of the new teachings.

8. It shall be shown that the shaman must have been the woman who is known by both the names Mary the Magdalene and Mary the Virgin. She was called Cephas (Peter) by Paul, a name which became confused with a second-generation figure, Simon, who was also given the name Peter. The Magdalene comes from the word for Tower and means the temple, whereas Cephas, the Rock, means the holy mountain. Both the Rock and the Tower feature in the Animal Apocalypse, written hundreds of years before the Jesus movement, as the two means by which God gives his message to the world.

9. In our quest for the origins of the Jesus movement, we must treat the gospels and other early Christian literature as historical documents. Our aim is to reconstruct the events that took place at the origins of the movement and the beliefs of those who founded the movement. We will see that the gospels are largely confused accounts based on a misunderstanding of enigmatic sources that were spiritual and mystic in nature.

10. However, the gospels also function as sacred literature. The story of the crucifixion and resurrection of the perfect god-man Jesus activates the "Easter Egg" of religious transformation. If we question the gospels, then we destroy their capacity to effect this transformation. This gives the dilemma that historical truth seems opposed to religious truth; we can have one or the other, but not both.

11. The first Christians did not have the gospels to activate the "Easter Egg". In the beginning, the transformation was effected on a personal basis by the shaman, who acted as "mother" in a disciple's spiritual rebirth. As the movement expanded, the function of "mother" was delegated to the apostles and others, but the induction was cumbersome. Converting the induction myth to the literal gospel story industrialised the process, permitting the rapid expansion of the movement.

Chapter 2

The Jesus of belief

If Christianity started out with a shaman bringing the spiritual revelations of Jesus to earth, then the gospels are a highly confused account. They have arisen not from eyewitness accounts but from misunderstanding the original mystical sayings and stories. It is time to look in some more detail at the traditional view and why it is necessary to reject it as literal history while at the same time recognising that the gospels did succeed in embedding much of the spiritual essence of the movement within their pages.

The Traditional Jesus

In the Traditional view Jesus was the heavenly logos, the second person of the Holy Trinity, who took the form of flesh and became man. His birth was humble, the son of a virgin mother Mary betrothed to a carpenter Joseph, who could yet trace his descent from King David. In a visitation from an angel, Mary was told that she would conceive by the Holy Spirit. She did conceive, and although Joseph was inclined to divorce her quietly, he was told by an angel in a dream to marry her. The birth of Jesus took place in Bethlehem where his parents had journeyed to for the purpose of a census. His birth was attended by portents; a star that moved in the sky guiding the Magi, the so-called "wise men", to bring rich gifts to the place where he lay; a visitation of angels to shepherds while they were watching their flocks telling them also to give homage to the new born King. Yet the baby Jesus was born in a barn and had a manger for a cradle. And his birth was marked by innocent deaths with the evil King Herod ordering the slaughter of all the infant boys of Bethlehem in an attempt to destroy the king whose coming had been foretold by the Magi. The baby Jesus became a refugee, taken by Mary and Joseph to Egypt on a donkey to escape the wrath of Herod until his death enabled them to return. After the tumultuous events of his birth his boyhood and early adult life would seem to have been uneventful. Jesus grew up in Nazareth, in Galilee, the apparent son of Joseph and became a carpenter in his own right. He had a number of brothers and sisters including James, who was to lead the Jerusalem church after his death.

When he was about thirty he went to John the Baptist to be baptised. John, seeing him approach, predicted that he was the one the people had been waiting for, the Messiah or Christ. As John baptised Jesus, the spirit descended upon him in the form of a dove, and a voice from heaven was heard affirming him as God's son. This marks the start of Jesus' mission that was to last for only a few years. On the shores of Lake Galilee, he recruited four fishermen as his first followers, including Simon, whom he was to rename Peter. He cast out demons from the synagogue in Capernaum and afterwards cured the mother in law of Simon, who was suffering a fever. He travelled throughout Galilee healing the sick and casting out demons. Gathering twelve of his followers together, he appointed them as his disciples and sent them out to travel and do the same. Jesus called himself the Son of Man and taught about something called the Kingdom of God or the Kingdom of Heaven. He told his followers to give up their belongings for the sake of the Kingdom, living one day at a time. He said that the poor and the humble, not the rich and the powerful, would inherit the earth. He told them to love one another and to love even those who hated them. If a man were to steal their coat, they should not seek revenge but should give him their shirt also. Although they were poor they were ready to feast and to drink wine; unlike the followers of John the Baptist they did not fast. Throughout his mission, Jesus performed healing miracles, restoring sight and hearing, curing leprosy, making the lame walk. There were also more spectacular miracles. One stormy night, his disciples were in a boat on Lake Galilee when they saw Jesus walking towards them. He joined them in the boat and quietened the waters. On two occasions he fed a great multitude of followers, starting with nothing more than a few loaves and fishes, and dividing the food up so that everyone was fed, and there were baskets of scraps left over. But the most impressive miracles of all were the raising of people from the dead including Lazarus, who had been dead for four days.

One Sunday a week before the Passover, Jesus entered into Jerusalem on a donkey and was greeted by the crowds laying branches before him. There followed an episode in which he expelled the moneychangers from the temple. The priests began to plot against him and persuaded one of his own disciples, Judas Iscariot, to betray him. On the night of the Passover feast, Jesus had his last supper with his disciples at which he predicted the betrayal of Judas. As Jesus broke the bread at that last meal, he told his disciples it was his body and as he passed them the wine he told them that it was his blood. Afterwards, they went to the garden of Gethsemane on the Mount of Olives to pray. It was there that the priests came to arrest Jesus. They brought with them Judas, who gave Jesus a kiss to identify him. There was a brief struggle in which a supporter of Jesus cut off the ear of the servant of the high priest and it ended with Jesus in custody and his supporters fleeing. There followed a trial by the Jewish Sanhedrin at night at which Jesus was convicted of blasphemy. He was taken by the Jews to Pontius Pilate, who not wanting to condemn Jesus offered the Jews a choice between releasing Jesus or one Barabbas who was guilty of insurrection and murder. The people chose Barabbas and demanded that Pilate crucify Jesus. Pilate did not want to arouse the people, so he agreed and had Jesus scourged and handed over for crucifixion. He was taken into the Praetorium where he was dressed in purple and had a crown of thorns placed on his head while the soldiers mock worshipped him as king of the Jews. He was then taken away to outside the walls of Jerusalem where he was crucified between two robbers. The crucifixion lasted a surprisingly short time, about six hours. At the ninth hour of the day, Jesus cried out "My God, my God why did you forsake me". Shortly after he gave a loud cry and yielded up the spirit and the veil of the temple was rent in two. At the same time, the bodies of many of the saints that had been dead came out of their tombs and went into Jerusalem.

The body of Jesus was requested of Pilate by Joseph of Arimathea who had it buried in a newly hewn tomb with a large stone rolled over the entrance. The next day was the Sabbath at which no work was permitted but in the morning of the day after, the first day of the week, some women including Mary the Magdalene came to anoint the body with oils, as was the custom. They found the stone rolled away and, entering the tomb, they were greeted by an angel who told them that Jesus was not there but had been raised and that they should go on to Galilee. The resurrected Jesus then appeared first to Mary the Magdalene before appearing to the eleven disciples who remained of the twelve, for Judas Iscariot had committed suicide. Jesus remained on earth in his resurrected state for forty days before being taken up to heaven, but he will return to rule a new heaven and a new earth at the end of time. In the meantime, he sends to those who believe in him the comforter, the Holy Spirit. By his sacrifice death has been overcome and those who believe in him and die before his coming will also be raised.

The above story has been compiled from the four gospels; no one gospel alone contains all the details and in places the gospels are contradictory. It is the version that is familiar to us but what is less well known was how long it took for this version to be accepted. For the first few centuries, the nature of Jesus was a subject of intense and sometimes violent controversy among Christians. Eventually one view, what we will call the proto-orthodox, won out, and became the doctrine of the mainstream church that led to the Roman Catholic and Greek Orthodox churches of the present day. The other perspectives were suppressed but not completely obliterated. Islam developed from a Jewish Christian group that had not accepted the gospels and preserved a view of Jesus which differed from that of the orthodox Christians. Other views lay dormant to emerge as heresies in the middle ages, through such movements as the Bogomils and Cathars. And traces of other Christianities survived within the obscure writings of the alchemists.

In the second and third centuries, there was an astonishing diversity of Christian beliefs. As well as Docetism we encounter Jewish forms of Christianity such as the Ebionites. But the main challenge to the proto-orthodox was a range of diverse sects that have been lumped together under the heading "gnostic" coming from the word gnosis, to know. It was not intellectual knowledge to which the gnostics laid claim but the spiritual knowledge of heavenly things. The gnostics did not believe in obeying a moral code laid down in scripture but in the direct experience of God through an ascent to heaven or entry into the "bridal chamber". For a long time, the gnostics were known mainly through the writings of the early church fathers who opposed them. Indeed, we have very little from the early proto-orthodox church apart from anti-gnostic writings which is testimony to the importance of the gnostics in this period. The most encyclopaedic account of the gnostics comes from Irenaeus, bishop of Lyons, in his "Against Heresies" which was written at around 180. So incredible did Irenaeus' descriptions of the gnostic sects appear that later Christians thought he was exaggerating. However, in 1945 a number of ancient books or codices were found buried in the Egyptian desert at Nag Hammadi. When the material was examined by scholars, it was identified as a large collection of gnostic writings from the fourth century including our only complete copy of the Gospel of Thomas. For the first time we could see the gnostics not through the eyes of their enemies such as Irenaeus but their own writings. It became clear that Irenaeus was not exaggerating although he did set out to make the gnostics' views seem absurd. The Nag Hammadi collection also revealed that there was a tremendous variation among the gnostics and that to apply the label "gnostic" was to group together a range of beliefs which in reality had little in common with each other. Although we may see the gnostics and the proto-orthodox church as being very different, they were in the beginning two wings of the same broad movement. There was considerable tolerance and diversity of belief in the second-century church, and it was only when some Christians, such as Irenaeus, attempted to define proto-orthodox doctrine that the gnostics began to be excluded. Irenaeus grouped together all the other versions of Christianity and presented them as opposed to the proto-orthodox. This enabled him to emphasise how the gnostics disagreed with each other compared to the unanimity of the proto-orthodox view. In reality, the proto-orthodox view was merely one among many types of Christianity and the apparent harmony of the proto-orthodox compared to the divergence of their gnostic opponents was a result of placing everything that did not agree with the proto-orthodox (as defined by Irenaeus and others) into the "gnostic" bin. The rise in the proto-orthodox went hand in hand with a new emphasis on Christian scripture and the gospel tradition. The gospels became accepted as an essentially true version of events, which enabled the anti-gnostic writers to portray gnosticism as having fallen away from the original simplicity of belief. There is no doubt that the proto-orthodox view became very popular, and its development was aided by the growing cult of martyrdom. And it has to be said that many forms of gnosticism did involve ridiculously over elaborate systems of angels and powers. Faced with the growth of the proto-orthodox church gnosticism began to decline in the fourth century.

Eventually, the proto-orthodox view won out. The victory was sealed when Christianity became the official religion of the Roman Empire under Constantine the Great, which gave the bishops sufficient political power to be able to impose a uniform structure of belief and to eliminate their gnostic opponents. The orthodox gospel view of Jesus then remained essentially unchallenged within Christian societies for over a millennium.

However with the Renaissance and the recovery of Greek culture and philosophy a new questioning way of thinking began to develop in the West. This new attitude was to lead to the progressive development of science. It became apparent that the intervention of God was not needed to explain the workings of the universe. Science developed beautiful and intricately interlocking theories set out in the precise language of mathematics which achieved unparalleled accuracy of prediction as measured by experiment. And it became increasingly apparent to scientists that much of the biblical account was simply wrong.

As an example, the bible implied that the Earth was quite young. It gave an account of the creation and the generations of men, starting with Adam and Eve and leading up to the time of Jesus. A number of individuals worked back from the bible and from known historical events to conclude that the world was created at around 4000 BC. Ironically among those who came to this conclusion were Kepler and Newton, two of the founders of modern physics and astronomy. The great biblical scholar Bishop Ussher went further than this and put the date of the creation more precisely as nightfall on the day preceding the 23rd October 4004 BC.[3] Ussher arrived at this date by considering the history of the world as consisting of six great "days" each a thousand years long, with the building of the Jewish temple exactly in the middle of this period at 1004 BC and the birth of Jesus at 4 BC coming exactly one great day after the temple. In this scheme, Jesus would be absent for two days and reappear at the start of the third, which would be a few years before the year 2000. These six great days of normal time would be followed by a final day of a thousand years for the new earth to be ruled by Jesus making up the perfect week, the seven days of the creation. Bishop Ussher has come under considerable ridicule in the modern era for his precise dating of the epoch of creation and yet his timetable is a work of surprising perception. We will see that it has uncanny similarities to the apocalyptic calendar that underlies the Jesus movement.

The new scientific knowledge did not support the conclusions of those who calculated the age of the earth from the bible, and it was evident to geologists that the young Earth implied by the bible was wrong. Geological processes worked slowly, and the Earth must be many millions of years old. As science developed the date was pushed further and further back until the current estimate is that the earth is over 4000 million years old. It would seem that the bible is out by a factor of one million!

It is not just the age of the Earth that is at stake. There are a number of other miracles in the bible that were in conflict with the developing scientific knowledge. Two of the more spectacular miracles in the Old Testament involved changing the course of the sun. The sun was stopped in its tracks to enable Joshua to win a battle,[4] and on a separate occasion the shadow on the sundial of King Ahaz was moved back ten steps.[5] When the universe was conceived as a series of concentric spheres with the earth at the centre and the sun a bright light revolving around it, stopping the sun or moving it backwards was not seen as a problem. But when Copernicus and Galileo argued that the sun was at the centre of the solar system and that the day was due to the rotation of the earth it became apparent that the earth would have had to suffer a violent deceleration for either of these miracles to have taken place. Such a deceleration would have involved massive earthquakes, thousand miles an hour winds and a tsunami to end all tsunamis. Clearly this did not take place, and the sun did not stop in the sky or the shadow of the sun move backwards on the sundial. The inconsistency of the heliocentric solar system and these miracles in the bible was behind the conflict between Galileo and the church. The church may have had the political power to put Galileo on trial and sentence him to house imprisonment but in the long term it was Galileo who won. It had been demonstrated that at least some of the miracles in the bible could not be true, and the idea of the inerrancy of the bible was broken. The floodgates were opened to other challenges to the biblical account.

The New Testament as well as the Old Testament came under scrutiny. Miracles such as Jesus walking on water or feeding the five thousand with a few loaves and fishes had always strained credulity and did not fit in with the new understanding of the physical world involving as it did quantifiable physical forces and the conservation of energy and matter. And as medicine and biology advanced the understanding of the human body it became clear that there was not some life force that could be poured into a person to restore them from death to life. The body was a biological machine, an intricate machine but still a machine. If the machine stopped for long enough that biological processes ceased, then it could not be restarted. The brain starved of oxygen would die within minutes. Once the immune system stopped working, microorganisms would rapidly reproduce and would inflict irreparable damage at the cellular level as they did so. There was no way that a person who had been genuinely dead for two days could be revived. The physical resurrection could not have happened.

Theories began to develop to explain such miracles in scientific terms. So the feeding of the five thousand was really the result of everyone sharing the food that they had brought with them. When Jesus appeared to be walking on water on the Sea of Galilee, he was really walking on a submerged spit of land that jutted out into the lake. And the resurrection was explained by the idea that Jesus had not really died but had swooned or been drugged so as to have seemed dead. He was rescued by someone who moved the stone from the tomb and after this "resurrection" he stayed in hiding, appearing to his disciples a few times until he disappeared to India or some such place. All such explanations destroy the religious significance of the phenomenon they explain. If Jesus were drugged or swooned on the cross, then he was a fraud who fooled his disciples into thinking he had come back from the dead.

An abundance of such scientific explanations has sprung up around the star of the nativity. It has been suggested that this was a comet, or a supernova, or two meteors. In fact, none of these objects can account for the way the star is described in Matthew. More recently a theory that the "star" was a close apparition of two planets or a planet and a star has become popular. The idea is that this rare event may have had astrological significance to the Magi, who were astrologers. However, all these theories follow the same approach in naively taking the description of the star at face value. We shall see that the star has a completely different meaning that relates to the myths of apocalyptic predecessors of the Jesus movement and not to any real astronomical or astrological event. The story of the star has been misunderstood and literalised by the author of Matthew.

But what we are interested in here is not the physical explanations of miracles, which takes us towards the Traditional Secular view of Christianity, but the phenomenon of belief. Most churches today hold to the belief in a physical resurrection as the foundation stone of Christian faith. Many Christians believe that God can simply intervene in the universe to suspend the laws of science if he wishes. To them, the scientific objections are irrelevant since God can do what he wills. Such explanations undermine the wholeness of science, its interconnectedness, and its internal consistency. You cannot have a heavenly finger poke down into the universe and change it. Anyone who has studied science in depth, and who has a real feel for it, knows this. However given the prevalence of scientific illiteracy even among the supposedly educated this is not much of an objection for many. To the scientifically illiterate the scientist's attacks on religion are "arrogance" akin to a person imposing their opinions on others. But science is not based on opinion but mathematically rigorous theories tested by experiment.

Christianity has always had its apologists who construct elaborate arguments to defend the religion against science. One strategy is an attempt to relegate science to just another preconception. The argument goes that each individual will approach something like the resurrection with their own preconceptions. These preconceptions may be religious, they may be sceptical, or they may be based on science. The apologist argues that regardless of their preconceptions a person should consider the evidence for the resurrection as it stands and be prepared to abandon their preconceptions if they conflict with the evidence. Such apologists believe that the evidence contained in the gospels and the letters of Paul is compelling and that the scientist should be prepared to accept that, in this instance, his or her scientific preconceptions are wrong.

The sleight of hand in this argument is to frame the issue so that it is presented as two alternatives, science or the resurrection, to which the reader or listener will instinctively assign roughly equal probabilities. The argument then considers the evidence in favour of only one of these alternatives, the resurrection. Science effectively becomes downgraded to just another opinion without allowing for the totality of evidence behind the scientific viewpoint. A bodily resurrection is scientifically impossible because it would violate laws across biology, chemistry and physics. A resurrection would require the creation of new energy from nowhere which is against the conservation of mass/energy. It would require very precise and detailed changes at the cellular and molecular level that would have to be repeated across the billions of cells in the body. And, of course, all the billions of microorganisms which would have begun breeding in the process of decomposition would have to be eliminated. For such changes to happen "spontaneously" and without any possible mechanism would require a massive decrease in entropy. These things cannot happen within the framework of science. We must abandon either the scientific viewpoint of the world or the bodily resurrection; we cannot have both.

When considering science against the bodily resurrection we need to consider the probabilities of each taking into account the quality and quantity of the evidence. Science is based on literally millions of experiments. It has a mathematically rigorous structure of theory and makes predictions of astounding accuracy. For example, the theory of quantum electro-dynamics predicted the anomalous magnetic moment of the electron which has been measured as being in agreement with the theory to fourteen significant digits. Such accuracy of prediction is beyond anything encountered in everyday life. However, scientific accuracy is very evident in everyday life through the machines and technologies that are the basis of an industrial civilisation. These technologies work because the laws of science are invariants and give fully repeatable results.

The evidence that the apologist offers for the resurrection consists of the letters of Paul and the gospels. The gospels were written a considerable period after the events described and are not first-hand eyewitness accounts. The letters of Paul are an eyewitness account as he lists himself among those who witnessed the resurrected Christ. But it is clear from Paul's letters that his own experience was spiritual; he regarded himself as being in regular spiritual communication with Christ, and never says he saw a bodily resurrected Jesus. Nor is there any evidence from Paul's letters that the others who witnessed the resurrection had experiences that differed from his. So the only evidence for a bodily resurrection actually comes from the gospels. Paul's letters provide evidence against such a bodily resurrection.

We can calculate the probability of a physical resurrection using Bayes' theorem. Assuming that we knew nothing at all about the evidence for the resurrection we would attach a low prior probability to the event due to its conflict with scientific laws behind which there is a huge amount of experimental evidence. Let us put this probability at one billion to one for the sake of argument. We then need two other probabilities. The first is the probability that if the resurrection had occurred it would give rise to the type of account that we can read in the gospels which we will put at 100%. The second is the probability that if a physical resurrection had not occurred we would also end up with the type of account we have in the gospels. Apologists put a lot of effort into arguing that this probability was low. We will, in fact, see how a spiritual Jesus is perfectly consistent with the evidence. But for this purpose of putting in some numbers, we will accept the apologists' argument and put in a low probability of 10%. We might think that this means that the resurrection has a 90% chance of being true, but this does not take into account our prior knowledge of the likelihood of such an event. Using Bayes' theorem gives the true probability of one million to one against.

This low probability relates to a bodily rather than a spiritual resurrection. It does not mean that the account of the resurrection in Paul, explainable as it is by a spiritual event, is invalid. We may interpret such a spiritual resurrection from a scientific viewpoint as being psychological in nature and having no meaning beyond that given to it by the individual. Or we may regard it as being true beyond and outside science, relating to an aspect of reality that is more fundamentally true than science. But however we interpret it a spiritual resurrection does not involve observable phenomenon that are inconsistent with the laws of science.

There is one argument advanced by the apologists that is valid. Had Jesus been nothing more than a peasant religious teacher crucified by the Romans, and had the experience of his resurrection by his followers just been spiritual then no one would have regarded him as the Son of God or the Messiah. A belief in ghosts was commonplace at the time, and spiritual experiences or hallucinations would not have been enough to centre a religion on Jesus. The argument of the apologists is that only a direct physical experience of a resurrection shared by many people as described in the gospels would have been sufficient to persuade good Jews to abandon their religious practices and accept a crucified Jesus as Christ. Only such a physical resurrection could have provided the direct evidence of God's purpose that would have been required as the justification of this course of action. The argument is perfectly valid in so far as it highlights the inherent contradiction between the religion we observe in the earliest times and the notion of Jesus as a crucified preacher. But we know that the bodily resurrection cannot have happened so instead we must resolve the contradiction by questioning the idea that Jesus was that preacher and that he was ever a man.

Key points

1. The traditional account of Jesus, as given in the gospels, works as a religion centred on the crucifixion and resurrection.

2. However, it is becoming increasingly difficult to believe in the gospel story. The development of science has contradicted many miracles in the bible including the bodily resurrection. Without belief in the resurrection, the power of Christianity fades.

3. To many Christians, the scientific objections are not relevant because they believe that God can intervene in the universe whenever and however he wants. This view is based on ignorance about science which is an interrelated whole with a deep mathematical structure.

4. Some Christians attempt to defend the bodily resurrection by casting science as just anther opinion or preconception. This argument fails to take into account the quality and quantity of evidence supporting the scientific viewpoint.

5. The only evidence for a bodily resurrection consists of the gospel accounts which were written long after the events by people who were not eyewitnesses, and which are ambiguous and inconsistent. The only evidence of someone who had directly seen the risen Jesus is from Paul's letters and Paul's experience was spiritual in nature. Moreover, Paul never implies that the other apostles saw Jesus in a different way to himself.

Chapter 3
The Jesus of the scholars

Scholars have long been trying to go beyond the theological Jesus to a historical Jesus, a Jewish teacher living and teaching in Roman occupied Palestine. Although their quest may seem rational, their conclusions are anything but rational. If Jesus had taught what they think he taught, Christianity would have died out very rapidly from sheer boredom. And no real religion could ever have featured the complete U-turns in belief that they describe. These are symptoms of a deep underlying problem. Starting with an assumption of a historical Jesus, it is impossible to develop a realistic account of the development of Christianity.

The Traditional Secular Jesus

The assumption behind the Traditional Secular view is that the gospels are ultimately derived from historical events, but those events have become obscured by exaggeration and theologising. There is no distinct dividing line between the Traditional and the Traditional Secular. Some people attempt to reconcile their faith to science by adopting so-called rational views of miracles and a spiritual view of the resurrection while maintaining the basic story of Jesus as set out in the gospels. Such a soft non-literalistic approach to belief will merge imperceptibly into the Traditional Secular. Yet in its hard scholarly core the Traditional Secular makes no concessions to belief but tends towards atheism.

The Traditional Secular began as an attempt to study the New Testament as historical documents written by real people rather than as sacred texts handed down by God. Very quickly it was realised that the gospels were not the eyewitness accounts that tradition would have them. It had long been recognised that three of the gospels, Matthew, Mark and Luke were so similar in places that one must have copied another. These three were called the Synoptic gospels, meaning with one sight. The accepted theory to account for the similarity was that Matthew was the first gospel to be written and had been copied by the other two. Mark is much shorter than Matthew and virtually everything within it is also found in Matthew, often word for word. So the theory went that Mark was constructed as an abridged shortened version of Matthew. Paper was expensive in the ancient world and documents had to be copied laboriously by hand, so the production of a shorter Matthew made sense. The Gospel of Luke shared material with both Matthew and Mark and so was believed to have been written by someone who had these other two gospels available as sources. The Gospel of Luke also added additional material not in the other gospels, and it was believed that this other material went back to other eyewitness accounts. The Gospel of John is clearly different from the three Synoptics and has from the start been recognised as a more spiritual account and accorded a later date. This traditional view of the priority of Matthew is called the Augustinian hypothesis after the church father who first formulated it, St Augustine of Hippo. Under this theory, Matthew was originally written in Hebrew and was an eyewitness account by the disciple Matthew, the tax collector. The Gospel of Matthew was then translated into Greek, which was used as a source by the authors of Mark and Luke and eventually John.

This traditional view was challenged in the nineteenth century by the development of the two-source hypothesis. Under this hypothesis, it was not Matthew but Mark that was the first gospel to be written. This concept of Marcan priority was supported by the newly developing discipline of textual analysis. Mark is a simpler and rougher gospel than Matthew and misses out significant elements of the story such as the nativity. Scholars realised that these very features were indications that it was older than Matthew. The author of Matthew took Mark and added to it while refining the original text of Mark and smoothing over a number of difficulties. But this meant that Matthew could not have been written by an eyewitness because no eyewitness would have based their gospel so closely on another gospel. Moreover, Mark contained a strong clue as to its date. In the little apocalypse in Mark 13, Jesus gives a prediction of the destruction of the temple that there "*shall not be left one stone on another*" *(Mark 13:2)*. The prophecy continues by saying that the followers should watch for the "*abomination of desolation spoken of by Daniel the prophet standing where it ought not*" *(Mark 13:14)* which has long been seen as a reference to the destruction of the temple by the Romans in 70. The original "abomination of desolation" mentioned in both 1 Maccabees and Daniel was the mid-second century BC erection of a statue of Zeus in the temple and the sacrifice of pigs at this altar by Antiochus IV Epiphanes. While the sanctuary of the temple was burning during the siege of Jerusalem in 70 the Romans echoed the actions of Antiochus IV by bringing their legionary eagles into the temple and giving sacrifice before them.[6] To Christians this fulfilment of the prophecy of Jesus seemed miraculous. But scholars studying Mark realised that the "miracle" had another explanation. The Gospel of Mark, or at least the references in it to the destruction of the temple, must have been written after the destruction of the temple itself and while these events were still fresh in the memory. It has become clear that the writing of prophecies after events and then predating them is a very common device in Jewish scripture and probably originated as a literary technique for explaining the divine meaning of momentous events. But if the prophecy had been written after the destruction of the temple then this suggested a date of the 70s or perhaps 80s for Mark, some forty years after the events described in the gospel. Although it is just about possible for Mark to have been written by someone who was a young adult when the supposed events of Jesus' life took place, it is very unlikely. Why would anyone wait so long before dictating their account? The old person near to death writing down the events they witnessed as a youth is a useful device for novelists but a romantic fiction; people do not suddenly become capable of producing a work such as the Gospel of Mark in old age. An old person could only have produced such a work if their mind was already trained to the task by composing extensively when younger. But then why did they not write the gospel earlier?

Most scholars do not believe that Mark was written by an eyewitness, and it shows no signs of originating in Palestine. It is written in Greek and incorporates a number of Latin loan words and Aramaic words which are explained for a Greek speaking Gentile audience. So instead of the original gospel being a Hebrew version of Matthew written by an eyewitness, scholars were forced to conclude that the first gospel was the shorter, and to most Christians less satisfactory, Gospel of Mark, and that even that gospel was a long way from being an eyewitness account.

Under the two-source hypothesis, the author of Matthew used not only Mark but also another source called Q from Quelle the German for "source". Under this theory, Q was also available to the author of Luke, who used it together with Mark as sources for their gospel. Scholars who believe in the two-source hypothesis have attempted to reconstruct Q by the joint material in Matthew and Luke. The reconstructed Q turns out to be a sayings gospel rather than a narrative gospel like Mark. It has received considerable attention from scholars because, if genuine, it must predate Matthew and Luke and potentially is earlier than Mark. But did Q really exist? It is strange that such an important text seems to have left no sign in history other than its influence on Matthew and Luke. No copy of Q has ever been found, nor is there any reference to Q in the voluminous writings of the church fathers and other early Christians, nor do any of these writings quote directly from Q. There is a simpler explanation of the relationship between Matthew and Luke that does not involve the hypothetical Q and that is the Farrer hypothesis that Luke copies both Mark and Matthew directly. Be that as it may, the majority of scholars still favour the two-source hypothesis and it is the presumed existence of Q that has dominated most of the recent scholarly work on the historical Jesus.

The secular account of the historical Jesus typically takes as its starting point this base of Mark and Q. There are many different versions, but they all go something like this. Jesus was an itinerant religious figure who was teaching an apocalyptic Judaism centred on the reign of the heavens. The Gospel of Mark preserved the nucleus of his story although even in Mark the story has become considerably embellished. The embellishment develops through the Gospels of Matthew, Luke and John with the depiction of Jesus departing ever further from the original and with the addition of fantastic elements, such as the nativity stories. These stories of the nativity of Jesus are found in both Matthew and Luke but the details differ so they could not have belonged to Q but must have been additions made by the gospel writers independently based on an earlier tradition.

In this secular account, Jesus abides by the Jewish Law. It has become a cliché of historical Jesus studies that Jesus is never shown as not being Law-observant in Mark even though he teaches his disciples to break the Law, and they do so. From this, it is concluded that Jesus obeyed the Law but that his disciples departed from the Law after his death and attributed this departure to the teachings of Jesus. (There is a completely different explanation of why Jesus does not appear to break the Law and that is because under the shaman paradigm his actions are not observable; he exists spiritually within the minds of the disciples. It is their actions that are observable and they are the ones who break the Law, who eat the corn on the Sabbath, and who do not fast but who celebrate while the bridegroom is within the bridal chamber.)

The secular approach to the resurrection is to regard the long ending of Mark as a later addition. Without the long ending, the Gospel of Mark ends before the resurrection with the women leaving the empty tomb in amazement after hearing the message of the angel and telling no one of what they have seen. In some theories, the empty tomb is a genuine memory of the stealing of the body of Jesus by the Romans or priestly Jews. In other theories, the empty tomb has been manufactured so as to combat those who claimed that the resurrection was spiritual rather than physical. Either way the more complete resurrection accounts in Matthew, Luke and John, are seen as later developments. Under the secular approach, the resurrection is all part of the elaboration of the story over time.

This secular view of Jesus does not work as a religion. It has lost the central mystery of Christianity, the resurrection. It has retained some of the trappings, the teachings and ethics, which even the sceptical respect, but it has ripped out the heart of the religion. It is like a car without an engine. It appears that Christianity needs the irrational elements of the story that have been taken out. Without these elements it cannot function, its adherents become lukewarm and drift away.

Of course the proponents of the secular view are not primarily interested in Christianity as a religion. They are interested in reconstructing the life of Jesus in a historically realistic way. Such a realistic reconstruction must deduct all the supernatural elements. But the failure of the reconstruction to function as a religion indicates the failure of the theory as history. Any theory must account for the phenomenon observed with the minimum of additional arbitrary assumptions. In the case of the Jesus movement the phenomenon we observe from the very earliest sources is a religion; a fully formed and intensely spiritual religion centred obsessively on the being of Jesus. The secular historical theories of Jesus simply cannot account for the existence of this religion without introducing a volume of arbitrary assumptions that is greater than the core theory itself.

Christians regard Jesus as the divine saviour of humanity and the Son of God, part of the Godhead itself. It is not possible that any mere man, yet alone a crucified peasant philosopher, would have been thought of in this way. It is common for prominent figures to become legends, but the process requires the retelling and evolution of stories over many generations. The belief in the divine Jesus did not emerge slowly over centuries but was there right from the beginning. It is present in all the earliest sources including letters written by Paul within twenty years of the accepted date of the crucifixion. In no other case does the process of becoming a myth go so far as it is supposed to have done with Jesus or so quickly.

Nor can the secular theory explain a Christian's inner spiritual experience of the risen Christ. This inner spiritual experience is so powerful that it enabled Christianity to grow from a handful of Jewish outcasts to conquer the mighty Roman Empire in a few hundred years. Christianity survived the collapse of the Roman Empire and continued to spread across the globe remaining dynamic and expanding for two thousand years. Today Christians speak as they did in the time of Paul of a profound personal transformation, of finding the Jesus within. There is a continuity of spiritual experience from the earliest days of the movement to the churchgoers of the present time. The secular theory cannot account for this inner spiritual experience. Under the secular view, Christianity is the accidental product of a series of haphazard events and not the result of a profound spiritual transformation.

This problem extends to the very first followers of Jesus. His disciples could not have experienced the interior Jesus when the real Jesus was there right in front of them as a living man, warts and all, and in their memories after death. The interior experience of Jesus requires him to be both God and man. There are many examples of human martyrs, but none of them induces the spiritual feelings that Jesus does.

And if Jesus had introduced a Eucharistic ceremony it cannot have had the meaning latter attributed to it, that the bread represented the flesh of Jesus and the wine his blood. Christians believe that by consuming the Eucharist, Jesus becomes present, that the bread and wine are transformed into his substance, that he is there with the participants. This is not something that Jesus could have taught.

The problem, in essence, is that for Jesus to have been the founder of Christianity he would have had to know about his own death and resurrection. Without this central foundation, his teachings become impossibly vague and inconsequential. Jesus in the gospels is teaching of the coming kingdom of God, and it is a kingdom that he will rule as Christ. All this makes sense under the traditional view because Jesus is divine and has foreknowledge. But when we switch to the secular view we can no longer believe that Jesus has foreknowledge because such an assumption is not scientifically reasonable.

So if we follow the secular theory, then we have to imagine an abrupt turn in the history of Christianity after Jesus died. The new converts must have believed and experienced something completely different from what their teachers believed and experienced. A gradual development towards a spiritual and divine Jesus might make sense, but there is no evidence for such a gradual development. Paul has the same experiences of the spiritual Jesus as Christians have claimed throughout history, just more intense. Nor is there any evidence that Paul believed anything different in this regard than the leaders of the movement in Jerusalem, the same individuals who in the Secular Traditional view were Jesus' own disciples. Paul has many disagreements with the Jerusalem "pillars" yet Paul's exalted view of the nature of Jesus, and his spiritual experiences of Jesus, are never the subject of controversy.

The about turn continues into the practices and beliefs of the early Christians. They must have chosen to abandon the Jewish Law. They must have renounced the dietary requirements, removed the distinction between clean and unclean, ceased to observe the Sabbath in favour of the new Sabbath. It is difficult to underestimate what a profound change this would have been for any Jew, nothing less than the complete abandonment of their religion. The Jews believed that Yahweh had ordained the Law through Moses. To remove the Law would have required a higher authority than Moses, a greater force than Yahweh.

No Jew would have regarded a crucified peasant philosopher as an authority for such a change, no matter how charismatic they might have been. God was greater than any man and crucifixion was an eloquent sign of divine displeasure. The early followers of Jesus were all Jews and would not have abandoned the Law simply because they believed they had been visited by a ghost. Nor is there any reason they would have wanted to abandon the Law if Jesus himself had not taught such abandonment.

And if it was Jesus who had declared the Law obsolete then what authority did he give for doing so? In the gospels, the authority Jesus gives is himself. In no other case do we find a religion that has been started by an individual who regards themselves as the ultimate divine authority.

We are left with a picture of the development of Christianity that resembles no other religion known to man. According to the Traditional Secular view the early followers of Jesus disregarded almost everything Jesus taught, practised, and experienced and replaced it with an entirely new set of beliefs, observances and spiritual experiences. This makes no sense. The Traditional Secular view must be wrong. This view has emerged by deducting from the traditional account all the supernatural and unrealistic elements. But what remains is not a coherent theory of Christian origins. When we deduct the apparently irrational elements from the traditional story, we do not end up with something that is credible or compatible with the development of other religions.

The irrational religious elements must be integral to Christian origins and not later developments. These religious elements by themselves make perfect sense. Jesus as the Son of God is essential because the early movement would only have abandoned the Jewish Law on the highest possible authority, an authority that is greater than Moses, greater than the angels who, the New Testament tell us, brought the law. The resurrected Jesus bringing revelations to the disciples is exactly what we would expect. It is not Jesus the Son of God or the resurrected Jesus that is the problem; it is Jesus the man, the wandering philosopher of wisdom, that is the difficulty. The early Jesus movement as evidenced from the earliest sources, such as the letters of Paul, fits in perfectly with the normal development of a religion. What does not fit in is the idea that there was a real living and breathing Jesus before this stage. The assumption of a historical Jesus creates the inconsistencies.

Nor can the secular historical Jesus account for the vast diversity of early Christianity. There must have been something in the origins of the movement to account for this diversity. A theory must account for how the origins could give rise at the same time to a wide range of gnostic sects, to the proto-orthodox church, to the church of Marcion and to Jewish-Christian sects from which Islam ultimately developed. Imagine that we were observing a Galilean Torah observant Jesus teaching his followers about the imminence of the end of the world and the coming kingdom of God, and teaching a social gospel of how the poor would be rewarded and the rich and the powerful would be overturned. Would we have predicted that from this teacher gnostic sects would emerge believing that Sophia had been cast out of the pleroma, the totality of the Godhead, and that as a result mankind was trapped in a world ruled by evil forces, and that Jesus had descended from the highest reality to redeem Sophia, and hence mankind, by his sacrifice? Would we have predicted the belief of such gnostics that attempting to change the world was futile and that only by renouncing the world could the disciple of Jesus overcome its evil and ascend into the higher reality? Or would we have predicted that a large proportion of the future follows of Jesus would belong to a church (that of Marcion) that taught that the Old Testament Yahweh was an evil tyrant and that Jesus had descended from a higher God to supplant him and end his rule? We would not have predicted any of these things, and the secular historical Jesus theories cannot account for such beliefs having arisen from the starting point of their reconstruction of Jesus. Somehow the origins of gnosticism must have been there from the beginning; there must have been something baked into the beliefs of the earliest Jesus movement that led to the gnostic sects and the church of Marcion, just as it led to proto-orthodox and Jewish forms of Christianity. Each of these Christianities has gone down a different path; each has chosen certain beliefs and aspects of the early movement to emphasise and develop, and each has caused other beliefs and aspects to atrophy. But all the paths lead back ultimately to the same starting point, and that starting point cannot have been the historical Jesus of secular theories.

And so we must consider the third view. If Jesus was not a man was he nothing more than a myth?

Key points

1. Most scholars believe in Marcan priority, meaning that the Gospel of Mark was written first and that both the Gospels of Matthew and Luke copied much of their material from Mark. In the case of Matthew, almost the whole of Mark has been copied and in places, this copying is word by word.

2. The Gospel of Mark is normally assigned a date in the 70s based on the prophecies of the destruction of the temple which took place in 70.

3. Almost all scholars have believed that the authors of Matthew and Luke also drew upon a hypothetical saying gospel that has been given the name "Q No fragment of this supposed gospel has ever been found nor is it mentioned by any of the early Church fathers. More recently opposition to the Q hypothesis has been growing with a significant minority of scholars now doubting the existence of at Q. The alternative theory is that the author of Luke has simply copied the so-called Q material from Matthew.

4. Most scholars who are not trying to defend the traditional religious view of Jesus, believe that Jesus was teaching a version of Judaism and that it was his followers who established a separate religion after his death. We have called this view of the historical Jesus the "Traditional Secular".

5. The problem with the Traditional Secular is it fails to explain what is unique about Christianity; that its prophet is also the subject of the religion. All the features that make Christianity what it is, that trigger the "Easter Egg" of religious experience, are removed. The Traditional Secular Jesus does not know of his coming crucifixion or his resurrection, his body is not the bread, nor his blood the wine, he does not believe that he is the Son of God or that he will come back to rule at the end of time.

6. After subtracting all the things that Jesus could not have taught under the Traditional Secular view, we are left with only a vague set of moral teachings. There is no explanation of how Christianity was able to evolve from such confused beginnings to a religion that made a profound spiritual transformation in the individual, and which expanded rapidly throughout the Roman Empire.

7. The followers of Jesus would have had to make an extreme U-turn by disregarding almost everything that Jesus taught and replaced it with a new set of teachings that he would have abhorred. Although a degree of evolution is to be expected given enough time, such a sudden and complete U-turn would be unique in the history of religion.

8. The idea that his followers had grief-induced hallucinations and so believed that he had risen from the dead does not explain the centrality of the resurrection to Christian belief. Such hallucinations were common and a belief in ghosts universal. Most people in the ancient world thought that the dead were able to return temporarily from the underworld.

9. If Christianity had started with a Jewish wisdom teacher who was preaching a version of Judaism, this would not account for the huge variation in beliefs that we find among Christians by the second century. It could not explain how the teachings of the Docetists, the many gnostic sects, or Marcion could have emerged from such beginnings.

Chapter 4

Jesus as myth

Although the vast majority of scholars have always believed in the historical Jesus, a few brave rebels argued that Jesus must have always been the Son of God and the idea that he was a man who lived in the first century was a mistake. They pointed to the many similarities between Christian belief and the myths of dying and resurrected Gods that were common in the ancient world. More recently the book "The Jesus Mysteries" by Freke and Gandy exposed this view to a wide audience, and in the age of the internet, many amateur researchers have taken up the mythical Jesus idea.[7] Although derided by professional scholars, the mythical Jesus view has become popular because it offers a more coherent explanation of Christian belief in the resurrection than the historical Jesus. So did Christianity emerge from the myths of the ancient world?

The Mythical Jesus

Jesus the myth turns the rational secular on its head. In this view, Jesus starts out as divine and becomes man. Jesus is originally a god-man located in some mythic time; a god-man who his been put to death by evil forces but who returns from the dead in triumph. Through his sacrifice, his followers shall escape death by sharing in his mystic life. However, some on the outer fringes of his movement misinterpret the stories told about him, locating them wrongly in the immediate past. So his death at the hands of other divine powers becomes death at the hands of earthly powers, the Romans and the Jewish establishment, and his resurrection becomes a quite literal physical resurrection. In the same way, other gods and goddesses in the original myth become transformed into characters in the Jesus stories. For example Mary the mother of god and Mary the Magdalene can be

matched to the mother goddess figure in her roles as divine mother and
fertility/love goddess.

Jesus as myth is the counter-culture equivalent of the rational view of
Jesus as man hypothesis. The scholars reject the Jesus as myth hypothesis
virtually to a man and woman. Many go further, disparaging the mythi-
cists as amateurs and internet conspiracy theorists. And yet you can sense
that under the surface they are troubled. The mythical Jesus is the ultimate
nightmare for anyone who has built their academic reputation on books
and peer-reviewed papers about the historical Jesus.

The Jesus myth hypothesis starts by noting the close connection between
the death and resurrection of Jesus and the death and resurrection of many
gods of the ancient world. These fertility gods were killed in the winter and
resurrected in the spring, reflecting the cycle of nature. They were symbols
of the corn and growing things on which life depended. They were often
represented by a human king who was appointed to rule for a term (often
seven years) and then ritually slaughtered.

One highly developed form of these myths was the Greek mystery religions that took the Roman world by storm and which were highly prominent at the time of Christ. The most influential of all were the Eleusinian
mysteries which celebrated the grieving goddess Demeter and her daughter Kore/Persephone. The early orthodox Christian writer Hippolytus reports that at a key point the celebrant of these mysteries cries out *"August
Brimo has brought forth a consecrated son, Brimus"* (Hippolytus, *Refutation of all
Heresies 5:3).*[8] Brimo is a name for Demeter and Brimus for Dionysus. The
innermost mysteries were a closely guarded secret, but Hippolytus has no
scruples in revealing them. He reports that those admitted to the highest
grade of the mysteries contemplate in mystic ecstasy *"an ear of corn in silence
reaped".*[9]

The mysteries of Dionysus himself seemed to have been as varied as the
god.[10] He was all things to all men; represented both by a great bull and by
an effeminate youth, he was the god of wine (Bacchus) and sexual ecstasy
but was also regarded by some as the image of the human soul. The myth
of Dionysus involves the god being torn apart and eaten, and the sacred
meal was a prominent part of his rituals. In some cases, this may have involved his followers tearing apart and eating raw meat but may also have
been represented more sedately by a good meal. (It is not surprising that a
religion that combined feasting and drinking with uninhibited sexual behaviour and admission to inner spiritual secrets should have been so popular.)

Of particular interest were the mysteries of the Orphics. In their myths Dionysus was eaten as an infant by the Titans, and it is from the Titan's flesh that the human race is generated. The Orphics believed that humans had a dual nature – a fleshy body represented by the Titans and the heavenly soul within from Dionysus. This is most eloquently represented by a hymn on a gold lamella from Thessaly (translation by Marvin W. Meyer):

I am parched with thirst, and perishing.
But drink of me, the ever-flowing spring on the right, (where) there is a fair cypress.
Who are you? Where are you from?
I am a child of Earth and of starry heaven, but my race is of heaven (alone).[11]

The purpose of the Orphic was to free the soul from its prison in the "tomb" of the body by a devotion to purity. The Orphics had a great influence on Plato and the Platonic conception of the soul.

The Egyptian mysteries of Isis and Osiris are closely related to those of Demeter and Dionysus.[12] Doubtless some of the similarities had resulted from convergence in Hellenistic times when Egypt became part of the Greek world. But the truth is that the religions of the eastern Mediterranean are close siblings having developed from common prototypes and in an environment of mutual influence. Osiris like Dionysus is killed, and his body is searched for and found by a grieving Isis. He undergoes a "resurrection" the precise nature of which is unclear. He comes back to life and although he seems to dwell in the underworld he influences life on earth, inspiring his son Horus to overcome his assassin and brother Set. It is through the resurrection of Osiris that the Egyptian would derive his hope of life after death. The elaborate procedures of mummification are given to the Egyptians to echo the reassembly of the body of Osiris by Isis. After mummification the dead are believed to be judged by Osiris and, if they have lived virtuously, are mystically joined to him to share his immortality.

Although originating in Egypt, the cult of Isis and Osiris spread throughout the Roman world and was immensely popular. The similarities with Christianity are obvious. Like Christianity, we have a dying God whose resurrection brings life after death for his followers.

There are also remarkable similarities between the attributes of Mary the mother of Jesus in early Christianity and the goddess Isis. This extends to the way that Mary and Jesus were portrayed. The familiar pose of Madonna and child with the baby Jesus held on the lap of his mother Mary goes back to Roman times. But these Roman representations of Mary and Jesus are almost indistinguishable from depictions of the infant god Horus on the lap of Isis!

One further mystery religion that has been advanced as a source of Christianity is that of Mithras.[13] The origins of Mithras are as a god of light in Indian and Zoroastrian literature. The real Magi, the supposed "wise men" bearing gifts in the Matthew account of the nativity, were a priestly cast dedicated to the worship of Mithras. In Roman times, Mithras had become, rather surprisingly, a bull-slayer. His mysteries had immense popularity with Roman soldiers and spread throughout the Roman world. His cult was so popular that it was a serious rival to the spread of Christianity.

The initiate to the cult would experience a form of baptism and tests of worthiness. Participation in the mysteries was intended to lead to the salvation of the initiate, and the mysteries themselves celebrated the redemption of the cosmos. The mysteries were carried out in a Mithraeum, a cave, or a building designed to mimic a cave, which was intended to represent the cosmos. The mysteries involved seven stations or gates which represented seven gates that the soul would have to pass through to leave the cosmos/cave and ascend to the divine realm.

Central to the Roman mysteries was the slaughter of the bull the sacrifice of which brings about the regeneration of the cosmos. The bas-relief from Heddernheim shows three ears of grain growing from the tail of this slaughtered bull.

Mithras is also associated with the Sun god and was believed to have been born on the 25 December. Mithras and the sun god have a sacred meal over the body of the dead bull which is reminiscent of the Eucharist. Mithras was believed to have been born from a rock, and afterwards an arrow is aimed at the rock from which flows a stream. These images are strikingly similar to an image used by Paul in 1 Corinthians where he compares Christ to rock from which flows spiritual water.[14] And the name of Jesus' principle disciple Peter means quite literally "rock".

Many of the parallels seem remarkable, but there is one problem. They come from a non-Jewish context, and we know that early Christianity was a Jewish phenomenon. What is needed is a missing link, a set of beliefs that can bridge the chasm between the mystery religions and Christianity. Remarkably we can find such a bridge in some of the accounts of the early church fathers concerning the gnostics. An example is the account of the Naassenes by Hippolytus of Rome.[15] He is writing around 225, and his Refutation of All Heresies is an invaluable record of the gnostic beliefs at the beginning of the third century. He records that the Naassenes regarded their teachings as having come down from James, the brother of the Lord, through Mary. But Hippolytus himself does not attribute them to James and Mary but as having come from the "Barbarian and Greek mysteries"![16]

The description by Hippolytus of the belief system of the Naassenes is a compendium of the pagan beliefs of the Roman world. Among other sources it draws on Homer, the myth of Osiris, and the beliefs of the Phrygians concerning the "Great Mother".[17] These pagan beliefs are used by the Naassenes to illuminate the nature of Jesus and the sayings of Jesus and Paul.

So has Christianity come from the mystery religions through proto-gnostic groups from which the Naassenes have developed? At a broad level, some of the parallels are remarkable but the devil as always lurks in the detail. One problem is that the account of the Naassenes by Hippolytus is almost two hundred years after the start of the Jesus movement. How can we project these beliefs back two hundred years without any intermediary evidence?

The early evidence that is sometimes quoted in support of the mythological interpretation is often taken out of context. Take for example Paul's reference to the rock that is Christ. If we look at this in the original context, then any link with Mithras becomes unlikely. Paul is drawing an analogy with the rock from which Moses drew water in the desert to sustain the Israelites. Paul is equating Christ to this rock and the members of the church to the Israelites. His source is not pagan religion but the Torah.

More generally there is a disconnect between the Jewish origins of the Jesus movement and the links made by the mythologists. Most of the evidence advanced is comparatively late in date, from the time when the church had thrown off its Jewish roots having become a Gentile phenomenon. Inevitably there were cross influences, conscious or unconscious, between Christian and pagan religion. Most members of the church would have been converted pagans themselves, and almost everyone in the church would have relatives and friends who were pagan. These influences, when they occur, seem strange to us because we have not grown up in a pagan world.

One example where pagan influence may have occurred is the date on which the birth of Christ is celebrated, the 25 December, a few days after the winter solstice. As the sun approaches the solstice, it sinks ever more southwards in the sky until the solstice itself, when the southwards motion ceases. At this point, the sun is "dead" and dwelling symbolically in the underworld. This is a time of great anxiety for primitive people. Suppose the sun stays where it is? There would be eternal winter, and all human life would cease. So the first detectable northwards motion, which occurs around 25 December, would have been greeted with great rejoicing. The worship of Sol Invictus, the unconquered sun, was popular with the Romans and they celebrated his birth on 25 December.

The fact that Christ's birth is also celebrated on this date has been advanced as an argument for the mystery religion interpretation; in the Jesus Mysteries, Freke and Gandy state that the birth of Mithras was celebrated on the 25 December.[18] This assertion is dubious; most likely there was not a separate Mithras tradition of the 25 December, but the Mithras celebrations were linked to those of Sol Invictus. A more fundamental problem for those seeking a connection with Jesus is that no one in the early centuries of the church regarded Jesus as being born on the 25 December or his birth having anything to do with the solstice! There is not one reference to the birth date of Jesus among the early sources, not the canonical sources in the New Testament nor in the non-canonical sources including the imaginative narratives of the infancy of Christ that mention just about every other story that must have been circulating at the time. When at the end of the second century Clement discussed the possible dates for Jesus' birth he does not even mention the 25 December.[19] The first reference to the 25 December as the birth date of Jesus is in a Roman church calendar from 336 which records the celebration of his birth on this day.[20] The traditional explanation of the takeover of the 25 December as a celebration of Christ's birth is that it dates from the time when Christianity was becoming the official religion of the Roman Empire. According to this explanation, it was necessary for the old pagan festivals to be replaced by Christian equivalents, so the celebration of Jesus' birth was located at the time of the old Saturnalia. Although this was undoubtedly a practical factor for the promotion of the 25 December, a better explanation for why the birthday was originally fixed on this date is that it was exactly nine months after the supposed date of the crucifixion. In the ancient world, there was a widespread expectation that great men would die on the same day of the year on which they had been either born or conceived. Since Jesus' conception was believed to be divine it made sense to suppose that he would have been crucified on the same day of the year that the holy spirit had first entered into Mary. Both the western and eastern churches fixed the date of the crucifixion in relation to the Passover from clues in the New Testament but they each came up with slightly different dates - 25 March in the west and 6 April in the east. They also celebrated Christmas on different days, 25 December in the west and 6 January in the east, but in each case Christmas was celebrated exactly nine months after the crucifixion. Taking the traditional nine months for a pregnancy, this would mean that the virginal conception would be dated to the same day of the year as the crucifixion in both the Western and Eastern churches.[21]

So the reason the 25 December was originally advanced by some to be Jesus' birthday was not connected to pagan religion or the solstice. However, the reason this day then won widespread acceptance may have been due to the advantages of setting up a Christian feast day to rival the pagan attractions of the birth of Sol Invictus and the feast of Saturnalia. (The reverse is also possible, that the cult of Sol Invictus adopted December 25 because the Christians had begun to celebrate the birth of Christ on that day.) This example demonstrates two problems with looking for connections between Christianity and pagan religion. The first is the role of coincidence. The second is that the culture into which Christianity was expanding was pagan so that interaction and contamination between the two were inevitable. Many of the apparent links between paganism and Christianity can be explained through these two causes.

There is though an aspect in which the Jesus movement is linked to paganism, and that is through Judaism itself. Monotheism evolved slowly from polytheism, which has left its mark throughout the scriptures. The monotheistic worship of Yahweh became centred in the southern kingdom of Judea and Jerusalem. The Jesus movement is closer to the religion of the northern kingdom of Israel which was more polytheistic. Judaism is descended from a Canaanite religion which is intimately linked to other religions in the eastern Mediterranean. They are branches of the same family. When the prophets in the scriptures preach against the whoredom of the Canaanites, they do so because the priests who were writing the prophecies were fighting Canaanite religion amongst the Jews. Canaanite religion did not die out but became subsumed into what we now know as Judaism. So the seventy gods of Canaan who ruled under the supreme God El became angels with El himself becoming merged into El/Yahweh.

There is little doubt that the mystical machinery of the Jesus movement has evolved from the myths of the dying and resurrected gods. The route though lies far back in the history of Israel and not in the pagan religions of the Roman Empire in the first century. We know that the worship of other gods was commonplace in the high places of Israel and Judah and even in the temple itself. In Ezekiel the prophet is shown the abominations of Judah, the worship of other gods, which are the reason for the destruction of Jerusalem and the exile. Included among these is a reference to Tammuz:

Then he brought me to the door of the gate of Yahweh's house which was to-ward the north; and, behold, there sat women weeping for Tammuz. (Ezekiel 8:14)

Tammuz is the same as the Sumerian shepherd God Dumuzi the consort of the goddess Inanna. The Ezekiel passage is evidence that Dumuzi was worshipped in Judea including in the temple in Jerusalem. The priestly authors of Ezekiel attributed the fall of Judea to such worship, but we shall see that the predecessors of the Jesus movement took a very different view.

We know about the myths of the Sumerians through cruciform tablets dug up from the sands of Nippur and other places in southern Iraq. These tablets are of incredible antiquity. The myth of the descent of Inanna is recorded on tablets dating from around 1750 BC, so that almost as much time separates the first century Jesus movement from these tablets as separates us from the first century. And when the tablets were first written the myths would already have been old. The myth of Inanna tells of how the goddess attempts the descent from the great above to the great below, from heaven to the underworld, in pursuit of wisdom. She has girded herself with heavenly protection, the crown on her head, the lapis beads around her neck, the double strand of beads falling to her breast, the royal robe around her body, the breastplate, the gold ring around her wrist, and the lapis measuring rod in her hand. But as she passes through the seven gates to the underworld she must give them up one by one until at the seventh gate she has her gown removed and enters the underworld naked. Now as a mere mortal woman she is judged, and the goddess of the underworld Ereshkigal strikes her down and turns her into a corpse, a piece of rotting meat hung upon a hook. She is rescued by her father Enki the God of Wisdom. He fashions two hermaphrodite creatures who infiltrate the underworld like flies and who persuade Ereshkigal to give them the corpse. They sprinkle the corpse with the water of life and food of life that Enki has given them and Inanna arises.

She cannot however leave the underworld without another being given in exchange. It is her husband Dumuzi whom Inanna fixes on to take her place. She pronounces the word on him, and the demons of the underworld seize him although he escapes and flees. He has only a brief respite; the demons hunt him down and capture him. They strip him of his crown, his sceptre and his garment, and when he is naked, they take him down into the underworld. Inanna, however, searches for Dumuzi and alerted by a fly finds him. She arranges that he will dwell in the underworld for only six months of the year and for the other six months will return above the ground to be replaced in his turn by his loving sister Geshtinanna.

There are clear links between the descent of Inanna to the underworld and the myths of Demeter/Persephone and Isis/Osiris. They are examples of a great meta-myth relating to death and life, the descent to and return from the underworld linked to the seasonal disappearance and reappearance of vegetable growth, of the corn and the wheat that human life depends upon. The myth of Inanna holds out a glimmer of promise, of the possibility of release from the underworld, at least for a goddess.

Inanna later becomes the Babylonian and Assyrian goddess Ishtar and is identified with the Semitic Astarte. It is probably Inanna, the Queen of Heaven, in the form of Astarte who is being worshipped in Jerusalem according to Jeremiah:

See you not what they do in the cities of Judah and in the streets of Jerusalem? The children gather wood, and the fathers kindle the fire, and the women knead their dough, to make cakes to the queen of heaven, and to pour out drink offerings unto other gods, that they may provoke me to anger. (Jeremiah 7:17-18)

The descent of Inanna is reminiscent also of the descent of the gnostic Sophia or Wisdom. In some gnostic systems, the disharmony of the cosmos results from a decision of Sophia to leave the pleroma, the totality of the Godhead to descend into the world. This descent of Sophia echoes the descent of Inanna from the great above to the great below. Through this descent, Sophia becomes dead and trapped in the world of matter, and it is to redeem Sophia that Jesus descends into the world and accepts crucifixion. In this myth Sophia represents not just Wisdom as an emanation of God, but also the human soul, that starts as divine, but which has become trapped in the material realm. Only the sacrifice of Jesus can release it to reascend into the heavenly sphere and immortality.

The parallel nature of Sophia and the human soul are the key to understanding some of the similarities between Jesus and Dumuzi. Just as Dumuzi is offered in substitution for Inanna, who is freed from the domain of death to ascend to the great above, so Jesus is offered as substitution for the soul of man, to enable the human soul to be freed from death and ascend from the underworld up to heaven. The judges of the underworld have passed judgment on Inanna, and she has been found guilty, yet Dumuzi who takes her place is apparently innocent; when he appeals to Utu the god of justice, Utu helps him escape by turning him into a gazelle although it does him no good in the end. So also the soul of man is guilty of sin but Jesus, who gives himself in substitution, is innocent and sinless.

There are other similarities. Dumuzi is the shepherd God, and Jesus is the good shepherd both in the gospels and in early representations such as those found in the catacombs of Rome. Dumuzi is king just as Jesus, the Christ, is king. Dumuzi would also seem to have been a fisherman; certainly in the Sumerian king list there are two early mythical kings called Dumuzid, one a shepherd and one a fisherman. Yet Jesus is also heavily associated with fishermen, and the fish is also an early symbol for him in parallel to the good shepherd.

Dumuzi is known as the bridegroom of Inanna just as Jesus is called the bridegroom. And there are similarities between the descent of Inanna and the mysticism of the early Jesus movement. Most significantly both Inanna and Dumuzi are stripped of their robes to enter the underworld. Those who would ascend to heaven in the Jesus movement reversed this process; they had to discard the garment of the body, either temporarily in mystic trance or permanently in death and put on the heavenly garment.

The worship of both Dumuzi and Inanna by Jews at around the time of exile is attested to by the opposition of the priests. And it is to this very time that the origins of the Jesus movement can be traced. And yet Jesus is not Dumuzi. The origins of the Jesus myth have developed from other sources than the Shepherd God of the Sumerians. Dumuzi is not crucified or hung from a tree. Dumuzi does not chose his fate or make his sacrifice willingly; he does not bring his followers into life, nor does he teach them the kingdom of God. The Jesus movement has been influenced by Dumuzi and Inanna, and by the Egyptian parallels of Isis and Osiris. But influence is not to equate Jesus to Dumuzi or Osiris. The worship of Jesus has evolved among those to whom the worship of Inanna and Dumuzi was part of daily life. The myths were ingrained. The Jews were polytheistic but were moving towards monotheism. In this process, the worship of other gods had to be subsumed within the worship of Yahweh. Religion is inherently conservative and would be innovators borrow shamelessly from their predecessors. The priests could offer no equivalent to the journey to the underworld of Inanna and Dumuzi, but the Jesus movement did.

The Jesus movement emerged from the mystics of the cult of Enoch. Their practices were based upon the attempt to ascend with Enoch to heaven. Yet there was something missing from the spirituality of the Enochians, and that was the descent to the underworld. The descent and mystic death is the basis of Shamanism around the world. The shaman must die to be reborn. They must make the journey to the realm of Ereshkigal and confront the terrors of that place. They must suffer death and desolation. And one must be given in their stead, a better and greater one than they, so that the shaman can escape and ascend into a new spiritual life. The Enochians were looking in the wrong direction, upwards rather than downwards. Their attempt to ascend to the great above was doomed until they had descended to the great below. The accounts in the books of Enoch of the ascent of Enoch to heaven, although fascinating, are fake. They read more like fantasies than genuine mystic accounts. If you want genuine spiritual insight, then you must look in other places such as the Gospel of Thomas or the letters of Paul:

I am crucified with Christ: nevertheless I live; yet not I, but Christ lives in me: and the life which I now live in the flesh I live by the faith of the Son of God, who loved me, and gave himself for me. (Galatians 2:20)

The difference between the Jesus movement and its predecessor, the cult of Enoch is that the Jesus movement was the real thing. The shamans of the Jesus movement had made the journey. The role of the shaman was already ancient, but it entered into a new fusion with the visions of Enoch and the monotheistic worship of Yahweh. And so the new reality that was Christianity was born.

It did not exist alone. In parallel, the priests were developing a new monotheism based on the Book. They had no time for mystics, for Enoch or the Queen of Heaven. The priestly establishment had their temple in Jerusalem. The Pharisees and the scribes, less fortunate, had to make do with the texts. But for both priests and Pharisee, religion was a question of being rational and exacting. The priests were occupied with the control and operation of the temple, the Pharisees with the understanding and exegesis of the Torah that had been handed down by Moses. For both Priest and Pharisee religion was intimately linked with the law. It was a question of the correct obedience, keeping records, making well-argued judgments. The mystics were a danger to this well-regulated world. If they had direct experience of God what was the point of the Book? If they had journeyed to heaven what use the temple? Were the priests supposed to subject themselves to the incoherent utterances of vagrants? What value then their monopoly? The answer was simple enough. The word of God was in the past. The present was a matter of studying the word, teaching the word and obeying the word. The mystics were liars, the cult of Enoch invalid, the vagabonds of the Jesus movement blasphemers to be suppressed.

The Jesus movement is the most radical expression of the meta-myth of the descent into the underworld. It is radical because the Jesus movement was as monotheistic as the religion of the priests. Jesus was not a God, but the Son of Man. He has come forth from the one and only ultimate God and yet he shares a common nature with men and women. He has gone to the underworld to rescue Inanna, to offer himself as her replacement; but his Inanna is not the Goddess of love but the human soul. It has been condemned to death, hung upon a hook, but he will feed it the bread and wine of life. He will resurrect it and raise it, and he will do so through his perfect sacrifice.

Key points

1. The crucifixion and resurrection of Jesus has close similarities to the death and resurrection of gods in much of the ancient world.

2. The mystery religions were of great significance in the Roman world at the time Christianity emerged. Prominent among these mystery religions were the Eleusinian mysteries which celebrated the grieving goddess Demeter and her daughter Kore/Persephone who returns from the underworld.

3. The mysteries of Demeter's son Dionysus were highly varied and immensely popular. He was the god of wine and unbridled sexuality, but he could also represent the human soul. In the Orphic mysteries, Dionysus was eaten by the Titans from whose flesh humanity was created. Because of this humans have a dual nature, a physical body from the Titans and a heavenly soul from Dionysus.

4. The mysteries of Isis and Osiris originated in Egypt but became prevalent throughout the Roman world. Osiris is killed by Set and his other brothers, and his body is searched for and found by his wife and sister, Isis. He then comes back to life, at least for a while, before reigning in the underworld. The Egyptians practiced mummification in the hope that the dead would revive like Osiris.

5. The cult of Mithras was another mystery religion with close parallels with Christianity. Mithras was a Zoroastrian god of light, who became a bull-slayer. The sacrifice of the bull enabled the redemption of the cosmos and the ascension of the soul to heaven. Mithras was believed to have been born on the 25 December, the time of the Saturnalia feast. The cult of Mithras became very popular in the Roman army, and it was a close competitor of Christianity in the early centuries.

6. A possible link between the Greek mystery religions and Christianity is through the gnostics. However, all the evidence for such a link is comparatively late and could be explained by cross-influence with Roman culture. The earliest sources show that Christianity emerged from a Jewish apocalyptic sect with no evidence of influence from the Hellenistic world.

7. The most plausible link with the mystery religions is through the Sumerian god Dumuzi and his consort, the goddess Inanna. It is known that Inanna and Dumuzi were worshipped in Israel and Judea, including in the temple itself. In the central myth, Inanna descends into the underworld where she becomes a mortal woman who is killed and hung upon a hook. She is rescued through the sacrifice of Dumuzi, who is taken into the underworld in her place. Inanna can then ascend into the great above, into heaven. Like Jesus, Dumuzi is a shepherd and a fisherman.

8. It is unlikely that Jesus was identified as Dumuzi. However, Christianity would have emerged in an environment where the worship of Dumuzi and Inanna was common, and it has borrowed, perhaps unconsciously, from the myth. In the Christian version, Inanna becomes the human soul trapped in matter and redeemed from the underworld by the sacrifice of Jesus.

Chapter 5

How do new religions arise?

Neither the historical nor mythical Jesus can explain Christian origins. We need a new starting point. It is unlikely that Christianity should be a special case with origins unlike those of any other religion. So we need to look at the ways in which new religions arise. We will consider a number of examples and find the same pattern. Religions are created by a prophet or shaman receiving a visitor from heaven.

The visitor from heaven

How do religions start? By far the most common pattern, repeated time and again, is that the founder of the new religion has a series of revelations from a higher spiritual authority. These revelations may take the form of possession by a spirit or god, they may occur through dreams, through hallucinatory experiences, or through mystical practices intended to put the adept in a state of spiritual receptivity. We will call this higher authority a "visitor from heaven". Normally the visitor from heaven comes down to earth although sometimes it is the shaman who is believed to have travelled to heaven. But in all cases it is the visitor from heaven that is the source of the message. The founder passes on to his or her followers the sacred teachings that have been revealed by the visitor from heaven.

Another pattern sometimes found is the literary form where the new teachings are contained in a written account that is ascribed to an esteemed figure who lived in the past. This may take a revelatory or fictional form, in which there is no deception intended, or at the other extreme it might involve the physical recovery of some supposedly hidden book that is presented to the founder's followers as a genuine historical discovery. The literary form is very common in Jewish and early Christian writings. Here it is not used so much to form a new religion as direct an existing movement in the direction the author desires. There is a mass of early Christian writings attributed to the apostles or such like including some which present revelations from Jesus himself. In some cases, such as the pastoral epistles of Paul in the New Testament, the writings can only be described as forgeries because their authors have taken great care to make them look genuine. In other cases, such as some of the gnostic discourses, we should probably see them more as a revelatory-literary genre in which the authors believed they were passing on genuine revelations in an accepted literary form.

Cases of possession by a visitor from heaven are almost commonplace. There are many examples of charismatic Christian preachers and mystics who regard themselves as being possessed by the Holy Spirit or by Jesus. In India, there are barefoot mystics who are seen as being possessed by a god or goddess and are addressed as the incarnation of that god or goddess. But it is useful to consider an example which fully developed into a successful religion. The Mormons today are a movement with around 15 million adherents spread around the world. Although based upon the foundation of Protestant Christianity, the Mormons are sufficiently different in their beliefs to characterise them as a separate religion rather than just a separate church. The founding of the Mormons by Joseph Smith gives us a good example of the typical development of a new religion and has the advantage of having occurred in more recent history than the origins of most religious movements and of being well documented.[22]

Joseph Smith was born in 1805 in Vermont but moved to western New York, an area that was swept by the religious revivals of the Second Great Awakening. In the 1820s, Smith had a number of visions including one in which an angel Moroni came and told him about the location of a sacred treasure. This included golden plates recording revelations from an ancient American Indian tribe descended from Jews who had fled Jerusalem before its fall to the Babylonians. After a number of attempts, Smith retrieved the plates from a hill near his home and began translating them with the aid of others. The plates themselves were supposedly written in a language called "reformed Egyptian" and were not seen by anyone other than Joseph Smith who did not even show them to his co-translators. Once translated they were published in 1830 as the Book of Mormon, which in style closely resembled the English of the King James bible. The golden plates disappeared a number of times and were eventually taken back by Moroni once the work of translation was complete, leaving no physical evidence. From the beginning, the existence of the plates was doubted and to address these

doubts Smith had eleven witnesses sign statements testifying to their existence. Three said that they had seen a vision of the angel Moroni with the
plates and eight others said that they had been shown the plates by Smith
and even allowed to hold them. All the witnesses were close confidants of
Smith, and the eight were members of two families including the Smith
family. Today most Mormons believe in the physical existence of the plates
as an article of faith, although few non-Mormons would regard them as
anything other than a fantasy.

The whole story illustrates many of the features of a new religion. Joseph Smith had visions of a visitor from heaven, the angel Moroni. He presented the teachings of Moroni to his followers, and some of them then had
conforming visions themselves; a number of others saw Moroni. The teachings that Joseph Smith passed on were recorded in a sacred book written
by Mormon and Moroni and supposedly translated by Smith and others.
Smith had other visions not involving Moroni that he also passed on to his
supporters. And Smith had regular "revelations" from the spirit that he
would utter as a medium. Smith never attributed himself as the ultimate
authority for any of his pronouncements, although he acknowledged that
some of his revelations were expressed in his own words. This is quite different from Jesus who never gives a source for his teachings but issues
them as edicts and who uses the Son of Man, that is himself, as an authority. One similarity between Smith and Jesus is that Smith suffered martyrdom, being killed by a mob at Carthage Jail. But this martyrdom was never
assigned any particular significance by his followers. Smith left behind him
a church that would thrive due to the belief, commitment, and mutual
support of its members who overcame almost unimaginable hardship. Under their new leader Brigham Young, the Mormons were led to the wilderness of Utah where they built new Zion with a temple at Salt Lake City.
Although Brigham Young was himself regarded as a prophet almost everything Mormons believe and practice goes back to Smith. Young did introduce open polygamy which was once widely thought to be his own innovation. But it is now known that polygamy was actually introduced by Joseph Smith as a secret teaching during the Nauvoo era and that Smith himself took no less than forty-three wives. Brigham Young did withdraw the
Mormon priesthood from black men in contradiction to the teachings of
Smith, but this is reversing a revolutionary policy of Smith and is in line
with the generally racist culture of the time.

There is always a whiff of the fraudulent about Joseph Smith, but that
does not mean that he was not a true prophet. Perhaps he simply saw more
clearly than most that the average believer lacked spiritual insight and

must have something "real" to latch onto. The golden plates have a mystical reality, brought by an angel and flickering in and out of existence, and yet Smith felt obliged to present them as dull physical plates of gold. He was forced to follow up this initial deception with hocus-pocus such as showing the plates to his friendly witnesses.

Turning to Christian and Jewish religious innovators we find extensive examples of both the revelatory and literary methods. Often the two are fused together as in the Mormons. The gnostics and Jewish mystics naturally passed on the revelations from their spiritual experiences whereas the Jewish priestly classes and the proto-orthodox Christians, neither of which groups had revelations or valued them in others, used the literary technique.

Looking at specific examples the great gnostic teacher Valentinus regarded his own teachings as having come from a revelation of the Logos who appeared to him in the form of a small child, as is described in this hostile account by Hippolytus:[23]

For Valentinus likewise alleges that he had seen an infant child lately born; and questioning (this child), he proceeded to inquire who it might be. And (the child) replied, saying that he himself is the Logos, and then subjoined a sort of tragic legend; and out of this (Valentinus) wishes the heresy attempted by him to consist. (Hippolytus, Refutation of All Heresies 6:37)[24]

The gnostic teacher Marcus, a follower of Valentinus, also traced back his teachings to a visitor from heaven. We know about it because his enemy Irenaeus wrote extensively about Marcus representing him as a fraud and conjurer:

He declares that the infinitely exalted Tetrad descended upon him from the invisible and indescribable places in the form of a woman (for the world could not have borne it coming in its male form), and expounded to him alone its own nature, and the origin of all things, which it had never before revealed to any one either of gods or men. (Against Heresies 1:14:1)[25]

The literary method of assigning beliefs to great figures who lived, or who were believed to have lived, in the past was a technique that was beloved of early Christians. A large proportion of books in the New Testament, including all the gospels, are assigned to individuals who did not in fact write them. In some cases this false attribution was probably not made

by the original author but by others as the book circulated. But there are
certainly works in the New Testament that are carefully constructed forgeries intended to deceive the reader as to their true authorship. These include
the false epistles of Paul, such as the letters to Timothy and Titus. Such
writings were intended to present the views of those who wrote them as if
they were from Paul or some other early figure and are often politically
motivated in the sense of trying to steer the early church in a certain direction rather than communicate spiritual revelations. It is not just in the writings of the New Testament that early Christians put words into the mouths
of the apostles and into the mouth of Jesus himself. There is a vast literature of works that have not been accepted into the cannon, both the so-
called Apocrypha and gnostic works, and most of these attribute their
teachings to prominent early figures.

The literary revelation method was also the principle way in which the
Jewish scriptures evolved. The approach was to read God's meaning in the
history of Israel by retro-writing the revelations of the prophets so as to
reveal the true meaning of events. The prophets warn the kings and people
what is about to happen and why. The first generations to read these
"prophecies" would have understood that they were intended to be a type
of inspired fiction which revealed God's intentions to those who are alive
after the event but who had been struggling to understand what the event
meant. Over time the people forgot that these prophecies had been written
after the events they foretold so that they became, in themselves, miraculous evidence of the existence of Yahweh and his plan for the Jews. The
scriptures evolved through a process by which layer upon layer was added
in this way, with the layers that had been inherited from the past being believed to be real.

There is no hard and fast distinction between the revelation and literary
channels. Many revelations involve a literary aspect, such as Joseph Smith
receiving the Book of Mormon, and much of the literary material would
have originated in revelation experiences or intuitive inspiration. The material is perhaps best seen as a spectrum ranging from a hot spiritual extreme where direct revelations are received by the charismatic from a
"heavenly messenger" and passed on to others, through the middle of the
spectrum where revelations are assigned to figures who lived in the past by
creatively rewriting the history of the past without necessarily a motivation
to deceive, right through to a cold rational end of the spectrum, the deliberate and manipulative rewriting of the past for political ends. We might
add an honest, cold extreme whereby a teacher undertakes exegesis of a

text to communicate to others their interpretation of the text but without any attempt to change the original.

What is a common factor in all these cases is that the person bringing the revelation always quotes some other person or agency as their origin. One reason is that no one would believe a person who gave him or herself out as being divine. Such a person would be treated as a lunatic, if not immediately put to death. More fundamentally the consciousness always sees such revelations as coming from the outside, from a higher authority than the self. We may call this outside heaven or an angel, or we may call it the unconscious, but it is never "us".

We can sum up the typical development of a new religious sect by a number of principles.

- The founder of the sect should assign their teachings to an authority that is either spiritual (a visitor from heaven) or historical (a prophet or wise man/woman who lived in the past).

- As the sect expands from its Charismatic founder, it should transmit the beliefs of the founder from generation to generation. Changes to these beliefs should be gradual and accretive.

- The religious practices of the of the sect should be derived from the founder and be passed down generation to generation changing only gradually. In particular any significant deviations in practice from the religious background from which the sect emerged can be traced back to the founder.

- The mythologizing of the founder should increase with the number of generations that have elapsed from the founder's life.

We have seen already that the secular historical theory of the Jesus movement does not satisfy these principles; that the sect embarks on the mother of all U-turns immediately after the death of the founder and yet on the other hand the mythologizing of the founder is already at an acute level in the earliest available texts. But what is of particular interest is the way that Jesus speaks of himself as if he were the ultimate authority.

As an example take a story near the beginning of Mark. When Jesus is at Capernaum, a crowd surround his house and four men who are desperate for him to heal a paralytic take the unconventional route of breaking through the roof. When Jesus sees the sick man, he says to him *"Son your sins be forgiven you"* (Mark 2:5). Some scribes who are present recognise that Jesus is taking authority to himself and think to themselves *"Why does this man thus speak blasphemies? Who can forgive sins but God only?"* (Mark 2: 7).

Although they do not say this aloud Jesus knows what they are thinking and answers them:

"Why are you reasoning these things in your hearts? Is it easier to say to the paralytic 'Your sins are forgiven', or to say, 'Arise, take up your mat, and walk?' But that you may know that the Son of Man has power on earth to forgive sins..." He said to the paralytic, "I say to you, arise, and take up your mat, and go to your home." (Mark 2:8-11)

The man does indeed get up and walk to the amazement of everyone. Shortly afterwards there is an episode where the disciples of Jesus eat ears of corn on the Sabbath. The Pharisees complain to Jesus about this:

And he said to them, "The Sabbath was made for man, and not man for the Sabbath. So the Son of Man is Lord also of the Sabbath." (Mark 2:27-28)

Here Jesus speaks as if he is the ultimate authority on Law observance and as if he needs to give no justification to abrogate one of the most essential elements of the Jewish Law, the respect for the Sabbath. Although both of these particular examples involve Jesus as the Son of Man, this assumption of an unquestionable authority is Jesus' normal manner. The reader of the gospels picks up on this subconsciously, and it gives the gospels much of their power. No human being could talk in this way. The reader understands this and begins to attribute to Jesus a nature that is more than human.

Under the traditional view, this is all explainable by Jesus' unique combination of human and divine nature. But if we believe that Jesus was a man and not divine then this manner of speech cannot go back to him. We then have only two alternatives; either it is a literary invention attributed to a real Galilean charismatic called Jesus but preserving almost nothing of his true speech; or it is spoken by a "visitor from heaven" through possession or revelation and communicated through a shamanic individual.

The first option, that of literary invention, can be ruled out through the other criteria, that the teachings and practices of the founder should be respected and passed down to succeeding generations changing only gradually over time. For Jesus to have been used by others as the literary mouthpiece for their own beliefs involves a dilemma. Jesus was either highly esteemed by his early followers or he was not but, in either case, he should not be functioning exclusively as a literary mouthpiece for others.

First suppose that Jesus was highly esteemed. If so then his followers should have faithfully followed his teachings and carefully transmitted them to later generations. This is the pattern we see with the Mormons and other religious movements. If his followers stayed loyal to Jesus' teachings then most, or at least a substantial amount, of the teachings that have come down attributed to Jesus must go back to Jesus. But in this material Jesus never uses an authority other than himself. If he had his own visitor from heaven then why does this not get passed on in the tradition?

Now consider the other possibility that Jesus was not so highly esteemed that his followers felt it necessary to pass down his beliefs. The problem with this case is that such a lowly Jesus could never have functioned as an authority for the disciples' own teachings. This is particularly so as Jesus suffered crucifixion that was a form of the cursed death of hanging from a tree. We might see a crucified person as a martyr, but the Jews would have seen his fate at the hand of the Romans as a clear demonstration of God's displeasure. It would have been interpreted as a sign that Jesus was not a valid prophet, and not the Christ, but had been cursed and disowned by God. No Jew would have used such a failed prophet as an authority.

We have logically ruled out the common idea among secularist historians that the sayings of Jesus that have come down to us are largely later literary inventions. With this, we can also rule out the idea of Jesus being a historical figure. We are forced to adopt the only hypothesis that makes sense of the data. Jesus is himself the visitor from heaven. He does not give anyone but himself as an authority for his teachings because he is the absolute authority, the divine Son of God, the Christ.

Jesus and the shaman

The spiritual Jesus was not a hologram or an apparition like a ghost. He has appeared through an intermediary, a great shaman who was the true founder of Christianity. The shaman has seen the resurrected Jesus and taught others to see him also. An experience of the risen Christ was normal in the inner circle of the Jesus movement and a qualification for being an apostle. In the Gospel of Thomas, the disciples are in regular spiritual communication with Jesus. These spiritual experiences of Jesus are not something that stopped suddenly but have continued throughout time. Indeed the spiritual experiences of Christians today, of the Christ within, go back in a continuous line to the shaman and differ only in intensity to the direct experience of Christ spoken of by Paul and in Thomas. The experience of the inner Christ did not arise accidentally, as in the Traditional Secular view, but was always a part of what it meant to be a Christian; there was no change between the days of the founder and subsequent development other than a gradual falling off in intensity.

The shaman paradigm also explains why Jesus gives himself as authority for his teachings. Jesus as the "visitor from heaven" is the ultimate authority. It is the shaman who is the human founder, and the shaman modestly disappears to such an extent that the founder's teachings are viewed as coming directly from Jesus. There is no need to explain why Jesus speaks like no other human, for he was not human, and no mystery of how a man became to be regarded as the Son of God, for he was not man but the Son of God from the beginning

Unlike the Traditional Secular theory, there is no need to evoke a U-turn in the practices and beliefs of the movement either. The shaman would have introduced all the great changes such as the abandonment of the dietary Laws, the moving the Sabbath to the Sunday and the introduction of the Eucharist. The necessary authority for these changes has come from the spiritual Jesus. Only someone above the giver of the Law can sanction its abandonment. The early Christians of the first century are not disregarding the founder's teachings but walking obediently in the radical path the shaman established.

Under the secular Jesus theory, Christianity would have to follow a development like no other religion. With the shaman theory, the development becomes typical rather than atypical. A shamanistic founder receiving revelations from a visitor from heaven and passing on the new laws and teachings to their followers is the norm for new religions. The break with the mother religion, in this case Judaism, is not accidental but an intrinsic and inevitable result of the introduction of a new spiritual authority which will never be accepted by most adherents of the established religion.

The shaman paradigm brings together a number of concepts that are not themselves new. Others have wondered if Christ was a spiritual rather than physical figure to the first Christians. Most significantly, the pioneering work of G.A. Wells was instrumental in the modern incarnation of the myth theory.[26] Wells showed how Paul in his letters seems to know nothing about Jesus' life on earth. The epistles are consistent with a Christ who was crucified on earth in the distant past and who had now been resurrected spiritually. These ideas were developed further by the Canadian humanist Earl Doherty in his *Jesus Puzzle* book and website.[27] To Doherty,

Jesus existed in the lower heaven where he was put to death by demons before being spiritually resurrected.

The idea that the sayings of Jesus were spoken in a state of shamanic possession has become quite popular among many who believe in the historical Jesus; but for them, the shaman is Jesus. This raises the question, who is it who is supposed to be possessing Jesus? Those who believe in the historical Jesus do not have an answer to this. They cannot take the logical next step that Jesus must be the possessing spirit, not the one possessed.

This book puts the concepts of the non-historical Jesus and the shaman together. It embarks upon a search for the first Christianity among Jewish mysticism rather than pagan myth. The *Shaman Paradigm* series will search both for the shaman and for what came before the shaman. The person in whom Christ was first resurrected did not exist in a vacuum but was part of a movement which had already existed for hundreds of years. Those in this movement looked for the resurrection of the Christ, but they expected that resurrection to come in the skies and not through a lowly prophetess.

Key points

1. The typical pattern for the creation of a new religion is that a prophet or shaman has a "visitor from heaven" who brings revelations or communicates a book. Sometimes the visitor is believed to be physically present, and sometimes the visitor is spiritual. Occasionally it is the shaman who journeys to heaven.

2. A well-documented example of the development of a new religion is that of the Mormons. Their prophet, Joseph Smith, received visits from a "visitor from heaven", Moroni, who revealed the location of a hidden book, the Book of Mormon, written on tablets of gold. Joseph Smith eventually recovered the book and had it translated, although even his co-translators were forbidden to see the actual tablets.

3. We find accounts of spiritual visitors among the gnostics. Valentinus apparently received revelations from a newborn child who was the logos (this could be confusion with the child of seven days). His follower, Marcus, received the Tetrad in the form of a spiritual female visitor.

4. The other common form of religious innovation is the literary, whereby new teachings are presented as coming from a respected prophet who lived in the past. This was very common among both Judaism and early Christianity. Sometimes this form is employed as a literary device with no intention to deceive, although later generations do not understand the de-

vice and accept the "prophecies" as being genuine. At the other extreme, this can be a cold-blooded attempt at religious deception.

5. In no case do we find a prophet or shaman giving themselves as the ultimate authority for their teachings. They are always the conduit and never the source. It would seem that it is psychologically impossible for people to regard themselves as a divine authority. Anyone doing this would be seen as mad.

6. In the gospels, Jesus gives himself as the authority. This is picked up unconsciously by the reader who then assigns a divinity to Jesus.

7. There are two explanations as to how Jesus could function as such a divine authority. Either he is the visitor from heaven who has appeared to a shaman or the gospel Jesus is a purely literary creation.

8. We can rule out a literary creation. If Jesus had been respected by his followers, they would not have rejected his teachings and substituted their own. And if Jesus had not been respected, then they would not have used him as the authority for their own teachings. In any case, no Jew would have used a crucified teacher as an authority because the cursed death of crucifixion was seen as a rejection by God.

Conclusion

Jesus must be the "visitor from heaven" and not the human shaman/founder.

Chapter 6

Signal and noise

The recovery of Christian origins is essentially a question of signal and noise. The signal is the original material both oral and written together with the events that took place at the beginning of the movement. We cannot observe this signal directly. Our observables are the surviving texts from the early centuries of the movement. Our problem is that these observable texts also have a large amount of added noise. Somehow we must distinguish the signal from this noise.

Filtering out the noise?

As the movement developed so did the myths and stories, the philosophy and political intrigue. For our purposes, all this subsequent development is noise that is added to the original signal. In an environment where teachings and stories are passed down from mouth to mouth the amount of noise will increase exponentially with time. Only when a source is written down and is transmitted as a text does the addition of noise moderate. Even then it does not cease completely for texts change and evolve with frequent editing and interpolations, as well as with copying and translation errors. As a rough rule, the lowest added noise texts will be those that were written earliest. This is the justification for seeking out the earliest texts to base our study on. Although this general correlation between the date of composition of a text and the signal to noise ratio is useful, it is by no means perfect. A text where the author is recording traditions and verbally transmitted material that have been passed down to him or her will have considerably lower noise than a text written at the same time that is an imaginative invention. Documents can also copy other documents so that a late written document may have sections with low noise where it uses an earlier document as the source.

To illustrate the concept of the exponential growth of noise suppose that the ratio of noise to signal doubles every thirty years. This means that a document written thirty years after events can be expected to contain something like 50% information and 50% added noise. But a document written 100 years after events will have 10% information and 90% noise while a document written 200 years after events will have 1% information and 99% noise. Clearly a document written two hundred years or more after events will not be very useful for the investigation and to the extent that it adds a great deal of noise will distract from the signal. This exponential increase in noise explains why it is pointless resorting to traditions that are first recorded many hundreds of years after the events to which they supposedly relate. Even if there are fragments of information here and there, they are lost in a sea of noise.

How can we recover the signal from the noise? The techniques that scholars use are basically attempts to filter out the noise. One such technique is the criterion of embarrassment, also called the criterion of dissimilarity. The idea is that an author is unlikely to invent details that were embarrassing to their view of Jesus or which contradicted the theology of their group. Where such embarrassing details occur, we can be sure (according to the criterion of embarrassment) that the information is an established tradition. The criterion of embarrassment is occasionally useful but suffers from some major disadvantages. First, it only applies to those things that are seen as being embarrassing to the early church. Since most things from the early movement would not have been embarrassing it will throw away much more genuine material than it accepts. Second, the things that it accepts, being the things that the early church did find embarrassing, are going to be an odd and biased collection.

There is another fundamental problem with the criterion of embarrassment. How can we know what early Christian authors would have found embarrassing? The problem becomes more acute the earlier we go back towards the origins of the movement. We have a good idea of what the later church fathers found embarrassing because they were part of an established church that left voluminous writings. But how can we decide what the author of Mark found embarrassing when the only writing he has left behind is the very gospel to which the technique is being applied? We do not know where the author of Mark lived, what group he was a member of, and we have no insight into the beliefs of that group other than what is in the gospel itself. This inevitable subjectivity means that, in practice, the method is applied not to the beliefs of the author of Mark, but to the beliefs of the later proto-orthodox church that developed from his gospel. So the criterion of embarrassment is applied to things that later Christians would have found embarrassing rather than things that the author of Mark would necessarily have found embarrassing.

This problem is compounded because those applying the criterion of embarrassment are working within a historical Jesus context. They make the assumption that there are real historical events that have given rise to the stories in the gospels. But if the shaman paradigm is correct then all these stories have arisen through a process of literalisation. There simply cannot be any original embarrassing events about a spiritual Jesus and all the embarrassing stories in the gospels must have arisen through the transition of a spiritual Jesus into a Jesus of flesh and blood. So although the embarrassing features may have their origins in early material, this material has been completely misunderstood. To give an example, it is embarrassing that the Gospel of Mark gives a mother of Jesus but no father. Using the criterion of embarrassment, we might conclude that this is telling us that Jesus was illegitimate. But under the shaman hypothesis it means no such thing because Jesus, as a spiritual being, will not have a human father.

These are the types of issues that apply to any attempt to filter out noise from the sources. Any such filter involves making subjective judgements about what is noise and what is signal. But these subjective judgements are inevitably based on the preconceptions of the person making the judgement. The result of the exercise will confirm these preconceptions as anything at variance with them will be filtered out and dismissed as noise.

All attempts to filter out noise suffer from this disadvantage that you need to know the answer before you can apply the filter. Instead of attempting to remove the noise at this stage we must take a fundamentally different approach.

Recovering the signal: redundancy

The problem of signal and noise is not something unique to early Jesus studies; it is present in all communications. For example, any radio transmission will involve added noise. No transmission will achieve 100% fidelity, and there will be inevitable noise including contamination from both manmade and naturally occurring radio sources. In analogue radio this noise contamination is an irritating problem but it is possible for digital signals to remove it completely. They do this by using redundancy.

The degree of redundancy expresses the amount of repetition in a message. In a message with high redundancy, the signal is encoded in the message several times. So a message with high redundancy takes more space and carries less information per bit than a message with low redundancy. But a digital signal that is encoded with high redundancy can be accurately reconstructed even if the transmission is poor. If the same signal is encoded without redundancy, then any parts of the message that are lost cannot be recovered, and noise cannot be distinguished from the signal. With enough redundancy, digital communications can achieve perfect fidelity even if the underlying transmission is of poor quality and full of noise.

The information from the early Jesus movement is not encoded in zeros and ones but stories and sayings. As they have been passed down, these stories and sayings will have been misunderstood, changed and reinterpreted. The stories and sayings should, however, exhibit redundancy. We would expect the original material to form an interlocking whole with the same concepts being expressed in different ways. We would also expect redundancy to come about as a consequence of multiple channels of transmission. A saying is not taught to one pupil but to many pupils, a story is not told to one person but many people. At any one time, there is a gene pool of versions of a saying or story in existence that have undergone various levels of mutation from the original. This gene pool has a high degree of redundancy and when the material is committed to writing this redundancy will be frozen into the texts. Different versions of sayings will be incorporated and different mutations of stories that may have changed to such an extent that they are not recognised as coming from the same source.

We would expect the material that comes down to us to have high redundancy, and we will see that this is the case. If redundancy is high then attempting to filter out the noise through such means as the criterion of embarrassment is not sensible because this will destroy the signal. The situation is like a jigsaw puzzle to which random extra pieces have been added (noise). The problem is that we cannot identify these extra pieces without completing the puzzle. Only when the puzzle is complete can we see what pieces represent noise because they will not fit, and we can discard them. The pieces that represent the original signal form a coherent whole because of redundancy. If we were to destroy the pieces we considered to be noise at the beginning, we would also throw away so many of the genuine pieces that the puzzle might then be impossible to complete.

Some scholars spend a great deal of time setting out methodologies for how they are going to select and fit the pieces together, yet this is to take the wrong approach to the problem. We must leave all the pieces on the table and attempt to put them together. You can never recreate the original picture by applying a set of rules. Instead, it is a matter of identifying the patterns that link together multiple pieces of evidence. This pattern matching requires the intuitive parts of the brain, and it requires the puzzle to be done as a whole. And yet the end results are not subjective. The thing about jigsaw puzzles is that once they have been assembled it is easy to see if they have been put together successfully. The same will apply to the recreation of the original Christianity. Once we have put the pieces together the pattern will make a satisfying whole; the beliefs of the early Jesus movement are consistent and compact; they could be written down in a few pages and yet they flow through all our different sources.

Leaving all the pieces on the table does not extend to including later texts because as we have seen the ratio of noise to signal increases geometrically with the date of the material within the work. There comes a point where including a text is not useful because it adds too much noise. We will limit our consideration mostly to the first two centuries with a strong preference for works that date to the first century or the early second century. We will not however apply a hard age cut off because some later works can embed early traditions. Ultimately this is a matter of judgement, and our main use of later works is to confirm something we have found in the early material.

Sources and the literalisation bow wave

So what are the main sources available to us? We will draw on a wide variety of sources, but it is worth setting out the sources that meet the criteria of the first century / early second century.

<u>Works included in the New Testament</u>

The genuine letters of Paul (50-60): Romans, 1 & 2 Corinthians, Galatians, 1 Thessalonians, Philippians, Philemon.

The Gospel tradition:
  Mark (70-80)
  Matthew (c80)
  Luke & Acts (90-100)
  John (c100)

The Book of Revelation (c90)

The secondary letter tradition (60-120):
Hebrews
James
Jude
1,2,3 John
1,2 Peter
Forged letters of Paul - 1 & 2 Timothy, Titus, Ephesians, Colossians, 2 Thessalonians

Works not included in the New Testament

The Gospel of Thomas (30-60)
Shepherd of Hermas (c100)
Odes of Solomon (80-150)

Although the above list is organised between those works within the New Testament and those without, we will attach no importance to this distinction. The New Testament was compiled by the proto-orthodox church and reflects the bias of that church. This list is largely based on commonly accepted dating although often this is inevitably subjective. The dating of the Gospel of Thomas is very controversial and will be discussed later. There is a useful piece of objective evidence, and that is the dating of the earliest physical texts and fragments. Larry Hurtado has summarised the texts from the second and third centuries[28] and a count of the entries on his list is given in the table below. I have excluded certain classes of texts, such as writings of the church fathers, magical and prayer texts, and fragments of unknown works.

Text	Count
Gospel of John	17
Gospel of Matthew	13
Shepherd of Hermas	11
Gospel of Luke	7
Acts; Romans	6

Text	Count
Revelation	5
Hebrews; 1 Peter	4
Ephesians; 1 Thessalonians; James; Gospel of Thomas	3
1 Corinthians; Philippians; 2 Thessalonians; Jude; Gospel of Mary; Acts of Paul	2
Gospel of Mark; 2 Corinthians; Galatians; Colossians; Philemon; Titus; 2 Peter; 1 John; 2 John; Odes of Solomon; Sibylline Oracles; Protoevangelium of James; Acts of Paul and Thecla; Apocryphon of Moses	1

Dating a manuscript is not an exact science, and although most of the manuscripts counted are from the second or third centuries, some may come from the fourth. The dating of the physical manuscript does not tell us when the original text was written except that this could be no later than the earliest available manuscript. Just because a text is not on this list, it does not mean that it was not in circulation in the second or third centuries. For example, the list does not include the Nag Hammadi codices because they date from slightly after the cut off date of 300. However, we know that most of the texts in that collection date from the second or third centuries.

The table has its limitations, but it does give some useful evidence of what texts that were popular in the second and third centuries. It tells us what the average Christian was reading around 200 without the esoteric bias that is introduced by a collection like Nag Hammadi or the proto-orthodox bias of the approved New Testament cannon. The most popular texts were some of the gospels that were to become part of the New Testament. The Gospel of John was the most popular followed by the Gospel of Matthew and with Luke not far behind. It is no surprise that Matthew was popular, but the position of the last written gospel John as the most popular of all is surprising. But the biggest surprise is that the first written gospel, Mark, only occurs in a single early manuscript. This is probably because Matthew includes practically the whole of Mark. Copying was a time-consuming and expensive business, and early Christians would not have seen the need to keep Mark as a separate document.

The book of Revelation features relatively highly as does Romans. The other letters of Paul are also present with no real distinction between the genuine and fake letters except that 1 and 2 Timothy do not appear in any early surviving manuscripts. Some of the most important letters of Paul appear in only one or two copies. This again illustrates that the number of copies in circulation at this later date is not a good guide to how early the work was written.

We can see that there is a broad correlation between the table and the books of the New Testament. The New Testament largely included the most popular works, and these are indeed among the earliest. But the correlation is less than perfect. The Gospel of Thomas is found in three papyri fragments, which puts it ahead of many of the works that were included in the New Testament. But the most notable exception is the Shepherd of Hermas, found in no less that thirteen early manuscripts, ranking only behind John and Matthew in popularity.

The Shepherd of Hermas is a dull work yet the manuscript count offers proof of its importance in the second and third centuries. And there is a confirming piece of evidence. When Irenaeus was writing Against Heresies at around 180 he quotes from the Shepherd and simply calls it scripture.[29] Irenaeus was no fool, and he had been a Christian since his youth having studied with Polycarp. He is not going to refer to a work as scripture unless he had been taught to think of it as that by his teachers. So the Shepherd must have been already well established and accepted when Irenaeus was young in the middle of the second century. This would place its date of composition to no later than the beginning of the second century which would date it as contemporary to, or perhaps slightly after, the gospels.

And yet despite its popularity and the fact that the Shepherd shows distinct moralising and proto-orthodox tendencies, it was still rejected for inclusion in the canon because it was considered heretical. The Shepherd's problem was that it was written too early. It does not reflect the later orthodoxy because that orthodoxy had yet to emerge. For us, it is an immensely valuable window into Christianity before the gospels.

One of the reasons the Shepherd was rejected was the concept of the "virgin spirits" who unite with men so that the spirit does not leave the man or the man the spirit. This would have been considered dangerously similar to the beliefs of some of the gnostic "heretics" such as Valentinus or Marcus. But in fact, we will see that this is a belief that goes back to the origins of the movement. Something else that goes back to the early movement is the concept behind an allegorical story involving the building of the tower on a rock. The Shepherd of Hermas tells us that the tower and the rock are the same. We will see that the tower is the Magdalene, and the rock is Cephas.

We can divide the sources into "streams". The gospels and Acts form one such stream because they are all closely related. Both Matthew and Luke are heavily based on Mark, and the author of John must have known all three of the other gospels. The letters of Paul form another such stream, as does the Gospel of Thomas. The Book of Revelation must be put into a stream of its own because it is so different from all the other early sources, and the same applies to the Shepherd of Hermas. The letters in the secondary letter tradition are placed together in a stream because they all share a common literary genre that is derived from the letters of Paul. However, there is wide variation between the letters and Hebrews in particular could be placed in its own stream. The Odes of Solomon is an early Christian poetic work that follows the hymn form of the psalms. It is one of the most beautiful works of early Christianity and deserves to be better known. It is placed in the list of sources because of features that show links to early material including the Dead Sea Scrolls. It probably dates from the late first or early second centuries.

The point about the definition of the "streams" is that they all show a large degree of independence from each other. There are clearly some streams that are earlier than others, such as the letters of Paul and most significantly the Gospel of Thomas, and these influence the later streams. But by and large we can envisage the streams as representing distinct traditions that are flowing in parallel to each other. Although there is some interaction between these traditions, it is comparatively minor.

This all changes with the development of the gospel stream. The development of literalism spreads out like a bow wave that steadily engulfs all the other streams. The early spread of literalism can be seen by the fact that the first gospel Mark is rapidly followed by the other gospels and Acts. As the literalism bow wave cascades over the other traditions, it diverts and swamps them. By the middle of the second century, there cannot have been a Christian anywhere who was not very familiar with the gospel account, and this applies to those who were gnostics as well as to the proto-orthodox.

However, the early sources from these other streams that date before the bow wave has hit them are not significantly affected by literalism. The Traditional Secular view of the historical Jesus draws its evidence overwhelmingly from just one stream, the gospel tradition. Why is it that none of the other streams have anything useful to say about Jesus as man?

If there is one stream that we would expect to provide us with information about Jesus and his teachings, it is the letters of Paul. Yet the silence of Paul about Jesus, the man, is notorious. Why is it that Paul tells us almost nothing about Jesus? The traditional explanation is that Paul was only interested in the redeeming spiritual Jesus. But surely Paul should have mentioned the teachings of Jesus or taught his parables. And as Earl Doherty has pointed out, even if Paul were not interested in Jesus the man would not his audience have demanded information about him? Jesus in the letters of Paul is a spiritual being with whom Paul is in contact. But this would hardly have satisfied the churches he was writing to if Jesus had been a man who had lived a few decades previously. They would have wanted to hear about Jesus' views on the many moral and practical issues that Paul deals with in his letters.

The spiritual Jesus is not unique to Paul. It is the spiritual Jesus who speaks the sayings in the Gospel of Thomas. The disciples do not know where this Jesus is but they want to go there: "*Show us the place where you are for it is necessary for us to seek after it*" (Thomas 24).

The other letters in the New Testament also tell us no stories of Jesus. For example, Hebrews is only interested in the theological Jesus as the "high priest". It starts with an explanation, which will seem bizarre to most Christians today, of why Jesus is superior to the angels.

Or suppose we turn to the Book of Revelation, written at about the same time as Luke and Acts and before John. We will find many things in Revelation, such as a woman arrayed with the sun and moon under her feet and a crown of twelve stars, or a beast coming out of the sea with seven heads and ten horns, but one thing we will not find is the historical Jesus. Revelation tells its stories through series of startling images. It is about events at the end of the world, the trials that Christians face, and the eventual victory, a new heaven and a new earth. It tells us only one factual piece of information about Jesus, and that is that he was crucified in a city that can be interpreted as either Rome or Babylon but which is certainly not Jerusalem. So the only fact that Revelation gives that could apply to the historical Jesus is in major contradiction to the gospels!

The Shepherd of Hermas is in some ways similar to Revelation in that both are told in the first person, and both are allegorical. Another similarity is that it also has no stories about Jesus' life. Jesus in the Odes of Solomon is as spiritual as in the Gospel of Thomas or the letters of Paul. In a few places there is overlap between the Odes and the gospels; in Ode 24:1 the dove hovers over the head of the Messiah, an echo of the baptism of Jesus in the gospels, but the relationship of the Dove and Jesus, with Jesus as the "head" of the Dove, is certainly not from the gospels and can be seen as going back to the relationship of Mary and Jesus. Mary also appears in the Odes as the virgin mother of Jesus. In Ode 33 she preaches and draws to her the elect.

This episode does not relate to Mary as she is depicted in the gospels but can be seen as going back to a genuine memory of the female shaman who started the movement.

So to return to the question, why is it that none of the streams other than the Gospel tradition tell us anything useful about Jesus the man? The traditional answer is that this is due to the development of a Christology in which Jesus the man became replaced by Christ, the divine Son of God. But this explanation cannot account for the lack of evidence for Jesus the man in all the streams apart from the gospels. The streams are very diverse and have arisen largely independently of each other. If Jesus had really lived as a man, then we would expect some, at least, of these other streams to reflect his life, even though distorted, in their mirror. But we only find Jesus the man in the gospel stream (remembering that all the gospels are closely related). The explanation that is consistent with the evidence is that Jesus the man is not present in the other streams because he did not exist until created by the Gospel of Mark. Scholars think they are doing history in their "historical" Jesus studies, but they are really studying the literary creations of the gospel tradition.

Thomas as exemplar

We will not treat all the early sources as equal. There is one that can be considered as an "exemplar", encoding and preserving the earliest beliefs of the movement. The Gospel of Thomas is perhaps the most amazing survival from the early Jesus movement, a list of sayings many of which we will see go back to the founder of the movement or beyond. The Gospel of Thomas will give us the clues to unlocking many of the secrets of the Jesus movement, and our reconstruction of the early Jesus movement would not be possible without it.

The dating of Thomas is more controversial than the dating of any other work in early Christian studies. Most scholars divide into two camps. There are those, the traditional, who regard it as "gnostic" and assign it a comparatively late date, typically in the mid second century. At the extreme in this camp are those who think Thomas is dependent on Tatian's harmony of the four gospels, the Diatessaron, and who date it as late as 200[30] even though this date conflicts with the physical evidence of the papyri fragments of Thomas. In the other more radical camp are scholars who believe the gospel to be early, that is first-century, and that some at least of the sayings might go back to the time of Jesus. The dichotomy is driven by the fact that there are links between Thomas and all four of the gospels. This could mean either that all the gospel writers knew Thomas or that the author of Thomas knew all the other four gospels and that it was written after them. Hence the tendency for either a very early, or a comparatively late date.

The best-known advocate for an early Thomas is Stevan Davies, whose book *The Gospel of Thomas and Christian Wisdom* revolutionised the academic study of Thomas.[31] Up to that point, Thomas had been seen as "gnostic" and therefore dated by scholars to no earlier than the second century. Davies pointed out that this characterisation of Thomas as gnostic was incorrect, as it did not share the developed gnostic features of other works in the Nag Hammadi corpus. Instead, he saw Thomas as being influenced by the early Jewish Wisdom tradition. In his two-part paper *Mark's use of the Gospel of Thomas* he demonstrates that the author of Mark used Thomas as a source, most significantly by showing how Mark 9:43 to 10:16 is dependent on Thomas 22.[32] Remarkably, this discovery seems to have been either ignored or marginalised by most other scholars. In conclusion, Davies dates the gospel to 50-70.[33]

Another proponent of a first-century dating is Stephen Patterson who argues that Thomas was not dependent on the Synoptics and suggests a date of 70-80 for the gospel.[34] Elaine Pagels, the scholar and best-selling author, argues in her book *Beyond Belief* that the Gospel of John was written in opposition to the Gospel of Thomas.[35] She follows George Riley in believing that the character of Doubting Thomas in the Gospel of John was intended to discredit the early Christians who looked to the Gospel of Thomas.[36] Her book brings out beautifully the many similarities in the way the concept of light is presented in Thomas and John, as well as the crucial difference that in Thomas the light is within the disciple, and in John the light is Jesus.

Some scholars take the view that the gospel we have today developed in stages. Probably the most notable proponent of this theory is April De-Conick. She dates an original kernel of sayings to the earliest years of the movement but believes that additional material was added to this kernel through a series of accretions of new sayings and elaborations of existing sayings.[37] The problem with this layer idea is that it is basically an attempt to filter out noise and to get to the original signal, in this case the kernel sayings. But any filter is, as we have seen, inevitably subjective and based on preconceptions. The effect of the filter is to allow through any evidence that confirms the starting preconceptions and to reject anything that goes against them. So such a filter will inevitably serve to reinforce preconceptions. This is the opposite of what we should be doing. The most valuable pieces of evidence are exactly those things that challenge our preconceptions and force us to abandon or modify them. Applying a filter will cause us to reject such challenging evidence as noise.

Looking at the criteria that DeConick applies we can see that they are subjective. Essentially she identifies the characteristics of what she sees as several layers of development and then applies those criteria to the sayings to sort them into groups that then confirm those layers. To give one example to illustrate her method, she allocates saying 43 as an accretion arising in the years 60-100 because Jesus condemns the Jews in this saying: "*Rather you are like the Jews for they love the tree but hate its fruit or they love the fruit but hate the tree.*" She assigns this to a time when the church was becoming Gentile and separating itself from its Jewish roots.[38] In doing this, she is following the academic consensus that the anti-Jewish elements that are such a feature of the early Christian writings could not go back to Jesus. If there is one theme that runs though modern scholarship on the subject, it is the Jewishness of Jesus.

However, by applying a filter, such as that any anti-Jewish saying must be Gentile in origin, we are simply confirming our preconceptions. The principle of redundancy tells us that we should instead leave all the pieces of the puzzle on the table until we have attempted to fit them together into a coherent pattern. We can then identify the redundant elements which repeat in different forms and which are the confirmation that the fit is correct.

In this book, we will take a very different approach towards Thomas. We will assume that it is largely original material going back to the days of the founder. Scholars working in the traditional historical Jesus school will tend to see Thomas as secondary because it is a spiritual gospel, and they think the spiritual Jesus evolved as a secondary development. However, under the shaman paradigm Jesus is spiritual in the beginning and only becomes literal in the gospels; it is the gospels that are secondary and which have developed later. So the links between Thomas and the gospels would be explained by the gospels developing their literalistic stories based in part on the spiritual sayings in Thomas. Which means that Thomas would predate all the gospels by a considerable margin. There would have been some changes and perhaps additions in the long centuries in which Thomas was copied and translated but such editing is probably far less extensive than generally believed.

An original Thomas gospel goes hand in glove with the shaman paradigm. The appreciation of the role of Thomas has been long held back by attempting to fit it in with the historical Jesus where it does not belong. Freed from this constraint, we can recognise Thomas for what it is, a depository of the early sayings of the movement that will give us an "exemplar" that is relatively uncontaminated by literalism. We will make the assumption that it is early, but the proof will be in the results. We will see that the gospels have used Thomas and how passage after passage in the gospels can be traced back to Thomas.

So we will take as our starting point these twin pillars of (i) the shaman paradigm and (ii) the Gospel of Thomas. However our sources will be much wider than Thomas and what we will be searching for is redundancy, the hidden river of meaning that flows through all the early writings. Redundancy is most impressive when it takes the form of multiple sources that look at first sight to be startlingly different but which turn out to be based on the same underlying pattern because this indicates that the pattern goes back long before the sources in which it is expressed.

The Martyrdom Source and the Deep Source

Up to now the discussion of redundancy has been conceptual. To illustrate what is meant we will turn to some impressive examples of redundancy. The first is the Martyrdom Source (considered later in this volume) and the other the Deep Source (considered more fully in the second volume).

The Martyrdom Source tells the story of the death of the shaman in Rome. It is reconstructed from a number of different "texts" being passages contained in works some of which are inside and some outside of the New Testament. These texts include passages in Revelation, Acts, the Apocalypse of Elijah, the Acts of Philip, and the Questions of Bartholomew. There are also links to the passion account in Mark and Matthew. The Martyrdom Source texts show a number of themes, such as the death and resurrection of one or two "witnesses", the appearance of a dragon/serpent who represents Satan, and the throwing down of Satan from heaven.

Normally, when scholars detect a link between texts, the texts are obviously related to each other, but in this case, they are very different and it is this difference that is key to the method. If the texts were minor variations on a story, then they could have been copied from each other (as took place with the stories in Matthew, Luke, and John) or from another closely related source. But if they are completely different stories then any link between them must go back to before these stories were created, to before the literalisation process. This means that the source is a window into the world before the gospels.

However, if the texts are so different, how can we be sure that the source is real? The number and the quality of the themes present in the texts is the evidence that they derive from one ultimate source. For the Martyrdom Source, we can identify between nine and eleven texts and ten different themes. The number of themes that occur in most of these texts is far above a random level.

The original source, the signal, has been transmitted through several different channels, written or oral, and each of these channels has added noise, giving rise to multiple variations. These variations have then been incorporated into the narratives in which we find them. To recover our source, we must distinguish the signal from the noise, both the noise added in transmission and the greater noise added by turning the source into a narrative story. The more texts we have, the better we can eliminate the noise to recover the signal. If we have only one text, then such a recovery is impossible. Fortunately, the more important a source was, the more variations we can expect to find. This is because the sources which were most important to the movement had a high probability of transmission, so we would expect to have multiple versions surviving.

The death of the shaman would have been very important to the movement, so it is no surprise to find the Martyrdom Source existing in several different texts. The themes allow us to attempt a reconstruction of the source. We will see that the Martyrdom Source records a conflict between the shaman and Nero in Rome. The conflict has cosmic significance because the shaman is believed to be the avatar of Christ and Nero the avatar of the devil, represented as a dragon. Although it appears that the shaman has been killed and defeated by the dragon, she has really been taken to a place of refuge from where she will return at the appointed time. This myth of the return of the shaman was necessary to explain how it was possible that Mary could be killed by Nero before the end times.

No source exists in isolation. The genuine beliefs, myths and stories of the Jesus movement form an interlocking whole. If the Martyrdom Source is genuine, it should tie in with other sources, and it does. We find other hints about the role of Nero in destroying "the temple". It is also significant that the early Christians believed that Nero was the anti-Christ, for the number of the beast in Revelation, 666, indicates his name.

The Martyrdom source illuminates a number of mysteries. It tells us why Revelation casts Nero in the role of the beast, the anti-Christ, and not

Tiberius, Emperor at the time of the supposed crucifixion of Jesus, or Pilate who supposedly ordered that crucifixion. It tells us why Revelation says that Christ was crucified in a place that must be Rome and not Jerusalem. And it tells us why Nero accused the Christians of starting the fire of Rome; some Christians at the time claimed that the shaman had destroyed Rome by bringing down fire from heaven.

The Martyrdom Source shows all the features we would expect from applying the principle of redundancy to recover the source signal from the added noise:

The source is identified from multiple passages.

The passages are very different from each other.

The source is confirmed by other evidence.

The source gives us surprising insights that clarify other problems/evidence.

The second example, the Deep Source is perhaps even more important than the Martyrdom Source. It is called the Deep Source because it goes back to the very origins of the movement, to a time when John the Baptist was still alive. The Deep Source tells of the coming of the "visitor from heaven" to the shaman. It is inferred from several apparently unrelated episodes in the gospels:

The baptism of Jesus and stay at Capernaum in Mark 1:1-31

Additions made to the baptism story in Matthew 3-4

The entry into Jerusalem and expulsion of the money changers from the temple in Mark 11:1-33

The baptism of Jesus, the wedding at Canna and expulsion of the money changers from the temple in John 1:19-2:18

The raising of Lazarus in John 10:23-11:57

The entry into Jerusalem in John 12:1-19

The story of the Samaritan woman in John 3:23-4:43

Under any conventional view, there would be no link between these passages. As we explore the early Jesus movement of the shaman, we will uncover the metaphorical code they used to express their spiritual beliefs. Using this code we can see that all the above passages represent part of the sequence of the coming of Jesus to the shaman:

The shaman witnesses/shares in the death of Jesus

The shaman mourns the death of Jesus

The shaman anoints Jesus

The shaman witnesses/shares in the resurrection

The substance of Jesus enters into the shaman

The Jewish Law comes to an end, and the old temple is replaced by the new temple (the shaman)

The shaman (the temple) is transformed and purified by the expulsion of the demons

The shaman enters into the divine marriage with Jesus

The shaman tells others and is not believed

Through the shaman, the others are reborn and experience Jesus themselves

The others believe and become the shaman's followers

We find evidence for this sequence in both the resurrection accounts and the Deep Source, for the two are closely linked. They exhibit mutual redundancy and go back to the earliest level of tradition in the movement. The sequence was of vital importance to the early movement, so the probability of transmission was high. Because of this high transmission, the tradition is successfully communicated through multiple channels giving rise to multiple versions. And because the sequence originated very early, when most transmission was oral, these versions exhibit wide divergence. The gospel writers have then literalised the different versions as quite distinct episodes in the fictional history of Jesus.

Can we be sure that the Deep Source existed? All the Deep Source passages are expressions of the sequence of Jesus coming to the shaman, but this link will be rejected by anyone who believes that Jesus was a historical person. However, in this case, we can offer further proof. There were details included in the Deep Source which act as "markers". These markers have frequently survived the process of transmission and literalisation and have been incorporated into the gospel passages. The existence of these markers demonstrates that the passages, even though very different, have all come from the same ultimate source.

One such marker is the name "Bethany" which must have been associated with the beginning of the Deep Source. The name has survived transmission, and we find that several of the passages start at a place called Bethany. This is not just a matter of geography since Bethany appears to move around - it occurs in different locations in different stories! Bethany was either a real place, the home of the shaman before the appearance of

Jesus, or a metaphor ("the house of misery") for the shaman's spiritual state at this time.

Another marker is that some of the sequences have an implicit reference or link to the dream of Jacob. In this dream, Jacob, lying asleep in the wilderness, sees the angels ascending to and descending from heaven. The story showed the crossing of spiritual forces from heaven to earth so we can understand why it should have been associated with the spiritual coming of Jesus to the shaman.

A third marker is a reference to Capernaum. (The significance of Capernaum to the Jesus movement will be explored in the second volume.) Capernaum occurs in multiple Deep Source passages, and there are two separate episodes where a sick person is cured of a fever in Capernaum.

The most significant marker of all concerns John the Baptist. All of the sequences are associated with an unfavourable comparison between John and Jesus. In all but one case this unfavourable comparison is the same; the water baptism of John is inferior to the heavenly baptism of Jesus. We shall see that the Jesus movement was in a highly competitive rivalry with the movement of John in the beginning. The Jesus movement at this time depreciated the water baptism of John by comparing it unfavourably to the spiritual baptism offered by the shaman. This deprecation of water baptism has found its way into the Gospel of Thomas where saying 89 rejects those who wash the outside of the cup rather than cleansing the inside. (In this saying, the cup represents the disciple and the cup maker is God. In the gospels, the saying has been literalised as the Jews cleaning their cups!) This rivalry with John ceased on his death which enables us to date the Deep Source to between AD 26-35, some forty years before the gospels were written.

There is one other marker, and it links back to the tree of the Jews in Thomas 43. In the Deep Source passages, a tree features three times. It is a fig tree blasted by Jesus because it yields no fruit, a fig tree under which Nathaniel sits until called away by Jesus, and a tree with no fruit in Matthew. This tree is the tree of the Jews. It represents the Law, which is rejected and will be destroyed because it does not yield the fruit of life, and this rejection is in the Deep Source. This shows that Thomas 43 does, in fact, go back to the very start of the movement. The scholars are wrong in thinking that the early Jesus movement had not rejected Judaism - they were heretics from the beginning.

It is simply impossible that so many features shared between the Deep Source passages should have arisen by chance. The Deep Source existed and takes us back to the very origins of the movement. The concept of redundancy has allowed us to penetrate the literalisation layer to see what came before. But it does more than that. The sequences in the New Testament that have arisen from the Deep Source are key passages. If all of these have come about through a misunderstanding of an original spiritual source, then the whole concept of the literal Jesus as man collapses. The Deep Source is the proof that the Secular traditional view of the scholars is incorrect.

High or low redundancy in the gospels?

We can only recover the original signal if there is redundancy in our materials. So how much redundancy is present in the gospels and other early sources? Traditional scholars would not put the question in these terms, but if they did, their answer would have to be low or zero redundancy. It is remarkable how few examples there appear to be of duplicated stories in the gospels; the story of the feeding of the multitude occurs in two versions in Mark, but there is little else. Low redundancy implies that the original stories about Jesus have been sparsely sampled; if we only have a small selection of the original material, then duplicates are less likely.

This state of affairs is suspicious because it implies a low probability of any particular story surviving to the time of the gospel writers. Did Jesus' early followers not treasure stories about him? There were certainly multiple channels in existence, many churches both scattered around the near east and further afield, as far as Rome itself. So why was there not a high probability of transmission for important stories, and hence multiple versions coming down to the gospel writers through multiple channels? The suspicious tidiness of the gospels implies that they are literary creations. We must drill back to before the literalisation level to find redundancy. Hence, the many passages derived from the Martyrdom Source and the Deep Source.

This book is based on the thesis that there is massive redundancy in the four gospels plus Thomas and the other early Christian literature. Uniquely in the ancient world, we have a vast amount of material from the early centuries of the Jesus movement. From the start Christians communicated their teachings and stories to each other, and almost from the start, they wrote then down and copied them; it seems that anything about Jesus was precious. Because of the efficiency of transmission we have an abundance of riches. We do not need to dig up some long lost codex to uncover the truth behind the Jesus movement. All the information we need is right in front of us, staring us in the face. We just have to be able to distinguish signal from noise, but because of high redundancy, the signal can be recovered.

In contrast historical Jesus scholars live in a state of poverty, a world of low redundancy and sparse sampling. In such a world recovery of the truth is impossible because there is no way to distinguish signal from noise. We should not be surprised that a deep pessimism lurks beneath the surface of the "quests" for the historical Jesus. Periodically there is a burst of optimism about a new approach, but this soon dribbles away, leading to the inevitable conclusion that the historical Jesus is forever unknowable.

There is one case in which the apparent lack redundancy is particularly significant, and that is between the Gospel of Mark and the so-called "Q" material in Matthew and Luke. Most scholars believe that Q and Mark originated independently of each other. Both are sizeable collections of sayings and stories about Jesus. If they both independently drew on early material then, even with sparse sampling, there should be a significant overlap between the two. And yet Q and Mark show basically no overlap. This is a clear sign that Q is not independent of Mark, but was complied by someone who intended to supplement Mark. So did Q ever exist independently of the Gospel of Matthew?

Key points

1. The recovery of Christian origins is a matter of signal and noise. The signal is what happened at the start of the movement and what the founders of the movement taught. These events and beliefs were transmitted, sometimes orally, sometimes in writing, to the time of the authors of the surviving texts such as the gospels. These authors added additional noise by "literalising" their sources into stories about Jesus as a man.

2. We can recover the signal if the surviving texts exhibit redundancy. Such redundancy comes from multiple passages that have come from the same early source or which reflect the same early belief.

3. It is a mistake to attempt to filter out the noise from the signal, as any filter will simply confirm our preconceptions. All the pieces need to be left on the table while we attempt to fit together the puzzle.

4. Noise increases exponentially with time, so it is the earliest sources that are most useful for our reconstruction. However, sometimes a later source can draw upon or have embedded within it an early source.

5. Most of the early sources are in the New Testament, but there are exceptions, the most significant of which are the Gospel of Thomas, the Shepherd of Hermas and the Odes of Solomon.

6. We can divide the sources into "streams". The gospels form one such stream because the later gospels (Matthew, Luke, and John) all draw upon the earlier gospels, starting with Mark. As the gospels increase in influence, they swamp all the other streams. They become the accepted view of the origins of Christianity even among those, such as the gnostics, who do not share their view of Jesus.

7. The idea that Jesus was a man is only found in the gospel stream. The early streams that arose in parallel to the gospels do not show knowledge of the gospel Jesus. These streams include the Gospel of Thomas, the letters of Paul, Revelation, the Shepherd of Hermas, the Odes of Solomon, and the other New Testament letters such as Hebrews.

8. The Gospel of Thomas will be regarded as an "exemplar" representing the earliest sayings of the movement. The proof that Thomas is indeed early will emerge from the results.

9. Two examples of the application of redundancy to the recovery of the signal are the Martyrdom Source and the Deep Source. Both are found from multiple similarities in a number of passages that appear, at first glance, to be very different from each other.

10. The Martyrdom Source tells of the death of the shaman in Rome on the orders of Nero. It explains why early Christians thought of Nero as the anti-Christ and why Nero believed that the Christians had caused the fire of Rome. It reveals a myth that the shaman was not truly dead but would return to life before the end times.

11. The Deep Source goes back to the very beginnings of the movement and reflects the sequence of the coming of Jesus to the shaman. The Deep Source is closely related to the resurrection accounts.

Chapter 7
Luke and Q

We are using Thomas as an exemplar, but we also have to consider Q as another potential exemplar. If Q existed as a separate text then it then it may be very early. But if Q did not exist, the Q material would have been composed as part of Matthew and so would date from around 80.

The existence or otherwise of Q is bound up with the relationship between Luke and Matthew. If the author of Luke knew the Gospel of Matthew, then there is no need to hypothesise another document Q. This leads to another question; who wrote Luke and Acts?

Did Q exist?

Under the two-source theory, the author of Luke was unaware of the Gospel of Matthew. He or she composed the gospel from Mark and Q, just as the author of Matthew did for his gospel. A flaw in the theory is immediately apparent; is it really likely that two authors should think of this rather odd method of construction completely independently of each other? It is much more probable that the author of Luke has simply used the gospels of Mark and Matthew. The reason many scholars do not believe that the author of Luke copied Matthew is that there are substantial differences between the two gospels including the order in which the Q material is used. Had the author of Luke copied Matthew directly we might expect the gospels to have resembled each other more closely.

This essentially is the mystery of the Gospel of Luke; how can it share so much material with Matthew and yet be so different? The conventional answer to the mystery is that the gospels were written independently, and both used the hypothetical source Q. What scholars term as Q is essentially nothing more than the joint material shared between Luke and Matthew that has not come from Mark. No copy of Q has ever been found, so it has to be reconstructed from Matthew and Luke.

The source Q has long been a foundation stone of New Testament scholarship but recently its very existence has been questioned, most significantly in *The case against Q* by Mark Goodacre.[39] There is, in fact, a complete lack of any direct evidence for Q. Not only does no copy of Q exist but no early author refers to it or quotes from it. It is as if Q disappeared from the face of the earth after being copied by the authors of Luke and Matthew.

The case for Q was boosted by the discovery of the Gospel of Thomas. The reconstructed Q was essentially a sayings gospel with some additional material and there was controversy over whether such a sayings gospel could have ever existed as all the other examples of gospels known at that time were narrative in structure. So the discovery of another sayings gospel seemed to vindicate Q.

However, if we consider more deeply the differences between Thomas and Q, then the case for Q is actually undermined by Thomas. First the evidence for Thomas is exactly what we would expect to have for Q. Thomas has been found in both a complete Coptic text and in multiple Greek papyrus fragments. It is both referred to and quoted in early writings. If this quantity of evidence for Thomas exists then why do we not have anything at all for Q? Even if the usage of Q declined after the gospels were written would a text that was so widespread that it was a foundation for both the gospels of Matthew and Luke really have left no trace?

Thomas undermines the potential existence of Q in a more fundamental way because it provides an example of how a real sayings gospel was used. What emerges is that the early authors were utterly confused as to what the Thomas sayings really meant. We get multiple and varied interpretations that clearly do not reflect the original meaning.

A good example is Thomas 22, an enigmatic saying in which Jesus compares little babies at the breast to those who enter the kingdom. When the disciples ask Jesus if they must then be like children to enter the kingdom he gives them an enigmatic answer:

[...] Jesus said to them: "When you make the two one, and when you make the inside as the outside, and the outside as the inside, and the upper side as the lower side; and when you make the male and the female into a single one, that the male be not male nor the female female; when you make eyes in the place of an eye, and a

hand in place of a hand, and a foot in place of a foot, an image in place of an image, then you will enter into [the kingdom]." (Thomas 22)

It is not surprising that early Christians struggled to understand this. But what is interesting is that we have at least three early uses of this saying and all of them are different:

1. In 2 Clement 12 the making of male and female into one so that the male is not male, and the female not female is interpreted as an exhortation to chastity.

2. In the Acts of Peter and the Acts of Philip, the saying has been read as a formula for reversing left and right and turning upside down. This has given rise to the story of the upside down crucifixion of Peter and Philip.

3. In the Gospel of Mark, the Thomas saying is the source for a whole narrative section from Mark 9:43 to 10:16. The first element involves Jesus giving the instruction to cut off a hand, foot or eye rather than sin so that the disciple may enter the kingdom rather than be cast into Gehenna and the fire. Next Jesus is questioned about divorce and in his reply he forbids divorce because a man and his wife should not be two but one flesh. After this, some people bring children to see him and his disciples try and stop them. But he tells the disciples to let the children approach and that they must enter the kingdom like a little child. All these elements come from the Thomas saying but have been drastically interpreted for the author of Mark's literalistic account.

The three different authors have completely different understandings of Thomas 22 and have also used the saying in different ways. In 2 Clement the saying is quoted and given a straightforward interpretation; in the Acts of Peter and the Acts of Philip the saying is quoted and used as the basis for a story; in Mark the saying is not quoted but has been developed into a series of teachings given by Jesus, which have been placed in a fictitious setting. Later we will be asking what the saying really means but what is important for now is the range of interpretations. The use of Thomas 22 is an example of redundancy, the generation of markedly different forms that go back to a single original. Each interpretation adds considerable noise and yet preserves aspects of the original. And this turns out to be entirely typical of the way in which early authors used Thomas. The lack of understanding gave wide latitude to the meanings and narratives that could be developed in the literalisation.

Yet when we turn to the supposed sayings gospel Q we find no such latitude. Although there are variations in the detail of the Q material between Matthew and Luke, the meaning of the sayings is always a constant between the two gospels. There is very little ambiguity and certainly not the huge variation we find with those authors who used Thomas 22. This straightforward clarity has been seen by some to commend the Q material in Matthew and Luke as compared to the "gnostic" Thomas. But it is really a sign that all is not as it should be. Confusion is inevitable if the gospel writers are using a real saying that has been transmitted in the wild without the addition of cosy interpretations and explanations. The absence of variation between the meanings of the sayings given in Luke and Matthew can only have arisen if the author of Luke has taken the sayings not from a genuine sayings gospel but directly from Matthew. The author of Matthew always supplies a context for the sayings and where necessary adds explanation so that his reader is in no doubt of their meaning.

We know that the early members of the movement did find the sayings obscure because we are told in the Gospel of Mark that only those who were in the kingdom could understand them:

"To you the mystery has been given of the kingdom of God. But to those who are outside everything is done in parables." (Mark 4:11)

We are faced then with a contradiction; in the gospels the meaning of the sayings is so plain that anyone can understand them. This clarity is a feature of the literalisation process where the parables were given a simpler and more superficial meaning. The original sayings are obscure because they are intended to engage a person's intuition and lead them towards the kingdom.

In conclusion, the existence of the real sayings gospel, Thomas, does not support the existence of Q. The close agreement between the meaning of the sayings in Matthew and Luke is evidence that the author of Luke has copied the sayings from a post-literalisation source, namely the Gospel of Matthew. Is there other evidence supporting the idea that Luke copied Matthew? Yes! At the very beginning of the gospel, we are virtually told that this was the case. The gospel starts with a preamble:

Insomuch as many have undertaken to draw up an account of those things which have been accomplished among us, even as they delivered them to us who

*from the beginning were eyewitnesses and servants of the word, it seemed good to
me also, having been acquainted with all things from the very first, to write to you
carefully and in order, most excellent Theophilus, that you might know the certainty of those things, wherein you have been instructed. (Luke 1:1-4)*

The introduction is addressed to one Theophilus who is called "most excellent" implying that he is of high rank. The idea of addressing a work to a
patron is an aspect of Roman aristocratic society. It shows that the author
of Luke was part of the Roman establishment and moved in aristocratic
circles. This is a world away from the Palestine from whence the Jesus
movement emerged.

The author tells Theophilus that many similar accounts are already in
existence. These many accounts have been derived from what has been
handed down by eyewitnesses and servants of the word. So we are to envisage gospels that have been written from earlier source material, either
written or oral, which the author of Luke believes to have been derived
ultimately from eyewitness accounts. However, under the two-source hypothesis, the author of Luke is only supposed to have Mark and Q as major
sources. And Q seems to be what the author of Luke would regard as an
eyewitness account rather than a narrative gospel. So what then are the
many gospels? The first gospel we know about other than Mark is Matthew. The Gospel of Matthew was influential from the start and rapidly
overtook Mark in popularity. It was transmitted widely and gave rise to
derivative works such as the Gospel of the Hebrews. The author of Luke is
writing at a time when there are many other gospels in existence so he or
she must be writing sometime after the Gospel of Matthew was written.
Given the author's wide access to sources, it seems highly unlikely that
they should be unfamiliar with the most popular gospel of all, that of Matthew. It is hard to imagine what "many gospels" could mean if they did not
include Matthew.

Why then should the Gospel of Luke be so different from Matthew?
There is a clue in the introduction to Luke. Although many gospels have
been written, yet those gospels are not good enough. The author of Luke is
"acquainted with all things from the very first" meaning not that they, the author, are an eyewitness but that they have acquired knowledge going back
to the beginning. The Gospel of Luke then has been written to offer a superior version of events to the other gospels that are extant, including the
Gospel of Matthew. And this gives us a clue as to the real reason for the
differences with Matthew. The author of Luke strongly disagrees with Matthew and wishes to supplant this gospel – but due to the lack of alternative

material they have no option but to use it as a source. Most likely this disapproval is because Matthew is a very Jewish gospel and was taken up by Jewish Christian groups that were antithetical to the Gentile and aristocratic Roman environment in which Luke was written. As the Gospel of Luke is intended to offer a superior account of events, it cannot just copy Matthew. So the author of Luke has deliberately changed the material in Matthew in a number of places so as to give what is supposedly a more accurate version. In truth, the author of Luke is a fantasist whose account bears very little relation to reality.

The evidence for Luke deliberately changing Matthew lies in the "same but different" pattern that runs through the gospel. The structure and contents of Luke are heavily influenced by Matthew and yet the detail of the content is often completely different. This is illustrated by the structural features which Luke shares with Matthew:

Matthew is based on Mark and copies that gospel closely.
Luke is based on Mark and copies that gospel closely.

Matthew adds to Mark the additional Q material.
Luke adds to Mark the additional Q material.

Matthew includes a genealogy of Jesus.
Luke includes a genealogy of Jesus, but it is different from Matthew's genealogy.

Matthew includes a nativity account.
Luke includes a nativity account although the events are different from Matthew.

These are not minor details but the elements that determine the structure of the two gospels. Such similarities are extremely unlikely to arise by chance. The only other gospel in the New Testament that was written after Mark, the Gospel of John, does not share a single one of these features. Nor is there any early gospel outside of the New Testament that shows anything like this level of similarity.

If we were to assign a probability to each of these features arising independently, it might be of the order of 1 in 10. Just deciding to base a gospel closely on Mark is unlikely to occur to two different authors independently. This is compounded by the fact that (according to the two-source hypothesis) both have decided to add to this gospel the same Q material. And then is it really likely that they would both independently decide to add a genealogy and a nativity story?

To calculate the probability of all four features arising together by chance we need to multiply the individual probabilities to give an overall probability of 10,000 to 1 against. The calculation is naive and may be an order of magnitude or two out, but it serves to illustrate just how unlikely it is that the gospels of Matthew and Luke have emerged independently of each other. There are two ways to explain the similarities:

1.   Luke has been influenced by Matthew.
2.   Both Luke and Matthew have been influenced by a third gospel (other than Mark) which is now lost.

We can rule out the second possibility because there is no evidence that such a gospel existed. If it did, it would have had to include both a genealogy and a nativity, and we would still have to explain why these are so different in Matthew and Luke if both authors copied the same source. So we can conclude that the data is best explained if the author of Luke has been greatly influenced by Matthew but has deliberately changed some details. This creates a "same but different" pattern that has perplexed scholars.

As an example, the Gospel of Luke follows the same basic structure of Matthew's nativity story but goes out of the way to change the details. Matthew has the story of the Magi following the star and Herod's slaughter of the innocents. Instead of the Magi, the Gospel of Luke has humble shepherds watching their flocks by night when a great angel of the Lord appears to them. He gives them good tidings of great joy about the newborn baby in the city of David who is the Christ. The shepherds decide to go and see the baby for themselves. In nativity plays the Magi (the so-called wise men) and the shepherds are on the stage paying homage to the baby in the manger at the same time, although they come from two different stories. This makes sense in the nativity plays because there is an innate similarity in the stories, another illustration of the "same but different" pattern. The Magi see the star as a sign of the newborn king of the Jews and search for him to give him gifts and worship. The shepherds are told about the newborn king by an angel and are also given a sign: *"And this shall be a sign to you; you shall find the babe wrapped in swaddling clothes, lying in a manger"* (*Luke 2:12*). Both Magi and shepherds then find the baby and pay homage. The stories are even closer than might appear to the modern mind because to the Jews of the time both stars and angels were "the host of heaven" and two aspects of the same thing. The author of Luke has followed the basic pattern set out by the author of Matthew but changes the details of the story considerably. We shall see later that both the authors of Matthew and Luke must have used the same ultimate source for the nativity and that the author of Luke has extracted different elements to make the story different from the version in Matthew.

The "same but different" pattern can be seen in another small but telling feature. To traditional commentators, one of the glories of the Gospel of Matthew is the Sermon on the Mount. The fact that this is not found in Luke is seen as strong evidence that Luke does not copy Matthew. But if we look closely at Luke the Sermon on the Mount is in fact there also. In Matthew the sermon begins with crowds following Jesus who goes up a mountain:

And his fame went throughout all Syria: and they brought to him all sick people that were taken with various diseases and torments, those who were possessed by demons, those epileptic, and those paralytic; and he healed them. And there followed him great multitudes of people from Galilee and Decapolis, and Jerusalem, and Judea, and from beyond the Jordan. And seeing the crowds, he went up into a mountain and when he had sat down his disciples came to him. And he opened his mouth, and taught them, saying, "Blessed are the poor in spirit: for theirs is the kingdom of heaven ..." (Matthew 4:24-5:3)

In Luke, Jesus goes up a mountain to appoint his disciples, as in Mark and then comes down to give the sermon:

And he came down with them and stood in the plain. A large crowd of his disciples, and a great multitude of people from all Judaea, and Jerusalem, and from the sea coast of Tyre and Sidon, who came to hear him, and to be healed of their diseases. Those who were troubled with unclean spirits were healed. And the whole multitude sought to touch him, because power was going out of him and healing them all. And lifting his gaze upon his disciples, he said, "Blessed are the poor, for yours is the kingdom of God ..." (Luke 6:17-20)

The author of Luke has followed Matthew in inserting the beatitudes at this point but has made Jesus give the sermon on a plain not on a mountain! We see the "same but different" pattern here with the author of Luke influenced by Matthew but changing the details. As ever, the author of Luke is trying to improve upon the earlier gospel. In Matthew, Jesus is being followed by a great multitude of people and goes up the mountain not to give a sermon to them, but to escape from them. That he is addressing his disciples only is clear by phrases such as *"You are the salt of the earth"* *(Matthew 5:13)* meaning that his audience are a select few and not the multitude. The author of Luke spots the flaw in this and reorganises things so that Jesus can give his speech to the crowd as well as the disciples. Because a multitude would not fit on a mountain, he or she has Jesus come down to the plain where the crowd must be gathered so that they too can listen to his sermon.

Another example of "same but different" is in the two completely different genealogies that the gospels of Matthew and Luke give for Jesus. The author of Luke is attempting to give an improved version over Matthew. Whereas Matthew starts the genealogy at Abraham, Luke takes it all the way back to Adam, the Son of God. The genealogy in Luke is also more "realistic" in that it has more names to cover long periods of time than does Matthew, where the number of generations is implausibly small. The author of Luke, however, has made a mistake in trying to improve upon that which he or she did not understand. The genealogy in Matthew has been derived from an earlier source that applied a structure of seventy generations, organised in "weeks", to the history of the world. This apocalyptic calendar was of great importance to those from whom the Jesus movement emerged. The genealogy in Luke violates this basic structure revealing that it is a later invention made up by the author of Luke and not something that went back to the early movement.

The "same but different" pattern eliminates the need for Q. The author of Luke must have known the Gospel of Matthew well, and there is no need to posit a third source for which there exists no evidence. The Q material is simply the additions to Mark made in Matthew, which have been picked up also by the author of Luke.

The female author of Luke and Acts

Who did write Luke and Acts? We can be sure of one thing, that it was not Luke the companion of Paul who is the true author of Luke. Quite simply the gospel is too late and too dependent upon other sources to have been written by someone as close to the action as Luke. The idea that it was written by Luke was probably suggested by the "we" passages in Acts that make it look as if the work were written by a companion of Paul.

Neither Acts nor Luke tells us the name of the author, the only clue being the name Theophilus to whom both works are dedicated, but this is almost certainly a pseudonym. To trace the real author we need to look at certain internal clues. One thing that is clear on any sensitive reading of the two works is that the author was a woman. By which we mean that the person overseeing the production of the work was female, although it is likely that she had considerable scribal assistance. Quite simply the work continually takes the female viewpoint. For example, the story of the nativity in Matthew is told completely from the male perspective of Joseph but in Luke it is told almost completely from the female perspective of Mary. There are other female orientated episodes, such as the meeting between Mary and Elisabeth at the beginning of the gospel, or the story of Martha and Mary. And then there is the habit that the author of Acts habitually falls into of giving more prominence to the female than the male, so very different to other ancient works in which the female fades to the point of invisibility. Of course, the gospel is presented as if written by a man but this is one with the framing of the gospel which mimics a learned Roman work.

Beyond the female authorship we will see that Luke and Acts was written by a member of the Roman establishment who hero worshiped Paul and who identified with Herod Agrippa II to the extent of structuring her work around him. Most significantly she knew Josephus personally. She was considerably influenced by his Jewish War and had advance prepublication knowledge of his longer work, Jewish Antiquities. She was even able to persuade him to include within Jewish Antiquities a brief section about Jesus that she had written, the so-called Testimonium Flavianum. The Testimonium has clear links to Luke and Acts which is evidence for a common origin. And yet there is also evidence that it really was original to Josephus and not a later interpolation.

As well as excellent access to Jewish sources the author had access to detailed information on the Roman governance structure that suggests she was able to call on the services of bureaucrats working within the structure. And finally she had superb access to Christian sources, although she takes appalling liberties with them. Indeed, she must have been highly influential among Christians to get her imaginative productions accepted as history. We are getting a picture of a woman who was very well connected and influential; a Roman matron, the leader of a house church, and probably the patron and protector of the church in a significant city. The link with Herod Agrippa and Josephus, who both made their home in Rome after the Jewish War, indicates that this city was none other than Rome. In the second volume we will consider the evidence in more detail and suggest that Luke and Acts were produced in the household of one of the most power-

ful women in the Roman Empire, and one moreover who is known to have
been a Christian.

Key points

1. Although the existence of the hypothetical sayings gospel "Q" has
been a foundation stone of the historical Jesus studies, this has recently
been questioned. Instead of the authors of Matthew and Luke both using
Q, the joint material in both gospels could be explained by Luke copying
Matthew.

2. The discovery of the Gospel of Thomas superficially boosted the case
for the sayings gospel Q. However, when we look at how early Christian
authors used Thomas we see a great deal of confusion. They did not understand the sayings and each interpreted them in their own way. We find no
such confusion between the so-called "Q" sayings in Matthew and Luke.
This is evidence that the author of Luke has taken these sayings from the
Gospel of Matthew where the meanings are explained.

3. The dedication of Luke to Theophilus states that there are many other
gospels in existence, but that the author has become acquainted with the
things that happened from the first. This shows that the author intended to
create a gospel that he or she regarded as superior to the existing gospels.
The most successful and influential of all the early gospels was Matthew,
which must have been written within a decade or so of the first gospel,
Mark, and which rapidly became very popular. The author of Luke is writing from a sophisticated Roman environment and has excellent access to
sources; it is inconceivable that Matthew would not be among the gospels
known by the author of Luke.

4. The Gospel of Luke shares a number of structural features with Matthew. These include basing the gospel on Mark, including the so-called "Q"
material, including a genealogy of Jesus and a nativity story. It is very unlikely that two writers working independently of each other would have
come up with gospels that share all these structural features.

5. Although the structural features are similar, the details are often very
different. For example, the genealogy in Luke is completely different from
Matthew, and the nativity story features shepherds instead of the Magi.
This gives rise to what we can call the "same but different" pattern of Luke
copying Matthew.

6. The "same but different" pattern suggests that the author of Luke is
heavily dependent on the Gospel of Matthew although they disagree with

it. They are deliberately changing certain features to create what they regard as a superior gospel intended to replace Matthew.

7. This tells us something about the author of Luke. They have supreme self-confidence which is not justified by their degree of knowledge. Although they use genuine sources, they invent narratives shamelessly around these sources and have such high status that they can get these inventions accepted by their local Christian community.

8. In the second volume, we will show from internal evidence in Luke and Acts that the author was a woman with high status in the Roman establishment, and that Theophilus was a pseudonym for her husband or another close male relative. The evidence points to this woman being one of the most powerful individuals in the Empire, the leader of a house church in Rome, and the patroness of Christians in that city.

Chapter 8

The search for the founder

The first step to uncovering the secrets of the Jesus movement is to identify the founder. Using the spiritual hypothesis we can deduce three things about the founder that must be true and these will lead to three lines of enquiry. All three are invariants that would have survived the process of literalisation. If all three lines lead to the same person, then we will be satisfied that that person is the founder. The three criteria are:

Prominence: the founder would have been revered above all others in the early church. The position of prominence and the feeling of reverence must have been passed down to the age in which the first writings are made. So we would expect the leader to be very prominent in the writings that have come down to us – we are not looking for an obscure character.

The first witness of the resurrection: under the spiritual hypothesis the founder must be the first witness of the resurrection. The shaman's experience of Jesus would surely have been preserved in the literature of the movement and from the stories of this experience we can uncover the name of the shaman. Under the Traditional Secular view the stories of the resurrection are a later accretion and so the identity of the first witness is not of special significance; but under the spiritual hypothesis the resurrection comes first, and the first witness is the heart of the movement.

The first leader: if Jesus was not the first earthly leader then the founder was. Find the identity of this first leader and you have the identity of the founder.

Starting with the first criterion, that of prominence, we do not have many candidates, and we can immediately eliminate one of the few, the apostle Paul. It is Paul who has left us the earliest eyewitness account of the Christian movement through his epistles. It is Paul who is often regarded as the person who changed the direction of the movement by deifying the human Jewish Jesus into the Son of God and starting a new religion in the process. But we must reject this charge. On the shaman paradigm, Paul could not have changed the movement in this direction since it was cast in these terms from the beginning.

Could Paul have started the religion? Could he have been the founder? After all, he had exactly the type of spiritual experiences we would expect from the leader including an intimate relationship with the risen Jesus and perhaps even a personal visit to the third heaven. He was energetic and boasted of his charismatic spiritual gifts. He was a revered figure; his writings were carefully preserved, and he was known in both the proto-orthodox and gnostic wings of the early church, being known by many as "the Apostle". Is not Paul the natural candidate for the leader?

The answer is no. Paul can be eliminated by the best possible evidence; his own firsthand account. It is obvious from his letters that he is a late recruit to a church that is already well established. Before his conversion, he has been involved in the persecution of the church. He puts himself last in the list of the apostles who have seen the risen Christ. He defers to the established leadership of the Church in Jerusalem visiting first for instruction and later to ask for approval of his teachings. The evidence is all the more persuasive because his acknowledgment of the pre-eminence of James and the brethren in Jerusalem is grudging and spiked with put-downs. If he were eulogistic, we might be suspicious. But no later forger would have written about the Jerusalem leadership in the exasperated tone which Paul uses. Yet it is clear from his account that despite his grumblings he accepts them as the acknowledged and proper leaders.

Eliminating Paul we must consider other potential candidates. The most obviously prominent follower of Jesus is the disciple and apostle Peter/Cephas (both forms of the name are used). In the gospels he is the most prominent of the disciples, although there are some curiously negative stories about him. He is also prominent in Acts of the Apostles where he shares the limelight with Paul. The same two apostles, Peter and Paul, were greatly esteemed in the early church. We have eliminated Paul, so Peter must now be considered at the top of the list for prominence.

Other than Peter there is James whom most scholars believe was the leader of the movement after Jesus' death. However, James does not satisfy the criterion of prominence despite the fact that he was the first of the Jerusalem pillars and is called "the brother of the Lord." The church as a whole did not have the same view of James as it had of Peter or Paul. In fact, he was obscure to the point of invisibility. This would be odd if he were really the shaman founder of the movement. Even those churches far from Jerusalem should have inherited numerous stories about him.

Beyond James, there are no other male disciples or apostles who come anywhere close to the prominence we would expect from the founder. We must turn instead to two women who both happen to be called Mary; Mary the Magdalene and Mary the mother of Jesus. In recent times, Mary the Magdalene has attracted a large amount of interest from the feminist contingent. They see in her a female apostle and teacher whose memory was put down and suppressed by the patriarchal leadership of the developing proto-orthodox church. In support of this notion, there are a number of works outside of the New Testament in which a "Mary" plays a key part. In the relatively late Pistis Sophia, the disciples ask questions of the risen Jesus. Of the forty-six questions, some thirty-nine are asked by this "Mary", who may have been Mary the Magdalene. Whoever wrote the Pistis Sophia regarded her as the most prominent of the disciples. The earlier, second-century Gospel of Mary features Mary as the disciple whom Jesus loved the most and the recipient of secret revelations, exactly as we would expect of the shaman. This Mary is probably the same as the Magdalene, although this is not explicit in the text. These works show that some groups in the second century and later looked to Mary as a source of revelation beyond the other disciples and apostles. There is also evidence of friction between these groups and the proto-orthodox church that claimed Peter as its authority. This conflict is portrayed in the texts as a conflict between Mary and Peter; in the Gospel of Mary it is Peter who questions the genuineness of Mary's revelations.

Any prominence in the early movement that Mary the Magdalene might have had is eclipsed by the other Mary, the mother of Jesus. Even today the Virgin Mary is revered in the two oldest churches, the Roman Catholic Church and the Greek Orthodox Church. In the Catholic Church she is called the Mother of God, the Queen of Heaven, the Mother of the Church, and even the Co-Redemptrix, the joint redeemer of humanity with Christ. In the Eastern Orthodox Church she is the Theotokos, the God-bearer. The breakaway protestant churches rejected the role that Mary played in Catholic worship as unscriptural and even blasphemous because it raised Mary onto a level with Christ. The answer of the Catholic Church was that scripture was incomplete; not everything was written down in the New Testament, but there was also living knowledge that was passed down from generation to generation through the church. This may have been truer than they supposed. For it is possible that the adoration of the Virgin dates from before the literalisations of the gospels. If so, then Mary has been transformed by these literalisations into the physical mother of a physical Jesus. Originally she must have been something different, something that has led the gospel writers to make this mistake. We have to consider the possibility that Mary was the shaman-founder of the Jesus movement. If so it would explain why the prominence of Mary was so widespread, why it was embedded not just in the churches of the East and West but also in Islam and the Koran where she is esteemed above all other women. The titles of Mother of the Church, of Co-Redemptrix and Queen of Heaven suddenly become fitting.

But were Mary the mother of God and Mary the Magdalene really two separate individuals? The name Mary is used a number of times, particularly in the crucifixion and resurrection accounts where all the women with the exception of Salome are called Mary. Traditionally there are at least three separate women involved including Mary the mother of Jesus and Mary the Magdalene. It is true that Mary was a very common female name among Jews of the time, but the occurrence of so many uses of the name points towards redundancy. It suggests that variations of a name belonging to one woman have come down through different channels and mistakenly given rise to different characters. If we turn to the earliest gospel, that of Mark, then we will see that there is no evidence against Mary the mother of Jesus and Mary the Magdalene being one and the same woman. In fact, there is only a single explicit reference to Mary the mother of Jesus in Mark and she is not mentioned in the crucifixion and resurrection story, although this is the only time the name Mary the Magdalene appears in the gospel. So even with a literalistic interpretation of the gospel, it is possible that the two are the same. Only in the later gospels do the mother of Jesus and the Magdalene develop as two distinct characters.

So we are left with two or maybe three main candidates who meet the prominence criterion. Peter and Mary the mother of Jesus have the prominence we would expect, whereas Mary the Magdalene had the right degree of prominence among certain groups but not for the movement as a whole. The criterion of prominence is powerful, but it is also high level, and it cannot be conclusive. The second criterion is more precise. We would expect to find the identity of the founder in one particular place in the story. Jesus has appeared first to the shaman/founder, and this event would have been of supreme importance to the Jesus movement. We would expect the identity of the founder to be preserved in the form this story takes in the literalistic gospel, the story of the resurrection. And so the question that should take us straight to the founder is simple; who was the first person to see the resurrected Jesus? It is a simple enough question but answering it will prove far from simple.

Chapter 9

Who first saw the risen Christ?

The resurrected Christ appeared first to the shaman. Stories of this first appearance would have been treasured to become part of the lore of the movement. Even when the story was literalised in the gospels, with Jesus living and dying in first century Judea, the identity of the founder as the first witness would have been preserved. So who first saw the resurrected Christ?

The search for the first witness

There are no less than five accounts of the resurrection appearances that go back to the first century or start of the second. These are contained in the four gospels and Paul's first letter to the Corinthians. Given such an abundance of evidence, it should be easy to determine if one person is singled out as the first witness. But there is a fundamental difficulty. The four gospel accounts are not independent as the gospels of Matthew and Luke copy Mark extensively, and John was probably written when all the other gospels were already in existence. To compound the problem the crucial part of the Gospel of Mark, the so-called long ending, is disputed with most scholars regarding it as a later addition.

But among all these accounts there is one tantalisingly direct piece of evidence in the form of Paul's first letter to the Corinthians. The letter is earlier than any of the gospels being dated to the 50s. Moreover, Paul was directly acquainted with those involved so his evidence is the nearest we can come to an eyewitness statement. As the earliest account of the resurrection it will be taken first:

For I delivered to you first, what also I did receive, that Christ died for our sins, according to the scriptures, and that he was buried, and that he was raised the third day, according to the scriptures, and that he appeared to Cephas, then to the twelve, afterwards he appeared to above five hundred brethren at once, of whom the greater part remain till now, although some have fallen asleep; afterwards he appeared to James, then to all the apostles. And last of all, as if to a miscarriage [or abortion], he appeared also to me. For I am the least of the apostles, and am not worthy to be called an apostle, because I did persecute the assembly of God. (1 Corinthians 15:3-9)

The meaning of "risen on the third day" seems plain enough and it is understandable that the author of the Gospel of Mark should have taken it at face value as meaning that Jesus died three days before his resurrection. But if the words are understood in the context of apocalyptic beliefs then a very different meaning of the "third day" becomes apparent. We shall see that the predecessors of the Jesus movement used an apocalyptic calendar in which a "day" stood both for a generation and, as in this case, for a week of seven generations. Jesus has been dead for two days, that is fourteen generations, and now at the beginning of the third day, the age for his resurrection has come.

The passage is crucial for read correctly it recounts the history of the Jesus movement. It shall be considered in depth later, but the question for now is the identity of the first witness of the resurrection. Paul's account gives us a completely clear and unambiguous answer; it was Cephas, the Aramaic form of the name Peter. Note also that there is no distinction between the appearances to Paul (which were clearly spiritual) and the appearances to the other witnesses. There is nothing to suggest that Cephas and the others saw Jesus in a different way to Paul.

Before relying on this piece of evidence, it must be asked if it was really written by Paul or has a later redactor been at work? There is one excellent piece of evidence that it is original. The author of Luke and Acts follows the sequence of the post-resurrection appearances given here by Paul closely, particularly in Acts. She must have had access to a copy of Paul's account that was very close to our version.

So the earliest written evidence points to Cephas. What about the next in order of writing, the Gospel of Mark? The story in Mark is very different from the laconic account in Paul. The story starts with a dramatic visit to a tomb and a mysterious messenger:

And the Sabbath having past, Mary the Magdalene, and Mary of James, and Salome bought spices, that they might come and anoint him. And early in the morning of the first day of the week, they come to the tomb, at the rising of the sun, and they said among themselves, "Who shall roll away for us the stone out of the door of the tomb?" And having looked, they saw that the stone had been rolled away, and it was very large. And entering into the tomb, they saw a young man sitting on the right hand, arrayed in a long white robe, and they were amazed. And he said to them, "Do not be amazed. You seek Jesus the Nazarene, the crucified. He is risen! He is not here; see the place where they laid him. Go, say to his disciples and Peter, that he does go before you to Galilee; there you shall see him as he said to you." And, having gone out, they fled from the tomb in trembling and amazement, and they said nothing to anyone for they were afraid. (Mark 16:1-8)

One immediate difference with Paul's account is the women. Paul makes no specific mention of women, although it is possible that women could be included among the groups of the five hundred and the apostles. But he certainly does not bring women in as the earliest witnesses. If women played an important role in the resurrection, why should Paul ignore them? He mentions women many times elsewhere and his letters are the main source of evidence for the importance of women in the early church.

In fact, if we read Mark carefully we will see that this part of Mark's account is not inconsistent with Paul's account because it does not identify the women as witnesses of the risen Christ. They see the empty tomb and the mysterious young man (whom in the other gospel accounts is explicitly called an angel). They are told Jesus has risen and are tasked with giving a message to Peter and the disciples; he will appear to them in Galilee. But the women do not see the risen Jesus himself.

There are no resurrection appearances in this part of Mark. But there is an implied sequence that is given in the young man's message. Jesus will appear to *"his disciples and Peter"*. Note how close this is to Paul's *"Cephas, then the twelve"*. Both times one individual is singled out; in Paul it is Cephas and in Mark it is Peter. But these are two versions of the same name.

This part of the Mark account ties in so well with Paul's letter that this letter is likely to have been the author of Mark's source for this information. Mark adds the intriguing detail that Jesus' appearance to the disciples is to be in Galilee. Nowhere in any of his letters does Paul even mention Galilee.

The final sentence is particularly puzzling -- the women *"said nothing to anyone for they were afraid."* Some see this as evidence that the story of the women was invented by the gospel writer in order to establish the empty tomb. His first audiences would have been unfamiliar with the story, so he needs to explain to them why they had not heard it before. However, if this were the true narrative purpose of the women's silence, then the gospel writer would have made the women tell someone their story to establish why he, the author, knew it. He would have had to write something like, "They said nothing to anyone at the time for they were afraid, but later they gave me this true account." But he does not do this.

The Gospel of Mark does not end here and what comes next changes everything:

> *And he, having risen in the morning of the first day of the week did appear first to Mary the Magdalene, out of whom he had cast seven demons. And she went and told them that had been with him, as they mourned and wept. And they, when they had heard that he was alive, and had been seen of her, believed not.* (Mark 16:9-11)

This is from the so-called long ending of Mark. It is found on most, but not all, early copies of Mark and is almost universally rejected by scholars as a later addition. The reasons for this rejection will be considered later, but we should note that this continuation shatters everything. We are now told that Jesus appeared first to Mary the Magdalene in stark conflict with Paul, who tells us he appeared first to Cephas and who never mentions the Magdalene. This is startling enough on the conventional view but on the shaman paradigm the first witness of the resurrection is also the founder of Christianity. So we have to consider the possibility that the founder is Mary the Magdalene.

However, according to many scholars the appearance to Mary is a literary invention. According to this view, the long ending is a later addition compiled from odds and ends found elsewhere in the Gospels. The women going to the tomb are not mentioned by Paul because they were invented by the author of Mark. He is trying to convince his audience that the resurrection is physical and not spiritual. So he has to rule out the possibility that the body is still in the tomb, to include witnesses who see that the body is gone. The young man's words give a clue as to why these witnesses could not be Peter and the other disciples. There must have been an early tradition that it was in Galilee that they saw the resurrection. After all Jesus had just been executed for sedition, and his followers were hardly likely to hang around Jerusalem. But if they are in Galilee then they cannot also be in Jerusalem to see the stone rolled to one side and the empty place where Jesus' body had laid. So the author of Mark falls back onto the secondary characters and uses the women whom the Gospel of Luke tells us tagged along after Jesus. It is women who would have anointed a body in death pouring over it fragrant incense to take away the shock of the stench. What could be more natural than for the female mourners to find the empty tomb?

It is all very plausible and quite consistent with the evidence, if the evidence is limited to a few lines in Mark. For ignoring the long ending does not solve the problem of the appearance to Mary the Magdalene. It merely pushes the problem back to the next gospel to be written, that of Matthew. In this gospel two women, Mary the Magdalene and "the other Mary" go to the tomb. They see an angel who tells them to tell the disciples that Jesus has risen and goes before them to Galilee. This part follows Mark closely but then Matthew inserts a meeting between the women and Jesus himself:

And they departed quickly from the tomb, with fear and great joy, and they ran to tell to his disciples. And as they were going to tell his disciples Jesus met them, saying, "Greetings!" And they having come near, laid hold of his feet, and worshipped him. Then Jesus said to them, "Fear not, but go and tell my brothers that they should go into Galilee, and there they shall see me." (Matthew 28:8-10)

If Mark has really invented the women at the tomb and if the long ending of Mark is not yet written, then from where has the author of Matthew got the idea that Mary the Magdalene met the risen Jesus on that first day of the week? The meeting serves no purpose in the narrative. The message that Jesus gives the women merely repeats what the angel has already told them. Yet at a stroke of his pen he diminishes the role of Peter and the other disciples, even though elsewhere the author of Matthew is keen to build up Peter as the Rock on whom the church is built. Surely Jesus should appear first to this Rock? Yet we are to believe that the author of Matthew changes the accepted appearance to Peter and substitutes an appearance to two women. By the time he is writing, the role of the early disciples must have been legendary within the church, and the first encounter with the risen Jesus cherished. We can imagine how stories must have been told and retold about this event. So how is the author of Matthew able to foster onto his readers the notion that a quite different person to the received first witness saw Jesus first? And why should he want to? The author of Matthew elsewhere shows himself loyal to his sources, particularly Mark. There must have been a strong reason to insert the appearance to Mary the Magdalene and "the other Mary" and there must have been a pre-existing tradition that Jesus appeared first to the Magdalene for this account to be accepted. And accepted it was. In the later Gospel of John, this meeting of

Matthew has become much more prominent. The other Mary has been dropped and Mary the Magdalene meets Jesus, whom she first mistakes for a gardener, alone:

Jesus said to her, "Woman, why do you weep? Whom do you seek?" She, sup-posing that he is the gardener, said to him, "Sir, if you did carry him away, tell me where you have laid him, and I will take him away." Jesus said to her, "Mary." She turned, and said to him in Aramaic, "Rabboni," which means "Teacher." Jesus said to her, "Do not touch me, for I have not yet ascended to my Father; but go to my brothers and say to them, "I am ascending to my Father, and your Father, and my God, and your God." (John 20:15-17)

So what was the author of Matthew's source for his story of the meeting between the two Mary's and Jesus? In fact, Matthew follows Mark quite closely at this point, but it follows it across the boundary and into the long ending which is not supposed to exist! After the angel gives the women the message, they feel *"fear and great joy"* and run to tell the disciples. In Mark, the women are afraid and filled with *"trembling and amazement"* and tell no one. We see that Matthew follows Mark but also makes the women's fear-ful first reaction more joyful. This smoothing of Mark's rough edges is en-tirely typical of Matthew. The long ending of Mark continues from this point with Jesus appearing on the first day of the week (the same day) to Mary the Magdalene and this is exactly what happens next in Matthew with Jesus meeting the women. Note that the long ending does not record the words spoken between Jesus and Mary. In Matthew, the speech of Jesus repeats what has already been said by the angel. If the author of Matthew's source had recorded Jesus' words, he would surely have included them in his gospel. The fact that he is forced to recycle the angel's speech shows that his source, like the long ending, did not include such words.

The question of the genuineness of the long ending is critical to under-standing the resurrection and hence understanding Christianity. If it is genuine, then it is an incredibly valuable witness to some of the earliest traditions that were circulating in the church. The long ending is the sim-plest and most natural way of explaining the resurrection appearance to Mary the Magdalene and "the other Mary" in Matthew. But regardless of whether or not the long ending is genuine, it is certain that there must have been an early tradition that the risen Jesus appeared to Mary the Magda-lene. The evidence is in Matthew, for if there had not been a strong Mary tradition the author of this gospel would never have sabotaged Peter's role as the acknowledged first witness.

There is one further gospel to be considered, and that is Luke, the last written of the three synoptic gospels. Like Matthew, Luke follows Mark quite closely with the women's visit to the tomb. This time the women are Mary the Magdalene, Joanna, Mary of James and *"other women with them"*. They find the stone rolled away from the tomb as in Mark, and they enter but this time they see *"two men in glittering apparel"*. The men give them a message:

"Why do you seek the living among the dead? He is not here, but is risen! Remember how he spoke to you, when he was yet in Galilee, saying, 'The Son of Man must be delivered into the hands of sinful men, and be crucified, and the third day to rise again.'" (Luke 24:5-7)

All this is similar to Mark, but there are some differences. The list of women has changed slightly with Joanna taking the place of Salome and the general "other women" added, which makes it seem like a large assorted group (is Salome supposed to be included in these other women?). Another change which seems inconsequential and yet odd is the doubling up of the angels; although Luke following Mark calls them men while the description makes their identity plain enough. The most striking change is perhaps the dropping of the message that Jesus will appear to the disciples in Galilee. The author of Luke has subtly changed the angels' words so as to make them recall a prophecy that Jesus made in Galilee. This enables her to site the resurrection appearances in Jerusalem without contradicting the angels' message.

The women tell the eleven and the other followers of Jesus about what they have seen but they are not believed. Note that neither Luke nor Matthew follows the supposed ending of Mark where the women tell no one. In Luke, Peter runs to the tomb and sees the grave clothes before going home wondering at what had happened.

This is followed by Luke's splendid story of the road to Emmaus. Two of Jesus' followers set off to Emmaus, a village outside Jerusalem. We learn that one of them is called Cleopas, but the second is unnamed. On the road, Jesus joins them in a form that they do not recognise. He asks them why they are sad, and they tell him about Jesus of Nazareth, how he was crucified and how they had hoped that he was the one to redeem Israel. They tell him about the women visiting the tomb and about the messengers and the grave clothes. The stranger then expounds to them the meaning of the scriptures, how it was prophesied that the Christ had to suffer. When they come to the place of parting, the two ask the stranger in for dinner. He

agrees, and it is at the table, as he breaks the bread, that they recognise him
before he vanishes. In the continuation the two hurry back to Jerusalem:

> *And having risen up the same hour, they returned to Jerusalem, and found the
> eleven, and those gathered with them, who said, "The Lord has risen indeed, and
> has appeared to Simon." And they were telling the things that happened on the
> way, and how he was made known to them in the breaking of the bread. And as
> they spoke these things, Jesus himself stood in the midst of them, and said to them,
> "Peace to you." (Luke 24:33-36)*

Luke's account is ambiguous. Who is the first witness? The two who
walk to Emmaus? We do not know the identity of one of them. Or is it Simon, presumably Simon Peter? Did he see Jesus before the two on the
road? In the flow of the narrative, it is the two who see Jesus first, and the
appearance to Simon is not even described. But from the information in
Luke the matter is unresolved. Deliberate ambiguity in a text is a modern
literary technique. When it appears in an ancient document, we may suspect evasion. The author of Luke is ambiguous because she does not know.
She is grappling with multiple traditions and fudges the issue.

One thing that is sure is that the author of Luke does not mention Mary
the Magdalene or any other woman as being the first witness. This is not
the same as saying that Mary could not have been the first witness in Luke.
For we do not know the identity of the companion of Cleopas on the road
to Emmaus and it cannot be ruled out that this person was the Magdalene.
Indeed, we shall see that there is evidence that could be interpreted as
meaning that Cleopas was her husband, although we will reject this interpretation.

Why does the author of Luke not mention Mary the Magdalene as one
of the witnesses? Is the author of Luke a misogynist who has reduced the
role of the women? This is to ignore the evidence that the gospel was written by a woman and consistently gives a female viewpoint. Or is the gospel
simply telling us the truth that Jesus did not appear first to Mary but Peter?
There is that one telling line *"The Lord has risen indeed, and has appeared to
Simon."* Does this put the Gospel of Luke in the same camp as Paul and the
short ending of Mark in putting Peter forward as the first witness?

But if so why does the gospel not make it clearer? Why not shout it from
the rooftops? Why not describe with all the imaginative colour normal for
Luke the first meeting between Peter and Jesus? The gospel is strangely
hesitant about the matter. And why introduce the two on the road to Emmaus? Why have Peter visit the tomb to see the grave clothes but not see

the resurrected Jesus? This is the natural place for Jesus to appear to Peter, but he does not.

To look for answers to some of these questions, we must turn beyond the Gospel of Luke to its companion work the Acts of the Apostles. It was written by the same person as Luke and picks up the story where the gospel leaves off. But there is a brief overlap; at the beginning of Acts some appearances of the resurrected Jesus are also mentioned. But there is a mystery about these appearances and solving it will reveal the pattern behind the Luke accounts.

The mystery of the ascension

The author of Luke and Acts wrote two accounts of how Jesus was finally taken up to heaven. The first, in the Gospel of Luke, is short:

And he led them out as far as to Bethany, and he lifted up his hands and blessed them. While he blessed them, he was parted from them and was carried up into heaven. And they, having worshipped him, did turn back to Jerusalem with great joy, and were continually in the temple, blessing God. (Luke 24:50-53)

When does this ascension take place? The appearance to two on the road to Emmaus, ending in the evening meal, is the first day of the resurrection. The two immediately hurry back to Jerusalem, a journey of a few hours. There Jesus appears to all the disciples before leading them out to Bethany. So, according to Luke, the ascension must take place on the second day of the week, the second day of the resurrection. However, in Acts the resurrected Jesus stays on earth for forty days:

To whom also he presented himself alive after his suffering with many proofs, being seen by them during forty days and speaking about the kingdom of God. (Acts 1:3)

Between Luke and Acts, the author has changed her understanding of how long Jesus was on earth. But the biggest mystery concerns those who witness the ascension in Acts. They are all "*assembled together*" when Jesus tells them they will be baptised with the spirit, and will witness to him not just in Jerusalem, but in all Judea, Samaria and to the ends of the earth.[40] This is followed by the ascent to heaven:

And after he had spoken these things they saw he was taken up, and a cloud hid him from their sight. (Acts 1:9)

As the disciples are gazing up into the sky, two men appear dressed in white. They tell them that Jesus, who has been taken up to heaven, will come back in the same manner. Afterward, they return to Jerusalem from the Mount of Olives which is *"a Sabbath day's journey"*, meaning the maximum distance a Jew could travel on the Sabbath. This distance was two thousand cubits or about a mile. In Luke, the ascension was from Bethany but now it is apparently from the Mount of Olives. But the biggest surprise comes when they return to Jerusalem.

Up to now our natural assumption would be that all the principal followers of Jesus are present at his ascension. After all, Jesus has given them vital information about the Holy Spirit along with the direct proof, by his ascension, of his divine nature. But when the group returns they go to an upper room where the main followers of Jesus are waiting for them! Those who have stayed behind are the eleven remaining disciples, including Peter and James, along with Jesus' mother and brothers. Why have none of them witnessed Jesus' ascension to heaven?

The resolution of this mystery lies with Paul's account of the resurrection. He tells us that Jesus appeared to Cephas (Peter), the Twelve, the five hundred, James and *"then to all the apostles"* before making a final appearance to Paul himself. What the author of Luke does in Acts is to follow this list in an absurdly literal manner. Working backward, Paul is the last person to see the risen Christ. So the author of Luke-Acts has Jesus return to put in one final special appearance to Paul on the road to Damascus. Before this, the risen Christ appears, according to Paul, *"to all the apostles"*, a group that must exclude Cephas, the Twelve, and James, who are listed as seeing the resurrected Christ earlier. And this is exactly how the author of Luke-Acts presents the ascension! Jesus' final appearance is to an anonymous group who exclude all those listed before "all the apostles" in Paul's list. The first two individuals listed by Acts in the upper chamber are Peter and James, the only two individuals named in Paul's list. The author of Luke is unsure if the James in Paul's list is one of the two disciples of that name or the brother of the Lord. So as well as naming James, she also names the brothers among those who do witness the ascension. This is to take an absurdly literal interpretation of Paul's statement since he would not have repeated a person in the list even if that person had seen Jesus multiple times.

All of which is important because it tells us two things:

The author of Luke knew of Paul's account of the resurrection.

The author of Luke attached great importance to it and modified her own narrative to make it consistent.

This confirms Paul's resurrection account as early and genuine. But it also gives us a vital clue to understanding the resurrection account in Luke. If the author of Luke has followed Paul's account in Acts, then she would have done the same in Luke. So those elements in Luke that support a first appearance to Peter cannot be regarded as independent of Paul. This would explain the statement *"The Lord has risen indeed, and has appeared to Simon"* meaning Simon Peter, which appears out of place in the narrative. Also, the absence of an explicit appearance to Mary the Magdalene cannot be regarded as positive evidence against such an appearance. The author of Luke is simply trying to follow Paul, and he does not mention Mary the Magdalene or any other woman.

Key points

1. Under the shaman paradigm, the resurrected Christ must have appeared first to the shaman. The stories of this event have been literalised in the gospels, but the identity of the person who first saw the risen Christ should be preserved.

2. There are five early accounts of the resurrection, but they are not consistent.

3. In the earliest account, that of Paul, Jesus first appeared to Cephas and then the Twelve. There is no mention of Mary the Magdalene or any other women.

4. The second earliest account is that in Mark. Three women, led by Mary the Magdalene, find the empty tomb. They see a man/angel who gives them a message to pass on to Peter and the disciples, that Jesus will appear to them in Galilee. However, the women are frightened and tell no one.

5. Up to this point, the Gospel of Mark is consistent with Paul. However most copies have a continuation, the so-called "long ending". This long ending bluntly states that Jesus appeared first to Mary the Magdalene, followed by two others in another form, and only then the disciples. Many think that the long ending was not original but was written much later than the rest of Mark.

6. Matthew follows Mark closely in the first part of the account, with two women including Mary Magdalene finding the empty tomb and an angel. But it also seems to follow Mark into the long ending. On the way back from the tomb the two women are met by the risen Christ, making Mary the Magdalene the first witness of the resurrection.

7. The author of Matthew must have had as a source either the long ending or a strong pre-existing tradition that Mary the Magdalene was the first witness. Otherwise, he would never have reduced the role of Peter by having Mary see the risen Christ first.

8. The Luke account is ambiguous. The role of the women is downgraded, there is a story of two meeting Jesus in disguise on the road to Emmaus, and there is also a statement that Christ was seen by Simon. Some of these features are due to the author of Luke trying to make her account consistent with Paul. It is clear from the beginning of Acts that the author of Luke knew of Paul's account of the resurrection and attached great importance to it.

9. The Gospel of John emphasises the role of Mary the Magdalene but is later than the other gospels.

Conclusion

The first witness, and hence the shaman, can only be one of two individuals; the person called Cephas/Peter or Mary the Magdalene. There is a fundamental inconsistency in the early evidence with separate strands pointing to each of these individuals.

Chapter 10

Is the long ending original to Mark?

Was the long ending original to the Gospel of Mark or was it added much later? This question is central to the search for the shaman. If the long ending is early then it contains the earliest evidence pointing towards Mary the Magdalene. But if it is late then we can disregard it in our quest.

The long ending

Most authorities reject the long ending, although this rejection is not universal. The arguments against the long ending being original to Mark are:

It is not included in all early copies.

Early authorities reject the long ending.

The best manuscripts exclude the long ending.

The language differs from that used elsewhere in Mark.

There are inconsistencies and lack of flow between the rest of Mark and the long ending.

The contents of the long ending have been almost exclusively copied from elsewhere.

Matthew and Luke follow Mark closely until the long ending and then diverge wildly.

None of these is a knockout blow on its own. It is the cumulative effect that causes the long ending to be rejected. The key point is whether the authors of Matthew and Luke knew the long ending; if they did, then this would make it earlier than these two gospels. But first we will consider the other objections.

It is not included in all early copies.

It is quite normal for ancient documents to have sections missing and it is quite normal for these missing sections to be the start or the end, as these were easily detached and lost. So the absence of the ending from some copies is not some unheard of and remarkable state of affairs but exists with many other documents. It is, however, significant that the version without the ending was perpetuated. If the omission originated with a mistake or accident, we would expect future copyists to revert to the version including the long ending with which they must have been familiar. So at least some of those copyists must have believed that the long ending was not original. We must, however, bear in mind that the great majority of surviving copies of Mark include the long ending, so it was more widely accepted than the version without the ending.

Early authorities reject the long ending.

The early church historian Eusebius (260-339) seems to have had doubts about accepting the long ending.[41] He says that nearly all the copies of Mark, or at least the accurate ones, omit the ending and end at verse 16:8. However, this is presented as just one view on Mark and not the universal opinion, or indeed his own opinion. It may also be significant that the context of this is an attempt to reconcile the timing of the resurrection of Jesus between the gospels of Matthew and Mark. The divergence between the various gospel accounts of the resurrection was a serious embarrassment for the early church. Matthew had become accepted as the definitive eyewitness account written by the disciple himself, so it was convenient to relegate the long ending of Mark as a later addition. Jerome (340-420) writing later has similar doubts, but these are probably derived from reading Eusebius.

Against these, there are a string of early witnesses who accept the long ending. Most significant is the early church father Irenaeus who quotes the long ending twice. The first is an oblique reference in Against Heresies about the Lord by his passion conferring on his followers the power *"to tread upon serpents and scorpions, and on all the power of the enemy"* (*Against Heresies* 2:20:3)[42] which is clearly based on the long ending even though the wording is not identical. The second reference is quite specific:

> *Also, towards the conclusion of his Gospel, Mark says: "So then, after the Lord Jesus had spoken to them, He was received up into heaven, and sits on the right hand of God". (Against Heresies 3:10:5)*[43]

Against Heresies was written around 180 so this provides an early dating for the long ending. Irenaeus was well informed and a critical reader. His writings provide the earliest evidence for what was to become the canon of accepted New Testament texts and he rejected the great mass of apocryphal material circulating in his time. He is not a person who was easily fooled, and he accepts the long ending without comment as part of Mark. This means that the long ending must have been circulating as an integral part of Mark for a considerable period. He would hardly have accepted some new addition to the Gospel of Mark that had been penned in his own lifetime! The version of Mark that had been taught to him by his respected teachers must have included the long ending, or he would have rejected it as a novelty. This would push the latest date for the long ending to sometime around the middle of the second century and probably earlier than that, say 130 to give sufficient time for it to have circulated widely and to have been accepted by the previous generation.

The mention by Irenaeus trumps the doubts of Eusebius almost a century and a half later. The statement that nearly all the copies of Mark omit the long ending is clearly an exaggeration. He is telling us no more than we already know from the surviving manuscripts, that the long ending is omitted from some early copies. Quite simply Eusebius does not know if the long ending is genuine or not because, even for him, it is all in the distant past.

The best manuscripts exclude the long ending.

This argument seems to come from the idea that good copies are either early copies or have been derived from early copies by a small number of steps. So if the good copies do not have the long ending, then the long ending could not have been present in the earliest manuscripts.

The flaw in this argument is that even if the long ending were added later, it is still very much earlier than any surviving manuscript. We know from the quote by Irenaeus that it was circulating as part of Mark at c180 and must have been composed significantly before that date. The earliest complete manuscripts of the gospels, the Codex Sinaiticus and Codex Vaticanus, both of which are missing the long ending, date from the fourth century, some two hundred years later. Considerations about the quality of these manuscripts are irrelevant because they can tell us nothing about the era in which the family tree of copies of Mark has diverged into the two branches; the branch of copies with the long ending and the branch of copies without. To put this another way, either the long ending was deducted from some copies of the original gospel or it was added to some copies. In either case, there is no reason to suppose that the remainder of the gospel was of differing quality between those texts with and without the long ending. So the survival of one branch or the other in the best quality manuscripts two hundred years or more later is a matter of chance.

Both Sinaiticus and Vaticanus are of the Alexandrian text type. It seems that the omission of the long ending originated within the Alexandrian context, which also happens to have given us the best surviving manuscripts. This is not evidence that the Alexandrian texts had access to an earlier version of Mark than the other manuscript branches.

The language used differs from that used elsewhere in Mark.
Inconsistencies and lack of flow between the long ending and the rest of Mark.

The difference in language is derived from studies of the vocabulary used by the long ending compared to that used by the rest of Mark. There are 16 words that occur in the 12 lines that are not used elsewhere in Mark. Of these 16 words 3 are used more than once in this short sequence. The problem is that the long ending is rather small to be used to derive statistically valid conclusions based on frequency of word usage. In fact, while the frequency of unique word use is higher than the average for Mark, it is lower than some other sections of Mark and not outside the range of variation for passages in Mark.[44]

More significant are stylistic differences between the long ending and the rest of Mark. The author of Mark has a well-known addiction to the use of the conjunction *kai* ("and"). The use of conjunctions in the long ending is odd compared to the rest of Mark, and the frequency of *kai* is lower than normal for the gospel, although again not without precedent in other passages in Mark.

The transition between Mark 16:8 and the start of the long ending at Mark 16:9 is awkward. Line 8 ends in the word *gar*, the only time the gospel ends a sentence in this way. The use of *gar* is abrupt, and some have argued that the sentence has been cut short. However *gar* is known as an acceptable sentence ending from other Greek works of the time. The start of the next line, 16:9, *Anastas de*, is more appropriate as the beginning of a new work than as a continuation of line 16:8. This can, however, be explained if 16:9-20 was initially intended to be a separate section.

Turning from language to the issue of contradiction and narrative flow, it is apparent from a casual reading that the long ending does not flow as smoothly from the rest of Mark as might be expected. This is illustrated by the first words of the long ending: *"And having risen early in the morning of the first day of the week, he did appear first to Mary the Magdalene, out of whom he had cast seven demons."* This seems to be in flagrant contradiction to the angels message of a few lines before, that Jesus will appear to the disciples and Peter in Galilee. But that is not all. It repeats the information about the first day of the week that has already been given in the story of the women visiting the tomb. And it tells us that Mary the Magdalene has had seven devils cast out as if she were being introduced for the first time even though she has been a witness to the crucifixion and the empty tomb.

Consider the piece of information that is repeated; that Christ was raised on the morning of the first day of the week. There is a difference in the way the information is used in the two places. In the first instance, it forms a logical part of the narrative flow. When the women go to the tomb, we are told that it is early in the morning of the first day of the week. This is part of the scene setting that helps us locate the subsequent events in space and time. In the second instance, the information serves no narrative purpose. The first occurrence makes eminent narrative sense, and this is the clue that it has been changed and assimilated into the story by the author of Mark. The second occurrence is a bare statement of fact and may lay closer to the original source of the information.

The cumulative effect of all these features is unavoidable; the long ending is heterogeneous to the remainder of Mark. It has been written by someone else other than the person who wrote the rest of Mark. This leaves open the possibility that the author of Mark may have appended it to his own composition. But this conclusion about the long ending style differing from Mark does not just apply to 16:9-20 but also to the line 16:8 with its anomalous ending "gar". This line comes before the start of the long ending proper and the fact that it does not seem to have been written by the author of Mark means that the long ending must have been appended to the gospel by someone other than this author and the extra line at 16:8 added at the same time. There are two ways to explain this state of affairs:

The long ending has been added relatively late (early second century) after Matthew and Luke were written

The long ending has been added early before Matthew and Luke were written.

It is critical to understand which of these two possibilities is correct. If the long ending is late, then it simply reflects the resurrection stories of Matthew and Luke and does not advance our search. If, however, it is early then it is most likely material that pre-dates the rest of the gospel and which has not been rewritten in the author of Mark's style. We would then have an incredibly valuable pre-Mark account of the resurrection. To distinguish between these two alternatives, we must consider the last two arguments against the long ending.

<u>The content of the long ending has been mostly copied from elsewhere.</u>

Most scholars believe that the long ending copies material from Luke, Matthew and Acts. If it does, then it clearly cannot be earlier than those works. But there is an alternative explanation, and that is that Matthew, Luke and Acts copy the long ending.

It is very easy to see that two texts share the same material and that one of them must have copied from another. It is very hard to determine which is original and which has copied, unless one document is already known to be earlier than the other. For example, Mark and Matthew share a great deal of material, and it is immediately clear that one has copied from the other. But which of the two came first is a question that has absorbed scholars for many years.

So to say that the long ending has copied material from elsewhere is to pre-judge the point based on the preconception that the long ending must be relatively late. It is equally possible that these other texts have copied the long ending. To decide between the two is a far from trivial question. But in two cases, it can be shown that the shared information is more likely to have been copied from the long ending.

Take first the fascinating information that Jesus had cast out seven demons from Mary the Magdalene. The long ending gives this information as part of the statement that Jesus appeared to her on the first day of the week. The same information is included in the Gospel of Luke:

And it came about afterward that he went through every city and village, preaching and proclaiming the good news of the kingdom of God. And the twelve

were with him, and certain women, who were cured of evil spirits and infirmities; Mary who is called Magdalene, from whom seven demons had gone out, and Joanna wife of Chuza, Herod's steward, and Susanna, and many others, who were ministering to him from their means. (Luke 8:1-3)

The positioning of the material in the long ending is odd, coming immediately after the initial resurrection appearance. Why draw attention here, of all places, to the fact that Mary the Magdalene was prone to hysterics? The positioning in Luke, on the other hand, seems very logical, situated in the Galilean mission when the exorcism must have taken place and putting Mary the Magdalene in the context of other women followers of Jesus. Indeed, this mention in Luke introduces the women followers and provides an explanation of why there were women around for the passion and resurrection. But this sort of narrative logic is often a sign of invention! Real early sources have a habit of not being logical; it is the gospel writers who twist them into the logic of their own stories. And indeed when we look at how Mary the Magdalene is mentioned in Mark and Matthew we notice something very strange.

In Mark, the name "Magdalene" only occurs in relation to the passion and resurrection story. The name does not appear once in the whole gospel before the passion.

Matthew also only uses the name "Magdalene" in connection with the passion and resurrection, and does not mention this name before.

In both these earlier accounts, the title of the Magdalene is associated with the passion and resurrection. So how is it that the author of Luke, writing later, has information about Mary the Magdalene in the Galilean mission, information that was not available when Mark or Matthew was written? The answer is that she does not. The author of Luke has either invented the story about the seven devils or taken it from somewhere else and put it in the place where she thinks it should logically go. If we accept that she is unlikely to have made up such a negative piece of information about the Magdalene, then it must have been taken from a passion or resurrection account. We find in the long ending the perfect source.

And if we look at the information given in the long ending we will see that it is not illogical after all, at least not under the shaman paradigm! The author of Luke believes Jesus to have been a man who lived in the recent past, so she positions the exorcism of Mary the Magdalene during his mission before his death. But on the shaman paradigm the apostles only knew the resurrected Jesus. So the exorcism from Mary the Magdalene must have happened after the resurrection and not before. In this case, the order preserved in the long ending is the original order. The resurrected Jesus appears to the Magdalene and then he casts out seven demons from her to purify her nature so that she is a fit dwelling for the spiritual Christ.

The second example relates to the signs that the resurrected Jesus tells the disciples will distinguish those who believe in him:

"And these signs shall accompany those who believe; they shall cast out demons in my name; they shall speak in new tongues; they shall take up serpents with their hands; and if they drink poison it shall not hurt them; they shall lay hands on the ill, and they shall be well." (Mark 16:17-18)

Speaking in tongues was practised by Christians from the earliest times, as is evident from Paul's letters. Casting out of demons and healing the ill are typical of the miracles performed by Jesus. Taking up snakes and drinking poison without being harmed are more curious. Why are these two, rather specific abilities included? The answer is probably that the author of the long ending has literalised a saying. A snake is a metaphor for a false teacher and the poison (literally deadly drink) is their teachings. An example of this use of "snake" is found in Matthew where the Pharisees, scribes and Sadducees are described as a "brood of vipers".[45] In Romans, Paul uses a metaphor that the words of sinners are like snake poison: *"Their throat is an open sepulchre; with their tongues they have used deceit; the poison of asps is under their lips" (Romans 3:13).* In the original source the tongue is like a snake and its words like poison: *"They have made their tongue as sharp as a serpent's, viper's poison is under their lips" (Psalm 140:3).* The original saying must have meant that the followers of Jesus will be immune to the snakes (the false teachers including the Jewish religious establishment), and can drink their poison (listen to their falsehoods) without being harmed because they have that within themselves that is proof against the blandishments of other philosophies. The person who wrote the long ending has not understood the metaphor but makes it literal, as applying to real snakes and real poison.

All this gets interesting because Acts has a story about Paul being immune to snakes. Paul is on his way in chains to Rome, but his ship has been shipwrecked on the island of Malta. To keep warm Paul and his companions build a fire:

Paul gathered a bundle of sticks, and having laid them upon the fire, a viper, having come out of the heat, fastened on his hand. And when the natives saw the creature hanging from his hand, they said among themselves, "No doubt this man is a murderer, whom, though he has escaped the sea, justice did not allow him to live." He then, indeed, having shaken off the creature into the fire, he suffered no injury. But they were expecting him to swell up, or to fall down suddenly dead. But after they had waited a long time, and seeing nothing unusual happening to him, changed their minds, and said he was a god. (Acts 28:3-6)

This story about Paul taking up a snake and being unharmed is clearly related to the long ending. Note how the long ending says that the believers will be able to take up snakes in their hands and how in the Acts story Paul lifts up the snake with the hand to which it is attached. So has this elaborate story been developed from the long ending saying in the normal novelistic manner of the author of Luke-Acts or has the long ending included immunity to snakes because its author is aware of the story in Acts? In this case, Acts must have done the copying because the idea of the apostles being immune to snakes has come about because of a misunderstanding of a metaphor. We have a three step process that would occur in a certain order:

Metaphor - The followers of Jesus will be immune from snakes (false teachers) and can drink their poison (their teachings) unharmed.

Literal - The followers of Jesus can pick up snakes and can drink poison without being harmed.

Literal specific – a particular follower of Jesus was bitten on the hand by a snake and was unaffected.

The literal understanding of the metaphor must come before it is applied to a specific person. The long ending is at the literal stage whereas the Acts story is literal specific. So the long ending is closer to the original source than the Acts story, and so could not have developed from the Acts story. Instead, the Acts story must have been based on something very like the long ending.

There is a second example of this saying applied at the literal specific level. Eusebius tells us that the writings of the second century church father Papias include a story about Justus Barsabbas (the disciple who according to Acts failed to win election as the twelfth apostle to replace Judas[46]) drinking poison and being unharmed.[47] This gives us, in parallel to the

Paul story, another example of the signs in the long ending being applied to a particular individual.

Returning to the Acts story it continues with Paul being received into the house of a landowner called Publius. The father of Publius becomes sick, and Paul cures him: *"Paul entered in, and prayed, and laid his hands on him, and healed him"* (Acts 28:8). This corresponds to the long ending where the picking up of snakes and drinking poison is followed by the sign *"they shall lay hands on the ill, and they shall be well"*. Notice how both have the laying on of hands. This coincidence of the snake incident being followed by the laying on of hands is further evidence that Acts is copying the long ending here. Going the other way from Acts to the long ending is unlikely. Why should the long ending copy this relatively obscure section of Acts to summarise the signs of belief in Jesus when there are much more spectacular miracles elsewhere?

There is, however, one thing special about the placing of these two stories: they are the last two miracles in Acts. The stay on Malta is followed by a miracle-free voyage to Rome and Paul's subsequent house arrest. Acts is full of miracles and signs, so is it significant that the author of Luke-Acts has chosen to end the story with these two particular miracles? Ancient writers loved chiastic compositions. Such compositions are symmetrical with the end mirroring the beginning. So if Acts ends its catalogue of signs and miracles with two taken from the long ending then how does it start?

Is the whole of Acts an elaboration of the long ending?

The first miracle performed by the apostles in Acts is in fact the speaking in tongues, the miracle which is found in the long ending list immediately before the handling of snakes. So it appears that Acts has taken miracles from the long ending and placed them in a chiastic structure at the beginning and end of the signs given by the apostles. This gives rise to the startling idea that the whole of Acts can be seen as a vast elaboration of the few lines of the long ending.

This is not as surprising as it may seem when we consider the extreme paucity of sources available to the author of Luke. The gospels take the story to the death and resurrection of Jesus. It is true that the author of Luke has access to the letters of Paul. But Paul's letters lack connection with the literalistic story of Jesus as presented in the gospels. What the author of Luke needs is a frame to connect the Pauline material to the gospel accounts. To supply this connection she must turn to the few lines in the prior gospels that refer to what happens after the resurrection. The author of Luke has at most two such sources; the speech that Jesus gives to the disciples on the mountain in Galilee in Matthew 28:18-20, and (assuming it was in existence at the time) the long ending. It is not surprising that the author of Luke-Acts does not use the Matthew passage. The Gospel of Luke has a "same but different pattern" in relation to Matthew; although Luke is heavily influenced by Matthew, it avoids as far as possible directly copying Matthew because it was written in opposition to Matthew. The basic idea of the Matthew speech, that the disciples should go out across the world spreading the gospel and baptising, is also found in the long ending. One thing not in the long ending but in Matthew is the formula of the Trinity, "*in the name of the Father and of the Son and of the holy spirit*" (*Matthew 28:19*), which was to later become of considerable theological importance but which is not a phrase that is taken up or used by the author of Luke-Acts.

So instead of Matthew the author of Luke-Acts draws upon the long ending which, according to most scholars, was not even written at this time. At the very start of Acts the author alludes to the material covered by the long ending:

The former account have I made, O Theophilus, of all that Jesus began both to do and teach, until the day in which, after he had given commands through the Holy Spirit to the apostles whom he had chosen, he was taken up. (Acts 1:1-2)

There is only one known source that may have been available to the author of Luke in which Jesus gives commands and is then taken up to heaven, and that is the long ending. This feature is not found in the rest of Mark nor Matthew, nor the letters of Paul. The detail that the commands were given through the spirit is interesting and ties in with the shaman paradigm that the apostles only knew Jesus through the spirit. The long ending does not tell us that the resurrection was spiritual, but there is nothing in it to contradict this idea.

It is worth reviewing the commands given to the disciples in the long ending to see how they match up with the account in Acts:

And he said to them, "Go into all the world, and preach the gospel to all creation. He that believes and is baptised shall be saved; but he that believes not shall be condemned. "And these signs shall accompany those who believe; they shall cast out demons in my name; they shall speak in new tongues; they shall take up serpents with their hands; and if they drink poison it shall not hurt them; they shall lay hands on the ill, and they shall be well." (Mark 16:15-18)

The final line of the long ending confirms that the disciples did indeed do these things:

And they went forth, and preached everywhere, the Lord working with them, and confirming the word with accompanying signs. (Mark 16:20)

This line can be taken as summing up the whole of Acts! Acts starts in Jerusalem and ends half way across the known world in Rome. In between these two poles, the apostles travel widely. Everywhere they go they preach, they give signs and perform miracles.

After the number of the apostles has been made up to twelve with the election of Matthias they are all together at Pentecost when the Holy Spirit descends upon them as tongues of flame. The apostles begin to speak in tongues and the Jews who are gathered in Jerusalem from many different nations each hear the men speaking in their own language. All are amazed, although some think them drunk. Peter begins to preach to them and quotes a prophecy from Joel "*And it shall come to pass in the last days, said God, I will pour out of my Spirit upon all flesh: and your sons and your daughters shall prophesy, and your young men shall see visions, and your old men shall dream dreams*" (Acts 2:17). He goes on to say that Jesus was "*a man attested by God among you by miracles and wonders and signs*" (Acts 2:22. He continues by urging them to "*Repent, and be baptised every one of you in the name of Jesus Christ for the remission of sins, and you shall receive the gift of the Holy Spirit*" and to "*Save yourselves from this perverse generation*". His preaching is successful: "*Then they that gladly received his word were baptised: and the same day there were added to them about three thousand souls*" (Acts 2:41). After which: "*And all that believed were together, and had all things common*" (Acts 2:44).

This episode reflects the long ending where it is necessary to believe and to be baptised to be saved and where belief and baptism are accompanied by signs and miracles. There is one thing that has been added by the author of Luke-Acts and that is that the ability to perform signs and miracles is achieved through the medium of the Holy Spirit, which is given to those who believe and who are baptised. What about the other promise in the long ending, that those who do not believe will be condemned? There is a hint of this when Peter warns his listeners "*Save yourselves from this perverse generation*" (Acts 2:40). To understand what he means, we must turn to the symmetrical passage at the end of Acts. Here Paul, imprisoned in Rome, gives a speech to the Jews of that city just as Peter gives a speech to the Jews in Jerusalem. He talks all day to them in his lodgings about the Kingdom of God. He is less successful in his persuasion than Peter: "*some believed the things which were spoken, and some believed not*" (*Acts 28:24*). As the Jews are about to go still arguing among themselves, Paul pronounces his verdict on them by quoting Isaiah: "*Go unto this people, and say, Hearing you shall hear, and shall not understand; and seeing you shall see, and not perceive ...*" (*Acts 28:26*). This is part of the passage in Isaiah that is the condemnation of the Jewish people before the exile. He adds: "*Therefore let it be known to you, that the salvation of God is sent to the Gentiles, and that they will hear it*" (*Acts 28:28*). From the beginning of Acts, where a vast number of Jews join the movement, the situation now has completely reversed. The Jews do not believe, and their generation will be condemned. It is Gentiles who believe and who are saved.

The twin speeches of Peter and Paul at the beginning and end of Acts are used to give effect to the words of the resurrected Jesus in the long ending. We have seen the same chiastic structure is used to represent the signs in the long ending. We start with the speaking in tongues by Peter and the other apostles, and this is followed by healing miracles performed by Peter. The casting out of demons is performed by Peter[48] and then by Paul, who casts out the spirit of divination of the slave girl.[49] At the end, we have the picking up of the snake by Paul followed by the healing of Publius' father by laying on of hands by Paul. The only sign in the list in the long ending not carried out in Acts is the drinking of poison without being harmed. Possibly the author believed this to be the same sign as the picking up of snakes, as both involve resistance to poison.

So the beginning and end of Acts have been written to give effect to the promises in the speech of Jesus in the long ending. These promises are represented by the first speech given to the Jews by Peter and the last speech given to the Jews by Paul and by the first miracles performed by Peter and the last miracles performed by Paul. There is clearly a movement from Peter, representing the Jews and the beginning of the church to Paul representing the Gentiles and the future of the church.

The following table summarises how Acts uses the long ending speech in a chiastic structure.

The long ending speech (Mark 16:15-20)	Acts
Frame - beginning:	
And he said to them, "Go in-to all the world, and preach the gospel to all creation.	<u>Beginning</u> *But you shall receive power when the Holy Spirit comes upon you, and you shall be witnesses to me both in Jerusalem, and in all Judea, and Samaria, and to the ends of the earth.* (Acts 1:8)
Believing theme:	
He that believes and is bap-tised shall be saved;	<u>Beginning</u> Peter preaches successfully to Jews in Jerusalem: *Then they that gladly received his word were baptised: and the same day there were added to them about three thousand souls* (Acts 2:41)
but he that believes not shall be condemned.	<u>End</u> Paul preaches unsuccessfully to the Jews of Rome: *Go unto this people, and say, Hearing you shall hear, and shall not understand; and seeing you shall see, and not perceive ...* (Acts 28:26).
Miracles theme:	
And these signs shall accom-pany those who believe;	Acts is all about the signs given by the apostles.
they shall cast out demons in my name;	The casting out of demons is spread through Acts.
they shall speak in new tongues;	<u>Beginning</u> First miracle in Acts: *And they were all filled with the Holy Spirit, and began to speak with other tongues, as the Spirit gave them utterance.* (Acts 2:4)

The long ending speech (Mark 16:15-20)	Acts
they shall take up serpents with their hands; and if they drink poison it shall not hurt them;	<u>End</u> Penultimate miracle in Acts: *But Paul having gathered together a quantity of sticks, and having laid them upon the fire, a viper, having come out of the heat, did fasten on his hand. (Acts 28:3)*
they shall lay hands on the ill, and they shall be well.	<u>End</u> Last miracle in Acts: *Paul entered in, and prayed, and laid his hands on him, and healed him* (Acts 28:8)
Frame - end:	
And they went forth, and preached everywhere, the Lord working with them, and confirming the word with accompanying signs.	<u>End</u> About Paul under house arrest in Rome: *Preaching the kingdom of God, and teaching those things which concern the Lord Jesus Christ, with all confidence, no man forbidding him. (Acts 28:31)*

This is the evidence that the author of Acts was well aware of the long ending and that it was attached to their copy of Mark. So the long ending must have been part of Mark at the time that the Gospel of Luke was written in the late first century.

The resurrection accounts in Matthew and Luke

There is one more potential objection to the long ending; that the resurrection accounts in Matthew and Luke do not follow it. Certainly the gospels of Matthew and Luke follow Mark closely up to the point of the long ending and then diverge widely, both from the long ending and from each other. The argument goes that if the long ending had been in existence when they were written, this divergence would not have happened. But we have already seen that there is at least one important instance, that of the first resurrection appearance to Mary the Magdalene and "the other Mary", where Matthew does seem to follow the long ending, and which is very hard to understand if the long ending were not available when Matthew was written.

In fact, the divergence of Matthew and Luke at the point of the long ending does not imply that they did not use the long ending as a source. If the long ending is in existence, then the authors of Matthew and Luke are faced with inconsistent sources. Mark with the long ending is internally inconsistent, as well as being inconsistent with Paul's account in 1 Corinthians. Faced with such inconsistencies the authors of Matthew and Luke have to make choices of which features to retain and which to reject, so divergence is inevitable.

To test whether the long ending was available in the composition of Matthew and Luke, we must turn the question around. We will assume for the moment that the other gospel writers did not have the long ending and that Mark ended at 16:8. The sources available to the authors of Matthew and Luke would then be consistent so we can predict the broad outlines of the story that they would generate from these sources. We might expect some embellishment, but we would not expect contradiction in such an important area. If there are such contradictions, then the authors of Matthew and Luke must have had another source available to them. The process is:

1. To identify how the story must have developed if only Mark to 16:8 and 1 Corinthians 15 were available.

2. To identify any features in either Matthew or Luke that contradict this story completion.

3. To identify any source that may have all or most of these contradicting features present.

So how would the story have been developed if the other gospel writers only had Mark up to 16:8 and potentially 1 Corinthians 15 as sources? In the shortened Mark, the fact of Jesus' resurrection is attested by the man in the tomb, but there are no resurrection appearances as such. This is the way the gospel would have ended:

"Go, say to his disciples and Peter, that he does go before you to Galilee; there you shall see him as he said to you." And, having gone out, they fled from the tomb in trembling and amazement, and they said nothing to anyone for they were afraid.

We must imagine a gospel writer sitting and reading this ending. The deficiencies are glaring so our gospel writer decides to take the action forward. How would he or she have continued the story?

It is not difficult to see how the story must end because it is so strongly implied by the young man's message. Jesus must appear in Galilee to Peter and the other disciples. There is, however, one little detail that may give our gospel writer pause, and that is the baffling last line that the women *"said nothing to anyone"*. As an ending this is bizarre. The women are given a message, they do not pass it on, and at this point the gospel ends! And if they do not pass it on, how can we be sure that Peter and the disciples kept their appointment in Galilee? However, the overall import of the ending is clear and unmistakable. The only difficulty lies in the last line, and this causes only brief puzzlement in the reader rather than suggesting any alternative ending. We can expect our gospel writer to either pass over this last line in silence or to change it to something more positive.

The other potential source is Paul's account in 1 Corinthians that Jesus appeared to Cephas and then the twelve. As long as our gospel writer thinks that Cephas and Peter are two forms of the same name, the two accounts are perfectly consistent. So it is only possible to continue the story with an appearance in Galilee to Peter and the twelve. Turning to Matthew we find what we would expect in the story at the end of the gospel:

Then the eleven disciples went to Galilee, to the mountain where Jesus had appointed them. When they saw him, they worshiped him, but some doubted. And having come to them, Jesus spoke to them, saying, "All authority in heaven and on earth has been given to me. Therefore go and make disciples of all nations, baptising them in the name of the Father and of the Son and of the Holy Spirit, teaching them to observe all things, everything I have commanded you. And behold, I am with you all the days, to the completion of the age." (Matthew 28:16-20)

There is nothing in Mark about a mountain, but neither is there anything to contradict this. There is, however, one detail that does not agree with what we would expect, and that is that Peter although implied to be present in the eleven is not mentioned separately by name. Why not? It would have been so easy to have the impulsive Peter chasing up the mountain to throw himself at the feet of his risen Lord, while his fellow disciples followed hesitantly behind. If the author of Matthew had inherited a strong tradition of Peter as the first witness, this is how he should have written it. Nor is this lack of a mention an oversight, for Peter has been written out of the earlier messages given by the angel and Jesus. The young man in Mark says that the women should tell *"his disciples and Peter"*[50] but in Matthew this has become *"his disciples"* with Jesus asking them to tell *"my brethren"*. We may note that this is inconsistent with 1 Corinthians which clearly singles out Cephas as the first witness before the others.

The Gospel of Matthew also inserts a whole episode of watchmen appointed by Pilate on the advice of the high priests and Pharisees to secure the tomb with a stone and to watch over it because Jesus has predicted that he would rise on the third day. The watchmen observe what has happened and when they report back the priests bribe them to say that the body was stolen by Jesus' disciples. The gospel adds *"this story is widely circulated among the Jews until this day"* (Matthew 28:15). The reason for this episode is plain. The author of Matthew is loyal to his source but does change Mark when there is a problem with that gospel. The problem with Mark here is that no one sees the stone being rolled away, and when the women enter the tomb they see only a man. The author of Matthew comes from a Jewish Christian group, and this group would have used Mark to proselytise among their fellow Jews. The comment about the Jews believing that the body has been stolen would reflect the argument that was thrown back at them when they tried to use the resurrection account to prove that Jesus was divine. There is nothing in Mark to say that the moving of the stone was due to supernatural agency or that the man in the tomb was divine. Some of the Jews must have read Mark carefully and come to the perfectly reasonable conclusion that it was Jesus' disciples who had arranged the disappearance of the body and who gave the women the message.

The author of Matthew addresses this problem in two ways. First he has the stone moved by an angel who also gives the message to the women. Then he supplies independent witnesses to the whole event (the watchmen) while also accounting for why the Jews maliciously put around the slander that the body was stolen. This whole episode is an embellishment of the Gospel of Mark's account but is not inconsistent with that account.

What is inconsistent with the Mark account is that the number of women who visit the tomb has been reduced from three to two by omitting Salome. The most important inconsistency with the implied ending, however, is that these two then see the risen Jesus. If the author of Matthew had only Mark without the long ending and perhaps 1 Corinthians then this added resurrection appearance is inexplicable; it contradicts both these sources and depreciates the role of Peter.

So there are all together three inconsistencies with what we would expect if the author of Matthew's version of Mark had ended at 16:8; the resurrection appearance to the two women, the writing out of Peter as a named witness, and the reduction in the number of women to two by leaving out Salome.

We would expect Luke to have an appearance to Peter and the other disciples. The author of Luke certainly knows of Paul's resurrection account and regards it as authoritative, and there is nothing in Mark up to 16:8 to contradict Paul's account. So it is very significant that Luke deviates considerably from a simple appearance to Peter and the disciples. The sequence of Luke's account is complex but is summarised below:

The women go to the tomb see two angels and are told that Jesus is raised.

They tell the others and are not believed.

Peter runs to the tomb and sees the grave clothes.

The two disciples on the road to Emmaus see Jesus but do not at first recognise him.

After they return to Jerusalem, they are told that the Lord was raised and seen by Simon.

Jesus appears to those gathered together in Jerusalem including the eleven.

Jesus leads them out to Bethany where he ascends.

In looking for inconsistencies with the implied ending of Mark we have to allow for the fact that the author of Luke probably had access to the Gospel of Matthew. However, consistent with the "same but different" pattern, Luke does not copy the specific details of the Matthew resurrection account. The general form of the accounts is similar with the empty tomb and angelic appearance to the women leading to a number of resurrection appearances culminating with an appearance to all the disciples. This, however, is also the form of the long ending of Mark so we cannot be sure if the author of Luke has been influenced by Matthew, by the long ending or by both.

The "same but different" pattern may be evident in the fact that the author of Luke follows Matthew in changing the number of women in Mark but has increased the number rather than reduced it. The expanded group is now Mary the Magdalene, Mary of James and Joanna along with other unnamed women. There seems no reason to make this change other than to downgrade the special role of Mary the Magdalene. Another change made by the author of Luke is the insertion of a new episode with Peter running to the tomb and seeing the grave clothes. The motivation would seem to be to enhance the role of Peter by having him observe the empty grave like the women.

The first clear inconsistency with the implied ending of Mark is that the resurrection appearances take place in Jerusalem and its surroundings rather than Galilee. If the author of Luke's sources are Mark without the long

ending and 1 Corinthians along with Matthew, then why does she make
this change? Paul does not mention a location and Mark without the long
ending strongly implies that the resurrection takes place in Galilee. The
author of Luke is aware of this problem because the message of the angel is
changed to remove all reference to Galilee. The argument that the disciples
are in Jerusalem so they can witness the descent of the Holy Spirit does not
seem sufficient reason to change the location. It is not far from Galilee to
Jerusalem and Acts allows forty days between the first resurrection appearance and Pentecost. Besides the Pentecost episode was invented by the
author of Luke and there is no reason it could not have been situated in
Galilee rather than Jerusalem. It would seem that the author of Luke has
some other source that indicates that the resurrection happened in Jerusalem.

The most significant inconsistency is that the author of Luke has introduced the whole new story into her narrative of the disciples on the road to
Emmaus. The story is long and takes up a large portion of the total resurrection account in Luke. It occurs at a key point in the narrative between
the angelic appearance to the women and the appearance to Simon and the
eleven and is the first time in Luke we see the risen Christ. There must have
been a very strong reason for the author of Luke to deviate so strikingly
from Paul's account.

The reported appearance to Simon does not count as an inconsistency
because Luke uses the name Simon in other places to mean Peter, who is
mentioned just a little earlier as seeing the empty tomb and the grave
clothes. This supposed appearance to Simon Peter is thus consistent with
the message of the angel in Mark and with 1 Corinthians 15:5.

In conclusion both the authors of Matthew and Luke deviate substantially from the implied ending of Mark and must have had access to at least
one other source in addition to the shortened Mark. It is worth summarising these inconstancies:

Matthew
The first appearance of the risen Christ is to the two women walking
from the tomb and not to Peter and the disciples.

Peter is eliminated as a named individual from the message of the angel
and the resurrection appearance.

The number of women is reduced to two with the omission of Salome.

Luke

The first appearance of the risen Christ in the narrative is to two who are walking to Emmaus - one is called Cleopas, and the other is unnamed.

The resurrection appearances take place in Jerusalem and its surroundings and not in Galilee.

The number of women is increased, and Joanna replaces Salome.

Can we find one or more sources that can account for these deviations from Mark up to 16:8? We do in fact have such a source, and that is the long ending! The most significant feature is that both Matthew and Luke have an extra appearance to two disciples coming between the message of the angel or angels and the appearance to the eleven. This then becomes the first appearance of the risen Christ. We can rule out the idea that Luke has copied Matthew (or vice versa) for the stories are very different and feature different individuals. So we can deduce that there must have been a common source which had an appearance to two disciples between the angelic message and the appearance to the eleven. We can further deduce that the two disciples in this source must have been unnamed because both Matthew and Luke assign them different identities. Additional evidence for this is that the Gospel of Luke does not even mention the name of one of them. We may suspect that the author of Luke has simply used the name Cleopas because it is floating around in one of her sources and because Cleopas is not one of the eleven/twelve to whom the risen Christ appears later. In the case of Matthew, the number of women has been deliberately reduced to two which is particularly significant as the author of Matthew does not change details in Mark without good reason. So we can conclude that the number two must have been specifically mentioned in the source.

The source we are looking for is the long ending:

After that, he appeared in another form to two of them, as they walked, and went into the country. And they went and told it to the rest: neither did they believed them. (Mark 16:12-13)

This comes between the appearance to Mary the Magdalene and the appearance to the eleven. Looking at the details we can see how the author of Luke has followed the clues in this passage while enormously expanding the story. The two in Luke are "walking in the country" on the road to Emmaus. They see Jesus *"in another form"* because he takes on another appearance until the end of the meal. This type of imaginative elaboration is very typical of the author of Luke, who is a natural novelist rather than a natural historian. In contrast, the author of Matthew is very loyal to his sources and is a much more reliable witness to those sources, although he is always ready to make changes to eliminate inconsistencies and remove negatives.

Both authors are grappling with the internal inconsistencies within the version of Mark containing the long ending, and they use different strategies to try and resolve the problem. The most glaring inconsistency is the tension between the young man's words that Jesus will appear to Peter and the disciples in Galilee and the almost immediately subsequent appearance to Mary the Magdalene. Although the long ending does not tell us explicitly where the resurrection appearances take place, we can deduce that the location must be Jerusalem. Mary the Magdalene sees Jesus on the same day as the discovery of the empty tomb so she must still be in Jerusalem. And she immediately tells the disciples, so they must be in Jerusalem also. This contradicts the message of the young man/angel that the appearance will be in Galilee. The Gospel of Luke resolves this difficulty by changing the message so that the resurrected Jesus will not appear in Galilee and situating all the appearances in Jerusalem and the surroundings. This explains the second inconsistency in Luke; the author is not deliberately changing the location but making a choice as to what locational clue to follow.

The author of Matthew makes different choices. He picks up on the message of the man-angel and sets his ultimate scene in Galilee. This leaves him the problem of dealing with the appearance to Mary the Magdalene and the two disciples walking in the country. He solves this by taking the liberty of combining the two into one; he writes in an appearance to two women immediately after the angel's message, and he makes one of the women Mary the Magdalene. In the long ending the two disciples are walking in the country or a field; in Matthew the two women are running from the tomb to tell the disciples and must also be in the country outside the walls of Jerusalem. The author seems to have had the idea of equating the initial appearance to Mary with the empty tomb and the message of the angel that Jesus has risen and is in heaven, so that the appearance to the two, as they leave the tomb, is *"in another form"*. He keeps the final appearance to the eleven as in the long ending, but he locates it explicitly in Galilee. He changes the meal which in the long ending is associated with a Jerusalem location and instead has Jesus appear on a mountain in Galilee. He probably has some other source for this mountain; we will see that the appearance of Jesus to disciples on a mountain makes perfect sense in terms of the metaphorical framework of the movement. The resurrection account in Matthew has all the important elements from the long ending in Mark;

the message of the angel, the first appearance to Mary the Magdalene, the appearance to two disciples, the final appearance to the eleven; all combined into a brief and consistent narrative.

The mystery of why the author Matthew writes Peter out of the resurrection is also solved. The long ending makes no specific mention of Peter, and the first appearance is to Mary the Magdalene. The promise of the young man in Mark that Jesus will appear to the disciples and Peter is thus a confusing detail as Peter plays no special role in what follows. So the author of Matthew has simply dropped the reference to Peter in the angel's message. It would seem that the author of Matthew is either unaware of Paul's account in 1 Corinthians or did not value it.

The one inconsistency that is not explained by the long ending is the increase in the number of women in Luke. The fact that both Luke and Matthew drop Salome is surely not a coincidence and we can see the author of Luke as being influenced by the Gospel of Matthew in changing the list of women. The problem that the author of Luke is facing is how to reconcile Paul's version of events of an appearance to Cephas and the twelve with the long ending. The author of Luke gives preference to Paul and so is forced to demote the appearance to Mary the Magdalene; the statement in the long ending that Jesus appeared to Mary is interpreted as meaning that she saw the empty tomb and received the message that Jesus had risen. This is a reasonable reading of Mark 16:9 if it is taken as summarising what has just happened. The increase in the number of women can be seen as a novelistic device to reinforce the primacy of Peter by taking the attention away from Mary the Magdalene while at the same time not being inconsistent with the long ending. Similarly, the author of Luke introduces the retrospective reference to Simon seeing the risen Christ to give primacy to Paul's account but without violating the sequence of the long ending. As for the introduction of Joanna, we shall see that it was the habit of the author of Luke to write into the story people she knew. Most likely Joanna was a member of her household and a co-worker on the gospel whom she rewarded with a cameo role.

In fact the account in Luke mostly follows the long ending closely, setting the appearances in Jerusalem as the long ending implies, developing the appearance to the two walking in the country into a major story, and having the final appearance at a meal (implied by Jesus asking them for something to eat). Another theme the author of Luke picks up from the long ending is the lack of belief. The women at the tomb are not believed by the disciples, and the two on the road do not at first recognise Jesus.

This lack of belief is a major theme in the long ending but does not appear in the other sources available to Luke; the short ending, Paul or Matthew.

There is one other small detail that occurs in the long ending and which is picked up by both Matthew and Luke and that is that the disciples who see the risen Christ at the climatic appearance are eleven in number. This contradicts the evidence of Paul in 1 Corinthians 15:5 that Jesus was seen by Cephas and then the Twelve.

The evidence in Matthew and Luke for the prior existence of the long ending is compelling. If the long ending did not exist, it would be necessary to invent it. Otherwise, we could not account for the deviations of Matthew and Luke from a Mark that ended at 16:8. But there is one further consideration, a consideration that turns on the mysterious last line of the short ending, that the women were afraid and told no one. It is this apparently inexplicable line that holds the final clue.

The mystery of the silent women

If the version of Mark without the long ending were the original gospel, then it preserves the original ending. We would expect it to end as an ancient document should end. If, however, the long ending has been ripped out from the original then we would expect a jagged edge. The shorter version will not end properly, and the ending will match up with what has been taken away, like a sheet of paper that has had a strip torn off it. This is a simple but powerful test to conclude whether or not the shorter document could have been the original gospel. Which of the two applies to the short ending? The short ending ends with the women saying nothing:

And, having gone out, they fled from the tomb in trembling and amazement, and they said nothing to anyone for they were afraid.

There is no ancient document that we know of that ends like this. As well as Mark we have five other books (excluding letters) in the New Testament, Matthew, Luke, John, Acts, and Revelation. Matthew ends with Jesus' commission to the disciples, Luke ends with the disciples witnessing the ascent of Jesus to heaven and returning to give praise in the temple, John ends with the many other things that Jesus did and which are too great in number to write down, Acts ends with Paul preaching and teaching for two years in Rome, Revelation ends with a warning that the book is not to be altered and a promise and a prayer that Jesus will come quickly.

In each case it is clear that the ending is an ending. Each ends on a note of triumph and hope. But the supposed ending of Mark ends in fear and silence. There are some who argue that this is a moving ending, but they are projecting modern preferences for sophisticated ambiguity into the past. Whoever wrote Mark was not a post-modernist. So the shorter version of the gospel fails to end as we would expect an ancient text to end.

So do we have a jagged edge? The last line is negative so we must ask why it is there, what purpose does it serve? Those secularists who believe that Jesus was just a man have an answer. The line is intended to hide a deceit. The story of the empty tomb has just been newly minted, so the author has to explain why his readers have not heard it before. So the purpose of the line, as they would have it, is to improve the credibility of the empty tomb story. If this is so then the author fails miserably for he does not address the obvious question of how he came to know the story.

It truth, the line is not intended to give support to the empty tomb. To understand its real purpose, we must place it into context with what comes after, the long ending, as well as what comes before. Look at the line in this whole context:

The young man tells the women to tell the disciples and Peter that Jesus goes before them to Galilee.

The women are afraid and tell no one.

Jesus appears to Mary the Magdalene on the morning of the first day.

The first and last points are glaringly inconsistent and cause the authors of Matthew and Luke immense problems when they come to write their gospels. The line about the silent women is sandwiched between these two inconsistencies. And this gives the clue as to its real purpose; it must be intended as a bridge between the two contradictory statements. Which is exactly what it does! Notice that the man-angel does not tell the women directly that Jesus will appear in Galilee but gives the women an errand, a message to pass on to "*Peter and the disciples*". It is this message that says Jesus will appear to them in Galilee. But the women "*said nothing to anyone*" – they fail to pass on the message! Because the women fail in their errand, Peter and the disciples would not have gone to Galilee to see Jesus appear. Mary the Magdalene and her companions have been afraid and showed lack of faith. It is because of this lack of faith that Jesus has to appear to Mary directly instead of appearing to the disciples in Galilee. The line bridges two inconsistent stories.

So the silence of the women is not an ending but a jagged edge. It only makes sense if followed by the long ending.

Key points

1. The long ending is missing in a few early manuscripts of Mark although most include it.

2. Eusebius (c300) is aware that some copies of Mark omitted the long ending and doubts if it were part of the original gospel. However, Irenaeus writing much earlier in the second century quotes from it as part of Mark.

3. There are a number of linguistic and continuity issues that suggest that the long ending differs from the rest of Mark and was not written by the same person.

4. These difficulties include line 16:8 which terminates those manuscripts that omit the long ending. If the long ending were not original then this line, in which the women are frightened and tell no one, is unlikely to be part of the original gospel.

5. The line 16:8 is not how we would expect an ancient text to end. All other early Christian writings end on a note of triumph and not with fear and despondency.

6. The line 16:8 performs an essential function linking the long ending to the rest of Mark and explains why Jesus did not appear to Peter and the disciples in Galilee. Because the women were fearful, they did not pass on the message and Jesus had to appear direct to Mary the Magdalene. Moreover, the fear of the women in Mark 16:8 ties in with the theme of doubt in the long ending proper.

7. There are similarities between Acts and the long ending that suggest that Acts was conceived as a vast expansion of the speech of Jesus in the long ending. Acts places elements from this speech in a chiastic structure. So the first and last miracles in Acts come from the long ending, and the two episodes of the speeches of Peter at the beginning and Paul at the end reflect Jesus' words in the long ending.

8. The resurrection accounts in Matthew and Luke do not continue as we would have expected if the long ending did not exist. Matthew introduces an extra appearance to two women, one of whom is Mary the Magdalene, whereas Luke adds a story of the appearance to two on the road to Emmaus as well as changing the location of the resurrection appearances to Jerusalem. All these features match elements in the long ending.

Conclusion

The long ending is not original to Mark. The gospel must have original-ly ended with the triumphant message of the young man at Mark 16:7. The long ending was added almost immediately after the gospel was written with 16:8 also added as a transitional line.

This version with the long ending was extensively copied and all surviv-ing copies derive from it, including those copies that subsequently lost the ending.

The authors of Matthew and Luke-Acts both had a version of Mark that included the long ending.

Chapter 11

The Gospel of the Long Ending

We have concluded that the long ending was not original to Mark but was added very early. All surviving texts of Mark have been derived from a copy with the long ending, but the ending was deleted in some copies.

But this leads to another question. Why should the long ending have been added so quickly to the newly written gospel and why, if it was an innovation, did it win such quick and widespread acceptance that it superseded the original version? The only answer that makes sense is that the long ending was based on a source that was earlier than Mark, and reflected a version of the story that the first readers regarded as authentic. We can go further and attempt a reconstruction of this original source, which we will call the "Gospel of the Long Ending". We will see that the author of Mark used this Gospel of the Long Ending as a source. The Gospel of the Long Ending has not been added just once to the gospel; it has effectively been added twice!

The twice-added ending

It is ironic that those who deleted the long ending must have done so from the belief that they were returning to the original, yet those who had earlier added it did so from the same motive. The first readers of Mark rejected the original ending because they believed that it deviated from the accepted story of the resurrection. And because these first readers had been Christians before the Gospel of Mark was written, the long ending, or something very like it, must already have been in existence when Mark was written. And so we come to the conclusion that the long ending is earlier than the rest of the Gospel of Mark and not later.

But if the long ending was earlier, then why should the author of Mark deviate from its version of the story? We already have the clue to answer this question. The author of Mark does not have one source for the resurrection but two. The first is an early form of the long ending and the second is Paul's account in 1 Corinthians. These two sources are inconsistent with each other! The author of Mark is trying to resolve these inconsistencies by combining the two into an account that does not contradict either source. Once we realise this, we can appreciate the subtleties of his empty tomb story. His basic approach is to downgrade the appearance to Mary the Magdalene but to do so in such ambiguous terms as to avoid a direct contradiction of the long ending. He combines the appearance to the Magdalene and the appearance to the two others into one episode involving three women.

When the women come to the empty tomb, they see "a young man" who tells the women that Jesus has risen. It is here that ambiguity enters into the account. Who is this young man, is he an angel? In Matthew he certainly is: *"And, behold, there was a great earthquake: for the angel of the Lord descended from heaven, and came and rolled away the stone, and sat upon it."* (Matthew 28:2) The author of Matthew tends to change Mark when he detects a problem with the earlier gospel. The problem here is that the young man is not impressive enough. Is he really an angel? Perhaps he is just a man or even Jesus "in another form" that the women do not recognise. This is exactly what happens in John. Mary the Magdalene comes across a gardener at the tomb whom she does not recognise at first but who is actually Jesus.[51] The Mark account is skilfully drafted so that, depending on whether we interpret the young man as an angel or as Jesus, we get back either to Paul's account or the long ending:

1. If the young man is an angel, then Jesus does not appear to the women. Instead, he will appear to Peter and the disciples later. This is consistent with 1 Corinthians 15 where Paul says that Jesus appeared to Cephas and the Twelve.

2. If the young man is Jesus, then the account is consistent with the long ending. Jesus appears to Mary the Magdalene on the first day of the week, he appears to two others in "another form" (as the young man) and later he will appear to all the disciples.

By keeping the status of the young man ambiguous, the author has been able to produce a story that does not directly contradict either source. However, most readers would not have appreciated the subtlety. They saw the young man simply as an angel and not as Jesus. The first readers would have been familiar with the tradition represented by the long ending that Jesus appeared first to Mary the Magdalene and they would have wanted this tradition reflected in the story. So they appended the long ending again to the gospel to make it clear that Jesus did appear to Mary first.

The following table shows the features in Mark 16:1-7 that correspond to details in the long ending.

Mark 16:1-7	Source (Long ending Mark 16:9-20)
And when the sabbath was past, Mary Magdalene,	... he did appear first to Mary the Magdalene...
and Mary the mother of James, and Salome,	After that he appeared in another form to two of them
And very early in the morning the first day of the week (mia ton sabbaton)	And [Jesus] having risen early in the morning of the first day of the week (prote sabbatou)
they came to the tomb	as they walked, and went into the country
they saw a young man sitting on the right side, clothed in a long white garment; and they were afraid. And he said to them "Be not afraid: You seek Jesus of Nazareth, who was crucified. He is risen, he is not here."	So then, after the Lord Jesus had spoken to them, he was taken up into heaven and he sat at the right hand of God.
But go your way, tell his disciples and Peter that he goes before you into Galilee: there you shall see him, as he said to you.	Afterward he appeared to the eleven as they reclined at the table

This shows that there are a number of features that match. One of the most specific is the "*first day of the week*", although the English disguises the fact that a different Greek phrase ("*one of the week*") is used in Mark 16:2 compared to Mark 16:9 ("*first of the week*"). The author of Mark is not making a word for word copy of the long ending, but rephrasing certain elements of it for his own account. We should note that the tomb would have been outside the city walls and so "in the country".

It is not just the areas of agreement that provide evidence for the author of Mark's use of the long ending. Equally important are the elements he leaves out. Where there is an element of the long ending that we would expect the author of Mark to use but he does not, this indicates that it was not in his source, but has been added when the long ending was appended to the gospel. We can be sure that changes were made to the long ending at this stage because Jesus appears to eleven disciples. We know from Paul that twelve disciples in addition to Cephas saw the resurrected Jesus; the idea that there were only eleven remaining disciples after the betrayal of Judas originates with the Gospel of Mark. When the long ending was added it was edited to replace the original "Twelve" or "the disciples" with the eleven.

If we remove those elements of the long ending that the author of Mark should have used but did not, then we can recreate the original source. We can then apply a test of whether this recreated source makes sense as a stand-alone document. Is it of lower entropy than the full version of the long ending as found in Mark? If the correspondences between the empty tomb story and the long ending were just coincidence, then we would expect this process to remove a random selection from the long ending. What is left should make less sense than the original; it should be at higher level of entropy.

The most significant features in the long ending that do not correspond to anything up to Mark 16:7 are:

1. The speech that Jesus gives to the eleven in Mark 16:15-18.
2. The last line, Mark 16:20.

Also Mark up to 16:7 does not have the "eleven" or the theme of doubt that pervades the long ending. It is difficult to see why the author of Mark would not use the speech of Jesus, which gives the disciples important instructions, or the last line which is a positive statement of the actions of the disciples after Jesus is removed to heaven. We can conclude that these elements were not in the version available to the author of Mark but were additions made when the long ending was added to Mark. On the other hand, the theme of doubt is something we would have expected the author of Mark to possibly omit because it is negative. Besides, although the theme of doubt is not in Mark before 16:7 it does appear in the transitional line of 16:8. The person who added that line is aware of the theme of doubt and is extrapolating it backwards. No one would have wanted to add the doubt theme if it had not already been in there. So we can conclude that the doubt theme was original and that the elements that have been added are Mark 16:15-18, Mark 16:20 and the concept of the "eleven". If we delete these, we can reconstruct what we will call the "Gospel of the Long Ending".

The Gospel of the Long Ending

And [Jesus] having risen early in the morning of the first day of the week, he did appear first to Mary the Magdalene, out of whom he had cast seven demons. She went and told those who had been with him and who were mourning and weeping. And they, having heard that Jesus was alive and that she had seen him, did not believe it.

After that, he appeared in another form to two of them, as they walked, and went into the country. And they went and told it to the rest: neither did they believe them.

Afterward he appeared to [the disciples/the twelve] as they reclined at table, and rebuked their unbelief and hardness of heart, because they did not believe those who had seen him after he was risen. So then, after the Lord Jesus had spoken to them, he was taken up into heaven and he sat at the right hand of God.

It is obvious that this makes sense as a stand-alone source. It has a simple and coherent form of three rising to a climax which is lost in the full long ending. It has a single central theme of the lack of belief in those who first witnessed the risen Christ until the witnesses had seen him themselves, and in particular a lack of belief in the first witness, Mary the Magdalene. The passage is also chiastic with the first line, the rising of Jesus, symmetrical to the last line, Jesus being received up to heaven. The appearance to Mary the Magdalene is symmetrical to the appearance to the disciples, with the belief of Mary contrasted with the lack of belief of the disciples. These features show that it is lower entropy than the version attached to Mark.

It is in fact exactly what we would expect from a genuine early source. It lacks the elaboration of the later development of the story, yet it stands alone as a powerful whole with a simple, coherent structure and message. Such a coherent form is not going to be produced by material selected at random. So the fact that it has emerged out of our analysis is strong evidence that the analysis is correct and that the author of Mark did have this Gospel of the Long Ending as a source for his resurrection account.

When this Gospel of the Long Ending was appended to Mark the central theme of lack of belief in Mary the Magdalene was lost. The transitional line, about the women being afraid and not passing on the angel's message, has been developed by extrapolating backward the doubt-theme in the Gospel of the Long Ending. The lack of belief now applies also to Mary;

because of her lack of belief, Jesus has to appear directly to her. The result is that Mary loses the unique role that she had in the original as the one who was not believed.

The Gospel of the Long Ending presupposes a backstory with Jesus as a man who had lived on earth and who had been known and loved in his earthly life by Mary and the disciples. But behind it, we can see the shaman paradigm, the idea that Jesus appeared first to Mary and that she was not believed by the disciples until they had the same spiritual experience. This short piece then is a bridge between the spiritual Jesus and the literal Jesus and is the very first known literalistic gospel.

The Gospel of the Long Ending and Paul's account in 1 Corinthians 15 are not quite the only information available to Mark. We can identify at least three other pieces of information that he gives that do not come from either of these sources:

1. There is nothing about the rolling of the stone away from the tomb entrance in the Gospel of The Long Ending. Paul does tell us that Jesus was buried[52] but does not mention a tomb or a stone.

2. The names of the other women with Mary the Magdalene (Mary of James and Salome) do not come from the Gospel of the Long Ending.

3. In the message of the young man, Jesus will appear in Galilee, a place that is not mentioned in the Gospel of the Long Ending or by Paul.

We will find explanations for all of these points when we consider the wider context of the resurrection stories.

The development of the resurrection stories

We can now summarise how the resurrection stories developed:

1. There were just two main sources, Paul's account in 1 Corinthians 15 and the Gospel of the Long Ending.

2. Faced with these two hopelessly conflicting sources, the author of Mark favours Paul's account but uses both in his story. By a clever use of ambiguity around the identity of his young man, he avoids contradicting either. His original gospel ends at 16:7, with the message of the young man.

3. The early readers of the gospel do not appreciate the ambiguity and some reject the ending because it conflicts with the tradition passed down to them that Jesus appeared first to Mary the Magdalene. So they append the Gospel of the Long Ending to the end of Mark. They add the line 16:8

about the women failing to pass on their message as a transition to explain why Jesus appears to Mary and not the disciples as promised. They also add additional material to the body of the Gospel of the Long Ending.

4. This expanded gospel circulates more widely than the original because the resurrection appearance to Mary the Magdalene satisfies the established belief of the early Christians. The expansion, however, is clumsy and makes the resurrection account in Mark appear inconsistent.

5. The author of Matthew has a copy of Mark with the long ending attached, and he smooths out the problems with the account while trying to stay close to his source. He introduces a meeting of the resurrected Jesus to the two women as they walk away from the tomb. This serves the double purpose of making sure that the first appearance is to Mary the Magdalene, in accordance to the long ending, and to satisfy the appearance to two others as they walk in the country, also in accordance with the long ending. For the appearance to the disciples, he takes his cue from the earlier words of the young man. He has Jesus appear to "the eleven" on a mountain in Galilee rather than at a meal in Jerusalem. In this way he preserves the long ending appearance in its essentials, whilst making it consistent with the promise of the young man. The words of Jesus to the disciples on the mountain are based on Jesus' speech to the disciples in the long ending.

6. The author of Luke, like the author of Matthew, is confronted by the inconsistencies in Mark but, as ever, chooses a different solution. Instead of situating the appearance to the disciples in Galilee she follows the story of the meal in the long ending and switches the location of the appearance to Jerusalem. The author of Luke gives primacy to Paul's account in 1 Corinthians. The doubling up of the angels is probably an attempt to explain Matthew's two appearances to the women, while making it clear that Jesus did not appear first to Mary the Magdalene. She does this because Paul does not mention women among the first witnesses. The appearance to two others in a different form is developed into the story of the road to Emmaus. Although the narrative follows the sequence of the long ending, there is a strong suggestion in Luke's account that the first witness is Simon Peter, to be consistent with Paul's Cephas, although the gospel does not explain how he came to see Jesus.

7. The author of Luke writes Acts as the story of how the apostles gave effect to the words of Jesus in the long ending. The message of Jesus found in the long ending of Mark is embedded in a chiastic structure at the beginning and end of Acts.

8. The resurrection story in John is drafted after the other versions and draws upon the other three gospels.

9. Later, a new version of Mark is produced with the long ending deleted but leaving the transitional line about the women being afraid which becomes the new ending. This is an attempt to return to the original and circulates alongside the version of Mark including the long ending.

The first witness conclusion

We have traced back the origins of all the surviving early resurrection accounts to two main sources:

The resurrection statement of Paul in 1 Corinthians
The Gospel of the Long Ending as found, with additions, in the long ending of Mark

With these two sources, the search for the first witness ends in a mystery. We have strong evidence from Paul that Cephas was the first witness. But there is equally good evidence from the Gospel of the Long Ending for Mary the Magdalene.

We have seen the evidence for the Gospel of the Long Ending being the first literalistic gospel and predating the remainder of Mark. On the standard view, the idea that the first gospel could have been a resurrection gospel makes no sense. If Jesus had been a man then the first gospel should reflect traditions based on stories about the man. But if the disciples only knew the resurrected Jesus then the gospel tradition must have developed backwards, starting with the resurrection, adding the passion and only then adding the life of Jesus on earth.

In the Gospel of the Long Ending, the only named disciple is Mary the Magdalene. The gospel's theme is the lack of belief, but it is a lack of belief in Mary rather than in Jesus. If Mary were the shaman this would all make sense. But then why does Paul tell us that it was Cephas who first saw the risen Christ? Why does he not even mention Mary? Paul knows what happened; he knew the "pillars" in Jerusalem, he stayed with Cephas for fifteen days. The idea that he swallowed Cephas' version of events and suppressed the competing claims of Mary does not make sense either. He is immersed in the early church, and he must have known the traditions that it was Mary who first saw the risen Christ, if such traditions existed. Why does he not mention her if only to rebut or qualify her claims? Even if he did not accept her as the first witness, surely he would have included her in his list of those who saw the resurrected Christ if there was a widespread tradition that that was the case? From the evidence of his letters, he is frequently at odds with Peter, James and the other pillars. So why does he not use Mary to take Cephas down a notch?

The silence of Paul is deafening and is telling us something very important. We have a contradiction, and it is always tempting to try and explain away such contradictions. But we must live with contradiction if we are to advance, for contradiction is often a sign that a deeper understanding is required. In this case the solution is staring us in the face, yet it requires us to take a profound step, a step that will strike many as absurd. But before we take such a step, we must consider the third criterion. The founder/shaman should be the first leader of the Jesus movement, so who is that first leader?

Key points

1. The long ending has been added twice to Mark. The author of Mark has used it as a source for his resurrection account, and it has then subsequently been added on to the end of the gospel in its entirety.

2. The author of Mark's other source is Paul's account in 1 Corinthians.

3. The author of Mark has used ambiguity to avoid contradicting either of his sources although he leans towards Paul. If the young man is an angel, then his account is consistent with Paul as the women do not see the risen Jesus, who will then appear first to Peter and the disciples. But if the young man is really Jesus "in another form" then his account is consistent with the long ending, with a first appearance to Mary the Magdalene and two others.

4. The early readers of Mark rejected his rewriting of the resurrection and preferred the long ending version. So the long ending was added back to the gospel with the transitional line of Mark 16:8.

5. The elements of the long ending that Mark does not use, including the speech of Jesus, must have been added at the same time it was appended to the Gospel. If we deduct these elements, we get back to the original "Gospel of the Long Ending" that existed before Mark.

6. The Gospel of the Long Ending has a simple structure of three appearances followed by Jesus being taken up to heaven. The main theme is that the disciples disbelieve Mary the Magdalene until they see the risen Jesus for themselves. This theme was lost when the long ending was added to Mark because the added transitional line of 16:8 makes it seem that Mary also showed lack of faith.

Chapter 12

Who was the first leader?

It is time to move on to the third criterion. The shaman would have been the first leader of the Jesus movement. So if we can identify this first leader, then we will have found the shaman. In this search, we must turn to the earliest sources. First, we will look at the Gospels of Mark and Matthew and the Acts of the Apostles. The authors of these works believed Jesus was a man, and their storytelling has added noise to their sources. We must look through this noise for the signal that points to the identity of the first leader. Who, of the followers of Jesus, is shown consistently in a leadership role? Who does Jesus appoint as the foundation of his church? Who takes charge of the movement after Jesus' death? Who gives the holy spirit to others and who revokes the Jewish purity Laws?

Mary the Magdalene

The first conclusion is that none of the early sources implies that Mary Magdalene is an early leader of the movement. Indeed, they say little or nothing about her. Paul never mentions the Magdalene explicitly. He makes only one reference to a Mary, and that is in the midst of a long list of greetings at the end of Romans.

Neither does Acts mention the Magdalene and we have already seen that Mark and Matthew only bring in the Magdalene in connection with the passion and resurrection. Nowhere do we find anything in the New Testament implying that Mary the Magdalene had a leadership role.

It is true that the Gospel of Thomas has two references to a Mary, but neither tells us that she was the leader. To get any evidence of a prominent role for the Magdalene we have to turn to later gnostic material such as the Gospel of Mary. This work fits uncannily into the shaman paradigm with

Mary as the privileged recipient of revelations from the risen Christ, which she then passes on to the other disciples. But the Gospel of Mary is second century rather than first century and the role it accords Mary may simply be a result of Mary's prominent role in the gospel accounts of the resurrection. This role is particularly evident in the Gospel of John and anyone who had listened to that gospel might see Mary the Magdalene as being specially favoured by the risen Jesus.

This silence about the Magdalene is surprising. Why does she pop up at a critical point and then disappear completely, until a later, possibly secondary, literature about her develops? But disappear she does, and we must move on to consider who it is that the early sources show to have been the first leader.

The Gospels of Mark and Matthew

Starting with the first gospel, Mark, who other than Jesus is in a leadership position over the disciples? It is well known that the gospel gives a list of twelve disciples, but it is less well known that most of these twelve receive no further mention. It is as if the gospel writer knows nothing at all about most of the disciples. The names themselves are suspect as the real identities of the twelve had faded into oblivion by the time the Gospel of Mark was written. Just a few individual disciples are prominent in the gospel. It is worthwhile setting out the main scenes in which the disciples feature in Mark:

The first four fishermen disciples are called on the shore of the Sea of Galilee; Simon, Andrew, James and John (Mark 1:16-20).

Jesus heals Simon's mother-in-law (Mark 1:29-31).

Jesus returns to the sea and passing the tax office sees Levi of Alphaeus and tells him to "Follow me" (Mark 2:14).

Jesus appoints the twelve disciples on a mountain in Galilee, and Simon is given the name "Peter" (Mark 3:13-19).

Jesus asks his disciples who they think he is, and Peter replies that Jesus is the Christ, a key revelation in the narrative of the Gospel of Mark (Mark 8:27-29).

A few lines later Jesus says to Peter "Get behind me Satan" (Mark 8:32-33).

Jesus goes to a mountain with Peter, James and John and appears trans-figured before them along with Moses and Elijah; Peter says that they should make three booths or huts (Mark 9:2-10).

James and John ask if they can take the seats next to Jesus in his glory on his right and left hand (Mark 10:35-40).

Peter, James, John and Andrew question Jesus on the Mount of Olives (Mark 13:3).

Judas Iscariot betrays Jesus to the chief priests (Mark 14:10-11).

Jesus says all the disciples will stumble this night; Peter declares "not I" and Jesus predicts that Peter will deny him three times before the cock crows twice (Mark 14:27-31).

Jesus takes three disciples Peter, James and John with him in the garden of Gethsemane (Mark 14:32-33).

Jesus finds Peter sleeping and says, "Simon, you sleep!" (Mark 14:37).

Judas comes with the chief priests and kisses Jesus to mark him out (Mark 14:43-45).

Peter goes to the hall below the chief priests house as Jesus is being questioned and denies Jesus three times as predicted (Mark 14:66-72).

The young man in the tomb tells the women about the resurrected Christ and tells them to tell "the disciples and Peter" (Mark 16:7).

The first four to be called are two sets of brothers; Simon and Andrew, James and John. The gospel tells us that Simon is also called Peter, although Paul never uses the name Simon for Peter/Cephas. Whenever a named disciple is mentioned in the narrative he is almost invariably one of just three disciples; Peter, James, and John. Andrew receives a few brief men-tions, and Judas Iscariot is a special case. But the other disciples are men-tioned only in the list of the twelve. Levi is an exception, as there is the sto-ry of him being called in the tax office, but then he is not included in the list of the twelve. It just so happens that Jesus' favourite three disciples have the same names as the three Jerusalem "pillars", James, John, and Peter, who feature in Paul's letter to the Galatians as the Jerusalem leadership. This coincidence is suspicious!

The three favourite disciples are not all equal. They have a de facto leader even if he has not been officially appointed. Peter is always men-tioned first in any list of the disciples, and it is Peter who plays the leader-ship role among the others whenever there is need. Peter is present at the significant points of the narrative, including the questioning of Jesus when Peter penetrates alone into the chief priest's house. Most significant of all are the words of the man-angel in the tomb that the women are to tell "*the disciples and Peter."* Note how in this phrase Peter is differentiated from the disciples.

So Mark does provide us with a very clear candidate for the position of early leader, and that is Peter, whom the author of Mark thinks, rightly or wrongly, is also called Simon. If Simon is not the same as Peter, then he must be a prominent discile in his own right, as Mark knows more than one story about him. There are also other stories about characters called Simon that could possibly go back to the same individual as Simon the disciple, although in Mark they are different persons. There is a Simon the leper, who like Simon the disciple owns a house, and there is Simon the Cyrenian, who bears Jesus' cross in a misunderstanding of a Gospel of Thomas saying.

The Gospel of Matthew follows Mark very closely. We can see a further development of the Simon/Peter theme with the compound name Simon Peter making its appearance for the first time. There is, however, one spectacular new addition that would seem to give us a definitive answer as to the identity of the first leader. It is controversial, partly because it does not seem to make sense in the traditional view, and partly because it has been used to justify the special position of the Catholic Church. The controversial section starts immediately after Peter recognises Jesus as the Christ and the Son of the living God:

And Jesus answered and said to him, "Blessed are you, Simon Bar-Jona, because flesh and blood have not revealed it to you, but my Father in heaven. And I also say to you, that you are Peter, and upon this rock I will build my church; and the gates of Hades shall not prevail against it. I will give to you the keys of the kingdom of heaven. Whatever you bind on earth will be bound in heaven, and whatever you loose on earth will be loosed in heaven." (Matthew 16:17-19)

Although Peter is addressed as Simon Bar-Jona (meaning son of Jonah) the play on rock (Peter/Cephas) makes it clear that this passage, if genuine, originally applied to Peter and the reference to Simon has been added by the author of Matthew. The saying gives quite extraordinary powers to Peter. He is given the keys of the Kingdom of Heaven, from which comes the popular cartoon depiction of Peter standing outside the pearly gates with keys in his hand. He has the power to bind and loose; the power to specify what is permitted and what forbidden. His decisions will be followed *"in heaven"* as well as on earth. He is the rock on which the church will be built, and it (not Jesus!) will prevail against the gates of Hades. Note also how *"flesh and blood"* has not revealed Peter's admission of Jesus as the Christ and Son of God but the Father, who is in the heavens. So Peter is the recipient of divine revelation.

Understandably those operating with the view of Jesus as a man have great problems with this passage and frequently reject it as a later interpolation into Matthew. For a start, they do not believe that Peter was the first leader after Jesus, so the idea of Peter being given this role here strikes them as being incorrect. Then the powers assigned to Peter are so extraordinary and spiritual in nature that this does not accord with their view of a realistic earthly Jesus. And the idea of one disciple being singled out to the extent that the church will be built on him alone does not accord with their view of early Christianity. So some think that it was added much later to justify the powers being assumed by a Roman Catholic Church that claimed Peter as its founder.

But under the shaman paradigm, the passage makes complete sense if it is Peter who is the shaman! It shows Peter not as a disciple but as the first leader of the movement. Of course, Peter is distinguished above the disciples and, of course, he is given extreme powers! He attains these powers through divine revelation with Jesus speaking through him in a state of spiritual possession. The church must be built upon the shaman because there is no one else. He has the keys to the kingdom of heaven because he shows others how to pass into the kingdom. He opens the gate, the gate that is Jesus himself. It is only through the shaman that the gates of Hades can be overcome.

The shaman paradigm has illuminated this saying, revealing a meaning that has been obscured by the growth of the literalist view of Jesus in which Peter is relegated to being a disciple. Equally, the saying reveals the identity of the first leader; it points more emphatically to Peter than anything in the Gospel of Mark, yet it also collaborates what has already been deduced from Mark. Is there anything that can confirm whether this was an original part of the Gospel of Matthew? There is an episode in Acts that although not directly related to the saying shows Peter exercising one of the powers granted him; the power to bind and loose.

Acts of the Apostles

Acts is where we should expect strong clues as to the identity of the first leader. It purports to give the history of the first followers of Jesus after his death. The problem is that Acts is a work of fantasy, albeit a fantasy written by an early Christian with excellent access to sources. Acts is essentially the tale of the two apostles Peter and Paul. The first half is concerned mostly with Peter and is followed by a second half devoted almost entirely to Paul. We know by the evidence of Paul's own letters that he was not a member of the movement in its earliest days and cannot have been the first leader. So Acts offers a clear candidate for the first leader, and that is Peter.

The evidence in Acts for Peter exercising the prime role in the movement is overwhelming. It is Peter who takes the lead in addressing the followers of Jesus at the beginning of Acts and arranging for a twelfth apostle to be elected. At Pentecost, when the Holy Spirit descends upon the apostles, it is Peter who addresses the crowd converting three thousand to their cause. It is Peter who addresses the Sanhedrin when he and John are arrested. So it goes on and on, with Peter taking the leadership at each key event until the story switches to follow Paul.

We can see the stories in Acts as being a largely fictitious narrative from the fertile imagination of the author of Luke. But the stories are improvisations around a kernel of early sayings and traditions, and some early material is visible beneath the gloss of invention. One of the fascinating aspects of Acts is that it repeats material found in the gospels but switches the subject from Jesus to the apostles, mostly Peter or Paul. This is evidence that early stories were originally attributed to both Jesus and the apostles which is understandable if Jesus was spirit, believed to be present in the flesh only through the medium of the apostles. This is particularly true of the stories told of Peter. The table shows the close parallels between the doings of Peter in Acts and Jesus in the synoptic gospels.

Peter in Acts	Jesus in the gospels
Peter cures a lame man (Acts 3:1-11). He cures a paralytic with the words "heal you does Jesus the Christ" (Acts 9:33-35).	Jesus cures the lame. In Mark 2:1-12 there is a miracle where Jesus cures a paralytic which is similar to Acts 9:33-35.
The people bring out their sick on couches and mats so that Peter's shadow might pass over them, and they be cured (Acts 5:13-15).	The people bring their sick on couches to wherever Jesus is so they might touch his garment and be cured (Mark 6:55-6).

Peter in Acts	Jesus in the gospels
A female disciple called Tabitha/Dorcas dies. Peter is sent for and finds her friends mourning for her. He brings her back to life with the words *Tabitha anastēthi* meaning "Tabitha arise" (Acts 9:36-43).	Jesus is called to cure a girl but when he arrives she is dead. Jesus brings her back to life with the words *Talitha koum* meaning "little girl arise" (Mark 5:41).
Peter is arrested and brought before the high priests and the Sanhedrim (Acts 4:1-22).	Jesus is arrested and brought before the high priests and Sanhedrim.
Peter is taken from prison by an angel (Acts 12:1-17).	Jesus is raised from the tomb

Two of these links come from back-to-back episodes in Acts. In Acts 9:33-35, Peter cures a paralytic in Jesus' name telling him to "*rise and make your bed*" whereas in Mark Jesus cures a paralytic saying the words "*rise and take up your mat*".[53] Acts has not copied Mark directly for the Greek words used are different although the meaning is the same. In the next story, Peter raises a dead girl called both Tabitha and Dorcas whereas in Mark, Jesus raises the dead daughter of Jairus. The name Tabitha in Acts is a misunderstanding arising from the words used to raise the girl in Mark, with "Talitha", meaning girl, being interpreted as a proper name. Again the author of Acts has not taken this directly from Mark because that gospel explains the meaning of the word. But Acts must be using a source about the raising of a dead girl in which the words spoken are very similar to those preserved in Mark as *talitha koum*. There is one other odd detail of interest in the story of Dorcas/Tabitha and that concerns garments. When Peter goes to the upper chamber where she lies he is met by the mourners: "*all the widows stood by him weeping, and showing the coats and garments which Dorcas made while she was with them*" (Acts 9:39). The reference to garments tells us that this was originally a mystical saying for garments reoccur repeatedly in the early Christian material and have a spiritual meaning. The author of Luke, however, interprets the reference to garments as if Dorcas were a dressmaker.

Perhaps the most interesting parallel between Peter in Acts and Jesus is the prison episode in Acts 12, which has similarities to Jesus' resurrection. Peter has been imprisoned by Herod and is in danger of his life. This imprisonment takes place at the time of the Passover, exactly the same time as

Jesus was crucified! Herod is holding Peter until after the Passover, so he spends the Passover, which is Easter, in a tomb-like prison cell. He sleeps between two soldiers echoing the two transgressors between whom Jesus is crucified. Although bound and heavily guarded an angel comes at night to free him:

And a messenger of the Lord stood by, and a light shone in the buildings, and having smitten Peter on the side, he raised him up, saying, "Rise in haste." (Acts 12:7)

This tells us that Peter is struck or "smitten" by the angel on the side - the word is normally used for killing. It seems a trifle heavy handed for waking a person. In the Gospel of John, the crucified Jesus is struck on the side by a soldier with a spear.

Peter is then "raised" by the angel who takes him out of the tomb like prison. They pass through a first and second ward of the prison before coming to an iron gate "leading to the city" that opens for them. This escape from the prison is filled with gnostic imagery around the ascent of the soul.

To the gnostic, the soul is trapped in the prison of the world from which it must escape. This escape may be either after death or, for a few, in life through a mystic ascent. Either way, the soul must pass through the lower heavens avoiding the jailer angels who guard these lower domains. In the Enochian Jewish worldview, there were three heavens with God dwelling in the third. So the ascending soul has to pass through the lower two heavens, the domain of the "jailers", just as Peter passes through two wards of the prison. He then comes to the gate into the city, Jerusalem. In early Christian imagery, the higher Jerusalem is a very common image for heaven.

In the Gospel of Philip, an early second-century gnostic gospel, there are insights into the concept of the gnostic escaping from "the powers" who rule the lower realms:

The powers do not see those who are clothed in the perfect light and consequently are not able to detain them. (Gospel of Philip 70:5-7)

Not only will they be unable to detain the perfect man, but they will not be able to see him, for if they see him they will be able to detain him. (Gospel of Philip 76:23-25)[54]

The Gospel of Philip is a ragbag collection of odds and ends, and it is likely that these two sayings, although now separated in the gospel, belong together and were taken from one original source. Now in Acts, when the angel comes to Peter the building (literally "house") is filled with light. This is followed by Peter being told to put on his garments. Note the similarity with the Philip saying that those who escape must be "clothed in the perfect light". In Acts, the garments are, of course, literal garments; but we can see behind it a source in which Peter becomes a man of light and puts on his garment to escape the powers.

The imagery about the ascent of the soul does not end there. After his escape Peter comes to the house of a woman called Mary. He knocks and a servant girl, Rhoda, hears his voice but does not open the door, instead running in joy to tell the others who react with disbelief:

And they said to her, "You are mad!" But she held that it was so, and they said, "It is his angel." (Acts 12:15)

A person's "angel" is a common Jewish image of the soul, the person's spiritual twin. It is the angel soul that escapes from the prison of the world and ascends through the two lower heavens that are guarded by the jailers, the heavenly powers that rule the world. The soul has to escape through the gate that leads into the Jerusalem of the third heaven. But there is a further aspect of this visit of Peter to the house of Mary. There are several points of similarity to the story of the resurrection in Mark.

There is an appearance to a woman called Mary.

The girl who first hears Peter is not believed when she tells the others. In the Gospel of the Long Ending Mary the Magdalene is similarly not believed.

The girl is told that it is "his angel". In the Gospel of Mark, an angel appears to the women in the tomb.

The traditionalist would doubtless emphasise the differences; that the Mary in this story is not Mary the Magdalene but Mary the mother of John Mark; that it is Rhoda and not Mary who tells the others and who is not believed; that an angel in Jesus' tomb is not the same as Jesus' angel. This viewpoint assumes that Acts records a history of events that actually happened rather than a series of stories invented around earlier sayings that were not fully understood. It assumes that there really was a Mary, the mother of John Mark, instead of this Mary being a character concocted to explain certain name forms that did not fit in with the Gospel narratives. It assumes that Rhoda was a real girl, serving Mary, rather than a name given by the author of Luke and Acts to an unnamed girl who was originally

Mary herself. To show that all these assumptions are not necessarily valid, we shall offer a reconstruction of the source for the Acts story:

He rose from his prison, and evaded his jailers, passing through the first and second domains, for he was clothed in the light, and they could not detain him. And the entrance to that place of death was unsealed and opened. He came to the place where Mary was. And the maiden did tell the others in joy but they believed her not. Yet she affirmed the truth. For it is said that she had heard his angel speak. But when the others saw him themselves then they believed.

The point is that this hypothetical source, constructed from the Acts story, could equally serve as a source for many details of the resurrection story in Mark! Note how the place of death, meaning the underworld, could be interpreted by the author of Mark as the tomb in which Jesus' body was placed. The opening of the entrance, being really the opening of the gates of hell, becomes the rolling away of the stone. The same place of death is misunderstood by the author of Acts as the prison of a tyrannical and murderous ruler (which in a sense it is). This is not to suggest that a passage actually existed in this precise form, only that there is a joint kernel of information in both stories that must go back to an earlier original.

So we have in Acts another version of the resurrection account. It is fascinating that this resurrection account is associated with two names and that these two names are the same as the two early traditions regarding the first witness of the resurrection; Peter and Mary.

The story in Acts is linked to both the gnostic ascent of the soul from the prison of the world and also to the death and resurrection of the Christ. How can it be both of these at the same time? The literalist mind cannot understand such contradictions. Hence, the early literalists constructed stories of a literal Jesus to make sense of gnostic mysteries that are not intended for the world of logic and the senses. But is clear from gnostic sources there is an ambiguity between the redeemer and the thing being redeemed. This ambiguity will need to be explored in its place, but just to say here that in some way the gnostic has to experience the death and resurrection of the Christ in order to free their soul from the lower realm. So the ascent of the soul and the resurrection of the Christ are in mystical experience the same thing, and it is only the literal interpretation of the Christ as a man that makes them appear different.

A link between the crucifixion and ascent of the soul is found in the Odes of Solomon, a collection of early Christian psalms that show similarities to the Gospel of John and which may date from as early as 100. In the

Odes, the mimicking of the crucifixion of Jesus by extending the arms is a form of prayer:

I extended my hands, and hallowed my Lord. For the extension of my hands is his sign. And my extension is the upright cross. Hallelujah. (Odes of Solomon 27)[55]

This is linked to the casting off of chains and the journey to heaven:

I raised my arms on high on account of the grace of the Lord. Because he cast off my chains from me, and my helper raised me according to his grace and his salvation. And I stripped off darkness and put on light. [...] And I was lifted up in the light, and I passed before his face. (Odes of Solomon 21:1-3 & 6)[56]

Compare also the role of the helper to the angel in Acts, and the replacing of the clothing (darkness) with a new clothing (light). The nature of the garment is made explicit in another Ode:

I was rescued from my chains and I fled unto you, O my God. [...] And I was covered with the covering of the spirit and I removed from me my garments of skin. (Odes of Solomon 25:1 & 8)[57]

Here the skin, the flesh, is replaced by the garment of the spirit. The experience is not in the flesh but in the spirit, and it is through the medium of the spirit that the follower of the way can visit heaven.

The story of Peter's ascent to heaven is not unique in the canonical sources. There is an explicit reference to an ascent to the third heaven in the letters of Paul. But there is a mystery in Paul's account as to the identity of the "man in Christ" who makes the ascent to the third heaven.

Who ascended to the third heaven?

Paul writes about the ascent to the third heaven in 2 Corinthians:

I knew a man in Christ fourteen years ago, whether in the body or out of the body I do not know, God knows, such a one being taken away to the third heaven. I have known such a man, whether in the body, or out of the body, I do not know, God knows, being caught away to paradise, and hearing unutterable words that it

is not lawful for man to speak. Of such a one I will boast, and of myself I will not
boast, except in my infirmities. (2 Corinthians 12:2-5)

The phrase "*in Christ*" is used in the same way that narrator of the Book
of Revelation says he was "*in the spirit*".[58] There is one circumstance that
immediately connects with the Acts story. Paul does not know if this experience was "*in the body*" or "*out of the body*"; that is whether it took place
physically or in a vision. In Acts we find identical uncertainty; during his
escape Peter does not know if it is really happening or if "*he saw a vision*".[59]

Given the link with the escape from prison in Acts is it possible that this
"man in Christ" is Peter? Most commentators would say no because they
think that the "man in Christ" is Paul himself. The case for it being Paul is
based upon the context of the story in 2 Corinthians. The story is related as
part of a longer piece where Paul is "boasting" as part of his defence against
accusations made by others who have questioned his status as an apostle
(Paul frequently needs to defend himself against such accusations). In this
context, so the argument goes, it would be pointless for Paul to give in his
defence the revelations of another. He must still be boasting by giving the
visions he has received as the sign of his apostolate. The clincher comes
when Paul, after recounting the vision, goes on to "boast" in his infirmity,
his "*thorn in the flesh*" that has been inflicted on him so that "*I might not be*
exalted overmuch by the exceeding greatness of the revelations" (2 Corinthians
12:7). Paul slips into the first person so showing, so goes the argument, that
the revelations must belong to himself. The problem with this is that it contradicts what Paul writes in verses 2 to 5, where it is clear from Paul's language that he is writing about another. How can this apparent contradiction be resolved?

First we need to understand the whole context. Paul's opponents are
some who have offered the Corinthians a rival teaching about Jesus. Paul
characterises them as "*false apostles, deceitful workers, transforming themselves*
into apostles of Christ". He goes on to say that even the Adversary changes
himself into an "*angel of light*" and so it is not surprising that the ministrants
of Satan change themselves into the "*ministrants of righteousness*" (2 Corinthians 11:13-15). They "*preach another Jesus whom we did not preach*" and offer
the Corinthians a spirit different from the one they received.[60] We learn
that these "false apostles" are Hebrews like Paul.[61] They accuse Paul of being a spiritual fake, which is clear from Paul sarcastically alluding to the
Corinthians asking for proof that Christ is really speaking through him.[62]

To this end Paul "boasts" by recounting his sufferings undertaken for the cause of spreading the gospel. He has endured floggings and beatings, shipwreck and stoning:

In journeyings often, in perils of waters, in perils of robbers, in perils by my own countrymen, in perils by the heathen, in perils in the city, in perils in the wilderness, in perils in the sea, in perils among false brethren. In labour and toil, in watchings often, in hunger and thirst, often fasting, in cold and nakedness. (2 Corinthians 11:26-28)

After this enumeration of his sufferings for the gospel, he comes to the crucial passage concerning revelations. To understand Paul's meaning we need to take this passage (2 Corinthians 12:1-11) step by step:

To boast, really, is not profitable for me. I will come to visions and revelations of the Lord.

Paul will stop boasting because it is not profitable, so we are not to interpret what comes next as "boasting". Instead, he is moving on to revelations from the Lord. This is followed by the journey to the third heaven, the "man in Christ" passage. Some early manuscripts have a variation in the above line that can be translated "*I must boast although it is not profitable*". The existence of such variations demonstrates that early Christians had difficulty following what Paul meant here. But either way what comes next makes it clear that Paul is not boasting of his own revelations:

Of such a one I will boast, and of myself I will not boast, except in my infirmities.

If Paul is hiding his own vision under a thin veil of modesty, then this sentence is a contradiction, as Paul would still be boasting about himself, although in disguise. The phrase "of myself I will not boast" would be a lie.

For if I may wish to boast, I shall not be a fool, for truth I will say.

Paul could give his own revelations without being a "fool" for he has truly received such revelations.

But I forbear, lest anyone may think me above that what he sees in me, or hears of me.

But in this case, he will not give his own revelations because they are so great that people will hold an exalted view of himself over and above what they see and hear with their own eyes and ears.

And that by the exceeding greatness of the revelations I might not be exalted overmuch, there was given to me a thorn in the flesh, a messenger of the Adversary, that he might buffet me, that I might not be exalted overmuch.

This is the crucial line. To balance the greatness of Paul's revelations he has been given some infirmity, the "thorn in the flesh", some moral or physical impairment. Are the revelations here the journey to the third heaven? No! They are the subjects of the previous sentence, the revelations that he could boast of if he chose to but does not. In the previous line, he does not boast of his own revelations less anyone thinks him above what he seems to be. Here he has been given the thorn in the flesh to stop him being "exalted overmuch". The two are the same and mean the same revelations, those Paul does not give.

Concerning this thing thrice I called upon the Lord that it might depart from me. And he said to me, "Sufficient for you is my grace, for my power is perfected in infirmity."

The infirmity is not lifted for in Christ weakness becomes strength.

Therefore I am well pleased in infirmities, in damages, in necessities, in persecutions, in distresses for Christ. For whenever I am infirm, then I am powerful. I have become a fool in boasting. You did compel me; for I ought by you to have been commended, for in nothing was I behind the very chief apostles, even if I am nothing.

Paul here recaps what he has been boasting about; the persecutions and hardships he has endured and his infirmity (not revelations!). He has become a fool for "boasting" but he has been pushed into it to defend himself against the accusations levelled against him by the "false apostles".

Paul's argument is a masterpiece. It is a wonderfully constructed whole, and we cannot fail to be moved by pity for his sufferings and admiration for his rhetoric. Paul is thoroughly humble with a humility that is the sign of a consummate egotist. He uses this humility as a weapon against his opponents, brilliantly turning their criticism on its head and using it against them. According to Paul, they accuse him of weakness while "boasting" of themselves. Paul responds by saying that although none should think of him as a "fool" yet he will be willing to seem a fool by boasting a little in reply.[63] But instead of boasting of his own spiritual gifts, as we might expect, he boasts instead of his weaknesses, in which he includes his sufferings and hardships undertaken for the sake of the gospel. When he comes to his own revelations, he boasts of his infirmities that have been visited on him to balance the revelations rather than in the revelations themselves. The argument is brought full circle by concluding that, in Christ, infirmity is power. So Paul's weaknesses are really strength and Paul is more of an apostle than those who oppose him.

It is necessary to Paul's argument that he does not give his own revelations, as this would be boasting in a positive rather than a negative sense. Instead, he boasts in the revelations granted to another, to the "man in Christ". Besides it is the authenticity of his revelations that is under attack, and it is the question of authenticity that he needs to answer. He cannot answer this doubt over authenticity by feeding his audience more incredible visions. If anything he has to reign back and be sober.

To understand Paul's defence, we must surmise that his audience knew more than we do. They must already have been familiar with the story of the journey to heaven and know the identity of the "man in Christ". We can also surmise that this person must have been an unimpeachable source, a high authority in the church, considerably above those who attack Paul. For Paul is using the "man in Christ" to trump his opponents. The accent in Paul's account should be read as "*I knew a man in Christ fourteen years ago*" – that is Paul has personally known this person and, fourteen years previously, this person has entrusted Paul with an account of the journey to the third heaven. This person is Paul's teacher, and he or she has initiated Paul into the secrets of heaven.

To picture this as a simple verbal exchange, a passing on of information, would be surely wrong. The apostles were mystics possessed by the risen Christ. We should picture instead the teacher passing into a trance in which they become possessed by Jesus, and reliving in Paul's presence the ascent, not just recalling it but experiencing it again with Paul as a silent participant. The things of heaven that cannot be spoken in human language would be spoken in the language of tongues. Note that Paul does not talk about what was seen but only of what was heard.

Paul starts his section by saying he is coming to "*revelations of the Lord*", and this is exactly what he gives us. The "*man in Christ*" is in a sense the

Lord since this person is the form in which the Lord was believed to have come to earth. They are the prototype for the spiritual possession that all the apostles, including Paul, share in. But this person is seen as being different from all the other apostles because this person has been specially chosen for the passage of the Christ into the world. They are the only person in the early church whom Paul regards as his spiritual superior; the first leader, the founder, the first witness of the resurrection.

Nothing else can make sense of Paul's passage. The link with the first leader is extremely clever and provides an argument for the authentication of Paul's own revelations that is all the more powerful for being subliminal and not explicit. Boasting in the founder's revelations is far more effective than if Paul were to boast in his own revelations, for then his opponents could simply say he was lying. Just look at what Paul's boasting in another achieves, if that other is the founder:

It emphasises that Paul was in privileged communication with the first leader. Subliminal message – the founder accepted me and my revelations and so should you.

It emphasises the first leader's extreme revelations and puts Paul's own revelations in the same category. Subliminal message – if you question my revelations, then you should also question those of our founder.

It hints at the greatness of Paul's own revelations by saying he could, if he chose, boast of revelations that are similar in nature. Subliminal message – I am like the founder in spiritual gifts and above my opponents.

Who could this person be who has gone to the third heaven? One clue is in the timing. Paul writes "*I knew a man in Christ fourteen years ago ...*" which dates the time when Paul knew of the event (or perhaps when Paul knew the person, in which case the "*man in Christ*" must have been dead for some years when Paul was writing). The expression "*man in Christ*" could cover a woman as well as a man for the word used (*anthropon*) means human being although later Paul talks about "*such a one*" in the masculine form.

There is one other occasion in his letters when Paul talks about fourteen years, and that is in Galatians, where fourteen years separate his first and second visits to Jerusalem. Here we have an apparent coincidence in that although Paul mentions the number of years between events that have happened to him only three times in his letters, in two of these cases he gives precisely the same period of fourteen years. And that is not the only coincidence. Paul's account in 2 Corinthians can be dated to around the time of the second visit to Jerusalem, and was most probably written as

Paul was about to embark on that visit. So we have the further coincidence that the two periods of fourteen years end at approximately the same time.[64]

The challenge by the other apostles fits into the larger conflict between Paul and elements backed by the Jerusalem leadership. This conflict is at its height around the time of the second visit to Jerusalem. This second visit of Paul to Jerusalem is intended to resolve matters, but although both sides seemingly come to an agreement it almost immediately breaks down.

It is unnatural for people to fix events in dates and terms of years. Instead human beings tend to remember things in relation to other prominent events in their lives (we might say "that happened a few years before our wedding" or "we visited that place a few years after the birth of our first son".) But it shall be seen that the term of fourteen years is highly symbolic to the Jesus movement. If Paul's first visit to Jerusalem was highly significant to him, then the fact that he was returning again after fourteen years would have appeared to him portentous. So the period of fourteen years, measured from the first visit, sticks in his mind. He uses it twice; first in 2 Corinthians as he is about to visit Jerusalem again, referring to something that happened on his first visit; and a few years later when he writes in Galatians about the second visit and relates it to the first.

So we can see the strong possibility that the "man in Christ" was someone Paul met in Jerusalem on this first visit. If this was Paul's first meeting with the founder, then we can imagine just how significant this must have been for him. But who was it that Paul met in Jerusalem? Paul's account in Galatians is specific; he went to meet Peter/Cephas and stayed with him fifteen days, seeing only James apart from him.[65] Note how Paul has remembered the precise number of days for this visit – nowhere else does he specify the length of a visit like this. It is Peter/Cephas who is the best candidate for the "*man in Christ*".

So we come full circle; in 2 Corinthians and Acts we have two journeys to a third heaven that can be seen as two very different descriptions of the same event. This event concerns Peter/Cephas, but there are also links in the Acts account with Mary. The event has parallels to the resurrection story which seems to come in two versions, one concerning Cephas and the other Mary. The evidence increasingly points to Cephas and yet we get these strange loose ends concerning Mary.

Peter and the spirit

There is one other revealing power attached to Peter in Acts; he is the focal point of the Holy Spirit. In Acts, the spirit is given by the twelve apostles by the laying on of hands. Later Paul has the same ability. All this is odd since we do not find in Paul's letters any of the elements of the Acts description:

Paul never says that a person can be given the spirit by human agency.

Paul never implies that the "twelve" or any other such group had the power or right of giving the spirit.

Paul never mentions the laying on of hands

In Acts, any of the twelve apostles can theoretically give the spirit but it is always Peter who actually administers the spirit. He is present at Pentecost when the spirit descends upon the apostles, and he lectures the crowd immediately afterwards promising them the spirit if they are baptised. In the fascinating episode of Simon Magus,[66] Philip goes to Samaria where he meets Simon the magician or Magus, who was there before him. Philip converts large numbers including Simon, but Philip does not have the ability to give others the Holy Spirit. It is only when Peter and John come and lay hands on the converted that they receive the gift of the spirit. At this point, Simon Magus tries to buy the authority to give the spirit, an offer that Peter scorns.

So why cannot Philip give the Holy Spirit? There is an apostle Philip, one of the twelve. But it seems that the Philip in Samaria is not this apostle but the Philip who Acts says was one of the seven "Hellenists" appointed to special roles after the apostles.[67] One motivation for including Philip in the list of the seven is that this explains why he cannot give the Holy Spirit. For this to be necessary, the story of the conflict between Philip and Simon must go back beyond Acts, along with the concept that the spirit was given through the agency of Peter.

The information about Simon Magus' beliefs comes from later sources, and it would be naive to assume automatically that such later sources reflect the teachings of the historical Simon Magus. However, the parallels between the sect of Simon Magus and the early church are striking and suggest that the two groups were intimately linked. But what we are concerned with now is what the story in Acts can tell us about the early apostles.

The first piece of information concerns Philip. There is a Philip in the list of the twelve disciples, but other than the bare listing of his name he does not feature any further in the three synoptic gospels. It is true that the name of Philip is used in the fourth gospel, but this can be seen as nothing more than adding a little narrative colour. For example, in the account of the first miracle of the loaves and fishes in Mark 6:35-44 it is simply "his disciples" who feature in the exchange with Jesus, complaining that it would take two hundred denarii to buy sufficient food to feed the multitude. The account in John 6:1-13 is dependent on the synoptic account of this miracle, repeating as it does the same details, such as the two hundred denarii and the five loaves and two fish. Yet in the Gospel of John it is Philip who asks the sceptical questions. The author of John is basing his account on the Synoptics and has replaced the generic "disciples" with the name "Philip" to give it verisimilitude. The little new information that the author of John gives about Philip is equally suspect. The gospel says that Philip came from the town of Bethsaida on the Sea of Galilee, as did the supposed fishermen Peter and Andrew.[68] If the author of John is looking for a hometown for the fishermen disciples, then Bethsaida is an obvious choice, as it is mentioned in Mark as a place in Galilee frequented by Jesus, and its name means "house of fish".

The Gospel of John was written after Acts and so cannot account for the role of Philip in Acts. No known texts from before Acts record any information about Philip other than his name. So the author of Acts must either have had access to other sources, since lost, or he is using Philip as a name for an essentially invented character. The evidence that the role of Philip has not been invented is in the clumsiness of the story. Philip converts Simon during his mission to Samaria, but the point of the story concerns Peter, who also travels to Samaria, at which point Philip drops out. If the story had been invented from scratch Philip would surely not be in it. So we can conclude that Philip must have been in the source the author of Acts is using.

Acts conveys some other information about the Philip who was in the seven. He was known as Philip the Evangelist, had a house in Caesarea, and had four virgin daughters "prophesying".[69] There is also a story in Acts about Philip after he has left Samaria converting a Eunuch.[70] From all this, we can see the outlines of a historical individual called Philip, probably from Caesarea, who was an early apostle and evangelist, and who at some stage visited Samaria. Although Acts sees this person as being distinct from the Philip in the Twelve, doubtless the author of Mark has used the name of the historical Philip for the disciple. We cannot conclude from the available information that Philip was definitely one of the Twelve, although this is quite possible. The information about the virgin daughters of Philip who prophesied is fascinating as is the story of the Eunuch. Later Philip was to become an important figure in gnostic sources.

The Acts story aims to debunk the spiritual claims made by the followers of Simon Magus in competition to the early Christians. That the two groups were linked can be seen by the representation of Simon as a baptised follower of Philip and hence an enemy from within. The story shows Simon as being active in Samaria before Philip and as having a large number of disciples who believe him to be *"the great power of God"*. Even the final condemnation of Simon is not absolute but holds the possibility of redemption. What information can we deduce from the episode of Simon?

There was a rival group based in Samaria lead by Simon and which, like the early Jesus movement, offered its followers the "spirit".

This rival group was linked to the early Jesus movement and in particular linked to the early apostle / disciple Philip.

The gift of the spirit is shown as originating with Peter.

The story attempts to debunk the movement of Simon by saying that their claim to offer the spirit derives from nothing more than a failed attempt to purchase it from Peter.

Whatever the true early relationship between Simon and the Jesus movement, the author of Acts portrays Peter as the source of the spirit.

Another time when Peter is involved with the gift of the Holy Spirit is the episode of the centurion Cornelius who has a dream and sends for Peter.[71] Cornelius and his household are Gentiles, but when Peter obeys his summons and begins to lecture the Gentiles about Jesus, the Holy Spirit descends upon them. From this Peter concludes that God has no favourites and so proceeds to order the baptism of these Gentile Christians.

The giving of the spirit to Gentiles is a profound development. The episode in Acts is clearly fantasy penned by the Gentile author of Acts to justify why Gentiles should be admitted to the church on the same terms as Jews. But although the details are in the novelistic genre of Luke and Acts, this does not mean that the story is not based on an earlier tradition. Under such a tradition, it is Peter who successfully gives the spirit to Gentiles; and Peter who, as a result, concludes that Gentiles should be admitted to the church. For a Jew, this is a breathtaking action that could only be taken by a truly revolutionary founder-leader.

The story of Cornelius is interlinked with an episode that has even greater consequences. For Peter does not just decide that Gentiles can be admitted to the church, he also abrogates the Jewish Law. This is a final parting of the ways, the separation of Christianity from Judaism, and the formation of a new religion. Such a separation was perhaps inevitable, but the visible abandonment of the Law is an act of provocation against the Jews among whom most of the early Jewish Christians lived.

The loosening of the prohibition on eating unclean foods is a radical act. Yet there is a mystery about it. For in Acts, it is Peter who loosens the prohibition on unclean foods following a revelation. But in the Gospel of Mark, the main source document for the author of Luke and Acts, Jesus himself has already declared all foods to be clean. This is the mystery of Peter and the blanket from heaven.

Peter and eating unclean food

Just before the centurion's servants come to him Peter goes on to the roof of the house he is staying in and being hungry wishes to eat. But there falls upon him a trance:

And he saw the heaven opened, and descending to him a vessel, like a great sheet, being let down to earth by four corners, in which were all the four-footed animals and crawling things of the earth and the birds of heaven. Then a voice came to him: "Having risen, Peter, kill and eat." And Peter said, "In no way Lord, for I have never eaten anything common or unclean." And a voice again came for a second time to him, "What God did cleanse do not you call common." This happened three times, and immediately the vessel was taken up to heaven. (Acts 10:11-16)

The story is naive and not without its amusing elements – the great sheet lowered from heaven and filled with all the animals of the earth is one of the less successful images in the New Testament. As always the author of Luke elaborates shamelessly. But the essentials show Peter loosing the prohibition against eating unclean foods based upon revelations received in a trance-like state. Peter is here exercising the power of "binding and loosening" given to him in the Matthew saying. Effectively Peter is elevated above Moses and has the power to rescind the Law of Moses. For a

Jew of today, this is unthinkable. But then the evidence is that the first Christians did not come from the Torah based Mosaic Judaism but from an Enochian school that set little value by the Torah. We can explain this assignment of powers to Peter if: (i) The author of Luke has read the *"rock on which I will build my church"* saying in Matthew, or (ii) she has another source that tells her that Peter pronounced all foods clean.

Either way supports the assignment of the power to loose and bind to Peter in the Gospel of Matthew; the first because it would be a witness that the "rock" saying is genuine and the second because it is an illustration of Peter using the power. But long before the author of Acts is writing, another gospel has already recorded that it was Jesus who declares all foods to be clean:

Do you not perceive that nothing entering from outside is able to defile a man? Because it does not enter into his heart, but into the belly, and goes out into the sewer?" Thus he pronounced all foods pure. (Mark 7:18-19)

This is the mystery of the sheet from heaven. Why does Acts have Peter pronounce all foods clean when Jesus has already done exactly the same? The author of Acts is very familiar with the Gospel of Mark, which serves as the major source for her Gospel of Luke. And if we look at motivation, she has a strong reason for boosting the case for abandoning the Law because she is Gentile and an enthusiastic follower of Paul. It is surely preferable to have Jesus as an authority for such a radical move. But Acts has Peter!

A partial explanation is that the author of Luke and Acts may not have known the passage in Mark. The episode of clean and unclean is in the long section from Mark 6:47 to 8:27 that does not seem to be used in Luke. One explanation is that it was missing from the copy used by the author of Luke. If this is so, it has the startling implication that the author of Luke may only have known about the Gospel of Mark from a single mutilated copy. It is true that Luke has an episode of Jesus not washing his hands that is clearly related to the disciples not washing their hands in the missing section of Mark. But the author of Luke could have been loosely copying the equivalent story in Matthew. The Gospel of Matthew was written by a Jewish Christian who was keen to emphasise that Jesus did not come to end the Law. So the conclusion in Matthew has been significantly toned down: *"these are the things defiling the man; but to eat with unwashed hands does not defile the man"* (Matthew 15:20). It is significant that the version in Matthew does not include the words *"Thus he pronounced all foods pure"* as does

Mark. If the Gentile author of Luke has read the Matthew but not the Mark version, then she would have thought it was about eating with unwashed hands and not about eating unclean foods.

It is still surprising that the author of Luke-Acts did not know of a tradition that it was Jesus who declared all foods clean. Instead, she had a tradition that it was Peter. Some of those working in the historical Jesus as man school find this evidence that Jesus himself was Law abiding, and the abrogation of the Law came after his death. After all, in the Gospel of Mark the key words "*thus he pronounced all foods pure*" are not actually spoken by Jesus but are in the narrative. In this view, the Gospel of Mark was written at a time when Law observance was a matter of controversy and conflict in the Jesus movement. Because the author of Mark supports the abrogation of the Law he puts this spin in his narrative, giving Jesus as the authority for a belief that is really the author's own. The author of Acts knows that the real authority is Peter, and she gives something closer to the truth in her version of events.

The problem with all this is that it makes the followers of Jesus more radical than Jesus himself. This is not how religions evolve. It is only the founder who has the status to make such radical departures from existing belief. If Jesus had been Law-observant, then his followers would have been so too. It is not psychologically possible that his followers would have pursued a line of development in complete conflict with the teachings of an earthly Jesus, in conflict with the beliefs they had been brought up in, and in conflict with their fellow Jews around them. If the early followers of Jesus were conventional Jews (as those in the historic Jesus school would have us believe) then they would have believed in Yahweh as the supreme creator of the universe, as the father who was both loving and vengeful. It would have taken more than a second-generation leader's vision of a blanket from heaven to cause them to put aside the Law of Yahweh and invite the terrible punishment that would, in their mind, have ensued.

The abrogation of the Law is not a minor technicality but the visible manifestation of a major realignment of the powers of heaven. For a Jew to dispense with the Law they had to believe that the Law had been overturned in heaven, either because Yahweh himself had rescinded it, or because he who the Jews thought was Yahweh was not the supreme ruler.

The traditionalist Christian can see this, believing as they do that the Law had been overturned by the perfect sacrifice of Jesus, and that subsequent to his resurrection Jesus ruled in heaven as regent. The Traditional Secular school cannot take this line because they do not believe that Jesus was divine. Jesus himself, as a man, could never have believed that he was the new ruler in heaven and could not have predicted his own death or seen it as a perfect sacrifice. So Jesus must have believed in the Law of Yahweh and could not have abrogated it. This was done by his followers, chiefly Peter and Paul, in a shrewd move to repackage the movement to appeal to the Gentile market. This view is possible because the Traditional Secular school exists among academics, and academics in the humanities have been heavily influenced by post-modernism that holds that there is no such thing as truth. Instead all texts are political documents that reflect the biases of their authors, who are driven primarily by self-interest. If the Law is inhibiting the spread of the new movement among gentiles then Peter and Paul, as the crafty leaders they must surely have been, will find a way around the Law.

Nothing could be further from the reality of religious belief than post-modernism. Whereas the post-modernist sees no absolute standard of truth, the religious person holds their god or gods as the fundamental source of all truth and power. It is precisely for this reason that religion is so incurably conservative with beliefs remaining unchanged for millennia. To overturn the Law of Yahweh in the mind of a Jew, the mountain of received belief would have to be moved. The postmodernist does not see this mountain because according to their theories and the evidence of their own un-religious minds it should not exist.

The problem here is Jesus as man. The abrogation of the Law must go back to the first leader, and that person must have believed that a fundamental realignment in heaven had taken place. These are both necessary conditions. Jesus is the subject of the religion and Jesus is the realignment in heaven. As the traditionalist could tell us, Jesus had made his sacrifice, been resurrected, and now had replaced the one the Jews called Yahweh as ruler. All these things must have been believed in by the first leader. The difference is that he or she would have located the death of Jesus in the distant past and believed that the resurrection, the rebirth of Jesus, had taken place spiritually through the medium of his or her own body.

With the shaman paradigm, there is no conflict in the abrogation of the Law being attributed both to Jesus and Peter. It is precisely what we would expect. If Peter is the founder, and on the evidence of Acts he surely must be, then Jesus speaks through him. That all foods are permitted can simultaneously be both a revelation given through Peter and a saying from Jesus. The new ruler of heaven pronounces a new law for man through the human lips of the founder, a law that is no law but the spirit.

So from the three sources of Mark, Matthew and Acts there is over-whelming evidence pointing towards Peter as the first leader. What is impressive is that all three, analysed separately, point to the same person. Given the prominence of Peter, it is therefore surprising to find that most scholars do not think that Peter was the first leader after Jesus. Instead, they believe that the first leader was another character who makes only fleeting and mysterious appearances in Acts -- James "the brother of the Lord". The evidence for James comes primarily from the earliest source in the New Testament, the genuine letters of Paul. Each of the three sources considered so far, Mark, Matthew and Acts were written by individuals removed in time and space from the scene of action. It is not as if they had first-row seats, or even that they were watching standing at the back of the theatre. It is more as if they were passers-by in the street hearing scraps of information from those who have talked to others who had witnessed the performance. But with the letters of Paul we come to an eyewitness who personally knew some of the prominent figures involved, including both Peter and James. Unlike the authors of the gospels, Paul knew the answer to the question we are trying to answer. The evidence of his letters must outweigh all other sources. But scholars are looking at them through the spectacles of their "Jesus as man" preconceptions. If we look at them through the fresh eyes of the shaman paradigm, can we make more sense of some of the puzzling features of these letters?

Key points

1. Although the Gospel of Mark names twelve disciples, most of them play no role in the narrative. Only three disciples are in any way prominent; Peter, James and John. Of these, it is Peter who is named first of the Twelve, and Peter who always plays the leadership role.

2. In the Gospel of Matthew, Jesus appoints Peter as leader of the church. He is the rock on which the church will be built, and he shall have the keys to the kingdom of heaven. Peter is given the power to loose or bind, meaning to revoke or make laws, and these laws will then be binding both in heaven and earth. This gives Peter a position ahead of Moses, the bringer of the Law, something no mainstream Jew could contemplate.

3. In Acts, it is Peter who leads the disciples after the death of Jesus. It is also Peter who gives the spirit to others.

4. A number of miracle stories are told about Peter in Acts, which are versions of stories told about Jesus in Mark. Most significantly, the story of Peter's arrest and escape from prison is another version of the death and resurrection of Jesus.

5. In Acts, it is Peter who pronounces all foods clean and who brings Gentiles into the church without circumcision. Both are revolutionary moves that could only be done with the highest, divine, authority.

6. The best candidate for the "man in Christ" who, according to Paul, visited the third heaven is Cephas/Peter. Paul is recalling an experience in which the shaman journeyed to heaven.

Conclusion

The Gospels of Mark and Matthew and the Acts of the Apostles all point to Peter as the first leader of the movement.

Chapter 13

Cephas and Peter

The letters of Paul are our best source for identifying the first leader. They are an eyewitness account by someone who must have joined the Jesus movement in the 30s and must have known the founder personally. Paul writes his letters in the 50s by which time James was the leader in Jerusalem. Yet it is clear that James could not have been the original shaman. He has come on the scene relatively late, and Paul does not respect him.

There is, however, a difficulty with Paul's letters. The surviving manuscripts use two different names, Cephas and Peter, both of which mean "rock"; Peter in Greek and Cephas in Aramaic. The conventional view is that these are two names for the same person. But is it correct that the shadowy figure that Paul calls Cephas is the same as the apostle Peter?

Two names, two people?

In the New Testament, the name Cephas is only used in two letters of Paul, 1 Corinthians and Galatians, and briefly in John 1:42 (written much later at around the year 100) which says that Cephas means "Peter". In the first of the two letters to be written, 1 Corinthians, all manuscripts use only "Cephas" with no occurrence of the name "Peter". But in Galatians there is a confusing situation as both Peter and Cephas appear in all early manuscripts. To make matters worse, some manuscripts will have Peter in a certain place while others will have Cephas. There is no obvious pattern why one manuscript should be using one name rather than another. It is as if someone has thoroughly jumbled up the names in Galatians. The two names mean the same, with Cephas being derived from the Aramaic word for "rock" and Peter from the Greek word for "rock". Cephas/Peter is a very unusual name, and the way it has been transferred from Aramaic to Greek is significant. When a name is taken from one language to another, it will be converted to something that sounds similar. So, in English, we use the word Peter to represent the Greek Petros. However, Cephas has been translated to preserve the meaning rather than the sound so it must have been the meaning that was important. It was not a person's name but a title, "the rock". The significance of this is that a title can be borne by more than one individual.

The mystery of Cephas and Peter in Galatians revolves around two issues. Did Paul really use both names in his letter? And if so, does this mean that they are two different people?

One thing is certain, that some early copyists changed between the names in multiple places. They did so for their own reasons, either to clarify things for their readers, or for their own doctrinal purposes. A popular approach is to attempt to reconstruct the original by guessing the motivations of these early copyists. The problem with this approach is that we can never be sure that we understand the motivations of unknown persons so distant in time. It is all too easy to project our own subjectivity into this type of exercise and get the conclusion we were looking for. So instead we will start with two facts:

Although Galatians has suffered multiple alterations in the names, no changes have been made to 1 Corinthians.

In all the letters of Paul, no name is ever changed by copyists except between Peter and Cephas in Galatians.

Why did the copyists only change between the names Peter and Cephas in Galatians? The best explanation is that Paul wrote both names in Galatians and the copyists thought they were two names for the same person, so they believed they had licence to change the names. We must remember that the copyists are working at a time when the literalistic gospels and Acts are fully accepted, and they know of only one "Peter", the fisherman-disciple and apostle.

In reality, Paul would not have done anything as confusing as using two names for one person in the same letter! There are two people bearing the title of "the rock" and Paul uses the Aramaic and Greek versions of the name to distinguish between them. Most likely we are looking at two individuals from two different generations of the movement, with Peter coming after Cephas. Paul only uses one name in 1 Corinthians because it is written earlier, and he does not need to refer to Peter but only to the original Cephas.

All of which is important because all the evidence for James being the leader above Cephas/Peter turns out to relate to the second Peter. The original Cephas could be the first leader and founder. To see that this must have been the case we need only turn to the earliest evidence of all, that of 1 Corinthians.

Cephas in 1 Corinthians

In 1 Corinthians, there are five mentions by name of any of the Jerusalem brothers or apostles. Cephas is mentioned four times and James once. The prominence of Cephas is telling, particularly as Paul has a habit of bringing his name in when it appears to have no direct bearing on the subject under discussion. The first mention of Cephas comes near the beginning of the letter when Paul is chiding the Corinthians for the divisions that have arisen among them because of the teachings of a rival preacher Apollos:

For it was told to me concerning you, my brothers, by those of Chloe, that there are quarrels among you. I mean this, that each of you says, "I am of Paul", "and I of Apollos", "and I of Cephas", "and I of Christ." Has Christ been divided? Was Paul crucified for you? Were you baptised in the name of Paul? (1 Corinthians 1:11-13)

How to interpret this passage? The explanation offered by many commentaries is that Paul is addressing four factions that have arisen among Corinthians. He describes each party according to their supposed leaders. But how could there have been a separate Christ party when all the others are teaching Christ? What comes later makes it clear that the true disagreement arises between the conflicting teachings of Paul and Apollos:

For when one may say, "I am of Paul" and another, "I of Apollos", are you not just human? Who then is Apollos? And who is Paul? Servants through whom you believed, even as the Lord gave to each. I planted, Apollos watered, but God gave growth. (1 Corinthians 3:4-6)

The exact nature of the relative teachings of Paul and Apollos is a fascinating subject. To summarise briefly, from the evidence of 1 Corinthians it would seem that Apollos is a fellow apostle to Paul who is teaching a more gnostic gospel than Paul. (The information about Apollos in Acts can be discounted as being mostly or entirely spurious. It is unlikely that the author of Acts, who is writing much later, had access to any information about the obscure Apollos other than what Paul had written.) Paul does not reject Apollos' teachings, although he attempts to belittle them while at the same time explaining that he could have taught the Corinthians the same mysteries had they been ready. Paul has fed them milk and not meat because they were still babes in Christ.

Once it is realised that the disagreement is really between those who look to Paul and those who have been influenced by Apollos, we can see that the initial list of four is a rhetorical device. The purpose is to make the disagreements of the Corinthians look absurd by exaggerating them. This is quite evident in the "*I of Christ*" that sounds absurd to us today but the "*I of Cephas*" is likely to have sounded equally absurd to Paul's original readers. They are absurd because they are meant to be absurd in the same way as the questions "*Was Paul crucified for you?*" and "*Were you baptised in the name of Paul?*"

We can see this rhetorical device in two ways. First, as a list in ascending order of importance. We start with Paul, who, as he says elsewhere, is the least of the apostles. It is entirely typical of Paul's outward modesty, the counterpart of his inner egotism, to put himself lower than his rival Apollos. The list ends with the highest possible authority, Jesus. Cephas is situated above the two apostles and immediately below Jesus. This position indicates his status. He is greater than the other apostles and lower only than the heavenly Christ. Cephas is the leader of the movement on earth.

The second way we are supposed to read the passage is as two pairings:

Paul and Apollos
Cephas and Christ

The subliminal message is that to divide into groups around Paul and Apollos is as absurd as forming groups around Cephas and Christ. "Has Christ been divided?" asks Paul and we may wonder what he means. This is one of three questions with the others intended to be absurd – "was Paul crucified?" and "were you baptised in Paul's name?" (Note how Paul implicitly criticises his own party in these two questions, a further demonstration of his outward modesty.) The dynamics of the passage are a *reductio ad absurdum* with the aim of making the Corinthian's divisions look ridiculous.

It is in this context that we must understand the question about the division of Christ that may sound odd to us today. It sounds odd because it is a fragment of the original Christianity that has been largely lost below the reinterpretation that started with Paul himself. We are fortunate today to have access to many of the original sayings through the Gospel of Thomas and in this gospel division is a recurrent theme, both explicit and implicit. (See for example saying 72 where Jesus asks ironically - "*I am not a divider, am I?*" a question that is a close parallel to Paul's.) The division in the Gospel of Thomas is both a division within a person and between persons, for there is no difference between the two. The division is a splitting of the individual, a divorce of that part of the person that is of God and belongs to God, and that part of the person that lives in the world, and is in danger of corruption from the rulers of the world. But those who realise the unity between the spirit and the flesh, the chosen, also become one super-personal entity and "stand as one". Or to use Paul's terms, the pneumatic elect are of one body, a spiritual whole. If the marriage of the spiritual part of the individual and Christ is sundered, then the individual is splintered into warring parts and the body of the elect is shattered.

The question "Is Christ divided?" is intended to shock, and it would have shocked anyone who had been inducted into the Jesus movement not from the gospels of the New Testament (for they had not yet been written) but from the sayings preserved in the Gospel of Thomas. Modern commentators have seen in Paul's words a metaphor for the divisions that have arisen in the Corinth community within the body of the elect. Although this is doubtless one level of meaning, it is an abstruse interpretation that would only occur to the reader with reflection, whereas Paul intends his direct question to have an immediate impact. In the Gospel of Thomas, division is primarily division within a person, not a division between the elect, and this is the clue to the meaning of the question. Under the shaman paradigm, if Cephas is the founder, then Cephas and Christ are one, and undivided. This oneness is the prototype for all the other apostles and elect who are also one with Christ, and through this identity, one with each other. This is the unity that cannot be split and at its heart are Cephas and Christ. Paul is telling us that Christ cannot be divided from Cephas.

Although the Cephas and Christ parties are doubtless an exaggeration for the purpose of Paul's argument, they must have had some foundation of reality or Paul could not have used them with credibility. So there must have been at least a few among the Corinthians who could be portrayed as a separate Christ party, as opposed to the Cephas party. What is the distinguishing characteristic of this Christ party? Not that they believed in Christ, for so did all the others. It must be that they alone rejected the resurrection of the Christ through Cephas! They are for Christ only and not for Christ and Cephas. Hence the retort from Paul – "has Christ been divided?" And with this clue we can understand that the Christ party must be a faction of the original apocalyptic movement that saw Christ as a spiritual messiah who had been crucified in the past and who expected his resurrection in the near future. Under the spiritual paradigm, we know that this earlier version of Christianity must have existed because the resurrection of the Christ through the founder cannot have happened in a vacuum. There must have been an earlier pre-existing Jewish sect who looked to the Christ as the redeemer who had been killed but who would return. The belief that the resurrection had already occurred was eventually triumphant, but originally it would have existed side by side with the belief that the resurrection was still in the future.

Paul himself clearly belongs to the Cephas movement, as do almost all of the Corinthians and his question "*Is Christ divided?*" is intended to be seen as absurd, a rejoinder to those maintaining that Christ is not manifest in Cephas. Although it might be tempting to place Apollos in this Christ party, Paul's defence against Apollos shows that Apollos must be teaching a spiritual, gnostic gospel in line with the Gospel of Thomas. He would seem to be a colleague of Paul,[72] which is by no means inconsistent with being Paul's rival. Most likely the Christ party has little real substance among the Corinthians but is an external influence from the Jewish Apocalyptic Christian groups that would have existed in parallel to Cephas Christian groups such as Corinthians.

The next reference to Cephas occurs near the end of Paul's section dealing with Apollos:

So then, let no one boast in men, for all things are yours, whether Paul, or Apollos, or Cephas, or the world, or life, or death, or things present, or things about to be. All are yours, and you of Christ, and Christ of God. (1 Corinthians 3:21-23)

How are we to make sense of this list? Again we have the three apostles listed in the same order; Paul, Apollos, Cephas. The conventional explanation is that Paul gives a list of the three parties in Corinth (now omitting the party of Christ!) saying that all the parties "belong" to the Corinthians. But we have seen that the early list can be thought of as two pairings Paul/Apollos and Cephas/Christ and that the whole section is about Paul and Apollos as rivals. Paul is quite explicit about this and tries to soften the implied criticism of Apollos:

Brothers, I have applied these things to myself and Apollos for your benefit, that you may learn from us not to go beyond what is written. (1 Corinthians 4:6)

Looking again at Paul's list we can see that the last four items are clearly two pairs of opposites, as are Paul and Apollos. Writing lists of opposed pairs is a favourite technique of Paul and we can see an example in 2 Corinthians where there are no less than ten opposed pairings:

... with the weapons of righteousness on the right hand and on the left; through glory and dishonour, through bad report and good report; as imposters and yet true; as unknown, yet well-known; as dying and, behold, we live; as being punished and yet not being killed; as being sorrowful yet always rejoicing; as poor yet making many rich; as having nothing and possessing all things. (2 Corinthians 6:7-10)

So what stops us interpreting the first list in terms of opposed pairs like the above passage? It is the awkward presence of Cephas in the initial threesome that breaks the pattern. But there is no evidence that Paul had such a threesome in mind! He repeatedly talks elsewhere about Paul and Apollos, not about Paul, Apollos and Cephas. Modern readers may put Cephas in the same group but neither Paul nor his audience would have done so. If Cephas were the founder, then they would have seen him as the human pinnacle of the movement far above Paul and Apollos. So perhaps the list was intended to be read as follows:

Paul / Apollos
Cephas / the world
Life / death
Things present / things about to be

If so then Cephas is paired with "the world" (*kosmos*) as opposites. Things of the *kosmos* are denigrated by Paul. The pairing of Cephas as the opposite of *kosmos* implies a view of Cephas as uniquely above the other apostles. But to fully understand Paul's list we must look at it in the context of Paul's whole argument that starts with the divisions among the Corinthians. He contrasts the wisdom of the wise with the apparent foolishness of those of the nascent church *"For the message of the cross is to those that perish foolishness; but to us who are saved it is the power of God." (1 Corinthians 1:18)* Here we have a statement of one of the themes that he will later summarise through the pair life and death. He goes on to tell us about those who perish and those who are saved:

Where is the wise, where the scribe, where the debater of this age? Has not God made foolish the wisdom of this world (kosmou)? For since in the wisdom of God, the world (kosmos) by its wisdom knew not God, it pleased God by the foolishness of preaching to save those who believe. (1 Corinthians 1:20-21)

Those who are wise through the wisdom of the world are perishing, those who know God through what is apparently foolish will be saved. Paul's argument is very subtle -- the wisdom of God (Sophia) has made it so that the world does not know God by its worldly wisdom. God has set up a test; those whose natures can recognise God in what appears to be foolishness will have life, whereas those whose natures are deceived by the things of the world, whether things of power or intellect or possessions, will fail to recognise God and will turn away from him in their hearts, and will perish. Paul then addresses the Corinthians to consider their own standing before they were called and how most of them were not wise according to the flesh, not powerful and not noble.

But God chose the foolish things of the world (kosmou) to shame the wise. God chose the weak things of the world (kosmou) to shame the strong. God chose the lowly things of this world (kosmou), and the despised things, and the things that are not, to annul the things that are. So that no flesh should boast before God. (1 Corinthians 1:27-29)

According to the world, the Corinthians are foolish, weak, and despised. But Paul then says something else that is more enigmatic; God has chosen that which is not, something which does not exist, to annul or bring to an end that which is, and which does exist. We should interpret this in the context of the passage where Paul is talking about things as they appear to the world. So when Paul says something does not exist, he means it does not exist in the eyes of the world. What is this thing? It is not God for there was essentially no atheism in the ancient world and almost everyone would have believed in some God or other. Paul tells us that it is the means by which God will annul the things that do exist. Later in 1 Corinthians Paul uses the identical Greek word to describe how Jesus will "annul" all worldly power on behalf of God: *"Then comes the end, when he shall have delivered up the kingdom to God, the Father; when he shall have annulled all dominion and all authority and power." (1 Corinthians 15:24)* So we can deduce that the thing that does not exist in the eyes of the world must be Jesus. It is Jesus whom Paul mentions in the very next line:

But because of him, you are in Christ Jesus, who has become for us wisdom from God, and righteousness and sanctification and redemption. (1 Corinthians 1:30)

The Corinthians are "in Christ", meaning that they have been possessed by his spirit, and he is their wisdom. Instead of boasting in themselves the Corinthians should boast of Jesus "the Lord". The idea that Jesus does not exist seems odd under the literal view of Jesus as a man who lived in the recent past, but it makes perfect sense under the shaman paradigm. The opponents of the movement would naturally have said that the spiritual Jesus did not even exist. Paul's response is that through Jesus, whom the worldly think does not exist, God will annul the powers of the world and bring in the kingdom that will replace the *kosmos*.

After this, Paul gives a discourse on the spirit, of how he appeared to the Corinthians not with eloquence and wisdom but with fear and trembling. In a crucial passage, to be considered later, he explains how the rulers of the age, the archons who are becoming useless, had crucified the Christ because they had not understood the mystery that had been hidden at the beginning of time. The mystery, the wisdom of God, is something that "*Eye has not seen, nor ear heard, neither has entered into the heart of man*" (1 Corinthians 2:9) -- it is invisible and untouchable. Is this mystery the same as the thing which does not exist, but yet will annul the things that are? Paul goes on to talk about how the person without the spirit does not accept the spirit and how to them it is foolishness. But the person with the spirit judges all things and is judged by no one. Paul finishes this section by saying that although no one can know the mind of God, "*we have the mind of Christ*" (1 Corinthians 2:16) again implying that the Corinthians are possessed by Christ.

After saying how he, Paul, had fed the Corinthians on milk and not solid food, he goes on to the section that will finish with the list of pairs. He starts with the rhetorical question relating to his first pair "*Who then is Apollos and who Paul?*" (1 Corinthians 3:5). Paul's answer is that they are both servants through whom the Corinthians have believed; "*I Planted, Apollos watered ...*" (1 Corinthians 3:6). He compares the Corinthians to a building; he, Paul, has laid the foundations but another (Apollos) is building on those foundations. The one who is building will be judged by the standard of his construction, whether he is building with gold, silver, precious stones, wood, hay or straw. When the day comes all will be tested by fire and if the building survives the builder will be rewarded but if it burns he will suffer loss. The implication is that Apollos is building at the wood, hay and straw end of the spectrum and the chances of his construction surviving fire are slim. But Paul realises he has gone too far in implying that his fellow worker Apollos will be condemned and rather lamely adds *"but he himself shall be saved; yet so as by fire"* (1 Corinthians 3:15). The odd thing about this addition is that the building itself, the Corinthians, will have gone up in flames, although the builder will be saved. This fire that will test the work of Paul and Apollos brings us to the last pairing, things present and things about to be. The present is the outwards seeming of things, the *kosmos*, but the future is the apocalypse, the fire in which the true nature of all things will be revealed. This also links to the third pair, that which survives the test will have life, and that which will fail will have death.

After comparing the Corinthians to a building under construction Paul now tells them that they are the temple:

Know you not that you are the temple of God, and that the Spirit of God dwells in you? If anyone destroys God's temple, God will destroy him; for God's temple is holy, which you are. (1 Corinthians 3:16-17)

Paul then returns to the theme he first started in 1 Corinthians 1:18 that the wisdom of this world and age, the wisdom of those esteemed wise is, in reality foolishness: *"For the wisdom of this world (kosmos) is foolishness with God"* (1 Corinthians 3:19). He tells the Corinthians that all things are theirs and summarises his discourse with the pairings; Paul/Apollos, Cephas/*kosmos*, life/death, things present/things about to be. We may suspect that the reader is intended to interpret the first three pairings so that the first thing is good and the second bad - Paul, Cephas and life as opposed to Apollos, *kosmos* and death. Paul then reverses the polarity with his last pairing; things present are bad, and things about to be good. This reversal enables the first item on the list, Paul, to be connected with the last item, things about to be, which are those things that will survive the fire. This reversal of polarity is actually typical of Paul; he does the same in the 2 Corinthians 6:7-10 passage quoted above, where in the first two pairings the good thing comes first before switching to the bad thing first for the remainder of the list.

We can see that the list of pairs summarises Paul's argument from 1 Corinthians 1:18 right up to 1 Corinthians 3:20. But in all this discourse there is one thing missing, there is no explicit mention of Cephas! If Cephas is opposed to the *kosmos* then Cephas must represent the wisdom of God as opposed to the wisdom of the world, that which is of little account but through which the *kosmos* is coming to an end. Cephas must be the means by which Jesus is coming into the world. And we may note that reference to the Corinthians being the temple of God coming immediately before Paul returns to the theme of the wisdom of the world. If Cephas is the means by which Jesus is coming to the earth then Cephas is the temple; he is the original of which the Corinthians possessed by Christ are the copies. So perhaps the temple is a veiled reference to Cephas, who is contrasted with the *kosmos*.

The next mention of Cephas makes his prominence clear. This is when Paul defends his position as an apostle:

My defence to those who examine me in this; have we not power to eat and to drink? Have we not power to lead about a sister, a wife, as well as other apostles, and as the brethren of the Lord, and Cephas? (1 Corinthians 9:3-5)

This is another key passage. The conventional explanation is that Paul is claiming the right to be supported by those he preaches to, and so to be able to eat and drink and support a wife as a companion. We shall see that this interpretation is incorrect and that Paul is talking spiritually and not about things of the flesh. The sister, the wife, is not a physical woman but a person's spiritual twin. But we are for the moment less concerned with the interpretation than with the list of people that Paul gives. The purpose of the list is to demonstrate Paul's credentials as an apostle and to give unassailable authority for the power to lead "a sister, a wife". In giving this authority, he mentions only one person by name and that is Cephas. This presents grave difficulties for anyone putting forward James as the leader of the movement ahead of Cephas. Why should Paul single out Cephas in this way unless it is he, and not James, who is uniquely prominent? An argument advanced by some is that Cephas was included as a particularly notorious example of a married Christian. But this is like saying that Cephas is put first in a list of two-legged people because he was a notorious example of a person with two legs. For just as having two legs is the overwhelming norm, so was marriage in the Jewish world and those who were single (such as Paul) the very unusual exception.

What information can we learn from the list? That Cephas was prominent, that Cephas is not included in the apostles as a group, and that Cephas is not included in the "brethren of the Lord", whoever they may be.

But there is something else. The brethren of the Lord, who are higher than the apostles, are listed after the apostles. So we are dealing with another listing in order of increasing status. But Cephas is given last and so must be of the highest status, higher than the brethren! We start with the group of apostles who are distinguished by having seen the risen Christ, who are spread out among the communities and who are the generals on the ground. We then have the group of the brethren of the Lord who are based in Jerusalem under James and who are the acknowledged leaders that Paul rails about elsewhere. And then we have Cephas, the founder of the movement and the highest human authority.

The final reference to Cephas in 1 Corinthians is also the most important; Paul's account of the resurrection appearances. We have already seen that Cephas comes first in this list and is distinguished from both the Twelve and the apostles. But full consideration of the list will deserve its own chapter.

Cephas and Peter in Galatians

It is in Galatians that we encounter confusion between the names Cephas and Peter, starting with Paul's first visit to Jerusalem when he stays with either Cephas or Peter for fifteen days; most early manuscripts have "Peter" but a few have "Cephas". Which is right? There are a number of criteria we can use to help decipher the confusion:

Consistency or otherwise with the position of Cephas in 1 Corinthians.
Internal consistency within Galatians.
The motivation of later copyists to change from either Cephas to Peter or from Peter to Cephas.

We know that Cephas in 1 Corinthians was the principal person in the movement. So for each time that Peter or Cephas occurs in Galatians, we can ask if the reference is consistent with the Cephas of 1 Corinthians. We can apply the same principle to internal consistency within Galatians.

Arguing from the motivation of copyists is more dubious. It is difficult to be confident of the motivations of a disparate group of people whose identities are unknown and who lived almost two thousand years ago. There are some things we do know. In the second and third centuries, the version of events in Acts and the gospels are widely accepted so our copyists will think of "Peter" as the chief disciple and apostle of Jesus and will be less familiar with the name "Cephas". They will also be concerned with anything that contradicts the four gospels or Acts which are accepted as a true account. The proto-orthodox church, to which the copyists belong, claims authority from Jesus through Peter. Anything that threatens the preeminence of Peter threatens this authority. Paul is potentially a danger-ous figure because he has a strong gnostic side and because many of the gnostic groups regard him as "the apostle" ahead of Peter. At the same time, he is highly respected because the proto-orthodox church has devel-oped from the gentile communities of which he was a prominent founder. All of which gives a strong political motivation for copyists to bridge the differences between Peter and Paul, showing that the authority of Paul was derived from Peter and that there was no disagreement between the two. A more subtle challenge to the authority of Peter exists in the obscure person of James who sometimes appears to be above Peter. Changing names from Peter to Cephas and vice versa is one way of dealing with these issues.

But different copyists will be motivated by different factors and we should not be surprised to find a random element to these changes that essentially adds noise to the incidence of the names. Changes are also more likely away from the name that predominates because there are more in-stances of texts with that name than texts with the other name. At the ex-treme, if the original name is in all texts at a given time, then any changes can only be in the direction away from the original.

The first encounter with the two names is Paul's visit to Jerusalem in Galatians 1:18-24. How consistent is this with 1 Corinthians? In the Gala-tians visit, Peter/Cephas is the most prominent individual in Paul's mind and the person he has gone to visit. The only other individual to be named, James, is mentioned as an aside. The strong implication is that Pe-ter/Cephas is the leader and has a status above that of James. This is com-pletely consistent with 1 Corinthians and "Cephas" must originally have stood in this passage. Turning to the motivation of the copyist, we can see a very strong motivation for changing Cephas to Peter and no motivation for changing Peter to Cephas. This passage gives the proto-orthodox church just what it needs to show that Paul was secondary to Peter and was in-structed by Peter.

The next mention of Cephas and Peter comes in the account of a second visit Paul made to Jerusalem after fourteen years. Following a revelation Paul went to visit James to submit his gospel to them "*lest I run in vain*":

Now of those esteemed to be something, what they were makes no difference to me, for God does not accept the appearances of man, those esteemed added nothing

*to me. But on the contrary, having seen that I have been entrusted with the gospel
of the uncircumcision just as Peter of the circumcision, for the one having worked
in Peter for apostleship of the circumcision, did also in me toward the Gentiles, and
having recognised the grace that had been given to me, James and Peter [or
Cephas] and John, those esteemed to be pillars, gave to me and Barnabas the right
hand of fellowship, that we should go to the Gentiles and they to the circumcision.
They only asked that we should remember the poor, the very thing that I was eager
to do. (Galatians 2:6-10)*

Paul's actions in submitting his gospel to James for approval are recounted in a later atmosphere of bitterness and recrimination, but they
demonstrate that Paul did accept James' leadership at the time of this second visit. The very fact that Paul felt the need to submit his gospel in this
way shows how poorly integrated he was into the rest of the movement.
The visit itself seems to have gone well with good will shown on both sides
but Paul's version of the conclusion is simply not believable. He states that
he Paul was to be apostle to the Gentiles, with Peter and James limited to
the circumcision in a sort of non-compete agreement. But if James were the
leader he would never have ceded a large portion of his authority in this
way to Paul. It seems that Paul has misunderstood James.

We do not have James' version of events but we can decipher what he
must have intended from his subsequent actions and Paul's misconception
of their agreement. James must have intended to keep the mainstream
church within Judaism by insisting on circumcision, but at the same time to
give Paul some limited freedom to establish semi-detached communities of
the uncircumcised among Gentiles. Paul has misread this as meaning that
he would be exclusive apostle to the Gentiles, whereas Peter and James
would limit themselves to the circumcised. But James had no intention of
limiting the expansion of his church in this way. Converted Gentiles would
be circumcised and so brought into Judaism when the time was right.
Paul's uncircumcised communities were to be a temporary and pragmatic
halfway house with a natural progression leading to them accepting circumcision -- as may have happened with Galatians. Doubtless all this was
expressed to Paul in diplomatic language. Paul has failed to read between
the lines and in his eagerness to win acceptance has taken James' diploma-
cy at face value and later felt betrayed.

So where does Peter/Cephas stand in all this? Although early manuscripts of Galatians are elsewhere in disagreement between Peter/Cephas,
in this one place all manuscripts agree on Peter in the first two occurrences
of the name: "... *as Peter of the circumcision, for the one having worked in Peter*

for apostleship of the circumcision, did also in me toward the Gentiles." Let us apply first the criterion of consistency with 1 Corinthians. In this line, Peter is described as an apostle whereas in 1 Corinthians, Cephas is twice listed separately from the apostles. Paul sets himself up as equal to this Peter but in 1 Corinthians, Cephas has a position of unique prominence well above Paul. Note how Paul emphasises the equivalence between himself and Peter rather than between himself and James. This is natural as Paul is submitting his gospel to James for approval and so he can hardly regard himself as being on the same level as James. The corollary is that this Peter must be of lower status than James and is not the Cephas of 1 Corinthians.

As to the motivation of the copyists, the use of Peter here is consistent with the portrayal in Acts of Peter and Paul as the two prime apostles (doubtless Acts has got its concept of the two apostles from this very place). In fact, this is the only place in Paul's letters that Peter is described as an apostle. Our copyists know from Acts that there were twelve apostles led by Peter and that Cephas is not one of the twelve. On grounds of consistency, they will have a strong preference for Peter instead of Cephas, which is reflected in the fact that all copies have Peter here. All this is consistent with Peter being originally written in these two places.

The next mention of the names is in the phrase *"James and Peter [or Cephas] and John, those esteemed to be pillars."* The manuscripts are not unanimous, with some having Peter and some Cephas and also with variations in the order in which James and Peter appear. Applying consistency with 1 Corinthians, Peter/Cephas is mentioned in the list of individuals present after James but before John. This shows that, in Paul's view, he was of lower status than James but higher than John. This Peter/Cephas is surely James' number two and the same person as Peter, the apostle to the circumcision, with whom Paul has just compared himself. But the Cephas of 1 Corinthians is of higher status than James, as is the Peter or Cephas that Paul stayed with on his first visit to Jerusalem. Even more telling is Paul's grudging remarks on the group of three who are esteemed to be pillars *"what they were makes no difference to me, for God does not accept the appearances of man."* There is no way that Paul would have talked about the founder in these terms. The justification of the Jesus movement depended upon the founder as being marked out as the leader by God. We conclude that Paul must have written Peter here. In what direction would our copyists have been tempted to change the names? There is a strong motivation to change from Peter to Cephas here as Peter/Cephas is shown as secondary to James. (There is also a possible motivation for going the other way, as Peter is more familiar to readers than Cephas.) In conclusion, Peter must have originally stood here and was changed to Cephas in some copies to avoid showing Peter as a subordinate of James.

The Galatians passage continues with the final mention of Peter/Cephas in the letters of Paul. It recounts a stormy encounter between the two in Antioch:

But when Cephas [or Peter] was come to Antioch, I withstood him to the face, because he was to be blamed. For before certain came from James he ate with the Gentiles: but when they were come, he withdrew and separated himself, fearing those who were of the circumcision. And the other Jews dissembled likewise with him so that Barnabas also was carried away with their dissimulation. But when I saw that they did not walk properly according to the truth of the gospel, I said to Cephas [or Peter] before them all, If you being a Jew, live after the manner of Gentiles, and not as the Jews, why compel the Gentiles to live as do the Jews? We who are Jews by nature, and not sinners of the Gentiles. (Galatians 2:11-15)

This is a fascinating and difficult passage. Paul here criticises Peter/Cephas to his face "before all" which, at first sight, seems to be thoroughly inconsistent with the role of Cephas in 1 Corinthians. However, the evidence of Galatians is that Paul had indeed fallen out with the founder at this time. In Galatians, Paul is very keen to stress his independence of the movement and the fact that his initial experience of Jesus did not depend upon any person. We would not expect this implicit denial of the founder if Paul were only in disagreement with James. The argument in Antioch would explain why Paul was angry with Cephas, who Paul saw as a hypocrite because he had given in to James on the subject of eating with Gentiles.

Another clue that this is Cephas and not Peter is that Paul criticises him as living in the manner of Gentiles. This does not fit the Peter in Jerusalem, who is described as the apostle to the circumcised. How could the person singled out as being, in particular, an apostle to Jews be said to live like a Gentile? And if he did live like a Gentile, how could he function in a Jewish environment where he would be seen, as Paul implies, as a sinner? Moreover, this Peter is one of the Jerusalem "pillars" and in the party of James; would James allow one of his own to live like a gentile? However, Cephas the founder is a different matter. We have seen how Peter as the founder has abrogated the purity laws and declared all foods clean. At this time, the founder must also have been based in Rome, where it would be much more natural to live like a Gentile.

There is also the reaction of the others in Antioch where everyone except Paul follows the example of Peter/Cephas. This Peter/Cephas must have been a person of the highest status in the movement. If this is the founder of the movement, then it would explain why no one, not even Paul's closest follower Barnabas, will side with Paul against Peter/Cephas.

Here there would seem to be a strong motivation to change from Peter to Cephas as the argument between Peter and Cephas disproves the image of harmony between the two that the proto-orthodox church was so keen to convey. Peter is shown in an unfavourable light and as being submissive to James. However, the motivations of copyists are diverse and difficult to assess and the process of change is partially random. Leaving the unfamiliar name Cephas here would raise a lot of questions in the reader's mind, as this person is obviously someone prominent and important who can exercise influence even over Barnabas. We would expect a natural tendency among copyists to identify this Cephas with the Peter who is mentioned just a few lines earlier as one of those esteemed to be pillars. So it is not surprising to find instances where the name has been changed to the more familiar Peter.

We will see later that there are very strong additional reasons for believing that Paul did originally write Cephas here. When we analyse the account of the Jerusalem visits in Acts, we shall uncover evidence of a major argument between Paul and the founder in Antioch. The conclusions for Galatians are summarised in the table below.

Passage	Reasons for choosing Cephas or Peter (C/P)	Conclusion - what did Paul originally write?
Galatians 1:18 – Paul meets Peter or Cephas in Jerusalem.	Consistent with 1 Corinthians; Paul seeks instruction from C/P; James only mentioned in an aside, so C/P is more important than James.	Cephas (P46: Cephas)
Galatians 2:7-8. Peter is apostle to the circumcised. *All manuscripts have Peter here.*	Inconsistent with 1 Corinthians; C/P is an apostle whereas Cephas is twice listed separately from the apostles in 1 Corinthians.	Peter (P46: Peter)

Passage	Reasons for choosing Cephas or Peter (C/P)	Conclusion - what did Paul originally write?
Galatians 2:9. Peter or Cephas is one of the three "pillars".	Inconsistent with 1 Corinthians; C/P is in an inferior position to James; Paul talks disparagingly of those esteemed to be pillars which includes C/P.	Peter (P46: Peter)
Galatians 2:11 & 2:14. Paul argues with Peter or Cephas "to his face".	C/P lives like a gentile which is consistent with the founder living in Rome but inconsistent with the description of Peter in Galatians 2:7-8 as apostle to the circumcision. Everyone except Paul follows the example of C/P, showing that C/P has high status.	Cephas (P46: Cephas. The name is explicit at 2:14 whereas 2:11 is in a missing section.)

The conclusion is that Paul meets Cephas both on his first visit to Jerusalem and in Antioch but meets another person he calls Peter on his second visit to Jerusalem. It cannot be a coincidence that two people have a rare name that means the same thing; it must be a title that has significance within the movement rather than a personal name or a nickname. All of which goes to explain a mystery of Paul's account of his first visit to Jerusalem. Paul is asserting his independence against the party of James and Peter, who have "*bewitched*" the Galatians. He claims that when he went to Jerusalem he kept apart from the church and that "*of the other apostles I did not see*". Yet bizarrely he seems to stress his stay with Peter. The truth is that Paul stayed with Cephas on his first visit, which he wants to stress because it legitimises his apostleship. Paul rejects the Jerusalem pillars of James, Peter and John but sees Cephas as being above this party of James

Is there any confirmatory evidence that this conclusion of which name Paul wrote in each place is correct? There is one very early source for Paul's letters; the papyrus called P46. This is a substantially complete text of Paul's letters, with the exclusion of the fake pastoral epistles. It includes Galatians and although there are damaged sections most of it is readable. The papyrus is dated to c200, which makes it much earlier than any other copy of Galatians. The table shows whether Peter or Cephas appears in each place for P46. In every case, the papyrus agrees with what we have concluded. Of particular interest is Galatians 2:9 where P46 is the only early witness for what must have been the original reading of "James and Peter". All other texts have either "Peter and James" or "James and Cephas". It is here we can see the real concern of copyists. The idea of James being mentioned first, and so being above Peter, drives a dagger into the heart of the authority of the bishops in the proto-orthodox church. This authority is derived directly from the earthly Jesus, who appoints Peter as the rock on which he will build his church. Acts shows Peter as carrying out the mission given to him by Jesus as leader of the twelve apostles and hence leader of the church. And yet here we have evidence from Paul's own letters, that Peter is subordinate to James, who is scarcely mentioned in the gospels. Moreover, this is a direct contradiction of the gospel that is most popular and considered most authoritative, that of Matthew, where Jesus explicitly appoints Peter to lead his church. The copyists address this problem in one of two ways; either they change the order to "Peter and James" to reflect what they think is the correct precedence or they change "Peter" to "Cephas". The very early P46 stands virtually alone in recording the original text, perhaps because it comes from an era in which the derivation of apostolic authority through Peter was not yet considered vitally important.

The only other changes the copyists make is to change from the obscure Cephas to Peter. There is no need to invoke any deep political motivation for this as Peter is the universally familiar form of the name. Ironically, the passage that modern readers might think the most embarrassing for the early church, the argument between Paul and Cephas in Antioch, does not seem to have bothered the copyists, some of whom have quite happily changed Cephas to Peter. This is probably because no important issue of theology or authority is concerned and because the Antioch passage does not contradict any other text considered authoritative.

Key points

1. The person Paul calls Cephas in 1 Corinthians has a prominence beyond anyone else in the early movement and a higher status than the apostles or the brothers of the Lord.

2. In a list of opposed pairs, Paul places Cephas in opposition to "the *kosmos*". The implication is the Cephas offers freedom from the *kosmos*, that is the world, and the heavenly powers that were believed to rule the world.

3. In Galatians, Paul must have used both the names, Cephas and Peter. He would not have done this unless Cephas and Peter were two separate people.

4. Paul certainly uses the name Peter for the person he meets on his second visit to Jerusalem. He describes this Peter as apostle to the circumcision, the Jews. This apostle Peter is under James in Jerusalem, and is part of the leadership group of three, the other being John.

5. As Peter is an apostle and below James, he cannot be the same person as Cephas, who is distinct from and above the apostles and the brothers of the Lord.

6. From the principles of consistency and motivation, we can deduce that Paul wrote Cephas in two places in Galatians; Paul stayed with Cephas for fifteen days on his first visit to Jerusalem, and much later had an argument with Cephas in Antioch.

7. The earliest manuscript of Paul's letters, P46, agrees with the results of this analysis.

Conclusion

Paul writes the name Cephas to mean the shaman and the first leader of the movement. He uses the name Peter for a second-generation figure who is part of the Jerusalem leadership under James.

Chapter 14

Paul's list of resurrection appearances

The final reference to Cephas in 1 Corinthians is also the most important; Paul's account of the resurrection appearances. Under the shaman paradigm this account assumes a critical importance. It is telling us the order in which people entered into the innermost spiritual mysteries of the movement. This makes it effectively a history of the development of the early movement. And then there is Paul's mysterious assertion that his own witness of the Christ was as if he were an "abortion". What does he mean by this? Under the conventional view it is inexplicable, but under the shaman paradigm, it gives us an insight into the nature of the spiritual induction that individuals must have undergone to see Christ.

Paul's account of the resurrection

For I delivered to you first, what also I did receive, that Christ died for our sins, according to the scriptures, and that he was buried, and that he was raised the third day, according to the scriptures, and that he appeared to Cephas, then to the twelve. After that he appeared to above five hundred brethren at once, of whom the greater part remain till now, although some have fallen asleep; then he appeared to James, then to all the apostles. And last of all, as if to a miscarriage [or abortion], he appeared also to me. For I am the least of the apostles and am not worthy to be called an apostle, because I did persecute the assembly of God. (1 Corinthians 15:3-9)

Even under the conventional Jesus as man school this accords an extraordinary place for Cephas in the Jesus movement. This list only includes two named individuals (apart from Paul); Cephas and James. The explicit naming of James indicates his prominence in Paul's world, particularly as there is nothing remarkable about his position in the list, coming as it does after over 500 people have already experienced the risen Christ.

Under the spiritual paradigm, the list becomes nothing less than a history of the movement, showing the order in which various groups become important in the movement by witnessing the risen Christ. We must understand the resurrection experiences not as happening over a short period of time but of being spread over decades. Note how the people familiar from Paul's letters, with the exception of Cephas, appear at the end of the list. This is because they are the contemporaries of Paul, whereas the earlier appearances happened years before to the previous generation. Let us reconstruct the history from this list.

We start with Cephas, who has the first resurrection experience. Cephas is the founder of the movement as we know it, although there must have been a precursor apocalyptic group who believed that the Christ had been put to death and were waiting for his resurrection.

Next comes the Twelve, who are represented in the gospels as the twelve disciples (wrongly including Peter/Cephas in their number). The author of Acts thinks these are the same as the twelve apostles, but this is clearly wrong as is shown by Paul's list. The apostles come on the scene later and are a completely different group. It would appear that the real Twelve have disappeared almost without trace. With a few possible exceptions, not even their names have been preserved. The list of the Twelve in Mark includes the names of the brethren who were prominent later. Most likely they were simply the first twelve followers of Cephas, who were rewarded with special status. The number twelve symbolises the twelve tribes of Israel. It would seem that Cephas attempted to make the Twelve into a leadership group, but their disappearance from the scene suggests that this was not a success and they were disbanded.

We then have the mysterious appearance to the five hundred that is not mentioned anywhere else. Paul's words give the impression that five hundred people were assembled together, and the risen Christ appeared before them. But such an assembly cannot have taken place in Roman-occupied Judea. So Paul has either worded this clumsily or, more likely, misunderstood something that had been told to him. The appearance to the five hundred at once must mean that there were five hundred people in the same place or region all of whom were seeing the resurrected Christ at the same time. The appearance of the Christ to each individual was not a one-off event, as is evident from Paul's letters. They were a prolonged series of experiences that occurred over a considerable time, and perhaps for life. So we are to picture five hundred converts, men and women, recruited at different times over a period of some years, each of whom is having concurrent and repeated experiences of the risen Christ. Paul says that some have died but the majority are still alive, which implies a dating of no more than about twenty years before he is writing. This is the first great expansion of the Jesus movement, from the original Cephas and the Twelve, to a total of five hundred followers in Palestine, all of them having charismatic experiences like the later apostles. The absolute numbers may be modest, but the compound growth rate is phenomenal, perhaps averaging something like 50% per year assuming that this expansion took about a decade.

This is followed by the appearance to James, who is surely only included as a named individual because of his later prominence. If the list can be read as history, then James has come on to the scene late. Yet he rises to the position of leader and is called brother of the Lord. How can this be explained? He must be a relation of Cephas, who belonged to a younger generation. This would explain why he does not appear in the list earlier; he is a child in the early years of the movement and is only admitted into its mysteries once he has reached adulthood. The other brethren of the Lord must also have a relationship to Cephas and would be from the same younger generation. James has seen the risen Christ some time before Paul, so even if were a teenager then, he must have been in his twenties by the time of Paul's conversion. When Paul is writing his letters, James is well into middle age.

The appearance to James is followed by "all the apostles" and it would seem that an apostle is defined as someone who has seen the risen Christ. In defending himself as an apostle, Paul uses the argument that he has seen Christ – *"Am I not free? Am I not an apostle? Have I not seen Jesus our Lord?"* *(1 Corinthians 9:1)*. The group of apostles is diverse and large, far from the group of twelve that the author of Acts envisaged. These are Paul's fellow workers in Christ who have spread out over the world teaching the gospel. They seem to belong to a new phase of the movement in which geographic expansion is an imperative.

Last of all is Paul himself. He says it were as if he were an abortion or miscarriage (*ektromati*). This is frequently mistranslated as "born out of time" to tie in with the conventional account of Paul seeing Jesus much later than the others. The reader of such a mistranslation is left with the impression that whereas the others saw the bodily raised Jesus, Paul was "born out of time" after Jesus had ascended to heaven, and so saw only the spiritual Jesus. This is an ingenious solution to the embarrassment caused by Paul's actual words. But whatever Paul meant it was certainly not this; a miscarriage or abortion happens earlier, not later than a normal birth. There is no ascent to heaven in Paul's account and nothing to suggest that all the others did not have a spiritual experience like Paul.

We should not see Paul as being special because he is last, for the list comes from Paul's own account, and subjective bias would account for the author's unique position. Paul has come in late and his claim to be the last apostle is rhetorical, an attempt to make the most of his unfavourable position in relation to the other apostles. It is unlikely that anyone else would have regarded him as the last apostle (many seemed to doubt that he was an apostle at all). Doubtless there were many who came later with as good a claim to be an apostle as Paul.

Regardless as to whether Paul was the last witness, the list does imply closure of the experiences of the resurrected Christ. It is certainly the interpretation of the gospels and Acts that the resurrection experiences took place over a certain period and then ended with the ascension to heaven. The Gospel of the Long Ending of Mark first mentions the ascension – *"The Lord, then, indeed, after speaking to them, was received up to the heaven, and sat on the right hand of God"* (Mark 16:19). Acts has the resurrected Jesus give to the disciples *"many certain proofs, through forty days being seen by them"* (Acts 1:3). In John the resurrected Jesus says to Mary the Magdalene - *"Do not touch me, for I have not yet ascended to my Father"* (John 20:17). These sources are not independent of each other. The author of the Gospel of the Long Ending (which came before Mark) believed that the time of the appearances of the resurrected Christ was long past. So we know that within a few decades of Paul writing there was a general sense that the resurrection experiences were over.

It is only Acts that gives a period in which the appearances occur – forty days, a traditional round number. The idea that the resurrected Jesus is on earth for forty days gets confirmation from an unexpected source, the Gospel of Mark. At the beginning of this gospel is the story of the baptism of Jesus by John. We shall see that this is a misunderstanding by the author of Mark of the "baptism of Jesus" which the author takes as a baptism applied to Jesus, to fit in with his literalistic gospel, but which originally meant the baptism of the disciple by the spirit of Jesus. Under the spiritual paradigm the spiritual baptism is the same as the resurrection experience. They would have both meant the descent of the resurrected Jesus into the disciple, and into the world (the wilderness). It is the literalistic version of the story that sees them as being quite different, with the "baptism of Jesus" taking place at the start, and the resurrection at the end of the story. In the Gospel of Mark following his baptism, Jesus is driven out into the wilderness using the same word *ekballei* which is used elsewhere in Mark for the casting out of demons:

And immediately the Spirit drives him out (ekballei) into the wilderness. And he was there in the wilderness forty days ... (Mark 1:12-13)

The wilderness stands both for the physical nature of the disciple and for the world. The duration of forty days is the same as Acts gives for the sojourn of the resurrected Jesus on earth. They must both come from the same original source that has been interpreted in two different ways by the two writers and applied at two different points of the literalistic story.

So we learn that the appearances of the resurrected Christ must have taken place for "forty days". It is clear from Paul's letters that the appearances of the Christ went on for many years, so "forty" days cannot mean forty literal days, although that is how the author of Acts interprets it. In fact the Jews made a very common habit of using "days" and "weeks" to describe much larger time periods. We shall see that the apocalyptic Jews who originated the Christ myth had an interpretation of day as a period of a generation. This cannot be the meaning here because it is clear that the appearances of the resurrected Christ were believed to have been confined to the first age of the movement and were already over by the time the first gospels were written. These constraints lead us to the most common metaphoric meaning of a "day" among the Jews, that it represents a year. So the real meaning of the "forty days" is that the appearances of the resurrected Christ on earth were for a period of forty years.

Forty years is very close to the length of a generation and it shall be seen that the apocalyptic precursor to the Jesus movement measured time in generations. There was no accepted length in years for a generation, although it was approximately half a human lifetime of three score years and ten, giving a figure of around thirty-five years. If the resurrected Jesus was supposed to stay on earth for a generation, then this could have been rounded to the significant forty years. What exactly is it that brings the resurrection appearances to an end?

Perhaps we should do as the Gospel of Thomas tells us to and look for the end where the beginning is. The resurrection appearances begin with Cephas, so do they end with Cephas also? Forty years would have been a long adult life time in the ancient world where a man was old by the time he was fifty and most people came nowhere near the seventy years of the hypothetical lifespan. Did the first Christians see Jesus as being so entwined with Cephas that the resurrection experiences would end when Cephas died?

This concept brings in focus the mechanics of the resurrection experiences. How was it that the Twelve saw the Christ after he appeared to Cephas? If we reject the crude supernaturalism of physical miracles, then it cannot have happened spontaneously. So many people do not just happen to have the same mystic experience at the same time. Instead, the experiences must have been induced somehow. Specifically they must have been induced by Cephas, for there is no one else at the beginning! But if Cephas has induced the Twelve then surely it has not stopped there. Many, perhaps all, of the others must also have been induced by Cephas. The numbers are quite manageable. Some five hundred people spread over ten years would be an average rate of one person a week.

We can picture how this would have happened. After preliminary training by others, a new convert who was thought ready for the inner mysteries would have been brought to Cephas. They would have listened to Jesus speak through Cephas' lips; and through the medium of Cephas they would have been born again in Christ, and baptised with his baptism, so that the spirit of Jesus descends into them, to fight the beasts and the adversary and to evict the demons. This is how they become witnesses to the resurrection of the living Christ.

And this brings with it a new perception of what it meant to be an apostle. We know that an apostle was the highest grade of teacher whose mission was to spread the gospel far and wide, taking the word over land and sea. Yet Paul tells us that all the apostles had seen the risen Christ so that this seems to have been the required qualification. Did the movement really give its highest level of authority to self-appointed individuals who said that they had seen the risen Christ? Such would have included many who were mentally unstable, spiritual wannabes or plain liars. And how is it that all those who saw the Christ towards the end of Paul's list received the status of apostles and the mission to spread the gospel, but those who saw the Christ earlier did not?

There must have been a degree of central control over who became an apostle and this is the clue that the experience of the risen Christ must have been induced by Cephas and that the apostles were personally selected and appointed by Cephas. Without some such central control, the new movement would have exploded in a mass of contradictory teachings (as was its fate soon enough) for it had in its genes the spirit of anarchy. Only the personal authority of Cephas could keep it on track, and only those endorsed by Cephas were to be the means of spreading the gospel.

James as successor in Thomas

There is one other intriguing early source that must be brought in, and that is a saying in the Gospel of Thomas which unambiguously names the successor to Jesus:

> *The disciples said to Jesus: "We know you will go from us. Who shall be great over us?" Jesus said to them: "In the place to which you come, you shall go to James the Just for whom the heaven and earth came into being." (Thomas 12)*

This reads oddly to modern ears because it uses a traditional Jewish praise formula. The meaning is something like "your new leader is James the Just who is to be respected." The Thomas saying ties in very well with the conventional interpretation derived from the letters of Paul as James as the first leader of the church after Jesus. But if James were the leader after Jesus the man, then how can we possibly explain the prominence of Peter in all the early sources? The resolution is offered by the shaman paradigm. In the Thomas saying it is the resurrected Jesus who is being addressed: *"We know that you will go from us"*. Under the shaman paradigm this resurrected Jesus has been reborn spiritually through the human medium of the first leader Cephas. We have seen that the resurrected Jesus was expected to be on earth only for one generation, corresponding to the lifetime of Cephas. Afterwards, there would a time before the second coming when the church would have ordinary human leadership. This leader would be James, who was to be the successor to Cephas/Jesus. The Thomas saying indicates James as the second leader and this interpretation is completely consistent with the letters of Paul.

We have seen that Cephas actually handed over the leadership to James in Jerusalem while still alive. The Thomas saying may reflect the situation when Cephas had nominated James as future leader but before making him leader, or it may have originated when James was nominally leader in Jerusalem but Cephas was still alive and regarded as the real leader by most in the movement. The purpose of the saying is to support James and confirm him as Cephas' successor. To achieve this, it could only have come from the founder.

When did Jesus first appear to Cephas?

We shall see that Cephas probably died in Rome as a result of the persecution by Nero in 64. If this is correct then if the spiritual experiences lasted forty years they must have started around AD 24. Assuming that Cephas has died relatively old and would not have had the resurrection experience earlier than his twenties, we can assign a birth date roughly in the range 6 BC to AD 4. This includes the traditional birth date of Jesus of c. 4 BC, which raises the suspicion that dates assigned to Jesus in the gospel may actually relate to the founder.

Under the shaman paradigm the ministry of Jesus begins with the appearance of Jesus to the shaman. The Gospel of Luke has a very interesting dating of this event:

> *Now in the fifteenth year of the reign of Tiberius Caesar, Pontius Pilate being governor of Judea, and Herod being tetrarch of Galilee, and his brother Philip tetrarch of Ituraea and of the region of Trachonitis, and Lysanias the tetrarch of Abilene, Annas and Caiaphas being the high priests, the word of God came unto John the son of Zechariah in the wilderness. (Luke 3:1-2)*

Although nominally dating the start of John's ministry, the whole John story in Luke is really to prepare for the baptism of Jesus in Luke 3:21-22. So we can assume that the purpose of this dating is to establish the date of this baptism and hence the start of Jesus' ministry. The information from Luke that the baptism took place while Pilate was governor is interesting. Under the spiritual paradigm, the baptism is the descent of the spiritual Jesus into the founder, which is also the same event as the resurrection. If the author of Mark had heard that the resurrection occurred under the rule of Pilate he would naturally have assumed that the crucifixion, taking place on the third day before the resurrection, would also have occurred under Pilate. This would then account for the specific role that Pilate plays in the gospels as the executioner of Jesus. Pilate was governor at the time that the founder had their baptism and resurrection experience and so, through a mistake, was to be ever branded as the killer of the Son of God. In a time before calendars people used to fix dates in relation to rulers. The Jews hated their Roman overlords, but they had a keen interest in who was chosen to rule over them for this could be quite literally a matter of life and death. They would have remembered who was governor at the time of an event, while the identity of the Roman Emperor was a distant and more abstract concept. So it is quite possible that it was remembered that the founder's experience of Jesus, which gave rise to the baptism and resurrection stories, took place while Pontius Pilate was governor. This would date the resurrection experience as no earlier than AD 26, a date only two years after the approximate AD 24 arrived at by deducting forty years from the assumed date of death of Cephas.

What about the further information in Luke dating the baptism to the fifteenth year of the rule of Tiberius? This Roman method of dating is typical of the author of Luke but very inappropriate to the Jews who started the Jesus movement. Even had they remembered a date they would not have remembered it in these Roman terms. So the author of Luke cannot have read the date as "*the fifteenth year of the rule of Tiberius*" in her sources but has translated the date of some event that was in the source into this Roman form. But how has the author of Luke managed to convert such an event into a precise Roman date? The author of Luke gets this sort of information from Josephus, who was writing about Jewish events for a Roman audience. So is there anything in Josephus that points to a date of the fifteenth year of the rule of Tiberius?

We find what we are looking for in a passage in the Jewish Antiquities about the governors of Judea:

> *After him came Annius Rufus, under whom died Caesar, the second emperor of the Romans, the duration of whose reign was fifty-seven years, besides six months and two days (of which time Antony ruled together with him fourteen years; but the duration of his life was seventy-seven years); upon whose death Tiberius Nero, his wife Julia's son, succeeded. He was now the third emperor; and he sent Valerius Gratus to be procurator of Judea, and to succeed Annius Rufus. This man deprived Ananus of the high priesthood, and appointed Ismael, the son of Phabi, to be high priest. He also deprived him in a little time, and ordained Eleazar, the son of Ananus, who had been high priest before, to be high priest; which office, when he had held for a year, Gratus deprived him of it, and gave the high priesthood to Simon, the son of Camithus; and when he had possessed that dignity no longer than a year, Joseph Caiaphas was made his successor. When Gratus had done those things, he went back to Rome, after he had tarried in Judea eleven years, when Pontius Pilate came as his successor. (Josephus, Jewish Antiquities 18:32-35)[73]*

Josephus tells us that Gratus was appointed governor by Tiberius who had become emperor on the death of Augustus in AD 14. After eleven years, Gratus was succeeded by Pontius Pilate who became governor in

AD 26. This would seem to point to Pilate becoming governor in the twelfth or thirteenth year of Tiberius' reign. However, there is a clue that we should not interpret the beginning of Tiberius' reign from the death of Augustus. The reign of Augustus is given as the very long period of over fifty-seven years. However, Augustus only became sole ruler in 30 BC. Josephus is counting the rule as commencing much earlier with the death of Julius Caesar in 44 BC although Augustus initially ruled as part of the triumvirate and alongside Antony. This is relevant because Tiberius had been appointed as joint ruler with Augustus in AD 12. So if a reader of this passage, such as the author of Luke, had attempted to date the start of Pilate's governorship in terms of Tiberius' rule he or she would have the example of Augustus to suggest that the rule of Tiberius should be counted from AD 12 and not AD 14. So the start of Pilate's term of governor would be dated to the fourteenth or fifteenth year of the reign of Tiberius.

Not only do the two passages point to the same date, it is immediately apparent that there are similarities between the Josephus passage and Luke 3:1-2. These similarities become more pronounced if we also consider the corresponding passage in the Jewish War of which the Antiquities passage is an expansion:

> But when the Roman empire was translated to Tiberius, the son of Julia, upon the death of Augustus, who had reigned fifty-seven years, six months, and two days, both Herod and Philip continued in their tetrarchies; and the latter of them built the city Caesarea, at the fountains of Jordan, and in the region of Paneas; as also the city Julias, in the lower Gaulonitis. Herod also built the city Tiberias in Galilee, and in Perea another that was also called Julias. Now Pilate, who was sent as procurator into Judea by Tiberius, ... (Josephus, Jewish War 2.168-9)[74]

We can see that all but one of the historical personages mentioned in the Luke passage are also mentioned in one or other of the two Josephus passages. We have Tiberius in relation to the start of his reign, Pontius Pilate, the tetrarchs Herod and Philip, and the high priests Annas and Caiaphas. This also explains the curious fact that Luke says that Annas is high priest as well as Caiaphas even though Annas had not been high priest for many years. Josephus mentions a number of high priests starting with Annas and ending with Caiaphas. The author of Luke seems to have summarised this sequence as Annas and Caiaphas, perhaps misremembering the passage because she has only heard it and does not have a copy. For Jewish Antiquities would not have been finished and published when the Gospel of

Luke was written although, as we will see, the author of Luke may have had privileged access to the work in progress.

It would be a very unlikely coincidence if the passages in Josephus that point to the same date as Luke 3:1-2 just happen to have many other similarities with Luke 3:1-2. We must conclude that this is not coincidence but evidence that the author of Luke has used the Josephus passages as the source for the dating. But this means that the event that the Josephus passages are pointing to must also be the event which the author of Luke's source is connecting to the baptism of Jesus. What is this event? Although Josephus is dating the start of the governorship of Pilate, the real event that he is recounting is something that happened very early on in Pilate's governorship, probably in the winter of late AD 26. The new governor brought into Jerusalem images of Caesar, either by mistake or as a deliberate trial of strength:

Now Pilate, who was sent as procurator into Judea by Tiberius, sent by night those images of Caesar that are called ensigns into Jerusalem. This excited a very great tumult among the Jews when it was day; for those that were near them were astonished at the sight of them, as indications that their laws were trodden underfoot: for those laws do not permit any sort of image to be brought into the city. Nay, besides the indignation which the citizens had themselves at this procedure, a vast number of people came running out of the country. (Josephus, Jewish War 2.169-170)[75]

Josephus recounts how after a standoff Pilate had his troops surround the protestors who came to Caesarea to petition for the removal of the ensigns and threaten them with death if they did not disperse. The people, however, bared their necks for the sword saying it was better to die than suffer the law to be transgressed. Faced with this passive opposition Pilate backed down and ordered the ensigns to be withdrawn. The reaction of the people shows the importance this apparently trivial matter had for the Jews. The ensigns bore the image of Caesar and so were considered idols and their presence in the holy city was a gross profanation. Such provocation had been carefully avoided by the predecessors of Pilate, and the fact that Pilate decided to back down suggests that he knew he was on weak ground.

This event occurring at the end of AD 26 would have taken place in the fifteenth year of Tiberius' reign as measured from AD 12. It would seem that the date of the baptism, the descent of the spirit of Jesus into the founder, happened at around the same time as this episode of the ensigns. But what is the connection between two such apparently disparate events, one being the spiritual experience of an individual and the other a political crisis triggered by the imperious actions of a Roman overlord? The answer lies in the apocalyptic mindset. The appearance of Jesus to the founder, and then the founder's followers, was not seen as a personal experience but as something of cosmic significance. Jesus had been dead for two great days, and now at the start of the third great day he was resurrected. Each great day was itself a week of seven days, and Jesus appeared to the founder on the first day of the final week. This great day would bring to a close the history of the world, it was the week of the apocalypse, and although Jesus had appeared in spiritual form at the start of this week, visible only to his chosen followers, by the end of the week he would appear to all, coming in glory at the time of the final judgement. The Gospel of Mark tells us the signal that will start the apocalypse:

> But when you shall see the abomination of desolation, spoken of by Daniel the prophet, standing where it ought not, (let him that reads understand), then let them that are in Judaea flee to the mountains: (Mark 13:14)

The author of Mark is writing shortly after the destruction of the temple by the Romans in 70. The Gospel of Mark develops the idea that this destruction was foreseen by Jesus, although we will see in the second volume that the supposed prophecy of the destruction of the temple actually related to the first temple which was the only temple considered valid by the early Jesus movement. The original "abomination of desolation" in the book of Daniel related to the much earlier conversion of the temple to the worship of Zeus by Antiochus IV Epiphanes. It would seem that the "abomination" was an idol of Zeus Olympus that was erected in the temple where sacrifices were made to it. However, later apocalyptic readers of the book of Daniel interpreted the "abomination of desolation" as a prophecy of something to come rather than something that had already happened. The Mark passage is evidence that it was used in this way among the Jesus movement long before the Gospel of Mark was written. Before the temple was burnt down by fire, it was desecrated by the Romans' sacrificing to their legendary standards within the temple.[76] This might be seen as fitting the original Daniel prophecy well, but it does not fit the saying as used in Mark. The Jews would not see "the abomination standing where it ought" because there would not have been any Jews around to witness the sacrifice to the legendary standards. And it would make no sense for those in Judea to flee to the mountains because the destruction was already at its peak, and the fate of all those within the city had been sealed for some time. The problem is that the Roman sacrifice in the temple was the culmination of the Jewish defeat and not the start of the war. It would seem that the author of Mark has used an existing saying that regarded the "abomination of desolation" as signalling the beginning of the apocalypse and has reused this saying by applying it after the event to the destruction of the temple. But if the original saying pre-dated Mark then it cannot relate to the Roman destruction because that happened only shortly before the Gospel of Mark was written. So instead the saying must have related to some other event that was seen by the early movement as signifying that the apocalypse had started. The only event that fits, and fits perfectly, is the episode of the bringing in of the ensigns to Jerusalem by Pilate. The ensigns would have been clearly visible to the people, they would have been "abominations" because they were idols of the imperial cult bearing the image of Caesar, and they would have been standing where they should not, in the holy city. A Jew of the time would have seen in all this a chilling echo of the time of Antiochus Epiphanes. Apocalyptic sects, including the predecessors of the Jesus movement, would have interpreted it as a clear indication that the end time was beginning. And yet the expected apocalyptic war did not break out in the years following AD 26. Gradually the excitement would have died down, and the apocalyptic significance that was once attached to the episode of the ensigns would fade from memory.

It did, however, leave behind a trace in some sayings from the early Jesus movement that must have been fashioned shortly after AD 26 and which were to be preserved in distorted form in the gospels. One of these sayings became Mark 13:14. The other was a source dating the "baptism of Jesus", the appearance of Jesus to the founder, to the same time as the raising of the ensigns in Jerusalem by Pilate. This second source was available to the author of Luke who interpreted it in terms of the framework provided by the Gospel of Mark where the baptism of Jesus is a water baptism carried out on Jesus by John. The author of Luke has looked up the episode of the ensigns in Josephus and used the Josephus passages as the model for her own impressive Roman historical style dating. She has then applied this dating to the start of the passage leading to the baptism of Jesus so that it becomes transferred to the beginning of the ministry of John the Baptist.

All of this gives a surprisingly precise dating for the appearance of Jesus to Cephas (if Cephas is indeed the founder). It must have happened at the end of AD 26 or at least close enough to the episode of the ensigns for the two to be connected in the apocalyptic mind. If Cephas has died in the Nero persecution of 64, then the time that Jesus was believed to be present in the world through Cephas would, in fact, be just under thirty-eight years. Such a number would not have appealed to the apocalyptic mindset and has been rounded up to forty years to correspond to the forty years that the Israelites spent in the desert after leaving Egypt. At the end of the same baptism sequence, the gospel gives the approximate age of Jesus:

And Jesus himself was beginning about thirty years of age ... (Luke 3:23)

Under the shaman paradigm, this cannot relate to Jesus. Does it relate then to the founder? There is no reason the precise age of the founder at this time should be remembered and there seems to have been little interest in the ancient world for such facts as a person's age.[77] However, the early Jesus movement attached great importance to the apocalyptic calendar and it is a necessity of that calendar that the founder's life span had to be split into two generations. The first generation is the length of the founder's life before the coming of Jesus and the second is the generation of Jesus living through the founder, a generation that starts when Jesus "begins" within the founder (note the odd expression in Luke above about Jesus "beginning" at around age thirty). It is likely then that the author of Luke has inherited a source that is less concerned with the founder's actual age at this time and more concerned with the split between the generations. Possibly this is the same source that dates the baptism of Jesus to the time of the ensigns. The age of thirty can in fact be deduced by deducting the forty years allocated to the second generation, the generation of Jesus, from the biblical human lifespan of seventy years. (It is unlikely that anyone would have known exactly how old Cephas was when he died.)

We can thus expect that the thirty years age of Cephas to be a symbolic age which meets the needs of the apocalyptic calendar rather than an actual age. However, it cannot be far out. If Cephas were much older than mid-thirties in AD 26, then Cephas would have been well into his seventies when he died in AD 64 (assuming that this was the date of death). Anything older would be improbably old for the ancient world for someone who would have had a tough life, particularly as they were still exercising a considerable influence on the movement. We can set a limit at the other extreme by applying the criterion that Cephas must have had a certain maturity at the start of the movement. The founder has to persuade people that their experience of the risen Christ is genuine and must then carry their followers with them through a series of radical departures from tradition. It is unlikely that a young person would be capable of this. So the early thirties is likely.

Dating the history of the early movement

We can date one other appearance in Paul's list, and that is the appearance to Paul himself. In 2 Corinthians, Paul tells how he had to make an escape from Damascus:

> *In Damascus the governor under the King Aretas was guarding the city of the Damascenes in order to seize me. But I was lowered in a basket through a window through the wall, and I escaped his hands. (2 Corinthians 11:32-33)*

King Aretas took control of Damascus in AD 37 and died in AD 40 so the episode of the basket must have taken place within those years. In Galatians 1:17-19 Paul tells us about his conversion and what he did afterwards:

> *But when it pleased God, who separated me from my mother's womb, and called me by his grace, to reveal his Son in me, that I might preach him among the Gentiles, immediately I did not consult with flesh and blood, not did I go up to Jerusalem to those which were apostles before me, but I went into Arabia and again returned to Damascus. Then, after three years I went up to Jerusalem to get acquainted with Peter/Cephas, and remained with him fifteen days, and other of the apostles I did not see, except James, the brother of the Lord. (Galatians 1:15-19)*

Paul's dramatic escape from Damascus cannot have happened in his first mentioned stay, after his conversion, because Paul conferred with no one. At this stage he has not started his work as an apostle and would not have annoyed the rulers of Damascus; nor has he made contact with the Jesus movement to help with an escape. So it must have happened when Paul returned to Damascus for a long stay having been to Arabia. Presumably the escape meant that he was unable to return to Damascus so it must have happened immediately before Paul went to Jerusalem to stay with Cephas. As this visit took place "after three years" we can date Paul's resurrection experience to AD 34-37 and his stay with Cephas to AD 37-40. It is this visit to Cephas that is the most likely source of Paul's information on the resurrection.

This means that Paul's list of resurrection appearances span about ten years. James comes towards the tail end and must have been a child in AD 26 when the resurrection experiences started. By the time Paul stays with Cephas, he would have been a young man, old enough to be inducted into the inner mysteries of the movement and mentioned by Paul although only in passing. When Paul is writing Galatians in the mid-50s, James is in full charge of the movement from Jerusalem and must have been of an appropriate age to be the leader. A date of birth of around AD 15 would meet these conditions with James about 20 years younger than Cephas.

We can set out an approximate timeline for Paul's account of the resurrection experiences as follows:

c5 BC	Cephas born
c15	James born
26	Cephas has the resurrection experience
26-27	The Twelve inducted
27-35?	Five hundred followers recruited and inducted
35?-37	James and the apostles inducted
34-37	Paul's conversion
37-40	Paul inducted

What is striking is the change that took place at around AD 35. Cephas seems to have switched from the indiscriminate induction of a large number of followers within Judea to a select group of "apostles" who would have the mission of spreading the movement far and wide. At the same time, Cephas would seem to have planned for a new generation of future leaders, moving away from the twelve to the group of "the brethren of the Lord" to be led by James. Was there some event that caused these changes? There was in fact something that happened at around this time that had a great impact on the movement. This was the death of John the Baptist. While John was alive, the Jesus movement was small and insignificant, constrained by John's much greater popular appeal. With the death of John, a vast number of new followers became available for recruitment. The founder made the pragmatic decision to make changes to appeal to these new potential followers, most significantly the introduction of water baptism which we can date from this time. It would seem that this change was spectacularly successful, and the movement expanded rapidly.

We shall see later the evidence that the Jesus movement arose in close proximity to John and was in a state of intense rivalry with John's movement. The Jesus movement was highly esoteric and appealed to a select few but in some ways it was modelled on John's movement. Just as everyone would be brought to John for baptism, so every new recruit was brought to Cephas for induction and the spiritual baptism of Jesus. This explains the large number of individuals inducted at the start of Paul's list, over five hundred, probably everyone in the movement at this time. At this stage, the whole movement was completely dependent upon Cephas.

Although the Jesus movement considered its spiritual baptism as greatly superior to the mere washing of the outside as practised by John, there were certain disadvantages that must have become increasingly apparent to Cephas. The spiritual baptism, unlike a water baptism, was a slow process with no guarantee of success. There must have been many who could not see Jesus, and many who simply pretended to see Jesus. Then there were the many who experienced something, but who did not have the depth of spiritual experience that Cephas intended. These were the "poor in the spirit" and they must have caused Cephas great unease. What to do about people who were well intended, who wanted to be part of the movement, who responded to the story of Jesus, but who were not spiritual enough for the full experience? The solution became apparent when after the death of John the movement began to adopt water baptism to appeal to the bereft followers of John. Cephas saw in this water baptism the perfect solution.

So the movement was re-engineered. No longer would new recruits be brought to Cephas for induction. Instead, the only condition for membership was that the recruit should avow that they believed in Jesus as Lord and receive a water baptism. They would then be instructed until ready to progress to the full spiritual baptism, to become what Paul calls the "perfect". So now there was a two-tier movement with a large and fast growing body of the baptised, "the called" and a smaller core of the perfect, "the chosen". The dependence on Cephas was removed; if the movement were to expand geographically, then new recruits could not be brought to one individual. So Cephas concentrated on the recruitment and induction of a group of apostles who would be responsible for taking the gospel across the Roman Empire. The apostles would set up churches wherever they went, and these churches would conduct their own baptisms and spiritual inductions. At the same time, Cephas prepared a younger group to take on the leadership role eventually. It is probably no coincidence that this leadership group belonged to the first generation to have grown up in the nascent movement, to have been completely moulded by Cephas.

The re-engineering was a tremendous success. A small esoteric group was changed into a great popular movement. The new structure was not just "scalable", capable of a vast expansion, it was also durable, lasting some two thousand years to date. Had these changes not been made the Jesus movement would most likely have faded out after the death of Cephas. The example of John the Baptist would have been very prominent to Cephas at this time. John was a great and popular religious leader but as soon as his head was cut off the movement he founded disintegrated. It was John who personally baptised and although the water baptism was far more efficient than the spiritual baptism of Cephas, it still gave a crippling dependence on one person's charisma. If the Jesus movement was to survive, it had to be about more than just one person. So Cephas began to withdraw from a central charismatic role and instead set up an organisation.

There were implications of the path adopted that would not have been foreseen. The eventual new leadership group under James was not a great success. It seems that James had not been moulded as fully into the new order as Cephas had thought. He had a mind of his own and that mind was inherently conservative. James tried to push the movement back towards mainstream Judaism. Resisting him all the way was the most successful of the apostles, Paul, who also must have caused Cephas much grief. Paul, the former Pharisee, was more educated than others in the movement; he was an eloquent writer, and very much a loose cannon. But the most significant issue was not a matter of personalities but an inevitable result of the two-tier structure and the rapid pace of geographical expansion. A mathematician could have told Cephas what would happen if you had two separate groups; the outer non-spiritual Christians whose numbers would expand at a fast rate; and a smaller inner spiritual group whose numbers could only expand at a slower rate. Very soon the non-spiritual would greatly predominate. And a student of human nature could have told Cephas that the non-spiritual would end up controlling the church and would reject the idea that their own faith was in any way secondary to the so-called chosen. We must remember that there was no outer sign of being in the inner spiritual elite. They did not wear a badge or have some special grade. It was not objective, this baptism of Jesus, although it was considered at the beginning of the Jesus movement as the ultimate reality.

In interpreting Paul's resurrection account, we must be careful of his subjective bias. The ending of the resurrection experiences with Paul will reflect both this bias and the date of his information which relates to his visit to Jerusalem in AD 37-40. We know Paul had his own experiences of Jesus throughout life, so his list relates to the time that new people had their first experience of Jesus and not to the total time that the experiences lasted. However, for Paul's assertion that he was the last of the apostles to have any credibility, the creation of new apostles must have largely related to a finite era of just a few years. Once the group of apostles had been assembled Cephas would seem to have more or less ceased new inductions.

Why does Paul call himself an abortion?

There is one known exception to this rule of induction by Cephas, and that is Paul himself. By his own account, Paul had a spontaneous revelation and did not owe his experience of the Christ to any other person. But again we must be cautious to allow for Paul's subjective position in interpreting his account. At the time Paul was writing Galatians, his relationship with James and Cephas was at a low point. Paul was furious at the way James was running the church and obliging Gentiles to be circumcised. He saw James as a backslider who was betraying the original philosophy of the movement. But his anger also extended to Cephas who had appointed James to his position and who was allowing all this to happen through what Paul saw as weakness. So in Galatians, Paul is very keen to stress his independence of the pillars in Jerusalem and to derive his own authority direct from the spiritual Jesus. One wonders if he was thinking at this time of splitting from the leadership of the movement and founding his own splinter movement. However, it seems that he did not have enough support for this and even the churches he founded looked to Cephas rather than Paul.

We must allow for Paul's state of mind in interpreting his account. Doubtless the basic facts he gives are correct but the meaning he derives from these facts suits his purpose at the time he is writing Galatians. Clearly Paul had a spontaneous conversion experience. As one who was persecuting the Jesus movement, he cannot have had any kind of induction at this early stage. He immediately went away from Damascus to spend some time in Arabia. When he returned to the city, he became sufficiently active in preaching the gospel to arouse the ire of the governor. During this time in Damascus, he must have had contact with the movement and after three years he sought out Cephas to regularise his position.

It is unlikely that famous "road to Damascus" revelation ever happened on the road to Damascus. The colourful account in Acts is a novelistic fiction developed from the bare bones of Paul's description. In Acts, Paul is struck blind by his vision until he is visited by Ananias, a disciple in Damascus. It is Ananias who lifts Paul's blindness and who baptises him. But

Paul does not mention an Ananias in his letter. On the contrary, he is quite specific that no one else was involved; *"I conferred not with flesh and blood"* he writes. Ananias has been introduced into the Acts story in a flagrant contradiction to Paul's own account. There must have been a strong necessity to write in such a contradiction to Paul's letter, and it is not hard to see what this necessity was. The early church would have felt deep disquiet about Paul's version of events. The proto-orthodox view was that Jesus was a man who lived and taught in Palestine and who appointed his disciples as Apostles to found the church and spread the word. Yet here was Paul, a persecutor of the church, having a vision and then going off to teach the gospel of Jesus without making any contact with the Apostles or anyone else in the church. He is doing his own thing without any reference to the central authority supposedly set up by Jesus. How does Paul know what Jesus taught? As a persecutor, he doubtless obtained a great deal of information about the movement but he never knew it from the inside.

To the proto-orthodox early church, this is all very odd. It is baptism, the physical laying on of hands, which passes on the magical essence of Jesus in an unbroken line originating from Jesus' physical presence on earth and passing through those who knew him, his disciples/apostles, and from them to all the subsequent Christian teachers and preachers and ministers, down to the individual believer's own baptism. But Paul himself would appear never to have been baptised. Nor did he bother to consult anyone in the church set up by Jesus' apostles before rushing off and converting others. Under the spiritual paradigm, the reason becomes clear. The apostles have never known Jesus in life but, like Paul, only in the spirit. Paul does not see their claim to divine authority as greater than his own.

Yet Paul does recognise their leadership and after a delay his position is regularised by an induction by Cephas. But what about Paul's strange admission that it was as though he was an abortion or miscarriage, *ectromati*? The implication of this word was that Paul's birth in Christ was irregular and premature and that Paul was not fully formed. The concept of the baptism of Christ as being a rebirth is clear from the Gospel of John:

Jesus answered and said to him, "Truly, truly I say to you, Except a man be born from above [or born again], he cannot see the kingdom of God." Nicodemus said to him, "How can a man be born when he is old? Can he enter the second time into his mother's womb, and be born?" Jesus answered, "Truly, truly, I say to you, Except a man be born of water and of the Spirit, he cannot enter into the kingdom of God. That which is born of the flesh is flesh, and that which is born of the Spirit is spirit." (John 3:3-6)

The reference to being born of water and the spirit is a reference to baptism. We can see that "water" has been added, as the rest of the saying is all about the spirit. The author of John has adjusted the original saying about spiritual baptism to make it also apply to water baptism. Removing this adjustment we get the original form:

Except a man be born of the spirit he cannot enter into the kingdom of heaven. That which is born of flesh is flesh and that which is born of the spirit is spirit.

In the original spiritual baptism it was Cephas who played the role of mother, Cephas who laboured until Jesus was formed in the one undergoing baptism, that they might be reborn of the spirit and enter into the kingdom of heaven. But Paul is outside the movement; he has not gone through this process of birth with Cephas but has been reborn spontaneously as if through a miscarriage. Talking about Cephas as a mother in labour may seem odd, but it is exactly the same terminology as Paul uses about his own relationship with the Galatians:

My little children, of whom I labour in birth again until Christ be formed in you ... (Galatians 4:19)

Although Paul is the mother in labour, Christ is actually formed within the Galatians and the same is true of the relationship of Cephas and the one being baptised. Should not his birth in Christ have been a miraculous and wonderful event for Paul, even if not mediated by Cephas? Elsewhere he uses the fact that he had a spontaneous experience of Jesus as a positive argument against James. So why should he describe it here using the word for the birth of a dead thing? Paul himself tells us the reason: "*for I am the least of the apostles, and am not worthy to be called an apostle, because I did persecute the assembly of God.*" At the beginning, Paul saw his unusual birth in Christ as a punishment for persecuting the early church. He is alone, cut off from Cephas and the rest. Later, as he comes into conflict with the "pillars", it becomes in his mind something more positive as demonstrating his independent relationship with Jesus.

In fact, we can trace Paul's use of *ektromati* to the Septuagint, the ancient Greek translation of the scriptures that Paul is familiar with and frequently quotes from. One of the two occurrences of *ektromati* in the Septuagint is highly relevant to Paul's situation. It describes what happens when the sister and brother of Moses, Mariam (Mary) and Aaron, oppose the taking of

a Cushite woman by Moses as a wife. All three are summoned to the tabernacle of meeting where Yahweh appears before them in a pillar of cloud. In
anger, he calls Aaron and Mariam to approach and when the pillar ascends
they see that Mariam has been afflicted:

> ... *and, behold, Mariam was leprous, white as snow; and Aaron looked upon
> Mariam, and, behold, she was leprous. And Aaron said to Moses, I beseech thee,
> my Lord, do not lay sin upon us, for we were ignorant wherein we sinned. Let her
> not be as it were like death, as an abortion coming out of his mother's womb, when
> the disease devours the half of the flesh. And Moses cried to the Lord, saying, O
> God, I beseech thee, heal her. And the Lord said to Moses, If her father had only
> spit in her face, would she not be ashamed seven days? Let her be set apart seven
> days without the camp, and afterwards she shall come in. And Mariam was sepa-
> rated without the camp seven days; and the people moved not forward till Mariam
> was cleansed. (LXX Numbers 12:10-15)*[78]*

Mariam's crime was speaking against her brother Moses for taking a
Cushite woman as a wife. Her anger against Moses is understandable for
the marriage appears to be contrary to the commands of Yahweh. But Mariam is punished by Yahweh himself for putting her interpretation of Yahweh's purpose above the revelation that Yahweh has made directly to Moses. The implication is that Yahweh has ordered the marriage to serve a
purpose he has not revealed to man.

Whatever the original author intended, this episode would have fascinated the later Jews who interpreted the scriptures through Midrash. The
marriage of Moses to a Gentile Cushite woman is highly symbolic for it
signifies the bringing in of Gentiles into the chosen people of Yahweh. Mariam is in the position of the conventional Jew, who opposes this bringing
in of the Gentile and so stands against the hidden purpose of Yahweh.

All of which is highly relevant to Paul's own situation. A remarkable
characteristic of the early church was its very openness to Gentiles whom it
sought to bring in on equal terms. Paul was a self-righteous persecutor of
the church and stands in the role of Mariam, a conventional Jew who opposes the bringing in of the Gentile. One of the most striking features of
Paul's ministry is that he, a former Pharisee, saw himself as having a special mission to the Gentiles. Nowhere does he tell us why he has this mission but in the story of Mariam we can see an explanation. Paul opposed
the church because it brought in the Gentile, and it is fitting that he should
be given his special mission to the Gentiles to make amends for his opposi-

tion. It is ironic that many in the early church, including the Jerusalem leadership, would come to see Paul as being far too pro-Gentile but then Paul would not be the first or last person to over compensate.

The points of similarity between Mariam and Paul are several -

Paul and Mariam have both had a meeting with God – Mariam has seen Yahweh in the pillar of cloud, Paul has seen the resurrected Christ.

As a result of her encounter with God, Mariam is made leprous like a *ek-tromati*. Paul describes himself as an *ektromati* following his encounter with Christ.

Mariam has opposed the marriage of Moses to a Gentile symbolising the acceptance of Gentiles within the Jews. Paul has persecuted the early church, a Jewish movement that has accepted gentiles as well as Jews.

Mariam's punishment is to be banished from the camp for seven days. Following his resurrection experience, Paul goes immediately into self-imposed exile from the early church.

Mariam's banishment lasts for seven days and if a day is taken as standing for a year as it does elsewhere, this would be interpreted as a period of seven years. Did Paul believe that his own banishment from the church should last seven years as his punishment for persecuting it? Paul actually made contact with Cephas/Peter after three years and not seven. But there are elements in Paul's account of this visit that are puzzling but which would be explained if Paul, in his own mind, remained in a state of self-imposed exile. He says how he was *"unknown by face to the assemblies of Judea, that are in Christ"* even after his visit. It seems that Paul visited Jerusalem almost in secret and kept apart from the main body of believers. The explanation that they feared and mistrusted him is not sufficient; he has by this time been a believer in Jesus for over three years and must have given ample proof of his conversion. A better explanation is that Paul sees himself in a state of punishment and exile. Yet Cephas does accept him into the movement for Cephas has an uncanny ability to read people. With Cephas as mother, Paul's birth in Christ becomes complete and he is made whole, becoming one of the chosen apostles.

Key points

1. Paul's list of the resurrection appearances can be seen as a history of the early movement.

2. It starts with Cephas, who must be the shaman.

3. The subsequent appearances of Jesus cannot have happened spontaneously but must have been induced by Cephas. The exception is the spontaneous and irregular appearance to Paul.

4. The first appearance to the shaman can be dated very precisely to the end of AD 26. This was when the new Governor of Judea, Pontius Pilate, set up ensigns (images of Caesar) in Jerusalem. The apocalyptic groups saw this as the *"abomination of desolation"*, the sign that was to signal the start of the end times.

5. The belief that Pilate had put Jesus to death arose because of the strong association between the resurrection and the episode of the ensigns. The author of Mark believed that only three days separated the crucifixion and resurrection. So if the resurrection took place under Pilate, then the crucifixion must have also.

6. After the shaman, the resurrected Jesus next appeared to the Twelve, who would have been the first followers of the shaman. Their identities have long been lost although the names of some may be included in the list of the Twelve in Mark.

7. After the Twelve, Jesus was seen by five hundred followers, who must have been inducted by Cephas over a period of around a decade. This first phase of the movement took place in Palestine.

8. There was then an abrupt change when the shaman stopped inducting all new members to the movement, but instead concentrated on a group who would go out and induct others. In the list of appearances, this new phase is marked by James and *"all the apostles"*. The new structure of apostles under James began an era of geographical expansion that was to take the Jesus movement across the Roman Empire.

9. The catalyst for this change would seem to be the death of John the Baptist, which took place at around the same time. The execution of John brought in a vast number of new converts, but it also provided a stark example of what happened to a movement that depended on the charisma of a single individual.

10. While John was alive, the Jesus movement practiced the spiritual baptism of Jesus through the medium of Cephas and depreciated water baptism. But after the death of John, water baptism was adopted, both to appeal to John's former followers, and to enable a rapid expansion under the new apostles. The intention was to follow up the "outer" water baptism by the "inner" spiritual, baptism. But the spiritual baptism was slow and only worked for some individuals. It became increasingly seen as elitist and "gnostic".

11. The induction was seen as a rebirth, with Cephas as mother/midwife. Paul calls his experience of Jesus an abortion or miscarriage because it did not take place in due time through Cephas, but was spontaneous, premature and incomplete.

12. Paul originally saw the nature of his rebirth as punishment for his persecution of the church. Just as Mariam, sister of Moses, was cast out of the Israelite camp for seven days, so Paul believed that he must stay outside the church for seven years. However, he actually visited Cephas in Jerusalem after three years, although he kept apart from other members of the church in this visit. On this occasion, Paul's birth in Christ would have been completed, and his position in the Jesus movement regularised. Later, when Paul was in conflict with James, he came to see the spontaneous nature of his experience of Christ as evidence that he had been specially chosen by God.

13. The total time of the resurrected Jesus on earth was forty days, meaning forty years. This is the approximate lifetime of the shaman after the first resurrection experience.

Chapter 15

Mary and Cephas

It is time to bring all the evidence together. Who was the founder of Christianity? And why do the sources appear to be inconsistent? The answer lies in something else that Paul tells us, something that might even seem to invalidate the shaman paradigm. For Paul says that Jesus has been "born of woman". Or does he?

Who was the founder?

We set out to find the identity of the founder beneath the layers of later literalistic accretions by three criteria:

Criteria	Individuals who satisfy criteria
Prominence	Mary, the mother of Jesus Peter (Cephas) (Mary the Magdalene has prominence among certain groups. There is the possibility that Mary the mother and Mary the Magdalene are the same person.)
First witness of the resurrection	Mary the Magdalene Cephas
First leader	Cephas

Two features stand out in this table. First that Cephas (either under that name or Peter) satisfies each of the criteria. We have seen the overwhelming evidence that Cephas was the first leader and hence the founder. We have the tradition from Paul that Cephas was the first witness of the resurrection, and we have seen that Peter has the right degree of prominence.

The second feature is the appearance of a woman called Mary under two of the criteria. We have seen the evidence for the alternative resurrection account, that it was Mary the Magdalene who was the first witness. And Mary, the mother of Jesus, has a prominence even greater than that of Peter. Indeed Mary the mother of Jesus evokes adoration in the early church exactly as we would expect of the memory of the founder. Under the spiritual paradigm, Jesus does not have a physical mother, so who is this woman? Is she a purely literary invention who from the meagre beginnings in the Gospel of Mark develops into a character to excite a feeling of love among Christians to rival the love they feel for Jesus? Or is the emotion of adoration there from the beginning and does it seed the development of the literary character from scraps of legend?

We have to consider the possibility that the two Marys are in fact one and the same. If so we have a clear rival to Cephas as the founder. We now have to consider this Mary, the mother of Jesus. How does she fit in? There is more evidence yet to consider, a clue in our earliest source, the letters of Paul, a clue that turns everything on its head and that will force us to reconsider the identity of the founder, a clue that may even cause us to reject the shaman paradigm altogether. For Paul appears to tell us that Jesus was born.

Christ born of woman

Paul is notoriously silent on the details of Jesus' life and teachings, and it is this very silence that has led a few academics to consider the Jesus as myth hypothesis seriously. In Paul's letters, there are only a few fragments that hint of Jesus having had a life on earth but these fragments must be taken seriously for they are potentially fatal to the shaman paradigm. The most specific is that James is described as "brother of the Lord". What this could mean if not a normal sibling relationship will be addressed later. But there are two other passages that would seem to cause the shaman paradigm most difficulty by saying that Jesus was "born of woman" and "born of the seed of David":

... while we were children, we were enslaved to the elements of the world. But when the fullness of time had come, God sent his son, born (genomenon) of a woman, born (genomenon) under the law, in order to redeem those who were under the law ... (Galatians 4:3-5)

... the gospel concerning his son, who is born (genomenou) of the seed of David according to the flesh and was declared son of God with power according to the spirit of holiness by the resurrection from the dead, Jesus Christ our Lord. (Romans 1:3-4)

According to the above translation these two passages tell us that Jesus was "*born of a woman*", a common phrase that simply meant that he was human, "*born under the law*", that is Jewish, and "*born of the seed of David*", a descendant of David as would be required of the Messiah. The actual word used in each case is *ginomai*. If Jesus was born, can the shaman paradigm be correct? To preserve the shaman paradigm this birth of Jesus would have had to have taken place in the distant, almost mythological, past when Jesus was believed to have lived on earth before his crucifixion. We cannot interpret Paul's words as applying to such a distant time because he says that Jesus being "*born of woman*" brings in the redemption of those under the law from the rule of "*the elements (stoicheia) of the world (kosmos)*". Under the shaman paradigm, this redemption must take place in Paul's own time through the resurrection.

What does the strange phrase "*the elements of the kosmos*" mean? The word *kosmos* means the universe rather than just the earth. Paul's argument is that an heir, while a child, may be placed under guardians and stewards until a time appointed by their father. Although they have to obey their guardians like a slave, the child is not a slave. So also mankind has been placed under guardians, the "*elements of the kosmos*", in a state of apparent slavery until Christ came to give us adoption as children. Many traditional commentators believe that by "*the elements of the kosmos*" Paul means the Jewish law. It is true that Paul's whole discourse is about freedom from the law and that in Galatians 3:24 Paul says that the law was our teacher until Christ came. However, if Paul meant the law then why does he not write the law here? Certainly the author of 2 Peter does not think these elements are the law, for he writes that at the time of the apocalypse the heavens will pass away, and the elements will be dissolved in a burning heat.[79] So the elements are something tangible that will be destroyed along with the heavens. These "*elements of the kosmos*" must, in fact, be the host of heaven, the angels or gods that were believed to be represented by the stars and planets. This is clear from the continuation of Paul's argument. He tells the Galatians to remember the time when they were pagans worshipping false Gods - "*Moreover when you knew not God, you were slaves to those which by nature are no gods*" (Galatians 4:8). He then asks them how can they turn again to the "*the weak and poor elements*" and so be enslaved again.[80] This makes it clear that the "elements" are the same as the so-called gods the Galatians used to worship as gentiles. Paul calls these elements weak and poor; in the Gospel of Thomas being in poverty means not being in the kingdom. As we shall see, this all makes sense in the context of the beliefs of the apocalyptic group from which the Jesus movement has come. They believe that Yahweh has appointed a group of seventy angels to rule the world. These angels are the same "*elements of the kosmos*" who are esteemed by the pagans as gods. Paul is trying to combine this apocalyptic belief in the angel rulers with his own Pharisee educated viewpoint in which the law is pre-eminent.

In 1 Corinthians 3:22, Cephas is paired in opposition to the *kosmos* implying that Cephas is the means of redemption from the *kosmos*. But here in Galatians we are told that redemption from the elements of the *kosmos* is through the son who is "born" of a woman. If Paul is really telling us that the Christ has been "born of woman" this would be a problem for the shaman paradigm. But Paul does not actually say this at all! The word *ginomai* does not mean to be born as it is frequently translated. It is not *ginomai* but *gennao* which is used elsewhere in the New Testament to mean to give birth or to be born. The word *ginomai* is very common and means to come, to become, to appear. The scrupulous translators of the King James Version never translate *ginomai* as "born". They render the Galatians passage as "*God sent forth his Son, made of a woman, made under the law*". The NAS version translates the word 487 times most commonly as "became"/"become", "came", "happened" and "done". In only five cases does it translate the word as "born" and three of these five are the above "born of woman" passages! In the other two cases "born" is not required and the same usage could be translated as "come" or an equivalent word. It would seem that the translators have been influenced by their beliefs, either consciously or subconsciously, to choose a word that reinforces those beliefs rather than one which conveys the true meaning of what Paul wrote.

It is not just translators who had problems with Paul writing *ginomai* instead of *gennao*. Paul's use of *ginomai* caused disquiet in the early church. Many copyists resorted to replacing *ginomai* with *gennao* which is found in many later copies. They did so because *ginomai* gave dangerous support for the heresy of Docetism, the belief that Jesus had come to earth in spiritual and not physical form.

So if Paul is not saying that Christ has been physically born what is he saying? The Galatians passage may be more correctly translated as:

... while we were babes, we were enslaved to the elements of the world [kosmos].
But when the fullness of time had come, god sent his son, come of a woman, come
under the law, in order to redeem those who were under the law ... (Galatians 4:3-
5)

Paul is telling us that the son of God has come to redeem those under
the law from the "*elements of the kosmos*", the angelic forces who rule the
cosmos. He has "*come of woman*" and "*come under the law*". Under the spiritual paradigm, Paul is telling us that the founder is a woman and that she is a
Jew among fellow Jews. The Romans passage can be translated as:

... concerning his son, who is come of the seed of David according to the flesh
and was declared son of God with power according to the spirit of holiness by the
resurrection from the dead, Jesus Christ our Lord. (Romans 1:3-4)

Paul is not talking here about two different events as the conventional
commentators and translators assume; the birth of Jesus to a descendant of
David and the subsequent resurrection of Jesus after his death demonstrating he is the son of God. No, Paul is talking about one event, the coming of
Jesus considered in both its worldly and spiritual aspects. Paul uses one of
his favourite and enigmatic phrases *kata sarka* "according to the flesh" to
indicate the physical human nature of this coming that is "of the seed of
David" in fulfilment of the prophecies of the Messiah. Meanwhile on the
spiritual level Jesus is the "son of God" by the resurrection from the dead.

The person through whom Jesus has come is the founder. That person
is:

A woman
Jewish
Of the seed of David

We can now put a name to the founder; she was called Mary the Magdalene and is also known as Mary the "mother" of Jesus, for the two are one
and the same. She was believed, by her supporters at least, to be a descendant of David. It is of no importance to ask whether she really was descended from the semi-mythical King David. What is fascinating is that she
can put forward a credible case for being a descendant which means that
her family before her had put forth such a claim and that this claim was
accepted by some. The time is one of great Messianic and apocalyptic ex-

pectations and claiming that you were of the seed of David is equivalent to saying that the Messiah might come from your family. Such a claim would not have been without its dangers in a time of Roman occupation, but the point was to impress a group of followers. The founder must have been born into a family of whom great things were expected, and although those great things were certainly not the spiritual appearance of the Messiah through a lowly female, the fact that she had these credentials must have been a major factor in her success in getting others to believe that her spiritual visitation was genuine. The picture we are forming is of a girl born into the leading family of an apocalyptic religious group, possibly even the daughter of the leader of the group.

We have now got the point of apparent contradiction, for we have not one founder but two founders. The case for both Mary and Cephas are backed by unimpeachable evidence. How can we reconcile this contradiction?

Mary and Cephas

We have seen that evidence points both towards Mary and Cephas. We have the early tradition represented by the Gospel of the Long Ending that Mary the Magdalene was the first witness of the resurrection, but Paul tells us it was Cephas. Peter and Mary, the mother of Jesus, are the two most prominent individuals in the early church with Mary receiving the adoration we would expect. The overwhelming evidence from the gospels, from Acts and above all from the letters of Paul is that Cephas/Peter was the first leader. And yet we have that phrase from Paul that the Christ has "come of a woman".

Is this evidence that Cephas/Peter made a sinister but successful takeover attempt for the Jesus movement? Was it Mary whose spiritual experiences started the movement and Cephas who has aggressively supplanted her? Has Cephas primed Paul with his own version of the resurrection story substituting himself as the first witness, although the alternative and older tradition that it was Mary survives elsewhere? This is this type of view that is beloved with the conspiracy theorists and feminists who project onto the early shadowy figure of Peter the male dominated characteristics of the church that was to emerge later. It is true that we have evidence of conflict between Mary and Peter in a few gnostic sources, but this evidence dates from the second century when gnostics looking to Mary the Magdalene were coming in conflict with the proto-orthodox church that had adopted Peter as its founder. There is no reason to believe that this supposed conflict between Mary and Peter went back to the individuals of those names in the early church.

There is, in fact, evidence against the takeover by Cephas theory. Paul tells us that Christ has "*come of woman*". If we believe the shaman paradigm, then it follows that Paul did realise that Mary had the special role of the person through whom Jesus had become manifest. Yet Paul also tells us that the resurrected Jesus appeared first to Cephas and nowhere does he mention Mary explicitly. What is going on? We would have to believe that Paul has not just been fed a story by Cephas but that he is a conspirator with Cephas in hiding the role of Mary. And yet when Galatians was written Paul had argued with Cephas. Why does Paul not write openly about Mary as the perfect weapon against Cephas and the "pillars"?

Is it possible that far from being enemies that Cephas and Mary were allies, perhaps even brother and sister? Did they jointly rule the early church with Mary having a special spiritual role and Cephas being the outward leader? Does Paul hide Mary's role because it was a secret for the elect and not to be babbled about freely? The problem is that Cephas and Mary cannot both have been the first witness. One person must have experienced the risen Christ first, and one person must have been regarded as the prime manifestation of Christ on earth. Yet the evidence points to both of them!

Neither the takeover theory nor the allies theory fit the evidence. We are forced to a conclusion that is both radical and simple; that ties all the loose end into one satisfying picture. Mary the Magdalene and Cephas must be the same person.

The immediate objection is that Mary is a woman, and Cephas is a man, so they cannot be the same. Certainly Paul talks about Cephas as a man, and Paul knows the truth for he has met Cephas. If Cephas is really Mary, then Paul is quite deliberately misleading his audience. But this would be justified if he has sworn to Mary/Cephas to keep her identity a secret. If Mary is Cephas, then Paul stayed with her on his first visit to Jerusalem. He saw James at the same time because he is her son, either biological or adopted, living in the same house. Paul has seen no one else in the Jerusalem church because he has remained in their house for the visit. It is at this time that he must have promised Mary to keep her secret and refer to her as Cephas as if she were a man. Paul is honourable and would keep his promise.

We know that the use of Cephas as an identity of Mary must go beyond Paul because traditions of Peter as the leader, independent of the letters of Paul, are found in the gospels and Acts. We have seen however that all the references to Peter as the first witness of the resurrection can be traced back ultimately to 1 Corinthians 15. So the resurrection experience stories must have circulated under Mary's own name with only Paul using the name Cephas. This is also true, as we will see, of the very early "Deep Source" which also tells of Jesus' coming to Mary. It would seem that Mary used the name Cephas to disguise her role as the leader but not her mystical experiences which were attributed under her own name.

And this brings us to the motives of using a false name. Paul's is not writing history after the event. His letters are dispatches from a war, to be written on the assumption that they may fall into enemy hands. For the Jesus movement is surrounded by enemies and those enemies hold all the power. At a surprisingly early stage, the movement was coming into conflict with the Roman authorities. But the first enemy was not the Romans, but the Jews. The beliefs of the Jesus movement would have been deeply heretical and blasphemous to the mainstream Jew. They abrogated the Jewish law, the Torah and abolished the power of the priests. They proselytised among Gentiles seeking to bring them in on equal terms, something which would have been regarded as a betrayal of the Jewish nation by other Jews. But worse of all was a deep blasphemy at the heart of their philosophy. They believed that the God of the Torah, the one the Jews worshipped as Yahweh, was not Yahweh at all but a great angel, the Angel of the Name. The Jews had never known the real, all-powerful Yahweh, who was untouchably distant and remote from man, and who could only be approached through the intermediation of Jesus. This ultimate Yahweh had sent Jesus to supersede the Angel of the Name and to render Torah obsolete. These beliefs were hidden deep within the sayings of the movement, sayings preserved today in the Gospel of Thomas. But it would seem that the Jews knew something of them. So the movement was persecuted, with the chief persecutors being those experts on the Torah, the Pharisees. We have an eyewitness account of this persecution by the ex-Pharisee Paul, but he would have been only one of many. Evidence for this persecution also comes from the gospels which single out the Pharisees for particular odium along with the small town scribes.

So the Pharisees and scribes set out to eliminate the Jesus movement. It is true that the Jews did not exercise civil authority in Judea, but this is a minor technicality, for the Romans would not have been on the side of the Jesus movement. They did not like religious innovations, and they liked those who aroused troublesome religious controversy even less. Even if the Jews could not conduct official executions, they could arrange beatings, "spontaneous" stoning and disappearances. The Romans could be expected to turn a blind eye provided the Jews were dealing with their own trou-blemakers. Those of the Jesus movement were vagabonds who were in no position to appeal to the Roman authorities and were far too poor to match the bribes their establishment opponents would be paying to Roman offi-cials as a matter of routine.

In seeking to destroy the movement, there was one target more valuable than all others, the founder and leader, the person whom Paul calls Cephas. This person would have been marked for death. Yet the evidence from Paul is that Cephas is not hiding in the wilderness but living in a house in Jerusalem. Would Cephas have lived openly in the midst of the movement's enemies? Cephas is a strange name for a Jew, the Aramaic for "rock" and not a traditional Jewish name at all. We can conclude that Cephas is not the real name of the founder but a title, a pseudonym behind which the true identity of the founder was hidden from the persecutors of the movement. Cephas can live in Jerusalem because the Pharisees do not know who he is.

The necessity for the founder using a pseudonym while operating in Ju-dea is clear. But now suppose that the founder is not a man but a woman. Would a woman leader use a male or a female pseudonym? It is a no-brainer that she would use a male pseudonym. She has one great ad-vantage, that being a woman she is below notice for most men, and for the religious leaders in particular. Even had she been known as a prophetess, they would have regarded her as a babbling woman and so relatively harmless, while they searched for the leader, for Cephas. But if she were to use a female pseudonym she would be immediately drawing attention to herself. A female leader would be easy for the Pharisees to find once they realised they were looking for a woman. And among the Jews there would have been an additional motive. Only men could fulfil a religious leader-ship role, and if it were known that the movement was led by a woman, this would lead to both ridicule and intensified persecution.

If Mary had been born a Roman or Greek the fact that she was a woman would not have stood in the way of her being a religious leader. Priestesses were a normal feature of the Hellenistic world. But to the Jews, a woman as religious leader would have been unthinkable. It is true that her mythical namesake from scripture, Mary, the sister of Moses, was a prophetess, but she was a special case from the distant history of the Jews. In the first cen-tury, religious matters were not discussed with women. Consider for ex-ample the words of Rabbi Eliezer ben Hyrcanus (late first century / early second century): "*Rather should the words of the Torah be burned than entrusted to a woman*" (*Jerusalem Talmud, Sotah*) and "*Whoever teaches his daughter the*

Torah is like one who teaches her frivolity (tiflut)" (Mishnah, Sotah 3:4). This continued to be the case in Judaism for long afterwards. We know of fringe sects, such as the Therapeutae written about by Philo, where women did participate along with men, and it is likely that Mary came originally from such a sect. But even the Therapeutae were organised along a strict male-female segregation with no suggestion that women were involved in any leadership role over men. The Jews of the time would have reacted with anger to a woman who put herself into the type of place Mary must have occupied in the Jesus movement.

Throughout history, some women have found themselves in the position of trying to penetrate a sphere of activity where women were simply not allowed to participate. For such women, the classic strategy is to become a "man" and adopt a male identity. Occasionally this may involve going to the lengths of donning male costume. More usually it stops at the adoption of a pseudonym. Many women have written works and engaged in correspondence with notable men under such a pseudonym without their readers ever guessing that they are dealing with a "she" and not a "he". Even in spheres where it was permissible to participate as a female, a woman would sometimes use a male pseudonym so as to avoid being considered purely as a woman. As an example from English literature, both the Bronte sisters (the daughters of thunder) and George Eliot used male pseudonyms in the Victorian age because they wanted their writing to be taken seriously.

We can see the motivation for Mary using a male pseudonym and that this is not anything unusual. We should note that Cephas is a title and not a real man's name so that the deception only extends to talking about Cephas as a "he" rather than a "she". But doubtless some readers will think it extraordinary that Cephas, who has given rise to the character of Peter in the gospels, should be the same as Mary the Magdalene, oft represented as a penitent prostitute. Extraordinary propositions require extraordinary evidence, so it is time to consider what evidence supports this identity. We will find that the evidence for Cephas being the same person as Mary is extraordinary; links between the two occur everywhere. If there is one thing that can be established beyond controversy it is the identity between Cephas and Mary the Magdalene.

We will start with the ground we have already covered. In 1 Corinthians Cephas is paired against the *kosmos* whereas in Galatians Paul tells us that redemption from the "elements of the kosmos" is through Christ who is *"come of a woman"*. The implication is that Cephas and Mary are the same. Then we have Paul's strange assertion that when he experienced the Christ it was as if he were an abortion or miscarriage. We have seen that this would be explained if normal birth in Christ was through Cephas as "mother", an induction which Paul eventually experienced when he stayed with Cephas. Paul's first experience of Christ though is abnormal and spontaneous, like a miscarriage or abortion, a birth before normal time and outside of the church. We have seen how Paul used similar "mother" language in describing how he had laboured to form Christ within the Galatians,[81] a strange way of looking at things that he must have taken over from Cephas. Again all this is perfectly understandable if Cephas is really Mary.

All of which reveals another very important trait of Mary; she repeatedly casts herself in the role of mother. She is mother to the movement and mother to the spiritual Jesus. This is all very odd to us because we are not used to seeing things through the eyes of a woman from a traditional society. In modern life, women are regarded in either their post-feminist incarnation as ambitious man-equals or in glamorised photographic form as sexual objects. We forget that this was not how women were seen through most of human history. Traditionally to be a woman was synonymous with being a mother. A girl would be married when barely out of adolescence (if not before) and would quickly start on the serious business of multiple childbirth. The worse fate that could befall a woman in Jewish and other traditional societies was to be barren, a fate which may have been the lot of Mary. A woman would derive status from her children and, in particular, her sons. It is likely that Mary was childless and that she endlessly compensates for this through metaphorical motherhood.

If Cephas was Mary, then this explains why Cephas, while still alive, appointed James as successor to lead the church from Jerusalem. Mary would have keenly felt the disadvantages that ensued to the movement from her leadership as a woman, disadvantages that were especially severe in Judea. So she decides to appoint James early and to move from Jerusalem to Rome. There are religious reasons why she chooses to relocate to the great centre of the Roman Empire but it also offers her freedom from the personal constraints that she faced in Jerusalem.

If Cephas is Mary, then this explains something else. Why does Cephas give in to those from James in Antioch? The Jews were an honour-shame culture that gave great respect to age. If Cephas were a man, then as the founder and elder he should not give in to the younger James. But if Cephas were a woman, then the situation is completely different. A woman came under the control of the man to whom she belonged, whether father, husband, brother or son. We know that for Mary this man was at one time

James, for the evidence is in one of her names, Mary of James, the name by which she would have been openly known in Jerusalem. She may have been the spiritual leader of the movement but to James she was also, on another level, a wayward female from his own household for whom he was responsible. In Rome this was academic, but in Antioch she was entering his sphere of influence, and he was losing face from her acting like a Gentile. So he sends messengers to her begging her to behave like a normal Jew, and she decides it is politic, while in Antioch, to obey his authority. And if Cephas were a man and founder of the movement would Paul really have the courage to confront him to his face? But if Cephas is a woman the dynamic is different.

Staying with Paul's letters the main evidence linking Cephas with Mary is the resurrection account. The formula that *"he appeared to Cephas, then to the twelve"* makes perfect sense if Cephas is the same person as Mary the Magdalene. But if not we have to explain why Paul never mentions Mary.

There is one further, direct, piece of evidence that Mary did adopt a male identity. This is a tantalising saying in the Gospel of Thomas that Mary had become male.

Making male

One of the most controversial sayings in the Gospel of Thomas is the very last one:

Simon Peter said to them: "Let Mary leave us, for women are not worthy of the life." Jesus said: "Behold, I shall lead her, that I may make her male, so that she will also be a living spirit resembling you males. For every woman who makes herself male shall enter into the kingdom of heaven." (Thomas 114)

You can depend on this saying being quoted whenever a defender of conventional Christianity writes about the Gospel of Thomas. Such Christians are in denial about the obvious use of Thomas by the four canonical gospels and seek any opportunity to buttress their collective delusion that Thomas is later than the four and not a "real" gospel at all. They will use this saying to discredit Thomas pointing out smugly that these gnostics were not as open to the equality of women as their modern supporters like to pretend. Here is Jesus supposedly telling women they must become male to enter the kingdom of heaven! They will then contrast this with some story of the "real" Jesus from the "real" gospels treating women even-handedly.

In the same way, you are sure to detect a distinct air of embarrassment from a Gospel of Thomas enthusiast when they write about this politically incorrect saying. They are likely to claim that it does not mean what the Thomas detractors think it means and that it is a late addition to Thomas and not part of the original gospel. There are in fact good reasons for this viewpoint. Some gnostics did interpret the world as being female (created by the fall of Wisdom/Sophia) and the spiritual realm as being masculine. Under this system, both men and woman are spiritually male. (Ironically, the origins of this view may come from Paul.)[82] If this is the meaning of the Thomas saying, then it is not anti-woman but is trying to affirm that a woman can enter the kingdom of heaven in equality to men. This feminine world/masculine spirit philosophy is, however, a second-century development that would be anachronistic in a first century Thomas gospel. The saying also reflects an anti-Peter viewpoint that dates from the second century when there was friction between the gnostics and the proto-orthodox church claiming authority from Peter. As an example of this friction, see the second century Gospel of Mary where there is a very similar story of Peter attempting to deny the validity of Mary's revelations. Finally, the saying is last in the gospel and where else would it be more natural to add a new saying?

However to reject this saying is to discard a vital piece of evidence. It is very easy to add a new saying anywhere within a sayings list rather than conspicuously on the end. And in fact, the Coptic gospel does have a structure in the form of two "bookend" sayings, 3 and 113, both of which are about searching for the kingdom and it not being found in a physical sense. If we look at this structure, we can see that it is chiastic, meaning that the end is symmetrical with the beginning:

Preamble and saying 1 - the secret words of the living Jesus written by Thomas - he who finds the meaning of the words will not taste death.

Saying 2 - seeking, finding, being troubled, being amazed and ruling over all.

Saying 3 - Start "bookend" - the kingdom not found in the sky or under the sea, but within and without.

[Main body of sayings]

Saying 113 - End "bookend" - the kingdom is not physically discerned but is spread out upon the earth and men do not see it.
Saying 114 - Mary must make herself male for the sake of the kingdom.
[End attribution - 'The gospel according to Thomas"]

The saying numbers were added by modern translators and saying 1 is really part of the introduction. The end attribution is probably not an original part of the gospel but is the form of divider between texts used in the Nag Hammadi codex. To preserve the chiastic structure, there should be something after the final bookend to balance what comes before the first bookend. So saying 114 is a necessary part of the structure.

The clue to the meaning of 114 may be a structure that is found a number of times in Thomas, where a saying consist of two parts where the second part contrasts, or even contradicts, the first part:

A leads to B;
B leads to the opposite of A

The key to this structure is that either A or B changes meaning between the two parts; typically one part has a spiritual meaning and the other a literal meaning. An example is Thomas 81: *Jesus said: "He who has become rich, let him become king, and he who has power let him renounce it."*

A (being rich) leads to B (becoming king)
B (having power like a king) leads to opposite of A (renouncing power, so becoming poor)

In this saying the first part is interpreted spiritually; one who has become spiritually rich enters into the kingdom of heaven and rules as king. The second part is interpreted literally; one who has entered the kingdom must renounce power in this world, and so become poor. We know that this is exactly what the first Christians did, that they renounced worldly power and gave up their possessions. The saying is stating the contradiction that to be rich is to be poor, to have true power means becoming powerless.

If a similar structure lies behind Thomas 114, then the saying should be interpreted as two parts with the meaning of "male" changing between the two parts. We should read it like this:

One said to him: "Let Mary leave us, for women are not worthy of the life." Jesus said: "Behold, I shall lead her, that I may make her male,

so that she will also be a living spirit resembling you males. For every woman who makes herself male shall enter into the kingdom of heaven."

The first part should be interpreted in a worldly sense. Mary as a woman is not eligible to go about with a group of men and discuss or study religion with them, yet alone to be their leader. Jesus, however, will "lead her" so that she becomes an honorary male. Cryptically this refers to Mary's alternative identity as Cephas.

The second half of the saying reverses the meaning of "male" from literal maleness to spiritual maleness, revealing a more profound spiritual meaning to the concept of Jesus making Mary male. The movement believed that the spirit of a woman was male, and the spirit of a man was female. If a woman makes herself male by becoming one and whole with her spirit, then she enters into the kingdom. Mary has become male through her possession by Jesus, and it is this spiritual possession that has changed her nature in a more essential sense than her adoption of the pseudonym of Cephas.

Did the first speaker in the original say that women were not worthy of life? This is a very harsh view that is not found anywhere else in early Christian sources. There is however evidence for being part of the original because it is necessary for the structure:

A (Mary/women not worthy of the kingdom) leads to B (Mary becomes male)

B (women become male) leads to opposite of A (women enter the kingdom)

We must remember that the view of the first speaker is not endorsed but rejected by Jesus. The purpose of the saying is to rebut this misogynist view and declare that women are indeed worthy of the kingdom. When Paul is writing his letters women are playing a full role in the church, and the view that they are not worthy of life would have been absurd. The saying then would be out of place in Paul's church of the 40s and 50s, but this position of full female involvement would not have been achieved without considerable struggle. The saying is recording this struggle and must pre-date the time of Paul, which places it in the first decade of the movement, the 20s or 30s. Specifically the saying is recording that Mary was rejected by some because she was a woman. The source of the opposition is internal; the first speaker says that Mary must leave "us" so both he and she belong to the same group. This group is not the Jesus movement as it was to develop, for this was made up of supporters of Mary, but rather its predecessor, the apocalyptic Christ movement, the remains of which are the party of Christ that Paul mentions in 1 Corinthians. The apocalyptic Christ movement was expecting the imminent resurrection of the Christ and while some accepted that this resurrection had occurred spiritually through Mary others, perhaps the majority, rejected her. The opposition to Mary must have been bitter as it is a consistent theme of the earliest sources such as the Gospel of the Long Ending.

Saying 114 records this opposition in the particular form of rejection of Mary as a woman. This is all one with the culture of first-century Judea. The Gospel of Luke has a group of women disciples following Jesus, listening to his words and supporting his needs.[83] This is complete fantasy. The author of Luke is a Gentile, writing far from Judea about sixty years after the event. The information about Mary the Magdalene has been taken from the long ending of Mark and the other names, which are not found in any other early source, have been written into the story. We shall see that the Gentile author of Luke has personal reasons for portraying this ardent group of women supporters of Jesus, but it has nothing to do with the reality of life as a Jewish woman in Judea. In Judea, it was not possible for respectable women to associate with men in public. The emphasis was on female purity both before and after marriage. A girl who was not a virgin would have no value as a bride and the theoretical penalty for a married woman committing adultery was death. If a woman had gone around with a group of men as in Luke she would have been classified as a whore. In particular, women are excluded from religious discourse with men as demonstrated in the quotes attributed to Rabbi Eliezer: *"Rather should the words of the Torah be burned than entrusted to a woman"*[84] and *"Whoever teaches his daughter the Torah is like one who teaches her frivolity"*.[85]

In requesting Mary's removal, the first speaker is reflecting the normal view in Jewish society that men and women should not associate with each other outside of the family. This is the reaction of the disciples in the Gospel of John when having left Jesus alone by a well they find that Jesus has been speaking to a Samaritan woman: *"And upon this came his disciples, and they wondered that he was speaking with a woman. No one, however, said, 'What do you seek?' or 'Why do you speak with her?'"* (John 4:27). We may ask why this line is included when the disciples do not even speak their concerns. Most likely the author of John is trying to rebut a source in which there is an implied criticism of Jesus for allowing a woman to be present. Could this source be either saying 114 or something derived from saying 114? In fact, this whole episode shows a number of similarities with saying 114. We shall see that this story of the Samaritan woman by the well is one of a number of sequences which are derived from what I have called the "Deep Source", a description of the coming of Jesus to the founder which is early than the literalisation layer and which goes back to the origins of the movement. The original of the Samaritan woman in the Deep Source is Mary. In addition to the Deep Source, the story draws upon saying 114 either directly or via an intermediary source. It is possible that this intermediary source has already convolved saying 114 and the Deep Source.

So what are the similarities between Thomas 114 and the John story? The Samaritan women is twice described as potentially unworthy to talk to Jesus; first when she is surprised that Jesus would speak to her as she is both a Samaritan and a woman; and second when the disciples wonder why Jesus is speaking to a woman. However, Jesus does speak to her and offers her "living water" which is a symbol for the spirit. He tells her that God is spirit and must be worshiped in spirit.[86] By his offer of living water Jesus is leading her to become a "living spirit" and so able to enter into the kingdom which is described here as the worship of God in spirit. It might be objected that the most remarkable element of saying 114, that of making male, is absent. This theme would be very hard to incorporate into the John story, but it is in fact there; when the woman asks for the living water Jesus tells her to "*Go call your husband and come hither*" (*John 4:16*) even though he knows she does not have a husband. The word for husband, *andra*, means man, so Jesus is telling the woman to summon her man. The way a woman becomes male is by union with her spiritual part, her spiritual husband, the inner man. The similarities are summarised in the table below.

Thomas 114	John 4:9-24
Let Mary leave us, for women are not worthy of the life.	John 4:9 "*How is it that you, a Jew, asks drink of me, a Samaritan woman?*" John 4:27 *And upon this came his disciples, and they wondered that he was speaking with a woman. No one, however, said, "What do you seek?" or "Why do you speak with her?"*
Behold, I shall lead her, that I may make her male	John 4:16 *Jesus said to her, "Go, call thy husband/man, and come here."*

Thomas 114	John 4:9-24
so that she will also be a living spirit resembling you males. *For every woman who makes herself male shall enter into the kingdom of heaven.*	Jesus offers the woman *"living water"*. John 4:14 *"the water that I shall give him shall be in him a well of water springing up into eternal life."* (Water = the spirit) John 4:21 *Jesus said to her, "Woman, believe me, the hour comes, when you shall neither in this mountain, nor yet at Jerusalem, worship the Father."* John 4:23-24 *"But the hour comes, and now is, when the true worshippers shall worship the Father in spirit and in truth: for the Father seeks such to worship him. God is a Spirit: and they that worship him must worship him in spirit and in truth."*

There is one thing missing; in the John story there is no mention of Simon Peter. The form of the name "Simon Peter" is used in John and the fact that Simon Peter is not mentioned at all in this story is evidence that the name was not in the version of the saying that came down to the author of John. The author of John goes out of his way to stress that the disciples did not say that the woman was unworthy to talk to Jesus which suggests that some thought that it was a disciple who had voiced this opinion. This is a perfectly reasonable conclusion from the original saying. The attribution to a disciple can be seen as a stage towards the substitution of Simon Peter for the unnamed man who rejects Mary. The name form "Simon Peter" originated from the Gospel of Matthew towards the end of the first century, so this change to the named disciple must have occurred in the late first century or second century. A second-century date is more likely because the supposed conflict between Peter and Mary dates from that time. This change is critical because it switches the view that "women are not worthy of life" from an unknown man in the audience to the chief apostle of the proto-orthodox church. The irony is that Peter is the same person as Mary and the way in which she becomes male.

There is another piece of evidence for Mary becoming male in a fascinating story in the fourth-century Acts of Philip. Jesus has told Philip to spread the gospel in the country of the Greeks. But Philip is cowardly and, once away from Jesus, bewails his fate. In the Acts, Mariamne (another form of the name Mary) tells Jesus about Philip's weakness, and Jesus sends her to accompany Philip:

And he said: I know, thou chosen among women; but go with him and encourage him, for I know that he is a wrathful and rash man, and if we let him go alone he will bring many retributions on men. But lo, I will send Bartholomew and John to suffer hardships in the same city, because of the much wickedness of them that dwell there; for they worship the Viper, the mother of snakes. And do thou change thy woman's aspect and go with Philip. (Acts of Philip 95)

Jesus calls Mariamne the "chosen among women". The title is a relic of her original status of the founder of the movement. She is told to change her "woman's aspect" - that is she is to change he women's clothes and to adopt a male disguise so that she can accompany Philip. Here we have a tradition that Jesus tells Mary, the "chosen among women", to become male so as to remain with the male disciples. It can be objected that this tradition is not necessarily early because the Acts of Philip is probably fourth century. We will see however that the Acts of Philip does preserve much earlier traditions and sayings in its literalistic stories. And this story is clearly linked to Thomas saying 114 and shows that there was a tradition to interpret Mary's becoming male not just spiritually but also literally.

At first glance, there is no mention of Peter in the Acts of Philip story. There are, however, two other places in the Acts of Philip where Peter is named and one of these is a very intriguing comment by Philip as he exhorts the others to purity:

"Therefore our brother Peter fled from every place where a woman was: and further, he had offence given by reason of his own daughter. And he prayed the Lord, and she had a palsy of the side that she might not be led astray." (Acts of Philip 142)

The story about Peter's daughter is found in the short Act of Peter and was probably an earlier part of the Acts of Peter (the Acts has not survived in its entirety). However, the idea that *"Peter fled from every place where a woman was"* is strange in relation to the depiction of Peter both in the Acts of Peter and elsewhere. According to the gospels, Peter has a mother in law and hence a wife. In the Acts of Peter, he gets into trouble because he is a magnet for the women of the Roman upper classes whom he converts to Christianity and chastity. So where does the idea that Peter avoided the presence of women come from? There is only one known source where such a concept is expressed and that is Thomas saying 114. It is interesting that the author of the Acts of Philip passes on the correct reason for the rejection of Mary by Peter, that it was improper for females to consort with males in this way.

So the author of the Acts of Philip must have a version of the saying in which the first speaker is named as Peter as in the Coptic version of Thomas. The earlier Gospel of John does not have Peter, showing that the name was inserted in the second or third centuries.

Key points

1. There is overwhelming evidence for Cephas as the first leader.

2. There are two early traditions for the first witness of the resurrection, Mary the Magdalene and Cephas.

3. The criterion of prominence points towards either Mary the mother of Jesus or Cephas/Peter. Although Mary the Magdalene appears to be less prominent, the "Magdalene" might be another name for the woman who is also known as the mother of Jesus.

4. Although Paul is often thought to have written that Jesus was "born of woman", what he actually wrote was that Jesus "appeared" or "came" of woman. The proto-orthodox church considered Paul's words as offering dangerous support for the idea of a spiritual Jesus and in many early copies the word for "born" was substituted.

5. Paul is telling us that the shaman through whom Jesus came was female, Jewish, and believed to be descended from King David.

6. The only solution that makes sense of the apparently conflicting data is if Cephas, Mary the Magdalene and Mary the mother of Jesus are all one and the same person.

7. Among the Jews, the priesthood and the study of the Torah were seen as exclusively a male preserve. There was a bias against women's involvement in religion in any capacity other than that of an ordinary worshipper, and it was unthinkable for a woman to be a religious leader. If the Jesus movement were founded by a female shaman, it would be a necessity, in Judea, to disguise her identity by using a male pseudonym.

8. If Mary the Magdalene is the same as Cephas, then this explains why Paul appears to make absolutely no mention of her in his resurrection account. She is there under her pseudonym Cephas. Substitute Mary for Cephas and Paul's account is similar to the Gospel of the Long Ending.

9. Direct evidence for Mary adopting a male identity comes in the saying at the end of Thomas. The saying records a controversy from the earliest days of the movement, as to whether it was proper for Mary, as a woman, to associate with the men, yet alone lead them. The solution proposed was that Jesus would "make her male", meaning that she should be treated, for the purposes of the movement, as if she were a man.

10. In the one surviving Coptic version of the Thomas saying it is Peter who expresses unease about Mary, and becoming male has been given a spiritual meaning. These changes indicate that the saying was lightly edited by second century gnostics.

11. The saying has left its influence in other sources. The Acts of Philip has a story about Mary adopting male disguise to accompany the apostles. In the Acts of Peter it is said that Peter would flee from the presence of women, indicating knowledge of the "Peter" version of the saying. Most significantly, the story of the Samaritan woman in the Gospel of John shows a number of affinities with Thomas 114.

Conclusion

The shaman was Mary the Magdalene. She used a male pseudonym, Cephas, meaning "the rock" and was also known as the "mother" of Jesus. Her followers believed that Jesus had "made her male", that is given her authority to lead the movement as if she were a man.

Chapter 16

Who wrote the Gospel of Thomas?

If the Gospel of Thomas is the earliest collection of sayings from the Jesus movement, then why is it ascribed to an obscure disciple, Judas Thomas? It is true that a rich literature about Judas Thomas developed in which he travels as an apostle to India. In this literature, he is even the identical twin brother of Jesus! However, this all dates from the third century. Why is it that Judas and Thomas appear to be two separate people in the earliest sources? Going further was there ever a disciple Thomas or is he a mirage created by those who wrote the gospels? Was the Gospel of Thomas originally called the Gospel of the Twin?

Didymus Judas Thomas

The Coptic Gospel of Thomas introduces its author thus:

These are the hidden words that the living Jesus spoke, and Didymus Judas Thomas wrote down. [1.] And he said this: "Whoever finds the meaning of these words will not taste death." (Thomas Incipit & 1)

The living Jesus spoke the sayings, but they come to us by way of "*Didymus Judas Thomas*". The end divider just has "*The gospel according to Thomas*" with no mention of Judas. The meaning of both Thomas and Didymus is "twin"; Thomas means twin in Aramaic and Didymus means twin in Greek. So "*Didymus Judas Thomas*" literally means "twin Judas the twin". The word "twin" has been translated twice and confused as a real name, Thomas.

The introduction is also found on Papyrus P.Oxy 654 dating from around 200. Unfortunately, the papyrus is damaged, and each line has a missing section. Instead of "Didymus Judas Thomas" it has ".... *called Thomas*" where the first name is missing. In translations, this first name is invariably recreated as Judas even though this word is not actually present on the papyrus. Another possibility that is just as likely is that the first name is Didymus. The name form "Thomas called Didymus" is used three times in the Gospel of John,[87] and there is no reason this should not be reversed on the papyrus.

Turning to the New Testament we find both Thomas and our Judas (whom we must be careful not to confuse with the more familiar betrayer Judas Iscariot):

Mark and Matthew include a Thomas in the list of the twelve but do not include a Judas other than Judas Iscariot.[88] They do include Judas as a brother of Jesus.[89]

Luke/Acts keeps Thomas in the list of the twelve but adds "Judas of James" in place of the obscure Thaddeus.[90]

John has both Judas (not the Iscariot)[91] and "Thomas called Didymus".[92]

The letter of Jude is supposedly written by Judas brother of James.[93]

The evidence is consistent with Judas being the brother of James and one of the "brethren of the Lord". There is nothing to suggest that Thomas and Judas are the same person, and both the gospels of Luke and John include them as separate individuals within the Twelve. Although it is possible that the disciple Thomas in Mark and Matthew could be the same as Judas, the brother of Jesus, there is no evidence for this. It is significant that when Luke adds Judas to the list of the disciples it is Thaddeus and not Thomas who is replaced. If the author of Luke believed that Thomas and Judas were the same person it would have been very simple for her to replace Thomas by "Judas of James, also known as Thomas" instead of blotting out poor Thaddeus.

Other than the Gospel of Thomas the most famous work involving Judas Thomas is the early third century Acts of Thomas. The Acts records the doings of "Judas Thomas called Didymus" who is sent by Jesus to India. This Judas Thomas is the identical brother of Jesus and at one point is confused with him.[94] This has given fuel to those who believe that Jesus survived the crucifixion and appeared a few times to his disciples before travelling to India under the name of Judas Thomas. Even if Judas Thomas were not Jesus but his twin, this would pose a challenge to the whole idea of the resurrection, not to mention the shaman paradigm!

However, the appearance of Judas Thomas in the Acts of Thomas and an early tradition about Judas Thomas in the Eastern Church are not independent evidence that he ever existed. They are both likely derived from the Gospel of Thomas itself. We know that by around 200, and probably long before, the gospel was being assigned to Judas Thomas. It would have been natural for the fertile imaginations of early Christianity to develop a secondary literature around this mysterious person. And if we look at the Acts of Thomas, we can see that the concept of the "twin" is repeated through the work and was originally spiritual in meaning.

Preserved in the Acts are two of the most beautiful works of early Christianity; the Wedding Hymn and the incomparable Hymn of the Pearl. The Hymn of the Pearl celebrates the spiritual twinning of the earthly person and the divine "garment". When the seeker of the pearl returns to his/her homeland he/she is given the robe again:

> *But suddenly, when I saw it over against me,*
> *The <splendid robe> became like me, as my reflection in a mirror;*
> *I saw it <wholly> in me,*
> *And in it I saw myself <quite> apart <from myself>,*
> *So that we were two in distinction,*
> *And again one in a single form.*
> *(The Hymn of the Pearl 76-78)*[95]

As for the Wedding Hymn, we can see that as going back to a poeticised tradition about Mary, descendant of David and bride of Jesus:

> *The maiden is the daughter of light,*
> *Upon her stands and rests the majestic effulgence of kings*
> *(The Wedding Hymn, Acts of Thomas)* [96]

In the Wedding Hymn are traces of genuine traditions about Mary such as her being surrounded by seven and twelve attendants:

> *Her groomsmen keep her compassed about,*
> *whose number is seven*
> *Whom she herself has chosen*
> *And her bridesmaids are seven,*
> *Who dance before her*
> *Twelve are they in number who serve before her*

And are subject to her,
Having their gaze and look toward the bridegroom
(The Wedding Hymn, Acts of Thomas) [97]

The twelve and the seven go back to the original leadership group of the Twelve and the seven brothers of the Lord who replaced them. In the Wedding Hymn, the *"princes"* at the feast (those who are in the kingdom) put on their royal robes and receive the light. They praise *"the Father of truth and the mother of wisdom"*. It is shortly after Thomas recites the Wedding Hymn[98] that the king demands that he blesses the bridal chamber of the newly married couple. This he does, and once everyone has left, the bridegroom lifts up the veil of the bridal chamber to go to the bride. He is shocked to find her talking to a man whom he takes to be Judas Thomas. But the man explains that he is really the Lord Jesus: *"I am not Judas who is also Thomas, I am his brother."*[99] Jesus then persuades the two to refrain from sexual intercourse so that they can become *"holy temples"*. If they do this, they will have *"living children"* and will lead an undisturbed life *"waiting to receive that incorruptible and true marriage ... and in it you will be groomsmen entering into that bridal chamber of immortality and light."*[100] The two cheerfully agree to this, much to the disgust of the bride's father when he realises the next morning that the marriage has not been consummated. There is much here that is absurd but beneath it is a genuine tradition in which Jesus is the "twin" of Thomas and enters into the bridal chamber with Mary for a marriage that is spiritual and not physical.

The Acts of Thomas has actually emerged from Syria and not India. The region of Edessa and East Syria was known as the daughter of Parthia, and there were trade links between India and Parthia.[101] The authors of the Acts would have known a little about India from these connections. In their work, India serves as the romanticised distant kingdom upon which the missionary activities of Thomas can be projected. There is no evidence of any genuine connection between India and Thomas.

The Thomas literature in Syria emerged towards the end of the second century and beginning of the third. This is the same area in which the Odes of Solomon were composed about a hundred years earlier. In Syria, early spiritual traditions held out for longer against the growing gospel based proto-orthodox view. These traditions were based around the name "Thomas" and the concept of the spiritual twin. We can see the figure of Judas Thomas as an attempt to reconcile this "Thomas the twin" tradition with the gospel account of a physical Jesus.

The evidence then points towards Thomas and Judas being separate in the first century and only being conflated into one character much later, towards the end of the second or beginning of the third centuries. It also points towards the Gospel of Thomas being originally attributed only to Thomas and not to Judas:

The gospel is always referred to as the "Gospel of Thomas" and never as the "Gospel of Judas".

The only time Judas is used in connection with the gospel is the fourth-century Coptic version of Thomas by which time it was accepted by many that Judas and Thomas were the same person.

The author of John knew of the Gospel of Thomas, but he never identifies Judas with Thomas.

Hippolytus mentions the Gospel of Thomas with no reference to Judas (Hippolytus, Refutation of all Heresies, 5:2).

Origen mentions a "Gospel according to Thomas" in his first Homily on Luke also with no reference to Judas.

The name people gave to the gospel is important because it is persistent. A copyist might add the name Judas to the introduction, but people are going to keep on calling the gospel by the name they are familiar with. At the end of the Coptic version the dividing header *"The gospel according to Thomas"* shows that it was called that by the monks who produced the codex.

All of this is suggestive, but the decisive piece of evidence comes from the Gospel of John. If we accept that the author of John knew of Thomas, then it cannot have been attributed to Judas Thomas at the end of the first century when John was written. This is because both Judas and Thomas feature in John and are clearly two separate characters. We will show later that the author of John certainly did know Thomas because he copies the gospel extensively.

The evidence from the first century of the movement is meagre but consistent. Judas was a real person, the brother of James and included in the group named "the brethren of the Lord". He is never called "Judas of Jesus" as we would expect if he were really the brother of Jesus (and his twin brother at that!). Instead, he is known in relation to James as "Judas of James" or "Judas the brother of James". We shall see that this is not the only case in which a person we would expect to be named in relation to Jesus is named in relation to James instead. In none of the early sources is Judas called a twin and he is never identified with Thomas. So it would seem that there is not a tradition for Judas being a twin at this early stage.

So how did Judas get to be Thomas? Someone in the second century has incorrectly deduced that Thomas was Judas from the evidence of the gospels. Thomas means twin and it would seem that there was a tradition that he was the twin of Jesus. So Thomas must be a brother of Jesus, but he is also listed among the disciples. There are only two disciples who, according to the gospels, are also brothers of Jesus, and they are James and Judas. James, the one-time leader of the movement, is too prominent to be credible as Jesus' twin. So, by elimination, the twin must have been the obscure Judas of James, about whom almost nothing is known. This conclusion would have been supported by the fact that although Judas is included in the list of disciples in Luke, he is missing in Mark and Matthew, suggesting that he is included in those gospels under his alternative name of Thomas. So the name Judas was added to the beginning of the gospel in some copies just as the name Didymus was also added.

The identification of Thomas with Judas and the subsequent development of a literature around Judas Thomas, the twin brother of Jesus, is a red herring. The gospel was originally called just the Gospel of Thomas. And this leaves us with the mystery that the second century Christians who identified Thomas with Judas were trying to solve. Who is this Thomas, twin of Jesus?

Who wrote Thomas?

If the Gospel of Thomas was originally known as "the Gospel of the Twin" was there ever a real person called Thomas? We have seen how the name Didymus attaches to Thomas in both the Gospel of John and the Coptic Gospel of Thomas. The word for "twin" has been translated and confused with a proper name. But if this happened with Didymus then why not with Thomas? Did Thomas ever exist or has he been created in the same way as Didymus by a conversion of "twin" into a proper name?

The origins of the disciple Thomas can be traced to the Gospel of Mark's inclusion of him among the Twelve. In reality, the identity of the original Twelve was long forgotten and whoever compiled the list was searching for names of disciples. When the Aramaic sayings in Thomas were written in Greek "the twin" became Thomas, which was confused as a name. So the compiler of the list of disciples would have concluded from the Greek version of the gospel that there was a disciple, Thomas, who wrote down the sayings that Jesus spoke. So Thomas is added to the list, but as no one knows anything about this Thomas, there are no stories about him in the gospel.

So what can "twin" mean if not a disciple who is a twin? The concept of twin-ship, the making of the two into one, runs like a thread through the Gospel of Thomas. Each person was conceived of as a twin; the physical person being one of the pair with the other being the soul/spirit. The concept of such twin-ship is explicit in early gnostic literature, but there is nothing specifically gnostic about it; to the Greeks every person had a daemon who was their spiritual twin. However, the immediate source of the gnostic twin was not Greek but a development of the Jewish apocalyptic movement. For a primitive representation of the idea of the spirit and body being joined together consider the parable in the Apocryphon of Ezekiel, a Jewish work that was quoted by numerous early Christian writers and which is thought to date from between 50 BC - AD 50. This parable has a blind man (the body) and a lame man (the spirit) who conspire to steal figs from the king's garden. The lame man rides on the blind man's shoulders to do the deed. When the king realises what has happened the two are joined together to be interrogated and punished. The lesson is that the spirit and body will be punished jointly for their joint acts. In this parable, the body and the spirit are the same sex. But a very common usage among the Jews was to refer to a man's soul as being female. It is this pairing of the physical person with a soul/spirit of the opposite sex, united in a divine marriage, that is normal in early Christian literature.

Under the spiritual paradigm, the "twin" must be interpreted in this spiritual sense. Jesus is not the physical person, but the spiritual, and so his sayings must be communicated through the medium of his physical twin who will write them down. The physical twin of Jesus is Mary, and so the "Gospel of the Twin" is really the gospel of Mary!

For confirmation of this conclusion, we will look again to Thomas 114. We have seen how the chiastic structure (itself an expression of twin-ship) implies that Thomas 114 is matched either with Thomas 2 only or with the whole introduction including Thomas 2. This is how Thomas starts:

These are the hidden words that the living Jesus spoke, and Didymus Judas Thomas wrote down. [1.] And he said this: "Whoever finds the meaning of these words will not taste death."

2. Jesus said: "Let him who seeks not stop seeking until he finds, and when he finds he will be troubled, and if he is troubled he will become amazed, and he will become king over everything." (Thomas Incipit & 1-2)

The words are hidden or secret, and the meaning has to be divined so that the reader "will not taste death". Thomas 2 then tells the reader the process that must be followed; not to cease seeking until he finds, and that when he finds he will be first troubled and then amazed before he will rule as king over the all, that is enter the kingdom of heaven. If we compare this with saying 114 we can see similarities in the form of each:

Initial state (not "life" but with an unrealised potential for "life")
Medium (Jesus)
Transformation (realisation of spirit)
End state ("life" = kingdom of heaven)

In each case, we start with an initial state that has the potential of life but in which that life is not realised. In each case Jesus is the medium for achieving a transformation; the hidden words that lead to life are spoken by the "living Jesus" and in Thomas 114 Jesus leads Mary to become a "living spirit". In each case the word for "living" is the same and Mary's "living spirit" is actually Jesus himself, so both involve the living Jesus. Through the medium of the living Jesus the individual undergoes a transformation which must lead to the realisation of the spirit and hence life. Once they have been through this transformation, the person is in the end state of the kingdom of heaven. Each of these stages is illustrated in the table below:

	Thomas Introduction	**Thomas 114**
Initial state (=not life)	*These are the hidden words ... Whoever finds the meaning of these words will not taste death*	*Let Mary leave us, for women are not worthy of the life.*
Medium (living Jesus)	*that the living Jesus spoke*	*Jesus said: "Behold, I shall lead her ... so that she will also be a living spirit*
Transformation (realisation of spirit)	*Let him who seeks not stop seeking until he finds, and when he finds he will be troubled, and if he is troubled he will become amazed*	*For every woman who makes herself male*

	Thomas Introduction	Thomas 114
End state (=life)	*and he will become king over everything*	*shall enter into the kingdom of heaven.*

The process of transformation is described in two different ways. In the introduction, it is a process of searching and finding. This is the process of seeking the spirit, and the first step involves finding something that invokes not joy but despair. Saying 114 summarises the same process in the female case by saying that a woman must become male. What is not stated, but implied, is that a man must become female. Both woman and man must find the spiritual part which is represented by a twin of the opposite sex, a twin who is simultaneously the seeker's brother/sister, husband/wife, and son/daughter. This process of entering the kingdom through the merging of the spirit and the person is also found in Thomas 22: "*and when you make the male and the female into a single one, that the male be not male nor the female female*".

So there never was a disciple Thomas. The prime collection of the sayings of Jesus is attributed to Mary as the earthly twin of Jesus. Does this mean that Mary authored the gospel? It is too early to be a fake. Unlike the gospels in the New Testament, it comes from within the inner core of the Jesus movement. The shaman would have exercised some degree of sanction and approval of the teachings of the movement. It is likely that Thomas began as an official authorised edition of the sayings of Jesus as spoken through the shaman. Although most of the sayings would go back to Mary, some may belong to the earlier "Christ" movement from which the Jesus movement emerged. The sayings would have originally circulated independently or in smaller groups. We will see evidence that it was not Mary herself but the person closest to her who collected the sayings together and put them into the current Gospel of Thomas at around the year 60. Because people in the movement were already very familiar with different versions of the sayings, the gospel as it was copied showed a high degree of variation.

As the movement expanded rapidly, the shaman grew old and was put to death, and all central control was lost. The movement went through a period of chaos in the second half of the first century, and it is no coincidence that it was at this time that the literalistic gospels were written. Order was gradually restored with the growth of the proto-orthodox church whose beliefs were based on the literalistic gospels. Having accepted the false gospels, the proto-orthodox church had no time for anything that contradicted the picture of Jesus in these gospels, and the first official gospel, Thomas, became heretical.

Key points

1. The Gospel of Thomas has always been known under that name. Thomas means "twin" and is not the real name of a person, so it should really be understood as the "Gospel of the Twin".

2. The association with Judas is likely to have been created by second century Christians who speculated on the identity of Thomas. Judas of James was one of the brothers of the Lord who is included in Luke as a disciple. Some thought he might be the same person as the disciple Thomas.

3. The growth of a literature about Judas Thomas is secondary and does not go back to any real figure living in the first century.

4. The gospel was not named after the disciple Thomas, but the disciple was created from the gospel. The author of Mark, knowing the Gospel of Thomas, assumed there must have been a disciple of that name.

5. The real author of the gospel is the earthly twin of the spiritual Jesus, who transmitted his sayings. This "twin" is the shaman Mary.

6. The identity of the author of the Gospel is indicated by the last saying, Thomas 114. This saying is paired in a chiastic structure with the gospel introduction and is also structured in parallel with that introduction. Thomas 114 is about Mary becoming male and a "living spirit", which is twinned with the "living Jesus" in the introduction.

Chapter 17

A female religion

The acid test of a theory is the insights it brings beyond the evidence it is attempting to explain. If the shaman is female, then it explains some otherwise very puzzling features of the Jesus movement. In its earliest days, Christianity was very open to women who participated at all levels. It was a religion of love, built upon self-denial and service to the other. It rejected violence, even to oppose the wicked, and commanded its followers to obey, rather then rebel against, the Roman oppressors. All of which is surprising because Judaism was obsessed by the law of Yahweh, regarded the careful study of scripture and the offering of proper sacrifices as the essence of religion and longed to overthrow the Romans. How did the Jesus movement turn from masculine Judaism to a set of beliefs that appealed very strongly to women?

A church of women

The Jesus movement spread like wildfire through the Roman Empire, and it did so in part because there was a ready supply of combustible material. The priests of other religions would seek out the rich and the socially elevated who were the most useful patrons. These religions were embedded in a social structure based upon the aristocratic right of those of good birth to rule. But the Christian movement turned all these things on their head. The movement was the opposite of the establishment, and it seemed to go out of its way to appeal to the lowest in society, the slave, the worker, the soldier, the dispossessed. But most of all it appealed to women. From the earliest stages it was popular among females, and where it made inroads into aristocratic society, it was through the female side of the household.

This was quite apparent to opponents of the movement who lampooned it as a religion of women and slaves.

What is remarkable about this is that the genetic background of the movement was so wildly unsuitable for such a popular religion. Judaism was male centred and focused on the exacting study of scripture (for the Pharisees) or the temple worship (for the Sadducees). It was intellectually focused and based upon the law which was endlessly expanded and commented upon. Of course, the Jesus movement came from the apocalyptic branch of Judaism that looked to Enoch rather than Moses. But this was equally masculine in approach. There is nothing, for example, in the rule of the Essenes as revealed by the Dead Sea scrolls, that would appeal to the female.

And yet from this most unpromising soil emerged a religion that would have wide appeal to women around the empire ranging from the household slave to the very highest aristocratic families in Rome. If the founder was a woman, we can begin to see how this was accomplished. The male centred religion of the Jews was changed through the spiritual insights of the founder into something of much more universal appeal. Barriers that separated individuals from the religion were dismantled one by one. When she saw that the spiritual elitism was preventing the expansion of the movement she introduced the water baptism to appeal to the "poor in spirit". She withdrew from her own special position as "mother" to introduce a structure of apostles, first under herself, and then under James, a structure which obliterated the geographical restrictions on the movement. She brought in the Gentile on equal terms to the Jew and she abrogated the law and temple worship, abolishing at a stroke the need for the whole Jewish religious establishment, from the high priest down to the humblest scribe. And she made the movement as open to females as it was to males.

Paul was heavily influenced by Cephas/Mary, and we can perhaps see her philosophy behind some of his words. In Galatians 3:28 Paul says that in Christ "*There is neither Jew nor Greek, there is neither slave nor free, there is neither male nor female*". When in 1 Corinthians 9:19-23 Paul says that he is a Jew to win over the Jews, under the law for those under the law, and not under the law to win over those not under the law, we can see an echo of the pragmatic approach of Mary.

There is abundant evidence from Paul's letters for the participation of females in active missionary roles. Often this was through male-female pairs consisting of a husband and wife, or brother and sister, a practical combination in a world where there were many threats to the safety of a single woman. The best evidence is in the long list of greetings in Romans

16 which gives us a snapshot of a group of Christians dwelling in Rome at this time. Paul starts by commending a woman called Phoebe who was probably the bearer of the letter and who he describes as a deacon. She is on some mission because Paul asks the Romans to give her any assistance she may need. He then greets Priscilla and Aquila, his fellow missionary workers and a husband and wife team. He goes on to mention Andronicus and a person called Julia or Junia or Junias, for the name is found in different variations. If, as is likely, the name is Julia or Junia then this person is a woman and probably the wife of Andronicus. This is important because Andronicus and Julia are described by Paul as "kinsmen", meaning Jews, as apostles and as being in Christ before Paul. This would put them among the group of apostles who were inducted by Cephas and gives the lie to Acts where the apostles are twelve in number and all men. Paul goes on to mention three more women, Tryphena and Tryphosa, and Persis, who have all worked hard for the Lord, meaning that they have been engaged in spreading the gospel. Paul's list includes other women; the mother of Rufus, the sister of Nereus and another Julia. It is clear that women were very important in the Rome church and on an equality with men. Woman must also have had a prominent role in the church at Philippi. In his letter to the Philippians, Paul pleads with two women who had both laboured with him in the gospel, Euodia and Syntyche, to put aside their disagreements.

The evidence is not confined to the letters of Paul. Acts gives evidence as equally abundant for the significant role of women in the early church and, in particular, the role of women from the richer classes as leaders of house churches that met in their households. We even have external evidence of the involvement of women in early Christianity in the form of correspondence between Pliny, the governor of Bithynia-Pontus, and the Emperor Trajan, that can be dated to around 111. Pliny is executing Christians who refuse to repent, to give the proper sacrifice to the Roman Gods and worship the image of the Emperor, but he is puzzled over what they are actually doing wrong. To find out more about this potentially dangerous new Christian sect, Pliny decides to torture two women who hold the position of "minister" in the church and who also have the misfortune to be slaves. Torture was the normal method of integration for slaves and Pliny seems to have taken full opportunity with these slave Christians. All he discovers, however, is *"depraved excessive superstition"*. Pliny's letter is evidence of the remarkably rapid spread of Christianity at this time. It also gives a surprising insight into the nature of church leadership. You could be a slave and female and yet still be a church leader.

All the evidence points to men and women participating as equals in the early church, with women occupying significant roles from apostles downwards. This was a revolutionary state of affairs, and it did not last. Paul's letters gave a dangerous precedent for the equal involvement of women that threatened the emerging male priesthood of the proto-orthodox church. To counter this threat, forged statements, supposedly by Paul, were added to his letters to make it appear that the apostle was against women as leaders and teachers. So in the forged epistle of Timothy there is a clear statement concerning the role of women:

Let the woman learn in silence with all subjection. But I do not let a woman teach, nor to use authority over a man, but to be in silence. (1 Timothy 2:11-12)

And even in the genuine 1 Corinthians the scribes have interpolated a passage to the same effect:

Let your women keep silence in the churches: for they are not permitted to speak; but they are commanded to be submissive as the law says. And if they want to learn anything, let them ask their husbands at home: for it is a shame for women to speak in the church. (1 Corinthians 14:34-35)

We can tell that this passage has been interpolated because it interrupts the flow of Paul's argument which is about everyone taking turns to prophesy in church and allowing others to prophesy also. In the line following on from this Paul asks rather alarmingly "*Or did the word of God originate with you, or has it come only to you?*" as if he were criticising the whole of womankind for daring to speak up in church. In fact this line makes perfect sense as the continuation of lines 32-33 where Paul says that prophecy should be kept under control because God is not the God of disorder but peace "*as in all the churches of the saints*". Paul is criticising the Corinthians for conducting unruly services, and his argument is not about women at all. In fact, some texts put these verses later at the end of verse 40 showing that some early copyists had exemplars that omitted the verses from 14:34-35. Besides, Paul has only just said in 1 Corinthians 11 that women should keep their head covered while prophesying! But how can women prophesy if they must keep silent?

The tragedy is that future generations believed that Paul had written these passages. And so by deceit the original balance of the church, with men and women participating equally and jointly in harmony, was lost so that a small minority of men could exercise power. In fact, one by one all of

Mary's innovations were reversed or their intentions undermined. So the introduction of water baptism for the poor in spirit was at first a great success but in time resulted in the elimination of the rich in spirit, the pneumatic Christians, from the church, a result which was certainly not what Mary had intended. Appointing James as leader turned out to be a mistake as he tried to unravel her abrogation of the law. Her attempt to reduce the importance of scripture in favour of the inspiration of the spirit also met with eventual failure. The problems started as early as Paul, who was unable to free himself from his Pharisee training in applying his considerable intelligence to the beliefs of the Jesus movement and who had a habit of falling back onto scripture to justify these beliefs. The example of Paul's letters gave encouragement to the church fathers and to the all-male priesthood of the proto-orthodox church who spent almost as much time studying Jewish scripture as did Jewish men. Even worse, the Christians added their own ragbag of mainly secondary writings which they called the New Testament and which they began to treat as if it were also God-inspired scripture. Like others who lived by the book, they began to worship the text rather than God, leading in time to absurdities such as the concept of biblical inerrancy, the complete opposite of the primacy of the spirit that Mary originally taught.

The reason Mary's initiatives eventually floundered is not because they were undermined by men but because both men and women are inherently conservative. The surprise is not the emergence of the patriarchy within the church but why this was not there in the beginning. The real mystery is how the female orientated environment emerged from the intensely patriarchal Jewish religious culture. The participation of both men and women on equal terms is an extraordinary state of affairs in the ancient world and requires an extraordinary explanation. If the founder of the movement, the person in whom the Christ has believed to have become manifest on earth and who led the church for a generation is a woman, then we have our explanation.

The religion of love

It is not just the openness of the Jesus sect to groups that were marginalised by mainstream religions that explains the dramatic spread of the movement. The fact is that the group gained followers from all echelons of society, from both men and women, rich and poor, slave and free. The reason was that the teachings of the movement were tremendously attractive to large numbers of people who lived in the Roman Empire. Instead of the disparate Roman gods, the movement taught of a single all-powerful God, one who was over all things and all times, a God who had originated the universe and who would soon bring it to a close. But most amazingly this God was a God of love. He did not want to punish mankind or control them but to save them. He had a secret plan for mankind, a plan that was now coming to fruition. The purpose of men and women was not to worship God in awe and fear, to present him with sacrifices, or to obey his law, but to accept his love. God had provided a path of redemption through the sacrifice of Jesus, the Christ. It was through Jesus that man could know God.

The monotheism came from Judaism, but where did the concept of God as love come from? Not from the God of the Old Testament for he is a wrathful and jealous God. He is the God of the Jews as a people, and is happy to exterminate non-Jews when they get in the way, as in the supposed (but probably imaginary) genocide of the Canaanites. Judaism revolved around the anticipated triumph of God's people, and they were essentially an ethnic group. It is true that the Gentile could convert and become a Jew but sufficient barriers were erected in his or her way that this was very rarely done. In reality, Judaism was a nationalistic religion and the Jews hated their successive Gentile oppressors with nationalistic fervour. The tragedy of the Jews is the contradiction inherent in the meta-narrative of being the people chosen by the creator of the universe and yet being only a small nation which is weak and relatively powerless compared to its larger neighbours. The Jews longed for the semi-mythical time of King David and Solomon when the united kingdom of Judea and Israel was strong, wealthy and successful. The prophecies of the Messiah promised a return to this golden age.

But above all, Jews of all types yearned for redemption from the Roman pigs. Messianic pretenders offering the illusive hope of such redemption were commonplace. The myth of the Messiah gave Jews the absurd and irrational hope that they could defeat the Romans. This hope led to the destruction of the temple in the Jewish War and, later, the effective elimination of the Jews from Judea as a result of the Bar Kokhba revolt. It was not just the hot heads who believed in eventual freedom from the Romans. The prudent shared the aspiration although they were less enthusiastic about translating it into action.

And yet when we turn to the Jesus movement, a Jewish sect led by Jews, we find that the desire for rebellion vanishes. The Messiah has come and he preaches peace, at least until the final battle; and when that battle comes it will not be a war of humans against humans, but of the Christ against the angelic rulers of the world. The Christian doctrine is to obey the powers and do your duty as a citizen provided this does not conflict with your greater duty towards Christ. It is true that the great allegory of the Book of Revelation reveals a rather different attitude towards the Romans, with Rome represented as a whore who rides upon the beast.[102] But then the book of Revelation was written later when the nascent Christian movement had suffered a great loss, the death of Mary, at the hands of the Romans. However, no Christian document, including the book of Revelation, ever incites Christians to rebellion. The Christian attitude can be summed up in the words of Paul:

Let everyone be subject to the governing authorities for there is no authority except by God. The authorities that exist have been instituted by God. Therefore one rebelling against the authorities is rebelling against what God has instituted, and those who resist will bring judgement upon themselves. (Romans 13:1-2)

We should bear in mind that this is a public letter that may fall into the hands of the authorities, so Paul is going to have to be careful what he writes. Perhaps if he were speaking in private, he might have given this a different emphasis. It is also unlikely that the founder would have put things in quite the same way as Paul. However, it probably does broadly reflect Mary's view because, as we shall see, Paul is writing Romans with Mary as an audience very much in mind. For Mary to believe in a philosophy of non-resistance is consistent with everything we know about the attitude of the Jesus movement to power. This philosophy is summed up succinctly in the early saying about paying taxes, in which Jesus says that what is Caesar's should be rendered to Caesar. Paul's statement that the authorities should be obeyed because God has appointed them reflects the original beliefs of the movement. Paul's words have been used to justify a divine status of kings, which is certainly not what he meant. The movement believed that the world was under the control of angels and that those angels, although evil, had been legitimately appointed. At the apocalypse Jesus would destroy the angels and their human accomplices, the rich and powerful, would receive the punishment that was their due. In the meantime, it was important, in a worldly sense, that they should be obeyed.

This philosophy of obedience enabled the movement to survive and thrive in the Roman Empire. Although Christians encountered persecution, this was mostly sporadic. Had the church been a movement of rebels it would have been quickly eliminated. When Pliny interrogates his Christians, he finds that they are meeting before dawn not to plot rebellion but to swear oaths to be better citizens. Pliny shares the puzzlement of many later Romans in knowing what to do about these Christians. On the one hand, they were atheists who refused to acknowledge the proper gods or give sacrifice to the image of the Emperor. On the other hand, they were law-abiding citizens who worked hard, paid their taxes and were loyal towards the Emperor.

How can we account for this change in attitude towards the Roman authorities from Jewish hostility and incipient rebellion to the willing and submissive obedience of the Christian? It might be thought that this change is due to the transition from a Jewish to a Gentile movement but that is to confuse cause and effect. This attitude is there from the beginning when the movement is Jewish and it is because of this attitude that the movement can appeal to Gentiles. There is no way that Gentiles would join a movement of rebellious Jews who sought the defeat of the Romans. The Gentiles were the Romans.

To the Jews, this philosophy of passive obedience would have seemed like craven cowardice verging on the treacherous. They would have despised it as unmanly, as the philosophy of women. And perhaps that is precisely what it was. The Jews who desired victory over the Romans shared one thing in common; they were men. Perhaps it took a woman to see things differently, to see the Roman powers not as hated oppressors but as men and women who had come under the control of evil forces but who were capable of redemption, of sharing in God's love. Perhaps it took a woman to see that the thing that the Jews loved, their nation, was in one respect just the other side of the same Roman coin and that the nationalism of the Jews was at heart the same evil as the nationalism of the Romans.

This attitude of obedience to the authorities was at one with the wider beliefs of the movement. This is best represented in the famous sermon on the mount in the Gospel of Matthew:

You have heard that it has been said, "An eye for an eye, and a tooth for a tooth." But I tell you not to resist the evil person; but whoever shall strike you on your right cheek, turn to him the other also. And if any man will sue you and take away your tunic, let him have your cloak also. And whoever shall compel you to go one mile, go with him two. (Matthew 5:38-41)

In this saying the principle of love is all encompassing. Evil must not be resisted on its own terms for to fight evil physically is to become it. Paradoxically you must surrender to evil to defeat it. Anything more at variance to the honour-shame culture of the ancient world cannot be imagined.

To the Romans, there was an equivalence between morality and masculinity. What was strong and courageous was good, what was weak and cowardly was bad. It was the morality of the soldier, the conqueror. All forms of weakness and submission were ultimately moral failings. Ironically in this, if in nothing else, Roman and Jew would have agreed. Both had the same masculine approach to life. For a Jew, even death was better than surrender. So what would the right-thinking male, Roman or Jew, have made of the command that if you were struck you should turn the other cheek to your assailant? And in fact how many times in the history of Christianity has this command actually been obeyed? How many Christian men would not hit back if another man came up in the street and struck him? It is virtually impossible for any man to act on this teaching for it is the very antithesis of masculinity, the negation of what it means to be a man. It is very difficult to see how any man could have originated this saying, but it is easy to see how a woman could have.

To Mary, the principle of love was all that mattered. Love flowed from her like milk from a woman's breast, and it flowed not to just one group but to the whole of humanity. The love she practised was more than human love; it was the love from Jesus, the love from God, absolute and all encompassing. It was the female principle of love that changed apocalyptic Judaism into the Jesus movement. Mary had no time for revenge, no time for rebellion, no time for war. The kingdom of heaven was the only kingdom that mattered and it was never a kingdom of this world. It was won not through a triumph of arms but a surrender.

The change from male to female is one of the conditions required for the religion of love. Although Mary would have regarded the inspiration as spiritual, with the authority and commands perceived to come from Jesus, a male founder would have been physiologically unable to give this inspiration the expression that Mary did. A female founder was necessary for the evolution of Christianity, which is not to say that Christianity is female, for Mary built upon the masculine foundation of apocalyptic Judaism, with the figure of the Christ at its centre. But with the female contribution the ingredient that is missing in Judaism, ever flowing love, is supplied and what was male only is made male-female and whole.

Key points

1. The early Jesus movement was remarkably open to women who participated in the church at all levels up to and including "apostle".

2. This is an extraordinary state of affairs for a church that had evolved from Judaism, a patriarchal religion which severely restricted female participation. The proto-orthodox church was soon to become patriarchal itself, so that women were not able to become priests or occupy any leadership position. However, this is an expected regression to cultural norms and it is the initial openness to full female participation that is unusual.

3. If a female shaman founded the Jesus movement, this openness to women is explained.

4. A female shaman founder would also explain another otherwise inexplicable feature of the Jesus movement; it was a religion of love. Although the Yahweh could at times be a God of mercy and forgiveness, there is nothing like the Christian concept of love in Judaism. Both apocalyptic and mainstream Jews longed for revenge against their gentile oppressors. Yet in Christianity, the thirst for revenge disappears, to be replaced by the ordinance to love absolutely. For the Christian, the Roman authorities were not to be overthrown, but obeyed.

5. As the religion of love that was fully open to women, the Jesus movement was attractive to women at all social levels. This was a key factor in its success, as Christianity was able to infuse itself even into some of the highest aristocratic households through the female side.

Chapter 18

Mary, daughter of Joseph

All Christians are familiar with the story of Mary, Joseph and the infant Jesus. However, if Mary were a shaman then the physical birth of Jesus never happened. So did Joseph exist and if so what was his relationship with Mary? The earliest gospel, Mark, does not know of any father of Jesus or husband of Mary. Clues can be found in the two genealogies in Matthew and Luke, which attempt to show how Jesus is descended from King David. But these genealogies have their own mysteries. Why are the two genealogies completely different? Why do they both trace the descent of Jesus through Joseph, even though Jesus is not supposed to be Joseph's son? Why does a group of Jesus' followers and brothers appear as his distant ancestors in Luke? Why is it that the Matthew genealogy names only five women, and those five are four whores and one virgin? And most strange of all, why is there a missing generation?

Birth and resurrection

The idea that Mary the Magdalene is the same as Mary, the mother of Jesus, may seem fantastic to the reader. A raft of distinct traditions has built up around both figures. Mary the mother of Jesus is the wife of Joseph, who rides pregnant on a donkey to Bethlehem. Mary the Magdalene is a much younger figure who is perhaps a prostitute or maybe the lover or even wife of Jesus. But all these stories have arisen as elaborations of a few brief mentions of the two women in the Gospel of Mark. The references to the Magdalene in Mark are meagre and relate exclusively to the crucifixion and resurrection story. The Magdalene only appears in her context as the first witness of the resurrection, and apart from this we are told nothing about her except that she had seven devils cast out of her by Jesus. If we learn little about the Magdalene from Mark, then we learn even less about the other Mary. Her story only develops in the nativity narratives in the later gospels of Matthew and Luke.

There is, however, an intimate connection between the two. Resurrection is rebirth. Both the mother and the Magdalene are the medium by which Jesus enters into the world. The idea of being born again to new life by first "dying" and then being resurrected is programmed deep in the human mind. It is a universal myth that is found again and again in human cultures and religions from all parts of the world. In archetypal form, it is represented by the dying and resurrected gods. The initiate achieves spiritual rebirth by sharing in the death of the god and being reborn through their resurrection. In the Christian story, it is Mary who is the medium of this rebirth and resurrection under her two identities.

It is only when the story is put into literalist terms that this unity between resurrection and birth is shattered. A literal physical Jesus has to have a literal physical birth that must take place long before his death and resurrection. So his mother is placed in an older generation than his "wife" the Magdalene. But originally the two were one. The Magdalene enters the womb-like tomb from which the stone sealing the entrance has been rolled away, and the dead Jesus is born again to life.

The concept of the birth of Jesus in spiritual form is found among the gnostics. In the mid-second century, Hippolytus recounts the opinions held by the school of the great gnostic teacher Valentinus as regards to the nature of Christ. Valentinus' followers in the West held that the body of Jesus was an animal one (that is a normal physical man in his unredeemed state) and that at his baptism Sophia as Holy Spirit descended on Jesus in the form of a dove and so "raised him from the dead". Here we have the concept of the resurrection of the Christ preceding his ministry. The physical birth is demoted to a normal human birth, and the real spiritual birth is identical to the resurrection. But what is really interesting is the idea held by Valentinus' followers in the East that Jesus never had a physical body at all and that the birth through Mary was spiritual in nature:

The Orientals, on the other hand, of whom is Axionicus and Bardesianes, assert that the body of the Saviour was spiritual; for there came upon Mary the Holy Spirit--that is, Sophia and the power of the highest. This is the creative art, (and was vouchsafed) in order that what was given to Mary by the Spirit might be fashioned. (Hippolytus, Refutation of all Heresies 5:15)[103]

The same belief among the Valentinians is attacked later by Tertullian who records that they believed about Jesus that:

He was produced by means of a virgin, rather than of a virgin! On the ground that, having descended into the virgin rather in the manner of a passage through her than of a birth by her, He came into existence through her, not of her -- not experiencing a mother in her, but nothing more than a way. (Tertullian:Against Valentinians, Ch. 27)[104]

The doctrine of Christ having a spiritual body is Docetism. The concept seems strange to the modern world because we picture this spiritual Christ as a sort of hologram floating over the ground, projected onto the world but not part of the world. However, we can see the origins of Docetism in quite different terms; that Christ was a spiritual being, who was invisible to the common eye but who communicated through the prophetess. It is telling that Docetism is consistently linked with Mary the virgin. If there is one individual whom we might expect to be de-emphasised in the Docetic worldview, it is the person who was regarded as the mother of the physical Jesus, but the opposite is the case.

We will see that the Docetic Christ born spiritually through Mary goes back to the foundation of Christianity and precedes the belief in a physical Christ. But for evidence we cannot rely only on the account of the beliefs of Valentinians given by the church fathers. How can we be sure that their beliefs were not a second-century development? Instead, we must go back in time and confront the earliest evidence about the mother and family of Jesus.

Daughter of David

Paul tells us that Jesus came *"of the seed of David according to the flesh"* (Romans 1:3). What is the evidence that Mary was regarded as the seed of David? None of the gospels tells us anything about the ancestry of Mary. The descent of Jesus from King David is traced in both Matthew and Luke through Jesus' supposed father Joseph and not through Mary, his real mother. However, the idea that Mary herself was descended from David was commonplace in the literature of early Christianity. For example, the popular infancy narrative, the Protoevangelium of James, dated to the second half of the second century, says of Mary *"she was of the tribe of Da-*

vid."[105] The Ascension of Isaiah contains an earlier reference to Mary being descended from David:

> *And I saw a woman of the family of David the prophet whose name (was) Mary and she (was) a virgin and was betrothed to a man whose name (was) Joseph, a carpenter, and he also was of the seed and family of the righteous David of Bethlehem in Judah. (Ascension of Isaiah 11:2)*[106]

Dated to the first half of the second century, much of this is dependent upon the Gospel of Matthew. But the information that Mary is of the family of David in her own right has come from somewhere else. So we have early traditions that a Mary is descended from the line of David. Scholars have an explanation for these traditions. They reason that these stories were an attempt to rebut criticism that the gospels do not prove Jesus' descent from David because Joseph is not the real father of Jesus. So, as an insurance policy, the idea that Mary also was descended from David was developed. There is no evidence for this explanation - it is based entirely on supposed motivation. To uncover the real truth we need to tackle earlier evidence than the Ascension of Isaiah. We need to go back to the source of the stories about Mary and Joseph in the gospels.

The missing father

The Jews like any patriarchal society attached great importance to a person's father and little importance to their mother. It is all the more shocking that the earliest source for the life of Jesus does not mention anyone as being his father but only gives the name of his mother:

> *Is not this the carpenter, the son of Mary, and brother of James, and Joses, and Judas, and Simon? (Mark 6:3)*

The author of the Gospel of Mark does not know who the father of Jesus was or was supposed to be! He gives only the mother's name in a place where any Jew would have given the name of the father. Some believe that this shows that Jesus was illegitimate. Under the spiritual paradigm, we have a better explanation for this lack of knowledge of the father of Jesus. He does not have an earthly father because he is a spiritual being appearing through Mary. His father is God, just as the gospels tell us!

But if Jesus did not have a father then from where did the author of Matthew get Joseph? It is time to confront the family of Jesus starting with the genealogies of Luke and Matthew.

One Jesus, two genealogies

At the start of the Gospel of Matthew a genealogy is given proving the descent of Jesus from Abraham through David. The Gospel of Luke also gives a genealogy, this time starting from Adam. However, much to the dismay of Christians over the ages, the two are completely different!

Matthew traces the descent of Jesus through Solomon, the son of David and is arranged in three blocks of fourteen names - or six blocks of seven. This structure is made explicit by the gospel writer although, as we shall see, the number of names does not quite add up. Luke also seems to have a structure of sevens but in this case it is implicit and no attention is drawn to it. Whereas Matthew traces the descent of Jesus from Solomon, in Luke's genealogy the descent is instead through Nathan, an obscure son of David. After David the two genealogies are entirely different, except that two names from the time of the return from Babylonian exile, Shealtiel and Zerubbabel, are repeated on both.

Both genealogies trace the line through Joseph even though, according to the gospels of Matthew and Luke, he is not Jesus' father! In Luke this is made explicit and the gospel states that Jesus is only "supposed" to be the son of Joseph. The traditional response to this bizarre feature is that for the Jews it was legal and not biological descent that is important. As Mary was married to Joseph he was Jesus' legal father even if Jesus was really the son of God.

Rather than accept the obvious, that the two gospels are in hopeless conflict, Christian scholars from the church fathers onwards have engaged in contortions to show how two entirely different genealogies are really the same. The most favoured explanation revolves around the idea of the levirate marriage. If a married man died without a son but has an unmarried brother, then that brother is obliged to marry the widow. The first offspring of this marriage was legally the child of the dead man. This would enable Joseph's true father to be Jacob (as in Matthew) but his legal father to be Heli (as in Luke) so that the genealogy passes through two separate routes. Another favoured explanation is that the Luke genealogy is really that of Mary and not Joseph. The argument goes that the comment about Jesus being the supposed son of Joseph was intended to be read as if in parentheses. This would remove Joseph from the genealogy and make Jesus the son of Heli, who would thus be the father of Mary.

The main problem with the Mary theory is that the natural reading of the texts is that it is Joseph who is called the son of Heli. Also, if Mary were married to Joseph, would Jesus really be called the son of Heli and not the son of Joseph, even if he were illegitimate? And if he was then why are there no explicit references to Jesus the son of Heli? There is also no early tradition among the church fathers of reading Luke as a genealogy of Mary.

But there is one potentially significant piece of evidence in support of the Mary theory; the earliest account of the life of the virgin Mary outside of the gospels gives the name of the father of Mary as Joachim, a variant of the name Heli! The early Christians were desperate for more information about the characters in Jesus' life than the gospels provided. To meet this demand, a number of romances and Acts were written around the figures in the gospels. One of the figures who most intrigued many early Christians was the virgin Mary, who conceived Jesus by the Holy Spirit. The story of Mary was developed in the Protoevangelium of James which was written in the second half of the second century and which became extremely popular and widely read. The Protoevangelium is clearly dependent upon the infancy narratives in Matthew and Luke. Neither of these gives any names to the parents of Mary but in the Protoevangelium they are named as Joachim and Anna. The name Joachim is a form of Eliakim or Eli, itself a variant of Heli.[107]

We are looking for a genealogy of Mary and here we apparently have evidence that such a genealogy, tracing the descent of Mary from David, did indeed exist. However, we should be cautious; the Protoevangelium is quite late to be used as a reliable source of evidence. Also Luke is inherently a less reliable witness of earlier traditions than Matthew, which tends to be far more loyal to its sources. The author of Luke has a habit of improvising shamelessly, developing involved narratives from mere scraps.

And when we look at the detail of Luke's genealogy we see a number of features which show that, whatever else it may be, it is not a genuine Jewish attempt to prove descent from David. Ironically, some of these details have impressed observers as evidence that the Luke genealogy is more "realistic". Consider, for example, the number of generations. Matthew has three groups of fourteen, or 42 generations, which seems an inadequate number to cover the span of time. The period from David to Jesus is covered by 28 generations compared to 42 generations in Luke. Consideration of the average time between generations would seem to favour Luke - but this is to ignore the real reason for Matthew's generations. We can trace back the timetable given by Matthew to the beliefs of the apocalyptic groups from which Christianity descended. It was a requirement for this "calendar of the apocalypse" that the history of the Jews should be organised in weeks of seven generations and that precisely fourteen generations should exist between the Babylonian exile and the coming of the Christ. The Matthew genealogy conforms to this timetable and is an indication that the genealogy goes back to the earliest days of the Jesus movement and beyond. However, the Luke genealogy attempts to improve upon Matthew by using a more realistic number of generations which shows that whoever wrote the Luke genealogy did not appreciate the requirement to have precisely fourteen generations; they are not part of the original Jewish apocalyptic movement but belong in a later Christian setting.

Another indication that the Luke genealogy is not early is that it traces the descent of Jesus from David through Nathan and not Solomon. The throne of David is established upon the descendants of Solomon *"forever"*.[108] No Jew would have traced a Messiah aspirant's descent through the obscure Nathan instead of through Solomon, the builder of the first temple. And it is pointless to say that this feature makes the Luke genealogy more "realistic". To say that a Jewish genealogy going back to King David is realistic is like saying that a modern Briton can claim a realistic genealogy going back to King Arthur. Both King David and King Arthur belong to the myths of their people. Once the myth of the throne of David became established, it was a requirement for anyone claiming to rule Judea to claim a genealogy going back to David. If lesser mortals wanted to claim Davidic descent, they did so by constructing a line going back to a ruler who was accepted to have been a descendant of David. All these genealogies would have gone through Solomon because the whole point of the exercise was to prove your worthiness to aspire to the throne of Solomon.

So why does Luke trace the descent through Nathan? One possibility is the type of idiosyncratic interpretation that could only be made by a Gentile and not a Jew. The author of Luke may have confused Nathan the son of Solomon with Nathan the prophet. In 2 Samuel, it is to Nathan the prophet that Yahweh gives a message for David concerning his seed: *"He shall build a house for my name and I have established the throne of his kingdom forever. I will be his father, and he my son."* (2 Samuel 7:13-14) This prophecy was about Solomon, but Christians also applied it to Jesus as a later descendant of David. The author of Luke is clearly aware of this prophecy as it is alluded to in the message of the angel to Mary.[109] It would seem that she developed the theory that it was actually spoken to Nathan, the son of David because it was intended to come true through him, and not through Solomon as the Jews thought. For a gentile Christian, like the author of Luke, this had the advantage of making Jesus' kingdom distinct and higher than that of Solomon. If the prophecy had been about Solomon, then Jesus would only be restoring the Solomon's kingdom, the kingdom of the Jews. But if the prophecy were about Nathan then the Jews would never have fulfilled it, and Jesus would be establishing an entirely new Christian kingdom among the Gentiles. Such an interpretation is typical of the imaginative author of Luke and evidence that the genealogy was assembled at the same time the gospel was written.

How to explain the only two names, after David, in common to both genealogies, Shealtiel and Zerubbabel? The second, Zerubbabel, is the leader who brought back the Jewish exiles from Babylon to Judea. The authors of both genealogies must have thought that it was vital to include him even though this return was not regarded as the true release from exile. As for Zerubbabel's father, Shealtiel, he would enter the genealogy on his son's coat tails because a Jewish man's name would include the patronymic; Zerubbabel son of Shealtiel.

The number of generations and the descent through Nathan are both indicators of the Luke genealogy being late in construction. But there is another feature that is even more surprising. Both genealogies are largely a king list and are taken from scripture. Only after Zerubbabel does the genealogy in Matthew depart from the list of kings. But in Luke the descendants of Nathan form a sequence that is not known from any other source. And in their midst is a list of several individuals prominent in the gospels:

Eliakim (of which Joachim and Heli are variants)
Jonam (a variant of John)
Joseph
Judas
Simon
Levi
Matthat (similar to Matthew)

Eliakim is the same as Joachim (the father of Mary in the Protoevangelium) and Heli (given in the same genealogy as the father of Joseph). Matthat and Matthew are closely related names and both mean "gift of god". With the exception of Eliakim all the names on this list are mentioned in Mark as brothers or followers of Jesus. Is it possible that this grouping of names is here by chance? As a control, we can compare the names of Jesus' brothers and followers with the names in Matthew's genealogy between David and Joseph. There is not a single name in common!

Not only do many names from Mark appear in the Luke genealogy but they are lumped together. This would seem to be an extraordinary coincidence and this can be confirmed by statistics. To minimise the dangers of bias, a simple, robust method has been used. This compares the two lists; (A) the followers and brothers of Jesus in Mark and; (B) the genealogy of Jesus in Luke after Nathan. The genealogy before David is not included because this is dictated by scripture and both Matthew and Luke are in close agreement up to this point. It is important that our comparison list (A) is unbiased so we have defined it in broad and simple terms - we are not making any judgement calls but simply reading the names from the first gospel to be written. We can then work out how unusual it is for the names from list (A) to occur in sequence in list (B) rather than scattered all about. With a narrow definition of what counts as the same name, we have a sequence of four names Joseph to Levi. There is a probability that the names would cluster in a sequence at least this long of 1 in 120. For a wider definition, we have the sequence of six names Jonan to Matthat and the corresponding probability is 1 in 180. A probability around 1 in 10 would normally be considered to be significant so in both cases the number of names in sequence is significant.[110]

This demonstrates a clear link between the names in the gospels and the genealogy of Jesus given by Luke. How can we account for it? The genealogy in Luke places these names of Jesus' supposed contemporaries alone in a group many hundreds of years before Jesus. They come shortly after Nathan in a remote period for which the author of Luke could have no information independent of the scriptures. The names are not found in scripture and so must have been either made up or, more likely, taken from some other source that has been misapplied.

What is the nature of this other source? One clue is that most of the names on the list can make some claim to be related to Jesus. In fact, out of all of the potential male relatives of Jesus there is only one glaring omission; James the brother of the Lord and one time leader of the movement. And this gives us the link between all the members on this list. They are all related to a James on the evidence of sources existing at the time the Gospel of Luke was written:

Joseph (Joses) , Judas and Simon are listed (in that order) alongside James as brothers of Jesus in Mark 6:3.

John is repeatedly called a brother of James. Jesus is often accompanied by his favourite disciples who include James and his brother John (according to Mark these are the sons of Zebedee). In Acts 12:2 (written by the author of Luke) we hear how "James, the brother of John" was killed with a sword.

Levi is called "Levi of Alphaeus" in the story of his being called from the tax office in Mark 2:14. There is a "James of Alphaeus" in Mark's list of the disciples which would make Levi a brother of James.

When Matthew repeats the story of the calling of Levi he calls him Matthew instead. From this there has been a long-standing tradition to regard Levi and Matthew as two names for the same individual particularly as Levi is not included separately in the list of the twelve. This would make Matthew a brother of James of Alphaeus.

If Joseph is included as a brother rather than as a father then the whole of the list between Jonan and Matthat would consist of individuals who could be considered brothers of James on the evidence of Mark and Matthew. So we have a list of the brothers of James (and hence brothers of Jesus) which has been incorporated into the genealogy. This list would seem to be an attempt to identify the "brothers of the Lord" who were seven in number. Paul tells us that one of these brothers is James and someone has complied a list of the other six from information available from the gospels of Mark and Matthew. We can tell that the list is not independent of these gospels because, as we will show, Levi and Matthew were not brothers of James and the very existence of Levi is due to a misunderstanding made by the author of Mark.

The position of Eliakim is not so clear. To admit him as a relative of James we would have to include the evidence contained in the genealogy of Luke itself. This gives Heli (Eliakim) as the father of Joseph so the same Heli would be James' grandfather. Because of these uncertainties Eliakim is not included in the above probability calculation (if Eliakim were included the possibility of the sequence arising by chance would become even more remote). However, it is unlikely that the name Eliakim appears at the head of a sequence of brothers of James by chance. And it is the presence of Eliakim that can explain why a list of the brothers of James appears in the genealogy at all. The list must have included the information that the brothers were descendants of Eliakim, who was a descendant of David. The author of Luke is looking to fill in the descendants of the obscure Nathan and does not recognise that Eliakim is the same name as Heli. So she interprets the list as a mini-genealogy which she then places in completely the wrong time frame to supply the missing descendants of Nathan.

The resolution of the mystery of the two genealogies lies with the author of the Gospel of Luke. She is a superb novelist and a complete fantasist with access to impressive sources of information. The author of Luke is not very interested in facts and makes daring and quite false imaginative leaps when dealing with factual information. She dislikes the Gospel of Matthew and misses no opportunity of trying to "improve" upon that gospel. So she extends the genealogy back to Adam, includes more names to give a more realistic number of years per generation and traces the descent through Nathan rather than Solomon, based upon confusion between Nathan the prophet and Nathan the son of David.

The virgin and the four whores

So we come to the other genealogy, that of Matthew. Is this genealogy older than the gospel in which it is found? It traces the descent through Solomon as would be expected of the Jewish Messiah. It has the structure of three blocks of fourteen generations which is a clear sign of its origins lying in the apocalyptic movement. But it also has some very odd features.

As with Luke, it is really a genealogy of Joseph who according to Matthew is not the real father of Jesus. Moreover, there is nothing about this Joseph in Mark. Even if Joseph is only Jesus' father in law through his marriage to Jesus' mother it is still an extraordinary state of affairs that (i) the Gospel of Mark makes no mention of him and (ii) the Gospel of Matthew traces the descent of Jesus through him. Was he known as Jesus' father or was he not?

Linked to this odd role of Joseph is something even odder. The genealogy says that Jesus was born to Mary:

... and Jacob begat Joseph, the husband of Mary, of whom was begotten Jesus, who is named Christ. (Matthew 1:16)

The Greek is quite explicit that Jesus is born of Mary rather than Joseph.[111] It is hard to overstate how odd this would have appeared to a Jew of the time when descent was always given through the male line. The sceptic regards this as further evidence that Jesus was illegitimate. In this view, the virgin birth story was developed to cover this illegitimacy. But looking at the circumstances around illegitimacy we will see that the virgin birth could not have fulfilled this function.

If Jesus were illegitimate then there would have been two possibilities. The first is that the illegitimacy was covered up, and the child was publicly accepted as Joseph's. This is quite possible, particularly if Mary came from a good family and Joseph from a relatively poor background; he could have been induced to overlook an indiscretion in his future bride. In this case, it would have been in everybody's interest to maintain the front that Jesus was the son of Joseph. But then he would have been called "Jesus son of Joseph" so why does the Gospel of Mark not know who his father was? There would have been no need for the virgin birth story since publicly Jesus would not have been illegitimate and to the ancient mind "face" was all that really mattered. If Joseph acknowledged him as his son, then he was his son.

The second possibility is that the illegitimacy was public because Mary was unmarried when Jesus was born. In this case, Mary would have been widely considered as a whore and subsequent marriage would have been difficult. If she were to marry Joseph, then there must have been a gap of time between the birth of Jesus and the marriage. It would have been impossible for Joseph to marry Mary while she was pregnant without acknowledging Jesus as his son. To do so would result in catastrophic loss of face. So in this second possibility, we have the situation where Mary is known to be a woman without virtue, Jesus is publicly known to be illegitimate, and Mary's marriage to Joseph would have taken place sometime after Jesus was born. This would be consistent with the evidence from Mark that Jesus' father was unknown. But it is not consistent with Matthew's tracing Jesus' descent from David through Joseph. Nor is it consistent with the virgin birth story. Jesus would have borne the stigma of illegitimacy throughout his life, and no one would have questioned the fact of his illegitimacy in his lifetime. Similarly, Mary would have long been accepted as a woman of dubious virtue. The Jesus movement would have had to live with these facts and develop strategies to adapt to them. To go back after Jesus' death and recast Mary as a virgin mother and Jesus as the son of God would have been laughable.

The virgin birth story is not a cover for illegitimacy. Rather it is an attempt to explain something that is in Matthew's sources, something that the author of Matthew does not understand. The author of Matthew has a source telling him that it is through Joseph that Jesus can claim descent from David. But he knows that Jesus is not Joseph's son!

There is a second intriguing feature about the Matthew genealogy that many regard as pointing towards illegitimacy. It is normal for Jewish genealogies to give only the male line and not to mention the mothers. Yet in four instances the Matthew genealogy gives the name of the mother also. And in each of these four cases, the women named are of dubious virtue; Tamar and Rahab both prostituted themselves, and Bathsheba was an adulteress. Ruth was a widow and a Moabitess, who goes to her kinsman Boaz when he is sleeping alone at night to persuade him to marry her.

All of the woman named would be seen, by the standards of the time, as whores. What can account for this strange pattern? Those who favour the illegitimacy theory regard it as pointing to the lack of virtue of the one other woman named in the genealogy; Mary herself. Perhaps the author is trying to link her to other women in the history of Israel who played key roles as mothers while at the same time being impure. But why would the author of Matthew, who first gives us the story of Mary as the virgin mother, connect her to women who were whores?

There is one other piece of evidence that would appear to support the illegitimacy argument, and that is a saying in the Gospel of Thomas:

Jesus said: "He who shall know father and mother shall be called the son of a whore." (Thomas 105)

Taken together with the four women in the genealogy it seems to be telling us that something is wrong about Jesus birth. But is this saying really about Mary at all? If it were about Jesus, why would such a negative saying be in the gospel? Even if Jesus were illegitimate, the sayings of the Jesus movement would not stress the fact! Also Thomas 105 talks about knowing "father and mother" which implies secret adultery. Neither the identity of the father nor the character of the mother is what we think it is. This does not fit the situation of an unmarried Mary becoming pregnant and subsequently marrying Joseph.

There is, however, a connection between the saying and the genealogy. In a normal genealogy only the male line would be named and we would know the fathers but not the mothers. However, in Jesus' genealogy, the mothers are also named in four cases. So for these four, and these four only, we know both father and mother, as the Thomas saying says. In each of these four cases, the mother can be thought of as a whore, and the offspring as "the son of a whore". The inclusion of the four mothers is a literal and pedantic expression of the Thomas saying!

What has happened is that someone has interpreted the Thomas saying as being about Jesus' ancestors. So, to explain the saying, they have put the four mothers who could be thought of as whores into the genealogy. Most likely this was done by editing an earlier existing genealogy at the time it was incorporated into Matthew. It certainly shows that the Thomas saying is earlier than the Gospel of Matthew.

The four women do not point towards Jesus' illegitimacy but are explained by the Thomas saying. This saying has been misapplied for it has nothing to do with Jesus or Mary. It is actually about the secret adultery of Eve, the mother of all humanity. The evidence for an illegitimate Jesus is evaporating. But we still have to explain the absence of a father in Mark, and why Matthew traces Jesus' descent through Joseph before maintaining in the virgin birth story that Joseph was not really Jesus' father. The resolution lies in another mystery; why is one generation missing in Matthew?

The mystery of the missing generation

It has already been pointed out that the number of generations in the Matthew genealogy has been fixed according to a pre-determined structure. The number of generations is enumerated immediately after the genealogy:

All the generations, therefore, from Abraham to David are fourteen generations, and from David to the Babylonian removal fourteen generations, and from the Babylonian removal to the Christ, fourteen generations. (Matthew 1:17)

This structure of three sets of fourteen generations is a sign that the genealogy is old and goes back to the apocalyptic movement that was the predecessor of Christianity. That the number of generations was important to the author of the genealogy is demonstrated by the fact that some names have been missed out so as to make the number of generations in the first two groups exactly fourteen. But there is a problem. In the final group, from the Babylonian removal to the Christ, there are only thirteen generations and not fourteen.

A number of solutions to this problem have been proposed. Perhaps a name has been missed out by mistake. But such an obvious error would surely have been spotted by the first readers of the gospels and corrected. Or perhaps David is supposed to be counted twice, at the end of the first group of fourteen and at the beginning of the second group which would enable the third group to steal an extra name from the second group. But this is contrived; however you look at it, David is only one generation. Another possibility is that perhaps Mary should be included in the list of generations. This would indeed make the number to fourteen. But the problem is that Mary is supposed to be married to Joseph and so is the same generation as Joseph.

However, with the realisation that the inclusion of Mary would make the number of generations come right, the solution is staring us in the face. Just look at the facts:

The father of Jesus is unknown by the Gospel of Mark

The Gospel of Matthew gives the descent of Jesus from David through Joseph even though Joseph is not supposed to be the father of Jesus.

The Matthew genealogy states that Jesus was born of Mary and not of Joseph

Matthew has the virgin birth story to show how Jesus was born from the holy spirit and Mary.

The Matthew genealogy has a missing generation, and this would be corrected if Mary is included as a generation

Everything comes out right if we make one small change; Mary must have been the daughter and not the wife of Joseph! This resolves all the problems:

The father of Jesus is not Joseph and is unknown to the author of Mark because Jesus does not have an earthly father.

The genealogy through Joseph is necessary to demonstrate that Mary is descended from David.

Jesus has been born of Mary because he has come of Mary and been spiritually resurrected and reborn through her agency. He is of the line of David "according to the flesh".

The virgin birth story tells us how the coming of Jesus was by the descent of the spirit to the virginal Mary and that the birth of Jesus did not involve the agency of man.

The number of generations is correct because Joseph and Mary are two separate generations taking the number to fourteen.

What has happened is that the original genealogy giving Mary as the daughter of Joseph has been changed so as to make her the wife of Joseph instead. Although the number of names has stayed the same, the change has eliminated a generation and given the wrong generation count. It has also caused the absurdity of tracing the descent of Jesus through Joseph, even though Jesus is not supposed to be the son of Joseph.

Why should the author of Matthew change a father into a husband? He tends to be loyal to his sources except where there is a difficulty that needs to be smoothed over or an inconsistency to resolve. In this case, he faces a number of difficulties that have arisen from the conversion of the spiritually resurrected Jesus into a man of flesh and blood. The first problem is that this fictional physical Jesus does not have a father, but only a mother inviting the suspicion of illegitimacy. This is the obvious conclusion of anyone reading the Gospel of Mark (even more obvious in the ancient world than it would be today). To address the problem he has to find a father, which he does in Joseph. The next problem is that Jesus is descended from David through his "mother" Mary. The genealogy is originally constructed to show that the spiritual Jesus is of the line of David "according to the flesh". The "according to the flesh" meant the shaman Mary; the genealogy is her genealogy and as such functions perfectly well. But when Jesus is turned into a physical man and Mary into his physical mother, the genealogy no longer works because you cannot trace the line of descent through the female. So there is another reason to make Joseph into Jesus' father so that the descent can be traced through him instead of Mary.

However, changing a father into a son is a big step and although it solves many of the problems faced by the author of Matthew he would surely not have done this without some source that told him that Mary was Joseph's husband. So how could a father be confused with a husband?

There is, in fact, an easy source of such confusion. Women were identified by the Jews in relation to the man who was the head of the family to which they belonged. Normally this man was their husband. However in the case of an unmarried girl or woman it would be her father. It seems likely that Mary was unmarried at the time when she had her vision of the risen Christ. Such a state would have been highly unusual in mainstream Judaism where girls married young. But Mary did not belong to the mainstream but was born into an apocalyptic group that looked to Enoch rather than to Moses. These groups eventually died out (except for Christianity!) and we know virtually nothing about their way of life and the roles that women could play within them. If Mary were the founder, then she must have been vastly better educated in religious matters than most Jewish women of the time, so her upbringing must have been very untypical. If there is any truth in the virgin birth story, it is likely that she had chosen or had been chosen, to devote her life to God rather than marriage. This may have been because she was a daughter of David and of the line of the Messiah so that she was considered, among her sect, to have a sacred role to play. She would not have been under the necessity to marry to preserve the line of David as this line could only be passed down through the male.

Remarkably, we do have a record of a Jewish sect from the time of Mary in which women participated equally with men in a monastery like existence and in which the women remained unmarried. This example is not from Palestine but Alexandria, the spiritual capital of the ancient world. Philo of Alexandria, writing in the first half of the first century, tells us about the Therapeutae (the word means "healers") in his "On the contemplative life" and intends them to contrast with the Essenes who represent the practical life. The Therapeutae lived a hermit-like existence in separate huts for most of the week but came together on the Sabbath for a community service. Both men and women participate, the two sexes being arranged in separate groups and being divided by a half-wall so that the women can follow all aspects of the service. On the seventh day of the seventh week, they have a special "feast" and after this they spend the night in a divine service. They first form two choirs, one for men, and one for women, singing hymns. Then the two choirs come together into one, imitating the coming together of the Israelites into one group to escape over the red sea from Egypt, with the men being led by "Moses the prophet" and the women by the "Miriam (Mary) the prophetess". Philo tells us that many of the women are virgins:

And the women also share in this feast, the greater part of whom, though old, are virgins in respect of their purity (not indeed through necessity, as some of the priestesses among the Greeks are, who have been compelled to preserve their chastity more than they would have done of their own accord), but out of an admiration for and love of wisdom, with which they are desirous to pass their lives, on account of which they are indifferent to the pleasures of the body, desiring not a mortal but an immortal offspring ... (Philo, De vita contemplativa 68)[112]

So we have an example here of Jewish women who remained unmarried in the service of God and who must have been as literate in their understanding of the scriptures as the men. This is not to say that Mary belonged to the Therapeutae - although there are fascinating parallels between them and the early Jesus movement. But it is evidence of a greater diversity of early Judaism than the writings of the later Rabbis would lead us to believe. Had Philo not written about the Therapeutae we would have known nothing about them, and he was only familiar with them because he happened to live in the same area. There were probably a number of similar small Jewish sects about which we know nothing. Such small groups would have been below the radar of an historian such as Josephus, a military man with no spiritual bent, who would have concentrated on the major power groupings such as the Sadducees, the Pharisees and the Essenes. It was from one of these small sects that Mary and the Jesus movement emerged.

Supposing that Mary had been unmarried, she would have been known as "Mary of Joseph". Even if she had been married, she might still occasionally have been called this, particularly if her father was very prominent, such as the leader of the group. But a mainstream Jew coming across "Mary of Joseph" would automatically interpret this as "Mary husband of Joseph"! And so the idea of her being married to Joseph could have arisen from an understandable misinterpretation.

Do we have any early evidence that Mary was in fact known as "Mary of Joseph"? The answer is that we do; moreover that this evidence comes in a context where it is closely associated with Mary the Magdalene. The source of this evidence is none other than the Gospel of Mark. For although that gospel does not appear to talk about Joseph we can, if we look closely, find the signs of his relationship to Mary.

Joses

We have already seen that a "Joses" is included in the list of the brothers of Jesus given in Mark 6:3. The name Joses is a shortened version of Joseph. As the brothers of Jesus are supposed to be the children of Joseph based on the evidence of Matthew and Luke, this gives the problem that Joses has the same name as his supposed father. It was not the custom of the Jews to name sons after fathers. After this brief mention, Joses disappears from the early writings (with the exception of the Gospel of Matthew's version of the Mark 6:3 story). We learn nothing more about this Joses brother of Jesus.

However, we do learn more about his mother. When the story of Jesus' crucifixion is told in Mark a group of female supporters from Jerusalem are looking from afar. We are given the names of three of them:

... *Mary the Magdalene, and Mary the mother of James the less and of Joses, and Salome. (Mark 15:40)*

Later as Jesus' body is placed in the tomb, this is observed by two women:

Mary the Magdalene, and Mary of Joses, were beholding where he is laid. (Mark 15:47)

There is one further reference to the names of the women when they go to the tomb:

And the Sabbath having past, Mary the Magdalene, and Mary of James, and Salome, bought spices ... (Mark 16:1)

We will consider Salome later, but we are interested now in the women called Mary. In Mark 15:47 we find what we are looking for: "Mary of Joses" which is to say "Mary of Joseph". This name is paired with Mary the Magdalene. In Mark 16:1 the same woman is called "Mary of James" and is again paired with the Magdalene. We have another occurrence of the name "Mary of James" in Luke 24:10. The author of Mark intends us to read these names as Mary the mother of Joses and Mary the mother of James. This is how he introduces them. But is this right? We are not primarily interested in the author of Mark's interpretations but in what his sources said. The only other time this woman is referred to in Mark is in the list of the brothers of Jesus:

Is not this the carpenter, the son of Mary, and brother of James, and Joses, and Judas, and Simon? (Mark 6:3)

So it is perfectly clear whom the author of Mark thinks this Mary is -- on the evidence of the Gospel of Mark this woman called Mary of Joses and Mary of James can only be the mother of Jesus! But this interpretation gives a major problem -- why is she not called "Mary of Jesus" or "Mary mother of Jesus"? Why should she be named instead after her lesser sons, Joses and James? And why is it that none of the three synoptic gospels names this woman at the crucifixion and resurrection as Mary of Jesus or refers to her as mother of Jesus?

We have already encountered another aspect of this problem in that another supposed brother of Jesus is called "Judas of James" and "Judas brother of James" but never "Judas of Jesus." And why for that matter is James never called "James of Jesus"? In fact, none of the family members of Jesus are ever called "of Jesus".

Under the spiritual hypothesis we have a simple explanation for this; Jesus never existed in flesh and blood. So we have terms like the "brethren of the Lord" and the mother of Jesus but what we do not find is a reference to Jesus in the names which his mother and brothers would be called in everyday life.

So what can be deduced about Mark's sources? The first thing is that the crucifixion and resurrection story in Mark does not call Mary the mother of Jesus even though the author of Mark clearly thinks she was the mother of Jesus. The reason must be that the author of Mark is using the names that his sources give for her.

The next point is that the names "Mary of Joses" and "Mary of James" are used without the "mother" being added; and that we have two examples of each of these forms of the names whereas "Mary the mother of James the less and Joses" only occurs once. Had the author of Mark started with "Mary the mother of James and Joses" he would have stuck with that to avoid confusion. So the names "Mary of Joses" and "Mary of James" are the starting point and must go back to his sources and the phrase "Mary the mother of James the less and Joses", occurring first in the narrative, has been added by the author of Mark to explain the names.

Whenever these names are used in Mark, they immediately follow on from Mary the Magdalene. The explanation is that they are alternative names for the same woman. The author of Mark does not realise this and thinks that the woman called "Mary of Joses" and "Mary of James" was a different person from the Magdalene, but he is wrong! We do not have multiple women witnessing the events - we have one woman whose story has come down under multiple names; Mary the Magdalene, Mary of Joses and Mary of James.

We have already concluded that the founder must have been the Magdalene, that she must have also occupied the role of the "mother" of Jesus and that she must have been daughter of Joseph so that she could claim descent from David. Like any woman she was named in relation to the important males in her family. Hence the name "Mary of Joses" after her father Joseph, the name under which she would have been known when she first had her experiences of the risen Christ. Later she is known as "Mary of James" after the male who was then the head of the family, James who was regarded as her "son" and whom she appointed as her successor as leader of the movement. These are the names she would have been called by those who knew her in everyday life. But within the movement she had another name, the Magdalene.

So where does Mary mother of Joses come from? The passage about the female followers of Jesus looking on to his crucifixion sets the scene for what comes next, the role they are to play in the resurrection. The crucifixion and resurrection were originally spiritual experiences of Mary alone, but in the literalisation of the story it becomes a public event, so Mark introduces a crowd of women looking on. He includes Mary of Joses and Mary of James telling us (rightly) that these were the same woman and that she was the mother of James and Joses. She was indeed in some sense the mother of James. But the author of Mark has extrapolated from "Mary of James" to conclude, wrongly, that "Mary of Joses" meant that she was also the mother of Joses. However, Mary would not have been known under the names of two of her sons but only after the eldest. The inclusion of Joses among the brothers of the Lord in the list of the brothers of Jesus at Mark 6:3 is most likely a consequence of this mistake. This misunderstanding explains a number of features:

It explains why we never hear about Joses the brother of Jesus again in the New Testament - he does not exist!

It explains why Joseph is never mentioned in Mark even though he plays a major role in Matthew and Luke. Joseph is in fact in all three gospels but in Mark he becomes Mary's son and in Matthew he becomes her husband.

It explains why Mary is called Mary of Joses in Mark even though James rather than Joses would have been the head of the family; Joses is her father and not her son.

Our conclusion is that Joses/Joseph is the father of Mary and not the husband or son and that the virgin Mary is the same as the Magdalene. We have seen how this resolves the problems of the genealogy of Matthew and establishes Mary, the founder, as a descendant of David.

The other father of Mary

Before we leave the genealogies, we must consider another candidate for Mary's father, Joachim/Heli. We have seen that the Protoevangelium of James gives the father of Mary as Joachim and that a variant of this name, Heli, is given as the father of Joseph in the Luke genealogy. A further variant of the name, Eliakim, appears at the head of the Luke "brother list" as a descendant of Nathan.

If Mary were really the daughter of Joachim, then this would disprove our conclusion that she was the daughter of Joseph. So how reliable is the Protoevangelium of James? It dates from the later half of the second century and is heavily dependent on the infancy narratives of Matthew and Luke. The idea that the father of Mary was called Joachim could have come from the additions to Daniel where the husband of Susanna is also called Joachim. The name of Mary's mother, Anna, is likely to have come from the Anna, who prays night and day in the temple in Luke. These influences do not inspire confidence in the Protoevangelium as a source of historically reliable information!

This does not mean, however, that the Protoevangelium did not have a source recording that Mary was the daughter of Joachim. It is significant that variants of the same name are found as the father of Joseph and as an ancestor of the brothers in the Luke genealogy. The resolution of this mystery lies in the far more reliable Matthew genealogy.

How did a family prove that they were descended from David? A long list of the descendants of David was known from scripture. To establish that you were related to David, you would need to link your own family tree back to one of these scriptural descendants. The Matthew genealogy does just this. It is divided into two; the first portion consists entirely of scriptural names running from David to Zerubbabel, who led the return from Babylon; but after Zerubbabel, all the names are unknown from scripture, and this later portion must be the family genealogy.

The first obscure individual is Abiud, who is supposedly a son of Zerubbabel. However, there is no Abiud in the list of the sons of Zerubbabel in 1 Chronicles 3:19-20 and so this must be the first name on the family genealogy. Although Abiud is indicated as a son of Zerubbabel, this could mean a more distant relationship, so some generations are likely to be missing at this point. We know that there are insufficient generations to cover the time span from Zerubbabel to Joseph so generations must be missing somewhere.

We can see how the Matthew genealogy has been put together. The family of Joseph derive their descent from a prominent ancestor who is reputed to be "a son", meaning a descendant, of Zerubbabel. In this way, they claim to be of the line of David. So is Abiud this prominent ancestor? We must actually move forward one generation. A Jewish male would always be called X son of Y. For this reason, the relatively obscure Shealtiel appears in both the Matthew and Luke genealogies because his much more famous son was known as Zerubbabel son of Shealtiel. The prominent ancestor must have been the person who comes after Abiud; Eliakim son of Abiud!

This gives the resolution of the mystery. Joachim/Heli/Eliakim is the father of the family, the distant ancestor through whom Mary, Joseph and the brothers of the Lord all derive their claim to be the seed of David. So Mary can be called a daughter of Joachim just as she is a daughter of David. Her real father is Joseph.

Key points

1. Mary was known as the mother in relation to Jesus' birth, and as the Magdalene in relation to his resurrection. The two were originally one; the myth of dying to be reborn is universal in the human mind and found in all cultures. As the literal story of Jesus developed, the birth and resurrection became two separate episodes, and so Mary was split into the characters of the mother and the Magdalene.

2. The Valentinians believed that Mary was not the mother of Jesus in the conventional sense, but the passage or way in which he had entered into the world.

3. Paul tells us that Jesus came of the seed of David "according to the flesh". There are early traditions outside the gospels that Mary was a descendant of David.

4. The Gospel of Mark does not mention Joseph or any other father of Jesus, but only his mother, Mary. This is against all custom for the Jews; a man would be known in relation to his father and not his mother. But as Jesus was spiritual in nature, he did not have a human father.

5. There are genealogies in both the Gospels of Matthew and Luke, but the two are markedly different. Both show the descent of Jesus from David through Joseph. However, Joseph was not supposed to be Jesus' real father!

6. There are features that indicate that the Luke genealogy was invented by the author of Luke. It does not follow Matthew's structure of three groups of fourteen generations, a structure that goes back to the apocalyptic origins of the movement. It also traces the descent from David through Nathan rather than Solomon, which indicates a Gentile origin and which would be explained if the author of Luke has confused Nathan the prophet and Nathan, the son of David.

7. There are seven individuals who appear anachronistically as descendants of Nathan, who could all be considered as relatives of James. This is explained if the author of Luke had a source which was an attempt at compiling a list of the brothers of James from the gospels. This source

must have stated that the brothers were descended from David. The author of Luke has wrongly made these "brothers" distant ancestors of Jesus.

8. The genealogy in Matthew is very unusual because, as well as the list of fathers, it gives the name of four of the mothers. Moreover, all the four women included can be seen as whores. Some see this as a veiled reference to the virtue of the other woman in the genealogy, Mary, and as evidence that Jesus was illegitimate. However, it is better explained as a literal, pedantic expression of Thomas 105, that *"He who shall know father and mother shall be called the son of a whore."* In truth, Thomas 105 is not about Jesus, but the secret adultery of Eve.

9. The Matthew genealogy says that Mary was mother of Jesus, and not that Joseph was his father as we would expect.

10. Although the Matthew genealogy is organised in groups of fourteen generations, the final group contains only thirteen fathers. This is evidence that it was altered when incorporated into Matthew. There are, in fact, fourteen names in total and if Mary were a separate generation from Joseph, the number of generations would be is correct.

11. All the problems with the Matthew genealogy are resolved if Mary is the daughter and not the wife of Joseph. The genealogy would then prove her descent from David through Joseph, and the number of generations would be correct.

12. There is evidence in the gospels for two names by which Mary would have been known in everyday life; Mary of Joses (Joseph) and Mary of James. They indicate that she belonged to the household of each of these men at different times. Joseph was her father, and James was her eldest son (either biological or adopted).

13. The family of Mary derived their claim to be descended from David through their ancestor Eliakim son of Abiud, who was reputed to be a descendant of Zerubbabel. For this reason, the family were known as the sons and daughters of Eliakim. This gave rise to traditions, that circulated under the variants of his name Joachim and Heli, that he was the father of both Mary and Joseph.

Conclusion

Jesus was spiritual and had a "mother", the shaman Mary, but no earthly father. Mary was the daughter of Joseph and through him claimed descent from David. However, when the story of Jesus was literalised it was necessary for Mary to have a husband. The author of Matthew made Joseph that husband because he misunderstood the name "Mary of Joses" to mean that

Mary was married to Joseph. To be consistent, he was forced to change an existing genealogy so that Joseph became the husband rather than the father of Mary, which left the "smoking gun" of a missing generation.

Chapter 19

Did Mary have sons?

At the time of Paul, the Jesus movement was led by a group in Jerusalem called the brethren of the Lord. This group was headed by James, "the brother of the Lord", whom Mary appointed as her successor as leader of the movement. Who were this group and why were they called brothers of Jesus? If they were Mary's sons, were they biological or adopted? And if Mary was not married to Joseph was she married to anyone else?

The brethren of the Lord

Motherhood was very important to Mary and she saw herself as the mother of the movement. She regarded the process of induction, of spiritual baptism, as giving birth to the new elect, with herself as "mother". She was also known as the mother of Jesus as well as his wife, sister and daughter. But there must have been a specific group of men (and possibly women) who were known as her "sons" and it is these who were the brethren of the Lord. We have concluded that James was the next generation from Mary, which means that the brethren must be of the same younger generation. There are two possibilities:

That they are her biological sons
That they are adopted into the role of sons and are probably Mary's nephews or other relations

In the "brother list" in the Luke genealogy, a supposed group of the brethren have been placed as descendants of Eliakim, who is in turn a descendant of David through Nathan. We have concluded that the family of Mary claimed descent from King David through this Eliakim. If the brothers were sons of Mary's brothers, or sons of cousins through the male line, then they would share the same claim as Mary to be descended from David. If, however, they were the biological sons of Mary then they would not inherit this claim of descent from David through their mother. So the information in the Luke genealogy supports the idea that the brothers were adopted rather than biological.

If the brothers are adopted, then they would not all have had the same father, and so they may not all have had this claim of descent from David. We have seen that the brother list is best explained as a list of brothers of James. So the information that they were descended from Eliakim probably related to James and has been applied to the other "brothers" by whoever compiled the list. This evidence points towards James at least being a nephew or cousin of Mary and able to claim descent from David, which would explain why Mary appointed him as leader.

If the sons were adopted, then Mary would either have been barren or an unmarried virgin throughout her life. This would explain the doctrine of the perpetual virginity of the Virgin Mary that was to develop in the second century. This would seem the most unlikely of beliefs because on the evidence of the gospels and the letters of Paul it is clear that Mary did, in fact, have a number of sons. It is possible to argue, relying on the Gospel of John, that the "brothers" were in fact Jesus' cousins and were the sons of Mary of Clopas whom the author of that gospel introduces standing next to the mother of Jesus at the crucifixion. Also, according to the gospels Mary is married to Joseph and although the birth of Jesus may be virginal there is nothing to suggest the two did not have a normal sexual relationship afterwards. Indeed to the Jews this was a moral and legal obligation on both husband and wife. In Matthew it is explicit that they did have such a relationship after the birth of Jesus: "*And he did not know her until she had brought forth her son*" *(Matthew 1:25).*

Given the evidence against the perpetual virginity of Mary, there must have been strong reasons for believing in this virginity. These reasons are not theological as the only important point was that Jesus should be the son of God; there is no reason he should not have earthly brothers. The concept of perpetual virginity would, however, be explained if Mary was believed to be a virgin before the gospels were written, and if there was a tradition that the "sons" of Mary were not real biological sons but younger relations.

Conventionally the idea of the perpetual virginity of the Virgin Mary is seen as arising from the fierce asceticism that developed in the church in the second century. This asceticism is evidenced in the writings of the period, for example in the various apocryphal acts of the apostles. These writings present the ideal of the female convert as renouncing all the evils of her former existence including most especially sexual commerce with her husband or lover. It is difficult to disentangle cause and effect, and if Mary had been a virgin throughout life, then this could have inspired the later asceticism. It is notable that the asceticism is common to both the proto-orthodox and gnostic wings of the church, which is a sign that it goes back to their common origin in the early years of the Jesus movement.

Is there any direct evidence for the brothers being adopted? There is, in fact, a "smoking gun"; the episode in the Gospel of John where Jesus gives his mother an adopted son. And this brings us to another mystery, why does the Gospel of John never name Jesus' mother?

The mother with no name

John is written later than the other gospels and demonstrates knowledge of all three, although its author does not copy any of them in a literal sense. It does not repeat the nativity stories, but that does not mean that its author is not fully aware of the stories! He makes Joseph the supposed father of Je-sus following Matthew/Luke:

The Jews, therefore, were murmuring at him, because he said, "I am the bread that came down out of the heaven." And they said, "Is not this Jesus, the son of Joseph, whose father and mother we have known? How then is it that he says 'I have come down out of heaven'?" (John 6:41-42)

The Jews think that Jesus is the son of Joseph, but he has really "*come down out of heaven*". Behind this we have a tradition that Jesus is not physi-cal but has descended from heaven, a Docetism that dare not speak its name. The author of John tellingly does not repeat the virgin birth suggest-ing he is unhappy with this story. But the thrust of this passage is that Jesus was not born normally of his "father and mother" as the Jews think. But there is something odd about John's account of the family of Jesus. The au-thor of John is familiar with all the other gospels and would know that Je-sus' mother was called Mary. In his own gospel the mother of Jesus is quite prominent and yet he never once gives her name. Why does he not name her as Mary? A clue can be found in his account of the women at the cross:

And there stood by the cross of Jesus his mother, and his mother's sister, Mary of Clopas, and Mary the Magdalene. (John 19:25)

Are there three or four women standing by the cross? It is not clear from the Greek whether Jesus' mother's sister and Mary of Clopas are intended to be the same person or not. Comparing this to the equivalent passage in Mark and Matthew, "his mother's sister" is equivalent to Mary, mother of Joses and James. To have "Mary of Clopas" as a separate person would give the absurdity of four women all called Mary! Moreover, a case can be made for the name Clopas being the same as Alphaeus, which is given in Mark as a name for the father of the disciple James (it will be considered later if Clopas is really the same name as Alphaeus). So Clopas/Alphaeus would be both the husband of Mary and the father of James supporting the idea that Mary of Clopas is identical to Mary, mother of James. So most likely there is one woman called both "Mary of Clopas" and "his mother's sister". She is the same woman called "Mary, mother of Joses and James" in the other gospels and must be the mother of Jesus's "brothers".

It is this single line in John that supports the doctrine of the Catholic Church that James, Joses and the other "brothers" of Jesus were cousins and not true biological brothers. Although it is true that the word for "brothers" can embrace cousins as well as direct brothers, this is not how anyone would interpret the list of Jesus' brothers in Mark were it not for the Gospel of John. And this interpretation is not supported by any of the gospels except John.

It is also only in the Gospel of John that Jesus' mother is explicitly present at the crucifixion. Yet she is implicitly there in the Gospels of Mark or Matthew. Both these gospels have Mary mother of Joses and James by the cross and, in these gospels, this woman is clearly the mother of Jesus. But the author of John breaks the link between the two and makes this woman into Jesus' aunt. So he has not got his tradition of the mother of Jesus being present directly from Mark or Matthew. As well as these two gospels, he must have another source which directly calls her the mother of Jesus, although it is possible that this other source is itself dependent upon Mark or Matthew. Because the tradition has come through two different routes with Mary described in two different ways the author of John has split her into two!

This split raises another question; can two sisters both be called Mary? The traditionalists have their answers of course. The most popular is also the earliest; that Clopas is the brother of Joseph and so Mary, the wife of Clopas, is the sister-in-law of Mary, the wife of Joseph. This is an ingenious explanation, but there is nothing in John to suggest that it is true. And if we read the Gospel of John on its own, rather than in conjunction with the other gospels, there is actually no problem because the mother of Jesus is never called Mary.

Christians today read the gospels as one part of a larger whole, the New Testament. But that was not how they were written! The author of John had no idea that his gospel would come to be presented to Christians alongside that of Matthew, Mark, and Luke. He was writing to supersede the other gospels, and the fact that he was writing a gospel shows that he considered all the others to be inadequate if not outright wrong. The same is true of the other gospel writers; Matthew is intended to replace Mark, which is virtually contained within it and Luke was written in opposition to Matthew. Each author takes pains to make their own gospel internally consistent but never considers consistency with the others.

So John presents a consistent picture as regards the two sisters. One, the wife of Joseph, is the unnamed mother of Jesus. The other sister, called Mary, is married to Clopas and is the mother of the cousins of Jesus. The Mary that the other gospel writers think is Jesus' mother is presented in John as her sister. In the whole of the Gospel of Mark the mother of Jesus is named only once:

Is not this the carpenter, the son of Mary, and brother of James, and Joses, and Judas, and Simon? (Mark 6:3)

This passage is highly problematic since it does not mention the father of Jesus, a feature that would immediately have struck the Jewish author of John as absurd. Neither does it say that this Mary is married to Joseph. So the author of John has come up with an ingenious theory. This woman is Jesus' aunt still living in Nazareth when his mother has moved on. Naturally the inhabitants of Nazareth, when confronted with Jesus, think of him in terms of his aunt Mary and his cousins who are still in their midst. They call Jesus her "son" in the wider sense as there is no separate word for "nephew". This aunt is the same as Mary mother of Joses and James, who appears at the crucifixion. The author of John concludes she must be married to Alphaeus/Clopas from the name "James of Alphaeus", which appears among the disciples in Mark and Matthew. So he includes Mary of Clopas, sister of the mother of Jesus at the foot of the cross. This explains why the author of John represses the name of the mother of Jesus so assiduously - to distance her from his newly created Mary, aunt of Jesus.

The author of John may have had theological reasons for believing that Jesus was an only child. Note in particular a line at the beginning of the gospel:

And the word became flesh, and did dwell among us, and we beheld his glory, glory as of an only begotten of a father, full of grace and truth. (John 1:14)

This was most likely taken by the author of the gospel from another source. Although father here clearly means "heavenly father" the author of the Gospel of John may also have interpreted it in an earthly sense so that Jesus was also "only begotten" as the only son of Joseph. This could be another motivation behind separating the mother of Jesus from "Mary of James and Joses".

The author of John's theory about this aunt of Jesus has confused many Christians down the ages who have sought to make this gospel consistent with the others. The continuation of the women at the foot of the cross is all of a piece with it:

Jesus, therefore, having seen his mother, and the disciple whom he loved standing by, said to his mother, "Woman, look, your son." Then he said to the disciple, " Look your mother" and from that hour the disciple took her to his own. (John 19:26-27)

If we look at the dynamics of this situation we see that shortly before his death Jesus is entrusting his mother to his beloved disciple. This means that the author of John believes:

His mother is husbandless and Joseph is long since dead.
She has no other sons except Jesus.

She is at a point of crisis since her only son is about to die, and she will then have no protector, no male to whose household she can belong. Jesus deals with the situation by giving her an adoptive son. The recent theory that the beloved disciple is really Mary the Magdalene is anachronistic. Our culture is blind to the inescapable relations between the female and the male that have existed throughout human history up until the last century or so. The beloved disciple, as represented in John, has to be a man. Jesus' mother needs a protector and to entrust her to a female would serve no purpose. (This is not to say that traditions derived from the Magdalene have not contributed to the "beloved disciple" as portrayed in John; they probably have. But the gospel writer clearly thinks that the beloved disciple is a man otherwise his narrative would not function.)

So who was the beloved disciple? The Gospel of John claims to be based on traditions received from the beloved disciple (but not written by the disciple himself as is clear from John 21:24). The gospel is traditionally attributed to John, who is regarded as the beloved disciple. And when we look closer at the identity of the "sons" of Mary we shall see that there is indeed evidence for a John who is a son of Mary, and who belonged to the "brethren of the Lord". Moreover, this John is missed out of the list of brothers of Jesus in Mark 6:3 whom the author of John believes are the cousins of Jesus. The evidence points to it being this John whom the author of the fourth gospel thinks is the adoptive son of the mother of Jesus and for whom his gospel was to be named. So we have evidence that there was a least one individual, John, who was known as a "son" of Mary and yet was not her biological son.

Was Mary married?

We have seen that Mary must have been the daughter and not the wife of Joseph. So did Mary ever marry? If we equate Mary with Cephas, then there would appear to be excellent evidence that she was married from the letters of Paul:

My defence to those who examine me in this; have we not power to eat and to drink? Have we not power to lead about a sister, a wife, as well as other apostles, and as the brethren of the Lord, and Cephas? (1 Corinthians 9:3-5)

If Cephas is really Mary, then Paul is meticulous in maintaining her identity. This would quite literally have been a matter of life and death for Mary while she was living in Jerusalem. If it had come to light that she, a woman, was the religious leader of the despised Jesus sect a stoning would have been the inevitable result. When Paul gives a list of those who have the power to lead "a sister a wife" he puts Mary as the supreme embodiment of this principle even though for her it would have been a husband and not a wife. This would have seemed much less odd to the ancients than to us. In situations applying to both males and females it was normal to state the masculine position only - it being implicitly assumed that the equivalent female situation would apply as well. This is similar to the traditional use of the English pronoun "he" to cover both male and female. It is only very recently that people have become conscious of the need to make the female explicit by saying something like "he or she".

So is Paul telling us that Cephas/Mary is married? We shall analyse the Paul passage later and show that this is not what he is saying. If we take the passage in its full context, it becomes clear that Paul is talking spiritually. He is giving a list of the spiritual powers of the apostles, one of which is the ability to have "a sister, a wife" meaning the spiritual twin, a sister-wife for a man and brother-husband for a woman. Paul is is defending his status as an apostle here, so he too must have a spiritual sister-wife even though he is unmarried in the worldly sense.

So this is not evidence that Cephas and hence Mary was married. Instead, we must look in the gospels. The most promising line of attack is by considering the name forms that have survived rather than the gospel writers' interpretations of the relationships between individuals. These name forms are less liable to be changed in the process of converting the spiritual Jesus into a literal man. We have already seen the example of the preservation of the name "Mary of Joses" even though this has been wrongly interpreted as first a son and then a husband. As both wives and sons were known by their husband's name, we should look for any example of both Mary and one of her "sons" being called by the same name.

There is only one such potential occurrence in the Gospels. The name of the woman at the foot of the cross in the Gospel of John is called Mary of Clopas. This Clopas is arguably the same name as Alphaeus in "James son of Alphaeus" given as one of the disciples in Mark. If so then we have evidence for both Mary and James being named in relation to Clopas/Alphaeus, which would be *prima facie* evidence that Mary was married to this man.

If the two are the same name, then they would derive from the Hebrew Cheleph meaning to exchange/to replace. The Aramaic name would have been translated into Greek into the two different forms Alphaeus and Clopas. However, experts are divided as to whether Alphaeus is derived in this way or whether it was a completely different Greek name.[113] Even though we cannot say with certainty on linguistic grounds alone that the two names are identical, it is significant that a respectable case can be made for their equivalence. Intuitively, if the names were not the same, it is unlikely that they would both be linked in the gospels and, at the same time, linked linguistically. We can put a mathematical probability on this using Bayesian inference. This combines the information from the Gospels suggesting that that Alphaeus might be the same person as Clopas with the probability that a potential linguistic link can be found between two random names (this probability has been taken as 1%). Even though both pieces of information, when considered in isolation, are uncertain, the combined probability gives us a higher degree of certainty. The results of this calculation is a 97% chance that the two are the same.[114]

We seem to have found what we have been searching for; evidence that Mary was married to Clopas and that this person was James's father. Moreover, this is collaborated by the writings of Eusebius, the early church historian of the early fourth century. He tells us that James was succeeded as the first "bishop" of Jerusalem by Symeon son of Clopas.[115] A Simon is listed as one of the brothers of Jesus in Mark, so this would appear to be evidence that another of the brethren of Jesus was fathered by Clopas. The source of Eusebius' information is Hegesippus, a writer whose works are now only preserved only in a few fragments, principally quotes made by Eusebius. Hegesippus gives us more information about the brothers saying that Jude had two grandsons who were arrested by Domitian (81-96) for being of the line of David. He also tells us that Symeon was eventually martyred under Trajan (98-117).

So have we found convincing evidence that Mary was married to Clopas? In fact, we will show that there was no such person as Clopas! The whole thing is based on a mistake made by the author of Mark and perpetuated in a sequence of steps made by subsequent writers.

We start with Hegesippus. How reliable an authority is he? There are two problems with taking his evidence at face value. He is writing quite late, in the second half of the second century, about a hundred years after the events he describes. And he is a historical fantasist of the same type as the author of Luke and Acts. This is apparent from the three stories given by Eusebius concerning the Jerusalem family of Jesus.

The first story concerns the martyrdom of James. Hegesippus' account, as related by Eusebius,[116] is a fascinating source of information, but cannot be read as history. In the story James, after preaching from the top of the temple, is cast down by the Jews. Miraculously he survives this ordeal but he is then stoned. It is, of course, absurd that a person would be executed in the temple in such a manner although there is doubtless something behind the story.

The second story is the arrest of the grandsons of Jude (Judas) after someone had informed the Romans that they were of the line of David.[117] The two are brought before the Roman Emperor Domitian who interrogates them and finds that they are just farmers with calluses on their hands. In a point of surprising detail, we are told that their assets are 9000 *denarii* and 39 *plethra* of land. Finding them beneath his notice Domitian releases them, and they later become leaders in the church. The idea of the Roman Emperor personally interviewing some Jewish peasants is another absurdity. However, the information that Judas had two grandsons, who were themselves farmers and leaders of the church and who were arrested and interrogated in the reign of Domitian is not in itself unrealistic. Whether there is any truth in it or not we cannot be sure given the fantastic elements. As for the grandsons being of the line of David, this would have been inferred from the gospels as Judas was regarded as a son of Joseph (or alternatively son of Joseph's brother - see below) whose descent from David is given in Matthew and Luke. But the story of the arrest for being descendants of David is unlikely to be true because after the Jewish rebellion the Romans would not have allowed potential Messiahs to live.

The third story is the martyrdom of Symeon[118] when Trajan was emperor and Atticus consular governor. The absurd element in this story is the age of Symeon which is given as 120! Whoever the "brothers of the Lord" were it is clear that they were contemporaries of Paul and that they were running the church when he was writing his letters in the early 50s. At this time they would have been middle aged. Yet Hegesippus would have us believe that Simon was still active as bishop of Jerusalem some sixty years later! Life was hard in the ancient world, and people grew old much quicker than they do now. The Jews reckoned old age as starting at fifty. Only a few would have survived to sixty by which time a person would have been considered ancient. We can estimate that a younger brother of James might have entered such an ancient age at around the year 70 (this is consistent with the information about the grandsons of Jude given by Hegesippus). It is just not credible that he could still have been active in the reign of Trajan.

So why does Hegesippus repeat this absurdity? He must be fully aware of it himself since he is forced to assign Symeon an age of 120. The only answer is that his source tells him that a Symeon "bishop" of Jerusalem has been martyred under Atticus consular governor. Hegesippus has identified this man with Simon brother of Jesus in Mark, but he is mistaken, for this Simon would have been long since dead. And this in turn raises doubts over whether Symeon really did succeed James to the leadership of the church or whether it is all a case of mistaken identity.

Hegesippus is a credulous individual who elaborates his sources by writing the type of Christian romance "history" typical for his period. But what could his source be for "Symeon son of Clopas and does it go back to a genuine early tradition? We learn from Eusebius that *"Hegesippus records that Clopas was a brother of Joseph"* (Eusebius, *Ecclesiastical History* 3:11:2). This has given rise to the theory of a Levirate marriage between Mary and Clopas. A Levirate marriage occurred when a married man died leaving no son, in which case an unmarried brother would have an obligation to marry his widow and raise any offspring as if they were his dead brother's children. One objection is that Jesus is supposed to be Joseph's son, so the Levirate marriage obligation would not apply. And if Jesus were instead illegitimate, no brother would have considered it honourable to marry Mary!

In any case, the real source of "Symeon of Clopas is staring us in the face. It is none other that the Gospel of John. By the time of Hegesippus, all four gospels were well known and accepted among Christians. The more learned expended a great deal of energy trying to make sense of the obvious contradictions between the four accounts. From the beginning of the second century, Christian scholars were trying to make sense of the relationships between the various members of Jesus's family based on the assumption that all four gospels were correct. This impossible labour has continued to the present day. Hegesippus clearly believed in the cousins theory for the brothers of Jesus. This comes from the line we have already considered at some length:

And there stood by the cross of Jesus his mother, and his mother's sister, Mary of Clopas, and Mary the Magdalene. (John 19:25)

Now we have pointed out how John suppresses the name of the mother of Jesus to remove the obvious contradiction of this line. But the second century Christian, well versed in all the gospels, knows without question that the name is Mary. And as two sisters cannot both be called Mary, the second century Christian is obliged to conclude that Mary of Clopas is the sister in law of Mary, the mother of Jesus. Hence the idea that Clopas must be the brother of Joseph. It is also natural to identify Mary of Clopas with Mary mother of Joses and James who appears at the same place in Mark and Matthew. And so this Mary of Clopas must be the mother of the "brothers of Jesus" in Mark, who include, as well as Joses and James, Simon and Judas. Hence, Simon must be the son of Clopas brother of Joseph. Hegesippus is not writing independently of the gospels, and his account cannot be taken as confirmation of the gospels. Instead, we can see that the gospels are the ultimate source of his information about the "uncle" of Jesus.

To summarise, Hegesippus has information about a Symeon bishop of Jerusalem, who was martyred early in the second century under Trajan. He probably also knows that this person was related to James and wrongly concludes that he was the same Simon who is given as a brother of Jesus in Mark, even though the timing is impossible. Hegesippus thinks this Simon is the son of Clopas either from his own reading of the gospels or from some intermediary source, itself dependent upon the gospels and John 19:25 in particular. So he creates the idea that Symeon son of Clopas succeeded James.

We must discount Hegesippus and turn back to the gospels as our only genuine early source of information on Clopas. Working back in time to the last of the gospels to be written we come to the "Mary of Clopas" in John. The question is whether this is independent of the information in the other gospels and in particular of "James of Alphaeus" in Mark. It would have been very easy for the writer of John to have taken the name from Mark by concluding that Mary of James must have been married to Alphaeus. The copying cannot, however, have been direct because the two gospels use two different Greek forms of the name. But this is all part of the pattern of the Gospel of John which shows familiarity with all the other gospels but never makes a direct literal copy of any of them. The author of John evidently does not have written copies of the other gospels available as he writes, but he has listened to all of them, either through direct readings or indirectly from secondary story telling. If the author of John has taken the name from "James of Alphaeus", then the name must have already been known to him in its original Aramaic or Hebrew and he simply writes it in Greek in a form that he considers preferable to "Alphaeus".

There is some other evidence that the name was in circulation. It may have been familiar to the author of Luke as one of the two disciples on the road to Emmaus is called Cleopas, a name that appears nowhere else. Cleopas is a Greek name, and although it is not the same as Clopas, it sounds very similar. The author of Luke is a Greek-speaking Gentile. If she has heard of a "Clopas", an unfamiliar Jewish name, then she may well have misunderstood it as "Cleopas". Those who see Clopas as the husband of Mary have speculated that Mary herself was the other disciple on the road (conveniently ignoring the question as to why the gospel writer should not tell us such an interesting fact). But we have deduced that the story of the road to Emmaus is a novelistic elaboration derived from the appearance to two disciples walking in the country in the long ending of Mark. The author of Luke does not know the names of the disciples and for the purpose of her story needs two "extras", being followers of Jesus who are not among the twelve. She hits on the name Cleopas for one of these extras. Whether this is derived ultimately from Clopas we cannot be sure.

Key points

1. The group who Paul calls "the brethren of the Lord" and who were headed by James must be either biological or adopted sons of Mary.

2. The inclusion of the "brother list' in the Luke genealogy is evidence that James, at least, was considered to be descended from David. This indicates he was adopted by Mary and was the son of a male relation of Mary.

3. If the sons were adopted this would explain the doctrine of the perpetual virginity of Mary, and the emphasis on chastity that is found in both the proto-orthodox and gnostic wings of the church.

4. The author of John did not believe that "the mother of Jesus" had other children and developed the theory that the Mary mentioned in Mark was really Jesus' aunt. For this reason, he avoids naming the mother of Jesus as Mary.

5. At the crucifixion in John, Jesus makes the beloved disciple the adopted son of his mother. This is evidence that the beloved disciple, John, was an adopted son of Mary.

6. Looking at name forms, we find one candidate for a husband of Mary. In John we have the name "Mary of Clopas" and in Mark, "James son of Alphaeus". It is likely that Clopas and Alphaeus are the same name and are derived from the Hebrew word *cheleph* meaning to exchange or to replace. If so, then this may suggest that Mary was married to Clopas/Alphaeus and that James was their son.

7. Hegesippus, writing in the later half of the second century, says that a Symeon son of Clopas succeeded James as leader of the Jerusalem church and was martyred in the time of Trajan. As a Simon is included among the brethren, this might be seen as supporting the idea that the brothers are the sons of Clopas. However, Hegesippus must have confused two different Simons. The Simon who was the brother of James and who worked alongside him in Jerusalem, could not have still been active in the reign of Trajan some fifty years later, as is demonstrated by the impossible age Hegesippus gives him of 120.

8. Hegesippus also says that Clopas was a brother of Joseph. However the idea that Clopas was brother to Joseph was an obvious way to make the account of the women at the crucifixion in the Gospel of John consistent to the other gospels.

Conclusion

There is some evidence that the brothers were adopted by Mary and were sons of male relations. The most plausible candidate for a husband of Mary is Clopas/Alphaeus. However, the evidence from Hegesippus that apparently supports this relationship cannot be regarded as independent from the gospels.

Chapter 20

The calling of Matthew

So was Mary married to Alphaeus/Clopas and was he the father of the brethren of the Lord? There is a further clue to consider; James is not the only disciple to be called a son of Alphaeus. In Mark, we have a story about Jesus' recruitment of a tax collector called "Levi of Alphaeus" as one of his disciples. The same story appears in the Gospel of Matthew, but there the disciple's name is changed to Matthew. By making this change, the author of Matthew is trying to correct a problem with the story in Mark; although Levi is called as a disciple by Jesus, his name is missing from the list of the twelve disciples. It is this clue that will help us to unravel the true meaning of "Levi of Alphaeus" and to show that there was no such person as Alphaeus.

Whom does Jesus call from the tax office?

The story of the calling of Matthew from the tax office is recounted in the Gospel of Matthew:

And Jesus passing by saw a man sitting at the tax-office, named Matthew, and said to him, "Follow me." And he arose and followed him. (Matthew 9:9)

The story is short but powerful. Matthew is a tax collector for the Romans. He would be despised by his fellow Jews, the type of person that people would hate so much that they would spit on the ground as he walked past. Yet Jesus ignoring all convention calls this one as a disciple. He summons him out of the dark tax-office and into the light. Matthew, despite his money-grabbing past, responds to the call and simply follows.

The story has become archetypal and has reverberated with millions of Christians down the ages who have seen themselves as being called from their equivalent of Matthew's tax office. In Caravaggio's famous painting "The calling of St Matthew" the Christ figure, half hidden in darkness, points dramatically at the surprised Matthew, who responds with a questioning finger at his own breast - clearly saying "you are calling me?"

It is generally accepted that this story has given the Gospel of Matthew its name. Apart from this one brief episode, Matthew plays no part in the gospels or Acts other than being included in the list of the disciples. Because Matthew is the subject of the story in this gospel, the idea came about that the gospel was written by Matthew. It is all the more surprising then to find that the earliest version of the tax-office story does not even mention Matthew. The same story appears in Mark, but now the tax gatherer is called Levi:

And passing by, he saw Levi of Alphaeus sitting at the tax-office, and said to him, "Follow me." And he arose and followed him. (Mark 2:14)

Luke also has Levi in his version of the story showing that Levi was in his copy of Mark. For some reason, the author of Matthew has changed Levi to Matthew. Why?

The traditionalist will answer that Levi must be another name for Matthew. In support, they will point out that the list of disciples in Mark does not contain a Levi but does have Matthew. Since Levi clearly should be one of the twelve, this shows that the Gospel of Mark has him down under his other name of Matthew.

This argument belongs to the approach that attempts to make one consistent picture out of all the gospels. But such consistency was not in the minds of the gospel writers as they were writing. When the author of Matthew incorporates Mark into his own gospel, he was attempting to replace that earlier, and in his eyes, imperfect production. So if he spots a problem with the story being about Levi, then he simply replaces Levi with another obscure disciple.

There are a number of reasons why we can rule out Matthew being the same disciple as Levi:

1. There is no reason the disciple should be known by two perfectly good Jewish names such as Matthew and Levi. Neither name is a nickname, nor is it the case that one is Greek and the other Aramaic.

2. If the author of Matthew thinks that Matthew and Levi are the same person why does he not tell us this? As he is copying Mark, which uses Levi in the story, it would be natural to write something like "Matthew, called Levi" but instead he removes all mention of Levi.

3. In a telling detail, the Gospel of Matthew suppresses the "of Alphaeus" used to describe Levi. As a result there is no connection in the gospel between Matthew and Alphaeus. If the author of Matthew thinks that Levi and Matthew are one and the same why should he remove the name of his father?

4. Why does the Gospel of Mark not tell us that Matthew and Levi are the same? If they are identical, then the failure to communicate this to the reader gives rise to a fundamental problem with the narrative of that gospel.

The root of this problem lies in the Gospel of Mark. The author of Matthew's approach is to be loyal to Mark except where there is a difficulty with the earlier gospel. The substitution of Matthew for Levi must be intended to fix the narrative and link the story of the calling of the disciple to the list of disciples. In reality, the author of Matthew knows nothing about either Matthew or Levi and gives us no new stories about either. Matthew as tax collector is a red herring.

The mystery of Levi of Alphaeus

Everything about the story of the calling of Levi in Mark leads us to believe that he is one of the twelve. Jesus first calls from their fishing boats the brothers Simon and Andrew, and then James and John. In each case, the disciples immediately follow Jesus. The story of Levi occurs shortly afterward and fits the same pattern of a call by Jesus with the disciple responding by immediately following Jesus. These callings all precede the appointment of the twelve by Jesus, at which time they are named. But when the twelve are listed there is no Levi among their number! There is a son of Alphaeus, but this is James, not Levi. The omission of Levi spoils the pattern of the calling and then the appointment of the disciples. The reader is left wondering why he is left out. Had Levi changed his mind and gone back to tax collecting? This deficiency was clearly felt in the first century otherwise the author of Matthew would not have substituted Matthew for Levi and made Matthew a tax collector in his list of the disciples.

Not only is Levi missing from the list of the disciples, he is also missing from the list of the brothers of Jesus. We have seen that there is a high probability that Clopas is the same name as Alphaeus, which builds the case for Alphaeus being the father of the "brothers" of Jesus. Yet Levi is not included in Mark's list of the brothers nor is there any tradition of Levi being a brother of the Lord. And nowhere do we find any indication that Mary is his mother.

Yet on the evidence of Mark, Levi of Alphaeus and James of Alphaeus must be brothers; the name Alphaeus is a rare one and could hardly have applied to the fathers of two disciples by chance. So why has Levi disappeared from both the disciples and the brothers?

There is one explanation that answers both questions. The Gospel of Mark must have been revised after its original composition to remove Levi as a disciple. The change must have happened very early because it is in all surviving copies of the gospel and the versions known to both the authors of Matthew and Luke. It was probably made by the same group from which the gospel first appeared. The nature of the change is indicated by the fact that a "son of Alphaeus" appears in the list of the disciples even though Levi is missing. We know that Levi son of Alphaeus must have originally been a disciple. So the "son of Alphaeus" in the list of disciples indicates where his name must have originally appeared. In the first version of Mark, it would have read "Levi son of Alphaeus" and not "James son of Alphaeus"! Someone has replaced Levi by James.

This explains why there is no Levi in the brothers of Jesus; the name "James of Alphaeus has arisen by a mistake. James and Levi were not related. If the name has been changed, why has "of Alphaeus" remained attached to James? Presumably because the persons making the correction thought that James may have been the same person as Levi. This is the same type of thinking that has led Christians traditionally to believe that Matthew and Levi are the same; they both appear in the same place in different versions of the same material. Whoever made the alteration is familiar with an established list of the twelve in which James appears in the place where the Gospel of Mark originally had "Levi of Alphaeus". The same list would have been the original source for Mark's list of the twelve. The author of Mark has edited this list by replacing the second occurrence of the name James (James of Zebedee has already been included) by "Levi of Alphaeus". Some of his early readers are familiar with the original list and conclude that the second James and Levi must be the same person. They naturally give precedence to the version that is well known to them, and "correct" the newly written gospel, as it is being copied, writing back

James into the list. They have no problem with Levi in the story of the tax-office because they do not know this story from any other source. But by changing the name in one place and not the other they leave the telltale evidence for their revision.

Whether or not it happened in exactly this way, it is clear that someone has changed Levi into James because they were not happy with Levi as a member of the twelve. But if "James of Alphaeus" has arisen by a mistake it must follow that Mary had no connection with Alphaeus/Clopas and that "Mary of Clopas" must have been derived by the author of John from the "James of Alphaeus" in Mark.

We will verify this explanation by showing that "Levi of Alphaeus" was definitely made up by the author of Mark and that there was neither a Levi nor a Clopas.

The real Levi of Alphaeus

The author of Mark knows absolutely nothing about most of the disciples. Any scraps that he can find about them must have been very precious. One such scrap is the story of the calling of four of the disciples from their fishing boats. These four are two sets of two brothers. The repetition in the calling of two brothers from their fishing boats is a clue that an original story has been doubled up; we may doubt that the original had anything to do with Simon, Andrew, James, or John or any other supposed Galilean fishermen. Such is the meagre information about the disciples available to the author of Mark. Being able to add the dramatic story of the calling of the tax collector Levi must have held great appeal to him, so much so that he is ready to write Levi into his list of the twelve. But has the author of Mark understood his source?

The answers lie in the name "Levi of Alphaeus". Consider first the name Levi which was a common name but to any Jew would have signified the priestly establishment, the sons of Levi. It was the tribe of Levi that had the right to officiate in the temple and to receive payment for their services. The appearance of Levi in the story raises the suspicion that it may have been intended to symbolise the priesthood rather than an individual.

We have seen that with high probability the name Alphaeus is identical to Clopas, in which case both names must have been derived from *cheleph/chalaph*.[119] This is a Hebrew word meaning to exchange or to replace. Those favouring the theory of the Levite marriage see it as a nickname meaning "replacer" because the bearer of the name has replaced his brother Joseph as husband of Mary.[120] But can we find a connection between *cheleph/chalaph* and Levi? The noun *cheleph* occurs only twice in the Old Testament, although the verb *chalaph* is more frequent. Both the occurrences of *cheleph* relate to the tribe of Levi:

> *And behold, I have given the sons of Levi all the tithe in Israel for an inheritance, in return [cheleph] for their service which they perform, the service of the tent of meeting (Numbers 18:21).*

And concerning the tithe made to the sons of Levi:

> *You may eat it anywhere, you and your households, for it is your compensation in return [cheleph] for your service in the tent of meeting (Numbers 18:31)*

These passages are the authority establishing the right of the "sons of Levi" to receive the tithe being the tenth of all the agricultural output and the rights to the firstborn of the flocks. They were to officiate at the tabernacle that was placed in their care and protection. It is from the Levites that the priesthood was derived. Later the tabernacle was superseded by the temple, becoming incorporated into Solomon's temple. The Levites retained the responsibility to serve in the temple, and it was from their number that the temple priests were recruited.

It is the above passages that establish the right of the priestly class, the sons of Levi, to be supported by means of a tithe or tax on all other Jews. Returning to the story of Levi in Mark, we can find three independent connections with the above passages from Numbers:

The two sources are linked by the word *cheleph* which is used in one case to describe the right to the tithe and in the other case is a potential source of the name Alphaeus.

Both sources have "Levi" as the subject - in one case Levi is the tribe and in the other case he is a disciple.

In both sources "Levi" is involved in collecting tax; in one case the tribe is given the right to collect the temple tax, in the other Levi is a tax collector.

Let us look again at the story in Mark. It is very short, taking no more than a line. Levi is sitting in a building, a tax office, and Jesus asks him to leave, "to follow me". The word used for tax-office means a place to collect customs, taxes or tolls. It fits in with Mark's story that Levi is collecting tax for the Romans and cannot be part of Mark's source if this did concern the priesthood. We can tentatively reconstruct this source by using the criterion that it must be capable of giving rise to the story of the disciple Levi by being misconstrued by the author of Mark, while at the same time being consistent with Levi as the priesthood and the tax being the tithe rights for temple service. The suggested reconstruction is that the source was something like this:

Jesus said "Levi of the exchange [cheleph] shall leave this house and collect the tax no more." [Reconstruction of the source behind Mark 2:14]

"House" is a common way of referring to the temple and *cheleph* must have been an expression derived from Numbers 18:21 and 18:24 to describe the rights of the tribe of Levi to collect the tax in exchange for their services in the temple. The author of Mark confuses it with a person's name and translates it as Alphaeus. The original source in Aramaic, although now lost, must have continued in circulation so that the Hebrew form of the name was familiar to the author of John who retranslates it into Greek as Clopas. We can now summarise the sequence of events that must have taken place:

1. We start with a story about Jesus evicting the priesthood, Levi, from their rights (cheleph) to collect the temple tax.

2. This is misunderstood by the author of Mark as the recruitment of a disciple Levi of Alphaeus (cheleph) from a tax office. He writes in this new disciple "Levi of Alphaeus" to an existing list of the Twelve by replacing the second occurrence of the name James.

3. The first copyists of Mark are very familiar with the existing list of the Twelve, and spot the change that the author of Mark has made. So they reinstate the second James into his rightful place in the list. They assume that Levi must be another name for James, and so they leave the "of Alphaeus" put in by the author of Mark.

4. The author of Matthew is concerned about the inconsistency between the story of the recruitment of Levi as a disciple and the non-inclusion of Levi in the list of disciples. He solves this by changing the tax office story to be about another disciple, Matthew.

5. The author of John believes that the brothers of Jesus are not biological brothers and seizes upon "James of Alphaeus" as the confirmation of this. He uses the name Clopas (*cheleph*) to describe the mother of this James

as Mary of Clopas. This name form must have originated in an Aramaic context from *cheleph* rather than taken directly from the Greek Alphaeus used in Mark and probably goes back to the original source.

6. The same source was available to the author of Luke, who confuses the name Clopas with the similar Greek name Cleopas.

The above chain of circumstance has been deduced as the only way of explaining the evidence of Levi, Alphaeus and Clopas in the gospels. We have been led to a radical reappraisal of the story of Levi and have reconstructed the source behind it. This source has proved to be revolutionary; it speaks of the expulsion of the priesthood from the temple and the repudiation of their rights to the tithe or tax. This is a direct challenge to the powerful Jewish establishment and shows how dangerous and subversive the Jesus movement would have appeared to this establishment. The test of any theory is whether it brings about insights beyond the problems that the theory was intended to explain. We have sought to explain Mary of Clopas and the disappearing disciple Levi, and we have ended up with a challenge to the very existence of the Jewish priesthood. The question now is whether this insight is confirmed by other material. Does it help us to understand anything that was not previously understood?

In the Gospel of Mark when Jesus is brought before the chief priest certain false witnesses testify against him claiming that Jesus said:

I will destroy this temple made with hands, and within three days another not made with hands I will build. (Mark 14:58)

This saying predicts that Jesus himself would destroy the temple! The author of Mark is understandably uncomfortable with this and includes the saying as an accusation made against Jesus. But confirmation comes in the Gospel of Thomas which has another variant of the same saying without "the three days":

Jesus said: "I will des[troy this] house, and none shall able to build it [again]." (Thomas 71)

The temple was referred to as the "house" so here we have a straightforward prediction that Jesus will destroy the temple. The Jesus movement is a spiritual religion. Such a religion has no need of temples made with stone or other places of worship. In the past, God has dwelled within the sanctuary of the temple. Now he is to dwell within the chosen. As Paul asks the Corinthians: *"do you not know that you are a sanctuary of God, and that the Spirit of God does dwell within you?"* *(1 Corinthians 3:16).*

The full meaning of the destruction of the temple will become apparent later. But we can see how consistent all this is with Levi of Cheleph being evicted from the rights to the temple tithe. If the sanctuary is now within, there is no need of priests and no justification for them to be supported by the hard work of the people. The priesthood and their taxes are obsolete.

The most spectacular instance of Jesus opposing the priestly establishment comes with the story of Jesus casting out the money-changers. The Gospel of John adds some fine novelistic detail and has Jesus first making a *"whip of small cords"* *(John 2:15).* The earlier version in Mark is more prosaic but just as revolutionary:

And they came to Jerusalem and Jesus having gone into the temple, began to cast out those selling and buying in the temple, and the tables of the money-changers and the seats of those selling the doves, he overthrew, and he did not allow any to bear a vessel through the temple. And he taught them saying to them, "Has it not been written - My house shall be called a house of prayer for all the nations? But you have made it a den of robbers." (Mark 11:15-17)

The traditional interpretation was that the temple has been corrupted by commerce and that Jesus wants to return the house of his father to its proper purpose. However, this is to misunderstand the actual workings of the temple. Those "selling and buying" were not engaging in unfettered commerce but were selling the sheep and oxen that were the offerings for the sacrifice. Similarly, the doves were a poor persons offering. These sellers were required so that the temple could function; if there were no sellers, there would be no offerings to Yahweh. They were, and always had been, an integral part of the temple operations. So why should Jesus be so angry with them?

The most telling class is the "moneychangers". These people were engaged in collecting the half-shekel temple tax that was obligatory for every Jew, an operation that would often involve money changing to give the correct coin. Again they are part of the temple function; they are the tax collectors necessary for the temple operation and doubtless as unpopular as tax collectors always are.

We have reconstructed the source of the Levi story as being about the expulsion of the priesthood from the temple and their rights to collect taxes in return for temple service. Here we have another story in which Jesus evicts tax collectors from the temple! The two are saying essentially the same thing; the taxes for the maintenance of the temple and the priesthood will no longer be paid. The author of Mark must actually have had two separate sources for his story of the moneychangers. One of these sources was a Deep Source sequence about the coming of Jesus to the shaman and the expulsion of the demons within. The other source is a variant of the Levi story about the expulsion of tax collectors from the temple.

We have seen that other sayings and stories in Mark and Thomas are entirely consistent with the reconstructed source being about the eviction of the priesthood from the temple. We would not expect such a close agreement if the interpretation of Levi of Alphaeus standing for the priesthood's right to collect taxes is not correct. It follows that there was never such a disciple as Levi nor such a person as Alphaeus/Clopas.

Key points

1. There are multiple problems with the story of the calling of Levi/Matthew from the tax office in Mark and Matthew.

2. In Mark, although Levi is called as a disciple he is then omitted from the list of the disciples.

3. The author of Matthew is aware of this problem because he switches Levi to Matthew. Although a person could have both a Jewish and Greek name, this cannot be the case here because Levi and Matthew are both Jewish names.

4. In Mark, Levi is called Levi of Alphaeus and there is also a James of Alphaeus in the list of disciples. This would imply that Levi and James are brothers, but there is no other evidence for this relationship and Levi is never included among the brethren of the Lord.

5. If Alphaeus is the same name as Clopas, then it is derived from *cheleph* meaning to exchange. Although *cheleph* is a rare word in the Old Testament, we find it in Numbers in a passage that gives the sons of Levi the right to the tithe in exchange for their service in the tent of meeting. This is the scriptural basis for the right of the tribe of Levi, the priests, to receive the temple tax.

6. In the original source, Jesus is not calling a disciple called Levi. He is expelling the priests from the temple and forbidding them the right to collect the temple tax.

7. The author of Mark has confused an expression for the right to collect the tax, something like "Levi of the exchange", as meaning that Levi was the son of Alphaeus.

8. The author of Mark has created the disciple Levi through this misunderstanding. He has put Levi of Alphaeus into his list of the twelve by replacing a second occurrence of the name James. Early copyists of the gospel did not accept this innovation and restored James to his rightful place in the list keeping the title "of Alphaeus".

9. The author of John has then picked up on "James of Alphaeus" in Mark to create the name "Mary of Clopas" for the mother of James.

Conclusion

There was no such person as Alphaeus/Clopas. He is a fiction and Mary could not have been married to him. The original saying behind the Levi story recorded that the priests were to leave the temple and give up their right to the exchange, the temple tax. This is consistent with other sayings and shows the revolutionary nature of the Jesus movement.

Chapter 21

The two requests of Salome

Our last candidate for a husband for Mary is Zebedee. Were the sons of
Zebedee the sons of Mary? And why do we have a link between the mother
of the sons of Zebedee and Salome? With the insight that Mary is the
shaman and founder of the movement, we can look afresh at a request for
the sons of Zebedee to sit on the right and left sides of Jesus. Is this telling
us something very important about the organisation of the early Jesus
movement? Most strange of all, we will see connections with a very different story, in which Salome, daughter of Herodias, performs a dance for
Herod that so inflames him with lust that he grants her request for the head
of John the Baptist. Has this dance any basis in fact or is it a misunderstanding?

Salome, the mother of the sons of Zebedee

We have eliminated Alphaeus/Clopas as a husband of Mary. There is one
other candidate, and that is Zebedee, the father of James and John. When
the two disciples are called from their fishing boats in Mark, they are
named as "*James of Zebedee and his brother John*" (*Mark 1:19*). Later, they are
included in the list of the disciples:

*And he gave Simon the name Peter; and James of Zebedee, and John the brother
of James, and to them he gave the names Boanerges, which means "Sons of thunder". (Mark 3:16)*

Traditionally, James of Zebedee is not regarded as the same as James,
the brother of the Lord. After all, if Jesus were really a man he would not
recruit his own brother in this way! However, under the shaman paradigm,

the list of disciples is a confused memory of the prominent early members of the movement. This view is supported by a coincidence in names. The first three individuals named in the Mark list have the same names as the three leaders of the movement whom Paul meets when he makes his second visit to Jerusalem in the early 50s. This implies that James, the brother of the Lord, is the same as the person included in the disciple list as James of Zebedee.

The author of Mark is not giving us the original Twelve because their identities had long been forgotten. His list starts with those who were leading the movement during the first great expansion in the 40s and 50s. One ambiguity is that the three names actually stand for four people, because the author of Mark thinks Cephas and Simon Peter are the same person. So Peter comes first because he represents the first leader Cephas. The second person listed is James, who is the second leader of the movement. The third person in the triumvirate is John the brother of James, who is also a son of Zebedee. We shall see that Cephas/Mary, James, and John were regarded as the three who had been divinely appointed to lead the movement. There is a Simon included in the list of brothers in Mark, and we can equate him to the apostle whom Paul calls Peter. So Simon Peter is also a brother of the Lord. It is becoming clear that the brothers were a leadership group under Mary/Cephas. The brothers were not all equal with James and John given preference over the others.

So we have evidence that two of the brethren of the Lord were known as sons of Zebedee. An objection might be that John does not appear in the list of the brothers of Jesus in Mark. But we know this list is imperfect because it includes Joses, who the author of Mark mistakes for a son of Mary rather than her father. This shows that the list has been put together by the author of Mark based on his imperfect understanding and does not reflect a source that goes back to the early movement. We will find ample evidence that John was, in fact, one of the brothers.

If two of the brothers were "sons of Zebedee" was Mary married to Zebedee? We find another clue in Matthew, where the mother of the sons is included among the women who look upon the crucifixion:

Mary the Magdalene, and Mary the mother of James and of Joses, and the mother of the sons of Zebedee. (Matthew 27:56)

The parallel passage in Mark has "*Mary the Magdalene, and Mary the mother of James the less and of Joses, and Salome*" (Mark 15:40). So Salome has been replaced in Matthew by "the mother of the sons of Zebedee". The author of Matthew clearly thinks that the "the mother of the sons of Zebedee" is called Salome. We know that the mother of the brethren is Mary, so this implies that Salome is another name for Mary. It was common for Jews at the time to have both an Aramaic and Greek name, so it is quite possible that Mary used the name Salome in Greek. However, "Mary" was soon translated directly into Greek, so that "Salome" became redundant. We shall see that Salome also has a religious meaning, in that it refers to Mary's mystical role as the new Jerusalem.

With the exception of Salome, all the names found in conjunction with the crucifixion and resurrection in Mark, belong to the shaman; Mary the Magdalene, Mary of Joses and Mary of James. Under the shaman paradigm, this makes sense because the crucifixion and resurrection are spiritual events that were first witnessed by the shaman alone. If Salome is also a name for Mary, then the one exception is removed.

Further evidence that the "mother" of James and John was Mary is found in Acts in the story of Peter's escape from prison. This is prefaced by an introduction about the death of *"James, the brother of John"* (Acts 12:1-2). After his escape from prison, Peter goes to the house of Mary *"the mother of John who is called Mark"* (Acts 12:12). The origins of this story are a mystic account of the ascent of Mary/Cephas to heaven. The Mary in this story is the founder, and she must have been known as the "mother" of both James and John, who was also called Mark. This is consistent with the Gospel of John where Jesus appoints the beloved disciple (John) as the adoptive son of his mother. The evidence points to John Mark being the favourite son of Mary, the one whom she kept constantly by her side.

There is one further story about the sons of Zebedee in Mark. They beg a favour of Jesus: *"Grant to us that we may sit, one on thy right hand, and the other on thy left hand, in your glory"* (Mark 10:37). Jesus replies that they may share in his baptism, but the left and right places are not his to give. The other disciples are indignant at this request of James and John, but Jesus replies: *"whoever would be great among you, shall be your servant, and whoever would be first shall be slave of all"* (Mark 10:43-44). Matthew repeats this story closely but with the variation that it is *"mother of Zebedee's sons with her sons"* (Matthew 20:20) who comes to Jesus to make the request. Why should the author of Matthew make this change? Could it be that he was embarrassed by this request and so makes it come from their mother, the weak female? This cannot be the reason because it is clear from the story that James and John are behind the request. Asking their mother to make the request makes them look childish as if they are afraid to ask for themselves. The Matthew version is more embarrassing than the Mark version, not less.

Using the criterion of embarrassment, we would expect the Matthew version to be original. It is the author of Mark who alters the source out of embarrassment. James and John are supposedly two grown men, disciples who Jesus has appointed to the twelve and who have been following Jesus in all his travels. How can they ask their *mother* to make this request for them? It is instructive to compare the two versions:

And James and John, the sons of Zebedee, come to him, saying, "Master, we desire that whatever we may ask you should do for us." And he said to them, "What do you desire me to do for you?" They said to him, "Grant to us that one of us might sit at your right hand and one at your left hand in your glory." (Mark 10:35-37)

Then came to him the mother of the sons of Zebedee with her sons, kneeling down and asking something of him. And he said to her, "What do you desire?" She said to him, "Say that these two sons of mine may sit, the one on your right hand, and the other on you left, in your kingdom." (Matthew 20:20-21)

The two accounts are very similar, with an initial request that a petition is granted, Jesus asking what is wanted, and then the request that the two brothers sit on the right and the left. Matthew uses the convoluted expression "*mother of the sons of Zebedee and her sons*" to describe the persons making the request whereas Mark has the simpler "*James and John the sons of Zebedee*". Both have the same phrase, "*the sons of Zebedee*" which must have been in the original. We can deduce that the original had "*the mother of the sons of Zebedee*".

That this request should come from the mother caused problems when the story was literalised. In the literal story, James and John are disciples, intimate companions of Jesus, who have left their father Zebedee far behind.[121] Their mother should not even be with them, yet alone be the one making the request. So the author of Mark changes the story to remove their mother. The author of Matthew has the original source and puts the mother back in while keeping the sons from Mark. He ends up with the clumsy expression "*mother of the sons of Zebedee and her sons*".

Under the spiritual paradigm, we can understand completely why the request has to be made through the mother. It is she, the shaman, who is in communication with Jesus. The purpose of the request is to confirm James and John in the two highest positions in the movement. James will sit on the right, the place of honour, as the leader, and John will sit on the left and be second in authority. This is consistent with the appointment of James as the leader in Thomas 12: "*you shall go to James the Just for whom the heaven and earth came into being.*" In the Mark story, the request is refused but in the original it must have been granted otherwise there would be no point to the saying. The version in Mark reads oddly with James and John asking Jesus to promise "*that whatever we may ask you will do for us*". The author of Matthew is always sensitive to problems in Mark and his version tones this down so as to seem less absurd.

The original would have been a petition formula in which Mary asks of Jesus, in his role of divine king, to grant her request. The purpose of the original saying would be to confirm the request by stamping it with Jesus' approval. It would seem that this appointment of James and John caused considerable dissent in the movement. In the Mark story, the other disciples are upset with the two.[122] We know that Paul was furious with Mary/Cephas at the appointment of James, and there is also evidence that he had a major argument with her about John Mark. Indeed, the preference that she showed to John may have been even more controversial than her advancement of James as leader; John was her special favourite who lived with her and accompanied her everywhere, and there may have been some who suspected that he was her lover.

The strategy for dealing with this controversy is given in the continuation of the Mark story: "*Whoever would be great (megas) among you shall be your servant, and whoever would be first shall be slave of all*" (Mark 10:43-44). This is Mary's philosophy that a leader should not lord it over his or her followers but should be a humble servant. James would seem to have understood this strategy for one of his titles is "*James the least (mikrou)*".[123] We often find *mikrou* paired as a contrasting opposite of *megas*, "great", as in "small and great".[124] So "James the least" is a veiled reference to his position as leader of the movement.

If Mary's two favourite "sons", James and John, were both known as sons of Zebedee, does this mean that Mary was married to Zebedee? If so, she would have been known as "Mary of Zebedee" but we never find this name, not even once. The Gospel of Matthew uses the clumsy "mother of the sons of Zebedee" rather than "Mary of Zebedee" or "Salome of Zebedee". It would be surprising that she is never called by her husband's name if Zebedee were her husband. There is also the evidence from the Gospel of John that the beloved disciple, John, is Mary's adopted son and that she is not his true mother.

Most likely, Zebedee is Mary's brother, which would explain her personal preference for his sons. It would also make James and John grandsons of Joseph and hence descendants of David. This would provide a strong religious reason for making James the leader even while Mary was still alive. The fact that Mary could make the claim to be descended from David shows that she must have been born into a leading family in her religious group. This gave her credibility; the movement was able to claim that Jesus was from the line of David, according to the flesh, through Mary. But the fact that she was a woman would have caused many Jewish followers disquiet. In contrast James, the eldest son of Zebedee, son of Joseph would have an exemplary claim to be the leader. We can only assume that Zebedee himself was not available to lead the movement, either because he was dead at this time or because he was not a follower of his sister.

If James and John were descended from David it would be fitting that they should take the left and right hand positions. However in the Mark story the request was refused. Can we be sure that Jesus did grant Mary's request in the original saying? We can because the author of Mark has unwittingly incorporated the story not just once but twice within his gospel. It is time to look at the other version of the request, a story which appears so different that few would link it to the request about James and John.

The dance of Salome and the head of John

The lurid story of the dance of Salome and the beheading of John the Baptist is well known. John had been imprisoned for speaking out about the marriage of Herod to Herodias, the wife of his brother. The Gospel of Mark[125] tells us that Herodias wanted John killed, but Herod refused as he liked to listen to John. Herodias bided her time until her opportunity came at a dinner party to mark Herod's birthday. At the party, Salome, her daughter from her previous marriage, danced for Herod and his guests. Her dancing must have been good, for Herod was so pleased that he made her the extravagant promise that she could have whatever she wanted up to half his kingdom. The girl asked her mother what to request and she told her to ask for the head of John. So Salome requested the head of John the Baptist on a platter. Herod was shocked, but he had made a royal promise in front of his guests, and he felt he had to keep it. He ordered the executioner to behead John and bring his head on a platter that was then presented to Salome.

Salome has become the archetypal femme fatale, a woman whose sexual attraction and power over the male brings death in its wake. The story was popularised by Oscar Wilde's play Salome and the subsequent opera of the same name. In these entertainments, Salome's dance became the dance of the seven veils, a striptease. In reality, there is no way that a Jewish princess would have performed an erotic dance at a public event. In Mark, it is simply described as a dance that pleased Herod.[126]

In the story in Mark, the dancing girl is not even named, but just called Herodias' daughter. We know this daughter was called Salome from Josephus in whose writings we can also find an independent account of the death of John.[127] Josephus says that the reason for the execution was the popularity of John and that Herod had him taken to the fortress of Machaerus where he was put to death. There is no mention of Salome or dancing, and the execution appears to be a cold-blooded political calculation on the part of Herod. If the salacious story of the dancing of Salome were really true then why did Josephus not remark on it?

In fact, there is much about the Mark story that is unbelievable. It is incomprehensible that Herod would offer Salome whatever she wanted, up to half his kingdom, for a mere dance. And would he really have felt obliged to honour a request for the head of John? But the thing that is most wrong about the story is Salome herself.

In broad outline, the story in Mark is consistent with what we can deduce to have really happened from Josephus. We know that Herod did have an incestuous obsession for a woman to whom he offered half his kingdom. This relationship caused Herod enormous political problems, including a war, and resulted in the beheading of John the Baptist. But the woman who caused all this was not Salome but her mother, Herodias. Josephus tells us that Herod the tetrarch was journeying to Rome when he stayed with his half-brother, also confusingly called Herod.[128] It was on this visit that he fell in love with Herodias, his brother's wife. He persuaded her to a secret agreement in which she would divorce his brother and marry him. But first he would have to divorce his own wife, the daughter of King Aretas, on his return from Rome. His wife, however, got wind of the agreement and flew to her father who soon made war on Herod. In this war, Herod's army was destroyed by Aretas' forces, which the Jews said was divine vengeance for the execution of John.

If we remove Salome from the story in Mark, then it begins to make sense. In any case, it is likely that Salome was married, with her own household and court, at the time she was supposed to be dancing for Herod. Josephus says she was married to Philip the Tetrarch, who died in 64. As a widow, she went on to marry Aristobulus and have three sons by him. We actually know nothing disreputable about her.[129]

So how did the story in Mark arise? We must start with a source about the dancing of a woman that results in Herod making her an extravagant offer leading to the death of John the Baptist. In the original this woman was Herodias. Herod offered her "half his kingdom" because if she became his wife she would share his kingdom. Herodias agreed, setting into motion a train of events that was to lead eventually to the beheading of John. Herod's marriage to his brother's wife brought upon him widespread religious condemnation including the opposition of John the Baptist. The account of Josephus makes clear that Herod's execution of John was a calculated act made out of fear of John's immense popularity. But the reason Herod had cause to fear that popularity was his incestuous marriage with Herodias.

When a man acts as foolishly as Herod did for Herodias, it was normal in the ancient world to attribute this to the seductive powers of the woman as much as the unbridled lust of the man. So it is easy to see how the story that Herodias inflamed Herod by dancing for him would have been so popular. It is possible that Herodias did dance at a party held in honour of Herod when he was staying with his brother on the way to Rome, and that it was her dancing that sparked Herod's infatuation. The occasion could even have been Herod's birthday. But equally, the dancing may never have happened. The story fits the archetype of the seductive woman so well that people would have believed in it regardless, particularly as it enabled them to condemn the unpopular Herodias for wanton behaviour. In reality, the two could simply have been hopelessly in love with each other.

This Herodias dancing source cannot explain the whole story. Why should the author of Mark bring in Herodias' daughter, Salome? The answer is that he had another source, a Christian source that was closely related to the request of the mother of the sons of Zebedee. The author of Mark has confused Salome, the mother of the sons of Zebedee with Salome, the Herodian princess.

Two stories, one Salome?

At first sight, the story of Salome's dance seems to have nothing to do with the request of the disciples James and John, but there are deep links between the two.

First, there are a number of links between James and John the Baptist. These links are surprising and suggest that early Christians confused the two. The beheading story describes John as a man "*just (dikaion) and holy*". One of James' titles is "James the Just (dikaion)" which is used for example in Thomas 12. To describe a person as just or righteous is quite common but to describe two people as having the skin of a camel is more unusual. Hegesippus, as quoted by Eusebius,[130] gives the curious detail that James prayed so much in the temple that his knees became hard like those of a camel. John the Baptist is also described as having camel skin: "*And John was clothed with camel's hair, and a girdle of skin around his loins*" (Mark 1:6). Has John's garment of camel-skin become associated with James and then confused so that it becomes James' own skin?

Turning to the story itself, Herod's promise to the dancing girl and the request of James and John are presented in very similar ways:

"Ask (aiteson) of me whatever you desire (theles) and I will give it to you." And he swore to her, "Whatever you may ask (aiteses) I will give to you, up to half of my kingdom (basileias)." (Mark 6:22-23)

"Master, we desire (thelomen) that whatever we may ask you (aitesomen) should do for us." And he said to them, "What do you desire (thelete) me to do for you?" (Mark 10:35-36)

Both Herod and Jesus are kings, and the language is that of a king granting a petition to someone who is very close to them. There are similarities in vocabulary in the two requests with words for "ask" and "desire" being key in both. In the story, Herod makes the offer spontaneously but it makes more sense that the offer is in response to a request. A further similarity is that the offer is for half the kingdom. In Matthew, James and John ask to sit on the right and left sides of Jesus "*in your kingdom (basileia)*". At the earthly level James and John would jointly rule Jesus' kingdom, just as Herodias would jointly share Herod's kingdom.

Turning to the identity of the person who is to have their wish granted, it is the daughter of Herodias in the John the Baptist story and the "*mother of the sons of Zebedee*" in the Matthew version of the James and John story. We have seen that both can be called "Salome".

The result of the request by the dancing Salome is the martyrdom of John the Baptist. The result of the request by the mother of the sons of Zebedee is the ultimate martyrdom of her sons. This is clear when Jesus asks the brothers if they are able to "*drink of the cup that I drink of, and with the baptism that I am baptised with to be baptised?*" *(Mark 10:38)*. They reply that they are able, and Jesus tells them that they shall drink from his cup and be baptised with his baptism. The cup and the baptism were not originally symbols of martyrdom. They were the sharing in the life of Jesus, which meant first sharing mystically in his death. But the author of Mark does not know this and in his story it is a prediction of martyrdom.

If we look at the method of martyrdom, according to Mark, the Baptist died by being beheaded with a sword on the orders of Herod.

We do not learn from Mark the circumstances of the martyrdom of James and/or John but as we have seen, the two appear in the story of Peter's escape from prison in Acts:

Now about that time, Herod the king stretched out his hands to persecute some of those of the church. He put to death James the brother of John with the sword. (Acts 12:1-2)

So the method of death for James is exactly the same as for John the Baptist; both have been killed on the orders of Herod by the sword. The similarities between the two accounts are summarised below.

Death of John the Baptist	James and John to sit at the left and right hand
The daughter of Herodias is to have her request granted. This daughter was called Salome.	The mother of the sons of Zebedee asks to have her request granted in Matthew. This woman can be equated with Salome (she is substituted in place of Salome at the crucifixion).
The Baptist is described as just/righteous	James is called elsewhere James the Just
Herod offers Salome to ask anything that she desires and says that anything she asks for will be given to her.	In Mark, James and John request that whatever they ask for will be given to them. Jesus asks them what it is they desire. (The same words for ask and desire are used in each case.)

Death of John the Baptist	James and John to sit at the left and right hand
Herod offers up to half of his kingdom.	In Matthew the mother asks for James and John to sit on the right and left sides in Jesus' kingdom; so each is to have a half share in the governance of the kingdom.
As a result of the request, John the Baptist suffers martyrdom.	As a result of the request, James and John will suffer martyrdom.
John is beheaded with a sword on the orders of Herod.	The brothers James and John appear in Acts as sons of Mary with the information that James was killed by the sword (that is beheaded) on the orders of Herod.

The similarities are too many in number and too specific to be chance. The similarities are a symptom of redundancy and are a sign that the same ultimate source is behind both stories. The author of Mark must have inherited two versions of this source (call them S and Z) that are sufficiently different that he has not recognised them as being the same. He has incorporated the two versions in two completely different episodes. In the one case, he has combined features from S with a historical account of the death of John the Baptist to derive his story of the execution of John. The elements that must have been taken from S include the involvement of Salome and the extravagant offer of Herod. The author of Mark has used the second source Z to compile the story of the request of James and John.

We can deduce the following:

The author of Mark has access to both S and Z, the author of Matthew has access to at least Z.

The sources involve a woman called in one case "Salome" (S) and in the other "the mother of the sons of Zebedee" (Z).

The author of Matthew has some reason for believing that the two women are the same. It may be that the source Z also mentions Salome. Or it may be that he has both Z and S and recognises that they are two variants of the same story without connecting either to the story of John the Baptist.

In both S and Z, a king (Jesus) makes this woman an extravagant promise, that he will grant her anything she desires if she asks for it.

In Z the woman's request is given in the form of sitting at the right and left side in the kingdom. In S the request must be phrased differently such as dividing the kingdom in two.

Both S and Z have an allusion to future martyrdom, but it would seem that Z does not give any details. In S, there is an allusion to one dying by the sword at the orders of Herod.

As well as Z and S, the author of Mark has access to the source originating from outside the Jesus movement that laments the death of John the Baptist, blaming Herodias, and saying that the dancing of a woman caused the death of John by inflaming the lust of Herod. He combines that with S in which a king makes an extravagant promise to a woman called Salome which results in Herod ordering an execution with the sword. The author of Mark thinks this Salome is the Herodian princess whereas she is actually the same Salome as appears at the crucifixion and resurrection.

What then about the source behind the two stories? We can reconstruct it by looking at the details of the Mark story, the changes the author of Matthew makes to this story and the promise of Herod to Salome. The Z source must have gone something like this:

The mother of the sons of Zebedee said to him "Will you grant me what I desire?" He said to her "Ask me for whatever you desire and I will give it to you". She said to him, "That these two sons of mine may sit, the one on your right hand, and the other on you left, in your kingdom". He said, "They shall drink of my cup and be baptised with my baptism. The right and left places are for those for whom they have been prepared." (Reconstruction of Z source)

The story is intended to give authority to the roles of James and John. To drink of the cup and be baptised with the baptism is to enter the kingdom and is a necessary prerequisite for sitting on the right and left sides. The statement that the right and left places are for those for whom they have been prepared could not have been intended as a rejection of the request as the author of Mark thinks. The real meaning must be that the request of Mary has been anticipated, and the places for James and John have already been prepared. The saying serves to confirm James and John in their positions, not only because Jesus grants Mary's request, but also because that request was preordained and their places prepared before time. This supports the idea that James and John were qualified by heredity, by being sons of David.

It is interesting that the saying envisages that the request is made before the baptism, the spiritual induction of James and John into the kingdom. This means that they must have been very young at the time of the request, perhaps still children. It seems that Mary made the decision that James and John would lead her movement very early. The saying is set in a time before James saw the risen Christ which dates it to the early or mid thirties around the time of the death of John the Baptist.

The S source has departed in a number of ways from the Z source, in the substitution of Salome for the mother of the sons of Zebedee, making the promise to James and John more obscure, and a reference to martyrdom. We can see S as a story about Salome which draws upon Z rather than another version of Z itself. The reconstruction of the S source is necessarily more speculative than Z because we have less data to go on. The following is intended to illustrate how it would be possible to have a source S that has developed from Z and which could serve as a source of the John the Baptist story:

Salome pleased him and shared his couch at table. And he said that she should ask whatever she desired, and he would give it to her. Even that two might share his kingdom he would grant to her. But to give what she asked one would have to be destroyed to enter the light and that one would be divided. So the Just one was beheaded by Herod. (Potential reconstruction of S source)

The information that Salome shared the couch of Jesus comes from Thomas 61: "*Salome said ... you have mounted my couch [or bed] and eaten from my table*". This would tie in with Herod giving a feast with guests reclining at table. The sequence from Thomas 61 and Thomas 62 has certain elements in common with Z and S including "*Salome*" and the concept of the right and left hand. It starts with "*two will rest on a bed, one will die and one will live*" which could have been taken as relating to the brothers James and John. Thomas 61 is obscure and incomplete but contains a phrase that could be interpreted as a prediction of the martyrdom of James "*when he should be destroyed he will be full of light when however he should be divided he will be full of darkness*". Given these similarities it has been assumed in the above that Z has been conflated with Thomas 61-62 by the author of S. Needless to say, the precise nature of S is conjecture, although we can tell it existed through the influence it had on the Herod story.

We can see from the above illustrative reconstruction how the author of Mark may have made a quite reasonable assumption that S was about John the Baptist. This relies on two coincidences, one significant and one minor. The significant coincidence is that both John and James were put to death by a Herod, although it must have been a different Herod in each case. We know that this coincidence did, in fact, happen from two independent pieces of evidence, the account of Josephus and Acts 12:1-2. The minor coincidence is that Herodias had a daughter called Salome. We would expect isolated coincidences to happen in the same way that you do not have to have many people in a room before finding that two share the same birthday. It is the list of coincidences between the brothers James and John of Zebedee and John the Baptist stories that are significant. Some of these coincidences are random background events which have caused the link to be made in the first place; others are the result of the link having been made.

Key points

1. A triumvirate of Mary/Cephas and two of her "sons", James and John Mark, ruled the Jesus movement. Another "son", Simon Peter, was an effective apostle who was in practice a fourth member of the leadership group. These are the individuals represented by the first three disciples in Mark's list of the twelve. Paul meets these three "sons" when he visits the leaders in Jerusalem.

2. The appointment of James and John to the right and left hand side in Jesus' kingdom is found in a story included in both Mark and Matthew. In Mark, James and John make the request, but in Matthew, it is made by their mother who is called "the mother of the sons of Zebedee". The version where the mother makes the request is is more embarrassing, and so by the criterion of embarrassment, is likely to be original. Although the request appears to have been refused in Mark and Matthew, the intention of the original source must have been to record that the request had been granted.

3. The request has to be made by the mother, because that mother is the shaman, Mary. The role of the mother was removed when the story was literalised in Mark because James and John were now supposed to be disciples travelling around with an earthly Jesus.

4. At the crucifixion, Matthew replaces Salome by the "mother of the sons of Zebedee", indicating that the two were believed to be the same person.

5. Salome must have been a Greek name used by Mary. This would also explain why Salome is present at the crucifixion and resurrection in Mark, as the other women supposedly present are all different names for Mary.

6. There are close similarities between the story of the request for the right and left hand places and the story of the dance of the daughter of Herodias, who requests the head of John the Baptist. These similarities are; (i) the person involved in the request can be identified as Salome in both cases; (ii) there are close similarities in the form and wording of the request/offer; (iii) in both cases the request/offer involves sharing in the kingdom; (iv) in both cases the request results in martyrdom; (v) in both cases the method of martyrdom is beheading with a sword at the orders of Herod.

7. There are multiple connections between John the Baptist and James indicating that they were confused together in early Christian sources.

8. The story of the death of John the Baptist in Mark makes sense if the role of Salome is removed so that it is Herodias who performs the dance. The story is then consistent with events as recorded by Josephus. A dance by Herodias at a party results in Herod becoming obsessed with her and making her the offer of half his kingdom. They agree to marry, even though Herodias is married to Herod's brother, and many will regard the marriage as incestuous. The dance leads eventually to the beheading of John the Baptist who opposes the marriage. The dance did not take place immediately before the execution of John as in Mark, but earlier, when Herod stayed with his brother on the way to Rome.

9. The story of the execution of John the Baptist as it stands in Mark is a conjunction of this Jewish tradition concerning the dance of Herodias and a Christian source, S, involving Salome. The source S is revealed to be a version of the source Z that lies behind the story of the request for James and John to sit on the right and left hand in the kingdom.

Conclusions

James and John, the sons of Zebedee, were Mary's adopted, rather than biological sons. Mary was not married to Zebedee, but he may have been her brother. James and John were appointed to the right and left hand sides of Jesus' kingdom, meaning they were given the two leadership positions on either side of their mother, Mary. These roles were said to have been prepared for them before time because the two brothers were believed to be descendants of David.

The story of the dance of Salome has originated by confusion between a Jewish source concerning a dance by Herodias, which led to the death of John, and the story of the appointment of James and John. Salome was a Greek name used by Mary in the early days of the movement.

Chapter 22

James and John

We have deduced that James and John, the sons of Zebedee, were the two foremost brethren and led the movement under Mary. We must now look for evidence that may contradict or confirm this view. There is an alternative tradition that James, the brother of the Lord, was killed by stoning. If true, this would mean that he was not the same James who was killed by Herod. We must trace the origins of this stoning tradition to see if it is valid. On the positive side, we will look at sources that record that revelations were passed through James and John. And the role of John as one of the two primary brothers, the one who was closest to Mary, explains something that would otherwise be very puzzling. Why are three of the major works of the New Testament attributed to John Mark?

The martyrdom of James the Just

The proposed link between the John the Baptist story and the source S depends upon James being killed by Herod with the sword. Although Acts does not specify which Herod killed James, it repeats a story derived from Josephus that this Herod later died by being eaten up by worms after his subjects acclaimed him as a god.[131] This identifies him as Herod Agrippa I, who ruled until his death from violent abdominal pains in AD 44 (Josephus does not mention the worms). However, Herod Agrippa I cannot have killed James the brother of the Lord who is active when Paul is writing his letters in the mid-50s. So conventional commentators distinguish between James the son of Zebedee, who was killed by Herod, and James brother of the Lord.

We have identified James the brother of the Lord as being the same as the son of Zebedee, so he could not have been killed by Agrippa I. It is significant that Acts does not name the Herod who killed James, implying that the source did not name him either, and the author of Luke-Acts may have wrongly blamed Agrippa I. There was another Herod Agrippa, son of the first, whose reign fits in very well with an execution of James in the late 50s or early 60s. Herod Agrippa II ruled various dominions from 48 up unto the 90s. He was an ally and collaborator of the Romans and even sent troops to aid Vespasian in the Jewish war. As such he must have been heartily despised by his fellow Jews. But Josephus tells us that he was an expert on Jewish customs, and he would have regarded himself as a good Jew; he insisted that the foreign princes who sought his sister Drusilla in marriage should be circumcised.[132]

Josephus was a close friend of Agrippa II and was in a very similar political position, being a turncoat Jew and a client of Vespasian and the Romans. Josephus portrays Agrippa II very positively in his writings, and the author of Luke shares this positive view of Agrippa II so that Acts shows him as a wise ruler; when Paul is brought before Agrippa and his notorious sister Bernice, Agrippa says that he is almost persuaded to be a Christian.[133] This is so ridiculous that some see Agrippa's words in Acts as intended to be ironic, but this is to misunderstand the position of the author of Luke, who is a member of the Roman establishment and a great admirer of King Agrippa II. Indeed, the continuation shows that it is not intended to be ironic; although Agrippa sends Paul for trial to Rome in Acts, he does so reluctantly, wanting to set Paul at liberty[134] but unable to do so because of legal procedure.

If the author of Luke has a source that records that James was killed by Herod, it would be unthinkable to assign this death to her hero Agrippa II. His father Agrippa I makes a convenient scapegoat, particularly as his manner of death demonstrated that he had incurred the displeasure of God. But by assigning the deed to the earlier Herod, the timing is shifted back by one or two decades. Another implication of the author of Luke's favourable view of Agrippa II is that she would never have invented the story of Agrippa sending Paul to trial. In fact, she goes out of her way to show that he wanted to release Paul. So she must have had a source for believing that Agrippa II did send Paul for trial, meaning that he was actually a persecutor of the Jesus movement.

Everything we know about Agrippa II makes him a likely candidate for ordering the execution of James and the arrest of Paul in the years leading up to the destruction of the temple. To remove the leaders of this potentially dangerous movement would please his Roman masters, who were al-

ways seeking to eliminate sources of trouble, it would satisfy his own orthodox religious views, and it would appeal to the Jewish establishment
whom he is trying to keep on his side. He has the power to have James executed, but Paul is a Roman citizen, so all he can do is send him to Rome for
trial.

An execution of James by Herod Agrippa II fits the historical facts but is
inconsistent with some other accounts of the death of James that have come
down to us which suggest that James was stoned. Either James was not
killed by Herod Agrippa II or these other accounts are wrong.

The earliest potential source for the stoning of James is contained in Josephus' Antiquities itself where the execution is attributed to the Jewish
high priest Ananus:

> *But this younger Ananus, who, as we have told you already, took the high
> priesthood, was a bold man in his temper, and very insolent; he was also of the sect
> of the Sadducees, who are very rigid in judging offenders, above all the rest of the
> Jews, as we have already observed; when, therefore, Ananus was of this disposition,
> he thought he had now a proper opportunity; Festus was now dead, and Albinus
> was but upon the road; so he assembled the Sanhedrim of judges, and brought be-
> fore them the brother of Jesus, who was called Christ, whose name was James, and
> some others; and when he had formed an accusation against them as breakers of the
> law, he delivered them to be stoned: but as for those who seemed the most equitable
> of the citizens, and such as were the most uneasy at the breach of the laws, they
> disliked what was done; they also sent to the king [Agrippa], desiring him to send
> to Ananus that he should act so no more, for that what he had already done was
> not to be justified; nay, some of them went also to meet Albinus, as he was upon his
> journey from Alexandria, and informed him that it was not lawful for Ananus to
> assemble a sanhedrim without his consent. Whereupon Albinus complied with
> what they said, and wrote in anger to Ananus, and threatened that he would bring
> him to punishment for what he had done; on which king Agrippa took the high
> priesthood from him, when he had ruled but three months, and made Jesus, the son
> of Damneus, high priest. (Josephus, Jewish Antiquities 20.9.1)[135]*

The episode can be dated to 62, and so fits the correct timeframe. The
majority of scholars accept this as being genuine, but there are two glaring
features that show it to be a Christian interpolation. First there is a reference to Jesus as the Christ, which assumes that the reader will immediately
know who this Jesus is. The subject of the Christ or Messiah is very sensitive to Josephus because of his prediction that Vespasian was the subject of

the Jewish prophecies of a world leader. He avoids using the term when talking about Messiah aspirants, and the only other possible use is in the famous Testimonium Flavianum about Jesus. This other reference is widely separated from the above passage in book 18, and the reader would not connect the two unless they were approaching the text from a Christian perspective.

The other glaring problem is that the text envisages a relationship between Judaism and the Jesus movement that contradicts every other piece of evidence from the period. We know from Paul's letters that the Jewish establishment set out to eliminate the Jesus movement and that Paul, a Pharisee, was one of the persecutors. This persecution seems to have been led by the Pharisees rather than the Sadducees; the evidence for this is not just Paul's account but also the anger directed at the Pharisees and scribes in the gospels. The gospels are uniformly anti-Jewish, and the most vitriolic hatred of the Jewish mainstream comes from the two most Jewish gospels, Matthew and John. It is clear that the authors of these gospels have personal acquaintance with persecution at the hands of their fellow Jews. Even in Acts, written by a Gentile who was quite favourably disposed towards the Jews, it is the Jews who continually ferment opposition to the Jesus movement. There must be some basis in fact behind this representation.

All of this is evidence of a civil war with the mainstream Jews regarding the Jesus movement as the heretical enemy within. As we probe the beliefs of the Jesus movement, we will see that the Jewish mainstream were quite correct in this view and that their actions were, in the terms of their own philosophy, justifiable. The Jesus movement was not a Jewish sect with wholesome law-abiding Jewish views that were subverted by Gentiles. It was a deeply heretical group who believed that the Jewish law was void, that the Jewish temple was not the real temple, and that the Yahweh that the other Jews worshipped was not the real Yahweh but a fallible angel. Any right thinking Jew who knew anything about the Jesus movement would want to destroy them.

And yet in the Josephus passage the chief priest Ananus has to wait craftily for the opportunity of the change in Procurator to take action against the leader, James, of this notorious sect. And when he does act his actions evoke such outrage that a delegation is sent to the incoming Albinus, and he is removed from the priesthood. All of which is absurd. As others have noted all we need to do is to remove a few words "*who was called Christ*" to make the passage make sense. Without these words, we would assume that James must be the brother of Jesus the son of Damneus, who is made high priest at the end of the passage. What we then have is a conflict between two factions of the establishment; an ultra-conservative wing who have control of the Sanhedrin and who are led by Ananus the high priest and a more liberal wing in which two brothers, James and Jesus, play a prominent role. Ananus seizes the opportunity of an interim between two procurators to have James put to death on the pretext that he has infringed a very strict reading of the law. However, he has gone too far, and his actions arouse widespread condemnation. His liberal opponents are able to have him disposed and to placate them the high priesthood is given to Jesus, the brother of the James who was killed.

The more reasonable Jews considered the stoning to be unjust, so Ananus must have had James put to death on a technicality. The Jesus movement had broken the law in far more than mere technicalities and if it were James the Just who was the victim, the good citizens of Jerusalem would have been celebrating. Indeed, the death of James by Herod at the request of the leading citizens makes far more sense than those same citizens intervening in grief at his death.

What has happened is that a Christian copyist has made the understandable mistake of thinking that James the brother of Jesus must be the same as the Christian James. Both names were common Jewish names and the occurrence of a James and Jesus as brothers in Josephus is the type of coincidence that can be expected to arise at random. The addition to the text may have originated as a marginal note by a reader to identify James ("the brother of Jesus called the Christ") which was then incorporated into the text by a later copyist as often happened with marginal notes.[136] It is also possible, of course, that the executed James was not the brother of Jesus son of Damneus and that the original identifier for this James has been replaced by "the brother of Jesus called the Christ" by someone embarrassed by the lack of mention of the early church in the works of Josephus. This would require a less innocent motive.

Did early Christians make changes to Josephus? There is one piece of evidence that suggests that they did. Eusebius reports that the Jewish historian Josephus said this about the causes of the siege of Jerusalem (and hence the destruction of the temple):

These things happened to the Jews to avenge James the Just, who was a brother of Jesus, that is called the Christ. For the Jews slew him, although he was a most just man. (Eusebius Ecclesiastical History 2:23:20)[137]

We find no such statement in our copies of Josephus. So was there a Christian redaction in Eusebius' copy of Josephus that has not come down in the copies that have survived to the modern age? There is one circumstance that suggests not. Although Eusebius normally gives the reference for his quotes from Josephus, he does not in this case. This implies he was either quoting from memory or had taken the quote from an intermediary source. It would be odd if he should quote a passage from memory in a section that contains many quotes from Josephus. While writing this section, he must have had the works of Josephus at hand, so why did he not look up the quote? Most likely he was using an intermediary source that contained the above quote attributed to Josephus but did not say from where it had been taken.

In fact, we can find something very like the quote in the works of Josephus, but it does not concern James but John the Baptist. Herod's divorce of his wife to marry Herodias led to war with King Aretas in which Herod's army was defeated. Josephus says this about the defeat:

Now some of the Jews thought that the destruction of Herod's army came from God, and that very justly, as a punishment of what he did against John, that was called the Baptist: for Herod slew him, who was a good man, ... (Josephus, Jewish Antiquities 18:116-117)[138]

The similarities between the two passages are shown in the table below.

James (Josephus quoted by Eusebius)	John the Baptist (Josephus Antiquities)
These things happened to the Jews to avenge	*Now some of the Jews thought that the destruction of Herod's army came from God, and that very justly, as a punishment of what he did against*
James the Just, who was a brother of Jesus, that is called the Christ.	*John, that was called the Baptist:*
For the Jews slew him,	*for Herod slew him,*
although he was a most just man.	*who was a good man, ...* (also note the word for "*justly*" (diakaios) above)

The passage in *Antiquities* about the defeat of Herod being due to his execution of John must have given rise to the idea that Josephus said that the later sack of Jerusalem resulted from the execution of James. Once again we have confusion between James, brother of the Lord, and John the Baptist. The easiest way to explain this confusion is if James the Just was also beheaded by a Herod with the sword. The false Josephus quote blames not Herod, but "the Jews", suggesting that, as we would expect, the Jewish establishment had a role in persuading Herod Agrippa II to execute James.

The next account that mentions a stoning of James is from Hegesippus, as again reported by Eusebius in Ecclesiastical History 2:23. This account is typical of Hegesippus in having many absurd elements. James preaches to the Jews from the pinnacle of the temple before being cast down. He is then stoned by the "scribes and Pharisees" before being hit over the head and killed by a fuller's club. The account is fascinating and contains many mystical elements that have been literalised. We can see that Hegesippus has inherited a number of traditions about the death of James, including one in which he is stoned. Hegesippus' account ends with Vespasian besieging Jerusalem that shows he was also aware of a tradition that the sack of Jerusalem was divine vengeance for the death of James. Most likely he has access to the same pseudo-Josephus source as quoted by Eusebius.

The martyrdom of James by stoning is also found in the second Apocalypse of James found in the Nag Hammadi codices. This is clearly linked with the Hegesippus account - the setting for both is the temple, and the stoning is provoked by a lecture that James gives the people. In the Pseudo-Clementine Recognitions (1:66-70) there is another account of James preaching in the temple after which he is thrown down. He is struck with brands although this time there is no stoning and James only appears dead, after which he recovers. Finally Eusebius mentions another account in Clement's Outlines, Book 8, which work is now lost, that: "*there were two Jameses: one called the Just, who was thrown from the pinnacle of the temple and was beaten to death with a club by a fuller, and another who was beheaded*" (Eusebius, Ecclesiastical History 2:1:4)[139]

All these various accounts of the martyrdom of James are closely related and must share the same ultimate source which is either Hegesippus' account or a source used by Hegesippus. Stoning is only one theme alongside James being cast down and struck with a club and does not even feature in some of the accounts. But is there a kernel of historical truth in these accounts and was James stoned? If Christians were confusing the James who was killed by Ananus with James, the brother of the Lord, then this would account for a tradition that James had been stoned. But there is a second possibility, and that is that the stoning of James in Hegesippus has been taken from the stoning of Stephen in Acts. The two accounts are closely related as the table below shows.

Hegesippus[140]	Acts 7:52-60
And he answered with a loud voice, "Why do you ask me concerning Jesus, the Son of Man? He himself sits in heaven at the right hand of the great Power, and is about to come upon the clouds of heaven."	*But he, being full of the Holy Ghost, looked up steadfastly into heaven, and saw the glory of God, and Jesus standing on the right hand of God. And said, "Behold, I see the heavens opened, and the Son of man standing on the right hand of God." (Acts 7:55-56)*
And they cried out, saying, "Oh! oh! the Righteous One is also in error." And they fulfilled the Scripture written in Isaiah, "Let us take away the Righteous One, because he is troublesome to us: therefore they shall eat the fruit of their doings." So they went up and threw down the Righteous One ...	*And they have slain them which foretold the coming of the Righteous One of whom you have now become the betrayers and murderers: (Acts 7:52)*
And they began to stone him, for he was not killed by the fall; but he turned and knelt down and said, "I entreat thee, Lord God our Father, forgive them, for they know not what they do."	*And they cast him out of the city, and stoned him: ... While they stoned Stephen, he was calling out saying, "Lord Jesus, receive my spirit." And he kneeled down, and cried with a loud voice, "Lord, do not hold this sin against them!" (Acts 7:58-60)*

It is clear that the Stephen account in Acts has been used as a source by Hegesippus for the stoning of James. But why should he apply this to James? The clue is in the word *dikaiou* meaning the "Righteous One" or the "Just One". In Acts 7:52 the Righteous One is clearly intended to mean Jesus; the prophecies foretelling the coming of the Righteous One are prophecies of the Messiah (see for example Isaiah 53:11 which calls the suffering servant the Righteous One and Jeremiah 23:5 about the "righteous branch" of David). Stephen is saying that the Jews have killed the Righteous One, by which he means the betrayal and execution of Jesus. However, Hegesippus thinks that the Righteous One is the person who is being stoned and so connects the account with James the Just. What must have happened is that Hegesippus has inherited the Acts story indirectly; either through another written source which quotes the Acts story or through a verbal account. This secondary account is sufficiently confused to cause Hegesippus to apply it to a different person, either because the name of Stephen has been detached from the story, or because he thinks Stephen was a Greek name used by James.

We shall see in the next volume that the Stephen story is a complete invention by the author of Acts and is intended to show the persecution of the early church by Saul (Paul). It is cobbled together from various sources and draws heavily on the trial of Jesus in Mark. The character of Stephen is imaginary and based upon someone who assisted the author in the composition of Luke and Acts. So the stoning of James is not historical but caused by confusion with the stoning of Stephen, which is itself imaginary.

There are two pieces of evidence that support this conclusion, one negative and one positive. The negative evidence is that if James were really put to death by stoning then why is this not mentioned anywhere in Acts? A stoning by the Jews would fit in very well with the anti-Jewish theme of Acts. The author of Acts must be unaware of the stoning of James because this idea had not yet been invented when Acts was written towards the end of the first century. The martyrdom of James by the sword is in Acts but it is obscured by the splitting of James into the two separate characters of James of Zebedee and James the Just and by the extreme reluctance of the author of Acts to attribute the death of James to the real culprit, Herod Agrippa II.

The second piece of evidence is an otherwise puzzling thing that is said to Mary, the mother of Jesus in Luke. When she brings the infant Jesus to the temple an old man Simeon makes a prophecy about Jesus. He then adds to Mary: *"a sword shall pierce through your own soul also"* (Luke 2:35). This is clearly a prophecy of a martyrdom by the sword. Who then does it apply to? There is no evidence to suggest that Mary was put to death by the sword. So it must concern someone else who was very close to Mary. It cannot be Jesus whose supposed death was not by the sword. But it makes perfect sense if it is James, the first of her adopted sons, who is killed on the orders of Herod by the sword. It would then be based on a real memory that Mary was heartbroken by the death of James. This means that the execution must have happened while she was still alive which is consistent with a date in the early 60s.

The Apocalypses of James

The relationship between James and Jesus is mentioned in two other texts, both called the Apocalypse of James. These are known to scholars as the first and the second Apocalypse according to the order that they appear in the Nag Hammadi codex. Although these texts are confused, they show a number of traditions about James as the brother of Jesus but not his biological brother. In the first Apocalypse, it is stated that Jesus is the spiritual brother of James: "*for not without reason I have called you my brother although you are not my brother materially*".

The second Apocalypse of James is probably earlier than the first and dates from the early or mid second century. In this text, James recounts how he met Jesus:

He said to me "Hail my brother; my brother hail." As I raised my [face] to stare at him (my) mother said to me "Do not be frightened, my son, because he said 'My brother' to you. For you were nourished with this same milk. Because of this he calls me 'my mother'. For he is not a stranger to us. He is your [ ]." (The second Apocalypse of James, 50:11-23)[141]

This can be explained as an attempt to reconcile the tradition (i) that James and Jesus were brothers; (ii) that they both had the same mother; and (iii) they were not biological brothers. So the author of the Apocalypse hits on the theory that James' mother was foster mother to Jesus.

This passage also passes down a tradition of a family relationship between James and Jesus; unfortunately, there is a lacuna in the text and the missing expression in brackets could be recreated in a number of ways, including stepbrother or cousin on the male side. The most likely recreation of the missing text, though, is that James' father was the brother of Jesus. We have seen that traditions about Mary are sometimes applied to Jesus, her spiritual twin. So this could go back to a genuine memory that James' father was Mary's brother.

The introduction to the second Apocalypse of James is confused and may have been corrupted in transmission. It recounts that the apocalypse was written down by one Mareim. In the Apocalypse, Mareim is presented as a male priest who is related to James' father.[142] However, the name would seem to come from Mariamne, which is the same name as Mary. The idea that revelations from James are passed through Mariamne is also found in the beliefs of the Naassenes according to the early church father Hippolytus.[143]

Turning to the first apocalypse, we find a complicated explanation of how the words of Jesus to James are to be handed down. James is to keep silent but *"you are to reveal these things to Addai"* (First Apocalypse of James p36). Jesus adds *"When you depart immediately war will be made with this land"* (p36) which ties in with the tradition that the fall of Jerusalem was a result of the death of James. Addai is to keep the things in his heart and in the tenth year write them down (p36) There is then a damaged section in which the name "Levi" is mentioned (p37) and a woman or wife who has some connection to Jerusalem - *"... Jerusalem in her ... "* (p37). He (Addai?) is then to beget two sons through this woman who are to inherit these things (the revelations). Of these two it is said - *"The smaller is the greater. And let these things be shared with him and hidden in him until he comes to the age of seventeen years"* (p37).[144]

The purpose of this complex and confused sequence is to explain to the reader how the revelations of Jesus to James were kept secret but were passed down to the gnostics who were writing the apocalypse. Who is the Addai who is charged with the transmission of the revelations? In fact, this is the same name as Thaddaeus, which is *Th(addai)os* in Greek. It is Thaddaeus whom the author of Luke replaces by Judas (Jude) of James, who was a brother of James. For Judas to be named in relation to his brother, he must be much younger. Who better to pass on the secrets than James' own young brother? It is unlikely that Judas was really called Thaddaeus. Judas was one of the brethren of the Lord, so it is unsurprising that the author of Luke wanted to include him among the disciples. She probably chose to replace Thaddaeus because he was the most obscure disciple on Mark's list of the Twelve. However, when Christians began to read the gospels together and reconcile their numerous differences, they would have equated Thaddaeus (in Mark and Matthew) with Judas of James (in Luke). So the second-century tradition of Thaddaeus being another name for Judas arises.

There is a second tradition present in the Apocalypse that the revelations were passed through a woman and her two sons. This group is clearly Mary, James, and John. The son who is smaller but greater is James who is called "the less"; he who would be great in the movement must be least! The idea that the revelations will be hidden in him until he is seventeen may confirm that James was chosen for his role as the future leader while still a boy and inducted into the movement when he attained manhood.

If we take the first Apocalypse at face value, then Addai is the father of the son of the woman, that is James. This is typical of the confusion that arises when separate traditions are spliced together.

Behind all this complexity, there is a pattern. We start with the memory that revelations coming through Mary have been passed down through her two special sons, John and in particular James. Some changed the order because the idea of James receiving revelations form his mother is inconsistent with the gospel accounts; so we find traditions that revelations passed from Jesus to James and then to Mary.

Traditions from John Mark

There is evidence that John Mark was closer to Mary than James. He accompanied her everywhere, and he functioned as her scribe and secretary. This made him the ideal authority for the written productions of later Christians. We find that no less than three of the major books of the New Testament are attributed to him:

The first gospel to be written has always been known as the Gospel according to Mark, although there is nothing within the gospel to indicate its authorship. Acts 12:12 tells us that John was called Mark in Greek.

The fourth gospel is supposedly based on the testimony of the beloved disciple (John 21:24) and has long been known as the Gospel of John.

The Book of Revelation, the only book in the New Testament that actually gives the name of its supposed author, is attributed to John.

All three date from a similar period between the year 70 and the beginning of the second century, a time when the original traditions were still remembered but were fading and becoming confused. It is doubtful that the unknown person who wrote Mark intended his gospel to be attributed to John Mark or indeed to anyone else. He is writing modestly and anonymously, but some of his early readers attached the name of Mark to his gospel. The other two works are more self-consciously attributed to John. The Gospel of John does not actually claim to have been written by the beloved disciple but to be based on traditions passed down by that disciple. Only in Revelation is the claimed authorship by John explicit.

Revelation is supposedly based on revelations received in the spirit on the Greek island of Patmos in the Eastern Mediterranean. The book does not say that John lived on Patmos but only that he was there *"for the word of*

God, and for the testimony of Jesus Christ" (Revelation 1:9) which could mean, as is commonly supposed, that he was exiled there, but more likely that he was engaged in a missionary journey. Patmos is close to the coast of modern Turkey, and it is entirely possible that John did visit the island. We know that he must have made a number of sea journeys between Rome and Jerusalem and in the Roman period boats did not venture far from land. It could be that he spent some time at Patmos on one of these journeys, either because he was waiting for a boat or because he was on a boat that had to take shelter. Perhaps he was forced to overwinter there; sea travel only took place in the summer months and being stranded somewhere inconvenient for the winter was a common hazard for the traveller. Such a visit would have been remembered by those in the local area including Ephesus on the mainland, some fifty miles distant by sea, and the first of the seven churches mentioned in Revelation. When at the end of the first century a Christian from this area was writing Revelation and needed a prominent early figure to attribute it to, he recalled the local association of John with Patmos. This would involve a degree of anachronism because John's visit must have taken place decades before the Book of Revelation was written to the seven churches in the 90s. But Revelation is a book of prophecy, and the purpose of prophecy was to interpret current events by putting them in the mouth of someone who had lived in the past.

Eusebius mentions some later traditions that connect John with Ephesus. He quotes a letter written by Polycrates, the bishop of Ephesus, to Victor bishop of Rome at around 190. In this letter, Polycrates says that one of the daughters of Philip was buried at Ephesus and goes on to add:

And moreover John, who was both a witness and a teacher, who reclined upon the bosom of the Lord, and being a priest wore the petalon. He also sleeps at Ephesus. (Eusebius, Ecclesiastical History 3:31:3)

Mostly though Eusebius quotes Irenaeus for information about John. He says that John wrote his gospel at Ephesus[145] and adds - *"Then, again, the Church in Ephesus, founded by Paul, and having John remaining among them permanently until the times of Trajan, is a true witness of the tradition of the apostles" (Against Heresies 3:3:4).*[146] This dating to the reign of Trajan (98-117) implies that John was alive until the very end of the first century or beginning of the second century. Irenaeus' main source of information about John is Polycarp, bishop of Smyrna, whom Irenaeus knew when he was a youth. He repeats a story about John that supposedly came from Polycarp:

There are also those who heard from him that John, the disciple of the Lord, go-
ing to bathe at Ephesus, and perceiving Cerinthus within, rushed out of the bath-
house without bathing, exclaiming, "Let us fly, lest even the bath-house fall down,
because Cerinthus, the enemy of the truth, is within." (Against Heresies 3:3:4)[147]

Elsewhere Irenaeus says that Jesus continued to teach and spread the
gospel until he was over fifty, the age at which old age begins. This is a
surprising statement because it appears to contradict the gospels, but he
gives as his source the authority of John:

But from the fortieth and fiftieth year a man begins to decline towards old age,
which our Lord possessed while he still fulfilled the office of a teacher, even as the
Gospel and all the elders testify; those who were conversant in Asia with John, the
disciple of the Lord, that John conveyed to them that information. And he remained
among them up to the times of Trajan. Some of them, moreover, saw not only John,
but the other apostles also, and heard the very same account from them, and bear
testimony as to the statement. (Against Heresies 2:22:5)[148]

What is fascinating about this is that it recalls a correct memory that Jesus remained in spiritual possession of Mary, teaching and spreading the
gospel through her, into her old age. And of this there could be no better
witness than her constant companion, John Mark. It would seem that the
churches in Asia (modern day Turkey) and at Ephesus, in particular, inherited a tradition concerning John which was probably based on a genuine
connection from the middle of the first century. This tradition led writers
from this area at the end of the first century and beginning of the second
century to ascribe their works to John; in particular both the book of Revelation and the Gospel of John probably originated in the vicinity of Ephesus. And this in turn led Christians from later in the second century to
think that the disciple John had been alive in Ephesus until the early second century.

Irenaeus thinks John was alive in the reign of Trajan because he believes
that Revelation was written by the apostle and disciple John towards the
end of the reign of Domitian, and there was a tradition that the author of
Revelation had survived that reign. What about Polycarp who, according
to Irenaeus, actually knew John? Does this not prove that John did survive
into the second century and passed down traditions through the proto-
orthodox church? It is time to consider Polycarp in more detail along with

another supposed early bishop revered by the proto-orthodox church, Ignatius.

Key points

1. It is not specified which Herod killed James with the sword in Acts, indicating that he was also unnamed in the source. However, Acts identifies him with Herod Agrippa I, who lived too early to have killed James, the brother of the Lord.

2. If James the brother of the Lord were killed by a Herod it must have been Agrippa II. He was a stickler for Jewish tradition, and there is evidence that he did persecute the Jesus movement by sending Paul for trial in Rome.

3. Herod Agrippa II was a hero of the author of Luke-Acts, and she would have been very reluctant to depict him as the executioner of James. As her source does not specify which Herod killed James, she attributes the deed to the Agrippa I, so moving the execution forward in time by a few decades.

4. Josephus appears to say that James was stoned on the orders of the high priest Ananus. However, there is evidence that a Christian has interpolated an existing passage about Ananus' execution of a brother of Jesus, the son of Damneus, who was then appointed high priest instead of Ananus.

5. In the Josephus passage, leading Jewish citizens interceded with the Roman governor in protest at the stoning of James. As a result of this intervention, Ananus was removed from the position of high priest. This is completely inconsistent with what we know about the early relationship between Christianity and Judaism and is evidence that the passage was not originally about James, brother of the Lord. All other sources indicate persecution of the Jesus sect by both the Jews and the Romans at this time.

6. According to Eusebius, Josephus wrote that the siege of Jerusalem was divine vengeance on the Jews for the execution of James. The source is a statement by Josephus relating to John the Baptist and is another example of confusion between John and James made by early Christians.

7. There are other sources that report that James was stoned, as well as being cast down from the pinnacle of the temple, and hit with a fuller's club. All these sources go back to the account of Hegesippus or a source used by Hegesippus. This account, in turn, shows close affinities to the stoning of Stephen in Acts and has arisen by a confusion of the "righteous

one" in the Stephen story (who is clearly intended to be Jesus) with James the Just.

8. There are traditions from the two Apocalypses of James that (i) Jesus was the spiritual brother of James, and (ii) that Jesus and James were foster brothers. This shows that although they were acknowledged as brothers with the same mother, it was known that this was not a biological relationship.

9. In the two Apocalypses of James, there are traditions about revelations being passed down through James, and through a mother and her two sons.

10. Three major works in the new Testament, the Gospel of Mark, the Gospel of John and Revelation, have been attributed to John although none of them were written by him. This is evidence of his importance in the early movement.

11. Irenaeus thinks that John was alive in the reign of Trajan (98-117), but he also believed, incorrectly, that John had written both the Gospel of John and Revelation. As Irenaeus knows when Revelation was written (and maybe also the Gospel of John) he thinks that John must have survived into that time.

12. Irenaeus reports that Polycarp claimed to have known John.

Conclusion

The tradition that James was stoned has arisen from an interpolation into a Josephus passage and confusion with the stoning of Stephen in Acts. We find multiple traditions of revelations and information passed down through James and John.

Chapter 23

Polycarp and Ignatius

If Polycarp knew the disciple John who had sat at Jesus' feet, and passed the knowledge gained from John to Irenaeus, then this would suggest that the shaman paradigm is wrong. After all, Irenaeus is strongly against a spiritual Christ and insists that Jesus was a physical man. And Irenaeus' views appear to be confirmed by the very early evidence of the Ignatius letters. Coincidentally, these also emphasise that Jesus on earth was a flesh and blood man who suffered, and was not spiritual in nature. But was it really possible for Polycarp, who lived in the second century, to have known the disciple John? And are the Ignatius letters genuine, or are they forgeries?

The link to the apostles

The developing proto-orthodox church believed in the view of Jesus promulgated by the gospels. However, the gospel view of Jesus as physical man was opposed by many who said that he had been spiritual in nature. If the proto-orthodox church was to emerge triumphant from this struggle, the opposition had to be discredited as heretics. One of the first to take up the battle was Irenaeus. His "Against Heresies", written around 180, was a seminal work in the development of the church and set out to portray all the various gnostic, spiritual and Jewish Christian groups as having deviated from the original, simple truth of the gospels. But there was a difficulty. The proto-orthodox, like Irenaeus, had to demonstrate that they had authority as the church appointed by Jesus if they were to defeat the "heretics". To do that, they had to show an unbroken line of succession from Jesus to their own leaders. The line started with the disciples Jesus appointed (according to the gospels) and who then became the apostles (according to

Acts). The apostles chose the first church leaders (called "bishops" or "presbyters") whose authority then passed to their successors, right down to those who were leading the church in Irenaeus' own day. All very nice in theory, but in reality there was no simple line of succession of church leaders. Indeed, as the church was run by an ill-defined group of people, no one really knew who was in charge, and everyone claimed that their own views went back to some early figure. What the proto-orthodox needed was a way of short-circuiting this complexity, to establish a simple, direct connection between their doctrines and the disciple-apostles.

By a happy chance, two such direct links were to emerge from the circle of Irenaeus. One link was put forward by Irenaeus himself. It turned out that his very own teacher, Polycarp, had studied under none other than Jesus' beloved disciple, John. If so, then the doctrines Irenaeus put forward in his writings were only one remove from the disciple who was closest to Jesus, and who had written both the Gospel of John and Revelation. So the figure who had the most influence on the developing proto-orthodox church had a remarkably direct connection (or so he said) with Jesus who supposedly lived 150 years earlier.

The second link was in the form of the letters of a very early bishop, Ignatius, who was a contemporary, friend and correspondent of Polycarp. This Ignatius was a saintly figure, an early martyr whose own enthusiasm for martyrdom agreed precisely with the cult of martyrdom as it was developing at the end of the second century. From the evidence of his letters, Ignatius would have met his death in the early decades of the second century, so it was reasonable to suppose that he had been appointed as bishop directly by the apostles. Ignatius gave the proto-orthodox just what they needed, a very early figure of authority whose views agreed with their own in every respect. Indeed, the letters of Ignatius attack the very same groups that Irenaeus was fighting much later at the end of the century.

The testimony of Polycarp and Ignatius would seem to provide definitive proof that it was the proto-orthodox church who were the true heirs of Jesus. After all, these early bishops had direct contact with the very disciples who had sat at Jesus' feet. So if they condemned those who taught that Jesus was spiritual and not physical, then clearly those who believed in a spiritual Jesus were heretics who had fallen away from the truth.

There is, of course, another explanation. Polycarp did not know John and the whole Ignatius correspondence is a forgery. It is time to look more closely at Polycarp and Ignatius.

Polycarp

According to Irenaeus, Polycarp was so old that he could bridge the gap between Jesus and his own time:

> *But Polycarp also was not only instructed by apostles, and conversed with many who had seen Christ, but was also, by apostles in Asia, appointed bishop of the Church in Smyrna, whom I also saw in my early youth, for he tarried a very long time, and, when a very old man, gloriously and most nobly suffering martyrdom, departed this life, having always taught the things which he had learned from the apostles, and which the Church has handed down, and which alone are true.*
> (Irenaeus, Against Heresies 3:3:4[149]

The supposed ancient age of Polycarp should immediately arouse our suspicions. People did not live long lives in the ancient world; old age was considered to start at fifty and few would have survived past their sixties. This can be illustrated by the lifespans of five long-lived individuals in the late first to second century whose ages we can be sure of; the five so called good emperors. These all lived to an old age and died of natural causes. The table below shows their age at death.

Emperor	Age at death
Nerva	67
Trajan	63
Hadrian	62
Antoninus Pius	74
Marcus Aurelius	58
Average	65

In interpreting this table it should be remembered that the emperors received a standard of care and nutrition that was far above that of the average citizen. Yet even among this group of five exceptionally long-lived and pampered emperors, the average age at death was only 65. The reality of life for most people in the Roman Empire was frequent malnutrition, disease and physically exhausting and damaging manual work. The age at death of the average citizen must have been several years younger than the Emperors, even ignoring the many who died young. And yet when we turn to the Christian literature of the time we find some amazing examples of longevity. In the apocryphal Martyrdom of Polycarp when the bishop is asked to renounce Christ he replies *"Eighty and six years have I served him, and in nothing hath he wronged me; and how, then, can I blaspheme my King, who saved me?"* This implies that it was 86 years since Polycarp's conversion which would make him over 100 at the time of his martyrdom (we may wonder how old he would have lived to had he not been martyred!) An even more remarkable example of old age comes from Hegesippus who says that Simon, bishop of Jerusalem, was 120 at his martyrdom.[150] And Anna the prophetess who, according to the Gospel of Luke, lived in the temple must also have been older than 100.[151]

We can see that the ancient prophet or teacher is a staple of Christian literature. We will consider the significance of Anna's age later, but in the other two cases the unrealistically advanced ages are an attempt to bridge the gulf of time that lay between later writers and the beginning of the Jesus movement. We have seen how the advanced age of Simon has arisen through a case of mistaken identity in which a Simon who endured martyrdom in the reign of Trajan has been confused with Simon the brother of the Lord. As for Polycarp's advanced age, it is a fiction that has been developed by someone who was well acquainted with the writings of Irenaeus. At the end of the Martyrdom of Polycarp is an account of how the letter came to be discovered. The discovery is attributed to Pionius, who had a vision which led him to find an old damaged manuscript that had been made by Isocrates of Corinth, who had in turn copied the manuscript of Gaius, who had copied the original from the papers of Irenaeus. Clearly the true author of the martyrdom lived long after the time of Irenaeus and has invented this sequence to explain how a hitherto unknown manuscript written by Irenaeus had come into his possession. Pionius the supposed discoverer of the manuscript (not the true author!) was, like Polycarp, a martyr of Smyrna, who was killed in 250. The author is intending to portray Pionius as being inspired by the miraculous discovery of the Martyrdom of Polycarp before his own martyrdom.[152] This means that the author must have been writing in the later half of the third century after the martyrdom of Pionius.

One of the remarkable things about the Martyrdom of Polycarp is that it is very specific about dates and ages which is not typical of the time. The Martyrdom tells us that Polycarp was martyred on the seventh before the calends of March in the proconsulship of Statius Quadratus. This date, 23 February, is the same day of the year on which the miraculous discoverer of the letter, Pionius, was arrested before his own martyrdom. Clearly the author of the Martyrdom has set the unknown day of the martyrdom of Polycarp to coincide with the known, and more recent day of the martyrdom of Pionius. The dating of the proconsulship of Quadratus enables us to date the year to 155. If the age of Polycarp is intended to be 86, then the author of the Martyrdom dated the birth of Polycarp to 69/70. Such a date agrees very well with the information in Irenaeus, that Polycarp knew John and would converse with him and other apostles; that John lived until the reign of Trajan (when Polycarp would have been thirty); and that Polycarp was martyred as a very old man. However, if it were intended that the 86 years be measured from the conversion of Polycarp then he would have been born c50, which is more in agreement with Irenaeus' report that he had talked with many who had seen Christ. Of course, the author of the Martyrdom knew nothing about the real date or age of Polycarp at his martyrdom because this was long in the past. His knowledge about Polycarp comes from Irenaeus, and he retrofits the dates to be in agreement with what he has read in Against Heresies.

So what can we say about the dates of the real Polycarp? There are a few things that Irenaeus says about him that we can date at least approximately. The most specific is a journey he made to Rome:

He it was who, coming to Rome in the time of Anicetus caused many to turn away from the aforesaid heretics to the Church of God, proclaiming that he had received this one and sole truth from the apostles - that, namely, which is handed down by the Church. (Irenaeus, Against Heresies 3:3:4)

This can be securely dated because Anicetus was bishop of Rome between 157-168. The sea journey between Smyrna and Rome would have been long and hazardous and would not have been undertaken by a very old man. It could certainly not have been undertaken by a dead man which is what Polycarp would have been had his date of martyrdom really been 155 as the Martyrdom of Polycarp would have it. The author of the martyrdom has blundered and set the date too early, while Polycarp was still very much alive.

The second episode that can be approximately dated is a meeting between Polycarp and Marcion. As Irenaeus writes: *"And Polycarp himself replied to Marcion, who met him on one occasion, and said, 'Do you know me? ','I do know you, the first-born of Satan.'" (Irenaeus Against Heresies 3:3:4)*[153] This meeting most likely took place in the same visit to Rome for Marcion was at his peak of prominence in Rome at the time of Anicetus. However, if it took place earlier, then it cannot have been before about 140 when Marcion first appeared on the scene.

The third thing that can be dated is Irenaeus' own account that he knew Polycarp when he was a youth. The problem with a precise dating is that we do not know when Irenaeus was born. He was a priest at the church at Lyon during the persecution of Marcus Aurelius (161-180) and was sent in 177/8 to Rome with a letter to bishop Eleutherius concerning Montanism. When he returned he was made bishop of Lyon, succeeding the previous bishop Pothinus, who had been killed in the persecution. It is around this time that he must have written Against Heresies. If we assume that he was somewhere between 40 and 55 when he became bishop, then he would have been born between 125-140. He heard Polycarp when he was still a youth - let us say when he was about 15. This would give the time that he knew Polycarp as anywhere between 140 and 155.

We can summarise our reliable date ranges below:

Polycarp journeys to Rome between 157 and 168.
Polycarp meets Marcion between 140 and 168 (most likely during Rome visit)
Irenaeus in his youth saw Polycarp between 140 and 155.

What is striking is how late all these confirmed dates are. Polycarp is a figure active in the middle of the second century and we hear no reliable stories about him that can be dated before 140. This makes the idea that he knew John Mark quite absurd - the last definite date on which we know that John was alive is c60.

As to his death, we know it must have occurred before 180, as Irenaeus speaks about his martyrdom in Against Heresies. Eusebius says that he was martyred during the persecution of Marcus Aurelius (161-180), which seems reasonable. The most likely date of his birth would be c100. This would explain why he arises to prominence around 140-150 when he is mature enough to become bishop. He would be around 60 when he makes the long journey to Rome and around 70 at his death, which make him seem very old for the ancient world. If we wanted an older Polycarp, we could push his date of birth back to around 90, but this would make him 70 when he takes the long and arduous return journey to Rome, which does not seem likely. However, even if were born in 90, there is no way he could as a young man have known the disciple John and others who had seen Christ.

What about the story that Irenaeus credits to Polycarp, that John the disciple fled from the baths when he saw Cerinthus? We should note that Irenaeus did not hear this direct from Polycarp but from others who had known Polycarp. We are thus getting the story at third or fourth hand. Nothing is known about Cerinthus other than from the writings of Irenaeus, but we can estimate the time he was active from something Irenaeus says about him:

John, the disciple of the Lord, preaches this faith, and seeks, by the proclamation of the Gospel, to remove that error which by Cerinthus had been disseminated among men, and a long time previously by those termed Nicolaitans, who are an offset of that "knowledge" falsely so called, that he might confound them, and persuade them that there is but one God, who made all things by His Word. (Irenaeus, Against Heresies 3:11:1)

It would appear from this that Cerinthus came long after the Nicolaitans whom we can date because they were the target of the author of Revelation which was written in the 90s. This would imply that Cerinthus could not have been active much earlier than c120. John Mark would have been around 100 at this time and would have to be a very sprightly old man to be taking baths and fleeing from heretics. In fact the story of John fleeing from Cerinthus is remarkably similar to stories told by Irenaeus about Polycarp himself. We have seen the account of the meeting between Polycarp and Marcion ("*the first born of Satan*") which resembles the story of John meeting Cerinthus ("*the enemy of truth*"). Even more relevant is Irenaeus' remark in the letter to Florinus about Polycarp's reaction to hearing the opinions of so called heretics: "*And he would have fled from the very place where he had been sitting or standing when he heard such words*" (*Eusebius Ecclesiastical History 5:20*). Fleeing from opponents was a wise strategy for such as Polycarp, who founded their authority on a supposed succession from the apostles. Not only did it show their revulsion at the heretical beliefs but it also saved them from being worsted in debate.

So behind the John story there is perhaps an original episode in which Polycarp fled from Cerinthus, which in repeated telling has become confused with Polycarp's stories about John. Cerinthus would appear to be a Christian who was prominent in Asia (Turkey) a little before Marcion. He taught a different version of Christianity than Polycarp and came into conflict with him.

Ignatius

There is one letter that claims to be from Polycarp and that is a letter to the Philippians. This is part of a series of letters supposedly written by Ignatius and Polycarp. According to the letters Ignatius was bishop of Antioch and Eusebius dates him to the reign of Trajan (98-117) which, if true, would make him very early.[154] There is, however, no evidence that Eusebius had any information about Ignatius which is independent from the Ignatius/Polycarp letters. His dating of Ignatius can be explained by the fact that, according to these letters, Ignatius was a contemporary of Polycarp and, according to Irenaeus, Polycarp knew John the apostle, who lived to the reign of Trajan. Eusebius is quite vague about the dating; Ignatius is introduced as a contemporary of Polycarp, who knew the apostles,[155] suggesting that this was the source of the dating.

We will show that the Ignatius/Polycarp letters are obvious forgeries, a pastiche on the letters of Paul. The sequence is based upon the idea that Ignatius is on his way to martyrdom in Rome just as in Acts Paul is sent to Rome for trial. Ignatius writes to the churches in various cities on the way to Rome in the manner of Paul. The purpose of the letter from Polycarp is to act as a framing device for the whole forged collection. It supposedly presents these collected letters to the Philippians:

The letters of Ignatius which were sent to us by him, and others as many as we had by us, we send to you, according as you gave charge; the which are subjoined to this letter; from which you will be able to gain great advantage. For they comprise faith and endurance and every kind of edification, which pertain to our Lord. Moreover concerning Ignatius himself and those that were with him, if you have any sure tidings, certify us. (Epistle of Polycarp to the Philippians 13)[156]

This both explains how the letters came to be gathered together (copies were sent by Ignatius to Polycarp, who then sent them to the Philippians) and at the same time endorses the letters (they have the approval of Polycarp). In this framing device, Polycarp asks for news of Ignatius, so as to suggest to the reader that the journey of Ignatius is still in progress.

All of which is completely unrealistic. In the letters, Ignatius has been condemned and is being sent to Rome for execution. Although a Roman citizen might appeal to be sent to Rome for trial (as did Paul) there is no way the Romans would have gone to such trouble for the execution of a condemned Christian. If Ignatius had been condemned for failing to sacrifice to the Emperor's image, he would have been executed in the arena of his hometown, Antioch. The only people sent to Rome for execution were prominent rebel and enemy leaders defeated by the Roman army whose parade and executions would be part of the victory celebrations.

Moreover, Ignatius is supposed to be heavily guarded and under condemnation for the crime of being a Christian, and yet is able to write letters to his fellow Christians at each stage of his journey. Why do his guards allow him to write such letters? Why do they not arrest the bearers of the letters because they are also Christians? He speaks about being bound to "ten leopards", that is Roman soldiers. How do these ten soldiers not notice what he is doing or try to stop him? It is true that Paul was able to write one very short letter from prison (Philemon) but that was a personal letter and was written before the Christians were sufficiently prominent to become a target for persecution. Ignatius writes a whole series of letters setting out doctrine to a number of churches. And while captive he is able to make copies of his letters so that he can send them to Polycarp in a nice authorised collected edition. Most remarkable of all he is permitted to receive visitors from the churches of the cities he passes near to.

A smoking gun for the forgery is Ignatius' letter to the Romans, in which he asks them not to intervene on his behalf and so deprive him of the fruits of martyrdom. There is no way that any real person of the early second century facing trial and death would write such a letter. It is clearly a literary production written by someone long after the actual martyrdom who wants to hold up Ignatius as an example for the martyrs of his own day.

The cult of martyrdom emerged gradually in Christianity. From the beginning, the followers of Jesus were ready to give up their lives if it proved necessary; yet they did not wish to die nor did they invite martyrdom but did anything to avoid it short of renouncing Christ, or betraying their brothers and sisters, or ceasing to spread the gospel. Probably the earliest instruction about martyrdom is a saying in the Gospel of Thomas which would have come originally from Jesus speaking through Mary:

Mary said to Jesus: "Whom are your disciples like?" He said: "They are like children dwelling in a field which is not theirs. When the Lords of the field come, they will say: 'Give our field back to us.' They strip naked in their presence to give it back to them, and they give their field to them." (Thomas 21a)

In this saying the field is the disciples' body/the world. The body and the whole physical world belong to the demons and fallen angels. It is they who rule the world exercising legitimate but evil power. They own the field and can demand it back by sentencing the disciple to death. If they do so, then the disciple must give up the field, their body, by accepting martyrdom. To give up the field they become naked, that is they surrender the garment of the body and are clothed in the spiritual garment of Jesus.

Many Christians in the early centuries were asked to yield their bodies to the owners to the field. Some recanted and denied Jesus, but many accepted death. Many pagans went to the arena to enjoy the spectacle of the executions but found themselves wondering at the patience and courage displayed by the Christians. Many witnessing such martyrdoms ended up joining the movement themselves. Persecution, far from destroying the movement, gave it increased impetus.

In such an environment, it is not surprising that a cult of martyrdom developed. Those who endured martyrdom were held up as the highest examples of discipleship; they had exchanged the things of this world for the things of heaven. And so the idea developed that by suffering martyrdom a Christian would earn eternal life. Such a concept is completely contrary to the true early beliefs of the Jesus movement where the kingdom of heaven is a state of being, a state of connection to God; if you do not possess the kingdom while living, you will not possess it when dead. But in the proto-orthodox church the kingdom becomes something to be earned by good behaviour, a reward to compensate the Christian for hardships suffered in the name of Jesus. And those who suffered the ultimate fate of the martyr had clearly paid the entry price for the kingdom in full.

So in a diseased development Christians began to welcome martyrdom, to enjoy the prospect of suffering tortures for Jesus, and, in the extreme, to precipitate their own martyrdom by giving themselves up to the authorities. Although the proto-orthodox church encouraged this cult of martyrdom, even they frowned upon those who effectively committed suicide by bringing martyrdom upon themselves. In the Martyrdom of Polycarp there is a Christian called Quintus who has come forward of his own free will but who ends up by taking the oath and denying Jesus. The Martyrdom concludes: "*we praise not those who deliver themselves up, since the Gospel does not so teach us*" (*The Martyrdom of Polycarp 4:1*).

This cult of martyrdom reached its peak in the third century. And yet in the letter of Ignatius to the Romans, which is supposedly written at the beginning of the second century, it is fully developed. In fact, the letter has some remarkable similarities to a short portion of the Martyrdom of Polycarp that precedes Polycarp's own martyrdom. The table below shows this section in full alongside corresponding passages in the letter of Ignatius to the Romans.

The Martyrdom of Polycarp [157]	Epistle of Ignatius to the Romans
2.1 *Blessed therefore and noble are all the martyrdoms which have taken place according to the will of God (for it behoves us to be very scrupulous and to assign to God the power over all things).*	4.1 *I write to all the churches, and I bid all men know, that of my own free will I die for God, unless you should hinder me. I exhort you, do not become an unseasonable kindness to me. Let me be given to the wild beasts, for through them I can attain unto God. I am God's wheat, and I am ground by the teeth of wild beasts that I may be found pure bread of God.*
2.2 *For who could fail to admire their nobleness and patient endurance and loyalty to the Master? Seeing that when they were so torn by lashes that the mechanism of their flesh was visible even as far as the inward veins and arteries, they endured patiently, so that the very bystanders had pity and wept; while they themselves reached such a pitch of bravery that none of them uttered a cry or a groan, thus showing to us all that at that hour the martyrs of Christ being tortured were absent from the flesh, or rather that the Lord was standing by and conversing with them.*	3.2-3 *Only pray that I may have power within and without, so that I may not only say it but also desire it; that I may not only be called a Christian, but also be found one. For if I shall be found so, then can I also be called one, and be faithful then, when I am no more visible to the world. Nothing visible is good. For our God Jesus Christ, being in the Father, is the more plainly visible.*

The Martyrdom of Polycarp [157]	Epistle of Ignatius to the Romans
2.3 *And giving heed unto the grace of Christ they despised the tortures of this world, purchasing at the cost of one hour a release from eternal punishment.*	6.1-2 *The farthest bounds of the universe shall profit me nothing, neither the kingdoms of this world. It is good for me to die for Jesus Christ rather than to reign over the farthest bounds of the earth. Him I seek, who died on our behalf; Him I desire, who rose again [for our sake]. The pangs of a new birth are upon me. Bear with me, brethren. Do not hinder me from living; do not desire my death. Bestow not on the world one who desires to be God's, neither allure him with material things.*
And they found the fire of their inhuman torturers cold: for they set before their eyes the escape from the eternal fire which is never quenched; while with the eyes of their heart they gazed upon the good things which are reserved for those that endure patiently, things which neither ear hath heard nor eye hath seen, neither have they entered into the heart of man, but were shown by the Lord to them, for they were no longer men but angels already.	7.2-3 *For I write to you in the midst of life, yet lusting after death. My lust hath been crucified, and there is no fire of material longing in me, but only living water which is speaking in me, saying within me, Come to the Father. I have no delight in the food of corruption or in the delights of this life. I desire the bread of God, which is the flesh of Christ who was of the seed of David; and for a draught I desire His blood, which is love incorruptible.* 6.2 *Suffer me to receive the pure light. When I am come thither, then shall I be a man.*

The Martyrdom of Polycarp [157]	Epistle of Ignatius to the Romans
2.4 *And in like manner also those that were condemned to the wild beasts endured fearful punishments, being made to lie on sharp shells and buffeted with other forms of manifold tortures, that the devil might, if possible, by the persistence of the punishment bring them to a denial; for he tried many wiles against them.*	5.3 *Come fire and cross and packs of wild beasts, cuttings and mangling, wrenching of bones, hacking of limbs, crushing of my whole body, come cruel tortures of the devil to assail me. Only be it mine to attain unto Jesus Christ.* 7.1 *The prince of this world would fain tear me in pieces and corrupt my mind which is towards God. Let not any of you therefore who are present abet him. Rather stand you on my side, that is on God's side. Do not speak of Jesus Christ and desire the world.*
3.1 *But thanks be to God; for He verily prevailed against all. For the right noble Germanicus encouraged their timorousness through the constancy which was in him; and he fought with the wild beasts in a signal way. For when the proconsul wished to prevail upon him and bade him have pity on his youth, he used violence and dragged the wild beast towards him, desiring the more speedily to obtain a release from their unrighteous and lawless life.*	5.2 *May I have joy of the beasts that have been prepared for me; and I pray that I may find them prompt; nay I will entice them that they may devour me promptly, not as they have done to some, refusing to touch them through fear. And if they do not do this willingly, I myself will force them to it.*

The author of the letters of Ignatius tends not to just copy his sources but uses them quite freely in developing his own writing around them. However, each section 2.1 to 3.1 of the Martyrdom corresponds to something in the letter to Romans. Moreover, some of these correspondences are quite specific and unlikely to arise by chance, such as the young man Germanicus pulling the wild beasts towards himself and Ignatius saying he will do the same. If the two are related, then the direction of copying must be from the Martyrdom to the letter to the Romans. This section of the Martyrdom is a short description of the sufferings of a group of martyrs of whom only Germanicus is named. Some details, such as the martyrs being flayed as far as the inward veins are gruesome and realistic, showing that they are based upon eye witness testimony. The supernatural elements such as Jesus standing and talking to the martyrs are not confused with the actual witnessed events - it is not said that the spectators could see Jesus but only that the courage of the martyrs was such that it was as if Jesus were talking to them. The Ignatius letter is very different, being a long convoluted and quite unrealistic theological elaboration of the desire for martyrdom. It is the letter to the Romans that must have used the Martyrdom passages as a source and not the other way around.

All of which is consistent with section 2.1 to 3.1 being earlier than the rest of the Martyrdom and dating to the second century when it could be used as a source by the author of the Ignatius letter. It is clear that the Polycarp/Ignatius letters are forgeries but when were they written?

The silence of Irenaeus

If we examine the Ignatius and Polycarp letters we find an amazing series of coincidences with the contents of Irenaeus' Against Heresies. Both Ignatius and Polycarp seem to have believed much the same things as Irenaeus and opposed the same "heretical" beliefs that were also opposed by Irenaeus.

In the letters of Ignatius, there are two overriding political themes. The first is the promotion of an authoritarian and hierarchical structure for the church led by the bishops. The second theme is opposition to certain groups of "heretics" and Judaizers. According to the letters of Ignatius, the members of the churches should be completely subject to the bishop, who should even have the power to approve or reject their marriage partners.[158] Although the power of the bishops is to be preeminent the letters also emphasise the importance of two other groups under the bishop; the deacons or ministers and the presbyters (elders). The main group of "heretics" that the author of the letters opposes are Docetists who believed that Jesus was spiritual in nature and did not have a material body and so did not suffer in a material sense.

These themes agree with Irenaeus' own concerns. Against Heresies was aimed against those that Irenaeus regarded as heretics, including those who had a Docetic view of Christ. And in this work Irenaeus promotes the idea of the authority of the bishops arising from apostolic succession[159] in order to refute the supposed special knowledge of the heretics. Irenaeus also promotes the authority of the presbyters,[160] who have received their knowledge passed down from the apostles, again using them as an argu-

ment against the heretics. According to Irenaeus, both presbyters and bishops have received apostolic succession and it is unclear how the two roles
related to each other. In the letters of Ignatius, the bishop is a single individual in charge of the church in a city, and this is also the way that Irenaeus uses the term. Against Heresies gives the succession for the bishop of
Rome, the pre-eminent church, in a passage that the Catholic church uses
to support the concept of the papacy.[161] However, in the earlier work 1
Clement, which is supposedly a letter written from the church in Rome to
the church in Corinth, the word bishop seems interchangeable with presbyter[162] and applies to a group within a church rather than a single individual. So there was a great deal of confusion and variation in the governance
of the early churches and the terms presbyters and bishops originally
meant more or less the same thing; a group of senior members charged
with the running of the church by the other members. The idea of a single
bishop arose from the fictitious concept of a single "monarch" appointed by
the apostles over each church which is first voiced by Irenaeus in order to
combat the plurality of beliefs that he called heresy.

In reality, the early Jesus movement was chaotic. It is true that there was
a structure of apostles appointed by Cephas, but the role of an apostle was
an itinerant one. The apostle would come to a place, recruit, set up a nascent church and then take up his staff and move on. The principle of
spreading the gospel by wandering applied not just to apostles but to all
those in the movement; as Jesus says in the Gospel of Thomas, "*Become
passers-by*" *(Thomas 42)*. The church was not conceived as a human structure
that would need governance and management but as the spiritual union of
all within the movement. However, what actually happened was that most
Christians did not wander but stayed put. As fixed churches grew and developed, they needed management, and this duty would fall haphazardly
on whichever individuals had sufficient influence to wield control. This
might be those who had been longest in the movement, the elders, or they
might be those who had access to resources or social status. Most churches
were house churches that would meet in the home of a prominent member,
who would effectively be the patron of the church and who would doubtless be the effective leader. The idea of a single bishop who ruled each
church is anachronistic to the time of Ignatius.

We can see how well the letters of Ignatius support the causes that Irenaeus fought for. Irenaeus is very keen to quote prior authorities in support
of his augments and Ignatius, the early martyr and bishop of Antioch,
would have been the dream authority as far as Irenaeus is concerned. And

he must have been well aware of the letters of Ignatius because he seems to quote from the letter to the Romans:

As a certain man of ours said, when he was condemned to the wild beasts because of his testimony with respect to God: "I am the wheat of Christ, and am ground by the teeth of the wild beasts, that I may be found the pure bread of God." (Against Heresies 5:28:4)

This quote is included in a section about the apocalypse. Irenaeus alludes to the Gospel of Matthew, where John the Baptist predicts about Jesus : "*he will thoroughly clean his threshing floor, and gather his wheat into the barn; but he will burn up the chaff with unquenchable fire*" (Matthew 3:12). Irenaeus equates the chaff with those he calls heretics and the wheat with the faithful. He then goes further and develops the theme of the faithful being like wheat which is processed into bread through martyrdom: "*And for this cause tribulation is necessary for those who are saved, that having been after a manner broken up, and rendered fine, and sprinkled over by the patience of the Word of God, and set on fire, they may be fitted for the royal banquet*" (Against Heresies 5:28:4). Both the wheat and the bread are images used by the early Jesus movement for the kingdom of heaven. The bread is specifically the substance of Jesus, which is consumed by the disciple so that the essence of Jesus will enter into him or her. But Irenaeus turns this metaphor around and makes the bread into the disciple. Being rendered, that is broken, and being burnt refers to methods of martyrdom, which he likens to steps in making bread. In this way, Irenaeus distorts the original meaning of the metaphors so that now it is martyrdom that leads to the kingdom of heaven. The quote from the "*man of ours*" conveniently extends this metaphor of the wheat turning into bread to martyrdom by wild beasts.

Not only does Irenaeus apparently quote from Ignatius he also directly mentions the very letter from Polycarp, which introduces the collected edition of the Ignatius letters:

There is also a very powerful Epistle of Polycarp written to the Philippians, from which those who choose to do so, and are anxious about their salvation, can learn the character of his faith, and the preaching of the truth. (Against Heresies 3:3:4)

Irenaeus would have read in this letter about the blessed Ignatius, about his martyrdom and his letters, including the endorsement from his former teacher and hero Polycarp: "*For they comprise faith and endurance and every*

kind of edification, which pertains to our Lord" (Polycarp to the Philippians 13:2).
Besides Irenaeus would surely have heard all about Ignatius from Polycarp
himself while studying under him. For given the glowing opinion that Polycarp has about Ignatius and his letters, how could he have not mentioned
them to Irenaeus?

And yet here is the mystery; Irenaeus never once mentions the name of
Ignatius anywhere in his writings. He does not mention him when discussing the bishops and the concept of apostolic succession, even though in
letter after letter Ignatius asserts the primacy of the bishop. Why would
Irenaeus not quote the early bishop of Antioch's view on this subject? He
does not mention Ignatius' name when discussing martyrdom and he does
not use him as an authority against the heretics. For example, in several
places Irenaeus attempts to refute those who believed that Jesus did not
really suffer physically but only in appearance.[163] It just so happens that
Ignatius also writes against these same beliefs; in the letter to the Smyrnaeans he states that Jesus truly suffered and not only in appearance as some
believed[164] and he repeats this in the letter to the Trallians.[165] And yet Irenaeus never uses these very clear statements from the early bishop of Antioch that agree so precisely with his own views. Why not?

The answer that best fits the data is that Irenaeus does not quote the Ignatius letters because they were not in existence when he wrote Against
Heresies. Indeed, it is possible that Irenaeus had never even heard of Ignatius. The letters are a forgery produced by someone who had read Against
Heresies and who was a strong supporter of Irenaeus' views. Origen, who
writes in the first half of the third century, is familiar with the letters, which
means that they must have been forged in the decade or two after Irenaeus
wrote Against Heresies, say around 180-200. As for the location of the forger, we need only look at the churches to whom the letters are addressed.
The letter to the Romans is written to the church at the ultimate destination
and is necessary to the storyline. But the other letters, those to Ephesus,
Smyrna, Magnesia on the Meander, Tralles and Philadelphia, are all addressed to churches in one small region of Anatolia. This is the area that the
forger is interested in, the place from whence he comes. In contrast, the
great city of Antioch, the home city of Ignatius, is shadowy; the forger frequently refers to the church in Syria[166] rather than the church in Antioch,
showing that he does not make the distinction between the area and its
principal city. We can even be more specific as to the forger's location; all
the letters with only one exception are either written from Smyrna or to

Smyrna. The central role that Smyrna plays in the letters indicates that it is the forger's home.

This area of Anatolia, and Smyrna in particular, is where both Polycarp and Irenaeus came from. For although Irenaeus is at Lyon when he writes Against Heresies, he listened to Polycarp as a youth, and so must have spent his boyhood in Smyrna. He would have surely retained many connections in the area. So it is understandable that the works of the bishop of Lyon should be read in Smyrna and that his words would fall on receptive soil. This is also the area of the Martyrdom of Polycarp part of which, as we have seen, is used as a source for Ignatius' letter to the Romans.

There is one more letter in the collection, other than that to Rome, that does not relate to this small part of Anatolia, and that is Polycarp's letter to Philippi in Macedonia. The fact that Irenaeus mentions this letter is held up as proof that the letter must be genuine. But there is another explanation; the letter we have is not the one that Irenaeus knew but has been put together by the forger based on the description in Against Heresies.

We would expect those who put store by Irenaeus' description of Polycarp as someone who had known the disciple John to take great delight in this letter of Polycarp. After all, here is someone who had gained their information directly from the disciple who had rested on Jesus' breast and is now writing a "very powerful epistle" about his faith and about the truth. What insights it should give into Jesus and early Christianity! And yet even the most orthodox commentator is disappointed in the letter of Polycarp to the Philippians. For it is a pastiche cobbled together from other writings, principally the letters of Paul, including the fake letters 1 and 2 Timothy, the Gospel of Matthew and 1 Clement. If Polycarp were really the listener of John and this is really his letter then why does it largely consist of phrases ransacked from other works? Why does Polycarp not simply report what John told him?

As well as writing about Ignatius, the letter also gives the Philippians advice about a former presbyter called Valens who, together with his wife, has been guilty of some financial misconduct. He tells the Philippians to forgive the two of them and receive them back into the church. The forger is very good at introducing such local colour into his letters, and they are sprinkled through with names and personal touches. This is one reason the letters are accepted as genuine; it is hard for honest people to believe that such details could have been made up in a deliberate attempt to deceive. But if the forger were writing some 80 years or so after the events he is describing, he is free to invent names and circumstances, as there is no living witness to contradict him. And we know that forging such details was part of a venerable tradition among proto-orthodox Christians; the technique is used, for example, in the letters of Paul to Timothy, letters which the forger of the Ignatius letters uses but which were, ironically, forged in their own right. In fact, the story about Valens and his wife bears a resemblance to two other sources which the forger would have been well familiar with; the story of Ananias and his wife in Acts, who sell a property having promised to give the proceeds to the church but who lie about the price and keep back some of the money;[167] and 2 Corinthians where Paul suggests that an unnamed person who has been publicly shamed and excluded by the Corinthians for sexual immorality should now be forgiven and welcomed back.[168]

Although the ostensible purpose of the letter is to pass on the letters of Ignatius, to ask after him and to give advice about Valens, the bulk of the letter has nothing to do with these subjects; it is a homily setting out the teachings of Polycarp. The key to understanding the letter is to put ourselves in the place of the forger. To get the fake Ignatius letters accepted he needs to give them endorsement and credibility. He comes up with the clever idea of using the Polycarp letter described by Irenaeus for this purpose. So the main purpose of his letter is to serve as the framing device for the collection of the Ignatius letters and to have Polycarp appear to praise Ignatius and his letters. The forger uses Paul's letters as his model throughout and here he adds the type of detail that Paul would include, such as the Valens incident and the personal touches. But he then also has to meet Irenaeus' description of the letter as setting out the *"character of his faith, and the preaching of the truth"*. Hence the homily expounding the teachings of Polycarp. He cobbles this together by going through accepted proto-orthodox works and extracting appropriate material, rephrasing some of this material to simulate Polycarp's own words. To explain why Polycarp should embark upon this homily, he uses the device that the Philippians have requested Polycarp to write to them about righteousness.[169] He is in fact taking Irenaeus' description quite literally; the letter is intended for those concerned about salvation who desire information about Polycarp's preaching.

As a forgery the Ignatius-Polycarp epistles are good but not perfect. It is difficult to forge a sequence of eight letters and not make an occasional error. The forger's most obvious slip happens in the Polycarp epistle. The epistle starts by rejoicing that Ignatius has just passed through Philippi and ends with an enquiry of whether there is any further news of him. However, in the middle the forger makes the mistake of lumping Ignatius together with Paul and the other apostles and speaking about him in the past tense as if he were already dead: "*they are in their due place in the presence of the Lord, with whom also they suffered*" (Polycarp to the Philippians 9:2). The forger's problem is that he is used to thinking of Ignatius as a person who is long dead, as Paul and the apostles, and falls back into this mode of thought when his attention slips.

If this is an unforced error, then the forger's other mistakes are due to the difficulties of his task. One of these mistakes is having Ignatius sent to Rome as a condemned man. If there is a kernel of historical truth behind Ignatius then he must have been an early first century Christian from Antioch who was a Roman citizen and who asserted his right to be tried in Rome, where he was found guilty and executed. However, it would not meet the literary needs of the forger to have Ignatius sent to Rome for trial; he has to show him as a martyr, as already condemned.

Another problem relates to the strange journey that Ignatius makes to Rome. This is not dictated by the physical practicalities of transferring a prisoner safely across a distance in excess of a thousand miles in the Roman world. Instead, it is dictated again by the literary requirements of the forger's story. He has to bring Ignatius into his home region of Anatolia and in particular to the city of Smyrna, so he has him travel the very long land route instead of sending him direct to Rome by sea. Would the Roman's really have sent ten soldiers on such a journey simply to guard one Christian? But sending Ignatius by road to Smyrna is not the least of it. The idea of using Irenaeus' mention of the letter from Polycarp is brilliant but brings its own difficulties. The problem is that Irenaeus says that the letter was to the Philippians. So to incorporate the letter into the forgery Ignatius and his long-suffering escort must pass through Philippi in Macedonia. They sail from Troas to Neapolis, the seaport of Philippi, which is the same journey as Paul makes in Acts 16:11. Paul, however, is travelling to Macedonia, not Rome.

Another error the forger makes is time compression. To tell his story in a brief exchange of letters, the forger has to compress events that would, in the real world, have taken considerable time to play out. This can be seen in the sequence of events in the letters:

Ignatius travels from Antioch to Smyrna. There he writes to the Ephesians, Magnesians, Trallians and Romans. He asks them all to pray for the church in Syria.

Ignatius has moved on to Troas from where he learns that they are to cross unexpectedly to Neapolis.

Somewhere between Smyrna and Troas he learns that the persecution of
the church in Antioch has ceased. He asks that all the churches send am-
bassadors, or at least letters, to Antioch to celebrate.

He crosses over the sea and passes through Philippi. The Philippians
write to Polycarp in Smyrna reporting on the passage of Ignatius and asking him if he will send their letter on to Antioch.

Polycarp writes back to the Philippians enclosing the "collected edition"
of Ignatius' letters and asking if there is any further news of Ignatius.

There are a number of absurdities in this storyline. First the ending of
the persecution of the church in Antioch is a severe case of time compression. The cessation of the persecution is represented as a sudden event,
which happens in response to the prayers of Polycarp and others. It is in
effect a miracle in which Ignatius' faithfulness unto death is rewarded by
the physical salvation of his flock. Moreover, it happens while Ignatius and
others are still on the way to Rome for execution and indeed sufficiently
quickly for Ignatius to receive news about it and have sufficient time to
organise a conference in celebration! Just think what this involves:

There is an event that signals the ending of the persecution.

Those of the church in Antioch are so confident that the persecution has
ended that they immediately send a messenger to Ignatius.

The messenger must travel faster than Ignatius otherwise it is impossible to overtake him.

Even if he travels faster the messenger can leave only a short time after
Ignatius, perhaps just a few days, otherwise he still will not be able to catch
Ignatius before he leaves Troas.

In reality a persecution would not end overnight. It would take time,
several months, perhaps even a year or two, before Christians could be
confident that the persecution had ended. Yet the letters of Ignatius represents the ending as a sudden event. What could this event be? Did the Roman authorities suddenly announce that they were ceasing persecution of
Christians and if so why? After all, Christians were still officially criminals.
Would the Romans really announce that a class of criminals would no
longer be prosecuted? Or if the event were the replacement of the local
governor how could Christians be sure that his successor would not continue the persecution? It is simply not possible that the church could have
come to the conclusion that the persecution had ended and determined to

send a messenger in such a short period after Ignatius had been condemned.

This is not the only absurdity. Ignatius' response to the news is to organise a conference. He writes to Smyrna and to Philadelphia urging them all to send delegates. He also writes to Polycarp (who would be at Smyrna) urging him not just to send his own delegate but to write to the churches ahead of Ignatius. When Polycarp writes to the Philippians he mentions their letter to Antioch.[170] What, we may wonder, is the purpose of all this effort? It is apparently nothing more than to celebrate the end of the persecution! Travel was laborious, expensive and dangerous in the ancient world. Would churches really send members all the way to Antioch for such a frivolous cause? If church members were willing to travel would they not be better employed in spreading the gospel? And we must remember that Ignatius and others have been very recently condemned to death at Antioch. Why would the churches send their own people into considerable danger for no good purpose?

If this is not enough, there is a smoking gun proof of forgery among Ignatius' invitations. In the letter to the Philadelphians he makes a very specific request that they elect a deacon to send to Antioch. In case they baulk at this request he engenders some peer rivalry: "*it is not impossible for you to do this for the name of God; even as the churches which are nearest have sent bishops, and others presbyters and deacons*" (*Ignatius to the Philadelphians* 10:2). We have already seen how impossible it is that Ignatius could have known that the persecution is over. But now we have to believe an even more remarkable thing, that he has sent out invitations and received the responses back in an incredibly short time. Ignatius only hears about the end of persecution somewhere between Smyrna and Troas. He would then have to write to a large number of churches, including those he mentions that are near to Antioch. While the messengers bearing these letters were covering the long distance back towards Antioch, Ignatius himself would be moving in the opposite direction and would be at Troas long before they reached their destination. The messengers would have to wait while the various churches debated the requests and then turn around and start back again all the way to Troas with the cheerful news that the churches were sending bishops, presbyters and deacons. We know that Ignatius could only have spent a short time at Troas because he does not have the chance to write to the churches ahead with the news of the end of persecution.[171] Yet somehow he has miraculously received the messengers back again before he leaves Troas, including those who have gone all the way to the churches nearer Anti-

och and back, because he mentions the results in his letter to the Philadelphians.

It might be objected that although Ignatius is organising the delegates
from the churches on his way, perhaps the delegates he mentions in Philadelphians have been organised directly from Antioch. If so Ignatius could
have heard about the intention to send delegates via the same messenger
who brought him news of the end of the persecution. However, this would
simply make the timescale for the messenger from Antioch even more impossible than it already is. For not only would the church at Antioch have
to hear about the instantaneous suspension of the persecution, but they
would also have to organise a celebratory conference before sending their
messenger to catch up with Ignatius. The letter to Philadelphians mentions
churches that are going to send bishops, churches that will send presbyters
and others that will send deacons. So we have several churches involved.
These would be spread out in different cities, and only some of them (those
that send bishops) are near to Antioch. It would take the church in Antioch
some months to arrange such a conference. They cannot start organising it
before they are certain that the persecution is ended, and they would have
to arrange the conference and receive messengers back before their messenger to Ignatius leaves. And yet this messenger somehow catches up
with Ignatius between Smyrna and Troas, even though Ignatius has spent
the whole time on the road to Troas moving at the speed of a contingent of
Roman soldiers.

Clearly this is all absurd. There is no way that the timescale would work
out in the real world. The conference is a purely literary invention. We can
even reconstruct the nature of the source that the author of the forgery is
using, which must have said something like this:

> *The persecution of the church at Antioch stopped after the trial of Ignatius and*
> *all the churches rejoiced with Antioch at the ending of the persecution.*

The forger takes this literally and so has Ignatius hear that the persecution has ended and organise the conference so that all the churches can celebrate with Antioch.

A supporter of the letters might argue that the fact that Irenaeus appears
to quote Ignatius as the wheat of God ground down by the teeth of the wild
beasts proves that the letters must have been in existence before Against
Heresies was written. But this can be explained better if the forger copied
Irenaeus rather than the other way around. When Irenaeus quotes from a
written work he normally gives the source of the quote. But in this case

Irenaeus does not give any source except that it was said by a *"certain man of ours"* who has been condemned for his testimony. If Irenaeus has taken it from the letter of Ignatius to the Romans then why does not he say that? This is all one with Irenaeus' strange silence about Ignatius. If we did not have the Ignatius letters we would assume that a *"certain man of ours"* meant someone in Irenaeus' own church of Lyons. This was a church of many martyrs. It had endured a horrific persecution shortly before Irenaeus wrote Against Heresies. In fact the quote fits Irenaeus' argument, that the martyrs are made into the bread of God through their suffering, so well that it is difficult to believe that Irenaeus himself has not himself coined it, although it was probably based loosely on something said by an actual Lyon martyr. The forger has picked on this particular quote because it was unattributed and has then incorporated it into the fake letter to the Romans extolling martyrdom.

The appendix to this chapter shows the many detailed connections between the Ignatius-Polycarp letters and Against Heresies. To summarise:

Both feature Polycarp and the letter from Polycarp to the Philippians.

All of the letters bar one are supposedly either written from or to Smyrna, which is also the hometown of Irenaeus.

The passages about heretics in the letters can all be linked to Against Heresies.

When Polycarp talks about three classes of heretics these can be directly linked to the description of three gnostics (Saturninus, Basilides and Carpocrates) in section 1.24-25 of Against Heresies where they occur in the same order and using similar vocabulary.

There are specific quotes that have been taken from Against Heresies, including "the firstborn of Satan" in the letter of Polycarp which are the words Polycarp uses against Marcion, and the description of Ignatius being the wheat of God ground down by the teeth of the wild beasts.

A number of the major themes of Against Heresies are reflected in the letters including;

-Opposition to Docetism

- Opposition to those regarded as Judaizers and, in particular, the Ebionites

- Stressing that Jesus had a physical existence, that he was born through Mary and the holy spirit and that he was really crucified under Pilate.

- The "impossible" virgin birth of Jesus.

- The reality of the sufferings of Jesus (which in turn validated the sufferings of the martyrs)

- The importance of the redemptive nature of the blood of Christ;

- The role of the Eucharist

The explanation of these links is that the letters were forged by a supporter of Irenaeus who was well acquainted with Against Heresies and who lived in the Smyrna area. The purpose of the letters is to provide historical validation of the doctrines set out in Against Heresies and to reinforce the power of the bishops. They mark a milestone in the development of the proto-orthodox church coming from a time when that church was separating itself from those it regarded as heretics. The philosophy of this separation was developed first by Irenaeus, with his formulation of the myth of the one true church going back to the apostles who vested their authority in the bishops and presbyters. The foundations of Irenaeus' reconceptualisation of the church was a group of texts that he regarded as genuine and which were eventually to form the New Testament, as well as the practical example of the martyrs who suffered in imitation of Christ. Irenaeus groups the other forms of Christianity that existed at this time together as "heretics", using their very diversity as an argument against them. The letters of Ignatius show that some in the proto-orthodox church were ready to produce complete forgeries to support this position. These forgeries were accepted as genuine by the many honest members of the church who were deceived into thinking that the proto-orthodox viewpoint went back to the origins of Christianity and that the authority of bishops was derived ultimately from Jesus.

Irenaeus himself did not stoop to forgery, but he was prone to exaggeration and distortion; for example, his list of the bishops of Rome or his account of Polycarp listening to the apostles. The real origins of the proto-orthodox church lay not with the apostles but with the written gospels. In reality, the time of Irenaeus is a time of great confusion; the origins of the movement had been obscured by the noise of many interpretations which had overwhelmed the original signal of historical truth. Christians of the time must have been bewildered by the sheer number of conflicting texts, sects and philosophies. The genius of Irenaeus was to give them what they desperately craved, a simple concept of the church that tied in with the popular accounts in the gospels. He did this by discarding all the beliefs that appeared to contradict the gospels, some of which in truth went back far beyond the gospels to the origins of the movement. By labelling these as heresies he was able to reject them as being made up by "gnostics" who existed in the recent past.

Polycarp lived too late to know John Mark and the traditions that link John to Ephesus are false. These traditions have their origins in Revelation and the Gospel of John, which both claim John as their supposed author or authority. It was natural for mid second century Christians to think that John must have been alive when these works were written in the Ephesus area at the turn of the century. We also know from Papias that a presbyter John was active in the same area.

There is evidence that John became a martyr long before the reign of Trajan. The last we hear of John is from Paul's last letter, Philemon, where a Mark is included in the list of those who send greetings. This is consistent with other evidence that John Mark is in Rome with Mary in the early 60s. As a prominent Christian in Rome, it is very unlikely that he would have survived the persecution of Nero which claimed both Mary and Paul. Would he have left Mary who by this time was an elderly lady?

That John was indeed martyred is indicated by the evidence of the story of the sons of Zebedee in Mark. The point of the story, as told by the author of Mark, is that both James and John will drink of the cup, meaning martyrdom. The Gospel of Mark was written in the 70s so both James and John must have been martyred by this time. We have seen that James was most likely executed by Herod Agrippa II, and a martyrdom of John in Rome under Nero would mean that both brothers died before Mark was written. So it would appear that John was dead in the mid-60s, some thirty years before Polycarp was even born.

Appendix: The Ignatius-Polycarp letters and Against Heresies

This appendix shows the similarities between the Ignatius-Polycarp letters and Against Heresies. There are eighteen areas in which we can see close similarities between the two. So many similarities cannot be coincidence but are explained if the letters are forgeries made by a supporter of Irenaeus who had access to a copy of Against Heresies.

Polycarp is prominent in both the letters and Against Heresies

In the Ignatius letters, Polycarp is used as an authority to validate the letters. But it is Against Heresies that is the only genuine source of information about Polycarp who was a teacher of Irenaeus.

A letter of Polycarp to the Philippians features in both the letters and Against Heresies

A letter of Polycarp to the Philippians is used to present and endorse the collected letters of Ignatius.

A letter of Polycarp to the Philippians is mentioned in Against Heresies 3:3:4 but with no detail of what it contained and no mention of Ignatius.

Both the letters and Against Heresies emphasise the authority of the bishops

The Ignatius letters emphasise the authority of the bishops, who are seen as a single individual in charge of a church.

This view of the bishop as a single "monarch" of a church was first set out in Against Heresies 3:3:1-3, which envisages the bishops as being appointed by succession from the apostles. Irenaeus gives the succession of the bishop of Rome as a list of individuals who ruled one after the other.

Both have a connection to Smyrna

All except one of the Ignatius-Polycarp letters are supposedly written either to or from Smyrna.

But Smyrna is also Irenaeus' probable home city.

A passage about three types of heretics in the Polycarp letter corresponds closely to a section in Against Heresies about three gnostic teachers

In the Polycarp letter, there is a condemnation of three types of heretics:

For every one who shall not confess that Jesus Christ is come in the flesh, is antichrist: and whosoever shall not confess the testimony of the Cross, is of the devil; and whosoever shall pervert the oracles of the Lord to his own lusts and say that there is neither resurrection nor judgment, that man is the firstborn of Satan. (Polycarp to Philippians 7:1)

But Polycarp's supposed condemnation corresponds so closely to section 1:24-25 of Against Heresies that there must be literary dependence. In this section, Irenaeus sets out the beliefs of three different gnostics, Saturninus, Basilides and Carpocrates. Each of the three types in Polycarp's letter corresponds with one of these three gnostics in exactly the same order as they appear in Against Heresies.

Irenaeus says about Saturninus: *He has also laid it down as a truth, that the saviour was without birth, without body, and without figure, but was only sup-*

posed to be a visible man (*Against Heresies 1:24:2*). Compare to the first type in the Polycarp letter: *"shall not confess that Jesus Christ is come in the flesh"*.

Irenaeus writes that Basilides did not believe in the crucifixion of Jesus but that another, Simon the Cyrene, was crucified in his stead. Compare to the second type in the Polycarp letter: *"shall not confess the testimony of the Cross"*.

Irenaeus says of Carpocrates and his followers: *"they lead a licentious life, and, to conceal their impious doctrines, they abuse the name [of Christ], as a means of hiding their wickedness"* (*Against Heresies 1:25:3*). Compare to the third type in the Polycarp letter: *"shall pervert the oracles of the Lord to his own lusts"*. Also, Irenaeus reports that Carpocrates believed in the transmigration of souls, that things are only evil or good in human judgement and that only when a soul had experienced every experience could it ascend. Compare to the Polycarp letter: *"there is neither resurrection nor judgment"*. Irenaeus also says that they were *"sent forth by Satan to bring dishonour upon the Church"* (*Against Heresies 1:25:3*). Compare to the Polycarp letter: *"is the firstborn of Satan"*.

The exact phrase *"the firstborn of Satan"* has been copied from Irenaeus' story about Polycarp meeting Marcion in Against Heresies 3:3:4.

Both the letters and Against Heresies are against Judaism and Christian Judaizers

Ignatius writes against Judaism and Christian Judaizers in Magnesians and Philadelphians. In Philadelphians 6:1 he says that they should not listen to anyone preaching Judaism: *"for it is better to hear Christianity from a man who is circumcised than Judaism from one uncircumcised."*

In Against Heresies 1:16 Irenaeus writes against Christians who were close to Judaism. This section, which follows on from the sections above, covers Cerinthus and the Ebionites. Although Irenaeus links the Ebionites to both Cerinthus and Carpocrates, they seem to have very traditional Jewish views. They repudiate Paul as an apostate and live by the law: *"As to the prophetical writings, they endeavour to expound them in a somewhat singular manner: they practise circumcision, persevere in the observance of those customs which are enjoined by the law, and are so Judaic in their style of life, that they even adore Jerusalem as if it were the house of God."*

Both the letters and Against Heresies say that the Jewish prophets predicted and waited for Jesus

Ignatius in Magnesians tells his readers not to live according to Judaism: *"for the divine prophets lived after Christ Jesus"* and *"being inspired by his grace to the end that they which are disobedient might be fully persuaded that there is one God who manifested himself through Jesus Christ his son, who is his word ..."* (Magnesians 8:2). Also: *"even the prophets, being his disciples, were expecting him as their teacher through the spirit."* (Magnesians 9:2)

One of Irenaeus' major themes is that the prophets predicted and expected Jesus (see Against Heresies 3:21; 4:7; 4:10; 4:11). He seeks to prove that the old and new covenants are both from the same God and that Jesus is the outcome of the old covenant. In 4:11:1 he says about the prophets and righteous men that they *"prayed that they might attain to that period in which they should see their Lord face to face, and hear his words"* (compare with *"even the prophets, being his disciples, were expecting him as their teacher through the spirit"*).

An identical quote from a martyr is used in both the letters and Against Heresies

Ignatius in Romans 4:1: *I am God's wheat, and I am ground by the teeth of wild beasts that I may be found pure bread of Christ.*

Irenaeus in Against Heresies: *As a certain man of ours said, when he was condemned to the wild beasts because of his testimony with respect to God: "I am the wheat of Christ, and am ground by the teeth of the wild beasts, that I may be found the pure bread of God."* (Against Heresies 5:28:4)

Both the letters and Against Heresies talk in similar forms about the complex gnostic systems of angels and rulers

In Trallians 5, Ignatius says that although he could tell his readers about heavenly things this would harm them because they are still "infants" and would "choke". One source for this is a cut and paste borrowing from 1 Corinthians 3:2 where Paul says that he has had to feed the Corinthians on milk because they are not ready for meat. In the following passage Ignatius talks about his own knowledge of profound mysteries: *For I myself also, albeit I am in bonds and can comprehend heavenly things and the arrays of the angels and the musterings of the principalities, things visible and things invisible - I myself am not yet by reason of this a disciple. For we lack many things, that God may not be lacking to us (Trallians 5:2).* Ignatius is claiming to be able to understand such things as gnostic mysteries but then claims that he is not a disciple on this account. In other words, Ignatius has the power to know mysteries but chooses not to know them, because to lack such knowledge means that God is not lacking in him. The author of the forgery is tying himself in knots because he is attempting to trump the gnostics by asserting two contradictory things at the same time; (i) that because of his impending martyrdom Ignatius has the power to have superior knowledge of the very heavenly things that the gnostics claim to have knowledge of; and (ii) that such "gnostic" knowledge is harmful and that the Christians who lack such knowledge are closer to God.

We find the same opposition to complex gnostic systems involving the angels and heavenly rulers in Against Heresies. The actual source that the Ignatius forger seems to have used is the very beginning of Against Heresies. Here Irenaeus talks about the gnostics leading astray the simple-minded by offering them heavenly knowledge, which then destroys their faith. This is very similar to Ignatius refusing to feed his readers such heavenly revelations because this food would choke them. Irenaeus goes on to claim both to be able to know and teach such mysteries and yet ironically implies that he and his readers are not able to understand them; *I have deemed it my duty [...] to unfold to you, my friend, these portentous and profound mysteries, which do not fall within the range of every intellect, because all have not sufficiently purged their brains. (Against Heresies 1:Preface:2)*

<u>Both the letters and Against Heresies insist that Jesus was physical and give the same proofs of his physical nature</u>

Ignatius repeatedly writes against Docetism insisting that Jesus was physical according to the gospel accounts -

... but be you fully persuaded concerning the birth and the passion and the resurrection, which took place in the time of the governorship of Pontius Pilate; for these things were truly and certainly done by Jesus Christ ... (Ignatius to Magnesians 11:1)

Stop your ears therefore, when any man speaks to you apart from Jesus Christ, who was of the race of David, who was the Son of Mary, who was truly born and ate and drank, was truly persecuted under Pontius Pilate, was truly crucified and died in the sight of those in heaven and those on earth and those under the earth; who moreover was truly raised from the dead ... (Ignatius to Trallians 9:1-2)

He is truly of the race of David according to the flesh, but Son of God by the Divine will and power, truly born of a virgin and baptised by John that all righteousness might be fulfilled by him, truly nailed up in the flesh for our sakes under Pontius Pilate and Herod the tetrarch ... (Ignatius to Smyrnaeans 1:1-2)

For what profit is it [to me], if a man praises me, but blasphemes my Lord, not confessing that he had a body? (Ignatius to Smyrnaeans 5:2)

For our God, Jesus the Christ, was conceived in the womb by Mary according to a dispensation, of the seed of David but also of the Holy Ghost; and he was born and was baptised that by his passion he might cleanse water. (Ephesians 18:2)

In Book 3 of Against Heresies, Irenaeus repeatedly argues that Jesus was really born from Mary and the Holy Spirit, was a physical man and was really crucified. Moreover, Irenaeus uses the same "proofs" in speaking about Jesus as physical man that Ignatius gives:

1. He was born of Mary and the Holy Spirit:

For the birth of Jesus through Mary and the holy spirit see for example Against Heresies 3:10:2-4,3; 16:1-5.

2. He was of the seed of David:

The descent of Jesus from David is also stressed in Against Heresies Book 3 - David is mentioned no less than 52 times in this book.

3. He was crucified by Pontius Pilate and Herod:

That Jesus was crucified under Pontius Pilate is also stated several times in Against Heresies. Herod is included with Pilate as one who has crucified Jesus in Against Heresies 3:12:5.

4. He descended to the depths and was raised:

See Against Heresies 3:19:3 for the idea that Jesus descended to the depths and rose to heaven.

Both the letters and Against Heresies talk about Jesus as the "one physician."

In Ephesians 7:2 Ignatius says about Jesus: *There is one only physician, of flesh and of spirit ...*

Against Heresies 3:5 uses exactly the same analogy of Christ as physician: *But that the Lord came as the physician of the sick, He does Himself declare* saying, *"They that are whole need not a physician, but they that are sick; I came not to call the righteous, but sinners to repentance." (Against Heresies 3:5:2)*

Both the letters and Against Heresies say that Jesus was from both Mary and God, being born and yet pre-existing, and hence impossible

The Ephesian passage continues that Jesus was *"born and unborn, God in man, true Life in death, Son of Mary and Son of God, first possible and then impossible, Jesus Christ our Lord." (Ignatius to Ephesians 7:2)*

By Jesus being both born and yet unborn Ignatius means that although he was born at a point in time he had pre-existence. We can find this same idea expressed by Irenaeus: *"For I have shown that the Son of God did not then begin to exist, being with the Father from the beginning; but when He became incarnate, and was made man, .." (Against Heresies 3:18:1)*

The idea of Jesus being of both God and Mary and hence "impossible" comes from Against Heresies book 3: *He therefore, the Son of God, our Lord, being the Word of the Father, and the Son of man, since He had a generation as to His human nature from Mary, who was descended from mankind, and who was herself a human being, was made the Son of man. Wherefore also the Lord Himself gave us a sign, in the depth below, and in the height above, which man did not ask for, because he never expected that a virgin could conceive, or that it was possible that one remaining a virgin could bring forth a son, ... (Against Heresies 3:19:3)*

Both the letters and Against Heresies emphasise that Jesus suffered in reality and not in appearance

But if it were as certain persons who are godless, that is unbelievers, say, that he suffered only in appearance, being themselves mere appearance, why am I in bonds? (Ignatius to Trallians 10:1)

For he suffered all these things for our sakes [that we might be saved]; and he suffered truly, as also he raised himself truly; not as certain unbelievers say, that he suffered in appearance, being themselves mere appearance. And according as their opinions are, so shall it happen to them, for they are without body and demon-like. (Ignatius to Smyrnaeans 2:1)

For if these things were done by our Lord in appearance, then am I also a prisoner in appearance. And why then have I delivered myself over to death, unto fire, unto sword, unto wild beasts? (Ignatius to Smyrnaeans 4:2)

That Jesus did suffer in reality is another major theme of Book 3 of Against Heresies (see 3:16; 3:18:4-7). For example:

For if He did not truly suffer, no thanks to Him, since there was no suffering at all; and when we shall actually begin to suffer, He will seem as leading us astray, exhorting us to endure buffering, and to turn the other cheek, if He did not Himself before us in reality suffer the same (Against Heresies 3:18:6)

But again, showing that Christ did suffer, and was Himself the Son of God, who died for us, and redeemed us with His blood (Against Heresies 3:16:9)

<u>Both the letters and Against Heresies emphasise that you should physically remove yourself from Heretics and stop your ears to avoid listening to them</u>

But I watch over you beforehand to protect you from wild beasts in human form -- men whom not only should ye not receive, but, if it were possible, not so much as meet [them]; (Ignatius to Smyrnaeans 4:1)

Stop your ears therefore, when any man speaks to you apart from Jesus Christ ... (Ignatius to Trallians 9:1)

This theme about not even listening to heretics appears in the story of John fleeing from Cerinthus at the baths (Against Heresies 3:3:4). It is also found shortly after this passage in Irenaeus' account of the Christians in barbarian nations: *If any one were to preach to these men the inventions of the heretics, speaking to them in their own language, they would at once stop their ears, and flee as far off as possible, not enduring even to listen to the blasphemous address. (Against Heresies 3:4:2)*

<u>The letter to Smyrnaeans and Against Heresies refer to the same gospel story of the disciples touching the risen Jesus</u>

For I know and believe that he was in the flesh even after the resurrection; and when he came to Peter and his company, he said to them, "Lay hold and handle me, and see that I am not a demon without body." And straightway they touched him, and they believed, being joined unto his flesh and his blood. Wherefore also they despised death, nay they were found superior to death. And after his resurrection he ate with them and drank with them as one in the flesh, though spiritually he was united with the Father. (Ignatius to Smyrnaeans 3:1-3)

The episode is taken from Luke 24:36-43, but with the difference that Peter is not specifically mentioned. Peter does, however, recount this same episode in Acts 10:40-43 in a passage that is referred to, and quoted from, in Against Heresies 3:12:7.

Both the letters and Against Heresies emphasise that it is the blood of Jesus that redeems

Let no man be deceived. Even the heavenly beings and the glory of the angels and the rulers visible and invisible, if they believe not in the blood of Christ, judgment awaits them also. (Ignatius to Smyrnaeans 6:1)

The theme of Christ's blood redeeming mankind is another major theme of Against Heresies found in particular in Book 5 where there are many mentions of the blood of Christ. For example: *the Lord thus has redeemed us through His own blood (Against Heresies 5:1:1).* In 5:2 Irenaeus discusses how it is the physical blood of Jesus that redeems and which is also the Eucharist.

The letter to Smyrnaeans says that the heretics abstain from the Eucharist, and Against Heresies says that they should abstain from the Eucharist

They abstain from Eucharist and prayer, because they allow not that the Eucharist is the flesh of our Saviour Jesus Christ, which flesh suffered for our sins, and which the Father of his goodness raised up. (Ignatius to Smyrnaeans 7:1)

Against Heresies 4:18:4-5 considers the Eucharist and how the synagogues of the heretics do not offer a pleasing sacrifice to God because they do not believe that Jesus was the son of the creator of this world. Irenaeus says that if they do not change their opinion they should *"cease from offering the things just mentioned"* (the Eucharist) which is the flesh and blood of the saviour.

Key points

1. If we take the reliable dates in which Polycarp was active, they cluster in the three decades 140-170. His likely date of birth is c100, far too late for him to have known John Mark.

2. Although Ignatius is supposed to have been active in the early decades of the second century, there is no reliable information about him dating before 180. Irenaeus, who wrote Against Heresies at that date, does not seem to know of his existence.

3. The view of martyrdom put forward in the Ignatius letters is a literary composition rather than an authentic first-person account of someone facing death. It agrees with the developing cult of martyrdom that became prominent around 200.

4. A prisoner such as Ignatius would have been sent to Rome for trial rather than execution. Yet in the letters, Ignatius has already been condemned.

5. The letter from Ignatius to the Romans shows close similarities to the beginning part of the Martyrdom of Polycarp which shows that the author was familiar with this document, even though it must have been written much later than the supposed dates of Ignatius.

6. The timeline of actions in the Ignatius letters would be impossible in reality. They suffer from time compression, which is a result of trying to express events that would have taken several months or even years to play out, in a sequence of letters supposedly written on the road to Rome.

7. The letters are also unrealistic in the ability of Ignatius to write and receive visitors. They take an absurdly literal interpretation of all the churches rejoicing with Antioch at the ending of the persecution.

8. The author of the letters makes the mistake in the letter of Polycarp of including Ignatius among those Christian martyrs who are already dead, even though he is supposed to be still traveling to Rome.

9. The letters have a close connection to Smyrna, which is also Irenaeus' hometown.

10. Irenaeus knows of a letter from Polycarp to the Philippians, but this is best explained if the original Polycarp letter has been lost and the forger has developed their own Polycarp letter from the description in Against Heresies. The letter of Polycarp is nothing like what we would expect from a genuine letter from an early figure; it is a pastiche assembled from a variety of sources, including the letters of Paul. Even the personal details show affinities to features in Paul's letters.

11. The Ignatius letters and Against Heresies are closely linked. There are 17 different areas of similarity. In some cases, the agreements are very specific, such as when Ignatius attacks three types of heretics using the same vocabulary and the same order as a much longer section in Against Heresies on three schools of gnostics.

12. The letters must have been forged by a supporter of Irenaeus using a copy of Against Heresies.

Conclusion

Polycarp was a mid-second century figure and could not have known John Mark. The Ignatius letters are forgeries that date from 180-200 and were written in Smyrna by a supporter of Irenaeus.

Chapter 24

Dove and Thunder

We have developed, in outline, a picture in which Mary and her "sons" are the leaders of the movement. One of these sons is called "son of a Dove" and another two "sons of Thunder". We will see that the Dove and Thunder are two interlinked titles of Mary, that can be traced to scripture and which describe the spiritual role of Mary as the consort of Jesus and the link between heaven and earth. We will also discover one of the most beautiful works in early Christianity which is associated with Mary's title of Thunder, and which is a complex riddle about the contradictory nature of the female narrator.

The sons of Mary

The evidence points towards the "sons" of Mary being adopted with the two principal "sons", James and John, being biological brothers. When Paul goes to Jerusalem, he meets with three pillars, James, Peter and John. Peter must correspond to the Simon in the list of brothers in Mark 6:3 and the disciple Simon, the brother of Andrew. We can summarise what we know of the brothers in the table below.

Brother	Family relationships	Titles
James	Son of Zebedee, brother of John	The right hand, Oblias, the less, the Just, High-priest, son of Thunder
John called Mark	Son of Zebedee, brother of James	The left hand, High-priest, the beloved disciple, son of Thunder

Brother	Family relationships	Titles
Judas (Jude)	Brother of James, son of Zebedee?	None known
Simon called Peter	Father unknown, brother of Andrew	Peter (the rock), son of the Dove, apostle to the circumcision
Andrew	Father unknown, brother of Simon	None known
Two others (brothers or sisters)	Unknown	Unknown

We shall see that there is evidence that the brethren of the Lord were seven in number and of these seven we can assign names to five which leaves two unknown. From the evidence of the brother list in Mark 6:3, Jesus also had sisters, so it is possible that these two unknown brethren were in fact female. We have at least two distinct groups of brothers; the sons of Zebedee including James, John and presumably Judas, and the sons of an unknown father, Simon and Andrew. It would seem that this second group were less favoured than the sons of Zebedee either because they were more distantly related to Mary or because they were sons of Mary's sister and so could not claim descent from David. The list in Mark 6:3 also has Joses as a brother, but this is a misunderstanding of the name "Mary of Joses". The author of Mark has wrongly included Joses as a brother when he was actually the father of Mary, and he has missed out the brothers John and Andrew.

The table above shows the father of Simon and Andrew as being unknown, although in the Gospel of Matthew the name of Simon Peter is given as Simon Bar-Jona[172] (Simon son of Jona). In the Gospel of John, this becomes "son of John".[173] Although the name Jona is known as a man's name from other sources, it is rare, and the author of John has confused it with "John". In fact, Jona is the same as the word for "dove", which is *yownah* in the feminine. In the gospels the dove is the symbol of the spirit. So was Simon's father called Jona, or is he being called "son of the spirit"? Probably neither, because the representation of the spirit as a dove comes from a misunderstanding. The original spiritual baptism involved the spiritual substance of Jesus entering into the disciple. The story of the baptism in the gospels comes from a memory of the first spiritual baptism, that of the shaman. In this baptism, Jesus and the Dove became one. But the Dove is not the spirit, it is Mary.

A Jewish man would never be referred to in relation to his mother as "son of X" - it is always the woman who is called "mother of Y". Mary though is a very special case, and her sons are deriving their status in the movement through their mother. It would seem that the name "son of Mary" is still avoided as something that would have been unnatural in the culture of the time. Instead, the sons have been named in relation to their mother less directly by using her sacred titles. So Simon is "son of the Dove" and we have another example in the mysterious name Boanerges that is attached to James and John in the Gospel of Mark and which, we are told, means "Sons of Thunder". Mary is both Dove and Thunder.

The sons of thunder and son of a dove

In the gospels, the spirit descends in the form of a dove at the baptism of Jesus by John the Baptist. The Jesus movement was, at its beginning, a struggling competitor to the highly popular movement of John. Early sayings disparaged John with faint praise. But his martyrdom at the hands of Herod changed all that and the former rival became highly esteemed. His water baptism was adopted for new recruits in an attempt to appeal to his many followers. The story of the baptism of Jesus by John was written much later when the spiritual Jesus was being literalised into a man.

We shall see that there is a connection between the baptism stories and the Deep Source. The Deep Source is revealed by the comparison of several sequences from the gospels which apparently tell quite different stories but which are linked by multiple features. The Deep Source takes us to a time before the literalisations of the gospels. It is a sequence that tells and celebrates the coming of Jesus to Mary and it is a close parallel to the resurrection accounts. The Deep Source contains a criticism of John the Baptist that his baptism was with water, whereas the baptism of Jesus is from heaven. The author of Mark struggled to understand "the baptism of Jesus" and concluded that it must refer to a baptism of Jesus by John the Baptist. Because he knows that the baptism is spiritual rather than with water he shows the spirit descending into Jesus:

And immediately coming up from the water, he saw the heavens dividing, and the Spirit as a dove coming down upon him; and a voice came out of the heavens, "You are my beloved son, in whom I am well pleased." (Mark 1:10-11)

But he has got it wrong. It is the spiritual Jesus who descends into the disciple. The name Simon Bar-Jona is evidence that the "Dove", Yonah, was a title for Mary. In the first baptism, Jesus descends into Mary, the Dove, and this original baptism is identical to the birth of Jesus and his resurrection. He abides in the wilderness (the world) for forty days, meaning forty years, the remaining lifetime of Mary/Cephas. For this time, the spirit takes the form of the Dove; not a literal bird but the prophetess who has been possessed.

There is a further clue that the baptism of Jesus is derived from an original story about the birth of Jesus. Most early copies of Luke repeat the words of the voice in a form very similar to Mark. But there is a variant supported by early witnesses that quotes Psalm 2:7: *"You are my son, today I have begotten you" (Luke 3:22 variant).*

But why should Mary be called Yonah? The most likely source is the Song of Songs (also called the Song of Solomon) where "dove" is a name given to the female figure. The erotic love poem of the Song of Songs sits strangely in the Bible and is seen by most commentators as a complex allegory, although they do not agree on its interpretation. The conventional Jewish reading is that the female figure is Zion, Israel, and the male "beloved" is Yahweh. In the Christian interpretation the beloved is Jesus and the female figure the church. But early Christian commentators saw Mary the Magdalene and the Virgin Mary as the Dove and the Song of Songs as being about Mary and Jesus, an interpretation that has not been lost upon those who see Mary the Magdalene as being married to Jesus. Under the shaman paradigm, there is a quite different interpretation of the love affair between Mary and Jesus, that of the divine marriage, with Mary as the bride and the spiritual Jesus as the bridegroom. This would make Mary the "dove" and Jesus the "beloved". In the baptism story Jesus is also called beloved. A reference to the dove occurs in the following passage:

O my dove, in the clefts of the rock, in the secret places [cether] of the steep way, let me see your countenance, let me hear your voice; for sweet is your voice, and your countenance is lovely. (Song of Songs 2:14)

As we follow the clues back to the original sources, we will find the same words and passages turning up again and again. Statistically, it is impossible that these coincidences are random, and they show that we are on the right track. In this one line of the Song of Songs, as well as "dove" we find two other key words; "rock" which is linked to the name Cephas and the Hebrew word *cether* that means secret place. The dove is in the clefts of the rock which is the secret place of the steep way. A second passage in which the female figure is the "dove" has the beloved knock on her chamber at night:

I sleep, but my heart wakes: it is the voice of my beloved that knocks saying "Open to me, my sister, my love, my dove, my undefiled: for my head is filled with dew, and my locks with the drops of the night. I have put off my tunic; how shall I put it on? I have washed my feet; how shall I defile them? (Song of Songs 5:2-3)

She is asleep without her garment on when her heart wakes to the knock of her beloved. But she hesitates to open to him. When she decides to open it is too late:

My beloved put in his hand by the hole of the door, and my insides were moved for him. I rose up to open to my beloved; and my hands dropped with myrrh, and my fingers with sweet smelling myrrh, upon the handles of the lock. I opened to my beloved; but my beloved had withdrawn himself, and was gone: my soul failed when he spoke: I sought him, but I could not find him; I called him, but he gave me no answer. (Song of Songs 5:4-6)

The sexual imagery is obvious, and the myrrh belongs to the bridal chamber. The dove searches for her beloved in the city and is confronted by the mysterious "watchmen":

The watchmen that went about the city found me, they smote me, they wounded me; the watchmen of the walls took away my veil from me. (Song of Songs 5:7)

In the whole episode, there are several links to the story of Peter's escape from prison in Acts:

Both the dove and Peter are awoken from sleep.
The dove is smitten by the watchmen and Peter is smitten in prison by the angel.
Both the dove and Peter must put on their garments.
They both walk through Jerusalem at night.
The dove is confronted by the watchmen and Peter must evade the guards.
The beloved knocks on the door of the dove and is not admitted first time, Peter knocks on the door of Mary and is not admitted the first time.

We have argued that the escape of Peter from prison has its source in the journey to heaven of Mary/Cephas and that this is in turn linked to the resurrection of Jesus. The Acts story is garbled with the roles of the parties being confused. Such confusion is inevitable when gnostic spiritual imagery is literalised. We can see from the above points of similarity that the role of Peter and the dove in the two stories is broadly the same. But we have also seen that the role of Peter in the Acts story bears many of the attributes of the role of Jesus. One of these is the "knocking on the door" which rightly belongs to Jesus/the beloved but which has been transferred in the Acts story to Peter.

To the early Jesus movement, the watchmen in the Song of Songs play the same roles as the guards of the prison. They represent the rulers of the lower realm, the demon angels. They strike the dove and unveil her, depriving her of her garment. This interpretation has evolved over time through a spiritualisation of the initial meaning. To those who first developed the allegory of the Song of Songs, the female dove is clearly Zion, the female personification of Israel. The watchmen who guard her walls are the nations which lie all around the boundaries of Israel and take the opportunity to strike and humiliate her. But the imagery of the beloved scarcely fits Yahweh the father, the all powerful and jealous God. It is better seen as an early version of the angelic Christ or Messiah, the son of Yahweh who is the bridegroom and spiritual counterpart of Zion. The union of the Christ with Zion will bring about a new stage in the history of Israel, a stage of spiritual completeness when the heavenly authority of the Christ is lovingly joined with the earthly obedience of the state of Israel. With this new authority, the Jews will rule over the nations with wisdom, setting a moral example for all the other peoples of the earth, who will come to them for instruction. This is the original bridal chamber, the union of the earthly and the heavenly. It is the kingdom of heaven in which Yahweh rules the earth through his regent and beloved son, the Christ.

If this interpretation is correct, then the Jesus movement has developed in part from those who produced the Song of Songs in its ultimate form. (It is possible that this final form was the development of an earlier erotic love poem.) They would never have conceived the extent to which their vision would become spiritualised or that their Dove, Zion, would ever become a real woman of flesh and blood such as Mary of Joses. A further reference to the dove sees her as being only one compared to the many "queens and concubines":

There are threescore queens, and fourscore concubines, and virgins without number. My dove, my undefiled is but one; she is the only one of her mother, she is the choice one of her that bare her. The daughters saw her, and blessed her; yea, the queens and the concubines, and they praised her. (Song of Songs 6:8-9)

She is here, like Jesus, an "only begotten", the only child of her mother. In the original meaning of the Song of Songs, the queens and concubines would have represented the Gentile nations who are traditionally held to be around seventy in number. Of course, if we add the queens to the concubines we get 140 but the Semitic poetical convention is that such expressions are parallel ways of referring to the same thing, so that the queens are the same as the concubines. The queens represent the Gentile nations because these nations are in a sense valid with rulers who exert legitimate authority. But in another sense these nations are concubines because they lack the spiritual authority that shall come from the betrothal of the dove to the beloved. If this is the correct reading, then their number is given as threescore or fourscore, which is about seventy. Israel is different from the other nations because she was born much later than the others who are descended from the sons of Noah. However, although she appears as the youngest, she is really the oldest as she was conceived before any of the other nations. In the same way, the Christ is simultaneously the youngest and the oldest son. The praising of the dove by the queens and concubines is part of apocalyptic tradition whereby the gentile nations will praise Israel. As to the dove's mother, this is perhaps Wisdom.

There is further imagery in the Song of Songs connecting the dove to Mary the Magdalene:

Your neck is like the tower (Migdal) of David built for an armoury, whereon there hang a thousand bucklers, all shields of mighty men. (Song of Songs 4:4).

Elsewhere her neck is a "tower of ivory" and her nose "a tower of Lebanon",[174] imagery that would not be to every woman's taste today. The same word *Migdal*, tower, is the root of "Magdalene". Overall, the evidence that Mary the Magdalene was Yownah, the Dove, is significant, explaining the appearance of the dove in the baptism and leading us to another key text in the evolution of Christianity, the Song of Songs. So Simon Bar-Jona would indeed appear to carry this title after his mother, Mary.

So if Mary was the Dove was she also Thunder? The name Boanerges is given in the Gospel of Mark to James of Zebedee and his brother John.[175]

The same gospel tells us that the name means "sons of thunder". Commentators frequently see this as a comment on the character of James and John as being fiery in temperament. In support, they mention an episode in Luke where the two brothers urge Jesus to call down the fire from heaven to consume a village that would not receive him, a request that Jesus refuses.[176] In fact, this little episode is an obvious novelistic development by the author of Luke of the "sons of thunder" designation in the Gospel of Mark. The author of Luke is puzzled by this title but thinks that it means James and John were given the power to summon thunder. In the listing of the disciples, the Gospel of Luke omits the name Boanerges even though the story of the fire from heaven clearly shows that the author of Luke knew about it from Mark.

The author of Luke may have been influenced by the Gospel of Matthew, which also leaves out Boanerges. The omission in Matthew is more significant because the author of Matthew is loyal to Mark and only makes such changes if there is some difficulty with what is written in Mark. So we can surmise that the author of Matthew saw some problem with Boanerges. And there is a problem because the name Boanerges does not mean "sons of thunder" as Mark says. Boanerges is a Greek rendition of an Aramaic name, and the most likely reading of the original is either *bne rgas* (sons of tumult) or *bne rgaz* (sons of anger). One small clue that the meaning is "sons of anger" comes from that Luke story. Although the calling down of the fire from heaven comes from "sons of thunder", the two brothers are represented as showing anger by desiring retribution for a small slight. This suggests that the author of Luke was aware that Boanerges meant literally "sons of anger" and tries to reflect both this and "sons of thunder" in her story.

But why would the author of Mark translate "sons of anger" or "sons of tumult" as "sons of thunder"? Has he made a mistake? This is very unlikely because Aramaic was one of the major languages of the Roman Empire at the time the gospel was written, and Mark is a member of a movement founded by Aramaic speaking Jews only a generation or two earlier. Whether or not the author of Mark could speak Aramaic himself, he clearly had access to those who could within the movement. He is certainly very ready to give Aramaic expressions and their translations in his gospel. Instead of making a translation mistake he must have read both the name Boanerges and the meaning "sons of thunder" in his sources and so passes both down in his gospel.

Instead of seeing thunder and anger/tumult as being alternatives we should perhaps see them as two ways of referring to the same thing. Whatever is the ultimate source it must involve the word "thunder" together with one of *rgas* or *rgaz*. If so then the Gospel of Mark is giving us the correct meaning even though it is not a literal translation of Boanerges. The word it uses for thunder is the Greek *bronte*, which is a feminine noun and so appropriate as a name for Mary. Perhaps this is the Greek form of a title in the same way that the Greek name Peter was used for the Aramaic Cephas.

We must look for a source containing both words. The Hebrew word Ra'am meaning thunder is used as a noun only six times in the Bible - a frequency of 0.3 per 1000 verses. Used as either a noun or a verb (to thunder) the frequency increases to 0.8 per 1000 verses.[177] The Hebrew *ragaz* *(rgaz)* has a frequency of 1.8 occurrences per 1000 verses.[178] The chance of ragaz occurring with ra'am as a noun in at least one verse in the whole of the Old Testament is 1.0%. Or if ra'am as a verb is also permitted then the chance increases to 3.4%. In other words, it is very unlikely that we should find a verse containing both words. But this is what we find in Psalm 77:

The sound of your thunder (ra'am) was in the heaven: the lightnings lightened the world: the earth trembled (ragaz) and shook. (Psalm 77:18)

The fact that the two words are also found together in the title Boanerges and the explanation "sons of Thunder" given by Mark means that there is a high probability that Boanerges is linked to this passage either directly or indirectly. To verify this, we must search for other links between the psalm and the early Jesus movement.

The psalmist is meditating on the wonders done by God of old and the lines apparently refer to the crossing of the Red Sea. Certainly the psalm is part of a sequence of psalms about the flight from Egypt. But we may wonder if these words belong to an earlier source that has been incorporated into the psalm. The continuation has God crossing the sea:

Your way is in the sea, and your path in the great waters, and your footsteps are not known. (Psalm 77:19)

But we can see that this is the source of the well-known story of Jesus walking on water! This is the original version given by Mark:

And evening having come, the boat was in the midst of the sea, and he alone upon the land. And he saw them struggling to row, for the wind was against them, and about the fourth watch of the night he came to them walking on the sea, and wished to pass by them. And they, having seen him walking on the sea, thought it to be a ghost, and cried out, for they all saw him, and were troubled. And immediately he spoke to them, and said to them, "Take courage, I am he, be not afraid." And he went up to them in the boat, and the wind ceased, and they were greatly astonished. (Mark 6:47-51)

In this story, the disciples are struggling against the sea and a few lines earlier in the psalm the waters are described as "troubled":

The waters saw you, O God, the waters saw you; they were afraid: the depths also were troubled (ragaz). (Psalm 77:16)

The word used for troubled is again *ragaz*. The Greek word used in the Mark story to describe the disciples as being "troubled" is the equivalent of this word (it is used in the Septuagint version of the psalm). In both cases, we have a commotion at sea followed by the walking of God/Jesus over the sea.

In the same episode in Matthew 14:24-31 Jesus is joined by Peter, who begins to walk on the waters before becoming afraid because of the storm. He begins to sink, and Jesus rescues him but rebukes him for not having enough faith. It is unlike the author of Matthew to invent such a story, and we can surmise that he had a source where it was Peter who was walking on the waters as well as, or instead of, Jesus. We are seeing that Thunder was an alternative name for Mary/Cephas and the passage in Psalm 77:18-19 first talks about thunder and then about the walking on the waters.

The meaning for the original Jesus movement would, of course, have been mystic and has been literalised into an absurdity in the gospels. Mary/Cephas as Thunder is associated with the crossing of the waters, being the mechanism by which that crossing takes place. After walking the waters, Jesus appears to the disciples who think that he is a ghost or spirit. The waters are intended to mark the divide between heaven and earth and after crossing the waters Jesus appears spiritually to the disciples. The disciples are "troubled" and then "amazed" echoing Thomas saying 2 where the one who finds will be first troubled and then amazed.

A further use of "thunder" in the Psalms is linked to another word we have already come across:

You called in trouble and I rescued you; I answered you in the secret place (cether) of thunder (ra'am); I proved you at the waters of Meribah. (Psalm 81:7)

Here thunder appears in conjunction with the same word *cether* that was used in Song of Songs to describe the Dove as being in the "secret place of the steep way". It is not that *cether* is a particularly common word, occurring with a frequency of 1.5 per 1000 verses in the Old Testament, so the coincidence of it appearing in these two verses is significant. If we want to find the meaning of the secret place of thunder we can find it in Psalm 18.

First we have an image of what seems to be a volcanic eruption:

Then the earth shook and quaked; and the foundations of the mountains were trembling (ragaz) and were shaken, because he was angry. Smoke went up out of his nostrils, and fire out of his mouth devoured; coals were kindled by it. (Psalm 18:7-8)

Note the use of the word *ragaz* to describe the trembling of the mountains. Then God descends from the heavens:

He bowed the heavens also, and came down with thick darkness under His feet. He rode upon a cherub and flew; and he flew quickly upon the wings of the wind. He made darkness his secret place (cether), his canopy around him, dark waters, thick clouds of the skies. (Psalm 18:9-11)

The presence of God is hidden in a "secret place" of darkness, a great mass of black clouds. The effects of God upon the earth are felt through his thunder:

From the brightness before him his thick clouds passed, hailstones and coals of fire. Yahweh thundered (ra'am) in the heavens, and the highest gave his voice, hailstones and coals of fire. (Psalm 18:12-13)

This is followed by the routing of enemies and a rescue from the waters:

He sent out his arrows, and scattered them, and he flashed out lightnings, and routed them. Then the channels of water were seen, and the foundations of the world were laid bare at your rebuke, Yahweh, at the blast of the breath of your nostrils. He sent from on high, he took me, he drew me out of many waters. (Psalm 18:14-16)

The story is the parting of the Red Sea and the escape of the Israelites from Egypt. But behind it is something older, a remnant of Yahweh as the god of sky and storm, descending from heaven yet with his majesty hidden by angry clouds as he shatters his thunder on the land and the waters. The power of the volcano, the earthquake, the tidal wave is in these words, the hammer blows of the gods in anger. Man before science does not understand the physics of the atmosphere and the earth. The patterns of nature are written deep in the human brain even though covered beneath the gloss of intellect. The thunder remains as a symbol, a word, representing a power beyond the physical, an entrance into a world obscured by the rational mind and unperceived by the scientist.

The three words *ragaz, cether, ra'am* all appear in the invocation of the sky god in this psalm. They form a logical progression. The secret place, *cether*, is the sanctuary of the god, in his tent or canopy of cloud, the place where his presence is hid. The thunder *ra'am* is the emanation of the power from the secret place, visible to man, and *ragaz*, is the effect of the thunder on the lower world of sea and earth.

The word *ragaz* is used to indicate a trembling, whether in rage or fear of god. It is so closely linked to *ra'am* that this word for thunder is occasionally used where we would expect *ragaz*. For example we have the picture of the kings and inhabitants of the coast being afraid:

All the inhabitants of the coast shall be astonished at you, and their kings shall be afraid, they shall be troubled (ra'am) in their countenance. (Ezekiel 27:35)

What is clearly meant is that they are trembling with fear, but instead of *ragaz* the writer uses *ra'am*. The same is true of the one use of the feminine form *ra'mah*:

Have you given the horse strength? Have you clothed his neck with thunder (ra'mah)? (Job 39:19)

Some translators, perplexed by this passage, have resorted to translating *ra'mah* as "mane"! But the description is of a war horse eager for battle, and it is surely the trembling of the horse in anticipation, a trembling particularly visible around the neck, that is meant by "thunder". Again we would expect *ragaz* to be used but the writer uses *ra'mah* to convey the same meaning.

In the Jesus movement the thunder is not literal but spiritual, an emanation of the divine that forks across the boundary between heaven and earth.

The ecstatic visionary trembles and shakes as their body reverberates to the shock of this heavenly thunder. A visible shaking is common among charismatic Christian movements - for example the Quakers who get their name from the "quaking" of their founders. In Acts we have a story about a group becoming afflicted with the spirit and shaking together:

And they having prayed, the place was shaken in which they were gathered together, and they were all filled with the Holy Spirit, and were speaking the word of God with freedom. (Acts 4:31)

Also in Acts Peter's escape from prison is accompanied by a shaking of the prison which flings open the doors. Cephas/Mary is escaping from the confines of their body to ascend to heaven and the escape is associated with trembling and shaking.

There is one other use of *cether*, the secret place, that is intriguing and that is a direct reference to *cether* as the tabernacle and temple:

One thing have I desired of Yahweh, that will I seek after; that I may dwell in the house of Yahweh all the days of my life, to behold the beauty of Yahweh, and to inquire in his temple. For in the time of trouble he shall hide me in his pavilion: in the secret (cether) of his tabernacle shall he hide me; he shall set me up upon a rock. (Psalm 27:4-5)

The secret place extends to the holy of holies, the dwelling place of Yahweh in the temple. In the Protoevangelium of James, Mary dwells in the temple as a young girl.

We have traced back the titles son of the dove and sons of thunder/Boanerges and shown how they relate to the psalms and the Song of Songs. But this is not all. It shall turn out the passages we have considered for *ra'am* and *ragaz* are also closely associated with the source of the names Magdalene and Cephas. All of Mary's titles, the Magdalene, Dove, Thunder and Rock will be shown to relate back to a consistent set of imagery derived from the apocalyptic movement and concerned with the emanation of God upon the world. Of all her names the rarest is Thunder, encountered in the New Testament only indirectly in the name Boanerges. But there is one other potential link between Mary and Thunder. This is one of the most beautiful and enigmatic of all the early Christian writings, a work normally called "gnostic" but which is really impossible to fit into any genre, a work that is supposedly the words of Thunder herself.

The Song of Thunder

The work in question is "Thunder: Perfect Mind". It was discovered among the Nag Hammadi codices and even among that collection is unique. In Thunder: Perfect Mind an enigmatic female figure makes a number of declamatory "I am" statements which form a series of antitheses. It is apparently Thunder or Perfect Mind who is talking, and it is not immediately clear whether these are the same individual or whether two separate works have been combined.

The date of composition of Thunder: Perfect Mind is uncertain. There are no allusions to historical events and only in one place are there potential links to other works. In its final form, it surely dates a century or two after the time of Mary and the person who assembled it clearly believed it to be about Wisdom or the spirit rather than Mary. But what is intriguing is the possibility that an earlier work has been incorporated into Thunder: Perfect Mind and that this earlier work was called "Thunder" and did relate to Mary. There is one section near the beginning that is distinctive compared to the rest of the work. There is a great deal of repetition in Thunder: Perfect Mind but this section is not repeated elsewhere. It is also this one section that is linked to some other gnostic works.

There are various theories as to who the female speaker of this section is but none fit the section as a whole. We shall take the liberty of calling this section the "Song of Thunder" and we shall see that it fits Mary as shaman perfectly. The following translation of Thunder: Perfect Mind (Codex VI 13:16-14:9) is by George W. MacRae.[179] It starts:

For I am the first and the last,

Mary was the first in that she was the leader of the movement yet she also stressed the idea that she was also the last or least in the movement. This revolutionary concept reverses the notion of kingship upon which the ancient world was based. The king was greater than any of his subjects who were his servants or slaves. However, among the Jesus movement the ruler was to be the least of all and the servant of those who were ruled. This is the same concept that is expressed by Jesus in response to the request that James and John sit on the right and left side - "*If any wants to be first, he shall be last of all, and minister (diakonos) to all*" (Mark 9:35).

The phrase is repeated in Mark: "*many first shall be last and the last first*" (Mark 10:31). This is similar to what is found in the Gospel of Thomas: "*For there are many first who shall be last, and they shall become a single one" (Thomas 4b).* Elsewhere it is the chosen that stand as one.[180] Although the chosen are "the first" they are also "the last" and their role is to serve their brothers and sisters, the poor in spirit, who have been called but not chosen. The proper role of the pneumatic or spiritual is not to boast or lord it over the others but to lead through a life of service. A deeper meaning is a message of hope for the non-spiritual Christians. They are not necessarily the least they would appear, but many shall also be among "the first" at the appointed time.

I am the honoured one and the scorned one

Mary was honoured by God through the descent of Jesus into her, and honoured among her followers as her titles indicate. Yet it would seem she was also scorned both among the Jews and perhaps among the general Christ movement who did not accept the validity of her resurrection experience. It is also possible that the "scorned one" is a reference to her origins in Samaria. The same concept is expressed in the stone the builders rejected which became the cornerstone.

It should be noted that each line has been skilfully constructed to link to both the following line and the previous line. So "honoured and scorned" echoes "first and last" and links in turn to the next:

I am the whore and the holy one,

Mary would become known in the character of Mary the Magdalene as a whore and in the character of the Virgin Mary as the holy one. It is obvious why she should be called the holy one but "whore" is harder to understand and shall be considered further below.

I am the wife and the virgin

The wife of the spiritual Jesus yet remaining a virgin dedicated to God.

I am the mother and the daughter

Both the mother of Jesus, through the spiritual rebirth, and the daughter of Jesus and Wisdom made before time to fulfil her role.

I am the members of my mother,

Mary is the *stoma* or body (limbs) of Wisdom, being the personification of the goddess. Jesus and Wisdom are the male and female aspects of one divine being. Mary is the earthly bride of the spiritual Jesus and so is the earthly presence of Wisdom.

I am the barren one, and many are her sons.

Mary was barren because she remained a childless virgin, but she had seven adopted sons. More widely the whole Jesus movement could be thought of as her sons.

However, this phrase is also found applied to Wisdom/Sophia. From the second century Gospel of Philip[181] we have: "*Sophia is barren [without] child*" followed shortly afterwards by the phrase "*her children are many*" with an unreadable section in between (*Gospel of Philip 59:31-60:1*). Also from the Gospel of Philip: "*As for Wisdom, who is called 'the barren' she is the mother [of the] angels*" (*Gospel of Philip 63:30-32*). Interestingly this is immediately followed by a famous section about Mary the Magdalene being the "companion" of Jesus, the disciple whom he loved the most and of him kissing her frequently on the ----, the manuscript having a missing word at this point, allowing free reign to the imagination of the reader. Although this has added fuel to those who argue that Jesus and Mary the Magdalene were married, it should be noted that elsewhere the Gospel of Philip tells us that: "*it is by a kiss that the perfect conceive and give birth*" (*Gospel of Philip 59:3*) the conception being spiritual and clearly relating to the mystic bridal chamber that is such a focus of the Gospel of Philip. The source of the Gospel of Philip story is not a real life relationship between Mary and Jesus but a tradition of the divine marriage of the spirit which has then been combined with the literalistic gospel (the author of Philip clearly knows of the gospels).

Does this line apply to both Wisdom and Mary or one or the other alone? The two are inextricably linked, and it may be that a phrase traditionally applied to Wisdom has been deliberately used for Mary. But it is an odd coincidence in Thunder: Perfect Mind the "barren one" is followed in the next line (see below) by the divine marriage whereas in the Gospel of Philip the "barren one" is immediately followed by a section on Mary the Magdalene being the consort of Jesus and the two kissing. This suggests that the two are linked and that the "Song of Thunder" itself has served indirectly as the ultimate source for the Gospel of Philip here. If so then the application of the "barren one" to Wisdom may have been a mistake occasioned by the previous line equating Mary with Wisdom, her mother. In other words, the barren one whose sons are many was originally Mary and was only later applied to Wisdom by association.

I am she whose wedding is great and I have not taken a husband

As bride to the bridegroom Jesus, yet remaining unmarried.

I am the midwife and she who does not bear,
I am the solace of my labour pains

As it shall be seen the concepts of the midwife, she who does not bear, and the birth without labour pains repeatedly occur in the literature around the virgin birth. It is said that Mary did not need a midwife, so she is her own midwife. The birth of Jesus is non-physical, so his mother does not bear and does not suffer labour pains. Mary was also the midwife or mother for others in the movement to be reborn and experience Jesus.

I am the bride and the bridegroom...

The bridegroom Jesus is the spiritual part of Mary, so she is both bride and bridegroom.

... and it is my husband who begot me.

Created before the beginning of time by Jesus/Wisdom although only being born in the world in due time.

I am the mother of my father, and the sister of my husband, and he is my offspring.

Mary is the mother of Jesus, who in another sense is her father, since (linking back to the previous line) she has been begotten by him before time. It shall be seen that it is common to refer to the spirit (in the case of a man) as sister, wife and daughter and mother. Jesus is the spiritual part of Mary and is thus her "brother" while also being her husband, and he is also her son.

Confirmation of Mary as wife, mother and sister of Jesus is found in one of the most famous descriptions of Mary as "companion", that is wife, of Jesus in the Gospel of Philip:

> *There were three who always walked with the Lord: Mary his mother, and her [his] sister, and Magdalene the one who was called his companion.*[182] *For Mary is his sister, his mother and his companion. (Gospel of Philip 59:6-11)*

To be consistent with the second sentence, the first should have "his sister" instead of "her sister". Most likely the copyist has been influenced by John 19:25 in making this mistake. The second sentence is normally translated as *"His sister and his mother and his companion were each a Mary"*[183] which is understandable if three separate individuals are intended. But as Richard Bauckham points out in Gospel Women, the above translation is more correct.[184] The authors of the Gospel of Philip have inherited many of the original beliefs of the movement but are also operating within the gospel tradition. Like others, they attempt to reconcile spiritual sayings with the narrative gospel account. The phrase *"For Mary is his sister, his mother and his companion"* does not make sense in the gospel tradition because it originates before the gospels were written. The first line is their attempt to explain this phrase as relating to three separate individuals all called Mary. In reality, there was only one *"who always walked with the Lord"*, the same Mary whom Jesus promises to lead in Thomas 114. The one and only Mary was sister, mother and wife to Jesus.

> *I am the slave of him who prepared me.*
> *I am the ruler of my offspring.*

It is Jesus who is the one who prepared Mary before time. It was common for members of the early Jesus movement to talk of being Christ's slave, in the sense of belonging to him completely. As for being the "ruler of my offspring", this may refer to her role as master (the meaning of Martha) of the movement who were her sons and daughters.

> *But he is the one who [begot me] before the time on a birthday.*
> *And he is my offspring [in] (due) time, and my power is from him.*

Mary was begotten by the Christ before time, but in due time he will be reborn through her. Her spiritual power comes from Jesus.

I am the staff of his power in his youth, [and] he is the rod of my old age.

Youth is one of the titles of the heavenly Christ. Mary is the *staff of his power* because she was the mechanism by which Christ expressed his power on the earth, building his church through her (note the link to "power" on the previous line). Jesus is the rod of Mary's old age because he gives her the strength to continue with her mission in her old age.

And whatever he wills happens to me.

Linking back to the previous line, although Mary is the *staff of his power* yet the ultimate power belongs to Jesus and whatever he wills happens to her.

The following line "*I am the silence that is incomprehensible, and the idea whose remembrance is frequent*" is poetic in its own right but does not refer to Mary and marks the end of the "Song of Thunder" section. The remainder of the Thunder: Perfect Mind has been written in a similar but not identical style by someone who has confused the narrator in the Song of Thunder with a goddess who represents a compound of Wisdom, the spirit as female and other goddesses of the East, such as Isis. It is a later addition to the song of Thunder.

The author of the original Song of Thunder knows the truth about Mary and is not affected by the version of events in the literalistic gospels. It belongs to an era where this truth was still remembered in some circles before it was lost beneath the ever increasing confusion within the movement.

There are two gnostic works within the Nag Hammadi codices that are linked to the Song of Thunder, the "Hypostasis of the Archons" and "On the Origin of the World". Both belong to the genre of a complex gnostic Midrash on the scriptures, in this case the story of the Garden of Eden in Genesis. They are clearly both quite late in composition. The two works have many similarities and must draw upon a common source. The Hypostasis of the Archons has words spoken about the spiritual Eve by Adam which have clear similarities to the Song of Thunder:

"*... you will be called Mother of the living. For it is she who is my mother. It is she who is the physician and the woman and she who has given birth.*" (*Hypostasis of the Archons* 89:15-18)[185]

The corresponding section in "On the Origin of the World" is longer and closely linked to the "Song of Thunder":

Now Eve is the first virgin the one who without a husband bore her first off-spring. It is she who served as her own midwife. For this reason she is held to have said:

It is I whom am the part of my mother;
And it is I who am the mother;
It is I who am the wife;
It is I who am the virgin;
It is I who am pregnant;
It is I who am the midwife;
It is I who am the one that comforts pains of travail;
It is my husband who bore me;
And it is I who am his mother;
And it is he who is my father and my lord.
It is he who is my force;
What he desires he says with reason.
I am in the process of becoming.
Yet I have borne a man as lord.

(The Origin of the World 114:4-15)[186]

Note the "she is said to have said" implying that these words of Eve have been taken from somewhere else. The story of the spiritual Eve in the two works is highly involved and contrived. The question we must answer is whether the Song of Thunder was one of the sources for this story or alternatively whether the Song of Thunder is an elaboration of these words of Eve and not about Mary at all. The gnostic tradition about Eve is already present within the Gospel of Philip and is traditionally associated with the Valentinian school of gnosticism. The origins of this tradition were in fact present in the earliest stages of the Jesus movement and have simply been elaborated upon by Valentinus and his successors. But if the author of Thunder: Perfect Mind has got the words of the female narrator from the Eve story, then the identity of the narrator would not be mysterious but would have been identified in this source as Eve. If so, then why should the author of the Song of Thunder add certain things that clearly do not fit the heavenly Eve:

Being the "last" as well as the "first"
The honoured one and the scorned one
The whore and the holy one
The barren one and many are her sons
Slave of him who prepared her
Ruler of her offspring
Staff of her offspring's power in youth/ rod in old age

Most of these are inexplicable in terms of a conscious elaboration of the Eve story. On the other hand, the identity of the narrator of the Song of Thunder is mysterious and could be easily be projected on the spiritual Eve, particularly as it opens with her being described as "the first". If we start with the Song of Thunder and eliminate all that which does not fit in with the heavenly Eve story, we would get to something very similar to the words of Eve within the Origins of the World. So it is more likely that the words of Eve have been extracted from the Song of Thunder than that the Song of Thunder has been elaborated from the words of Eve.

In fact, there is a fragment of the Song of Thunder in an earlier work where it occurs with no association with Eve. We have already seen how the Second Apocalypse of James from the Nag Hammadi codices draws upon traditions about James. It is believed to go back to a Greek original with a possible date in the first half of the second century. In this gnostic gospel, James the Just (the brother of the Lord) preaches to the Jews in the temple in Jerusalem about the Christ. One description of Jesus links into the Song of Thunder:

He was the Holy Spirit and the Invisible One who did not descend upon the earth.
He was the virgin and that which he wishes happens to him
I saw that he was naked and that there was no garment clothing him
What which he wills happens to him.
(The second Apocalypse of James 58:14-24)[187]

Note how Jesus is the "*Invisible One who did not descend upon the earth*" so that he is spiritual in nature. The link with the Song of Thunder is that Jesus is described in one line with two terms that apply to the female narrator - as "*the virgin*" and as "*the one to whom (what) he wishes happens*" with this being repeated a second time - "*what he desires happens to him*". After this section, James talks about *"your house"*, clearly meaning the temple, and how he (or Jesus) shall tear it down. This is an echo of the Gospel of Thomas where Jesus says that he will destroy the temple. Although the Second Apocalypse of James is gnostic in nature, it contains no signs of the later elaborate gnostic systems. So some of the material of The Song of Thunder was present very early and predates the Valentinian context of the spiritual Eve.

One key difference between the words of Eve and the words in the Song of Thunder is that Eve is not described as a whore. However, while the Origins of the World presents the spiritual Eve as pure and undefiled, it also contains the evidence of a clear tradition in which Eve is a whore.[188] The *"rulers"*, the angelic forces in charge of the earth, attempt to *"cast their seed"* into the spiritual Eve but she, laughing at them, escapes into the tree of acquaintance leaving her *"likeness"* with Adam. The rulers, who are seven in number, mistake this likeness for the spiritual Eve and have intercourse with her, from which intercourse she bears a number of sons. In this way, they think they have defiled the spiritual Eve but they *"erred, not knowing that it was their own body they had defiled."* None of this is in the Genesis story of Adam and Eve, so it must have come from another tradition that has contributed to the gnostic Midrash. As another sign of separate traditions being combined, the story in Origins of the World is confused, so that first it appears that Eve's sons are from the rulers, then that the sons are different types of Adam, and then that they are apparently from Adam.

The same gnostic system is evidenced in the writing of Irenaeus as belonging to the school of Valentinus:

But the others coming and admiring her beauty, named her Eve, and falling in love with her, begat sons by her, whom they also declare to be the angels.

.... while Anthropos and the first woman (the Spirit) existed previously, this one (Eve) sinned by committing adultery.
(Against Heresies 1:30:7)[189]

What is remarkable is that there is a fragment in the Gospel of Philip talking about Mary in very similar terms to Eve in this story:

Mary is the virgin whom no power defiled. She is a great anathema to the Hebrews who are the apostles and [the] apostolic men. This virgin whom no power defiled [...] the powers defile themselves. (Gospel Philip 55:27-32)[190]

Note how the powers cannot defile Mary but instead *"defile themselves"*, whereas in the Origins of the World, the rulers, failing to defile the spiritual Eve, end up be defiling their own body.

The traditions regarding Eve, Mary and Wisdom, seem hopelessly entangled with the same stories and sayings appearing about each of them. To make progress, the knot must be broken. Mary is a real woman; she was called by the names Mary of Joses and Mary of James, was personally known to Paul, and had a number of "sons" of whom her favourites were James and John. She is not a mythical, spiritual principle or a goddess. There is little doubt that this real woman was described as a whore as well as a virgin. It is necessary to find out why.

Key points

1. We can identify five out of the probable seven "sons" of Mary; James, John called Mark, Simon called Peter, Judas (Jude), and Andrew.

2. Simon is called "son of Jona", which is probably derived from *yownah*, meaning "dove".

3. The dove appears as the form of the spirit in the baptism story in Mark. This can be seen as a misunderstanding of the original spiritual baptism of Jesus, by which Jesus entered into Mary, the Dove so that the two became one. The author of Mark, who believed that Jesus had been a physical man, had to change the story so that the Dove became the spirit that descended into Jesus.

4. The scriptural basis for "the dove" is the Song of Songs, in which the dove is the consort of the "beloved". The original meaning was an allegory about the love affair between Zion and Yahweh, but the Jesus movement applied it to Mary and Jesus.

5. In the Song of Songs, the dove is associated with certain words that were important to the Jesus movement; the rock (Cephas), the secret place (*cether*) and the tower (*migdal*), from which comes the title of "the Magdalene".

6. In the Song of Songs, when the beloved knocks on the dove's door she does not admit him. Afterward, she goes and looks for him in the city but is assailed by the watchman. In the original this is about the nations, seventy in number, who surround and assault Israel. To the Jesus movement, the watchmen were the seventy fallen angels who rule the world, each one of

whom represents a nation. This story in the Song of Songs is closely linked to the story of Peter's escape from prison in Acts.

7. In the Gospel of Mark, the title Boanerges is given to James and John, the sons of Zebedee. The gospel tells us that the title means "sons of thunder (ra'am)" but it actually comes from either *bne rgas* (sons of tumult) or *bne rgaz/ragaz* (sons of anger). We find *ragaz* and *ra'am* together in Psalm 77 which is also the source of the story of Jesus walking on water.

8. As well as Psalm 77, Psalms 18 and 81 also contain the same vocabulary of *ragaz*, *ra'am*, and *cether*. The words relate to imagery of Yahweh as sky God. He is in the secret place in the midst of the storm clouds (*cether*) from where his thunder (*ra'am*) issues forth, to cause a reverberation or shaking on the earth (*ragaz*). Applied to Mary, the title of Thunder indicates her role as the shaman in bridging the gap between heaven and earth, and her ability to penetrate the secret place of the presence of God.

9. Jesus crosses the waters between heaven and earth to appear to the shaman and the shaman's followers. The shaman also has the ability to cross the waters in the other direction. So in the Gospels, both Jesus and Peter are shown walking on water.

10. Thunder: Perfect Mind in the Nag Hammadi codices contains a section that can be seen as going back to an early source that knows Mary as Thunder. This section is quoted in gnostic works which have incorrectly identified the female figure with Eve.

11. This "Song of Thunder" is a teasing riddle that declares a number of contradictory aspects of the narrator. She is first and last, whore and holy one, virgin and wife, she is barren and has many sons, her wedding is great and she has not taken a husband, she is the midwife and she has not given birth. All of these features relate to aspects of Mary. It continues that she is the mother of her father, the sister of her husband and he is her offspring. This is the mystic formula that the spirit is a woman's son, father, brother, and husband. In Mary's case her spirit is Jesus, and so he is both her son and her husband, as well as her father and brother.

12. The description in the Gospel of Philip of Mary as the sister, mother and companion of Jesus is another example of the mystic formula by which Mary is the sister, mother and wife of Jesus.

Conclusion

Mary was the "Dove" from the Song of Songs and "Thunder" as the bridge between heaven and earth. Her sons are known as Simon son of the Dove, and James and John, the sons of Thunder.

Chapter 25

Was Mary a whore?

Traditionally, Mary the Magdalene was a penitent prostitute, and she has long been depicted thus in Western art, remorseful and yet showing a satisfying amount of décolletage. More recently it has become fashionable to argue that this identification of the Magdalene as a whore was completely unjustified, an attempt on the part of the male-controlled church to discredit a dangerously "feminist" figure. In truth, it would have been all but impossible to invent such a negative tradition about the Magdalene once she had been accepted as a revered character, as she certainly was in the gospels. And we can find early sources that do indeed suggest that Mary was a whore. So was the shaman a woman of dubious virtue, or has the meaning of the "whore" been misunderstood?

Eve the whore

Mary has a number of "sons" but there is no evidence that she was married to their fathers. We have deduced that these sons were most likely adopted. However, there is an alternative that may have occurred already to the reader, which is that Mary scorned traditional morality in these matters and took her sons' fathers as lovers. This would explain why she had a persistent reputation as a whore. Neither is it inconsistent with the virgin birth, as she could in her younger life have been a virgin dedicated to God, but later with the authority of the spiritual Jesus and her own group of followers decided that she was authorised to dispense with this constraint, just as she dispensed with other aspects of the Jewish law.

But there are problems with this picture. If Mary were a libertine, we would expect this to be reflected in the morality of the early Jesus movement which should have a reputation for promiscuity. But the opposite is the case. In both the proto-orthodox and gnostic wings, an extreme asceticism and rejection of sexuality became the norm. This is particularly true for women, who are repeatedly portrayed in a chaste ideal in which they renounce sex altogether. Of course, all this is alien to our own materialistic and sexually based culture, and there are repeated attempts by some to try and pretend that Jesus and his followers really had very modern attitudes to these matters. But this is to project our own culture on the past.

The early Jesus movement's attitude to marriage can be divined from the letters of Paul. He recommends that those who are unmarried, like himself, should remain in this condition, but he also emphasises that this is not a command but only his own thoughts on the matter. He then addresses those who are married but this time he makes clear that he is giving a command of "the Lord" and not just his own opinion. This is one of the very few instances in the whole of Paul's letters where he does give Jesus as an authority for a teaching:

And to the married I tell you, not I but the Lord, let not the wife depart from her husband. But if she does depart, let her remain unmarried, or be reconciled to her husband. And let not the husband put away his wife. (1 Corinthians 7:11)

Those who are married are to remain married and together but if a wife must depart from her husband then she is to remain unmarried. It is possible that Paul has got this from Jesus through his own mystic experiences, but it is striking how he singles out this one instruction as coming from the Lord in the midst of a lengthy discourse on marriage. More likely this is a revelation from Cephas that constitutes "official policy" which Paul has then developed with his own thoughts. If so, it demonstrates a strong respect for marriage originating from Cephas whom we have identified with Mary.

All in all it seems very unlikely that Mary could have been promiscuous. But if not then how did she get a reputation as a whore? The earliest evidence for the whore has been traced back to Thomas:

Jesus said: "He who shall know father and mother shall be called the son of a whore." (Thomas 105)

We have seen how this saying has given rise to the inclusion of the mothers in the Matthew genealogy and so must be older than that gospel. This is not the only place where the saying has affected the gospels. In John, there is an episode in which Jesus confronts some Jews accusing them of doing the deeds of their "father":

"I speak that which I have seen with my Father: and you do that which you have heard with your father." (John 8:38)

The Jews are puzzled and tell him that their father is Abraham, but Jesus rejects this saying that if they were the sons of Abraham they would do the deeds of Abraham. Their reply to Jesus is telling:

They said to him, "We were not born of prostitution. We have one Father, God." (John 8:41)

Jesus then reveals who is their real father:

"You are of your father the devil, and you want to carry out the desires of your father. He was a murderer from the beginning, and abode not in the truth, because there is no truth in him." (John 8:44)

In this exchange, the Jews do not know who their father is until Jesus tells them. Once they know who their father is, it follows that, in their own words, they are *"born of prostitution"*, that is they are sons of a whore. But this is the Thomas saying, that he who shall know father (and mother) shall be called the son of a whore!

The Jewish Christian author of John knows the Thomas saying and applies it to the mainstream Jews, whom he hates, saying that their true father is the devil. In all this, there is nothing about the mother and certainly no application to Jesus himself as *"son of a whore"*. The use of this saying in John demonstrates its internal dynamics. There are three parties, not one, and the saying is about all three and not just a statement that the mother is a whore. Instead, we have a secret adultery with the father not being who we think he is and the son being *"son of a whore"*. This is extremely derogatory; the author of John recognises that it is the condition of the son that is the point of the statement. The saying must have been included in the early collection of sayings of the Jesus movement, being preserved in Thomas and available to both the authors of Matthew and John. This shows that it was generally accepted within the movement that Mary founded. It follows that Mary cannot be the mother in the saying. For her son or sons would have to be (i) Jesus, or (ii) the brethren of the Lord, or (iii) the Jesus movement as a whole. But a negative statement about any of these three could not have found an accepted place among the early sayings of the movement.

Neither can we accept the author of John's interpretation that it is about the Jews, as this reflects the civil war that developed between the Jews and Jewish Christians. If we step back to the start of the movement and its Jewish roots the most natural identification of "father" and "mother" is with Adam and Eve. We have seen the later gnostic understanding that Eve was a whore. From John, we have the concept that the adulterous father is the devil. So we would have a myth where Eve has been impregnated not just by Adam but by the adversary. As a consequence mankind, in general, are the sons of a whore. This is supported by the accusation in John that the Jews' father was "a murderer from the beginning" which would seem to tie the adultery back to Genesis and the murder of one of Eve's sons by the other. The implication is that Eve's oldest son Cain was the son of the adversary rather than the son of Adam. All of this is implied by a statement in the Gospel of Philip:

First adultery came into being, afterward murder. And he was begotten in adultery, for he was the child of the serpent. So he became a murderer, just like his father and he killed his brother. (Gospel of Philip 61:5-10)[191]

We see here the serpent being identified with the adversary unlike the later works, such as Origin of the World, where the serpent becomes the instructor of the fleshy Eve. By the illicit intercourse of Eve with the fallen angels, mankind has been corrupted and is no longer wholly in the image of God (see Genesis 1:26-27) but also contains within the likeness of the adversary. This corruption is alluded to in another earlier saying preserved in the gospels and Thomas:

Jesus said: "The kingdom of the Father is like a man who had [good] seed. His enemy came by night, he sowed a weed among the good seed. The man did not allow them to pull up the weed. He said to them: 'So that you do not go to pull up the weed, and pull up the grain with it.' For on the day of harvest the weeds will be visible and will be pulled up and burned." (Thomas 57)

The good seed of the father has been corrupted by the bad seed of the adversary. As a result, the two are hopelessly intermingled until the "harvest". At this point, the weeds are destroyed. The normal understanding is that the harvest is the apocalypse that sorts out the good seed (the children of the father) from the bad seed (the children of the adversary). But a better reading is that the "harvest" is the moment when the individual comes into spiritual fruition. At this point the bad seed, the weeds within them, will be destroyed. These weeds are the demons that will be cast out following the individual's experience of the resurrected Jesus.

All of this is consistent with the spiritual baptism. Mankind is seen as being intrinsically defiled by the inner presence of demons and a person is only purified by the spiritual baptism, being the pouring out of Jesus into the disciple, whereby the inside of the cup is cleansed, and the person becomes pure. At this point the demons are cast out - it is what comes out of the mouth, the demons, that defile and not what comes into the mouth.

The source of all this does not lie in Mosaic Judaism and the story of the Garden of Eden. It lies in the Enochian tradition from which Christianity is descended. In the book of Enoch, the descent of evil into the world does not emerge from the disobedience of Adam and Eve but in the descent of the fallen angels to earth. Once descended they rule and corrupt mankind, taking human women as wives, and spawning the Nephilim, the giants, and the demons who wander the surface of the earth. Because of the intercourse between the angels and humans the seed of the fallen has entered into mankind. At some point, this Enochian tradition has hybridised with the story from Genesis and made the original sin of Eve into adultery with the angels.

Mary, as a daughter of Eve, was seen as coming to undo the sin of Eve. Like Eve, she is called a whore but unlike Eve she attains the purity that Eve lost. So with Mary we must see the process in reverse; she starts as whore and becomes virgin, whereas Eve starts as virgin and becomes whore. As the Christian tradition develops, the two become hopelessly confused because both are whores who are also virgins and mothers.

Mary the whore

So we have two whores rather than one. But was Mary a whore at all or is it all a case of mistaken identity? Mary the Magdalene did, of course, have a reputation as a whore, but some argue this was a later development that emerged from the confusion of certain gospel passages. They mutter darkly about patriarchal intrigue in diminishing the reputation of a woman who was seen as dangerously prominent and a role model for aspiring female leaders. All of which is to project the obsessions of the present into the past. Feminism did not exist in the ancient world, could never have been conceived in the ancient world, and if by chance it had been conceived, would have been quickly eliminated by the forces of natural selection that govern human culture as much as they do human genes. Feminism is only possible in industrial societies with excess food production and low child mortality. Feminism is about perceived fairness between men and women, and considerations of fairness do not exist under conditions of necessity. The ancient world was all about necessity for men as well as women, and the relations between the sexes would have settled into the ecologically optimum condition that maximised the number of surviving offspring. The ecological optimum involves both men and women being cast in what to us would be traditional roles - traditional because they have applied throughout history, up until the industrial revolution, as the optimal division of responsibilities between the sexes. And for both men and women these traditional roles would have involved working to the point of exhaustion with no time or freedom for anything else other than caring for and feeding their families.

Early Christians broke this pattern of necessity not through excess production but by limiting consumption and (frequently) eliminating reproduction. It is not for nothing that Paul advises those who are not married to remain unmarried. Only if the iron grip of necessity can be loosened is a person free to express in their life the kingdom of God. The morality of the early Jesus movement was to encourage the followers of the way to repudiate their responsibilities; in the words of the Gospel of Thomas, to become passers-by. Those around them would have been shocked by this behaviour, the abandonment of family responsibilities, of mothers and fathers, perhaps younger brothers and sisters, to the charity of others if not starvation. By this relaxation of necessity, both women and men had the freedom to be what they could not otherwise have been. But to escape necessity was the lot of a few, and only a few would have been willing to pay the price.

In fact, it would have been impossible to invent an adverse tradition about Mary the Magdalene after the gospels had been accepted. For in the gospels, she is portrayed as one of the holiest figures in the movement and the special person to whom the resurrected Jesus first appears. Once this picture was accepted, there would be great reluctance to think of this woman as a whore unless there was a pre-existing tradition to this effect. Nor is it sufficient to say that she would have been diminished because of the attitude of men towards a female figure; those same men were elevating the Virgin Mary, and there is no reason why Mary the Magdalene could not have developed in a similar way. The truth is that both Mary the Magdalene and the Virgin Mary go back to the same person, and different aspects of her have been split out into the two. The Magdalene has taken the title whore and the mother of God the title virgin.

Nowhere in the New Testament is Mary the Magdalene called a whore, although there is one episode that has been used to suggest she was. This is the story of the anointing of Jesus by a woman that is repeated in all four gospels but with striking variations. The first appearance is in Mark, immediately before the betrayal and last supper:

And he, being in Bethany, in the house of Simon the leper, reclining [at table], there came a woman having an alabaster box of ointment, of pure (pistikos) nard, very precious, and she broke the alabaster box, she did pour it on his head. (Mark 14:3)

Some of his disciples argue that she should have sold the perfume and given the proceeds to the poor, for it is very precious being worth three hundred denarii but Jesus rebukes them:

"For the poor you have always with you, and you can do them good whenever you wish, but you do not always have me. She has done what she could. She has come beforehand to anoint my body for burial. Truly I say to you, wherever the gospel shall be proclaimed in the whole world, what this woman did shall also be spoken of, in memory of her." (Mark 14:7-9)

There is no immediate connection to Mary in this form of the story, but there are two implicit connections. The final statement that the woman will be spoken of wherever the gospel is proclaimed gives a clear indication that she is Mary, the founder of the movement whose memory will be inseparable from the gospel.

The other connection is that there is another episode where women intend to anoint Jesus in Mark, an episode that occurs shortly after the anointing of Jesus by the woman with the alabaster jar. This is when Mary the Magdalene, Mary of James and Salome go to anoint Jesus in the tomb. These are all alternative names for Mary, and the original story is about Mary and Mary alone. We may think that she does not succeed in the anointing, but that is because the author of Mark has broken the narrative and placed the story of the actual anointing earlier. Jesus tells us that the woman with the alabaster jar "has come beforehand to anoint my body for burial" indicating that originally this anointing belonged to the resurrection story. The author of Mark cannot put it in its proper place because, in his literalistic version, Jesus is supposed to be risen and the tomb empty!

There are two possibilities for where the anointing belonged in the original story; either Mary goes to the dead Jesus and anoints him before he is
brought back to life or the anointing occurs after the resurrection. The second case ties in much better with what know about Jewish customs of
anointing with perfume. It was used in particular at weddings and in connection with the bridal chamber. Mary first witnesses the resurrection and
then anoints Jesus signifying the marriage or union between the two. The
bridegroom has entered into the bridal chamber.

Perfumes are much used in the imagery of the Song of Songs, particularly in connection to the Dove. Her breasts are compared to a mountain of
myrrh and a hill of frankincense.[192] When the beloved compares "*my sister,
my bride*" to a garden locked, again nard, myrrh and frankincense are used
in the imagery along with other perfumes.[193] And it is not just the female
Dove for whom perfume imagery is used but also the beloved himself.[194]
When the beloved knocks on the door of the Dove she initially hesitates but
when she does open the door to her chamber perfume imagery is again
used: "*and my hands dripped with myrrh, and my fingers with sweet smelling
myrrh, upon the handles of the lock*" (*Song of Songs 5:5*). This is all about the
bridal chamber which would be anointed with expensive perfume. The
significance is that this episode in the Song of Songs has served as a source
of imagery connected to the journey to heaven specifically in the version of
Peter's escape from prison. It is the bridal chamber, the destination of the
journey to heaven that is anointed.

In the second century an anointing was one of the five key "mysteries"
used by the Christians who wrote the material in the Gospel of Philip, the
five being baptism, chrism (anointing), Eucharist, redemption and bridal
chamber.[195] Although the anointing was probably with oil (see also Gospel
of Philip 98 where the bread, the cup and the oil are spoken of) it is also
connected to perfume. The use of anointing as a mystery among early
gnostic groups may have evolved from the shaman anointing Christ in the
original resurrection. The gnostic sources of the Gospel of Philip looked to
the anointing as a superior form of baptism and in some respects the
anointing and bridal chamber are interchangeable. The specific connection
to perfume occurs in two contexts where reference is made to those excluded from the inner mysteries. We can see this relating to the two wings of
the church, the proto-orthodox literalistic Christians, and those who are
gnostic and spiritual in outlook. These passages are a warning to the proto-
orthodox not to exclude the gnostics from the churches:

Spiritual love is wine and fragrance. All those who anoint themselves with it take pleasure within it. While those anointed with it are present those nearby also profit (from the fragrance). If those anointed with ointment withdraw from them and leave then those not anointed, whom merely stand nearby, still remain in their bad odour. (Gospel of Philip 77:35-78:7)[196]

Similar terms are used to speak about those excluded from the bridal chamber who cannot see the bride: *"but let the others yearn just to listen to her voice and to enjoy her ointment..."* (Gospel of Philip 82:19-21).[197] In other words, the non-spiritual Christians of the proto-orthodox church will benefit from the presence of the spiritual, but if they exclude the spiritual they will be in *"bad odour"*.

As to the nature of the perfume in the original source of the Gospel of Mark, a clue is perhaps to be found in the word usually translated as "pure" in "pure nard". This word *"pistikos"* is found only in the context of this story in the New Testament. However it is the adjective form of the female noun *pistis* that is used over two hundred and forty times in the New Testament and which is normally translated as "faith". It is also a name given to Sophia/Wisdom as in the title of the gnostic work Pistis Sophia and earlier in Eugnostos the Blessed.[198] The ointment of the bridal chamber is perhaps *pistis*, loving faithfulness and purity, described by analogy with precious perfumes as in the Song of Songs. The author of Mark has literalised this to his *"pure nard"*. As for the alabaster box, this is the usual container for precious ointments in the ancient world and is likely to be a novelistic detail added by the author of Mark.

In the development of the story by the other gospel writers, the author of Matthew, as normal, is faithful to the version in Mark, whereas the author of Luke, as normal, changes it shamelessly. It is clearly the same story with the same alabaster box containing ointment but instead of taking place in the house of Simon the leper the incident now takes place in the house of Simon a Pharisee. This time the woman uses her hair to wash Jesus' feet before anointing them with perfume. The most significant change, however, is that the woman is now a *"woman in the city who was a sinner"* *(Luke 7:37).* She is a prostitute, a high-class courtesan. Simon is shocked that Jesus allows the woman to touch him, but he rebukes Simon telling him that she loves him all the more because she, like a debtor with a large debt, has more to be forgiven. The question is whether the woman is a whore in a pre-existing tradition or whether the author of Luke has made it up to spice up the story. Although the author of Luke is inherently unreliable she also repeatedly demonstrates an excellent access to sources. In this regard, two things should be noted about the woman:

She does not stop kissing Jesus (Luke 7:45)
She has loved Jesus much, whereas others such as Simon have loved only a little.

The kissing gives us a motive for the author of Luke to change the attention to Jesus' feet. She clearly cannot have a story where a whore enters and kisses Jesus repeatedly on the head or mouth! These two extra details added by Luke are consistent with what other sources say about Mary and Jesus. The Eugnostos the Blessed says that Jesus loved Mary the Magdalene more than all the disciples and used to kiss her often.[199] The same idea of Jesus loving Mary more than the other disciples is repeated in the second century Gospel of Mary. So we can make a case for these features of the Luke story belonging to an earlier source where the woman is (i) called a whore, (ii) kisses Jesus often and (iii) loves Jesus more than all the others. The last two indicate the mysteries of the bridal chamber with Jesus as the spiritual husband of Mary.

The woman is finally given a name in the version of the story in John, and we learn that she is called Mary. John has copied features of his story from both Mark/Matthew and from Luke. So he has the anointing of Jesus' feet as in Luke and a disciple saying that the ointment should have been sold as in Mark. In John's version, this disciple is the bad guy Judas. The major change John makes is to relocate the story to Bethany and have the anointing performed by Mary of Bethany, sister of Lazarus. Such characters are of course fictions developed from repeated storytelling around the original names.

Put it all together and we have a story of the anointing of Jesus after his resurrection in the bridal chamber by Mary that has been taken out of its place by the author of Mark and which has been developed in novelistic fashion in Luke and John. The intriguing extra information that the woman involved was a whore comes from Luke only.

To find the origins of why Mary should be called a whore we have to go back to Eve. We have seen that the apocalyptic group from which the Jesus movement emerged had a myth that Eve had been a whore with the adversary, who had taken the form of the serpent, and that this myth goes back in turn to the Enochian descent of the fallen angels who take women as wives. The adultery of the women, symbolised by Eve, sows the seed of the devil into mankind. This seed is the demons. This is evidenced by a saying in Thomas that we know is old, certainly going back before the gospels of Matthew and John. The Valentinians had a more developed form of this myth in which Eve is an adulteress with seven of "the powers" and yet somehow escapes and remains pure. But there is an earlier saying in the Gospel of Philip that applies key elements of this story to Mary and not Eve. So perhaps the Valentinian form of the myth originated with Mary and was applied to Eve through confusion between the two "whores".

The demon husbands

We find that Mary is indeed associated with seven powers or demons. In the long ending of Mark, she had seven demons cast out of her after the resurrection of Jesus! This brings a completely new insight as to why Mary could be called a whore. Are the seven demons her "husbands" with whom she consorts before Jesus comes to her? This would mean that just as Jesus becomes her spiritual husband, so previously she has been a spiritual whore with the seven demons. This state is wiped clean by the resurrection after which Jesus expels the demons. She then enters the bridal chamber as a newly cast virgin, undefiled and clean. Indeed in her inner essence she has always been undefiled for the demons have occupied her flesh and not her spiritual being.

We can find evidence in early gnostic sources that demons were regarded in exactly this way. From the Gospel of Philip 65:1-26[200] we have a section describing demons as illicit lovers of the opposite sex:

The forms of the evil spirit include male ones and female ones. The males are they that unite with the souls that inhabit a female form but the females are they which are mingled with those in a male form through one who was disobedient.

This is telling us that the evil spirits are contra-sexual, the males going into women and the females into men. They are intermingled into mankind through "*one who was disobedient*", that is the adultery of Eve. It continues:

And none shall be able to escape them since they detain him if he does not receive a male power or a female power, a bridegroom or a bride. One receives them from the mirrored bridal chamber.

Only those who have united with a bridegroom or bride in the bridal chamber can escape the demons.

When the wanton women see a male sitting alone they leap down and play with him and defile him. So also the lecherous men when they see a beautiful woman sitting alone they persuade her and compel her wishing to defile her.

The demons are lecherous lovers who will go into a woman and "*persuade her and compel her*".

But if they see the man and his wife sitting beside one another, the female cannot come into the man nor can the male come into the woman.

Marriage protects against the demons but this is the spiritual marriage of the bridal chamber, as the next line makes clear:

So if the image and the angel are united with one another, neither can any venture to go into the man or woman.

So Mary's lecherous lovers, the seven demons, are expelled when her angel, Jesus, the beloved, knocks at her door and after being first refused finally enters the bridal chamber.

Similar imagery is repeated in "The Exegesis of the Soul" in the Nag Hammadi codices. This is concerned with the soul, seen as female, who becomes a prostitute when she enters into the world until she is redeemed in the bridal chamber. The work was most likely composed in the late second or early third century. It quotes widely from the New and Old Testaments as well as from Homer. What is of interest is not so much the work itself but the earlier sources it may have used. Some sections are similar to the Gospel of Philip and could be strikingly applied to Mary herself. The soul is deceived by the adulterers who deceive her "*pretending to be faithful true husbands*" (Exegesis of the Soul 128:14). Of particular interest is this section on the soul, who after abandoning her prostitution becomes purified in the bridal chamber:

Then she will begin to rage at herself like a woman in labour who writhes and rages in the hour of delivery. But since she is female by herself she is powerless to beget a child. From heaven the father sent her her man, who is her brother, the firstborn. Then the bridegroom came down to the bride. She gave up her former prostitution and cleansed herself of the pollutions of the adulterers and she was renewed so as to be a bride. She cleansed herself in the bridal chamber; she filled it with perfume; she sat in waiting for the true bridegroom. No longer does she run about the marketplace, copulating with whomever she desires, but she continued to wait for him - (saying) "When will he come?" - and to fear him, for she did not know what he looked like: she no longer remembers since the time she fell from her father's house. But by the will of the father ... And she dreamed of him like a woman in love. (Exegesis of the Soul 132:2-23)[201]

This combines imagery from both the virgin birth and the bridal chamber. Note how the bridegroom is sent from heaven and is her brother as well as her husband and also "the firstborn", which links him to being the offspring of the marriage. Note also the idea of the female figure being cleansed of the pollutions of the adulterers so that she is turned from whore to virgin. There is a clear link in this passage with the Song of Songs and the picture of the dove waiting in her perfumed chamber for the bridegroom and dreaming of him.

The mystical experiences that underlie the Jesus movement are expressed in contradictory terms that short circuit the defences of the rational mind. So the coming of Jesus to Mary is at the same time the nativity of Jesus, his resurrection and his entry into the bridal chamber. A few works, such as the Song of Thunder and the Hymn of the Pearl, capture these contradictions brilliantly, but most struggle with plodding logic to explain the contradictions through a contorted narrative. The Exegesis is of this plodding genre but retains within it glimpses of the earlier movement.

One of the weird features of the Exegesis is that the womb of the soul is described as being on the outside of her body, and so liable to pollution, until it is turned inward by baptism. This is linked in with the idea of the soul having children, another odd concept that indicates that the material in Exegesis of the Soul did not originally apply to the soul, but to Mary. Her "spiritual womb" is in reverse as Jesus is not born into the outward world, as for a normal birth, but is born inward into Mary herself.

The Exegesis tells us further[202] that a married couple in the world have to content themselves with intercourse after which they turn away from each other. So, no matter how much they may want to, they cannot become one whole except at the brief moment of joint ecstasy itself, an ecstasy that is only of the flesh. However, in the marriage of the bridal chamber *"[once] they unite [with one another] they become a single life"* so that they become whole and complete losing their individual identities within each other.

Mary and Jesus are essentially one being. As Paul asks about Cephas and Jesus - *Can Christ be divided?*

Of the offspring of the marriage the Exegesis tells us:

> *Thus when the soul [had adorned] herself again in her beauty [...] enjoyed her beloved and [he also] loved her. And when she had intercourse with him, she got from him the seed that is the life-giving spirit, so that by him she bears good children and rears them. (Exegesis of the Soul 133:31-134:4)*[203]

The children are clearly spiritual children, and this would apply to Mary, the barren one whose children are many. The children are the spiritual offspring of Mary and Jesus, those who are the chosen.

We can see that concept of demons being false husbands and adulterers is certainly circulating in the second century. We have also seen that there may be an earlier source behind the Exegesis of the Soul that related to Mary as whore, mother and bride and that this earlier source has been misapplied to the soul. But to be confident that this is the true meaning of "whore" we need earlier evidence that the demons were indeed regarded as Mary's husbands. We will find this evidence in two stories in the gospels.

The first is the story of the Samaritan woman in John 4:1-42. This is one of the "Deep Source" sequences which are sections of the gospels that go back to a single source that originated very early in the movement. We have already seen how the story of the Samaritan woman also used a version of Thomas 114 as a source. But it is worth now considering the story as a whole to see how it draws on traditions about Mary. Jesus goes into Samaria to a place called Sychar where there is a well of Jacob. He rests by the well while his disciples go on into the town and there he meets a woman. He asks her for a drink and she replies:

> *"How is it that you, a Jew, ask a drink from me, a Samaritan woman? For Jews have no dealing with Samaritans."*

Jesus responds that if she had known who he was then she would have asked for living water. This puzzles her as the well is deep, and he has no vessel to draw the water up. Jesus replies:

> *"Everyone that drinks of this water shall thirst again; but whoever may drink of the water that I will give him, shall not thirst ever again; and the water that I will give him shall become in him a well of water, springing up to eternal life."*

The woman responds to this by asking for the water "*that I may not thirst, nor come hither to draw.*"

Up to this point, we have the "baptism of Jesus" being the coming of Jesus into the person expressed by the metaphor of water, a life-giving well. Jesus offers the baptism and the woman, intuitively recognising it, accepts. But now something strange happens:

Jesus said to her, "Go, call thy husband, and come here."

Why does Jesus ask her to get her husband when the baptism is personal to the individual? The woman neither needs to ask her husband's permission nor can she answer for him. And, even stranger, it turns out that she does not have a husband:

The woman answered and said, "I have not a husband." Jesus said to her, "Well do you say that you do not have a husband. For five husbands you have had, and he whom you have now is not your husband."

The implication is that the woman has played the whore, either by having a succession of "husbands" to whom she is not married or by having five previous legitimate husbands and now living with a lover outside of marriage. With this revelation she acknowledges Jesus as a prophet. When the disciples return, they are surprised to see him talking with a woman. The woman leaves her water jug, symbolising that she has drunk of Jesus' life-giving water so no longer needs to draw from the well, and returns to the town. There she tells everyone about Jesus, and many in the Samaritan town believe in him. They go to see for themselves, and he stays with them for two days.

At the core of this story we again have the three inextricably linked aspects of the baptism of Jesus, the resurrection and the journey to heaven. In the original source the woman, although unnamed, is clearly Mary the Magdalene although the author of John has not recognised her identity. It is Mary who drinks the life-giving water that becomes a bubbling well within her. It is she who witnesses the resurrection, and she who spreads the gospel. The most obvious connection between the Samaritan woman and Mary is that they are both whores, but there are many other more subtle links. After the woman has had her encounter with Jesus at the well she goes and tells the town folk, and many believe in Jesus on the strength of her testimony:

And from that city many of the Samaritans believed in him because of the word of the woman testifying, "He told me all the things that I did."

Jesus knows everything that has happened to the woman. Change the tense to the future and this is the same as the Song of Thunder: *And whatever he wills happens to me.* The woman testifying to the Samaritans about Jesus is parallel to Mary, who, having experienced the spiritual resurrection of Jesus, testifies to the disciples. Mary as prophetess and first witness of the resurrection would have met with a great deal of disbelief as is evident from the Gospel of the Long Ending. The movement was built on her testimony, but it seems that it did not gain momentum until others had been inducted by her into the resurrection and had experienced Jesus for themselves. The author of John sanitises this and takes a more positive line about the reaction to the woman's testimony. Yet we can still see the outlines of the original disbelief that is dispelled by the experience of Jesus. When Jesus stays in the town, we are told that many more in the town believe in him, implying that initially they must have been sceptical. And it is these new converts who tell the woman:

"No more do we believe because of your speaking; for we ourselves have heard and known that this is truly the saviour of the world, the Christ."

The sceptics in the story did not actually believe her and are only won over by the experience of Jesus. Behind all this we have another version of the Gospel of the Long Ending, with the first witness of the resurrection being disbelieved. Nor is it just the town people who are sceptical. When his disciples return they are shocked to find him speaking with a woman:

And upon this, his disciples came and were amazed that he was speaking with a woman. No one, however, said, "What do you seek?" or "Why do you speak with her?"

We have seen how this is related to Thomas 114 and the idea that Mary is not worthy. It is also related to the Gospel of Mary where after Mary is visited by the spiritual resurrected Jesus, she tells her revelations to the disciples. Andrew and Peter are sceptical with Peter saying *"Did he then speak privately with a woman rather than us and not openly?"* The disciples originally disbelieved Mary and doubted that Jesus spoke through her. To begin with this doubting tradition was not linked to any particular disciple but during the second century it became fixed to Peter who had come to represent the proto-orthodox church as opposed to Mary the Magdalene who represented the gnostics. Ironically, these were two names for the same person, the founder from whom both wings of the church traced their descent.

The setting of the story of the Samaritan woman is highly symbolic. The place name Sychar means "drunken" and is an obvious reference to the water of life. The well in the story is called "a well of Jacob". The reference is to the story of Jacob in Genesis, and nothing could be more symbolic to the Jewish proto-gnostic. It starts in Genesis 28 with Jacob being sent to his uncle Laban to seek a wife. He stops for the night at a place on the way with stones for his pillow. It is here that he dreams of the ladder to heaven, resting on the earth with its top in heaven and with "*messengers of God going up and coming down by it*" (Genesis 28:12). And it is here that Jacob is promised the land for himself and his seed. When he wakes he is fearful and says - "*this is nothing but a house of God, and a gate of heaven*" (Genesis 28:17). This place at which the ascent to heaven could be made would have had special importance to spiritual Jews who were seeking to make just this journey.

Jacob goes further on and comes across the well. Some herdsmen are waiting around the well unable to water their flock because it is sealed by a stone. When he asks if they know of Laban they tell him that an approaching shepherdess is the daughter of Laban called Rachel. When Jacob sees her, he moves the stone so that she can water her flock. He kisses her and tells her that he is her father's nephew. Later Rachel will be his wife.

We can see the obvious link with the Samaritan story where Jesus meets the woman at the well and offers her the opportunity to drink. It is also linked with the resurrection story where Mary, under her names of the Magdalene, Mary of James, and Salome, asks: "*Who shall roll away for us the stone out of the door of the tomb?*" The resurrection and the baptism of Jesus are the same and the story in Genesis has served as one of the sources for the gnostic Midrash behind the Jesus movement. In this Midrash, Mary is cast in the role of Rachel. Although Jacob wants to marry Rachel he must first work for Laban for seven years: *Jacob serves seven years for Rachel and they are in his eyes as some days, because of his loving her* (Genesis 29:20). Note the correspondence of seven years and seven days, the same correspondence that is to cause the forty years for which the resurrected Jesus appears through Mary/Cephas to be termed forty days. But Laban tricks Jacob and gives him his unfavoured eldest daughter Leah instead. To marry Rachel he must "*fulfil the week of this one*" by working for another seven years. This Jacob does, and so he eventually marries Rachel after a wait of fourteen years. This figure of fourteen years shall be seen to be of key importance to the Jesus movement, foretelling the period from the death of Christ on earth to his resurrection and spiritual marriage to Mary.

Rachel is the original of the "barren one whose children are many", the designation that applied to Mary. It is said that *"Rachel is barren" (Genesis 29:31)* although later she conceives and bears Joseph and later Benjamin so her descendants are many. Mary is both the wife and mother of Jesus and Rachel is the wife of Jacob, who stands in the Midrash for Jesus, and the mother of Joseph, who also represents Jesus. The links between Joseph and Jesus are numerous and in one fascinating early Jewish work, Joseph and Aseneth, Joseph is given a Christ-like role being called the son of God and his firstborn son.[204]

The key element of the story though concerns the husbands. We know that Mary was possessed by seven demons so she should have seven husbands, but apparently only five are numbered. However, if we read the narrative carefully, we can see that the woman in the story does, in fact, have seven husbands:

The five husbands whom Jesus says the woman has had (John 4:18)

The one whom she lives with now but who is not her husband (John 4:18)

The mysterious husband whom Jesus asks her to call and who is not one of these other six (John 4:16)

This last husband is the one by which she will become male as in Thomas 114. The source for the author of John's information about the husbands must be something like this:

She had seven husbands and played the whore before she found her true husband with the coming of Jesus.

This would really be about Mary with the seven husbands being the demons with whom she plays the whore. But the author of John misreads it in literalistic fashion. Because a woman cannot have seven husbands at once, he interprets it as being sequential with seven husbands one after the other. So he makes the seventh husband the same as the true husband, which means she must have played the whore with the sixth husband. This leaves five previous husbands as in the John story. Note how the Samaritan woman, who has had many husbands, responds to Jesus' asking her to bring her husband with the response "I have not a husband." This contradiction recalls the song of Thunder where the female narrator who has a husband is also said to have "taken no husband."

As for the woman being a Samaritan this may have been suggested by the physical location of the well of Jacob in the northern kingdom of Israel, the first century Samaria. However, there is evidence that Mary was from Samaria and was considered a Samaritan by some Jews. It is significant that in the Gospel of John the Jews at one point call Jesus a Samaritan[205] as well as being possessed by a demon[206] and say that he is around fifty.[207] If Mary came from Samaria, then all of these would have been true of Mary. The apparition of Jesus on earth took forty years so that Mary must have been teaching at her prime when she was around fifty, and probably around seventy when she died. Supporting the idea that the Gospel of John may have been drawing on a valid tradition is a statement from Irenaeus that Jesus was a teacher into old age and over fifty when he died.[208] This is in flagrant contradiction with the synoptic gospels where Jesus dies in his early thirties. There are other points of evidence in favour of a Samaritan origin:

The only saying in the Gospel of Thomas that explicitly mentions a geographical setting is set in Samaria. That is saying 60 about a Samaritan carrying a lamb into Judea.

The gospels are favourable about Samaritans (e.g. the story of the Good Samaritan).

The picture of the Jesus movement derived from the shaman paradigm shows startling similarities to what we know of the movement of Simon Magus indicating that the two shared a common origin. The movement of Simon Magus came from Samaria.

The Jesus movement was descended from Jews who rejected the validity of the second temple in Jerusalem. The Samaritans rejected this temple.

The early Jesus movement emerged from an anti-establishment sect with Enochian apocalyptic beliefs that rejected Judaism of the type practised in Judea. Such a sect was more likely to find the freedom to operate within a religiously chaotic area such as Samaria rather than in Judea itself. Monotheism was never so established in the northern kingdom of Israel as in the southern kingdom of Judea, and the Jesus movement gives evidence of the survival of early polytheistic beliefs.

There is one other place in the gospels where a woman has seven husbands and this is in the Gospel of Mark when the Sadducees, who do not
believe in resurrection, ask a trick question of Jesus:

"Teacher, Moses wrote to us, that if any one's brother may die, and leave a
wife, but leave no children, that his brother should take his wife, and raise up seed
to his brother. There were then seven brothers, and the first took a wife, and dying,
he left no seed. And the second took her, and died, not having left seed. And the
third in like manner. And the seven left no seed. Last of all, the woman also died.
In the resurrection, when they rise, of which of them will she be the wife? For the
seven had her as wife." And Jesus answering said to them, "Do you not because of
this go astray, not knowing the Scripture, nor the power of God? For when they
rise out of the dead, they neither marry nor are they given in marriage, but are like
angels in the heavens." (Mark 12:19-25)

There is something wrong with this story as recounted in Mark. The
Sadducees' question is a good one, but it is made absurd by the sevenfold
levirate marriage. A simple example of a man marrying his brother's widow and then dying without child himself would suffice to illustrate the
question -- of which brother would she be the wife? Why then did the author of Mark bring in the sevenfold marriage? It must have been in the
source that he was using, a source which was originally about Mary, but
which he has misunderstood. Notice the similarities:

The woman has seven husbands whereas Mary has seven demons.
After the resurrection, none of the woman's seven husbands shall be her
husband. The seven demons are cast out of Mary when Jesus is resurrected.
The woman, like Mary, is childless.

The husbands are compared to the angels who do not marry. In the
book of Enoch, the rebellious angels sin by lusting after the women on
earth and descending to marry them. The progeny of these unions are the
demons who haunt mankind.

Behind this story, we have another saying about a woman who is barren
yet has seven husbands but who will be married to none of them after the
resurrection because it is sinful for the angels to take wives. The woman is
again Mary and the husbands the fallen demons/angels. The author of
Mark concocts the story of the Sadducees' question to set the otherwise enigmatic saying into the context of his narrative. The two stories of the Samaritan woman and the woman with seven husbands both go back to the

same tradition and were originally about Mary, who was a whore with her seven demons before the coming of Jesus.

We have seen that behind these traditions are two whores who have become confused. In a hybrid of the Enochian and Mosaic stories of the origin of sin, Eve, the mother, was believed to have committed adultery with the serpent and so sowed the seed of the devil into mankind. Mary as a daughter of Eve has inherited the sin of Eve in the form of her seven demon husbands until the coming of Jesus into the bridal chamber casts out the demons and cleanses her back into her pristine undefiled and virginal state. Later these traditions about Mary were to be incorporated into the gnostic story of Eve developed by the Valentinians where seven angels attempt to defile Eve but only succeed in defiling the body of flesh while the spiritual Eve escapes them.

Key points

1. Thomas 105 speaks about a secret adultery so that one who knew mother and father would be *"son of a whore"*. The saying alludes to the secret adultery of Eve with Satan. This interpretation is backed up by the Gospel of John, where the Jews are "sons of prostitution" because they do not know their true father, the devil. Also, the parable of the good and bad seed is about this adultery.

2. The Jesus movement believed that because of the adultery of Eve, the demons were sown within mankind. So all men and women are "sons of a whore" because, as descendants of Eve, they are infected by demons.

3. Mary is represented as a whore before the coming of Jesus, which has caused confusion between Mary and Eve. But Mary comes to undo the sin of Eve and restore her "sons" and "daughters" to a state of purity.

4. Mary is represented having seven demon husbands before Jesus, her true husband. Jesus expels these demons to purify Mary. The seven husbands occur in the story of the Samaritan woman in John, and in the sevenfold levitate marriage in Mark.

5. The Gospel of Philip confirms the idea that demons of the opposite sex will unite with and defile a person who is not "married" to their true spiritual husband or wife.

Conclusion

Mary, before Jesus came to her, was a "whore" but this referred to her spiritual state. Humanity, as the sons and daughters of the adulteress Eve, was corrupted by demons, the seed of the devil. Mary was said to have had seven demon "husbands" who were expelled by Jesus, her true husband.

Chapter 26
What is the meaning of the virgin birth?

The shaman paradigm casts a new light on the story of the virgin birth. It is not a mistake from a naive reading of prophecies of the Messiah, nor is it an attempt to cover up Jesus' illegitimacy. Instead we can see it as expressing a fundamental spiritual truth of the movement that has become an absurdity when Jesus became a physical man.

The virgin birth

The virgin birth is one of the most contentious parts of Christian doctrine. For the Catholic and Orthodox churches, it is an article of faith that is central to the mystery of the incarnation. Among Protestants it is something of an embarrassment, to be passed over quickly smacking as it does of the Catholic Church's deplorable cult of the Virgin Mary. Outside the circles of the devout, it is regarded as an absurdity.

The most common scholarly view is that the virgin birth story originated with the author of Matthew who misunderstood a prophecy of the birth of the Messiah based on the Greek Septuagint translation in which the original Hebrew word meaning "young woman" is translated into the Greek word meaning virgin. The virgin birth is not found in the earlier Gospel of Mark, which is notoriously silent as to Jesus' father. Some see this as proof that Jesus was illegitimate, and the virgin birth story was designed to hide this illegitimacy as well as to show Jesus as the fulfilment of Messianic prophecy.

In fact the conventional explanation is inadequate; the author of Matthew would not have made up anything as unlikely as the story of the impregnation of Mary by the holy spirit on the flimsy basis of a single translated word in a prophecy. The Jewish author of Matthew quotes the Septuagint because he is writing in Greek and because the Septuagint version suits his purpose. Regardless as to whether he could read Hebrew himself, he came from a culture where Hebrew literacy was commonplace; he is not going to be fooled by a loose translation of a word in a passage that would have often been read and discussed. Besides to any Jew, the Septuagint version would have essentially meant the same thing as the original, that a virgin would come to the bridal chamber, and there conceive the Messiah by her husband.

The author of Matthew has something in his sources that tells him that Jesus was born to a virgin and that this birth was in fulfilment of the prophecies. We can only understand this source through the concept of the spiritual Christ. In the gospel, the angel reassures Joseph that "*that which is begotten within her by the spirit is holy*" (*Matthew 1:20*). Mary is the shaman, and God has conceived through her the Christ, who is reborn and resurrected into the world. The birth of the Christ is internal to Mary and spiritual. The absurdity of the Matthew virgin birth story comes from the literalisation of this spiritual birth into the birth of a physical baby.

In fact, the Matthew story is not alone and must be interpreted alongside several other early sources that hint at the non-physical nature of the birth of Jesus. The virgin birth was a reality, but it was a reality that was docetic, a spiritual conception and a spiritual birth. Mary is the virgin and the mother; she is the mother whose womb did not conceive and whose breasts did not give suck and she suffered no labour pains. It is time to explore the virgin birth story starting with the nativity in the Gospel of Matthew.

The Matthew nativity

The Gospel of Mark has no account of Jesus' nativity nor does it offer a genealogy. We only learn that Jesus has come from Nazareth. The gospel does not know of a father but only of a mother called Mary. In short the gospel knows virtually nothing of the origins of Jesus.

Such a deficiency must have been painfully obvious to the author of Matthew and as normal he corrects it. Instead of the silence of Mark we now have a wonderful nativity tale; the virgin birth, the visit of the Magi (often mistranslated as "kings" or "wise men"), the slaughter of the innocents by Herod and the escape to Egypt. The author of Matthew has actually taken many of these elements out of their proper place; the Magi, the slaughter of the innocents, and the escape to Egypt did not originally belong with the virgin birth story and will be considered later. Here we will focus on the birth itself.

Although the Gospel of Mark has Jesus coming from Nazareth the Gospel of Matthew has Jesus born in Bethlehem. It tells us that Jesus grew up in Nazareth because Joseph settled there after the return from Egypt:

And he came and dwelt in a city called Nazareth: that it might be fulfilled which was spoken by the prophets, "He shall be called a Nazarene." (Matthew 2:23)

What is odd about this is that there is no prophecy in Scripture that the Christ would be called a Nazarene. The closest we can get is a prophecy in Isaiah:

And a rod has come out from the stock of Jesse, and a branch [netzer] from his roots is fruitful. The spirit of Yahweh has rested on him, the spirit of wisdom and understanding. (Isaiah 11:1-2)

This has long been interpreted by Jews as a prophecy of the Messiah, who will be a "branch of Jesse" because he is descended from David, son of Jesse. The image is of a tree having been cut down, the crashing down of the throne of David at the Babylonian axe, but re-sprouting from the stump. The word for branch, *netzer*, is the root of the words "Nazarene" and "Nazareth". It cannot be a coincidence that a key prophecy of the Messiah is related in this way to the word Nazarene, while Matthew tells us that Jesus was called a Nazarene in fulfilment of prophecy. However, Matthew cannot be referring to Isaiah 11:1-2 directly but must have some other source that uses the title of "the Nazarene" with the meaning "of the branch" for the Christ. That the Nazarene was an early title of Jesus is shown by the fact that "Jesus the Nazarene" is used in several places in Mark[209] rather than "Jesus of Nazareth". This title would have meant originally that Jesus had come to fulfil the prophecy of the branch. But the author of Mark interprets it wrongly as meaning that Jesus came from Nazareth: "*And it came to pass in those days, that Jesus came from Nazareth of Galilee, and was baptised of John in Jordan*" (Mark 1:9).

The author of Matthew thus inherits two sources. An unknown source based on Isaiah 11:1-2 that says the Christ will be the Nazarene and the Gospel of Mark, which says that Jesus came from Nazareth. He combines both sources in his statement that Jesus came from Nazareth to fulfil a prophecy that he would be called the Nazarene.

It is too much of a coincidence to believe that Jesus could be called the Nazarene both because he came from Nazareth and because he was the Christ. The story about Jesus coming from Nazareth must have come from the title the Nazarene and not the other way around. This is important because it undermines the idea that Jesus came from Galilee. We shall see that the Nazarene is not the only title that has been projected onto a town in Galilee and that in truth the Jesus movement had no connection with Galilee.

Although Matthew has Joseph settling in Nazareth, Jesus is born in Bethlehem. The implication of the gospel is that this is Joseph's home town. The author of Matthew gives this explanation of why they did not return to Bethlehem:

> But when Herod was dead, behold, an angel of the Lord appeared in a dream to Joseph in Egypt, saying, "Arise, and take the child and his mother, and go into the land of Israel. For those who sought the child's life are dead." And he arose, and took the child and his mother, and came into the land of Israel. But when he heard that Archelaus did reign in Judea in place of his father Herod, he was afraid to go there. Having moreover been warned in a dream, he turned aside into the district of Galilee. (Matthew 2:19-22)

We see here an attempt to reconcile a number of traditions. The author of Matthew's main source is the Gospel of Mark and anyone reading Mark would think that Jesus had simply been born and grew up in Nazareth in Galilee. The author of Matthew, however, gives a complicated explanation of why Jesus came to live in Nazareth. One reason is that he wants to locate the birth of Jesus in Bethlehem so that the prophecy of the coming of the Messiah is fulfilled. This will mean that Jesus is born in Judea to a Judean family. However, there is one fascinating aspect of the angel's message, and that is that he does not tell Joseph to return to Judea or to go to Galilee, but to return to Israel. The old northern kingdom of Israel was now known as Samaria, and we will see that this is the place from which the Jesus movement really originated. So the author of Matthew is trying to reconcile no less than three different traditions and sources. He has a tradition that the family of Jesus originates from Israel, a source that indicates Bethlehem, and the Gospel of Mark that says that he came from Nazareth in Galilee. We may note the half-hearted attempt to explain why Joseph ended up far to the north in Galilee: "*having moreover been warned in a dream*". The author of Matthew is trying to bring Galilee into the picture in contradiction to his sources outside Mark. The problem arises because the idea that Jesus came from Galilee has originated with the Gospel of Mark.

The Gospel of Matthew tells us why the birthplace of Jesus must be Bethlehem. As the Magi tell Herod, it had been prophesied that that the Christ would come from Bethlehem:

And you, Bethlehem of the land of Judah, you are by no means the least among the leaders of Judah, for out of you shall come a leader who shall feed my people Israel. (Matthew 2:6)

The reference would seem to be to Micah:

And you, Bethlehem Ephratah, though you are little among the clans of Judah, from you to me he comes forth, to be ruler in Israel. And his comings forth are of old, from the days of antiquity. Therefore he does give them out until the time she who brings forth has brought forth, and the remnant of his brethren return to the sons of Israel. (Micah 5:2-3)

This is included in a key passage that prophesies the return from exile and the coming of the Messiah, a section that was of vital importance for the Jesus movement. In the passage above it is told how the ruler shall come from Bethlehem and how "*his comings forth are of old, from the days of antiquity*". This is exactly the understanding of the Jesus movement, that the Christ has come forth into the world before, and that on a previous coming he was put to death. His latest coming waits until "*she who brings forth has brought forth*" this one being for the Jesus movement Mary. The author of Matthew is aware of this passage applied as it was to the "birth" of Jesus through Mary and so situates that birth in Bethlehem. This brings us to the account in Matthew of the birth itself which is brief:

For his mother Mary having been betrothed to Joseph, before their coming to-gether she was found to be pregnant from the holy spirit, and Joseph her husband being righteous, and not willing to publicly disgrace her, did wish to privately di-vorce her. (Matthew 1:18-19)

We have seen how the idea of Joseph being the husband of Mary is a misunderstanding of "Mary of Joses (Joseph)", meaning Mary, daughter of Joseph. It is under this name that she is known when she experiences the resurrection/birth of Jesus. The author of Matthew has inherited two traditions:

That it is Mary of Joses who is the mother of Jesus.
That she was a virgin and the conception was spiritual in nature.

To reconcile these two traditions, Matthew comes up with the story of Mary being betrothed to Joseph when she is impregnated by the Holy Spirit. In the continuation of the story, Joseph is visited in a dream by an angel who tells him *"that which is begotten [gennao] within her by the spirit is holy.* The word *gennao* is common in the New Testament meaning to be born or begotten. But in this one place only it is normally translated as "conceived" which gives a subtle shift in meaning. What the words really say is that Jesus has been born within Mary. Under the spiritual hypothesis this is exactly what has happened; Jesus has been born in the spiritual sense internally to Mary. But among those with the literalistic worldview it is has been read as meaning that Jesus was conceived within her. The fact that the words do not fit in comfortably with the author of Matthew's story indicates that he must be copying from one of his sources at this point. It is possible that the dream of Joseph goes back to an early tradition that Joseph was inclined to have Mary put away to somewhere private because of her claim to be the medium for the risen Christ; but then he had a dream that Mary's visions were valid and that Christ had indeed been reborn within her through the spirit. We may wonder at the reactions of her family to her revelations and specifically the reaction of her father who, as a supposed descendant of David, would have been prominent within the apocalyptic group awaiting the return of the Christ. Her claims that the Christ had risen and had appeared through herself, a mere woman, must have been regarded within the group as highly blasphemous if not a sign of madness. There is some support for this in Mark 3:21 where the "people" of Jesus, meaning his circle, kin or family, seek to restrain him on the grounds that he is "beside himself" – a phrase signifying madness. This could go back to a tradition about Mary whom must have been thought mad by many. But the relationship between father and daughter must ultimately remain a matter for conjecture, and we cannot be sure that Joseph was alive at this point.

The angel also tells Joseph that the baby is to be called Jesus *"for he shall save his people from their sins"* an allusion to the meaning of the name Jesus which is "Yahweh saves". This is followed up in typical Matthew fashion by quoting a prophecy fulfilled:

And all this came to pass, that it might be fulfilled that was spoken by the Lord through the prophet, saying, "Lo, the virgin shall conceive, and she shall bring forth a son, and they shall call his name Emmanuel" which means "God with us." (Matthew 1:22-23)

The quotation is from Isaiah 7:14. Ahaz king of Judea is threatened by two rival kings Rezin and Pekah, who are advancing on Jerusalem. At this point, the prophet Isaiah receives a commission from Yahweh to reassure Ahaz that the two "*stubs of smoking brands*" will not succeed in their aim. Although Ahaz does not want any prophecies, yet Isaiah gives him one:

Therefore the Lord himself gives you a sign. Lo, the virgin conceives, and brings forth a son, and has called his name Emmanuel. Butter and honey he does eat, when he knows to refuse evil, and to fix on good. For before the youth knows to refuse evil, and to fix on good, forsaken is the land you are vexed with, because of her two kings. (Isaiah 7:14-15)

It should be understood that the prophecies in the Old Testament were written long after the events they described and were intended to recast historical events as unfolding according to the prior plan of Yahweh. In this case, the prophecy was not originally about the Messiah but about events in the time of Ahaz and the reasons for the coming destruction of Israel. The birth of the child is a poetic allusion, the mother most likely being Zion. The name of the child Emmanuel meaning "God be with us" gives the game away. The child represents a godly remnant in Judea who will refuse evil and fix on good, and who will, as a consequence, eat "butter and honey" a reference to the land of milk and honey, the promised land. The prophecy is saying that the land of the two kings threatening Ahaz will be "forsaken" before this time. The kingship of Ahaz will survive, not because of the king himself, but because of those who will be godly in Judea. In fact, the prophecy of Emmanuel is one of a doublet. A little later the birth of a second boy is mentioned:

And I draw near to the prophetess, and she conceives, and bears a son. And Yahweh says to me, "Call his name Maher-shalal-hash-baz, for before the youth knows how to cry, My father, and My mother, the wealth of Damascus and the spoil of Samaria shall be taken away before the king of Assyria." (Isaiah 8:3-4)

This time instead of the "virgin" or young woman we have a "prophet-ess". In Isaiah "prophet" is used to signify false prophets and liars, in contrast to Isaiah himself, who is the true prophet. A description "prophetess" adds to this meaning of liar the additional suggestion of a female dabbling in magic. The prophet approaches her casually, and she conceives – signifying that she is a whore as well as a prophetess. After this allusion to the child being "son of a whore" the metaphor goes on to compare the child's father and mother to the lands of the two kings, Damascus and Samaria. The implication is that the northern kingdom of Israel (Samaria) is both politically and spiritually a whore. The child's name Maher-shalal-hash-baz means "swift is booty, speedy is prey" and is symbolic, foretelling the fate that will befall the land of the two kings, and Samaria in particular.

The story of the two boys Emmanuel and Maher-shalal-hash-baz symbolise the contrasting fates of the two sides at war. The godly Emmanuel will eat butter and honey whereas the ungodly Maher-shalal-hash-baz will be defeated and plundered. The meta-narrative is about making sense of the destruction of the northern kingdom of Israel (Samaria) by Assyria. In this meta-narrative the king of Assyria is co-opted as a servant of Yahweh by making him an instrument of the will of Yahweh. In this recasting of events, Israel is not defeated because it is weak but because it is ungodly. The northern kingdom of Israel was notorious for being more polytheistic than the southern kingdom of Judea and is represented by Maher-shalal-hash-baz the son of the whore prophetess, a female of falsehood and false gods. The southern kingdom of Judea survives because of a godly remnant represented as the son of the virginal Zion. This meta-narrative is written after the destruction by the Assyrians and has been projected backwards to the time of Ahaz and put in the mouth of Isaiah.

Most traditional commentators interpret Emmanuel and Maher-shalal-hash-baz as being real boys despite the obvious play on words in their names which is as true for Emmanuel as for Maher-shalal-hash-baz. The prophecy continues with the threat that the river of the Assyrian invasion will flood the land of Judea up to its "neck", being Jerusalem, and will cover "*the breadth of your land Emmanuel*" *(Isaiah 8:8)*. Although nations may conspire, and gird themselves (in armour) and plan against Judea yet they shall "*be broken*" for "*God is with us*" *(Isaiah 8:10)* being the same as the name Emmanuel. This links back into the opening of the prophecy, the threat to Ahaz from the two kings and links this to the later threat of the Assyrians who overrun Israel and threaten Jerusalem. Emmanuel is an obvious representation of Judea in its God respecting aspect.

The mother of Emmanuel is Zion, the personification of Jerusalem and Judea. That she is called a virgin does not mean that there is present in Isaiah the idea of birth without conception. Rather it signifies the bride is entering the bridal chamber as a virgin, pure and undefiled. Zion is represented as the bride of Yahweh and "God is with us", Emmanuel, is their child. The prophecy is applied in the Gospel of Matthew to Mary and her son Jesus. Once we realise that the father of Emmanuel in Isaiah must have been Yahweh, we can see how close the Matthew story is to this original. In both cases a virgin bears a son by Yahweh and in both cases the son is called Emmanuel. The difference is that in Isaiah the birth is nothing more than a poetical metaphor while in Matthew it has become literalised as a story that is presented as history.

Behind the Matthew story is an earlier Midrash on the Isaiah passage, a Midrash that goes back to the origins of the Jesus movement. In this Midrash, Mary is identified with Zion. We have already seen this identification in the Midrash on the Song of Songs where Mary is equated with the dove, an allegory of Zion. We shall see this same identification of Mary with Zion again and again. Mary is the virgin Zion through whom the Christ will be born of God the Father. The Midrash has been used by Mary or her early followers to justify her role as the route through which the spiritual Jesus is "born" into the world.

Much play has been made of the different words used to describe the mother of Emmanuel in the Hebrew and the Greek Septuagint versions of the Isaiah prophecy. The Gospel of Matthew, written in Greek, uses the same word as the Septuagint, *parthenos* whereas the Hebrew uses *almah*. It is frequently said that *almah* means a young woman of marriageable age while *parthenos* means virgin. The idea is that the story of the virgin birth came about because the author of Matthew was using the Septuagint version of Isaiah and misunderstood it as implying that a virgin, *parthenos,* would give birth whereas in fact the Hebrew original had a young woman, *almah.* But the distinction between *almah* and *parthenos* is an oversimplification. Until very recently there was no difference between a marriageable young woman and a virgin, it being implicit that the former implied the later. So the same word would be used for both even in circumstances where a woman's virginity was pretty nominal. In practise, the words *almah* and *parthenos* would have conveyed a similar meaning. But in any case no one would have taken a saying like "a virgin shall conceive and bear a son" as implying a virgin birth even if they interpreted virgin literally. It simply means that the woman was a virgin when she came to the marriage bed from where she conceives.

Although many Jews would have been familiar with the scriptures through the Septuagint it is very unlikely that the exact words used in this Greek translation would have influenced beliefs. Knowledge of Hebrew was widespread, and an interpretation based on the Greek in contradiction to the Hebrew would surely not have prevailed. The idea of the author of Matthew or another Jewish Christian originating the idea of the virgin birth because of the word *parthenos* in the Septuagint is unrealistic. What is more realistic is that the author of Matthew inherited a prior tradition of a virgin birth and then quoted the version of scripture that gave the most support to this tradition.

The prophecy of Emmanuel became regarded by the mainstream Jews as a prophecy of the Messiah. They certainly did not expect the Messiah to be conceived in any other manner than normal relations between husband and wife. But we have seen that the original Emmanuel is born of the virginal Zion by Yahweh. This original meaning has come down to the apocalyptic group from which the Jesus movement has descended with the additional Midrash that Emmanuel represents the Messiah. This has then been applied to Mary so that she, in place of Zion, conceives from the father and gives "birth" to the Messiah. The author of Matthew, writing much later, has picked up on this interpretation of the prophecy and twisted it very slightly for the purpose of his literalistic narrative.

The Gospel of Matthew makes clear that Mary does not remain a virgin after Jesus' birth. It says that Joseph "*did not know her until she brought forth her son*" (*Matthew 1:25*). This has doubtless been added by the author of Matthew to account for the brothers of Jesus. In his original source, Mary is simply a virgin.

This cannot be accepted by the historical Jesus school who attempt to fashion history from the fantasies that the gospel writers wove around the original mystical insights of the Jesus movement. Many of them believe that the virgin birth must have arisen from the historical kernel of the illegitimacy of Jesus. In this interpretation, Matthew retains a toehold on historical reality by implying that Mary did not remain a virgin. In later developments this toehold would be lost as the mystical role of the virgin was elaborated, and the idea of the perpetual virginity of Mary took hold.

But we can reverse this process and see the perpetual virginity of Mary as coming first and the literalistic story of Jesus as being the development. In its original form, it was not just the conception that was spiritual in nature but the birth as a whole. This is the only possible interpretation of certain clues preserved in early sources. And in the Gospel of Thomas we have a saying that is earlier than the Gospel of Mark and which speaks directly of the non-physical nature of the motherhood of Jesus.

The Luke nativity

There is a nativity in Luke as well as Matthew, and it follows the typical "same but different" formula in relation to the Matthew account; the two are intimately linked and yet the author of Luke seems to go out of her way to change the details. Although Mark says that Jesus came from Nazareth we have seen how Matthew locates the birth in Bethlehem. The implication from Matthew is that Jesus' family came from Bethlehem and that they only relocate to Nazareth on the return from Egypt. The author of Matthew is trying to claim Jesus as coming from Judea as you would expect from a descendant of David rather than from disreputable Galilee. But the author of Luke, who does not care where Jesus comes from, completely undermines this. She has noticed the inconsistency between Mark and Matthew and attempts to explain it while showing off her historical knowledge with the story of the census at the time of Quirinius, governor of Syria. She tells us that Joseph had to travel to Bethlehem to register because he was of the house of David and his family was based in that city. It is the Luke version that has won out over the centuries because it neatly explains why Jesus of Nazareth should be born in Bethlehem. But the author of Luke has got it wrong; there was no census at the time she claims and in any case people would have registered in their hometown and not been obliged to travel to some supposed ancestral home.

The imaginative author of Luke greatly amplifies the story of the virgin birth setting it in a longer novelistic narrative. First is the story of the conception of John the Baptist to two elderly parents, Elizabeth and Zechariah. Needless to say, the author of Luke knows nothing whatever about the origins of John. The movement of John originally rivalled the Jesus movement, and the earliest sayings about John and baptism are critical in nature. The author of Luke is far removed in time, distance and culture from the genuine John the Baptist. We do not know who the parents of John the Baptist were but the Luke story is pure fantasy and we can be pretty sure they were not called Zechariah or Elizabeth.

The angel Gabriel visits Zechariah first and then, after Elizabeth miraculously conceives, he visits Nazareth and the house of a virgin called Mary who is betrothed to Joseph. Gabriel tells her that she will conceive and give birth to Jesus "*the son of the Highest*". Mary is doubtful as she has not known a husband. (This echoes the Song of Thunder where the narrator also has taken no husband.) The messenger replies:

The Holy Spirit shall come upon you, and the power of the Highest shall over-shadow you, therefore also the holy one being born shall be called Son of God. (Luke 1:35)

Afterward, Mary visits her kinswoman Elizabeth and stays with her for three months. In the type of absurdity that is typical of second-century Christian romances the baby John within Elizabeth's womb leaps in gladness at the greeting of Mary. Elizabeth praises Mary, and Mary responds with the "Magnificat" in which she gives thanks to God for her blessings.

One of the most telling parts of this story is a phrase that Luke includes in the message of the angel "the *power of the highest shall overshadow you*". The word for overshadow, *episkiazo,* is used four other times in the New Testament. One of these is in Acts when the shadow of Peter falls on the sick and heals them. The other three are in the three versions of the transfiguration on the mount. Jesus has taken Peter, James and John up the mountain where Jesus is transfigured with his garment becoming shining white. There Jesus speaks to Moses and Elijah. And this is where they hear a voice:

And there was a cloud that overshadowed (episkiazo) them, and a voice came out of the cloud, "This is my Son, the beloved; hear him." (Mark 9:7)

The transfiguration is yet another version of how Jesus appeared to Mary, but this time under the name of "Peter". The appearance on a mountain has been interpreted wrongly by the author of Mark as a literal mountain. We have already come across the mountain as a metaphor for the kingdom of God, and we will see more about the true meaning of the "mountain" later. The overshadowing of Mary to conceive and the over-shadowing of Peter at the transfiguration are one and the same event. This mystical experience has been retold as birth, resurrection, baptism and transfiguration by those who have literalised the story. The transfiguration story is obviously linked to the baptism story which uses very similar words:

And a voice came out of the heavens, "You are my Son, the beloved, in you I am well pleased." (Mark 1:11)

The source of the "overshadowing" is linked to the imagery in Psalms and other sources which give Mary her title of Thunder. This imagery goes back to the sky god who is hid in the "secret place", *cether,* in the midst of the clouds his presence only felt on earth through his thunder. Mary / Peter are overshadowed by the cloud and enveloped by it, before coming to the secret place in its midst where the birth / resurrection of Jesus takes place.

We have seen that some manuscripts of Luke have an alternative version of the words spoken by the voice from heaven at the baptism of Jesus:

"My son are you, today I have begotten you." (Luke 3:22)

This implies that the baptism and the birth of Jesus are the same; both concern the manifestation of the Christ into the world. Clement of Alexandria mentions that the followers of Basilides celebrated the baptism and the birth of Jesus jointly on 6 January or 10 January. This may have been an early form of the feast of Epiphany, which is celebrated on 6 January. Certainly Epiphany seems originally to have been a celebration of both the birth and baptism of Jesus. Later the nativity began to be associated with Christmas on 25 December, leaving the celebration of the baptism on Epiphany, as is still the case in the Eastern Church. The alternative version of the words of Luke is actually a quote from the second Psalm:

"I have set my king upon Zion, My holy hill." I declare the decree of Yahweh, he said to me, "You are my Son, today I have begotten you. Ask of me and I give the nations as your inheritance, and the ends of earth as your possession." (Psalm 2:6-8)

This is one of the prophecies of the Christ, the anointed one. He has been anointed upon Mount Zion "my holy hill" and has been begotten. In the Midrash of the early Jesus movement, Mary was equated to Zion. So Jesus is born on Mount Zion, meaning born through Mary. The image of the appearance of Jesus upon the mount in the transfiguration is no more than an alternative version of this birth / resurrection of Jesus.

She who gave birth and did not give birth

Turning to works outside the New Testament we can see fragments in several places that point towards the spiritual birth of the Christ. In the second-century Acts of Peter, there is a discourse by Peter in chapter 24 where he quotes from "prophets" concerning the Christ, several of which point towards the spiritual birth:

"Who shall declare his generation?"
"And we saw him and he had no form or beauty."

These are from Isaiah 53:8 and 53:2 the "suffering servant" section of Isaiah that was so important to the early Jesus movement. Under the spiritual hypothesis, we can see a Midrash on this text as being used to justify the appearance of the spiritual Christ through Mary. The prophecies quoted by Peter continue:

In the last days a child shall be born of the Holy Spirit; his mother knows not a man and no man says that he is his father.

There is no known source of this prophecy, and it must have been taken from an earlier Christian work now lost. It would seem that we have here an alternative version of the virgin birth story that does not involve Joseph. Note how this is consistent with the Gospel of Mark where the father of Jesus is unknown.

She has given birth and has not given birth.

As shall be discussed below this line is a quote from the *Apocryphon of Ezekiel*. Here we see that the birth, as well as the conception of Jesus, is spiritual in nature. His mother has not gone through the normal mechanism of giving physical birth, a theme we find repeated again and again. The concept of she who has given birth yet has not given birth is also found in a line in the Song of Thunder: *I am the midwife and she who does not bear.* The list of prophecies in the Acts of Peter continues with:

Is it a small thing for you to weary men? Behold in the womb a virgin shall conceive.

The reference would seem to be to Isaiah 7:13-14 and is the prophecy of the birth of Emmanuel. The writer would have known of the application of this prophecy to Jesus from the Gospel of Matthew.

And another prophet said honouring the father "We neither heard her voice nor did a midwife come."

The reference is to the Ascension of Isaiah 11:13 and is considered in more detail below. Again this quote develops the theme of the birth not being physical.

Born not of the womb of woman but descended from a heavenly place.

The source for this prophecy quoted by the Acts of Peter is unknown indicating it must have been another early Christian work now lost. The quotation completes the birth prophecies and sums up what has gone before. We are now told explicitly that Jesus did not have a physical birth from "womb of woman" but was spiritual, descending from heaven. However, the author of the Acts of Peter does not distinguish this descent of Jesus from the "birth" through Mary. We are to suppose that somehow Jesus has been born through Mary and yet has not come forth from her womb. Under the conventional view, this makes no sense, but it is exactly what we have deduced from the shaman paradigm.

An earlier source than the Acts of Peter is the Apocryphon of Ezekiel from which the Acts gives the quote regarding she who has given birth and yet has not given birth. Unfortunately, the Apocryphon has not survived as a complete work but only in some fragments. The longest fragment is a parable of the lame man (the soul) and a blind man (the body) who conspire to steal some figs from a king's garden by the lame man riding on the blind man's back. Each claims that they cannot be held responsible for the act, the blind man because he cannot see, the lame man because he cannot move, but the king reunites them and punishes them together. It is made clear that the story is intended to be a parable about the resurrection at which time the soul will be reunited with the body and the two judged together. This story is precious early evidence for Jewish beliefs about the resurrection and the soul. But it is another fragment that is quoted by the early Christian father Tertullian that gives more evidence about the birth that is not a birth:[210]

We read also in the writings of Ezekiel concerning that cow which has given birth and has not given birth. (Tertullian - De carne Christi 23)

The same fragment is found quoted by other early writers -

And again in another place he says, "And the heifer gave birth and they said,
"She has not given birth" (Epiphanius, Panarion Haeresies 30:30:3).

Behold, the heifer has given birth and has not given birth (Gregory of Nyssa,
Against the Jews 3).

The quote in the Acts of Peter suppresses the reference to the cow that
was in the original. The reasons for not comparing the holy mother to a
cow are obvious. Yet this omission demonstrates that the author of the Acts
of Peter did not understand the symbolic meaning of the heifer. In the Animal Apocalypse of the book of Enoch, a work that will be shown to be of
crucial importance to the Jesus movement, the Messiah is represented as a
white bull. It follows that the heifer represents the Messiah's mother and
that it is the Messiah, the Christ, who has been born and yet not born. The
Apocryphon of Ezekiel was certainly in existence in the first century and
seems to have been originally a Jewish work. Yet it was popular with
Christian writers and the fragments that have come down may have been
subject to Christian reduction or addition. For example, the parable of the
lame man and the blind man is available in both Greek from a Christian
source and in Hebrew from the Jewish rabbinical literature. The Christian
version has subtle differences from the Jewish version that are best explained by an influence from the parable of the feast.

The saying of the heifer is quoted by Christians to support the virgin
birth. It depends upon the bull symbolism of the Animal Apocalypse and
so must be early. It records how Mary has given birth to the Messiah and
yet not given birth. We will see that other aspects of the nativity story are
also derived from the Animal Apocalypse. Later, as the literal story of Jesus
in the gospels wins out, the Animal Apocalypse is forgotten, so that by the
time the Acts of Peter is written the reference to the cow is an embarrassment that is discreetly dropped.

Another early work quoted by the Acts of Peter is the Ascension of Isaiah. This is originally a Jewish work but has Christian additions. These additions are dependent upon the nativity Gospel of Matthew and most likely
date to the first half of the second century. We are first introduced to Mary
who, following Matthew, is betrothed to Joseph but is also herself of the
family of David:

> *And I saw a woman of the family of David the prophet whose name (was) Mary and she (was) a virgin and was betrothed to a man whose name (was) Joseph a carpenter ... (Ascension of Isaiah 11:2)[211]*

We have seen how Jesus was originally believed to have been of the line of David through Mary and this confirmation suggests that the author of the Ascension of Isaiah had access to valuable early traditions. What follows is a strange little story about the birth of Jesus:

> *And after two months of days, while Joseph was in his house, and Mary his wife, but both alone, it came about, when they were alone, that Mary then looked with her eyes and saw a small infant, and she was astonished. And after her astonishment had worn off, her womb was found as it was at first, before she had conceived. And when her husband, Joseph, said to her, "What has made you astounded?" his eyes were opened and he saw the infant and praised the Lord, because the Lord had come in his lot. And a voice came to them, "Do not tell this vision to anyone." But the story about the infant was spread abroad in Bethlehem. Some said "The virgin Mary has given birth before she has been married two months." But many said "She did not give birth; the midwife did not go up (to her) and we did not hear (any) cries of pain." (Ascension of Isaiah 11:7-14)[212]*

In interpreting this story it must be remembered that the author is heavily influenced by the Gospel of Matthew. So following Matthew he has Mary betrothed to Joseph who in reality was her father. If we take out the elements that have come from Matthew we can isolate what has come from other sources:

The notion that Mary gave birth after two months
The non-physical nature of the birth
The birth being of the nature of a vision
The saying that Mary had "given birth" and yet "she did not give birth"
The saying that "the midwife did not go to her and we did not hear any cries of pain"

Some of these themes have been already encountered. Again Mary has "given birth" and not "given birth" just as in the Apocryphon of Ezekiel. This birth is non-physical although this is represented in the story by the absurdity of the baby suddenly appearing after which Mary is still an intact virgin. But the voice makes clear what is happening – *"Do not tell this vision to anyone"*.

The idea of Mary giving birth after only two months is new and at first glance seems unaccountable. But this timescale fits in perfectly with the "calendar of the apocalypse" of the early Jesus movement. In this symbolic timescale, the Messiah returns (is reborn through Mary) at the beginning of the ninth week – that is after day sixty-three. This symbolic period has been interpreted as literal days by the author of the Ascension additions so that he has Mary give birth to Jesus after "two months of days".

The concept of Mary needing no midwife (or being her own midwife) and of having no labour pains is another recurring theme that points towards the non-physical nature of the birth. Again we can recall two lines of the Song of Thunder:

I am the midwife and she who does not bear,
I am the solace of my labour pains (Thunder: Perfect Mind 13:25-27)[213]

The same imagery of the virgin not requiring a midwife occurs in the Odes of Solomon, a work which is certainly early and which may date from the first century (translation by J.H. Charlesworth[214]). Ode 19 describes how the breasts of the Father are milked by the Holy Spirit, a hermaphrodite image that appears shocking to those brought up with a masculine idea of God. The milk is clearly intended to be spiritual:

She gave the mixture to the generation without their knowing,
And those who received are in the perfection of the right hand.
(Odes of Solomon 19:5)

The Ode continues by saying how the milk flowed into the womb of the virgin:

The womb of the virgin took it,
And she received conception and gave birth.
So the virgin became a mother with great mercies.
And she laboured and bore the Son but without pain,
Because it did not occur without purpose,
And she did not seek a midwife,
Because he caused her to give life.
She bore a strong man with desire (or will),

And she bore according to the manifestation,
And possessed with great power.
And she loved with salvation,
And guarded with kindness,
And declared (or manifested) with greatness.
(Odes of Solomon 19:6-11)

Here Mary "*laboured and bore the Son but without pain*" and "*she did not seek a midwife*" because "*he caused her to give life*". She bore a strong man with "*will*" according to "*the manifestation*" and "*possessed with great power*". All of this points towards the spiritual nature of the birth. The end of the Ode gives attributes to Mary that go far beyond those of a physical mother. She "*loved with salvation*", indicating that it is through her that salvation has come, and most significantly "*declared with greatness*". What does this "declared with greatness" mean except that it is Mary who has brought the good news, the gospel, and declared it to mankind? This gives her a role far beyond that attributed to her as the mother in the traditional viewpoint.

Note also that what Mary has received into her womb is the same as that received by those who are in "*the perfection of the right hand*". It is spiritual, the gift of heaven, rather than physical. So far none of the sources advanced for Mary having given birth and not given birth has come from the earliest strata of the writings of the Jesus movement. The conventional view is that these sources are Docetic and belong to a secondary development of the virgin birth story in the gospels. Docetism is seen by the historical Jesus school as emerging in the early church as the earthly Jesus became forgotten, and the spiritual risen Christ became predominant. This view of Docetism would be a logical necessity if there was a human Jesus of flesh and blood. However, under the shaman paradigm there was never a fleshy Jesus and Docetism would represent the original earliest Christianity. If this is the case can we find any evidence predating the literalistic gospels for Docetism?

Such evidence exists in fact in the gospels themselves. The virgin birth story in Matthew and Luke with Mary conceiving by the Holy Spirit is clearly part of the Docetic view of Jesus. However, traditionalists view Docetism as a heresy and so, by definition, in their view the virgin birth stories in the gospel cannot be Docetic. The historical Jesus school, on the other hand, holds that the virgin birth story originated with the confusion between *parthenos* (virgin) and *almah* (young woman). We have already seen how this is inadequate to account for the virgin birth, which is just one element of a whole complex of sayings pointing to the spiritual generation of Jesus.

Key points

1. The virgin birth story would not have developed from the Septuagint version of Isaiah, which uses *parthenos* (virgin) to translate the Hebrew *almah* (young woman). In reality, the two words meant much the same thing, and the prophecy that the Messiah would be born of a virgin would have been interpreted as meaning that he would be conceived by a virgin bride.

2. The author of Matthew must have had a pre-existing tradition for the virgin birth which he regards as miraculous confirmation of a hidden meaning in the Isaiah prophecy.

3. The title of the Nazarene is derived from the prophecy that the Messiah will be "a branch" (*netzer*) of Jesse, meaning that he will be descended from David. However, the author of Mark has misunderstood the title as meaning that Jesus came from Nazareth. The author of Matthew tries to reconcile these two inconsistent interpretations by inventing an imaginary prophecy that the Christ will be called a Nazarene.

4. There is an alternative version of the baptism in Luke, in which the words from heaven say: *"My son are you, today I have begotten you."* Originally the birth of Christ, the baptism, and the resurrection were all one and the same, but they become separate events with the development of the literalistic story.

5. There are allusions to the birth of Jesus in a number of early works, including the Acts of Peter, the Apocryphon of Ezekiel, the Ascension of Isaiah, the Odes of Solomon and Thunder: Perfect Mind.

6. The allusions emphasise the contradictory nature of the birth as if posing a riddle. She has given birth and has not given birth. She has given birth, and yet no midwife came. She gave birth, yet endured no birth pains. These are similar to the teasing contradictions of the Song of Thunder.

7. In the Apocryphon of Ezekiel, it is a heifer which gives birth and yet does not give birth. This form must go back to the origins of the movement because it uses imagery from the Animal Apocalypse, where the Messiah is a great white bull.

Chapter 27

The womb that did not conceive

We have seen evidence that the origins of the virgin birth story lay in traditions that the mother of Jesus had not given physical birth. It is time to look at a saying in Thomas that is perhaps the earliest source of this tradition. This saying has influenced the authors of Luke and Mark and it may be the source of the virgin birth story in Matthew. Using the principle that a theory should explain more than the data used to frame it, we will see how the saying gave rise to the story of the miraculous birth of John the Baptist and provides a clue as to why Paul was believed to make tents.

Thomas 79

The best evidence for the origins of the virgin birth story is a saying that is earlier than all the literalistic gospels. It was used as a source by the author of Mark and so must predate Mark. This saying speaks directly of the mother of Jesus as having given birth and not given birth. The saying is found in Thomas:

A woman in the crowd said to him: "Blessed is the womb which bore you, and the breasts which nourished you." He said to her: "Blessed are they who have heard the word of the Father and have truly kept it. For there shall be days when you will say: "Blessed is the womb which has not conceived, and the breasts which have not given suck." (Thomas 79)

The conventional view sees this saying as a compound of two sayings found in Luke. There is no doubt at all that the saying we find in the one surviving Coptic copy of Thomas has been influenced by Luke. But it was common for translators and copyists to alter an unfamiliar form of a saying to something closer to the familiar gospel form of the saying. It must be remembered that the Coptic Thomas is comparatively late, dating from two or three centuries after the original gospel, and has suffered in places from the process of translation and editing.

The evidence that an original saying has been corrupted by additions from Luke can be found in Luke itself. For when we look at the form of the two sayings in Luke it is clear that the author of Luke has originally copied them from Thomas! The sayings are:

And it came to pass, as he spoke these things, a certain woman of the company lifted up her voice, and said to him, "Blessed is the womb that bore you, and the breasts which you have sucked." But he said, "Blessed rather are they that hear the word of God, and keep it." (Luke 11:27-29)

But Jesus turning to them said, "Daughters of Jerusalem, weep not for me, but weep for yourselves, and for your children. For, behold, the days are coming, in the which they shall say, Blessed are the barren, and the wombs that never bore, and the breasts which never gave suck." (Luke 23:28-29)

Although separated by twelve chapters there is one strong connection between the two contexts in which they appear; they are both linked to apocalyptic warnings by Jesus. The first is immediately followed by a long passage on the coming apocalypse, and the second saying is a warning of the apocalypse. The arguments for both sayings being copied from a Thomas original are:

The two sayings appear only in Luke and not in any of the other gospels. The author of Luke has got them from somewhere.

The key elements of the two sayings, "the womb that bore, the breasts which you have sucked" and "the wombs that never bore and the breasts which never gave suck" belong together as an antithesis demonstrating that they have both been taken from an original saying. They are found together in Thomas 79, a clear indication that this is the original.

The conclusion of the first saying in Luke is identical to the conclusion of another story found in all the synoptic gospels and Thomas. This is about the family of Jesus waiting in the outer chamber and being rejected by Jesus (see below for a discussion of this story). The ending in Luke 8:19-21 is virtually identical to the ending that has been added to *"the womb that bore you and the breasts which you have sucked."* There are two possible ways to explain this coincidence. Either the ending has been taken by the author of Luke from the family saying and added to the saying about the blessing given to Jesus' mother. This is quite possible because the family saying rejects the mother and brothers of Jesus in favour of those who do God's will. But another possibility is that this coincidence belongs to the originals and we have two closely related sayings that exhibit redundancy.

In attempting to reconstruct the original of Thomas 79, we must remove the words "*For there will be days when you say*" for these have been taken from apocalyptic context supplied by Luke 23:28-29. We then have two versions of the saying depending on whether or not the expression "*Blessed are those who have heard the word of the Father (and) have kept it in truth*" was original:

A woman said to him: Blessed is the womb which bore you, and the breasts which nourished you. He said to her: Blessed is the womb which has not conceived, and the breasts which have not given suck. (Version A of Thomas 79)

A woman said to him: Blessed is the womb which bore you, and the breasts which nourished you. He said to her: Blessed are they who have heard the word of the Father and have truly kept it. Blessed is the womb which has not conceived, and the breasts which have not given suck. (Version B of Thomas 79)

Most likely both versions were in circulation before Luke was written. Version A is taut and brings out the striking contrast between the two halves of the saying. The second version reduces the impact and introduces the "father" which breaks the link between the woman who has given birth and the woman who has conceived. However, there is strong evidence for version B. For a start, it requires fewer changes to generate the two sayings in Luke and the version found in Coptic Thomas. The author of Luke would have taken her first use of the saying (Luke 11:27-29) complete from the first half of Thomas 79. She would then have taken the second half of Thomas 79 for the second saying (Luke 23:28-29) adding only the "daughters of Jerusalem" passage to give it a context. Similarly, the translator/copyist of Thomas would only have to add the few words about the days that are coming to give the version we find in Coptic Thomas. And there is a common factor in both these changes in that they resolve the obscurity of the last line: "*Blessed is the womb which has not conceived, and the breasts which have not given suck*". Under the gospel tradition, this cannot be interpreted as a reference to Mary giving birth and yet not giving birth because she does give birth physically to Jesus. Those encountering this say-

444 The Rock and the Tower

ing must have wondered to whom it applied. The later translator or copyist of Thomas has the benefit of the Gospel of Luke to supply the context and so adds a few words to make this context clear.

Did the author of Luke also have some earlier source to supply a context? The answer is yes! There is a very similar saying in Mark where Jesus is also talking about the coming apocalypse:

"And woe to those with child, and to those giving suck, in those days; and pray you that your flight may not be in winter." (Mark 13:17-18)

The parallel to Luke 23:28-29, addressed to the "daughters of Jerusalem", is striking and shows that it is this Mark line that must have suggested the connection with the apocalypse. The author of Luke has noticed the obvious link between:

"those with child" / "the womb that does not conceive"
and also -
"those giving suck" / "the breasts which have not given the suck".

The pairings are opposites, but the first is cursed and the second blessed, making the two expressions equivalent. The author of Luke connects the original version of Thomas 79 with the apocalyptic warning of the Gospel of Mark. She decides that the Thomas saying is about the apocalypse, which fits well the second part but not the first which is clearly about the mother of Jesus. The author of Luke deals with this problem by splitting the two halves and interprets the first as being similar to the story about the rejection of Jesus' mother and brothers. After this rejection, Jesus then goes on to give apocalyptic warnings. The second part of the original is placed much later in the gospel and is turned into an apocalyptic speech given by Jesus.

But what about the remarkable similarity between the warning in Mark and the second part of Thomas 79? How can this connection, so obvious to the author of Luke, be explained? The answer is that the author of Mark also had a version of Thomas 79. And just like the author of Luke he is puzzled by it. We know that the original meaning of Thomas 79 is related to "she who gave birth and did not give birth" but such an interpretation makes no sense in the Mark literal gospel. The author of Mark is forced to think of another explanation of the saying and interprets it as an apocalyptic warning.

We should note how the blessing of the second part (of the woman who has not given birth) is reversed in Mark by expressing "woe" for the woman who has child and those who have given suck. This suggests that he did have both parts of version A available and has interpreted it as meaning that the woman who has given birth and given suck is not blessed. There is, however, no reference to those who have heard the word of the Father suggesting that the author of Mark had the A form rather than the B form.

So did version B ever exist? The answer lies in the Gospel of Luke. It is Luke that uses Thomas 79 in such a way that suggests that the author of Luke had the B form of the saying. And it is in Luke that we find another, surprising, use of the saying. For Thomas 79 has found its way into Luke not just once but no less than three times; not only has the author of Luke split the saying into two but she has included a whole long story that has been suggested by Thomas 79. The table below shows how someone familiar with Matthew could have interpreted Thomas 79:

Thomas 79 Form "B"	Post-Matthew interpretation
A woman said to him: Blessed is the womb which bore you, and the breasts which nourished you.	Mary, the virgin mother of Jesus, is blessed.
He said to her: Blessed are they who have heard the word of the Father and have truly kept it.	Those to whom God has sent a message and who believe that message are blessed.
Blessed is the womb which has not conceived, and the breasts which have not given suck.	In addition to Mary, there is another barren woman who will be blessed.

Where can we find all these elements together in one story? The answer is the story of Mary and Elizabeth the mother of John the Baptist! In this story Mary is blessed, a barren woman conceives so that her shame is lifted from her, and a theme runs through the story that those who hear the word of God and believe are blessed. We can follow the reasoning of the author of Luke in constructing this story. She starts with the "womb that bore you and the breasts which nourished you" which can only be Mary, and this directs her to the nativity account in Matthew. She then asks herself what does it mean that those are blessed who hear the word of the father and who keep it? She will immediately think of the message of the angel given to Joseph in the Matthew nativity story:

Then Joseph being raised from sleep did as the angel of the Lord had commanded him, and received his wife. And he did not know her until she had brought forth her son, and he called his name Jesus. (Matthew 1:25)

Joseph hears the word of God through the angel and keeps it. The author of Luke now has her theme, the faithfulness to God's word through belief. But what about the other woman, the one who is barren? She gets her idea for the identity of this woman from a combination of Thomas and Matthew. In the Gospel of Thomas saying 79 is immediately preceded by another saying about "a reed shaken by the wind":

Jesus said: "Why did you come out to the field? To see reed shaken by the wind? And to see a man clothed in soft garments [like your] kings and your powerful ones? These are clothed in soft garments and they cannot know the truth."(Thomas 78)

The ancient reader of Thomas did not have the benefit of numbered sayings. Indeed, it is far from obvious what constitutes an individual saying in Thomas, and some of the modern numbering divisions have been put in the wrong place. So it would be quite natural for the author of Luke to read Thomas 79 as the continuation of Thomas 78 rather than as a completely separate saying. Now, she thinks that Jesus is talking about John the Baptist in Thomas 78 because of the parallel passage in Matthew:

And as they departed, Jesus began to say to the crowds concerning John, "What did you go out into the wilderness to see? A reed shaken with the wind? But what did you go out to see? A man clothed in soft raiment? Behold, they that wear soft clothing are in kings' houses. But what did you go out to see? A prophet? Yes, I say to you, and more than a prophet." (Matthew 11:7-9)

The author of Matthew has misinterpreted the saying which does not apply to John at all, but the author of Luke does not know this! So she thinks that the woman praising the mother of Jesus is in the crowd listening to Jesus talk about John, and that when Jesus replies he is still talking about John. What could be more natural than that Jesus would respond to praise of his mother by praising the mother of the man he has just elegised? In fact, there is a close parallel to the continuation of Matthew 11:7-9 where Jesus says about John: "*Among those that are born of women there has not risen a greater than John the Baptist*" (Matthew 11:11). So the author of Luke concludes that the woman who has not conceived is the mother of John the Baptist.

The author of Luke now has all the ingredients for her story. In the Matthew nativity the angel visits Joseph, and it is he who shows his faithfulness to God by obeying the angel's message. However, the female-centric author of Luke is not going to give the limelight in the nativity story to the male! Quite rightly she thinks this is woman's business. So she changes the story so that the angel comes twice.

She starts with the elderly couple Zechariah and Elisabeth: *"And they had no child, because that Elizabeth was barren, and they both were well advanced in years" (Luke 1:7).* The first message is to John's father, Zechariah, who is burning incense in the temple when he sees the angel Gabriel on the right-hand side of the altar. The angel tells him that he will have a son and that he is to be called John. Notice the similarity of the message to that given by the angel to Joseph in Matthew; in both cases the men are told their wives will have a son in incredible circumstances, one an old barren woman, the other a virgin, and in both cases they are given their son's name. However Joseph, in Matthew, believes and obeys whereas Zechariah expresses a quite reasonable doubt as to how this could be true[215] and as a punishment for not believing is struck dumb until the prophecy comes to pass. When Elizabeth realises she is pregnant she shows a different attitude to her husband:

Thus has the Lord dealt with me in the days wherein he looked on me, to take away my disgrace among men. (Luke 1:25)

The male is sceptical and doubting, and it is the female who shows faith and belief. But the real contrast comes with the second message when Gabriel appears to Mary to tell her that she, a virgin, will conceive and give birth to a son to be called Jesus. Ironically, Mary shows an almost identical scepticism to Zechariah: *"Then said Mary to the angel, 'How shall this be, seeing I know not a man'?"* (Luke 1:34). Gabriel though reacts very differently, giving her the reassurance rather than striking her dumb, so that Mary is able to express her faithfulness:

And Mary said, "Behold the handmaid of the Lord. May it happen to me according to your word." And the angel departed from her. (Luke 1:38)

After this Mary goes to visit Elizabeth and when she enters her house Elizabeth is moved by the spirit to bless Mary. We can here see a close similarity with Thomas 79 in our form B recreation.

Luke - speech of Elizabeth to Mary	Thomas 79 Form B
And she spoke in a loud voice and said, "Blessed are you among women, and blessed is the fruit your of womb." (Luke 1:42)	*A woman said to him: Blessed is the womb which bore you, and the breasts which nourished you.*
"And from where is this to me, that the mother of my Lord should come to me? For behold, as the voice of your greeting came to my ears, the baby in my womb leaped in joy." (Luke 1:43-44)	*[...] Blessed is the womb which has not conceived, and the breasts which have not given suck.*
And blessed is the one having believed that there will be a fulfilment to the things spoken to her from the Lord. (Luke 1:45)	*He said to her: Blessed are they who have heard the word of the Father and have truly kept it.*

After this comes the Magnificat, which is spoken either by Mary (most early texts) or by Elizabeth (a few Latin texts). Some think the Elizabeth reading makes more sense because it is modelled on the song of Hannah in 1 Samuel 2:1-11 in which the formerly barren Hannah gives thanks for her son Samuel. Yet we will see how closely 1 Samuel 2:1-11 relates to Mary, suggesting that the author of Luke has used an existing Christian Midrash on the 1 Samuel passage in composing the Magnificat. One of the elements not in 1 Samuel is that the speaker is blessed:

For he looked upon the humiliation of his handmaiden. For behold, from henceforth all generations shall call me blessed. (Luke 1:48)

We can see how the author of Luke has interpreted Thomas 79 in the light of the Matthew account of the nativity to generate this story of the fictional parents of John the Baptist, Zechariah, and Elisabeth. But this means that the Gospel of Luke has used Thomas 79 twice in two completely different ways; first to give this pre-nativity story and second to split the saying up to give the two sayings at Luke 11:27-29 and Luke 23:28-29. This dual use of one saying may be a sign of multiple authorship of the gospel or the incorporation of texts into the gospel that were written earlier and which at one time had an independent existence. Rather than the production of a single author it might be better to think of the Gospel of Luke and Acts as the joint production of a house church under the control of its powerful female patron and leader who sets the direction and contributes some of the writing but who also draws on the contributions of others.

There is one further possible use of Thomas 79 in the gospels, and that is the Matthew nativity story. It is possible that the author of Luke was correct in spotting a link between Thomas 79 and the Matthew nativity. If the author of Matthew, like the author of Luke, has Thomas 79 in its B form then this could be one source of the story of the virgin birth. We have seen how the middle part of the saying, *"Blessed are those who have heard the word of the Father and have kept it in truth"*, is reflected in the Matthew nativity by Joseph hearing the word of God through the angel and keeping it. The first element *"Blessed is the womb which bore you, and the breasts which nourished you"* is a reference to the birth of Jesus through Mary. But then Jesus cryptically replies *"Blessed is the womb which has not conceived, and the breasts which have not given suck."* It is possible that the author of Matthew interpreted this to mean that Jesus is implying that Mary was a virgin and that her womb had not conceived from man. If so then he has evolved the story of the virgin birth from Thomas 79.

The use of Thomas 79 by Matthew is less certain than its use by both Mark and Luke; but the fact that it was available to the authors of Mark and Luke enables us to place it in the earliest strata of the movement. Most likely the original saying was version A, and it acquired the middle element of version B by association with the family saying which is very similar. Thomas 79 version A is an early form of the "barren one whose children are many" and "she who gave birth and did not give birth". The saying speaks of how Jesus' mother had a womb that has not conceived and breasts that did not give suck – she was either a virgin or barren. And now we must consider in more detail the Magnificat in Luke, which is spoken by Mary and based on an original by a barren woman.

Why does Mary sing the Magnificat?

One of the most beautiful parts of Luke is the young Mary's hymn of praise, the Magnificat, which starts:

"My soul does magnify the Lord, and my spirit rejoices in God my Saviour."
(Luke 1:46-47)

Here to magnify means to make great, to praise. It has long been recognised that the Magnificat is closely based on the song of Hannah in 1 Samuel.[216] Hannah was one of the two wives of Elkanah. He loved Hannah, but she was barren and tormented by her rival wife Peninnah who had many children. Eventually, she approaches the temple of Yahweh and is filled with the spirit so that the priest thinks her drunk. She begs Yahweh that she might have a child and her wish is granted so that she conceives and gives birth to Samuel, who is to be king. There are several points of similarity between the song of Hannah and Luke, and these similarities are not just in the words of Mary but also in the words of Zechariah.

The situation of Hannah closely resembles that of Elizabeth, who is also barren until she miraculously conceives John the Baptist. So we would expect Elizabeth to sing the Magnificat, but she does not! Instead, it is Mary. The problem with this was very evident to early Christians; in some early Latin manuscripts it is indeed Elizabeth who sings the Magnificat. However, it is Mary who speaks the words in all early Greek manuscripts. So why are the praises of a barren woman given to Mary, who, according to the gospels, had no problem conceiving?

We have seen the answer. It is Mary whose womb had not conceived but whose children are many, and it is she who is the subject of Thomas 79. So the song of Hannah, in which an anointed one comes through a barren woman, was very appropriate to Mary. The author of Luke has probably inherited a Midrash that applies the song of Hannah to Mary, and she has incorporated this Midrash into her gospel with one significant omission. She excludes references to the barren one because this would not fit the character of the mother of Jesus as developed in Mark and Matthew.

We can see that the Song of Hannah was important to the early Jesus movement. The song was probably an earlier psalm that has been absorbed within the Samuel story. So we must bear in mind the possibility that it came down to the apocalyptic movement in a different context and with different associations from the version we have now. However, the text in 1 Samuel will suffice to show the similarities to the beliefs of the Jesus movement:

My heart rejoices in the Lord, mine horn is exalted in the Lord: my mouth is enlarged over mine enemies; because I rejoice in your salvation. (1 Samuel 2:1)

This beginning is repeated in the Magnificat in Luke, and the concept of the horn being exalted is repeated in the speech of Zechariah *"and did raise an horn of salvation to us, in the house of David his servant"* (Luke 1:69). It is clear that the author of Luke identifies the horn as the Christ.

There is none holy as the Lord, for there is none beside you. Neither is there any rock like our God. (1 Samuel 2:2)

It shall be seen that the rock and the horn are used as imagery in other texts key to the Jesus movement signifying that all these texts originally evolved together.

... The bows of the mighty men are broken, and they that stumbled are girded with strength. They that were full have hired out themselves for bread; and they that were hungry cease. (1 Samuel 2:4-5)

The themes of the weak becoming strong and the strong weak, of the poor becoming rich and the rich becoming poor, occur again and again in the Jesus movement.

So the barren has born seven; and she that has many children has become feeble. (1 Samuel 2:5)

This is another reference to the barren one whose children are many. The line is particularly appropriate to Mary because she had seven adopted sons. There is a clear link to the previous reversals of weak/strong and poor/rich. This line may be why the psalm has been turned into a song of Hannah and is key to the Midrash applying it to Mary.

The Lord kills, and makes alive: he brings down to the Sheol, and raises up. (1 Samuel 2:6)

Here immediately after the reference to the barren one whose children are many we have a line that would serve as a source for the death and resurrection of Christ. Sheol is the underworld or grave, and the line would be interpreted as a prophecy that one who was dead and in the grave would be raised to life.

Yahweh dispossesses and he makes rich, he makes low and he makes high. He raises from the dust the poor, from a dunghill he lifts up the needy. (1 Samuel 2:7-8)

This continues the theme of the reversal of rich and poor.

... Broken are the adversaries of Yahweh, against them in the heavens he thunders. Yahweh judges the ends of earth, and gives strength to his king, and exalts the horn of his anointed. (1 Samuel 2:10)

Here we have mention of "his king" and the "horn of his anointed", the anointed being the same word as the Messiah or Christ. The themes of the anointed king and the barren one fit the story of Samuel, but the fit is contrived. In the flow of the psalm, the contrast between the barren one who will have many children and the bringing low of the mother of many is simply one of several reversals. There is nothing to indicate that it applies to the psalmist. And there are signs that the story of Hannah and her rival Peninnah has been given a spin so as to fit the psalm. In the story, Peninnah has been elevated to an enemy of Hannah which fits in with a major theme of the psalm, the overthrowing of enemies, which would otherwise be completely out of place in the mouth of Hannah. Yet Peninnah seems to be guilty of no more than a little bitchiness.

There is another clue that the psalm did not originally belong to Hannah. The last line tells of how the horn of his anointed would be exalted and matches the beginning of the psalm where the horn of the psalmist is exalted. The inescapable conclusion is that the psalmist is intended to be the anointed; surely not Samuel but King David. We are dealing with a literary composition of a psalm of David that has later been incorporated into the story of Samuel because of the coincidence of the reference to the barren one and the anointed king.

But the psalm could also be interpreted as a prophecy of the Messiah, and the evidence from Luke is that this is how it was interpreted in the Jesus movement. What makes the psalm special is the reference to one being raised out of the dead, a source of the concept of the dying and resurrected Messiah. Add to this the reference to the barren one who will have seven children and we can see how important this would have been to the Jesus movement. They would have applied it as a prophecy that the Christ would be resurrected through the barren one whose children are many.

The barren woman with many children

Another reference to the "barren one" occurs in a key piece of scripture for the early Jesus movement – the suffering servant section of Isaiah. The reference comes immediately after a section that was very important for the Jesus movement, describing how the suffering servant will be numbered among the transgressors and will bear the sin of many.

> *Sing, O barren one, she who has not borne! Break forth with singing, and cry aloud, She has not given birth! For more are the sons of the desolate than the sons of the married one, said Yahweh. Enlarge the place of thy tent, and the curtains of your tabernacles stretch out. Restrain not, lengthen your cords, and make strong your pegs. For you will break out to the right and left, and your seed will possess the nations. (Isaiah 54:1-3)*

The Jewish interpretation is that the "barren one" is Zion or Jerusalem. She is barren after the exile but will be redeemed and will sing again. At this time, she will have many sons and will spread out across the earth bringing the nations into her tent. However, the Jesus movement equated Mary with Zion, so that Mary is the "barren one".

This very same Isaiah passage is quoted by Paul in Galatians 4:27 in a section that is linked to the mother of Jesus. It is worth looking at the whole of the passage to understand the context. Paul is addressing the Gentile Galatians who have been bewitched by the Judaizers, who want to have them circumcised. Although Jesus has been crucified in front of their eyes (mystically) they are considering becoming Jews. Paul's argument is that they are children of Abraham by faith rather than law so circumcision is a backward step that would place them under the law. He tells the Galatians how they were children under the elements of the *kosmos* until they came under their inheritance and were adopted as sons:

> *And I say, as long time as the heir is a child, he does not differ from a slave, though being the owner of everything. Instead, he is under guardians and trustees until the time set by his father. So also, when we were children, we were held in bondage under the elements of the world (kosmos). But when the fullness of time had come, God sent his Son, come of a woman, come under the law, in order to redeem those who were under the law, that the adoption of sons we may receive. (Galatians 4:1-5)*

The insight that the woman mentioned by Paul here is the founder of
the movement is key to understanding Paul's argument that follows. All
those in the early Jesus movement, and not just the brethren of the Lord,
were in a wider sense regarded as Mary's "sons". Because the Galatians
have received the adoption as sons through Mary, and because Mary was
born under the law, the Galatians are also children of the promise, not bio-
logically like the Jews but through faith and grace. The male case, "sons",
can be taken as including the female; Paul does not normally bother to distinguish the two. The issue of circumcision was more vital to the men, but
the wider issue of law obedience applied to the women also.

Paul goes on to berate the Galatians for having turned against him before using the unusual image of conception and birth to describe his relationship with them:

*My little children, of whom I labour in birth again, until Christ be formed in
you. (Galatians 4:19)*

We have seen how Paul has borrowed this image from Mary/Cephas; it
is Mary who travails in birth, although without pain, and who brings forth
the Christ formed within her. Mary then acts as a midwife or surrogate
mother to induce the same experience in her followers including the five
hundred that Paul mentions in 1 Corinthians. Later she appoints the apostles to induce others; so Paul stands in the same relation to Galatians as the
founder does to the movement, a relationship which Paul subtly emphasises through this imagery.

After giving this surprising image of giving birth, Paul develops another
argument based on motherhood. Here Paul draws on a Midrash to develop
an argument against his Judaizing opponents. He points out that Abraham
had two sons; one by the maidservant (or slave) and one by the free woman. In Genesis, the story is given how Abraham's wife Sarah was barren,
and so Abraham took her maidservant Hagar to bed, and she gave him a
son Ishmael. Later, the elderly Sarah conceives and bears Abraham another
son Isaac. Paul identifies his fellow Jews with Ishmael, who has in fact been
circumcised. Because they are sons of the slave woman, according to the
flesh, they are under the Law. But those of the Jesus movement are sons of
the free woman according to the spirit, and so the Law does not apply to
them.

We can understand this argument by understanding that Mary is equated with the free woman, Sarah. Both Mary and Sarah are "the barren one

whose children are many". In the story of Abraham's sons, it is the second son who is the son of the promise, and this was applied in Midrash to the Jesus movement compared to the mainstream Jews. Although the Jews came first, it is the Jesus movement who are the sons and daughters of the free woman Mary. They have the freedom of the spirit whereas the Jews remain, in a spiritual sense, slaves under the Law. The most important part of Paul's argument is when he compares the two women in metaphor:

These things are in allegory, for these are two covenants: one indeed from Mount Sinai, bearing children into slavery, which is Hagar. Now Hagar is Mount Sinai in Arabia and corresponds to the present Jerusalem, for she is in slavery with her children. But the Jerusalem above is free, who is our mother.(Galatians 4:24-26)

Hagar is here compared to Mount Sinai, the place from which Moses received the Law. Paul then tells us that Hagar is also the Jerusalem below whereas the children of the free women are the Jerusalem above. Paul is intending his readers to equate the Jerusalem church to the "Jerusalem below". In this way, he subtly suggests that James is not a true son of Mary but still a slave under the Law. Mary is the heavenly temple (the Magdalene) and the rock (Cephas) that stands for the heavenly mount Zion on which the temple is built. As both temple and Zion, she is also the heavenly Jerusalem. In the Midrash, she is the free woman Sarah and her children are free from the Law to which the children of the slave Hagar are subject. After talking about the free woman *"who is our mother"*, Paul goes on to give the quote from Isaiah:

For it has been written: "Rejoice O barren woman, the one not bearing; break forth and call aloud, the one not in labour; because many more are the children of the desolate woman than of her who has a husband." (Galatians 4:27)

We have seen the affinities of this passage with Thomas 79. In his argument, Paul is concerned with two mothers: Hagar the mother of the flesh: and Sarah, who, although barren, is the new spiritual Jerusalem and mother of the movement. The depreciation of literal motherhood in favour of spiritual motherhood is also the subject of Thomas 79. We also have the connection with the "suffering servant" section of Isaiah, which was of vital importance to the Jesus movement's belief in a suffering Messiah. All of these connections point towards Isaiah 54:1-3 being a key text for the Jesus movement.

Paul is not making his argument up from scratch; he is using an existing Midrash constructed by the movement to support the role of Mary. Paul adjusts the Midrash for his own purpose, to demonstrate freedom from the Law. But the original still shines through:

Then, brothers, we are not children of the slave woman, but the free woman. (Galatians 4:31)

The brothers and sisters of the Jesus movement are all the spiritual children of Mary, "the barren one whose children are many".

Did Paul really make tents?

From Thomas 79 we have been led to a key passage in Isaiah, and this link has been confirmed by Paul's use of the same passage. A test of a theory is what it explains in addition to the data from which it was derived. The Isaiah passage involving "the barren one" explains some of the major changes that Mary made to the movement, changes which were instrumental in driving the expansion of Christianity across the globe. But it also explains a small detail which, although insignificant in itself, is a sign that we are on the right track. This detail is the curious idea that Paul was engaged in the manufacture of tents.

When the Jesus movement applied Isaiah 54:1-3 to Mary, they appropriated the prophecy to themselves and took it into their hearts. They believed that it was a command to them from God. It was not only a prophecy of what would happen; it was an instruction of what they must do. They were to enlarge the tent of the "barren one", the church, and spread out its pegs. It was promised that they would inherit the earth as indeed they did. Mary interpreted the prophecy by expanding the movement vigorously out of Palestine to the whole of the Roman Empire and beyond. It was also promised that the seed of the "barren one" would possess the nations, meaning that the Gentiles would become sons and daughters of Mary. What distinguished the early Christians from all other Jewish movements of the time is the extent to which they proselytised among Gentiles and brought them in on equal terms to the Jew. We can find the reason for this in the explicit instruction in Isaiah 54:1-3.

The instruction that they were to expand on "the right and the left" brought about another major change. The movement interpreted the right and left spiritually; the right were the "rich", the spiritual Christians who were the elect, while the left were the "poor", the unspiritual Christians who were called but not chosen. Previously the movement had only appealed to those of the right hand, but God was now giving Mary an instruction to expand the tent to cover the left hand also. Just as the Gentile was brought in on equal terms to the Jew, so the unspiritual were to be brought in on equal terms to the spiritual. The mechanism for achieving this was water baptism.

It is significant that the changes that correspond to Isaiah 54:1-3 were all made at around the same time and can be dated to around AD 35. It was at this time that Mary moved to a structure of leadership under the brethren of the Lord and appointed apostles to begin an expansion away from Judea and into the great cities of the Empire. It was also at this time that Mary switched from the spiritual baptism administered by herself to a water baptism administered by many. We have seen that a practical driver of these changes was the death of John the Baptist. But the passage in Isaiah gave Mary the authority and confidence she needed to make such radical innovations.

What should we make of the tabernacle or tent? This image clearly comes from the movable tabernacle that the Israelites carried with them in the desert and which held the Ark of the Covenant. The tabernacle evolved into Solomon's temple built on Mount Zion in Jerusalem, and it is this temple that is referred to by metaphor when Zion/Jerusalem is told to spread out over the face of the earth. Mary is the temple because Jesus dwells within her, and all her daughters and sons, in wider sense, become temples of the living Christ also. This temple is to be enlarged to cover and shelter all in the Jesus movement, including the gentile and those of the left hand.

Unfortunately, the author of Luke did not understand the metaphor of the tent. So in Acts she tells us that Paul spent his days making tents:

And after these things, he left Athens and went to Corinth. And having found a certain Jew named Aquila, a native of Pontus, and Priscilla his wife, recently having come from Italy because of Claudius having commanded all the Jews to depart out of Rome, he came to them. And because he was of the same trade, he stayed with them and worked. For they were tentmakers by trade. (Acts 18:1-3)

Priscilla and Aquila were prominent apostles who are mentioned more than once by Paul, most significantly in Romans:

Greet Priscilla and Aquila, my fellow workmen in Christ Jesus who have for my life laid down their own necks, to whom not only I give thanks, but also all the churches of the gentiles. Likewise [greet] the church that is in their house. (Romans 16:3-5)

It is Priscilla who is mentioned first by Paul in violation of the convention of listing the husband first, showing that she was more prominent than Aquila in the movement. The two are described as "fellow workmen in Christ" meaning that the three of them were involved in the work of preaching the gospel. Paul says that all the assemblies of the nations should give thanks for Priscilla and Aquila, so they must have been involved in taking the gospel to the Gentiles and probably came to this work before Paul.

The author of Luke interprets all this literally. She misunderstands Paul's reference to Priscilla and Aquila as "fellow workmen" to mean that they all worked together at the same trade as Paul. And she must have a source that says they were all engaged in spreading the tent, and so she turns them into three tent-makers.

Key points

1. Thomas 79 contrasts *"Blessed is the womb which bore you, and the breasts which nourished you"* with *"the womb which has not conceived, and the breasts which have not given suck"*. Although many conventional scholars believe that Thomas 79 was put together by combining two sayings in Luke, this cannot have been the case. The two parts of the saying match perfectly as a contrasting pair, showing that the author of Luke must have split the original saying into two.

2. The original saying is reconstructed as circulating in two versions, with the second including the line about blessing those who hear, and keep, the word of God. The saying preserved in Coptic Thomas is based on this second form, with the addition of a few words from one of the Luke sayings.

3. The saying was also used earlier by the author of Mark, who turned it into a prediction of the apocalypse.

4. The saying is also the source of the story in Luke about Elizabeth and Zechariah, the supposed mother and father of John the Baptist.

5. The link with John the Baptist would have been suggested because the saying comes immediately after Thomas 78, which was applied to John the Baptist by the author of Matthew. Because there is no separation between Thomas 78 and 79, it would have been easy to conflate the two into

one saying. This would mean that the woman in the crowd who speaks the first line of Thomas 78 has been listening to Jesus talk about John. So when she praises Jesus' mother, he replies by praising John's mother. So the author of Luke believes "the womb that has not conceived and the breasts that have not given suck" is a reference to the mother of John.

6. Based on Version 2 of Thomas 79, the author of Luke develops a story in which Mary, mother of Jesus, is blessed and in which the barren Elizabeth, conceives John the Baptist. The theme in Thomas 79 about hearing and keeping the word of God is expressed by contrasting the faithfulness to the word of God shown by the two future mothers with the doubts of Zechariah.

7. The Luke story interprets Thomas 78 in relation to the nativity story in Matthew. However, it is possible that the virgin birth story has itself been derived from Thomas 78. If so, then the author of Matthew has taken "the womb that has not conceived" as an allusion to the virgin nature of Mary.

8. The hymn of praise in Luke, the Magnificat, is based on the song of the barren Hannah when she knows she will be a mother; it is not given by Elizabeth, as we would expect, but by Mary. This shows that a Midrash applying the song of Hannah to Mary, the barren one, was in existence before the Gospel of Luke was written.

9. We can find a scriptural link with Thomas 79 in Isaiah 54:1-3, which is part of the "suffering servant" section of Isaiah. This passage says that the barren one will have many sons and will enlarge her tent to the right and left, and that her seed will possess the nations. The Jesus movement applied this to Mary and took it as an instruction. So Mary appointed a group of her "sons" to lead the movement. At this time, the movement began to expand geographically across the Empire and to proselytise aggressively among Gentiles.

10. The "right" and "left" were interpreted spiritually; the "right" being the spiritual elect and the "left" the "poor in spirit". Mary broadened the movement's appeal to the less spiritual "left" by introducing water baptism.

11. All these changes can be dated to around AD 35.

12. Paul along with two missionary companions, Priscilla and Aquila, was involved in enlarging the tent by taking the gospel to Gentiles. The author of Luke misinterprets this to mean that all three were engaged in the trade of tent making.

Conclusion

Thomas 79 predates the gospels and was used by both Mark and Luke. It may also have been the source for the virgin birth story in Matthew. The original meaning of the saying was that the true mother of Jesus had not given birth.

Chapter 28

Why does Jesus reject his family?

We have seen how early sayings that relate to the spiritual birth of Jesus through Mary have given rise to the story of the virgin birth. We have concluded that the references to Mary as mother do not relate to a real physical mother but to the prophetess who founded the movement. But there are other early sayings that appear to speak of the family of Jesus. If Jesus had a physical family then was he not a man? But if he was a man, then why does he reject his original family in favour of another "family" in these sayings? And if Jesus has rejected his real biological family, then why is that same family apparently ruling the movement from Jerusalem?

The family sayings in Thomas

As the successive gospels are written, and the post-gospel literature develops, the myth of the family of Jesus develops to satisfy the craving from Christians for literalistic detail. The more complete a picture we have of the family of Jesus the more false that picture becomes. We need to strip back to the earliest level of sayings that have been preserved from sources that predate the literalistic developments. The early sources available to us are the genuine letters of Paul, the Gospel of Thomas and the Gospel of Mark. What do they tell us about the family of Jesus?

The letters of Paul have two references to the woman through whom Jesus "appeared". Paul also talks of James as "brother of the Lord" and of a group in Jerusalem leading the church who are called the brethren of the Lord. We have seen how all this is consistent with the picture we have been building.

Turning to Thomas, there are a number of sayings that could relate to the family of Jesus. There is Thomas 12 appointing James the Just as the next leader although it does not say James is Jesus' brother. As for Thomas 105, that he who knows the mother and father will be son of a harlot, we have seen that this is not about the family of Jesus at all. Another saying that could conceivably be about the family of Jesus is Thomas 55:

Jesus said: "Whoever does not hate his father and his mother cannot be my disciple, and whoever does not hate his brothers and his sisters and take up his cross like me, he shall not be worthy of me." (Thomas 55)

However, the father, mother, brother and sisters are specifically those of the disciple and not of Jesus. Behind this saying, there is probably an Aramaic original for the same Aramaic word can mean both "hate" and "put aside". The original meaning was that the disciple was to leave rather than hate his or her family. In the ancient world, the family was more important than the individual. The Jesus movement could not develop unless it could get its followers away from the suffocating embrace of their conventional Jewish families. The same saying is found in Matthew (and also Luke):

He who loves father or mother above me, is not worthy of me, and he who loves son or daughter above me, is not worthy of me, and whoever does not take his cross and follow after me, is not worthy of me. (Matthew 10:37-38)

Note how this version of the saying is toned down from Thomas. By the time of the Gospel of Matthew, Christians are having their own families and a saying telling the disciple to "hate" their father and mother becomes very problematic. The author of Matthew does what he normally does with difficult sayings and skilfully smooths out the difficulty by saying that the follower of Jesus should not love his mother or father above Jesus.

In Mark 10:29, Jesus tells the disciples how those who have "*left house, or brothers, or sisters, or father, or mother, or wife, or children, or fields*" for his sake will be rewarded. So the disciple is told to leave their spouse and children, which contradicts Paul, who says that marriage was to be respected even when the husband or wife was a non-believer. The Thomas saying, which omits wife/husband and children, represents the original position. The aim was to get the disciple away from their biological family who could exercise influence over them, and into their new family, the brothers and sisters of the Jesus movement. It would have been counterproductive to separate disciples from these whom they had influence over, such as children, the next generation of believers. We can conclude that the saying as it appears in Mark is a secondary development.

In all of these variants, it is the disciple and not Jesus who leaves his family. What Jesus does is "take up his cross". There has been controversy as to whether this means the crucifixion which is mentioned nowhere else in the Gospel of Thomas. The phrase "take up his cross" was a common saying of the time, meaning to take up a heavy burden. However, the death of Jesus is clearly signalled in another saying in Thomas, about the tenant farmers, the two servants and the son. It is also clear from many sayings in Thomas that it is the resurrected Jesus who is speaking. So the Gospel of Thomas sayings are written from a perspective after the death of Jesus, and we have no reason to believe that Thomas 55 is not talking about Jesus' crucifixion.

The silence of Thomas about the death of Jesus is relative to other sources that make a great deal of the crucifixion. But this relative silence does not mean that the crucifixion was unimportant to the first Christians who used Thomas. We find the same absence of the crucifixion in the earliest surviving Christian images such as church and catacomb frescos. Early Christians did not use the symbol of the cross which only develops much later. The most profound innermost mystery of Christianity was originally the mystical crucifixion and resurrection of Jesus as is evident from the letters of Paul. We would have expected these innermost mysteries to have been shrouded in secrecy, to be shared only with the new believer when they reached a certain stage in their initiation (which seems to have existed among the Galatians for Paul reminds them that Christ was crucified in front of their eyes) and perhaps not to be written down. We can conjecture that most of the sayings in Thomas originate from this era and preserve the veil over the mysteries.

However, one person operating among gentiles did write about them, although only in letters intended for congregations of believers, and that is Paul. As his letters get copied and distributed more widely, the crucifixion becomes public knowledge. Then the author of Mark writes a gospel that reimagines the crucifixion as a historical event in the recent past. Christians forgot that the crucifixion and resurrection were ever considered as mysteries until eventually the cross is used as a very public symbol of the faith which was never true in the early centuries. So the Gospel of Thomas' apparently strange reluctance to mention explicitly the death or resurrection of Jesus is perhaps the remnant of a time when it was still regarded as a "mystery".

So far none of the sayings considered in Thomas means that Jesus has a real biological family. But there are two sayings that do seem to imply just this. Saying 101 is a variation on Thomas 55:

Jesus said: "He who shall not hate his father and: mother like me cannot be my [disciple], and he who shall [not] love [his father] and his mother like me cannot be my [disciple]; for my mother [. ..] but my true [mother] gave me life." (Thomas 101)

Thomas 101 goes further than Thomas 55 in that it is Jesus, rather than the disciple, who rejects his own father and mother. The gospel versions of the saying agree with Thomas 55 and not with Thomas 101. However, it is possible that there was a genuine early saying behind 101. The apparent contradiction of the first part is very typical of Thomas:

If you do not hate your father and mother in my way, you cannot be my disciple
If you do not love your father and mother in my way, you cannot be my disciple

The low entropy compactness of this form suggests that this was originally a stand alone saying. At some point it has been combined with another saying which has a lacuna but is in the form:

My mother [ ] but my true [mother] gave me life

This implies that the first mother is rejected in favour of a second mother. The rejection of one mother for another would make Thomas 101b very similar to Version A of Thomas 79, where the woman who blesses the womb that bore Jesus is contradicted by Jesus blessing the womb that has not conceived. The second saying that clearly implies a family is Thomas 99:

The disciples said to him: "Your brothers and your mother are standing outside." He said to them: "Those here who do the will of my Father, these are my brothers and my mother; these are they who shall enter into the kingdom of my Father." (Thomas 99)

Here we apparently have the biological family of Jesus, his mother and brothers, standing outside the room where Jesus is teaching his disciples. He rejects his earthly family in favour of those in the room, his true family *"those who do the will of my Father"*. Should we accept Thomas 99 as genuine or is it derived from the picture of Jesus conveyed in the gospels? We shall leave this question for a little later, to first consider the Gospel of Mark before reviewing all the earliest evidence about the family of Jesus.

Was Jesus a carpenter?

In Mark, as in Thomas, the family of Jesus receives remarkably little attention. The most complete story is when Jesus travels to his "home country" and teaches in the synagogue. The people are amazed but offended:

Is not this the carpenter [tekton], the son of Mary, the brother of James, and Joses, and of Jude, and Simon? And are not his sisters here with us? And they took offense at him. And Jesus said to them, "A prophet is not without honour, but in his own country, and among his own kin, and in his own house." And he was not able to do any miracles there except lay his hands upon a few sick and heal them. (Mark 6:3-5)

We have already considered this passage, but we must now look at the overall structure of the story. It is a rare example of the power of Jesus being limited – he is unable to perform any miracles except heal a few of the sick. This would have been embarrassing to the author of Mark, so by the criterion of embarrassment, we might conclude that it goes back to a real episode when Jesus visited his hometown with disappointing results. But we would be wrong! Stevan Davies shows that the source of this story is a saying in the Gospel of Thomas:[217]

Jesus said: "No prophet is acceptable in his village; a physician does not heal those who know him." (Thomas 31)

This saying is clearly linked to the story in Mark although it is much shorter. It is normally easy to see when two sayings or stories are related; it is much harder to determine which of the two is original. The first point to note is that the Thomas saying is low entropy. It packs in a large amount of meaning in a few words. The saying expresses one concept in two different ways, which is a standard characteristic of Semitic poetry. The prophet who is not acceptable in his village is like a physician who does not heal those who know him. Note that the prophet is not supposed to be the same as the physician; the two are parallels that express the same principle. The saying attests the truth of the first statement about prophets by linking it to the generally accepted truth about physicians.

The second aspect of low entropy is that the saying should be highly relevant in the context in which it was first used. As people become unfamiliar with this original context, they adjust the saying to fit the new meaning they give to it, and the entropy increases. Most people try to interpret Thomas in terms of the familiar New Testament gospels, but when Thomas was written those gospels were not in existence! If you take the story in Mark as your starting point, then the saying in Thomas appears to lack the colour and historical detail of the original story. This is because the original context of Thomas has been lost. We must restore the context by placing the saying in the early years of the Jesus movement. It is clear from Paul's letters that even the ordinary members of the movement were regarded as "prophets". So the saying is not about Jesus at all. It is an instruction to a new convert that they should leave their home village or town and spread the gospel in new lands. This was exactly what the early Christians did, taking their message far and wide over the seas, desert, and mountains. There are other sayings in Thomas with just this imperative, such as Thomas 52 *"Become passers-by"* and Thomas 14 telling the disciples that when travelling they should waive the clean/unclean distinction and eat what is set before them. This makes perfect sense; the movement ejected converts from their comfort zone and removed any safety net from beneath them. It would have been very tempting for a new follower to practise their new religion in their homeland, but this would leave them in the suffocating embrace of their wider family. They might start with the best intentions, to convert those closest to them, but they would be hopelessly outnumbered and subject to relentless pressure to give up their "sect". By leaving home, they would put these pressures behind, to express through their life the imperative of the kingdom of heaven. We have already seen the instruction for the disciple to "hate" (put aside) their father and mother and to take up their cross. Thomas 31 is expressing the identical concept in a different way.

Restoring the original context demonstrates the low entropy nature of the Gospel of Thomas version of the saying. Turning to the Gospel of Mark, the entropy increases as the saying is interpreted in the fictitious setting of the life of Jesus. The oddness of Jesus being unable to accomplish miracles is an indicator of this increase in entropy. The author of Mark has misapplied this saying to Jesus and interpreted it literally rather than metaphorically, so Jesus becomes both the prophet and the physician; Jesus is not accepted as a prophet and fails as a physician. He is unable to perform the wonderful healing miracles he could do elsewhere *"except lay his hands upon a few sick and heal them"* as the author of Mark adds lamely. The link between the prophet and the physician is present in Thomas in a low entropy state as a tightly interlinked metaphor, but in the literalisation of Mark it occurs in a higher entropy state as an odd, inexplicable detail in the story.

So the story is fiction and does not go back to an original anecdote about Jesus. But how about the additional detail that Jesus is a carpenter? Matthew has *"Is this not the carpenter's son?"*,[218] the version that is familiar to most Christians. The word *tekton* has a wider meaning than the English "carpenter" and refers to a craftsman or artificer. However, a *tekton* would normally work with wood, as opposed to a stonemason working in stone. One possibility is that the word as applied to Jesus is related to the role of God as the maker of the world. In Proverbs, Wisdom is described as a workman accompanying God in his labours at the creation of the world:

Then I was beside him, as a master workman. And I was daily his delight, rejoicing always before him. (Proverbs 8:30)

The links between the Jewish Wisdom movement and the Jesus movement are clear, and Jesus is sometimes portrayed as the male aspect of Wisdom. So from this equation of Jesus with Wisdom could come the concept that Jesus also was the master workman assisting at the creation. Evidence for this link comes in the words that lead up to Jesus being called the workman/carpenter in Mark:

"And what wisdom [sophia] was given to him, that also such mighty works through his hands are done? Is not this the carpenter ..." (Mark 6:2-3)

Note the reference to Sophia, Wisdom, being given to Jesus and that mighty works are done "through his hands" - an image appropriate to an artificer or craftsman. It could be that the author of Mark has interpreted quite literally a source derived from Proverbs 8:30 that equates Jesus with the master workman. But there is another source that could also have served for the information that Jesus was carpenter and that is Thomas 77b which is found in both Coptic and Greek versions:

"Split a timber, I am there. Raise up the stone, and you shall find me there."
(Thomas 77b)
"Lift the stone and there you will find me, split the wood and I am there."
(Thomas 77b from P.Oxy. 1)

We have seen that resurrection stories can be explained from just two sources, the Gospel of the Long Ending, and the resurrection account in 1 Corinthians. There are however a few details not in either source, and one of these details is the rock rolled away from the entrance to the tomb (Mark 16:4). The only source we know that has a similar detail is Thomas 77b: "*lift the stone and there you will find me*". But if the author of Mark has used this part of the saying in his resurrection story, then what has he done with the other part: "*split the wood and I am there*"? A person who splits timbers and wood is called a carpenter, so this could have given rise to the idea that Jesus was a carpenter. If so, Thomas 77b has been interpreted as a cryptic reference to Jesus' life on earth as a carpenter and his coming life after the resurrection.

The story of Jesus' visit to his hometown in Matthew 13:54-58 is virtually identical to the Mark version except for the detail that it is Jesus' father who is the *tekton*. The author of Matthew has surely made this change to remove the embarrassment that the Mark account makes no mention of the father of Jesus. It is the author of Matthew who makes Joseph into the father of Jesus. A son would almost invariably follow his father's trade so the author of Matthew comes to the reasonable conclusion that Joseph would also have been a carpenter. It is also possible that the author of Matthew has a separate source saying that Jesus is the son of the *tekton*, a source whose real meaning is that Jesus is the son of the Yahweh who made the world.

The two families of Jesus

We must reject the story in Mark 6:1-5 as giving any genuine information about the family of Jesus. But is there any other family story in Mark that could go back to the early days of the Jesus movement? There is one and only one. This occurs after Jesus has appointed his disciples on a mountain, and he comes down to a house to take bread. His "friends" think he is mad, and the scribes say he has been possessed by demons. It is at this point that his family comes to him:

Then came his brothers and mother, and standing without, they sent into him, calling him. And a crowd was sitting about him, and they said to him, "Behold, your mother and your brothers are outside seeking you." And he answered them, saying, "Who are my mother, or my brothers?" And having looked around on those who were sitting in a circle around him, he says, "Behold, my mother and my

brothers! For whoever does the will of God, he is my brother and sister and moth-
er." (Mark 3:31-35)

We should not be fooled by the skilful placing of this story in the narrative of Mark. The fact is that the author of Mark does not know the original
context of the story. In the whole of the Gospel of Mark, the only information about the family of Jesus, other than their names, which could conceivably be early is this one story. What is remarkable is that we have got
back to the same place from Mark as we did from Thomas.

The two versions are close, although the version in Mark is longer and
more filled out, and would probably appeal more to most readers. But this
does not mean it is the original! The Mark version has been developed to fit
it into the gospel narrative. The version in Thomas is more compact and
expressed as a saying by Jesus with a typical structure. A disciple (or perhaps just an onlooker) makes a statement, and Jesus replies with an answer
that echoes the original statement but which also contradicts it. This version is low entropy because it is written tightly around this structure which
it shares with other sayings in the Gospel of Thomas.[219] The same structure
is present in the Mark version but at higher entropy. This structure is now
obscured by extraneous material that has been added to give the story
more literary colour. It is the low entropy Thomas version that is original,
and the Mark version is the development of this saying into a story.

The same story is found in Matthew 12:46-50 and Luke 8:19-21. The Matthew version is virtually identical with Mark accept that Mark has "*does the*
will of God" at the conclusion and Matthew "*does the will of my Father in heav-*
en". Thomas has "my Father" and we can see why the author of Mark
would have changed this to "God"; the absence of Jesus' earthly father in a
saying about the family of Jesus is conspicuous. Matthew is closer to
Thomas but adds "in heaven" just to make sure that his audience does not
get confused with Joseph. Luke has an interesting variation in the reply of
Jesus:

Answering he said to them "My mother and my brothers are these who hear the
word of God and do it." (Luke 8:21)

All the other three, Thomas, Mark and Matthew have "*do the will of*
God/the father" but Luke has "*hear the word of God and do it*". The significance
is that "*hear the word and do it*" also appears in our reconstructed version B
of Thomas 79 - *Blessed are those who have heard the word of the Father and have*

kept it in truth. We know that the author of Luke had access to this saying and uses it at Luke 11:28. The wording of the story of Jesus' family in Mark and Thomas is very similar to Thomas 79, and the author of Luke has used the later form in her version of the family saying while keeping "God" as found in Mark.

And this leads us to the most remarkable aspect of the early family sayings. Not only are they so few, they are also very similar. The table below summarises all the family sayings that we have concluded are original.

Reference	Saying	Used in gospels?
Thomas 79	*A woman said to him: Blessed is the womb which bore you, and the breasts which nourished you. He said to her: Blessed is the womb which has not conceived, and the breasts which have not given suck. (Version A)* *A woman said to him: Blessed is the womb which bore you, and the breasts which nourished you. He said to her: Blessed are they who have heard the word of the Father and have truly kept it. Blessed is the womb which has not conceived, and the breasts which have not given suck. (Version B)*	Used by Mark 13:17, Luke 11:27-29, Luke 23:28-29, & the Luke story of Elizabeth and Mary
Thomas 99	*The disciples said to him: "Your brothers and you mother are standing outside." He said to them: "Those here who do the will of my Father, these are my brothers and my mother; these are they who shall enter into the kingdom of my Father."*	Used at Mark 3:31-35
Thomas 101a	*Jesus said: "He who shall not hate his father and mother like me cannot be my [disciple], and he who shall [not] love [his father] and his mother like me cannot be my [disciple];*	Not used.

Reference	Saying	Used in gospels?
Thomas 101b	*for my mother [. ..] but my true [mother] gave me life."*	Not used.

All of these sayings share the same form, and that form involves Jesus in having not one but two families:

Family I is rejected and replaced by Family II

The fact that all the potentially early family sayings take this form is evidence of redundancy - we are uncovering something that was very important to the early Jesus movement and which was expressed in several different ways. We can summarise the parties involved in each Family:

	Family I (rejected)	Family II (accepted)
Thomas 79 Version A	Mother	Mother
Thomas 79 Version B	Mother	Mother and father
Thomas 99	Mother and brothers	Mother, brothers and father
Thomas 101a	Father and mother	Father and mother
Thomas 101b	Mother	Mother

The implications are:

Every saying involves two mothers.

The mother who is accepted in Family II is "the womb that has not conceived and the breasts that have not given suck".

The mother who is rejected in Family I is "the womb that bore you and the breasts which nourished you".

The father in Family II is clearly God and is distinguished from the mother and brothers in Family II.

The mother and brothers in Family II do the will of the Father (God).

By implication the mother and brothers in Family I do not do the will of the father.

We know that "womb that has not conceived and the breasts that have not given suck" is a reference to Mary, the barren one whose children are many. So Mary must be the mother in Family II, and this means her seven adoptive "sons" must be the brothers (and possibly sisters) in Family II. It is Mary, James, John, Simon Peter, Jude, Andrew and the others who "do the will of the father". The evidence of Paul's letters shows that it is the group of James, John and Peter who are ruling the movement from Jerusalem and Thomas independently verifies James as the second leader. The brothers in charge of the movement are those whom Jesus accepts not those he rejects!

Of course, the traditional view is that Mary, James and the others are the biological family of Jesus and so Family I. But if the movement is led by the biological family of Jesus then why does every early saying reject them? The normal theory to explain this anomaly is that the family of Jesus originally rejected him before being converted to his teaching. There is no evidence whatsoever for such a conversion. Had the family originally rejected Jesus, and been rejected by him, we would have expected at least some hint of this in the sections of Paul's letters that were written when he was in conflict with James. And if the family of Jesus did convert then why did such negative sayings continue to be transmitted? Again it should be emphasised that every single one of the early family sayings rejects family I. If Jesus had rejected his brothers in such strong terms how could they had been accepted by the movement as its leaders? And if he had rejected Mary his mother then why was she venerated?

The problem for the traditionalists is that they believe Jesus was a man. As a man, he must have had a human family. But if this family is not Mary, James and the others then we get the absurdity that after rejecting his unknown real mother and brothers he adopted a whole different group as his mother and brothers. But under the shaman paradigm, Jesus was not human. If he has a human mother and brothers then they must be Family II and not Family I! Jesus is heavenly and his original Family I must also be heavenly. They are gods and angels.

There is no mystery about the identity of the heavenly brothers of Jesus. They are the sons of God, seventy or seventy-two in number, who started as gods in Canaan and who were downgraded to angels by the monotheistic Jews. We shall encounter the seventy fallen angels time and time again. The early Jesus movement called them the Morning Stars and the Sons of God; they were the origin of all evil, the rulers of the nations and the brothers and executioners of Jesus.

In contrast to the brothers, the heavenly mother occurs in only a few sayings in Christian literature. Still there can be little doubt as to her identity; she must be the goddess Asherah. Originally a Canaanite goddess and consort of El, it is now widely accepted that Asherah was at one time regarded as the wife of Yahweh. In Canaanite mythology, she was the mother of El's seventy or seventy-two sons. The Israelite god Yahweh was originally just one of the many gods of Canaan and was himself under the supreme God El. But as the Jews struggled to separate themselves from their fellow Canaanites their tribal God Yahweh began to take over the attributes and role of El. The worship of Asherah continued in the form of a pole representing a tree that was kept in the sacred places including the temple. But gradually the priests of Yahweh succeeded in phasing out the worship of Asherah and her sons. Her positive aspects became subsumed into Wisdom, who like Asherah is the companion of Yahweh. But the old beliefs persisted where the reach of the priestly cast was more limited, such as in the domestic rituals of the common people, in the northern kingdom of Israel, and among the apocalyptic cults of the Enoch movement.

The sayings about the two families of Jesus have cosmic significance. It is not about the rejection of a biological family in favour of the disciples but the rejection of gods in favour of man. Always man has been below, subject to the heavenly powers, but the sayings turn this relationship on its head. There is one God above all and that ultimate God has, through Jesus, accepted humans above the other "gods" and angels. Human beings may appear low in the cosmic order, but they were created in the image of God and have been adopted as daughters and sons.

Can we find confirmation of this reversal between humans and angel/gods that we have deduced from the family sayings? It explains something that Paul tells the Corinthians: "*Do you not know that we shall judge the angels?*" *(1 Corinthians 6:3)*. Man is so much higher than the angels that he has been given the power of judgement over them. It is not just the seven adopted sons of Mary who are the brothers of Jesus; in a wider sense, this applies to all the men and women in the movement, who are "sons" of Mary. As Paul says in Galatians 4:5, God sent his son come of woman that the "*adoption of sons we may receive*".

If Mary is the mother in Family II then logically she is the wife of the father who is the ultimate God. This might be thought an absurd concept but is exactly how Mary is portrayed in the gospels of Matthew and Luke. As Mary is told in Luke "*the power of the Highest shall overshadow you*". It is true that it is God's intermediary, the Holy Spirit, which is represented as actually doing the deed, but then we must remember that the conception is spiritual and certainly never intended to be physical. And in the Gospel of

Philip we find a much more graphic description of the highest god descending for spiritual intercourse with a woman:

> He who [was begotten] before everything was begotten anew. He [who was] once [anointed] was anointed anew. He who was redeemed in turn redeemed (others). Indeed one must utter a mystery. The father of everything united with a virgin who came down, and a fire shone for him that day. He appeared in the great bridal chamber. Therefore his body came into being that very day. It left the bridal chamber as one who had come into being from the bridegroom and the bride. So Jesus established everything in it through these. (Gospel of Philip 70:36-71:13)[220]

Jesus was born before everything, but was to be born again. He had been anointed as King but was to be anointed again. He had come to Earth before, had been redeemed (after suffering death) and was now returning to redeem others. The rebirth takes place in the great bridal chamber following conception between the ultimate god, the father of all, and a virgin who had "come down" or "fallen". It is Mary who is the virgin through whom this rebirth is accomplished; it is Mary who anoints Jesus as Messiah. The birth is instantaneous with the conception; Jesus appears in the bridal chamber. In a mystical sense that defies common logic, Jesus is also the bridegroom who unites with Mary in that chamber.

All of this is consistent with a heavenly Jesus being reborn and redeemed from death by spiritual conception between Mary and the highest God. It is also consistent with Thomas 101b where the mother in Family II gives Jesus life.

The only evidence for a father being included in the rejected Family I comes from Thomas 101a. As this saying is not used in the gospels, we cannot be sure that it is early. However, it has a similar structure and theme to the other family sayings and the principle of redundancy suggest that it is an expression of the early beliefs of the movement. The implication of this saying is that there is not one but two fathers. The rejected father is not the ultimate Yahweh, the true God of all things, but the lower Yahweh who gave the Law to Moses, and who is also called the Angel of the Name and the Ancient of Days. We shall find considerable evidence for belief in this lower Yahweh among the early Jesus movement. Unlike the mother and brothers, he was not regarded as being evil. However, as the conflict between the church and Judaism intensified, he develops into the autocratic Jewish God of Marcion and the gnostic Demiurge, the artisan or craftsman who ill-fashioned the physical universe.

Our quest for the family of Jesus in the earliest sources available to us has concluded with not one but two families, one heavenly and one spiritual, and neither of them is biological. There is one ultimate father who has come down and cast his spiritual seed into a mortal woman. His earthly consort, Mary, is the one whose womb did not bear and whose breasts did not give suck but who is nevertheless the mother of many. She has given birth to Jesus, reborn from death, and is the spiritual mother of her many sons and daughters. She has become Queen of Heaven replacing Asherah, the Goddess and wife of Yahweh, whose very name is almost forgotten. We are getting a view of Mary, the Virgin, the Magdalene, which begins to illuminate the special place she has long held in Christianity and Islam.

Key points

1. The story in Mark about Jesus' unsuccessful visit to his home town has come from Thomas 31, about a prophet not being acceptable in his own village. The real meaning of Thomas 31 is that the new convert must leave their home and travel, spreading the gospel.

2. This ties in with the saying about the disciple "hating" his or her mother, father, brothers and sisters. In the original Aramaic, this would have meant "to put aside" or leave rather than "hate".

3. The idea in Mark that Jesus was a carpenter has probably come from a misunderstanding of Thomas 77b, which says that Jesus can be found where the wood is split. It may also have been influenced by Proverbs 8:30 about Wisdom being a master workman assisting God at the creation. The author of Matthew attempts to develop the fictitious role of Joseph as Jesus' father, by changing Mark so that it is the father of Jesus who is the carpenter.

4. There is only one story about the family of Jesus in Mark that goes back to an original source. This is when his mothers and brothers attempt to visit Jesus while he is teaching, and are rejected by him in favour of his true mother, brothers and sisters who are present listening to him. The same story, in a simpler form, is also found in Thomas.

5. The other family sayings in Thomas are Thomas 79, about the woman who did not conceive, and perhaps Thomas 109 which is a compound of two sayings rejecting (i) the mother and father and (ii) the mother of Jesus.

6. In total, there are between two and four family sayings that may be original. Every single one of these sayings has the same form; there are two families of Jesus, with the first family rejected in favour of the second. We

are told the second family are those who do the will of the father, implying that the first family do not do his will.

7. Under the conventional view of Jesus, there is no satisfactory explanation for these sayings. If Jesus were a man, then the rejected first family must be Mary and the brothers including James. Yet we find James and the brothers in charge of the movement in Jerusalem and Mary venerated beyond any other person with the exception of Jesus himself.

8. Under the shaman paradigm, it all makes sense. Jesus does not have a biological family because he is not a man. Mary and the brothers are his spiritual family, the second family who do the will of the father. The first family who are rejected are Jesus' heavenly family.

9. We can identify the heavenly brothers of Jesus as the seventy or seventy-two "sons of God". To the Jesus movement, these are the same as the fallen angels in the Book of Enoch. They are the heavenly archons who are in charge of the world and who crucified Jesus.

10. The heavenly mother must be the Goddess Asherah who was originally the consort of Yahweh and who was at one time worshipped at the temple. Asherah was the mother of the Seventy.

Conclusion:

The family sayings record a momentous change in the ordering of heaven. People are to be placed above the gods/angels because they are closer to the ultimate God. Jesus rejects his divine family in favour of his new human family led by Mary.

Chapter 29

The Rock and the Tower

We have seen that Cephas and Mary the Magdalene are one and the same person. It is time to look more closely at the origins of the names Cephas, "the rock", and the Magdalene, "the tower".

Cephas and the Magdalene

Both the names Cephas and Peter come from the Aramaic and Greek for "rock", and the Magdalene comes from the Hebrew *migdal* meaning "tower". But why should a person be called after a rock and a tower? The New Testament offers no clues for either name.

The commonly accepted explanation for Mary being called "the Magdalene" is that she must have come from Magdala in Galilee. The place name Magdala is not recorded in the New Testament; although some manuscripts have the name at Matthew 15:39 this seems to have been a confusion with the name Magadan that appears in the best early manuscripts. The Jewish Talmud mentions two places called "Magdala" one of which *Magdala Nunayya*, the "tower of the fishes", is located about four miles north of Tiberias on the coast of Lake Galilee.[221] This town had a reputation for moral depravity and the Talmud records that it was destroyed by the Romans. Josephus mentions a town called Taricheae which was close to Tiberias and which was attacked and taken by the Romans during the Jewish revolt.[222] He does not give the Hebrew name of the town, but its Greek name associates it with its fisheries industry. Taricheae has been excavated and is now regarded as the same town as Magdala Nunayya.

The alternative explanation is that the Magdalene title is derived directly from *migdal* and means that Mary was "the tower". If so, then the existence of a town named from *migdal* may be coincidence. After all, it was common to name places after "tower" just as many English place names end in "bury", the old word for castle or fortification.

However, the connection between "the Magdalene" and Magdala/Taricheae must be deeper than random coincidence. Magdala/Taricheae is situated on the shores of Lake Galilee between Tiberias and another place that Josephus mentions, Capernaum. According to the Gospel of Mark, this is the precise location where Jesus recruited his first disciples! The Gospel of Mark starts with Jesus being baptised by John in the river Jordan and then being cast into the wilderness. After John is imprisoned, Jesus travels to Galilee. Walking by the shore of the lake, he meets two sets of fishermen brothers. First he sees Simon and Andrew fishing, and then James and John of Zebedee tending their nets. When Jesus calls them, all four follow Jesus, and they pass on to Capernaum.

The recruitment of Jesus' first disciples is the beginning of his ministry, and this key event happens on the coast of Lake Galilee a little before Capernaum. If you were to travel from the Jordan to Capernaum in the first century, you would first pass through Tiberias before coming to Magdala and then Capernaum. The fit is exact; the disciples must have been recruited around Magdala. The town had its own harbour and was the centre of the local fishing industry. Although we might picture a lonely lakeside setting from the Mark account, it is more sensible for fishermen to be based close to the fish processing industry. So Jesus starts his ministry in Magdala.

The link with "the Magdalene" cannot be coincidence. So did Mary come from this town? If Jesus were a man, then there is a problem with this. Why should Mary alone be singled out as coming from Magdala? If Jesus were based in this area he would have had many followers coming from the same town. If you were in New York you might know someone as "John from Zambia", but if you were in Zambia that is not what you would call him.

In fact, we have a perfect parallel to the association between "the Magdalene" and Magdala. Jesus was called "the Nazarene" because he was "the branch" of the house of David, meaning the Messiah. But the Gospel of Mark puts forward the wrong explanation that this title means that Jesus came from Nazareth, a small village in the hill country of Galilee. The connection with Nazareth has been invented to explain the title, and the same must have happened with Magdala. In reality, the Jesus movement was not from Galilee. This connection has been made up from a combination of the prophecies in Ezekiel and a theory that was evolved by literalistic Christians to explain the titles of the Nazarene and the Magdalene by associating them with Nazareth and Magdala.

When the Gospel of Mark was written, Magdala/Taricheae would have been well known throughout the Empire. During the Jewish war, the town was taken by Titus in one his most heroic exploits of the war.[223] This victory would have been well publicised because Titus' father Vespasian became Emperor, and Titus himself was awarded the title of Caesar, the second in command of the Empire. Titus received an extravagant triumph for the Jewish War in Rome in 71, in which his victories were celebrated and reenacted. Mark was written shortly after these events and while Titus' star was very much in the ascendant. So it is unsurprising that the author of Mark would have connected "the Magdalene" with the famous town of Magdala.

When we look at the beginning of Mark in more detail in the second volume, we will see that it is one of the "Deep Source" sequences. The Deep Source tells of the coming of Jesus to Mary, her purification by the expulsion of the demons, her divine marriage and unification with Jesus, the recruitment of the disciples and the spiritual Jesus teaching others through her. The Deep Source is closely linked to the resurrection stories; like the Gospel of the Long Ending it shares the same theme of disbelief in Mary. In Mark, the coming of Jesus to Mary becomes the story of the baptism of Jesus and his casting out into the wilderness. This should be followed by the purification of Mary, but for the sake of his literalistic story the author of Mark moves the recruitment of the disciples forward to before the casting out of demons. The names of the four disciples whom Jesus recruits do not belong to the original Twelve, but to the later leadership group, the brethren of the Lord; it is no coincidence that the four are two pairs of brothers. The Deep Source did not contain the names of the disciples, so the author of Mark has had to take these names from elsewhere, and confuses the brethren with the forgotten Twelve.

If Magdala was central to the author of Mark's story, then why does he not name the place? The problem he faces is that his source contradicts the literalistic story. The Deep Source would have recorded that Jesus recruited his disciples through the medium of "the tower", the Magdalene. If Jesus were a man this makes no sense, so the author of Mark has interpreted it as meaning that Jesus recruits the disciples in Magdala. However, if he were to name explicitly the town, then this would draw attention to his interpretation and risk attack from those who did not agree that "the tower" meant Magdala. We must remember that, unlike us, his first readers would be familiar with his sources. So he suppresses the name while reflecting the location in his story. We can see a similar subtle tactic in his resurrection account. Here, faced with two contradictory accounts of the resurrection, he favours Paul's. Yet he is careful to make his story ambiguous; he does not identify the "young man", leaving open the possibility that he is Jesus "in another form", which would make his account consistent with his other source, the Gospel of the Long Ending.

The tower

The word *migdal* appears some 50 times in the Old Testament mostly in connection with wars or the fortifications of cities. These are of little interest in tracing the name of the Magdalene and we must focus on the non-military uses of the "tower". The references that are most intriguing are concentrated in just a few books of the Old Testament. From Genesis, we have the following account of the building of the tower of Babel:

And they said, "Go to, let us build us a city and a tower (migdal), whose top may reach unto heaven" (Genesis 11:4).

The story of the Tower of Babel is the famous account of how the different nations of the earth came to be, of how all men spoke one language until they attempted to build a tower that reached to heaven. Yahweh saw their tower and was afraid of the power of men; if they were united there was nothing to restrain them. So he confounded them by splitting them into many tongues and scattering them across the earth.

The connection with the Magdalene is the link between heaven and earth. We have seen that Mary is the prophetess through whom the heavenly Jesus descends and that she is a bridge between heaven and earth. The tower of Babel is also such a bridge, with its base on the earth and its top in the heavens. This is not to say that the Magdalene would have got her name directly from the story of Babel. But is shows how *migdal* also meant a temple in the form of a tower that reached up to heaven. The common form of temples in the near east was the Ziggurat, which was a raised platform with a number of tiers linked by flights of steps. They enabled the priests and kings to ascend and get closer to the gods, to bridge the gulf between heaven and earth. It is such temples that have given rise to the myth of the Tower of Babel.

Another occurrence of *migdal* in Genesis occurs immediately after the death of Jacob's wife, Rachel. After Jacob (who has been renamed Israel) erects a pillar over her grave we learn that:

And Israel journeyed, and spread his tent beyond the tower of the flock (Migdal-eder). (Genesis 35:21)

It is not clear whether Eder is the name of a place, in which case Migdal-eder should be read "the tower of Eder" or whether it should be left as "tower of the flock". There is a remarkable comment on Migdal-eder in the Targum of Jonathan, the ancient Jewish translation of the Hebrew bible into Aramaic:

And Jacob proceeded and spread his tent beyond the tower of Eder, the place from whence, it is to be, the King Messiah will be revealed at the end of the days. (Targum Jonathan, Genesis 35:21)

Here is an assertion from Jewish sources that the Messiah will be revealed at Migdal-eder at the time of the apocalypse, the end of days. The first Christians believed that the Messiah had been revealed through Mary who was called Magdalene, a title derived from *migdal*. The correspondence is exact, and we have here a strong reason she should be called the Magdalene. The Targum Jonathan cannot be dated with confidence as being early and may not have been written until some centuries after the time of Mary; but coming from Jewish sources independent of Christian influence it is evidence that there was an early belief that the Messiah would be revealed in the "tower of the flock".

But this is not the only time we come across Migdal-eder. It also occurs in Micah 4 which starts with a prophecy:

In the last days the mountain of the house of Yahweh will be established as the highest of mountains, and it shall be raised above the hills; and people shall flow to it. (Micah 4:1)

This is the source of the sayings concerning the moving of the mountain with faith. This mountain, Mount Zion on which is built the temple, meant the Kingdom of God for the early Jesus movement. After the raising of the mountain of the house in Micah 4 comes the reference to the "tower of the flock":

And you, O tower of the flock (Migdal-eder), the strong hold (ophel) of the daughter of Zion, unto you shall it come, even the first dominion; the kingdom shall come to the daughter of Jerusalem. (Micah 4:8)

Here the "tower of the flock" is called the stronghold of the daughter of Zion, who is also the daughter of Jerusalem. In the original meaning, the daughter of Zion/Jerusalem clearly represents the Jewish people, as the continuation makes clear:

Now why do you cry out aloud? Is there no king in you? Is your counsellor perished? For pangs have taken you like a woman in labour. Be in pain, and labour to bring forth, O daughter of Zion, like a woman in childbirth. For now shall you go forth out of the city, and you shall dwell in the field, and you shall go even to Babylon. There shall you be delivered. There Yahweh shall redeem you from the hand of your enemies. (Micah 4:9-10)

The daughter of Jerusalem crying aloud in labour represents the pain of the Jewish people as they are led to exile in Babylon. But this pain is represented as birth pangs, for from this pain will bring forth the King, the Messiah. This passage envisages that the kingdom of the Messiah, the kingdom of God, is to be established by a military victory over the nations. The daughter of Zion/Jerusalem is used in Zechariah 9:9 in a prophecy of the Messiah: *"Rejoice greatly, O daughter of Zion! Shout, O daughter of Jerusalem! Behold, your King comes to you; he is just, and having salvation, lowly and riding upon a donkey, on a colt, the foal of a donkey."* In this passage, the daughter of Zion/Jerusalem is clearly intended to represent the nation of the Jews. It is this prophecy that gave rise to Jesus entering Jerusalem on a donkey in Mark 11:1-11. This passage in Mark is one of those derived from the Deep Source; the original is about the spiritual entry of Jesus into Mary, who is Jerusalem and the temple. When it has been literalised it has been combined with Zechariah 9:9 to give the idea that Jesus rode into the physical Jerusalem on a donkey. Matthew mentions this prophecy explicitly but makes the mistake of having Jesus ride on both a donkey and a colt. The author of Matthew does not realise that the verse uses the poetic tradition of repetition, so that the donkey and the colt are supposed to be one and the same.

But it is Mary to whom all this was applied to by the early Jesus movement. She is the daughter of Jerusalem to whom the first dominion, the kingdom, will come. It is she who is called the Magdalene after the "tower of the flock". We have seen how she is the one who gives birth and does not give birth. The early sources go out of their way to tell us that she experiences no birth pains and requires no midwife in contrast with the Micah passage which emphasises the birth pangs of the daughter of Jerusalem. The contrast of opposites is itself a link. The labour of the daughter of Jerusalem in Micah is the exile to Babylon, whereas the painless labour of Mary is the return of Babylon and the coming of the kingdom. It is the contrast between defeat and victory. The reason the sources emphasise the painless nature of the motherhood of Mary now becomes clear for this is a mark of her victory, a sign that the labour of the exile is over.

The Micah passage is also surely the clue for the source behind the Targum Jonathan addition to Genesis 35:21 that the Messiah will be revealed at Migdal-eder. It would make no sense for the Messiah to appear at a small obscure place such as Migdal-eder. The author of the Targum Jonathan has some source (perhaps an interpretation of the Micah passage itself) that states that the Messiah will come to the "tower of the flock". He has then assumed that this is the Migdal-eder as in Genesis.

All of this leaves the puzzle as to what "tower of the flock" actually means. Perhaps a clue comes from the previous line that talks of Yahweh reigning in Mount Zion forever. Is there some connection between Mount Zion and "the tower of the flock"? We have seen that Mount Zion is for the early Jesus movement a symbol of the kingdom and that Mary is herself compared to Mount Zion. We must continue the search for relevant passages using *migdal* in the Hebrew Scriptures.

We have already seen how the tower is used as imagery of the "dove" in the Song of Songs giving the connection to another name associated with Mary. Another image involving *migdal* occurs in Psalm 61:

Lead me to the rock that is higher than I. For you have been a shelter for me, and a strong tower from the enemy. I will abide in your tabernacle forever: I will trust in the covert of your wings. Selah. (Psalm 61:2-4)

Here we find the first reference to "rock" used in conjunction with "tower". The Hebrew word for "rock" used here, *tsur,* is not the same as the root of Cephas, but the conjunction is still potentially significant with both "rock" and "tower" used to describe the same thing and this is also linked to the tabernacle, the predecessor of the temple. The rock, tower and tabernacle are all places of refuge in God.

Cephas is Aramaic and Peter is Greek, which suggests that Cephas is the earlier form being in the language that would have been spoken by Mary and the first disciples. The corresponding Hebrew word is *keph* meaning rock, and it is used in two places in the Old Testament. In Job 30:6 we read about outcasts who "*dwell in the cliffs of the valleys, in caves of the earth, and in the rocks [keph]*." It is clear that the rocks here must be quite large for people to dwell among them; certainly not stones, but at least large boulders and perhaps rocky outcrops. In Jeremiah 4:29 we read of a whole city that shall flee so that "*they shall go into thickets, and climb up upon the rocks [keph]*". The rocks are a hiding place, a landscape upon which people will climb. Again the rocks must be sizeable boulders. In both passages, a rocky landscape is conjured up, strewn with large boulders and with shelter or hiding places between or under them.

The reason why the size of the rock is important is whether Cephas could be the "*rock that is higher than I*" and hence the same as the "*strong tower from the enemy*". Here we have imagery of a rock on which a fortress or at least a tower could be built. In Matthew, we read that Peter is the rock on which would be built the church and this implies that the rock of Cephas is larger than a boulder. The meaning of the word is not definite as regards to size yet *keph* does not seem to suggest a large rock on which a fortress could be built, unless this is a metaphor.

If we widen our search to permit words other than *migdal* and *keph* that could mean tower or rock we find some even more intriguing connections. In Psalm 18 (also essentially repeated in 2 Samuel 22) there is a reference to tower and rock together:

Yahweh is my rock (sela), and my fortress, and my deliverer; my God (El), my rock (tsur), in whom I will trust; my shield and the horn of my salvation, my high tower (misgab). (Psalm 18:2)

We have already come across this Psalm as one of the few places with vocabulary associated with other sacred names of Mary; the sky god is shrouded in the secret place *cether* and lets out his thunder *ra'am* so that the mountains shake *ragaz*. It would be a remarkable coincidence if by chance the same material also combined rock and tower when these are also titles of Mary. Psalm 18/2 Samuel 22 is thought to be among the earliest strata of material in the Bible and contains imagery related to Baal, which has been assimilated by the cult of Yahweh.[224] The coincidence in the names does not mean that the titles of Mary have been copied from Psalm 18 where they are applied to Yahweh. More likely this Psalm copies material from sources that were also used by the Enoch movement from which the Jesus movement was to develop.

The combination of *misgab* (tower/defence) and *tsur* (rock) are found elsewhere. In Psalm 62:1-2 they are used as metaphors for the Elohim, the plural of El, meaning God or Gods. Psalm 94:22 has Yahweh as the tower *misgab* and the Elohim as the rock *tsur*. The word *misgab* is a parallel to *migdal* and means a high place of defence. In Psalm 48, *misgab* is used as imagery associated with the temple and Jerusalem. The Psalm starts with praising Yahweh in *"city of our God (Elohim), in the mountain of his holiness"*. We have seen how this mountain, Moriah/Zion is used by the early Jesus movement as an image of the kingdom of God. The Psalm continues:

Beautiful for situation, the joy of the whole earth, is mount Zion, on the sides of the north, the city of the great King. God is known in her palaces for a refuge (misgab). (Psalm 48:2-3)

Here the *misgab* is in "the palaces" presumably the temple that was built on Mount Zion. Again we have a link with the temple as the habitation of God.

The cornerstone

Another place where "rock" and "tower" are used is Psalm 144:

Blessed be Yahweh my rock (tsur) which teaches my hands to war, and my fingers to fight. My goodness, and my fortress; my high tower (misgab), and my deliverer; my shield, and he in whom I trust; who subdues my people under me (Psalm 144:1-2).

Here we have the standard combination of *tsur* "rock" and *misgab* "tower" applied to Yahweh in war-like aspect. The psalm continues with imagery similar to Psalm 18, with the sky god sending down his lightning to earth and causing the mountains to fire. As in Psalm 18 there is a reference to being rescued from water – *"Send your hand from above; rid me, and rescue me out of great waters, from the hand of strange children"* (Psalm 144:7). We have seen how this rescue from the waters is linked to the story in Matthew of Peter being rescued out of the water by Jesus. It is clear that Psalm 144 and 18 are closely related. But Psalm 144 then takes a new tack with a new song.

The psalmist again asks to be delivered from the hand of the "strange children" or foreigners. Who are these strange children? Perhaps originally the Egyptians, but they became more widely the oppressors, those who held the flock in exile. We shall see later what they became to the Jesus movement. The Psalmist then asks for the benefits of freedom from the "strange children":

That our sons may be as plants grown up in their youth; that our daughters may be as cornerstones, polished after the likeness of a temple. That our garners may be full, affording all manner of store: that our sheep may bring forth thousands and ten thousands in our streets. (Psalm 144:12-13)

The most important aspect about this is the use of cornerstones or corner pillars to describe "our daughters". The cornerstone knitted the structure of the building together and was elaborate and decorated on prominent buildings. The description as applied to women would mean that they were strong and upholding while at the same time being beautiful and graceful. But here we have a phrase that could have been applied by the early Jesus movement specifically to Mary. The cornerstone occurs in both Thomas and Mark.

Jesus said: "Show me the stone which the builders rejected; it is the cornerstone." (Thomas 66)

Mark has virtually the same saying:

"And have you not read this scripture: 'The stone which the builders rejected is become the cornerstone. This was the Lord's doing, and it is marvellous in our eyes'?" (Mark 12:10-11)

The quotation that Mark makes here explicitly, but which is also implicit in the Thomas version, is Psalm 118:22-23. It is significant that both Thomas and Mark site this saying in exactly the same place after the parable of the tenants. As Thomas is a list of sayings, the placing of one saying after another would not necessarily be expected to have any significance. Mark, however, is a narrative, and the cornerstone is tacked on to the conclusion of the parable where it looks out of place. The conjunction of the tenants and the cornerstone in our two earliest sources cannot be coincidence. Either Thomas is copying Mark, or Mark is copying Thomas, or both Mark and Thomas are copying a third unknown source. The loose nature of the combination of the cornerstone and tenants in Mark is evidence that the author of Mark has taken this combination from elsewhere without understanding it.

There is a strong implication from the Mark version that the cornerstone is Christ. This comes about because in Mark the cornerstone saying is conjoined with the parable of the tenants, the subject of which is Christ. The Thomas version of the saying is more enigmatic, and the only link with the tenant saying is that they come one after the other in the list of sayings. Perhaps the author of Mark has got the saying from an early version of Thomas and has made a mistake in linking it with the previous saying about the tenants. If so then the cornerstone may not be Christ.

Psalm 144 suggests another interpretation of the cornerstone; that it is "a daughter", namely Mary herself. The Psalm compares the daughter/cornerstone to the likeness of a temple. We can see that the Jesus movement has interpreted Psalm 144 as a prophecy foretelling that a woman will become the cornerstone, the foundation of God's new kingdom, and the image of the new temple. This has been combined with Psalm 118 as a prophecy that the stone rejected will be the cornerstone. Whoever wrote the original of Thomas 66/Mark 12:10 must have felt that this applied particularly to Mary. Was this because she was a woman and hence excluded from participation in Jewish religion at a serious level by the "builders", the scholars and priests? If so, then the saying is ironic; although women were excluded from the old religion it is a woman who would be nothing less than the chief pillar and foundation of the new kingdom. All of which fits in with our modern culture but not the culture of the first century. We must understand the past in terms of its own culture and not project our culture onto it. Feminism was thousands of years in the future and no one at the time would have seen women as being excluded.

There must be a quite different reason Mary was regarded as rejected. In the song of Thunder her state as the "scorned one" is contrasted with her also being the "Holy one", which is a similar concept to the rejected stone being the cornerstone of the temple. Perhaps Mary was "rejected" because she was a childless woman who was yet to become the mother of many and the cornerstone of the Jesus movement and the new kingdom.

There is a further link to Cephas from this interpretation of the "cornerstone". Cephas is the rock upon which the church will be built whereas Mary is the cornerstone of the temple. The two are parallel statements of the same concept that the church/temple shall be built upon the foundation of Mary/Cephas.

The vineyard

We have seen that the best explanation of "the Magdalene" comes from Micah where it is prophesied that the kingdom will come to the "tower of the flock". We have also seen how the combination of "tower" and "rock" repeatedly occurs applied to Yahweh, El or the Elohim in Psalms associated in other ways with the early Jesus movement. Finally, we have found a link to the "cornerstone" sayings in Mark and Thomas. The question remains what does "the tower of the flock" mean? The answer can be found in one other use of *migdal* in the Old Testament, and that is the parable in Isaiah about the vineyard. We know this parable was important to the early Jesus movement because it is the basis of a parable used by Mark, the same parable of the tenants which is connected to the cornerstone saying in both Mark and Thomas. These continual inter-connections are signs that we are on the correct trail in identifying the material that was important to the early Jesus movement. We shall start with the vineyard parable in Isaiah 5:1-7:

Now I will sing to my well-beloved a song of my beloved touching his vineyard. My well-beloved has a vineyard on a very fruitful hill. And he fenced it, and gathered out the stones, and planted it with the choicest vine, and built a tower (migdal) in the midst of it, and also made a winepress.

The vineyard is surrounded by a hedge and has a tower built within it. The tower would be like a rustic watchtower rather than a military structure. The word used here for "beloved" is the same as used in the Song of Songs as the lover of the Dove. The parable continues:

And he looked that it should bring forth grapes, and it brought forth wild grapes. And now, O inhabitants of Jerusalem, and men of Judah, judge between me and my vineyard. What could have been done more to my vineyard than I have done in it? So why when I looked for it to bring forth grapes, did it bring forth wild grapes? And now I will tell you what I will do to my vineyard. I will take away the hedge, and it shall be eaten up; and break down the wall and it shall be trodden down. And I will lay it waste: it shall not be pruned, nor dug, but there shall come up briers and thorns. I will also command the clouds that they will not rain upon it.

The vineyard has not produced the fruit that the beloved was hoping for despite his loving care. So he will destroy it. The meaning of the parable is then made clear:

For the vineyard of Yahweh of hosts is the house of Israel, and the men of Judah his pleasant plant: and he looked for judgment, but behold oppression; for righteousness, but behold a cry.

The parable is about the exile and the destruction of the kingdoms of Judah and Israel. The beloved has planted these two kingdoms so that the Jews would want for nothing. But they have not yielded the wine of loving obedience. Instead, they have become "wild-grapes" divorced from the law of God. So the vineyard, their home, will be destroyed. The parable has been written after the fact of this destruction in the Jews' attempt to make sense of their crushing military defeat and humiliation at the hands of the Babylonians.

More specifically the vineyard represents Jerusalem. The hedge/wall represents the walls of Jerusalem overthrown by the Babylonians. So what does the tower represent? A clue is given by the version of the parable in the Isaiah Targum of Jonathan. This talks directly of how Israel is like a vineyard and was given "an inheritance in a high mountain". It continues:

I propped them up as a precious vine; and I built my sanctuary in the midst of them; and I gave also mine altar to make an atonement for their sins; and I thought that they should do good works before me, but they did evil works. (Targum Isaiah 5:2)

In place of the tower, the Targum has the sanctuary, the temple. And instead of the winepress the Targum has the altar. The altar stood before the temple just as the wine press stands before the tower. The Jews brought to the altar the offerings of the people whereas in the parable the winepress should be brought the grapes that the vineyard is expected to yield but does not. The parallel is exact, and the tower in the parable stands for the temple and the winepress for the altar. The fate of the tower is not given in Isaiah, but the fate of the sanctuary is given in the Targum:

I will break down the house of their sanctuary, and they shall be for a treading down. (Targum Isaiah 5:5)

The temple will be destroyed, as it was indeed by the Babylonians. If we believe the Isaiah Targum, then the meaning of the tower *migdal* is nothing less than the temple. By calling Mary "the Magdalene", the early Jesus movement are claiming that she is the new temple. In support of this we have already seen that the cornerstone saying compares the "daughters" who are the cornerstones, interpreted by the Jesus movement as Mary, to the likeness of a temple. The "hill" in the Isaiah parable represents the mountain on which the temple is built - that is the mountain or hill called variously Zion or Moriah. We have also seen how Mary was compared to Mount Zion. So the mountain and temple are both used to describe Mary.

Is this also the meaning of "tower of the flock"? The temple would fit the description in Micah 4:8 as the tower as the "stronghold of the daughter of Zion". The temple is a stronghold because the Jewish people, who in the original meaning were "the daughter of Zion", would metaphorically take refuge in it coming under the protection of Yahweh. This links the meaning into the Psalms where it is Yahweh himself who is the refuge, tower and rock. To the early Jesus movement, it was Mary who was the "daughter of Zion" and the "tower of the flock".

The temple

Proof that the "tower of the flock" really is the temple is found in a quite different source. The predecessors of the Jesus movement were not what we think of as mainstream Jews but looked to Enoch rather than Moses. The chief witness of this Enochian movement that has come down to us is the Book of Enoch which survives complete only in Ethiopian translations. It is a composite made up of several ancient works written at different times that have been assembled into one "book". One of these components is called the Dream Visions, which itself mainly consists of an embedded work known as the Animal Apocalypse. Fragments of this work along with others in the book of Enoch have been found among the Dead Sea Scrolls proving that this is an ancient text. It can be dated on the basis of internal evidence to no later than 165-161 BC.

The Animal Apocalypse is the Rosetta stone for decoding Christian origins and the most important text preceding the production of the Gospel of Thomas. Those who wrote the Animal Apocalypse were the intellectual and spiritual ancestors of the Jesus movement that was to arise almost 200 years later. Indeed, Mary and others in the early Jesus movement may well have been the physical descendants of the writers of the Animal Apoca-

lypse, for such groups survived by passing down their teachings generation to generation.

In the Animal Apocalypse, the animals represent humans whereas the
humans who appear in the story represent angels. The Animal Apocalypse
contains the earliest evidence of the Messianic movement so it is no coincidence that a group looking to the Messiah, the Christ, should be descended
from it.

In the Animal Apocalypse, the first humans from Adam onwards are
represented by cattle. Later mankind splits into numerous different animal
types, with Israel, from Jacob onwards, represented by the flock of sheep.
When the final end times come, the sheep will be turned into cows and
ruled by a rather fearsome bull with black horns, the representation of the
heavenly Messiah.

The confirmation of the meaning of the "tower of the flock" comes in the
account of the building of the first temple. The predecessor of the temple
was the movable tabernacle and is represented as a "house" which Moses
builds and in which the flock take shelter. After a ram, King David, has
defeated the other animals the house is enlarged:

*And that house became great and broad, and it was built for those sheep: and a
tower lofty and great was built on the house for the Lord of the sheep, and that
house was low, but the tower was elevated and lofty, and the Lord of the sheep
stood on that tower and they offered a full table before him. (1 Enoch 89:50)*[225]

The Lord of the sheep is Yahweh, and the tower is intended to represent
the temple. Here we have the meaning of the "tower of the flock" -- it is the
temple built in Jerusalem, exactly as we have already concluded! The Animal Apocalypse goes on to relate how the flock abandoned the tower and
how as a result the Lord of the sheep withdrew from the tower and gave
the flock over to slaughter, and how eventually the tower was destroyed.

It should be noted that the tower is the first temple and not the second
temple that was rebuilt after the return from exile and which was radically
remodelled by Herod. It is this second temple that Jesus supposedly visits
in the gospels, and it is the veil of this second temple that splits in two
when Jesus dies. The Animal Apocalypse gives a very different perspective
on this second temple. It tells of how the sheep attempt to rebuild the tower
but the offerings that were placed on a table before the tower were polluted
and impure. So the Lord of the Sheep does not visit the new tower -- it is a
false, empty temple! To the authors of the Animal Apocalypse the exile

does not end with the return to Jerusalem; it is about the withdrawal of the favour and protection of Yahweh from Israel. The physical temple may have been rebuilt but it is not the real temple because it is not visited by Yahweh. But if this is the case then the depiction of the temple in the gospels makes no sense. Why should the veil be torn in two when it has no greater significance than any other piece of cloth and when the holy of holies knows not the presence of Yahweh? Why should Jesus visit and teach in this false temple? Why should he cast out the moneylenders who pollute his father's house? Why should he predict the fall of the temple when it has already fallen and not been rebuilt?

In fact, we have seen that in Thomas 71, Jesus predicts that it will not be rebuilt, exactly the attitude of the Animal Apocalypse, but an attitude that applies to the first temple! In Mark, according to the witnesses at the trial of Jesus, he goes further and predicts it will not be rebuilt by human hands:

We heard him say, "I will destroy this temple made with hands, and within three days another not made with hands I will build." (Mark 14:58)

In the Gospel of Mark, this is placed in the mouth of those who held false witness against Jesus, a placing that indicates unease with the saying by the author of Mark. The saying must be well known, so he cannot exclude it entirely, but he wants to discredit it. The reason for his discomfort is obvious enough. Mark is writing some forty years or more after the supposed crucifixion of the Christ and the prediction that the temple will be destroyed has just become startlingly true. The Gospel of Mark makes a great play of this as a proof of the divinity of Christ. However, this saying is a major embarrassment. It predicts that the temple will be rebuilt in three days, which has not happened. It also predicts that Jesus will destroy the temple, which again has not happened.

The author of Mark deals with this embarrassing saying by making it hearsay given by false witnesses. In this way he makes it ambiguous - we cannot be sure if it was really uttered by Jesus or not. The author of Mark uses such ambiguity when he wants to de-emphasise earlier material without directly contradicting it. At the same time, he makes it clear earlier in his narrative (Mark 13:1-2) that Jesus did make an explicit prediction of the destruction of the temple.

In Thomas 71 Jesus says he will "*destroy this house, and none shall be able to build it again*", a version that is somewhere between Mark 13:1-2 and Mark 14:58. That Mark 14:58 is a genuine version of the saying is made clear by what happens next. The author of Mark hedges his bets; after putting it in the mouth of "false witnesses" he then makes it comes true after all! When Jesus dies, the veil of the temple is rent in two. In one sense, we can see that this is a clever move that leaves the stones of the temple intact to be destroyed in due course by the Romans. But this anticipation of the coming destruction is still inconsistent with the author of Mark's interpretation of the prophecy, that it was fulfilled in his own time by the Romans. We can conclude that again he must have had a good source to put this element into his story, a source that links the destruction to the death of Jesus. It is only this connection that can make sense of the "three days" which is clearly meant to be the time between the death and resurrection of Jesus. The destruction of the temple must be linked to the death of Jesus, and the rebuilding must be linked with the resurrection.

Is the temple that is destroyed and rebuilt the body of Jesus as most commentators and theologians like to think? This cannot be right as Jesus clearly states that he will destroy the temple. If his body were the temple, then Jesus would be a suicide and his sacrificial death would be self-inflicted and without meaning. In Mark the destruction of the temple, represented by the veil, happens simultaneously with the death of Jesus but the veil is not the body of Jesus.

The author of Mark is repeating earlier sayings and traditions but had no clear idea of what they meant. His conclusion that Jesus is prophesying the destruction of the temple by the Romans is false. So what does the temple saying mean? The saying was circulating in at least two forms:

Jesus will destroy the temple, and none will rebuild it.
Jesus will destroy the temple built by human hands and will rebuild another after three days not made by human hands.

We have seen how well the first of these fits in with the Animal Apocalypse. The temple is destroyed and despite the attempts of man is not rebuilt. We must surmise that this temple is the first temple of Solomon. It is this first temple, located deep in the history of Israel that Jesus will destroy.

The second version is an elaboration of the first. The temple that is destroyed will be replaced by another not made by human hands. The timescale of three days means that the second temple must be linked in with the resurrection. However, the three days cannot be three actual days because the period from the destruction of the first temple to the resurrection of Jesus among the early Jesus movement is several hundred years. We shall see that the three days are three symbolic great days measuring out the history of the world. It is this mistake of the interpretation of days that causes the author of Mark to set the life of Jesus in the recent past; he knows when the resurrection happened, but he does not know when Jesus was alive on earth. The temple saying tells us that the early Jesus movement believed that Jesus was alive at the time of the destruction of the first temple. If we believe that Mark repeats an earlier tradition by making the symbolic destruction of the temple, in the form of the veil, simultaneous to the death of Jesus, we can go further and date the death of Jesus to the same timeframe as the destruction of the temple. The destruction of the temple and the death of Jesus sunder the connection between man and God. After this destruction Israel and all mankind are in a state of exile. Although man might attempt to rebuild the temple he has no power to accomplish this. Only Jesus can do this deed, but he is dead; symbolising the death of man in God. The state of exile can only end with resurrection and the rebuilding of a new temple by God and not by human agency.

We have already seen what this new temple is. It is the tower, the Magdalene. She becomes the holy vessel that will receive the new wine of the resurrection. She gives birth and does not give birth. God returns to his temple to rule the world in a new interior sense. He will now be alive within Christians, not dwelling in a dead construction of stone.

The rock

The pursuit of the tower has led us to the temple. God dwells among his people through the Magdalene. The rock, Cephas, is the Magdalene in male guise; the name through which she outwardly leads the movement. If the tower is a cipher symbolising her role in the new kingdom then surely the outer name, Cephas, has significance too. We have already seen a hint of this in the parallel between the cornerstone and the rock on which the church will be built.

The tower has also led us to the Animal Apocalypse. If this is the ancient literature that was important to the Enoch group from whom the Jesus movement developed, then is the clue to the rock in the same writings? In the Apocalypse, the tower is the means by which God descends to earth and communicates with man. The Lord of the sheep stands on the top of the tower and receives the offerings of the altar. There is one earlier instance in the Apocalypse where God appears before the people. This occurs after the sheep (the Israelites) have escaped from the wolves (the Egyptians). The sheep who represents Moses communicates with God:

And that sheep ascended to the summit of that lofty rock, and the Lord of the sheep sent it to them. And after that I saw the Lord of the sheep who stood before them, and His appearance was great and terrible and majestic, and all those sheep saw him and were afraid before his face. And they all feared and trembled because of him, and they cried to that sheep in their midst saying "We are not able to stand before our Lord or to behold him." (1 Enoch 89:29-32)[226]

The rock in the story stands for Mount Sinai and plays the same role as the tower! God descends onto the rock (the mountain) and onto the tower (the temple) to communicate with the people. The reason why Cephas is the rock on which the church is built, even though it means no more than a large boulder, becomes clear. In the parable of the animal apocalypse all things are reduced and the boulder represents a mountain.

Jesus descends into the Magdalene/Cephas just as God would once descend onto the mountain and the temple. But this was before the exile to Babylon. The pillar of fire and cloud has long ceased to cast its terrible pall upon the mountain top and the temple is no more and shall not be rebuilt. But God has granted mankind a new temple, a new mountain, and she is the woman who bears the names of the Magdalene and Cephas.

The mountain is not just Mount Sinai. It is mountain in the collective memory of the Canaanite peoples, the mountain of God, the geographical location of which changes from tribe to tribe, locality to locality, but which represents a mystic mountain that is ever constant. It is the mountain that stands for the kingdom, the mountain that moves, the realm where God and man meet, halfway between earth and sky. It is mount Moriah on which the temple is built, one of the hills that make up Mount Zion. To the Jesus movement it is Mary who is Zion; the temple and the mountain are one, the tower and the rock, the Magdalene and Cephas.

It is on the mountain that Jesus appears transfigured to Peter, James and John in Mark 9:1-9; a scene that is connected through the words spoken by God to both the baptism and birth of Jesus. The meaning of the mountain is Peter, the rock and Jesus descends onto the mountain to speak to Mary/Peter mystically. The mountain appears elsewhere in the gospels. When Jesus appoints the disciples, he does so on the mountain:

And the unclean spirits, when they saw him fell down before him and cried out "You are the Son of God". And he strictly charged them that they might not make him known. And he goes up to the mountain, and called whom he would, and they came to him. And he appointed twelve, that they should be with him, and that he might send them forth to preach, and to have power to cast out demons. (Mark 3:11-14)

Jesus appears on the mountain (Mary/Cephas) and chooses his disciples. There is a hint here also of the Deep Source sequence, of the casting out of the demons from the Magdalene before she tells the disciples of the risen Christ and reveals Jesus to them.

In Matthew, the appointment of the disciples on the mountain is repeated a second time. After the resurrected Jesus appears to Mary, the eleven disciples go *"to the mountain which Jesus directed them"* where they also meet Jesus and receive a commission to teach and baptise (Matthew 28:16-20). This is all very similar to the original appointment of the disciples in Mark because it is derived from the same story. The author of Matthew knows about the prediction of the angel in Mark that Jesus will appear to his disciples in Galilee, and he links this with another story available to him, a story about the resurrected Jesus appearing to the disciples on a mountain and appointing them to teach. What he does not realise is that this is the story behind the original appointment of the disciples in Mark.

In Matthew, when Jesus gives his great discourse on moral teachings he does so from the mountain – the Sermon on the Mount. The author of Matthew has heard of Jesus speaking his teachings from the mountain, but does not realise that the mountain signifies Mary/Cephas.

A story in Matthew, which is repeated in Luke, links the temple and the mountain together, and this is also a Deep Source sequence. When Jesus is in the wilderness for forty days and nights, he is tempted by the devil. The forty days is the same period given by the author of Luke/Acts as the stay of the resurrected Jesus upon the earth. We have seen how this stands for forty years, the time for which Jesus was believed to have dwelt within Mary/Cephas. It should, therefore, be no surprise that the gospel repeats a story of Jesus being on both the temple and the mountain during this period in the wilderness:

Then the devil takes him to the holy city, and sets him on a pinnacle of the temple, and says to him, "If you are the Son of God, cast yourself down." (Matthew 4:5-6)

Jesus is tempted by the devil (the accuser) on the top of the temple. This is the high tower that is the temple, the Magdalene. Jesus rebuts this temptation and is tempted again:

Again, the devil takes him to a very high mountain and shows to him all the kingdoms of the world and their glory. And says to him, "All these things I will give you, if you will fall down and worship me." (Matthew 4:8-9)

This time Jesus is on the mountain, meaning Cephas, when he is tempted. Note how the kingdoms of the world must belong to the devil if he is able to offer them to Jesus. After this temptation, Jesus sends Satan away:

Then said Jesus to him, "Get you hence, Satan!" (Matthew 4:10)

The dismissal is virtually identical to the words addressed by Jesus to Peter in Mark 8:33: "*Get behind me Satan!*" Behind both stories is a memory of Jesus being tempted on the mountain and dismissing the devil or demon that is within Mary / Cephas.

Key points

1. The root of the title "the Magdalene" is the word *migdal* meaning "tower". The root of Cephas is the word *keph,* which means a large boulder or rocky outcrop.

2. The conventional explanation of "the Magdalene" is that it means that Mary came from the town of Magdala in Galilee. Magdala is normally identified with the town of Taricheae, which Josephus states was on the shores of the lake between Tiberius and Capernaum.

3. The place in which Jesus recruits the disciples in the Gospel of Mark is unnamed but is located in the precise position of Magdala / Taricheae. This would be explained if Mary is actually being called "the tower" which the author of Mark misinterprets as a reference to the town of Magdala. A parallel case is "the Nazarene" which he interprets wrongly as meaning that Jesus came from Nazareth.

4. The beginning of Mark is derived from a Deep Source sequence that tells of the coming of Jesus to the shaman. The author of Mark has interpreted this sequence as the baptism followed by the recruitment of the disciples and the visit to Capernaum. The source must refer to Jesus coming to the disciples through "the tower" which meant the Magdalene, but which was interpreted by the author of Mark as the town of Magdala. The fact that he does not name the town indicates that the author of Mark is aware that his interpretation could be attacked. In such situations, he tends to use ambiguity to avoid conflict.

5. In Genesis, the word *migdal* is used for the mythical Tower of Babel. This was a Ziggurat temple that was supposedly tall enough to reach up to heaven.

6. Also in Genesis, there is a place called *Migdal-eder* ("tower of the flock" or "tower of Eder") where Israel (Jacob) spreads his tent. In the Targum, it is said that the Messiah will come from Migdal-eder.

7. In Micah, there is a prophecy that the Migdal-eder is the stronghold of Zion, the daughter of Jerusalem, to whom will come the kingdom. It is promised that "the daughter of Jerusalem" will return from exile and give birth to the Messiah.

8. In the Psalms "the tower" and "the rock" are associated with each other and used to describe the stronghold or refuge that is God. The same sources are linked to vocabulary associated with the Dove and Thunder, two other titles of Mary.

9. Psalm 144, which has the tower and rock, also features the "cornerstone"; it says that the daughters of Israel will be like cornerstones and polished temples. Both Thomas and Mark have a saying about the stone that is rejected being the cornerstone. Mark applies this to Jesus, but the original would have applied to Mary.

10. The parable of the vineyard in Isaiah reveals the meaning of the "tower". In this parable, Israel/Judah is compared to a vineyard, with a tower and a winepress. The tower is the temple, and the winepress is the altar that stood before the temple.

11. This interpretation is confirmed by the Animal Apocalypse in the Book of Enoch. In this parable there is a tower built among the flock for the "Lord of the sheep". The tower clearly stands for the temple.

12. In Thomas, there is a saying that Jesus will destroy "this house" (the temple), and it will not be rebuilt. In Mark, Jesus also predicts that he will destroy the temple and rebuild a new one after three days "not made by hands". The temple that is destroyed must be the first temple.

13. In the Animal Apocalypse, the rock is the means by which God comes to the people before the tower is built. A sheep (Moses) ascends a large rock to communicate with God. The rock stands for Mount Sinai but also, more generally, the holy mountain, the point at which heaven meets the earth.

14. There are a number of stories in the gospels about the disciples seeing Jesus on a mountain. These include the transfiguration of Jesus, the appointment of the disciples in Mark, and the resurrection appearance to the disciples in Matthew. The source of these stories is a remembrance of Jesus appearing to the disciples through Cephas.

15. The story of the temptation of Jesus in the wilderness in Matthew (which is also copied by Luke) features Jesus being taken by the devil to the tower of the temple and the mountain. This recalls the tradition that Jesus took the form of the tower (the Magdalene) and the mountain (Cephas) while in the wilderness (the world) for forty days (forty years). His first act is to expel the demons from the Magdalene/Cephas.

Conclusion

The title "the Magdalene" comes from *migdal*, "the tower" and means the temple. Mary, the shaman, is the temple because Jesus dwells within her. She is the temple "not made by hands" that supersedes the first temple, which Jesus destroys. Cephas, the rock, stands for the holy mountain in the Animal Apocalypse. Like the tower, it is the means by which God communicates with the flock of Israel.

Chapter 30

The Shepherd and the Tower

The "Shepherd of Hermas", which dates from around the time the Gospel of John was written, was immensely popular with early Christians. Hermas was included in early canonical lists but was excluded from the New Testament in its final form because it contained elements that were considered heretical. Much of the imagery of the gospel goes back to the early movement, although it was placed in a moralising context. Among this imagery, we will find representations of Mary and a parable about the rock and the tower.

The Shepherd of Hermas

The Shepherd of Hermas was beloved by the proto-orthodox. More early papyrus copies of the Shepherd have been found than any other Christian work with the exception of the Gospels of John and Matthew. To Irenaeus, the first compiler of the list of books that was to become the New Testament, it was scripture. It is also included in the Muratorian fragment, a list of canonical books that is believed to date from about 200 or before. It says about the Shepherd of Hermas that "*Hermas wrote the Shepherd quite lately in our time*" for he was the brother of Pius the bishop of Rome. Another list of Canonical books, the Codex Claromontanus includes the Shepherd as the longest book in the canon.

The information that Hermas was the brother of Pope Pius is clearly untrue and may be a case of mistaken identity. Hermas, the brother of Pius, has probably been confused with Hermas, the supposed author of the Shepherd. The true author of the Shepherd is unlikely to be called Hermas. We know that the work was a literary creation intended for publication because Hermas is repeatedly urged to write down and communicate to the church the revelations that have been granted him. Yet it contains a number of personal details about Hermas that would never have been put in a public document. For example, we learn that Hermas is a former slave of Rhoda, and he tells of his lust for Rhoda after seeing her bathe. We also learn how reprobate Hermas' offspring and wife are. The ancient world was very concerned with face; if Hermas were the author's real name, the work would not have included such personal details.

The Shepherd can also be dated by a reference to a "Clement" to whom Hermas is to send his writings so that they can be distributed to the foreign cities.[227] This is surely Clement of Rome, who was active towards the end of the first century. So either the Shepherd was written at the end of the first century, or it was written later and set back in time to the first century. Pius became bishop around 140-155 so his brother would have lived much later than the end of the first century. Setting works in the past was a very common feature of early Christian literature, but no one is going to set a book several decades in the past and then write it openly under their own name! So either way, Hermas brother of Pius could not have been its author.

The common practice was to write such a work as if it came from some figure mentioned in the letters of Paul or some other early work. Often a minor character is used. We find just what we are looking for in Romans 16:14 where Paul includes one "Hermas" in his greetings to the Romans. At the very beginning, the Shepherd introduces Hermas as living in Rome! Most likely the Hermas in the Shepherd is supposed to be Paul's Hermas writing his book as an older man some decades later in the time of Clement. The actual date of composition would be early in the second century.

The Shepherd is at first reading a dull work written by an author with an absence of literary talent. However, it repays close study as a fascinating window on the early church. It is thoroughly proto-orthodox in tone and gives an insight into the development of the literalistic church from the original spiritual beginnings. The author of the Shepherd is concerned with establishing the authority of the church leaders. Although he does not name the gnostics, he is against the "sorcerers" and others whom he sees as having fallen away from simple belief. He eulogises the martyrs and those who have suffered for the Christian faith. Again this is very typical of Christianity as it entered its second century. The church was being actively persecuted, and those who endured torments and who gave up their life for Jesus began to be regarded as the highest exemplars. But the main obsession of the Shepherd of Hermas is much more personal to the average believer. It is the question of what happens to those who had been baptised but who had subsequently sinned.

Theoretically, a person who had gone down into the water had had their sins forgiven and had been reborn. The problem was that the baptised continued to sin. So was it possible to gain remission of sins after baptism? Hermas is in this condition both through his desire for Rhoda and through the sins committed by his family which reflect on him as head of the household. A series of visions and revelations improve his spiritual state as he is taught about the opportunity for repentance. The Shepherd of the title is the angel of Repentance, who is guiding Hermas.

The Shepherd of Hermas is written for a simple, unsophisticated audience and at times it is excruciatingly pedestrian. For example, in one parable the believers are each given a willow rod by an angel. When the angel retrieves the rods, the condition of the rod indicates that person's spiritual state. We might expect a pattern of three here but the author of Hermas manages to enumerate no less than thirteen different types of rods according to the proportion withered or cracked, each one of which relates to a type of Christian. Dull it might be, but it became immensely popular because it answered in a straightforward fashion the burning questions that the ordinary faithful were asking themselves.

The Shepherd tells us about the direction the church was taking but also reveals from where it was coming. It was written as proto-orthodoxy was developing and because it was written early suffers from not being orthodox itself. The author of Hermas cannot reflect the orthodox position because that position has not yet been defined. It is for this reason that the Shepherd was ultimately rejected from the canon, but it is also this which makes it of great interest to our quest for understanding the origins of the movement.

Beneath the surface of Hermas can be seen the tracings of earlier teachings and imagery. To extract this earlier stratum of information we have to get past the author's interpretations of his material. The Shepherd would seem to be a composite of two writings by the same author that have been joined. The first revelations are made by a female figure, and this is probably the earlier work. The female figure then disappears to be replaced abruptly by the Shepherd. The Shepherd portion of the work is a much longer development of the same themes and is likely to have been written later. As will be seen both parts draw on the same central image.

The old lady and the virgin

The Shepherd starts with Hermas, in a vision, being accused for his lust by Rhoda, who has been taken up to heaven for the purpose. Hermas is grieving on the difficulty of being saved if even such a small sin is held against him when a woman appears: "*and there came a woman, old and clothed in shining garments with a book in her hand*" *(Shepherd of Hermas 2:2)*.[228] She gives him some advice about controlling his wayward family. In the second vision a year later, the aged lady appears again. This time she gives him a book. After a while, he finds he can read the book and that it is about his sinful family. It also sets out the theme that repentance for the elect is possible up to a certain pre-ordained time but after that time no repentance will be acceptable. This theme will be developed further throughout the work.

Later a young man appears to Hermas in a dream and reveals that the old lady is the church. The image of an elderly lady seems curiously inappropriate for the church which is in its infancy. When Hermas asks why she should be old, the answer is that "*she was created the first of all things*" *(Shepherd of Hermas 8:1)*.

The Christians of the early second century inherited imagery of a female figure who was the temple, but struggled to place it in the context of the story of Jesus from the gospels. Who is this woman who occupied such a central and powerful role in the traditions that had come down to them? It was not just Mary who was a temple; all of her "sons" and "daughters", meaning everyone in her church, were also "temples" of Christ. So it was only one small step to see the woman as an abstraction, an allegory of the church.

In truth, this old lady is not an abstraction but a representation of Mary towards the end of her life. We know that she lived to be an old lady and she would have been remembered as such by the young people who would eventually become the elders and leaders. By the time the Shepherd is written, these younger people are themselves dead, and Mary has receded into myth. As for the church being created before all things, we find exactly this applied to Mary in the "Song of Thunder":

But he is the one who [begot me] before the time on a birthday.
And he is my offspring [in] (due) time, and my power is from him. (Thunder: Perfect Mind 14:1-5)[229]

The third vision takes place in the country. The aged lady appears again to Hermas this time sitting on a couch. She invites him to sit and he asks if he can sit at her right side but is told that this is reserved for those who have suffered *"Stripes, imprisonments, great afflictions, crucifixions, wild beasts"* (*Shepherd of Hermas 10:1*).[230] Originally the right side meant the spiritual elect, the perfect, but now among the proto-orthodox in the early years of the second century, it has shifted to mean the martyrs. The Shepherd continues with the lady showing him a great tower being built upon the waters by six young men who have accompanied her. When he asks the meaning she tells him:

> The tower which you see being built is myself the Church. (*Shepherd of Hermas 11:3*)[231]

We have another picture of Mary and this time she is a tower! The old lady is the Magdalene, the temple, reinterpreted as the church. The parable goes on to illustrate the different natures of the stones who make up the church and who stand for the faithful, including those who are put to one side, requiring repentance, but who eventually find a place in the tower. In the vision, the tower is built over the waters, an odd image. In the Shepherd, the waters stand for baptism, but we have seen the waters as marking the division between heaven and earth. Mary, the shaman, has the power to walk on water and cross the divide.

At the end of this vision, we learn that the lady has appeared to Hermas in three forms, becoming progressively younger each time, reflecting Hermas' reviving spiritual condition. This comes as a complete surprise to the reader. Up to this point she has been portrayed uniformly as an old lady. Parts of Hermas were written at different times, and it is likely that this depiction of the lady becoming younger was written after the earlier sections. It is necessary because we are about to be given another image of Mary. First Hermas sees a great beast pass by, but he shows faith and is not harmed. He then sees the lady again, this time in the form of a virgin:

> ... there meets me a virgin arrayed as if she were going forth from a bridal-chamber all in white ... (*Shepherd of Hermas 23:1*)[232]

Mary, the Virgin and the bride is coming forth from the bridal chamber. This makes absolutely no sense in terms of the literalistic Jesus of the gospels. So again, imagery relating to Mary must be transferred to the church. And the author of Hermas now has to make the church into a young lady.

After this, the lady disappears from the narrative and is not mentioned again and the Shepherd who gives the work its name appears abruptly. It would seem that something has been lost at this point. For the remainder of the work, the Shepherd instructs Hermas through commandments and seven parables, culminating in a reworking of the tower image. The lady is no longer present, and the tower is no longer built upon the waters. Instead in the middle of a plain surrounded by mountains is a great white rock with a gate hewn in it. It is on this rock that the tower is built.

In the Gospel of Matthew, Jesus tells his disciples that the church will be built upon the rock that is Peter. It is not clear if the author of Hermas knew of this gospel but, like Matthew, he has the church built upon a rock. It is certain that he does not intend his rock to be Peter as portrayed in the gospels. The stones that are placed in the towers base include forty for the *"apostles and teachers of the preaching of the Son of God"* and these come after thirty-five representing the first and second generations of the righteous, and a further thirty-five representing *"God's prophets and ministers"* (*Shepherd of Hermas 92:4*). This arrangement has a distinctly Jewish flavour and does not build the Church on the base of the first Christians but positions seventy stones, being Old Testament prophets and patriarchs, before them (seventy is a very significant number). The Peter of the gospels would be in the forty and certainly not the rock on which the whole structure is built.

What has happened is that the author of Hermas has inherited his imagery of the rock, the tower and the gate from older traditions and material that are also known to the author of Matthew. The author of Hermas develops the interpretation that the gate is the Son of God, the rock is also the Son of God, and the tower is the church. Matthew has a different explanation, that the rock is Peter. As we have seen the rock is really Cephas and the tower is Mary. The gate is Jesus, who comes through Mary/Cephas and through whom all who would be saved must pass.

The rock represents the mountain of God, and the tower the temple. The holy mountain is first mount Sinai but later becomes mount Moriah on which the Jerusalem temple was built. The combination of rock and tower, being mountain and temple, represent the heavenly Jerusalem, the kingdom of God. Those who enter the kingdom become temples themselves and part of the one temple. So they are joined spiritually with Mary, who came first. The Gospel of Thomas says the chosen shall stand as one (Thomas 22) and Paul talks of the faithful as being of one body. The Shepherd has the image of the faithful being stones that make up the tower and so become one whole.

The deeper understanding is that the rock and the tower are one. This is indicated in the Shepherd of Hermas by the tower being one with the rock:

For this reason you see the tower made a single stone with the rock. So also they that have believed in the Lord through His Son and clothe themselves in these spirits, shall become one spirit and one body, and their garments all of one colour. (Shepherd of Hermas 90:5)[233]

Beyond this image of the tower and rock being one is a remembrance of Mary and Cephas being one person. But it is also about all the chosen becoming one body through the "spirits".

The spirits

The spirits are a feature in the Shepherd of Hermas that gave disquiet to the orthodox and are one reason it was not included in the New Testament. They are represented as virgins who stand around the tower and who must hand the stones if they are to form part of the tower structure. It is true that the author of the Shepherd himself offers the mundane explanation that the spirits are virtues with names such as Faith and Continence. But this explanation does not sit easily with his description of the spirits which is drawing upon quite different earlier "gnostic" traditions. Hermas asks about the virgins:

"And these virgins, who are they?" "They," said he, "are holy spirits; and no man can otherwise be found in the kingdom of God, unless these shall clothe him with their garment; for if you receive only the name, but receive not the garment from them, you do not profit." (Shepherd of Hermas 90:2)[234]

This is the spiritual garment that occurs again and again in the early Christian literature. We have found it associated with the journey to heaven where the garment of the body must be replaced by the garment of the spirit, and here it is represented by the virgins. The Shepherd gives a description of the role of the virgins in enabling those who have died to become part of the tower:

"Because these first," said he, "bore these spirits, and they never separated the one from the other, neither the spirits from the men nor the men from the spirits, but the spirits abode with them till they fell asleep; and if they had not had these spirits with them, they would not have been found useful for the building of this tower." (Shepherd of Hermas 92:6)[235]

The entering into the kingdom of heaven after death is dependent upon the person being joined with the "spirits" in their life and after death. In the Shepherd, there is a curious scene where Hermas spends the night with the virgins. This scene serves no narrative purpose, and the author of Hermas is clearly embarrassed about some aspects of it for he goes out of the way to stress that everything is chaste and proper. But this is inconsistent with his description. Hermas is reluctant to spend the night with the virgins but they insist:

"You shall pass the night with us," say they "as a brother, not as a husband; for you are our brother, and henceforward we will dwell with you; for we love you dearly." (Shepherd of Hermas 88:3)[236]

There follows what can only be described as a scene of erotic dalliance:

And she who seemed to be the first of them began to kiss and embrace me, and the others seeing her embracing me began to kiss me themselves, and to lead me round the tower, and to play with me. I, too, had, as it were, become young again, and began to play with them myself, for some were dancing, others were gavotting, others were singing, and I walked in silence with them round the tower, and was merry with them. (Shepherd of Hermas 88:4-5)[237]

Again Hermas wants to leave but the virgins refuse to let him go so he spends the night with them *"for the virgins spread their linen tunics on the ground, and made me lie down in the midst of them" (Shepherd of Hermas 88:7)*. It is true that in the Shepherd they do nothing but pray but it is the bridal chamber and the divine marriage that lies behind all this. The author is drawing upon earlier traditions that he must have regarded as too important to omit.

The virgins here are represented in the plural but this is likely to be a misunderstanding by the author of Hermas of the meaning of the "spirits" being joined to men, for the bride is always singular in other sources. The spirit should be singular with one spirit belonging to one man. The image gives the form of a man's spirit and not a woman's, for the Shepherd is thoroughly masculine in its approach and does not consider the female case. When the believer is tempted, it is in the form of twelve beautiful women clad in black and with loose hair. These are equivalent to the seven demon husbands of Mary before she was united to Jesus, her true husband. For we learn in the Gospel of Philip that the demons that inhabit a man take female form and those that inhabit a woman take male form, and that the demons are cast out by the union with the spiritual bride or bride-groom.

The virgin spirit is both the bride and sister of the chosen. The Shepherd of Hermas makes it clear that only those with a spirit bride/sister will enter the kingdom. It is this spiritual wife and sister that Paul regards as the sign of an apostle.

We have seen how the Shepherd of Hermas uses the rock and tower im-ages and how they relate back to the titles of Mary and beyond her to the earliest meaning; the temple and the holy mountain. There is more to be learned from Hermas, not least concerning the Shepherd himself. But first we must follow the lead of the temple.

Key points

1. The Shepherd of Hermas was one of the most popular early Christian writings and was included in early lists of canonical texts.

2. The narrator Hermas is most likely intended to be the same Hermas who Paul greets at Romans 16:14. It was common to write works as if com-ing from an early Christian and Paul's letters provided a rich cast of minor characters.

3. The Shepherd of Hermas contains imagery of a female figure that goes back to Mary. Because this imagery conflicts with the literalistic story of Jesus from the gospels, it has been sanitised by changing the woman into an allegory of the church.

4. The mysterious female in Hermas is both an old lady and a young bride emerging from the bridal chamber. The old lady goes back to a genu-ine memory of Mary as she was in Rome towards the end of her life. The young woman is Mary in her sacred role as virgin and bride of Christ.

5. The lady shows Hermas a tower built over waters. She says that the tower is herself, the church. We can see this image going back to Mary as "the tower", the Magdalene. The tower is built upon the waters because the shaman was able to cross the waters and bridge between heaven and earth.

6. The image of the tower is developed further in the climatic parable of the Shepherd. The tower is built upon a rock through which a gate has been hewn. It is made up of many stones which represent the believers. In the interpretation of Hermas, the tower is the church, the gate is Christ, and the rock is also Christ. However, it makes no sense for both the rock and the gate to be Christ. Behind the parable, we can see the two identities of the shaman, the Magdalene (the tower) and Cephas (the rock), acting as a gate for Christ. The culmination of the parable is that the rock and the tower are one whole.

7. The image of the tower built on the rock is imagery that goes back to the Jerusalem temple built upon mount Moriah.

8. One feature of the Hermas that caused particular disquiet to the proto-orthodox is the role of the female spirits. These unite with Hermas in what is clearly a "divine marriage". It is said that men cannot be part of the tower unless they join with the spirits. This spiritual union with the female is very close to gnostic beliefs. There are also dark female spirits, corresponding to Mary's demon husbands.

Conclusion

The Shepherd of Hermas is an early second-century work that draws on sources and traditions going back to Mary and the origins of the movement. Although it presents these traditions in terms of the developing proto-orthodox belief, it is relatively uncontaminated by the gospels. It gives us confirmation of Mary's role as "the tower" and tells us that the rock and the tower are one.

Chapter 31

Were James and John both Jewish high priests?

One of the strangest early traditions is that both James and John were called high priests. There are even those who have suggested that they may actually have both been the Jewish high priest. If Mary is the new temple "not built by hands" does this explain this puzzling tradition? And what about the strange title "Oblias" given to James?

James and the temple

One of the seven adoptive sons of Mary was called by her own sacred title, Simon called Peter, the rock. If Simon has been honoured in this way, then what about the two principal sons, James and John Mark? They have been appointed to the right and the left side, so should they not also be honoured with sacred titles? Can we find a connection between them and the temple or the mountain?

We do indeed find strong links between James and the temple. The main source of the stories about James is Hegesippus as quoted by Eusebius in Ecclesiastical History 2:23.[238] Hegesippus reports how James used to pray daily in the temple. This has been interpreted by many as evidence that Christianity was not separate from Judaism at this time. However, the stories told by Hegesippus are absurd. They do not indicate the real practice of James but have arisen through the literalisation of mystic traditions. Hegesippus first describes James in terms that indicate a Nazarite:

He was holy from his mother's womb; and he drank no wine nor strong drink, nor did he eat flesh. No razor came upon his head; he did not anoint himself with oil, and he did not use the bath.

The clue as to why Hegesippus thinks James is a Nazarite is contained in what follows:

He alone was permitted to enter into the holy place; for he wore not woollen but linen garments. And he was in the habit of entering alone into the temple, and was frequently found upon his knees begging forgiveness for the people, so that his knees became hard like those of a camel, in consequence of his constantly bending them in his worship of God, and asking forgiveness for the people.

We have seen that James has become confused with John the Baptist and that this accounts for him having skin like a camel. However, the other elements do not come from confusion with John. What is meant by the "holy place"? The idea that James alone could enter suggests that this is the holy of holies which only the high priest could enter and then only once a year. This would place James in the role of high priest which is clearly absurd in a literal sense. However, "holy place" would normally suggest the temple as a whole. In Ezekiel, we can find a description of the Levitical priests in the imaginary second temple:

And it shall come to pass, that when they enter in at the gates of the inner court, they shall be clothed with linen garments; and no wool shall come upon them, whilst they minister in the gates of the inner court, and within. They shall have linen caps upon their heads, and shall have linen undergarments upon their loins; they shall not clothe themselves with anything that causes sweat. And when they go forth into the outer court, even into the outer court to the people, they shall put off their garments wherein they ministered, and lay them in the holy chambers, and they shall put on other garments; and they shall not sanctify the people with their garments. Neither shall they shave their heads, nor suffer their locks to grow long; they shall only trim their heads. Neither shall any priest drink wine, when they enter into the inner court. (Ezekiel 44:17-21).

The temple in Ezekiel is a prophetic vision of the temple that will be built to replace the first at the end of exile. In Ezekiel, the priests are to wear linen and not wool if they enter the inner temple court. From the same source, we get the information that priests are not to shave or drink wine which Hegesippus has interpreted as meaning that James is a Nazarite. If we believe Hegesippus, then only James could enter the temple, meaning he is high priest. However, he is not the high priest of the second temple in Jerusalem but the prophetic second temple of Ezekiel.

The prophecy of the temple in Ezekiel is not some random passage. It was a key text for the Jesus movement that comes up again and again. To the Jesus movement, the Ezekiel temple is not a building but a person, Mary. Through Mary, James can enter into the presence of God. He becomes a high priest serving at the temple. In this, he is not alone. Just as James has been given the place on the right hand, his brother John has been given the left hand. And there are traditions that John also was high priest.

James and John, wearers of the petalon

The person who was chosen as high priest had a sacred headdress that they wore when serving in the temple. This headdress included a golden band inscribed with the letters of the Tetragrammaton (YHWH), which represented the name of God. It was called the *petalon*. Only the high priest was allowed to wear it.[239]

There is one thing that Hegesippus says about James serving in the temple that was not repeated by Eusebius but was fortunately included by Epiphanius.[240] This is the information that James wore the *petalon*. More clearly than anything else this marks James as high priest. It also invalidates the reading of the Hegesippus passage as evidence of a reconciliation between the Jesus movement and Judaism. Unless we believe in the absurdity of James as the Jewish high priest, the source behind Hegesippus reveals a bitter conflict with mainstream Judaism. For if James were the true high priest, then the Jesus movement must have denied the validity of the Jewish high priest. This is all one with the rejection of the physical second temple by the Jesus movement.

It is not just James who wore the *petalon*. Eusebius quotes Polycrates, bishop of Ephesus, as saying that John became a priest wearing the *petalon*.[241] Again, this can only be interpreted as meaning that John was high priest. In John 18:15 the beloved disciple appears to know the high priest. A John is also listed among the family of the high priest in Acts 4:6. This has been interpreted by some as meaning that John came of a priestly family and eventually became high priest himself.

Needless to say, there is no evidence from outside the Jesus movement supporting the high priesthood of either James and John. We have seen the real explanation. It is Mary who is the temple, and James and John, at her right and left hand, serve as high priests.

James and Ananias

James' title of "high priest" may have left its mark in a curious episode in Acts 22:30-23:22. When Paul returns to Jerusalem, he comes into contact with the Jews and is arrested by the Romans. To find out what the argument is about, the Roman commander effectively places Paul on trial before the Sanhedrin. Paul's defence is simply to state that he has fulfilled his duty to God. When he says this, the high priest Ananias orders him to be struck on the mouth. A furious Paul curses the high priest: *"God will strike you, you whitewashed wall! You sit to judge me according to the law, yet you violate the law by commanding that I be struck!" (Acts 23:3)*. Those who are nearby Paul are shocked and accuse him of insulting the high priest. But Paul replies that he did not realise he was the high priest: *"I did not know, brothers, that he is chief priest: for it has been written, 'You will not speak evil of the ruler of your people'" (Acts 23:5)*. Paul then craftily starts an argument between the Pharisees and Sadducees concerning the resurrection and the meeting ends in tumult. But this is not the end of the affair. Forty Jews take a vow not to eat or drink until they have killed Paul. They arrange with the high priests to lie in wait for him when he is summoned to another meeting. However, Paul is warned about the plot by the "son of Paul's sister" who also informs the Roman commander. The Roman commander arranges for Paul to be transferred under heavy escort before the plotters can strike.

There is much that is melodramatic and absurd in this story. The idea of a Roman commander arranging a trial in front of the Sanhedrin is completely unrealistic. The story is a romantic, novelistic creation by the author of Luke, but she does normally have a source for her extravagant creations. We can identify one such source in the gospel account of the trial of Jesus before the Sanhedrin. It is this that has given rise to the striking of Paul on the orders of the high priest, whereas the high priest being a "whitewashed wall" comes from the scribes and Pharisees being "whitewashed tombs" in Matthew 23:27.

However, the story as whole cannot be explained by these sources, and there are some telling details that do not fit. But there is an event that could serve as a basis for the story, an event that the author of Luke has already used twice in Acts. This event is the so-called council in Jerusalem in which Paul submits his gospel to James and the others for judgement, and which led to a fierce disagreement between Paul and James, and the argument between Paul and Cephas in Antioch. In an example of redundancy, multi-

ple versions of this story have been incorporated into Acts. Two of these
are clear; the account of the council in Acts 15, and a second episode when
James gives judgement on Paul's mission in Acts 21:17-25. It is possible that
the author of Luke had a third source which she does not recognise as being about James because in this source he is called "the high priest". So she
unwittingly transforms James into Ananias and makes the argument into a
more thrilling episode involving an attempted murder. This explains the
otherwise very odd detail that Paul does not recognise the high priest
which is not something the author of Luke would have included unless it
had been in her source. It would be explained if the source contained a criticism of Paul that he did not recognise James as high priest and did not
obey the leader of the movement. The trial before the Sanhedrin would be a
distorted memory of the council in Jerusalem and its aftermath. The forty
who lie in wait for Paul would be those whom James sends to Antioch after
the council (the author Luke tends to exaggerate numbers). The purpose of
these messengers is to persuade the Jews with Paul not to eat or drink with
Gentiles, whereas the forty take a vow not to eat or drink. The accusation
that Paul hurls at Ananias, that he does not obey the law himself, does not
make sense in the Acts story. By ordering Paul to be struck on the mouth
for blasphemy, Ananias is carrying out the law, not breaking it. But this
accusation is essentially the accusation Paul makes against Cephas in Antioch, that they force the law on to others but do not obey the law themselves. As for Paul's sister, we can see this as a reference to Mary, who is his
sister in the Christian sense. This would make "the son of Paul's sister" either James or most likely John Mark, who was also central to the argument
in Antioch.

We can see how the main events of the story each correspond to an element in Paul's account in Galatians. The bitterness of the argument between James and Paul was such that it has been transformed into this story
of murderous rage, with James cast as high priest. The continuous recy-
cling of the events in Jerusalem and Antioch shows the importance of the
split between James and Paul. But the chief significance of the story lies in
something else, the way in which James has been confused with Ananias.
For this confusion will happen again in a very different episode, when Ananias appears to play a vital role in the conversion of Paul.

James as "Oblias"

Hegesippus' account of James continues:

Because of his exceeding great justice he was called the Just, and Oblias, which signifies in Greek, 'Bulwark of the people' and 'Justice,' in accordance with what the prophets declare concerning him.

This title Oblias has long puzzled scholars. Hegesippus tells us that it means a "bulwark of the people" and "justice" but his translations of the term do not make sense. The closest we can come to a source that could give Oblias and be roughly translated "bulwark of the people" is *ophel am* meaning "stronghold of the people".[242] The title clearly dates from much earlier than Hegesippus, who struggles to understand it. Does it fit in somehow with the titles given to Mary? The answer is that if Oblias does come from *Ophel am* then it is found in the very line from which the title "Magdalene" has been derived. We have traced back *migdal*, the tower, to a passage in Micah:

And you, O tower of the flock [Migdal-eder], the stronghold (ophel) of the daughter of Zion, unto you shall it come, even the first dominion; the kingdom shall come to the daughter of Jerusalem. (Micah 4:8)

We have seen that the tower of the flock here must stand for the temple. However, the same thing is described as *"the stronghold of the daughter of Zion"* using the word *ophel*. The word *ophel* means fortified hill. In Jerusalem, the hill Ophel is a promontory that extends southwards from Temple Mount. Excavations have revealed that it was the site of the original city of David. The location of Solomon's temple is unknown, and although most archaeologists would expect it to have been built on Temple Mount, Ophel is also a possible site.

If Oblias comes from *ophel am* then it is parallel to the rock and the tower; it means the temple or the temple mount or Jerusalem. Moreover, its origins lie long before the first century, which is another clue that the Jesus movement draws on traditions deep in the history of Israel. So we have evidence that James did have a title, Oblias, that is a parallel to "Peter" and which can be traced back to the same line of scripture as "the Magdalene". Note how Hegesippus adds after his explanation of Oblias that it is *"in accordance with what the prophets declare concerning him"*. If the title is derived from *ophel,* then this scriptural prophecy is Micah 4:8.

There is one further link to the temple in Hegesippus. Some people from the "seven sects" of Judaism ask James, "Who is the gate of Jesus?" and

James replies, "He is the saviour". Translations normally have "what is the gate of Jesus?" in an attempt to make more sense of the question, but it is better translated "who".[243] This odd question "tell us who is the gate of Jesus?" is repeated before James is cast down. In the Shepherd of Hermas, there is also a gate of Jesus. There the tower is built on a rock, and the rock has a gate in it. The author of the Shepherd tells us that both the rock and the gate are the Son of God. But we can see differently, that the rock (Cephas) and the tower (Magdalene) are both titles of Mary and represent the temple built upon the mountain. Of course, the temple must have a gate in it to allow Jesus to enter, and this is the "gate of Jesus". In Ezekiel the glory of God enters into the future temple through the east gate:

And the glory of Yahweh came into the house by the way of the gate which faces east. (Ezekiel 43:4)

The Jesus movement would have interpreted the glory of Yahweh as meaning Jesus. If the temple is a person and not a building as the Jesus movement believed then the question "Who is the gate of Jesus" makes perfect sense. We know the answer, it is Mary/Cephas who is the gate of Jesus, the means by which Jesus has come into the temple and entered into the world. The imagery of the gate is also found in Palm 118:

This gate of Yahweh into which the righteous shall enter. (Psalm 118:20)

Two lines later comes the important cornerstone line:

The stone which the builders refused is become the head stone of the corner. (Psalm 118:22)

We have seen how the cornerstone was applied to Mary as the cornerstone of the temple and the church. So it is reasonable to see the gate as also applied to Mary, so that she becomes the gate which enables the followers of the way to enter into the temple, into the presence of Yahweh. The gate has also by extension been applied to James as the successor of Mary.

A further connection is that elements of Psalm 118 have been applied to James in the Hegesippus story. In line 13 the psalmist says, "*I was pushed hard so that I fell*" from which is probably derived the detail of James being pushed from the temple. It continues with line 17: "*I shall not die, but live, and declare the works of the Yahweh"*. So James having been pushed survives and preaches.

Key points

1. Hegesippus speaks of James in terms that suggest he was a Nazarite. He says that James was able to enter the temple alone because he wore linen garments. These features are derived ultimately from the description of the priests of the theoretical second temple in Ezekiel.

2. Hegesippus also says that James wore the *petalon*, the headdress bearing the name YHWH, which was only worn by the high priest. There is a parallel tradition from Polycrates that John also wore the *petalon*. These traditions indicate James and John's special roles as high priests on the right and left of the temple, Mary.

3. The story of Paul before the Sanhedrin and his argument with the high priest Ananias can be seen as being derived from Paul's argument with James and Cephas after the Jerusalem council. In the source, James must be referred to as the "high priest" and the author of Luke confuses him with Ananias.

4. James is given the title Oblias by Hegesippus. This is probably derived from *ophel am* meaning "stronghold of the people". Ophel was the mount on which the old city of David was built and which adjoined the temple mount. It is linked to the Magdalene (*migdal*) by the line of prophecy in Micah 4:8 which says that the kingdom will come to the "tower (*migdal*) of the flock" and "the stronghold (*ophel*) of the daughter of Jerusalem".

5. Also in Hegesippus, the Jews ask James "who is the gate of Jesus?" The same image is found in the Shepherd of Hermas where there is a gate in the rock on which the tower is built. The image of the gate goes back to the temple of Ezekiel where the glory of Yahweh enters the temple through a gate. To the Jesus movement, the glory was Jesus and the gate Mary, the shaman.

Conclusion

The multiple links of James with the temple are evidence that James, like Simon Peter, was called by titles that were parallel to those attaching to Mary.

Chapter 32

The Lord will come into his temple

The Gospel of Mark opens with two prophecies. We shall see how, to the Jesus movement, these predicted the coming of Jesus to the Magdalene, and how the opening section of Mark developed the story of this coming. And we will decode an enigmatic saying from Thomas about two lions which also alludes to the coming of Jesus into his temple.

The beginning of Mark

The Gospel of Mark starts abruptly with the baptism of Jesus by John the Baptist. There is no nativity story, no Magi, no angels, no account at all of Jesus' earlier life. For those looking to the nativity stories in Matthew and Luke, it is an embarrassment that the first gospel lacks all mention of the miraculous circumstances of Jesus' birth. Some have argued from the abrupt start that the true beginning of the gospel is missing. They write wistfully of a Mark version of the nativity story that became detached. Although ancient texts did sometimes lose their beginning or end, there is not a shred of evidence that this happened to Mark. And viewed using the shaman paradigm the beginning of Mark makes perfect sense!

The author of Mark starts his gospel exactly where he should, with the coming of Jesus to Mary. He is using a "Deep Source" text and has prefaced it by two quotations from scripture which, for the Jesus movement, predicted this coming. The structure would have been clear from his sources but has been obscured by his literalistic story. The table below reconstructs how the sources made a coherent whole.

The beginning of Mark	
1. The gospel title	
The beginning of the gospel of Jesus Christ, the Son of God (Mark 1:1). (Note: "the Son of God" is not in all copies.)	This title was probably not part of the original gospel, but a division marker to separate the work from others that were bound together with it.
2. Two prophecies from Scripture	
As it is written in Isaiah the prophet, "Behold, I send my messenger before your face, who shall prepare your way." (Mark 1:2)	This is, in fact, from Malachi 3:1. The Jesus movement interpreted *"my messenger"* as meaning Jesus, the Christ, who is *"the lord whom you seek"*. The continuation of the line is that he *"shall suddenly come to his temple"*, meaning that he will appear in the temple, the Magdalene.
The voice of one crying in the wilderness, "Prepare the way of the Lord, make his paths straight." (Mark 1:3)	This comes from Isaiah 40:3. The one preparing the way in the wilderness (the world) is Jesus, and he prepares the path for the ultimate God. The Isaiah passage is about the return from exile. A female figure (possibly Zion/Jerusalem) is to ascend a mountain (the rock, Cephas) and declare the "good news", that is preach the gospel.
3. The Deep Source sequence shows how the prophecies came true	

John baptises in the wilderness. Jesus comes to John, and the spirit descends upon him as a dove. (Mark 1:4-11)	This is the beginning of the "Deep Source" sequence. The association with John the Baptist comes from a criticism of John in the Deep Source. In the original Deep Source, the baptism of Jesus was the descent of the spiritual Jesus into Mary (the Dove) and her followers. In Mark, Jesus is a man and so the baptism has to be reversed with the Dove descending into Jesus.
Jesus is "cast out" into the wilderness by the spirit where he stays for forty days. (Mark 1:12-13)	Jesus is cast out into the wilderness (the world) using the word that normally means demonic exorcism. This is a clue that in the source Jesus was spiritual. He abides in the wilderness for "forty days" meaning the forty years for which he is believed to abide in the world through Mary, the temple.
Jesus comes to Galilee where he recruits two sets of fishermen brothers as his first disciples. (Mark 1:14-20)	This is part of the Deep Source that has been placed out of sequence (it should come after the purification of Mary). In the Mark story, Jesus recruits the disciples in the exact location of Magdala. In the original Deep Source, the Twelve are recruited through the Magdalene. The author of Mark does not know the identity of the Twelve, so he substitutes the names of the principal brothers of the Lord.

They go to Capernaum where Jesus teaches in the synagogue. There Jesus casts out demons from a man with unclean spirits. (Mark 1:21-28)	In this continuation of the Deep Source, "the temple" has been interpreted as the synagogue. When Jesus comes to the Magdalene, he purifies her by casting out her seven demon husbands. He then teaches in the temple, meaning through the Magdalene.
They come to the house of Simon and Andrew where the mother-in-law of Simon is lying ill with a fever. Jesus cures her, and she then ministers to them all. (Mark 1:28-31)	This is the end of the Deep Source sequence in this part of Mark. The "mother-in-law" of Simon is really Mary, who was the "mother" of Simon although not his biological mother. She is cured of her sickness (demonic possession) and raised to life by Jesus. She is then able to minister to the Twelve, and eventually to all in the movement. In the context of the Jesus movement, "to minister" meant to feed with the bread, wine and fishes that were the substance of Jesus.

It is worth looking at the two quotations at the start of the Gospel in more detail. The first does not in fact come from Isaiah, but the book of Malachi:

Behold, I will send my messenger, and he shall prepare the way before me and the lord, whom you seek, shall suddenly come to his temple, even the messenger of the covenant, whom you delight in: behold, he shall come, said Yahweh of hosts. (Malachi 3:1)

The Gospel of Mark starts with the prophecy that the lord will come into his temple! The lord in the Malachi passage is the same as the messenger, the angel, of the covenant "*whom you delight in*". The messenger/lord is an angelic being who stands in for Yahweh himself and who will come, enter into the temple, and rule on behalf of Yahweh. The author of Mark thinks the messenger is John the Baptist, but he is wrong! The messenger is the

Messiah, the Christ. The Jesus movement interpreted this as the descent of Jesus into Mary, but this meaning is obscured because the author of Mark is forced to omit the second half of the line that does not fit his story about John. So he only has the messenger and not the lord entering into the temple.

The second of the two quotations really does come from Isaiah:

A voice is crying "Prepare the way for Yahweh in the wilderness; Make straight in the desert a highway for our God". (Isaiah 40:3)

The way is prepared for Yahweh, not Jesus. The Malachi passage starts with "*I will send my messenger...*" where the "I" is Yahweh. The two quotes are perfectly consistent. The messenger is the one who will enter into the temple and the one who will prepare the way in the wilderness for Yahweh. This one is Jesus, not John the Baptist.

Isaiah 40 is all about the promise of the return from exile. It gives comfort to "Jerusalem" who has sinned and yet has now been punished double for her sins. All flesh is like grass and goodness like a flower of the field; withered has the grass, faded the flower. Yet now there will be joy and the word of Yahweh triumphs:

O Zion, bringer of good news, get you up into the high mountain; O Jerusalem, bringer of good news, lift up your voice with strength; lift it up, be not afraid; say to the cities of Judah, Behold your God! (Isaiah 40:9)

There is an alternative translation of the passage that has the good news being brought to Zion, which might make more sense in the original. Whether it is Zion declaring the good news or whether the good news is being brought to Zion, the feminine is used and the one who is to declare the good news is female. It is from this passage that the idea of the Christian gospel is derived because "gospel" means "good news". The female Zion (Mary) is to go up a high mountain (Cephas), to declare the good news (preach the gospel), and to say to the cities of Judah "Behold your God!". The passage continues:

Behold, the Lord God will come with strong hand, and his arm shall rule for him: behold, his wage is with him, and his work before him. (Isaiah 40:10)

The "arm" of God is the Christ, who shall rule for Yahweh. We then have a depiction of Christ as the good shepherd:

He shall feed his flock like a shepherd: he shall gather the lambs with his arm, and carry them in his bosom, and shall gently lead those that are with young. (Isaiah 40:11)

The strong arm is the one who will clear the way for Yahweh and the shepherd who will rule for Yahweh. He comes through Mary who tells the people "Behold your God!" The voice shouts about preparing the way through the wilderness for Yahweh, but the author of Mark interprets this as meaning that the voice is shouting from the wilderness. He portrays John the Baptist as a wild man living in the wilderness.

It is clear that the real subject of the two quotations is Jesus. So why does the author of Mark apply all this to John? In reality, John was a rival to the Jesus movement whose supporters were recruited into the movement after his death. The idea of John being the precursor and baptiser of Jesus has been invented by the author of Mark. The story of the baptism of Jesus marks the start of the Deep Source sequence proper. The Deep Source contained an unfavourable comparison of the baptisms of John and Jesus, and this has given the author of Mark the false idea that Jesus was baptised by John. In the Mark story although John baptises Jesus with water he is then baptised spiritually by God. In the original baptism of Jesus, the spiritual Jesus descended into the disciple, and it was the disciple who was baptised.

Although the author of Mark has misunderstood the criticism of John in the Deep Source, his inclusion as a predecessor of Jesus also solved the difficulty of a prophecy at the end of Malachi:

Lo, I am sending to you Elijah the prophet, before the coming of the day of Yahweh (Malachi 4:5)

The problem is that Elijah had not come before Jesus. So the author of Mark develops the remarkable theory that John the Baptist is Elijah as is apparent from Mark 9:11-13 and Mark 8:28. The link between John and Elijah has probably been suggested by the fact that John's opposition to the marriage of Herod and Herodias is reminiscent of Elijah's opposition to Ahab and Jezebel.

Behind the story of the baptism of Jesus in Mark, some aspects of the original spiritual baptism can be seen. The quotation from Isaiah is that the Messiah is to *"Prepare the way for Yahweh in the wilderness"*. This is reflected in the Mark story immediately after the baptism:

And immediately the Spirit drives him out into the wilderness. And he was there in the wilderness forty days ... (Mark 1:12-13)

Jesus is "driven" into the wilderness using the same word as the gospel uses for the expulsion of demons. The wilderness is the world in a state of exile, subject to the angelic powers to whom it has been made over. Jesus is in the wilderness for forty days, meaning forty years, the time for which he is present within Mary.

The two quotations at the start of Mark lead to two key passages of Hebrew scripture, passages that were among the small number that were vitally important to the Jesus movement. The importance of these passages to the Jesus movement would have long predated the Gospel of Mark. It is also likely that the two quotes belong together and that the author of Mark has recycled an existing source and completely misunderstood it. Perhaps the fact that he has taken these two quotes linked together from a previous source is the reason the author of Mark has misattributed both to Isaiah when one comes from Malachi.

The lion that became man

We have seen that Mark opens with quotations from two prophecies; one that the Lord will come into his temple and the other promising a return from exile for "the daughter of Jerusalem". We will see how the same concepts are expressed in an enigmatic saying in Thomas, which, on the face of it, does not appear to have anything to do with Mary, or Jesus or the temple or the exile. This is the lion saying:

Jesus said: "Blessed is the lion which the man will eat, and the lion become man. And cursed is the man whom the lion will eat, and the lion become man." (Thomas 7)

This is a puzzling saying; not only does the lion eat the man but the man eats the lion! One idea might be that the "lion" represents the lower animal nature and the "man" the higher spiritual nature. This might make sense of the first half of the saying; if the animal is absorbed by the spiritual it becomes spiritual and so is "blessed". It would also fit the idea that the man eaten by the lion is cursed because the animal nature then destroys the spiritual person. The problem is that the second half of the saying ends with the lion becoming man. If the animal nature predominates, the man should become lion. This shows an apparent flaw with the saying in that both halves end the same way. Some translations assume this is due to a scribal error and change the last phrase to "and the man become lion".

However, it is dangerous to put such apparent inconsistencies down to errors. That which is inconsistent indicates where our understanding may be inadequate. Suppose that this is not an error. We must then discard the explanation that the lion represents the animal nature. Can we find any source for the lion becoming man? The lion was the largest and most powerful predator in the eastern Mediterranean so we would expect lion imagery to be very common in Jewish writings, and it is. The lion represents both positive and negative qualities; on the one hand, the lion is brave, powerful and strong and on the other, it is a cruel ravaging beast. Both aspects are represented in the scriptures.

What we might not expect to find is a lion changing into a man, but we find just this in a passage that was vitally important to the Jesus movement. This is when Daniel sees a vision representing four great kingdoms or kings that would successively rule the world. They appear as four beasts that emerge from the sea. Of the first Daniel says:

The first was like a lion, and had eagle's wings: I beheld till the wings thereof were plucked, and it was lifted up from the earth, and made stand upon the feet as a man, and a man's heart was given to it. (Daniel 7:4)

The lion represents the Babylonian kingdom and, in particular, the empire of Nebuchadnezzar, the king who conquered Jerusalem, destroyed the temple and took the Jews into exile. The lion has eagle's wings because of the speed of his conquests. The plucking of his wings is the revolts of the Medes and Persians which were to halt his progress and which mark the start of the decline of Babylon. He stands on his feet as a man and is given the heart of a man indicating the decline of Babylon from its powerful lion-like state. The Daniel dream continues until the Ancient of Days appears and the final kingdom is established under the son of man:

I saw in the night visions, and, behold, one like the Son of man came with the clouds of heaven, and came to the Ancient of days, and they brought him near before him. (Daniel 7:13)

It is hard to overestimate the importance of this passage to the Christ movement. It is predicting the kingdom of God and the arrival of the Mes-

siah coming "*with the clouds of heaven*". When during Jesus' trial in Mark the
priests ask him whether he is the Messiah he replies "I am" and repeats this
prophecy from Daniel.[244] Finding a lion that becomes a man in such a crucial passage cannot be a coincidence.

The lion is also used elsewhere as imagery for Nebuchadnezzar and the
Babylonians. In Jeremiah 4:7 the Babylonian invaders are compared to a
lion: "*A lion has gone up from his thicket, And a destroyer of nations is on his
way*". Another example comes from yet another key passage for the movement. We have seen the importance of the parable of the vineyard in Isaiah
5:1-7. The vineyard is Israel, and that parable tells how the vineyard shall
be uprooted and destroyed. In the continuation the prophet predicts how
Yahweh will summon the nations from afar to wreck his vengeance upon
Israel (the prediction was of course written after the event):

*Their roaring shall be like a lion, they shall roar like young lions: yea, they shall
roar, and lay hold of the prey, and shall carry it away and none shall deliver it.
(Isaiah 5:29)*

This tells us that the lion of the Babylonians shall carry away the prey of
Israel. The carrying away of Israel in the mouth of the Babylonian lion is
the exile. But after this, the lion becomes a man. It loses its lion-like courage, strength and ferocity and becomes fallible and human. The lion is an
instrument of God, and once it has fallen upon Israel, it has served its purpose as the means of God's punishment.

The lion who consumes must surely be Nebuchadnezzar and the Babylonians. But who is the man who is eaten? Does he signify Israel? This does
not fit another feature of the saying – that the man is cursed. Although Israel is taken away nowhere is it written that Israel shall be cursed. On the
contrary, the promise is that the exile will end, and Israel shall be redeemed.

If the man is not Israel then who is he? There is another possibility. We
have seen how the myth of Christ crucified must have predated Mary. It is
shared by the party of Christ mentioned by Paul who did not accept the
validity of the resurrection through Mary/Cephas. We have also seen how
this crucifixion must have been originally dated to the time of the destruction of the first temple. This suggests that the man devoured by the lion
was Christ. This is supported by the detail in the Thomas saying that the
man was cursed. The Jews believed that any man hung upon a tree, which
included crucifixion, was cursed:

For he that is hanged is cursed by God. (Deuteronomy 21:23)

Paul says quite explicitly that this includes Jesus who was cursed as a result of his crucifixion:

Christ has redeemed us from the curse of the law, being made a curse for us: for it is written, "Cursed is everyone that hangs on a tree." (Galatians 3:13)

To the Jews, a crucified Messiah was a contradiction because a crucified man was cursed by God. So being crucified was a sure sign that the person was not the true Messiah. In 1 Corinthians, Paul talks about one in the spirit not being able to curse Jesus:

You have known that when you were pagans, to the dumb idols you were led, as being carried away. Therefore, I make known to you that no one speaking in the spirit of God says "Jesus is cursed [anathema]," and no one is able to say "Jesus is Lord," except in the holy spirit. (1 Corinthians 12:2-3)

Note the apparently unconnected way in which Paul passes from the worship of idols to cursing Jesus. However, there is a connection, and that can be found in words Paul uses to describe how the Corinthians before their conversion, were led and carried away to the idols. Paul is using the terminology of exile. He is saying that just as the Jews were carried away by the Babylonians into captivity so were the Gentiles carried away into idol worship. This is interpreting the exile in cosmic terms as applying to the whole of humanity. In this cosmic exile, the Babylonians stand for the demons and fallen angels who lead the whole of mankind astray. This exile is also the death of Jesus, and it starts with his crucifixion. Through the whole period of exile, Jesus lies dead and cursed. The return from exile is the resurrection, and the resurrection undoes the curse. The new life of Jesus is the pledge that the curse has been revoked. Those who exist in the spirit share in this new life and so cannot say that Jesus is cursed. However, those who are not in the spirit, who are still in exile, see Jesus as dead. So they call him cursed and cannot call him Lord.

The idea that Christians cannot curse Jesus is also found in the remarkable correspondence between Pliny the Younger, Governor of Bithynia 111-113, and the Emperor Trajan (Pliny Epistles 10:96-97). Pliny says that the "Christians" are becoming so numerous in his province that the worship of the Roman gods is declining. He asks the approval of Trajan for his method of dealing with those accused of being Christians. Pliny tells of how he gives the accused three chances to recant. If they do not, then he orders their execution unless they are Roman citizens, in which case he orders them transferred to Rome. If they deny their former religion, then he makes them offer prayer and wine to the image of the Emperor and orders them to curse Christ because, as he reports to Trajan, this is something Christians cannot do. If an outsider like Pliny has heard this detail about cursing Jesus, then it must be widespread within the movement by the early second century. We cannot be sure whether this is a direct result of 1 Corinthians 12:2-3 or because Paul is quoting something that was an already widespread belief in his own day.

In 1 Peter there is a reference to the devil as lion:

Be sober, be vigilant. Your adversary the devil prowls around as a roaring lion, seeking whom he may devour. (1 Peter 5:8)

To see the link between this and the lion saying in Thomas, we must understand that the King of Babylon also represents the devil (see Isaiah 14). Again the lion is being interpreted at the cosmic level, not just representing the man Nebuchadnezzar and his armies, but more profoundly the power in heaven that they represent on the human stage, this power being the adversary, the devil. Just as Babylon has swallowed up Israel in exile, so the devil has swallowed up Jesus.

If the second Lion represents the Babylonians and their king then what is the first lion? This cannot be the same lion because it is blest, and the Babylonians/the devil cannot be blessed. So we are dealing with two quite different lions. The connection between the two halves of the saying must be the man and not the lion. In the second half the man, Christ, is eaten but in the first half it is he who does the eating. We have seen how it was a common belief that the disciple had to eat and drink the substance of Jesus, the bread and the water/wine, for Jesus to enter into them and for the disciple to share his life. But in this case, it is Jesus who consumes. There is an example of this in Thomas 11 where the spirit has to eat that which is dead for it to become alive. The body, being corruptible and belonging to the lower world, is unable to inherit the kingdom of heaven. By consuming the lower person, the spirit transforms what is fleshy into what is spiritual. A person who has been consumed by the spirit is possessed by that spirit. The person can then share in the eternal life of the spirit.

If this is the correct interpretation, then the person in question must be Mary for she is the one whose spirit is Jesus. The spiritual Jesus consumes

Mary so that she becomes him. He speaks his sayings through her lips and builds his church through her. Is there any evidence that Mary is the first lion in the Thomas saying, the one who is blessed?

The evidence comes from the Jewish Rabbinical literature where attention is drawn to the fact that Nebuchadnezzar and the temple that he destroyed are both called lions. To quote the Jewish Encyclopaedia:

The Talmud (Mid. iv. 7) points out that the Temple -- that is, the Hekal -- resembled a lion in being broad in front and tapering toward the rear. Concerning the name Ariel, a Midrash remarks that the Temple is called "lion" (Isa. l.c.), and so also is the house of David (Ezek. xix. 2-7) and Judah (Gen. xlix. 9). Nebuchadnezzar, likewise, is called "lion" (Jer. iv. 7); and it was this lion that destroyed the Temple, deposed the house of David, and carried Judah into captivity (Ex. R. xxix. 9). (Jewish Encyclopaedia entry for Ariel)

The key text, however, for the identification of the temple to a lion is the reference to "Ariel", meaning "the lion of God", in Isaiah 29:

Woe to Ariel, to Ariel, the city where David dwelt! Add you year to year; let them kill sacrifices. Yet I will distress Ariel, and there shall be heaviness and sorrow: and it shall be unto me as Ariel. (Isaiah 29:1-2)

The context makes it clear that it is Jerusalem that is called Ariel, the lion. Elsewhere Ariel is used for the altar of the temple[245] and the Jews also interpreted Ariel as meaning the temple itself. Mary is called the temple/tower, and she is also Zion/Jerusalem. So Mary is a lion just as much as the King of Babylon.

The symmetry of the Thomas lion saying now becomes clear. It contrasts the two lions; the one through who came about the end of exile (Mary) and the one through who came about the beginning of exile (the King of Babylon). Both are placed in relation to Christ. The King swallowed up Christ, which means to kill him, and by his death, Christ was cursed. Mary, however, was consumed by Jesus until her corruptible nature was turned into the spiritual nature that was Jesus himself (she became man). By being consumed, she was blessed and granted life.

Key points

1. The beginning of the Gospel of Mark follows a coherent structure that has been obscured by the literalistic story. In this structure, the "Deep Source" sequence tells of the coming of Jesus to Mary. This is prefaced by two quotations/prophecies that predict this coming.

2. The quotations are misapplied by the author of Mark to John the Baptist. For this reason, he is forced to suppress the parts of the prophecies that do not fit John. The first prophecy, in full, predicts that the Lord (Jesus) will come into his temple (the Magdalene). The second is about the return from exile. The messenger (the angelic Messiah) is to make a way for Yahweh in the wilderness (the world), and a female figure (Mary) is to preach the gospel from a mountain (the rock, Cephas).

3. The quotations are followed by a section of Mark that is derived from the Deep Source. This is no coincidence, as the Deep Source develops the themes of the quotations. The Deep Source is about the coming of Jesus into his temple, Mary, her purification by the expulsion of demons, and her recruitment of the disciples and teaching.

4. The Deep Source dates from the time the Jesus movement was in rivalry with John the Baptist and contained a criticism of John. The author of Mark misunderstands this criticism and develops his baptism story around it. The role of John also served as the fulfilment of the prophecy in Malachi that Elijah will return first (the author of Mark equated John with Elijah).

5. The lion saying in Thomas is another expression of the lord coming into his temple as the end of exile. It hinges around the fact that both the King of Babylon and the temple were represented as lions. One lion eats the man (Jesus) who through his crucifixion becomes cursed. This lion then becomes man, reflecting the prophecy that the Babylonian lion will lose its lion nature and be given the heart of a man. The other lion (the temple, Mary) is eaten by the man (Jesus), and so becomes blessed. This lion becomes man because her nature is unified with Christ so she "becomes male".

Chapter 33

Two and one

The Jesus movement believed that Jesus was the male spiritual component of Mary so that in a sense they were one and the same. Moreover, the Mary-Jesus unity was the archetype for all who achieved the spiritual state of "the kingdom of heaven". The movement believed that all humans were essentially male-female, but that only one component was born into the world, the other remaining in heaven. We will trace the origins of this belief and show it originated long before the Jesus movement.

The wife of your youth

We have seen how the first quotation in Mark, that from Malachi, is a prophesy that the "the Lord whom you desire" (the Christ) will enter into the temple (Mary). If we look closer at Malachi, we can find other clues that this book was linked to the predecessors of the Jesus movement. Most obviously it shares with the Animal Apocalypse a withering contempt for the second temple. The language it uses is at times shocking, such as this curse addressed to the priests:

Behold, I will corrupt your offspring, and spread shit upon your faces, even the shit of your solemn feasts; and one shall take you away with it. (Malachi 2:3)

This is the background to the prophecy that the lord will come into his temple. The writers of Malachi believed that the restart of temple worship after the exile was invalid and that Yahweh was not present in the physical second temple. We have seen that this is exactly the belief of the Jesus movement who also rejected the second temple. The temple that had been destroyed will not be rebuilt but replaced by one not made with hands, the human temple represented by Mary and the others who are chosen.

It is true that the reasons given in Malachi for the rejection are procedural – that the correct sacrifices had not been offered. But the venom displayed is hardly proportional to the reasons given. The author of Malachi was not an Enochian Jew, but there is some connection between Malachi and the Jews who were to give rise to the Jesus movement. Malachi is normally dated before 400 BC, much earlier than the Animal Apocalypse. However, the beliefs of the group from which the Animal Apocalypse emerged will go back further in time than the Apocalypse itself. In particular, the rejection of the validity of the second temple by this group must have started with the building of that temple. So it is possible that the author of Malachi was influenced by the group that was later to produce the Animal Apocalypse.

It is also possible that additions were made to the original text by the predecessors of the Jesus movement. Read, for example, the section on the worship of Yahweh among the nations, the gentiles:

For from the rising of the sun even unto the going down of the same my name shall be great among the nations; and in every place incense shall be offered unto my name, and a pure offering: for my name shall be great among the nations, said Yahweh of hosts. (Malachi 1:11)

It is taken from a passage in which the Jews were being criticised for not giving a "pure offering" and in which it is said that their offering will be refused.[246] In other words, Jews are being rejected in favour of gentiles! This is all very reminiscent of the early Jesus movement which expanded aggressively among the gentiles and included many gentiles among the chosen even while most Jews were regarded as being rejected.

The reason all this is important is one very curious passage on divorce that immediately proceeds and leads into the Malachi quotation given at the start of Mark. This is normally interpreted as being about the question of divorcing foreign wives. The Book of Ezra, that many would regard as approximately contemporary to Malachi, is very concerned about this question of non-Jewish wives and is adamant that they should be divorced. The book of Malachi, however, is both against the "*daughter of a strange god*" and against divorce. One interpretation is that the writer was both against foreign marriages and against divorcing a foreign wife once married. But this does not fit in with the passage either. The prohibition against divorce speaks in mystical terms about the "*wife of your youth*" and being joined into one whole, a union that is inconsistent with the condemnation of the daughter of the strange God.

Clearly we are not supposed to read the passage literally. Perhaps the meaning is metaphorical with the original faith, represented as the wife of your youth, being rejected for the "daughter of the strange God". Going further there is a clue that spiritual meaning is intended; the passage includes the word for spirit, *ruwach*, the feminine noun literally meaning breath, no less than three times. And there are distinct similarities with the Shepherd of Hermas. There the spirit is represented by a virgin wife and sister to whom a man must be joined if he is to enter the kingdom of God. At the same time, he is tempted to reject this virgin by beautiful women in black. If he succumbs to this temptation, he will lose his place in the kingdom unless he later repents, rejects the women in black, and becomes joined again with the virgin.

The section on divorce, Malachi 2:11-16, has caused extraordinary difficulty because it appears contradictory, and even nonsensical. But interpreting it spiritually in the light of later Christian writings it makes beautiful sense. It starts simply enough:

For Judah has profaned the holiness of Yahweh which he loved, and has married the daughter of a strange god.

We must read this not literally as meaning a foreign wife, but spiritually, as meaning that the men of Judah have spiritually strayed from the pure love of Yahweh. It continues that the one who marries the daughter of the strange God will be cut off and his offering refused. This daughter of the strange god would be equivalent to the women in black, the demon wives.

And this have you done again, covering the altar of Yahweh with tears, with weeping, and with crying out, insomuch that he regards not the offering any more, or receives it with good will at your hand.

Yahweh rejects their offerings because of this marriage. The equivalent in the Shepherd is where those who accept the women in black are rejected from the tower which originally stood for the temple.

Yet you ask "Why?" Because Yahweh has been witness between you and the wife of your youth, against whom you have dealt treacherously: yet is she your companion, and the wife of your covenant.

The "wife of your youth" is clearly wife before "the daughter of the strange God". That is why it is a question of divorce. In contrast to the daughter of the strange God, the "wife of your youth" must be the daughter of Yahweh and she is the true companion and wife of the covenant.

And did not he make one? Yet he had the residue of the spirit. And why one? That he might seek a godly seed. Therefore take heed to your spirit, and let none deal treacherously against the wife of his youth.

This line goes back to the story of the creation in Genesis. The last part equates a man's spirit to the "the wife of his youth". What this line seems to be saying is that God had a "residual of the spirit", that is enough spirit to make two, yet he chose to make one. So what happened to the residual spirit? It stayed with Yahweh and is the "wife of your youth"! When Yahweh breathed on Adam only part of the spirit entered into his body to animate it; the other part stayed behind. The two parts were still intimately joined although physically separated. They were brother/sister and wife/husband. The reason Yahweh did this was that he might have a "godly seed". The union of spiritual wife and physical man would produce the fruit that was pleasing to God because the spirit was the daughter of Yahweh and had remained with him.

For Yahweh, the God of Israel said that he hates putting away: for one covers his garment with violence, said Yahweh of hosts: therefore take heed to your spirit, that you deal not treacherously.

The "putting away" is divorce. In this passage, we come across the garment that recurs so many times in early Christian literature. The phrase "covers his garment with violence" can also be read "covers violence with his garment" although the first reading is preferred here. The spreading of a man's garment over a woman as a sign of marriage was a Jewish custom and seems to have started very early. When Ruth comes to Boaz secretly at night and asks him to cover her with his garment[247] she is asking him to marry her. We must take this one stage further and identify the garment with the spiritual wife herself. A man must not divorce his spiritual wife and so give violence to his "garment" but must take heed of his spirit. In the Shepherd the virgin spirits are closely associated with a garment to the extent that the spirits and the garment can be regarded as one. We know that in the Christian literature the garment stands for the spirit and so it does in Malachi!

If this reading of Malachi is correct, then the concept of the spirit as wife and garment must predate the Jesus movement by hundreds of years. It is true that we cannot be sure precisely when this part of Malachi was written. But if it is original, the idea that part of the spirit, the breath that Yahweh breathed into Adam, remained in heaven, would have evolved over four hundred years before the Jesus movement.

We can see that the early Christians did interpret this Malachi passage spiritually from a quotation by the fourth-century work, the Constitution of the Apostles. The author of the Constitution had access to early sources as is shown by his faithful copying of the first or early second century Didache. At one point, the Constitution uses the Malachi passage in a discourse against divorce:

You shall take care to thy spirit, and shall not forsake the wife of thy youth; for she is the partner of your life, and the remains of your spirit. I and no other have made her. (Constitution of the Apostles Book 6:14)

The quotation is not exact but reflects an interpretation of the Malachi passage. It is specific that the "wife of your youth" is "the remains of thy spirit" as we have concluded above. The Constitution equates "the wife of your youth" with a man's wife. But the quotation is likely to come from an earlier source as it supports the interpretation that the "wife of your youth" stands for a man's spirit and not his wife.

Two and one

In fact, the image of the spirit wife being left with God is not as strange in a Jewish context as it may seem. The Malachi passage draws upon the creation of Adam by God, but this is the second account of the creation. The first account speaks of man being created as "male and female":

So God created man (Adam) in his own image, in the image of God created he him; male and female created he them. (Genesis 1:27)

The difficulty is the inconsistency with the second creation account where Eve is formed after Adam from his rib. This inconsistency gave rise to the idea that Adam, the first man, had been made hermaphrodite combining both male and female in one whole. This is after all what Genesis 1:27 literally says. Some would then have asked what became of the female element. Some think that she is a female demon called Lilith who wanders the earth in disembodied form. However, this is a medieval legend first encountered in the Alphabet of Ben Sira, and there is no evidence that the story of Lilith goes back to ancient times.

One explanation is that the female element of Adam somehow passed into Eve during her creation. But the Malachi passage is evidence of another interpretation; that Adam's spirit was first created male-female; and that in the second creation the male element was breathed into the body of clay by Yahweh leaving the residual, the female element, to remain with Yahweh. The first creation is then a spiritual creation and the second an earthly creation. Certainly, this is the viewpoint of many gnostics who viewed the worldly creation as being inferior to the first spiritual making.

In this view the spirit that animates a person within, what we might think of as the rational and emotional person, is only one part of a whole. There is a second spirit that is intimately joined with the first and yet which has its existence outside the body, in the realm of God. The two are twins and to find completeness, to produce the fruit or seed that is the yield of the kingdom of heaven, the two aspects must be reunited.

All of this is quite explicit in the second century Gospel of Philip:[248]

If the woman had not separated from the man, she should not die with the man. His separation became the beginning of death. Because of this, Christ came to repair the separation, which was from the beginning, and again unite the two, and to give life to those who died as a result of the separation, and unite them. But the woman is united to her husband in the bridal chamber. Indeed, those who have united in the bridal chamber will no longer be separated. Thus Eve separated from Adam because it was not in the bridal chamber that she united with him. (Gospel of Philip 70:9-22)

When Eve was still with Adam, death did not exist. When she was separated from him, death came into being. If he enters again and attains his former self, death will be no more. (Gospel of Philip 68:22-26)

To show that this is a remembered tradition and not a product of second century gnosticism, it is necessary to trace it back to the first century. We can do this by showing that the separation of the two aspects was a major theme of the Gospel of Thomas and that a key saying concerned with this theme was clearly used by the Gospel of Mark. Since the Gospel of Mark was written shortly after 70 it follows that the Thomas saying must date sometime before this, say no later than the middle of the first century. This will prove that the male-female aspect of the person-spirit is not an invention of the second century but belongs with the origins of Christianity.

The reuniting of that which has been split is an obsession of the Gospel of Thomas, the very name of which means twin. In one saying the disciples ask Jesus how their end will be. Jesus gives a surprising reply:

The disciples said to Jesus: "Tell us how our end shall be." Jesus said: "Have you discovered then the beginning, that you seek after the end? For where the beginning is, the end will be also. Blessed is he who will stand in the beginning, and he will know the end and not taste of death." (Thomas 18)

The end is where the beginning is. The apocalyptic end state of the kingdom of God is the same as the creation in Genesis before it was corrupted. If a person returns to their spiritual state of the first creation, they will live in the end state of the kingdom of God. The same theme is continued in the first part of the next saying:

Jesus said: Blessed is he who was before he came into being. (Thomas 19a)

Adam is created first spiritually and then bodily. The spiritual state that existed first is the blessed state of completeness. Combining the two into one is linked with the moving of the mountain, the symbol of the kingdom of heaven:

Jesus said: "When you make the two one, you shall become sons of man, and if you should say: 'Mountain, be moved', it shall be moved." (Thomas 106)

The key saying though is Thomas 22, which tells the disciples how to reach the kingdom:

Jesus saw some little ones at the breast. He said to his disciples: "These little ones at the breast are like those who enter into the kingdom." They said to him: "Then if we be little ones, shall we enter the kingdom?" Jesus said to them: "When you make the two one, and when you make the inside as the outside, and the outside as the inside, and the upper side as the lower side; and when you make the male and the female into a single one, that the male be not male nor the female female; when you make eyes in the place of an eye, and a hand in place of a hand, and a foot in place of a foot, an image in place of an image, then you will enter into [the kingdom]." (Thomas 22)

In the first part, Jesus tells the disciples that they will enter the kingdom like infants. A similar saying is behind the story in Matthew. After a young child is brought to him Jesus says: "*Truly I say to you, except you be converted, and become as little children, you shall not enter into the kingdom of heaven*" (Matthew 18:3). However, we would not guess how young the child is from the Matthew story; in Thomas it is a baby still at breast. The author of Matthew does not understand how the disciples can become like babies so he makes the baby into a young child. The way they can become like babies is to be reborn, to return to their initial spiritual state. When the disciples ask whether they shall enter the kingdom as children Jesus replies cryptically with a series of opposites.

When you make the two one,

The person and their spirit sister/brother, wife/husband, must be rejoined into a whole.

and when you make the inside as the outside, and the outside as the inside

The spirit within and without must be made into one.

and the upper side as the lower

The spirit below, in the body, and above, in heaven, must be made one.

and when you make the male and the female into a single one, that the male be not male and the female female;

The male and female elements of the spirit that have been separated must be recombined. The person who enters the kingdom *is* the divine marriage. Through the marriage, they become again hermaphrodite just as man was made in the beginning. This is not to say that a man becomes effeminate or a woman masculine. Rather what we think of the person becomes one element of a greater whole, and this greater whole is hermaphrodite combining both masculine and feminine aspects.

when you make eyes in the place of an eye, and a hand in place of a hand, and a foot in place of a foot, an image in place of an image, then shall you enter [the king-dom].

We should think here of two bodies being merged into one. The person puts on the garment, the spiritual body, and their physical eye, hand and foot is replaced by the spiritual eye, hand and foot.

Entering the kingdom does not just involve joining with the spirit. It in-volves the redemption of the spirit from its state of prostitution. This re-demption, or change of state, is the "image in place of an image". The fallen state of the spiritual twin is the soul which is replaced upon redemption with the living spirit. The state of the fallen spiritual twin is referred to in Thomas 84:

Jesus said: "The days you look upon your likeness, you rejoice; but when you look upon your images which came to be before you, they neither die nor become manifest, how much will you bear?"

The best explanation of this saying is that Jesus is addressing his mes-sage to those who are seeking but have not yet found the Kingdom of Heaven, as is normal with sayings in Thomas. It starts with a person taking delight in their own reflection; the reader is supposed to imagine the say-ing addressed to a young and attractive person. The beauty of the physical reflection is contrasted with the spiritual "image" that came into existence long before they were born, the image of their first creation. When the per-son sees their physical reflection they rejoice but if they were able to see this spiritual image they would have much to bear. The spirit that was formed by God has been corrupted by demons and is in a state of prostitu-tion. Yet it neither dies nor is it made manifest. The corruption is invisible yet will endure for all time, long after the sensual beauty has faded. The fallen spirit is in the state that Christians would later call "hell". However, this is not punishment for wrongdoing but the way that all human beings naturally are before they have entered into rebirth.

Of all the sayings in Thomas, saying 22 sounds like one of the weirdest and most "gnostic". Does this mean that it is a later addition and not one of the original collection of sayings? We have already seen how it is used by the Acts of Philip and the Acts of Peter in the upside-down crucifixion. But we can date it a good deal earlier than this for it was copied by none other than the Gospel of Mark which means that it is older than any of the four gospels. The copying was discovered by Stevan Davies.[249] He noticed that a long passage in Mark consisting of three apparently separate stories was all derived from the Thomas saying. The first part of this section talks about hand, foot and eye being cut-off:

"And if your hand causes you to stumble, cut it off; it is better for you to enter into life crippled, than having two hands to go into Gehenna, into the unquenchable fire. And if your foot causes you to stumble, cut it off; it is better for you to enter into life lame, than having two feet, to be cast into Gehenna. And if your eye causes you to stumble, cast it out; it is better for you to enter into the kingdom of God with one eye, than having two eyes, to be cast into Gehenna, where 'their worm does not die, and the fire is not quenched.'" (Mark 9:43-48)

The author of Mark is struggling to understand what the Gospel of Thomas means by "hand in place of a hand". The original meaning is that the bodily hand, foot and eye are replaced by a spiritual hand, foot and eye. The author of Mark has some inkling of this but he makes it all absurdly literal. The bodily, and hence sinful, hand, foot and eye are cut off to be replaced by the spiritual equivalent after death. Note that Mark here has the same three; hand, foot and eye, as Thomas. There is clearly a link.

After this, Jesus is asked a question about divorce by the Pharisees. Jesus forbids divorce and gives as his reason the creation account in Genesis:

"But from the beginning of the creation, 'He made them male and female.' 'For this reason, a man shall leave his father and mother, and cleave to his wife. And they two shall be one flesh.' So they are no longer two but one flesh. What therefore God has joined together, let not man put asunder." (Mark 10:6-9)

This is in remarkable agreement with our conclusions on the meaning of the Thomas saying; at the beginning of creation man was made male and female and so shall return to a state of being one and not two. This shows that not only did the author of Mark have access to the Thomas saying but that he also has enough understanding of its meaning to connect it to the creation of Adam in Genesis. However, in his literalistic worldview he interprets it as being about marriage, the union of the flesh. After the passage on divorce, Jesus is brought some little children:

And they were bringing little children to him, that he might touch them. But the disciples rebuked them. And having seen, Jesus was indignant and said to them, "Permit the little children to come to me and do not hinder them! For to such belongs the kingdom of God. Truly I say to you, whoever does not receive the kingdom of God as a child will never enter into it." (Mark 10:13-15)

The connection to the start of Thomas 22 where Jesus says that the infants are like those who enter the kingdom is obvious. We have three successive stories in Mark that are all closely linked to the same saying in Thomas. We have seen that Thomas 22 is about spiritual rebirth, a return to the original state of the male-female spiritual union that Adam (mankind) existed in before his spirit was split into two. The author of Mark, however, does not understand the meaning and unity of Thomas 22. He takes three sections from the saying and constructs three stories around them, each one of which misses the point of the original. He places these three stories one after another in his gospel. It is here that we get an insight into the true nature of the Gospel of Mark. It is made up fiction based on a misunderstanding of genuine early traditions and sayings.

Those who are alive shall not die

There is one final saying in Thomas that talks about the two and one and it is as enigmatic as Thomas 22:

Jesus said: "This heaven shall pass away, and that which above it shall pass away. And the dead are not alive and the living will not die. In the days you were eating that which is dead you were making it alive. When you come into the light, what will you do? On the day when you were one, you were made two. But when you have become two, what will you do?" (Thomas 11)

The Jews believed in three heavens with the first being this world and the third being the abode of God. If we dwell in the first heaven then who dwells in the second heaven? It must be the spirit in its fallen state for it is not a physical inhabitant of the lower world, and neither does it dwell anymore with God. The middle heaven is a dangerous place for it is the home of other supernatural beings with designs upon the spirit, the wife of man. In Isaiah, there is a reference to the end of earth and heaven. It is in a section that promises vengeance upon "all nations":

And all the host of heaven shall be dissolved, and the heavens shall be rolled together as a scroll: and all their host shall fall down, as the leaf falls off from the

*vine, and as a falling fig from the fig tree. For my sword shall be bathed in heaven:
behold, it shall come down upon Idumea, and upon the people of my curse, to
judgment. (Isaiah 34:4-5)*

The passage is aimed against the "host of heaven" who originally were
the Canaanite deities and who became Yahweh's angels (the ancient mind
made no distinction between stars and gods). The host will be dissolved,
and the sword will be bathed in heaven before descending upon the earth.
It may seem odd that the host of heaven are being attacked in a passage
that is supposedly about vengeance upon the Gentile nations, but we shall
see that it will, in fact, make perfect sense. The host are among the "dead"
in the next line. They are the corrupters of the spirit and their habitation is
the middle heaven.

The Thomas saying talks about the two heavens passing away and the
natural interpretation is that this means the apocalyptic end times. Elsewhere, the gospel talks of the kingdom of heaven being spread upon the
earth and of the "rest" of the dead as having already come. Some see this as
evidence of "layers" in the Gospel of Thomas with different sayings written
at different times. In this interpretation, the idea of the kingdom being already present emerges relatively late as a response to the non-appearance
of Jesus in the second coming. However, the Gospel of Thomas is not inconsistent. Instead, it presents something extraordinary for the ancient
world – a reinterpretation of time itself. At the spiritual level, time is an
illusion and for a person in the spirit time does not exist. The end is the
same as the beginning, and the apocalypse has already occurred. The perfect stand as one and they stand both in the state before the creation and in
the end times of the kingdom of God. We must understand this concept of
time to make sense of this saying. Although the end times are not necessarily imminent in the time of the world they have in a sense already happened and are relevant to the disciple now.

If a person died before the end times, then the apocalyptic groups believed that they were placed in a kind of suspended animation before being
resurrected at the time of judgement. However, if all times exist in simultaneity then there is no need for any wait and the moment of a person's death
is effectively the moment of judgement. The spirit of a dead person would
proceed to the final kingdom in the same way that a person alive at the second coming would be taken up spiritually. However, while a person is
alive, their spirit is already able to enter the kingdom. The saying continues:

And the dead are not alive and the living will not die.

The living and the dead are not those literally living or dead, but those who have entered into the life of the kingdom and those who have not. At the end times, those who are not saved will be dead, but because all times exist in simultaneity, their deadness extends to the present and their life on earth. They may seem to be alive, but they are spiritually dead. Those who are alive spiritually in this world shall not die at the end times but stand in the kingdom. Saying 111 in Thomas makes clear that this is the meaning of "they that live will not die":

Jesus said: "The heavens shall be rolled up and the earth in your presence, and he who lives in the Living One shall not see death" (Thomas 111a)

The idea of those not living in the kingdom being "dead" is also found in the gospels. When Jesus is asked by a would-be follower if he may bury his father Jesus replies *"let the dead bury their dead"* (Matthew 8:22). The Thomas saying continues:

In the days you were eating that which is dead you were making it alive. When you come into the light, what will you do?

The play on alive and dead continues from the previous line. In that line, the state of being alive or dead does not change in the end times. But here we do have a change of state; the living becomes alive by being eaten. When a person eats a dead animal, the flesh of that animal becomes part of the substance of a person and so in a sense becomes alive again. The question posed is what happens when a person comes into the light, either at the end times or when they die. At this time the person's body is "dead". It is flesh and belongs to the lower heaven that is passing out of existence. Like an animal that is dead and eaten by a living man, so the body can only become alive again by being "eaten" by the spirit and so becoming spirit. This recalls the first part of the lion saying in Thomas 7: *"Blessed is the lion which the man will eat, and the lion become man."* The lion which is eaten is the temple, Mary, whose fleshy nature is consumed by the spiritual Jesus until she becomes one with him. Thomas 11 continues:

On the day when you were one, you were made two.

This is part of the larger theme of two becoming one. A person becomes complete by the marriage of the spirit and entering the bridal chamber. The irony is that in attaining this completeness and becoming "one" a person for the first time appreciates that they are in fact "two", and that they have a spiritual wife/husband, sister/brother.

But when you have become two, what will you do?

The person will again become two at the dissolution of the physical person, by death or the ending of the whole physical world. The question is posed "what will you do"? How will the dead body "survive"? Note the parallel structure of the last two lines:

In the days when you were eating that which is dead/ On the day when you were one, you were made two
When you come in the light, what will you do?/ But when you have become two, what will you do?

The theme of the saying is what will happen to the union of spirit and body when the world is dissolved. If the body is destroyed how is the Christian to attain immortality? By merging their existence completely with the spiritual twin through a perfect union so that the twin preserves their identity. Such is the implication of the Shepherd of Hermas which says about those who are resurrected into the tower: *they never separated the one from the other, neither the spirits from the men nor the men from the spirits, but the spirits abode with them till they fell asleep (Shepherd of Hermas 92:6).*[250]

In Paul's letter 1 Corinthians, there is a section where he addresses exactly the same question. It follows immediately after the crucial account of the resurrection appearances. Some in the Corinthian church are saying that there is no resurrection of the dead.[251] It will seem odd to the modern reader that early Christians should doubt the resurrection while still being part of the church. But it is easy to see how such doubt could arise from the philosophy behind the Thomas saying. The person will "become two" so that their spiritual wife/husband will survive but not their body. Some would have questioned whether such a state was a resurrection at all. Paul raises the question as to the form in which the resurrection occurs:

But someone will say, "How are the dead raised up? And with what body do they come?" (1 Corinthians 15:35)

Paul's answer is that something sowed cannot come alive unless it first dies. The seed that is sowed is not the living body that will be but just a grain that is "dead". He applies this analogy to the resurrection of the dead – "*It is sown in corruption; it is raised in in-corruption*" (1 Corinthians 15:42) and "*It is sown a natural body; it is raised a spiritual body*" (1 Corinthians 15:44). He compares this to the first Adam, who was fleshy representing the physical body and the last Adam, which is Jesus, who is spiritual in nature. It is in the image of the spiritual that the dead will be raised. Paul adds:

As is the earthy, such are they also that are earthy: and as is the heavenly, such are they also that are heavenly. (1 Corinthians 15:48)

He concludes:

Now I say this, brothers, that flesh and blood is not able to inherit the kingdom of God, nor does the perishable inherit the imperishable. (1 Corinthians 15:50)

He goes on to talk about the transformation of the living and dead at the end times:

Behold, I tell you a mystery: We will not all sleep, but we will all be changed, in a moment, in the twinkling of an eye, at the last trumpet. For the trumpet will sound, and the dead will be raised imperishable, and we will be changed. (I Corinthians 15:51-2)

He adds that once the corruptible has been changed to the incorruptible "*Death is swallowed up in victory*" (1 Corinthians 15:54).

The Gospel of Thomas and the letters of Paul appear to be so different in style and content that you might suppose them to have come from two different religions. However, we will repeatedly find that they are dealing with the same core concepts and coming to the same conclusions. So it is here. The Thomas saying is brief and enigmatic. It will infuriate the sensible literalistic person and will delight the intuitive, which is an alternative name for the spiritual. In fact, they are more enigmatic to the modern reader than originally intended. In the early church, a student studying the sayings would surely have done so with the aid of a teacher who would have helped elucidate them. This crucial knowledge of the context of the sayings has long since been lost and has to be painstakingly recreated before we can begin to understand them.

Paul's letters are very different. They are intellectual, written by a well-educated Jew, a former Pharisee, who is on the edge of the movement. They are designed to be read to the whole of a church and not just to the perfected. Mostly Paul's letters are easy to understand because they are designed to be understood by the generality of his listeners. It is when Paul becomes obscure that he gets really interesting. Obscurity in Paul indicates mysteries; an area that he is not at liberty to explain clearly.

But we must always be aware when reading Paul that he is not the foundation stone of the movement nor the source of the spring. He is a former Pharisee struggling to develop an intellectual religious philosophy for the movement. We can never be sure with Paul whether what he is telling us is what he has been taught or his own additions.

Both Paul and the Thomas saying are dealing with the situation at the end times when the dead and the living will enter into the kingdom. Both agree that the bodily person will not survive and that the resurrection will be spiritual. In both cases, the mortal man or woman will need to be transformed. For the Thomas saying it is a question of being consumed by the spirit and joining with it in indissoluble union. For Paul, the body will be transformed from an earthly to a heavenly body.

There is one aspect that is different between Paul and Thomas. We have seen how in Thomas the person and the spirit is a male-female pairing. Moreover, the spiritual body has existed since the beginning and is joined with the body of flesh to attain the completeness that is the kingdom of heaven. For Paul, the spiritual body seems to come into existence to replace the earthly body "in a twinkling of an eye". In general Paul de-emphasises the existence of the kingdom here and now. From his writings, it appears that Paul believed that the kingdom is something that only happens at the time of the second coming. But it may be that he was unwilling to talk about this aspect in letters that were intended for public distribution within the church. As he says at the beginning of 1 Corinthians, he is feeding his audience on milk and not talking wisdom to the perfected.

Key points

1. The Jesus movement believed that humans were created twice, first as spiritual beings and then as a physical man or woman. This is represented in Genesis as the two separate stories of the creation of Adam. The first Adam was hermaphrodite and spiritual, being both male and female. In

the second creation, Adam was breathed into clay and made a physical man.

2. In the physical creation, the male-female completeness of the original spiritual person is shattered. Either the male or female component becomes the physical person while the other component remains spiritual and in heaven. This spiritual component is in mortal danger because it exists in a state of corruption in the realm of demons. To be saved a person has to be reborn through Jesus so that the spiritual can be redeemed and the person become a male-female whole again.

3. There is evidence for the belief in the male-female nature of the individual hundreds of years before the Jesus movement. In Malachi "the wife of your youth" is the female spirit of a man, the part of the spirit that remained with Yahweh and that was not breathed into Adam.

4. There is some connection between those who produced Malachi and the predecessors of the Jesus movement. Both believed that the second temple was invalid and looked for the genuine new temple. They also believed that Yahweh would accept worship by Gentiles, but would reject many of the Jews.

5. The Jesus movement believed that to enter the end state of the kingdom of God a person had to go back to the beginning, the state in which they were first created. Thomas 18 says that one who stands at the beginning will know the end and will not die.

6. The critical saying is Thomas 22 which first compares the kingdom to a baby. It then says that to enter into the kingdom of heaven the disciple has to make the two into one, the inner as the outer, the upper as the lower, the male and female into a single one, so that the male is not male and the female not female.

7. There is a section of the Gospel of Mark (9:43-10:15) that has been derived from Thomas 22. This means that the Thomas saying must be considerably earlier than Mark, which was written in the 70s. So the concept of entering the kingdom of heaven by uniting male and female aspects belongs to the earliest decades of the movement and is not a second century gnostic development.

8. Another key saying is Thomas 11 which addresses the issue of what happens at the end of time or upon death. The answer is that people will remain in the same state after their physical death as when they were physically alive; those who are dead have never been alive, whereas those who have life will not die. The saying alludes to the idea that only the spiritual survives after death, and the physical person will die. If the spiritual and physical have been combined into a union, so that the male-female compo-

nents are one, then that person has life and will survive after death through the spirit. If a person has not achieved this union, then their existence is rooted in the physical, and they will die with their body.

9. The idea that a person will not be physically resurrected but can only exist after death in spiritual form is found also in Paul.

Chapter 34

Paul and the three powers

If the concept of a person and their spirit, as a male-female pairing was central to Christianity, then can we find it in the letters of Paul? The answer is that we can, in a passage that would otherwise be obscure.

Paul and the three powers

Of all Paul's letters, it is 1 Corinthians that gives us the greatest insight into the spiritual nature of the movement. It is no coincidence that in this letter he is having to defend himself against those who accuse him of teaching a false, unspiritual gospel. By his own admission, he has fed the Corinthians on milk and not taught them the wisdom spoken among the perfect. He attempts to correct this in his letter by hinting at his secret spiritual knowledge. A key section is when Paul defends himself against those who say he is not even an apostle:

> *Am I not free? Am I not an apostle? Have I not seen Jesus our Lord? Are you not my work in the Lord? If I am not an apostle to others, at least I am to you; for the seal of my apostleship are you in the Lord. (1 Corinthians 9:1-2)*

Paul is "free" because he is free from the Law and he has seen Jesus spiritually. These are two signs of the perfect. Even if others doubt him as an apostle, he should still be an apostle to those in Corinth because of the role he played in the development of their church. What exactly was this role? Paul sees the church at Corinth as being largely his own work. In Acts 18, Paul stays with Aquila and Priscilla at Corinth while talking in the synagogue and converting many Corinthians but also arousing the wrath of the Jews. The impression from Acts is that Paul virtually starts the Corinth church single handed, although we should note that Aquila and Priscilla are at Corinth before Paul. But Acts is a fiction concocted from the letters of Paul and other scraps of information. The idea that Aquila and Priscilla were in Corinth is likely to have come from the greeting that they and their household send to the Corinthians.[252]

What is more intriguing is that Paul says that of all the Corinthians, he only baptised Crispus, Gaius and the household of Stephanas, although he admits that he may have forgotten a few others.[253] If Paul really developed the church in Corinth single-handedly then who baptised everyone else? Paul calls the household of Stephanas the *"first fruits of Achaia"*[254] meaning that they were among the first converts in the Roman province of Achaia which covers most of Greece including Corinth. Although we may wonder if Paul is exaggerating a little here because of his own role in baptising Stephanas, it is evidence that Paul was part of the very first mission to Corinth and Greece. However, he cannot have been alone. You cannot start a church with three converts; there must have been many more and someone must have baptised them all.

We would expect this person to be the most senior member of the church available. If this were Paul then more or less everyone in this first wave would have been baptised by him. But they were not, so Paul must have taken them to someone else for baptism. All of which makes perfect sense if Corinth was the start of Paul's mission to the Gentiles. He has just been accepted into the church after his meeting with Cephas in Jerusalem. But he is on probation having persecuted the church as a member of the Jewish establishment. So he is sent on a distant mission among Gentiles where he can do little harm to the church should he revert to his past behaviour. Paul is not on his own on this mission but is part of a small group and he is not the leader of that group.

We have the name of Paul's likely senior at Corinth. In Romans, Paul commends a woman called Phoebe who is described as a minister of the church at Cenchrea. The word for "minister" is in this one place rendered as "servant" in most translations because Phoebe is a woman, but there is no reason to believe that her role was any different from male ministers. The case of Phoebe has become prominent as an argument for the ordination of women priests, but we are more interested in Phoebe herself. Her mission in Rome must be something important because Paul writes her a blank cheque calling on the church in Rome to do whatever she asks them to:

And I commend to you Phoebe our sister, a minister of the church that is in Cenchrea that you may receive her in the Lord, as does become saints, and may assist her in whatever matter she may have need of you. For she has been a leader (prostatis) of many, and of myself also. (Romans 16:1-2)

The last phrase uses *prostatis* the feminine form of a word that usually means a person who is placed over others but which here is usually translated as a succourer. The conventional commentators and translators cannot accept the possibility that a woman was placed over others in the church and certainly not over Paul, one of the two pillars of the church. So they make her Paul's patroness, giving him lodgings and seeing that he is fed and his clothes mended. But Paul's words literally mean that she was at one time his leader. Paul does not seem to have any problems with this and neither should we.

In fact, in the context of Paul's letters it all makes perfect sense. Cenchrea is the eastern seaport of Corinth. And there is a data point that places Paul in Cenchrea. In Acts, we read that *"he shaved his head in Cenchrea for he had a vow" (Acts 18:18)*. In the narrative, this occurs as Paul is leaving Corinth for Syria with Aquila and Priscilla, but behind it must be a source that has Paul fulfilling a Nazarite vow in Cenchrea. Such a vow involved the person growing his hair long until the fulfilment of the vow. Theoretically the hair should be cut in the Jerusalem temple but as this was inconvenient for Jews who lived aboard they would fulfil the vow wherever they happened to be.

Although it is natural to see the church at Cenchrea as being subsidiary to its much more prominent sister in Corinth, this is not necessarily the historical order. The first Jesus missionaries would have arrived at Cenchrea by sea from Palestine. They were foreign Jews teaching a strange new religion and would have stood out a mile in the hedonistic Greek city of Corinth. Surely Cenchrea was a much better place to establish a beachhead. The seaport would be filled with people from all over the Roman Empire and the Jews would have blended in better. And they would have been right there by the ships, able to serve their fellow missionaries who might arrive at the port and to receive and pass on the news from Jerusalem and other places. They would also be well placed to make a quick escape if necessary.

Phoebe is a Greek name and she is likely to have been a Jew of the diaspora like Paul himself. It would be natural to send diaspora Jews on a mission to Corinth because they would be more attuned to Gentile culture than Jews from Palestine. Phoebe is likely to have travelled with a male relative, such as her husband or brother and Paul would have been a member of their small group. It is possible that the account in Acts 18 of Paul working in Corinth with a Jewish couple who were already in the movement is based on a memory of this courageous little group. If so, the author of Acts has wrongly identified the couple as Aquila and Priscilla because of the greeting in 1 Corinthians 16:19. The group set up their base at Cenchrea under the leadership of Phoebe and Paul took a Nazarite vow there not to cut his hair until he had developed the church in nearby Corinth. Although Phoebe was nominally the leader, it was Paul who proved to be more talented and dynamic. He succeeded in his vow and was on his way to being the self-styled apostle to the Gentiles. By the time that he wrote his letter to the Romans, he had travelled widely having played a prominent role in the establishment of several churches whereas Phoebe had remained at Cenchrea.

In Acts 18, the mission to Corinth occurs quite late in Paul's career but if he were under Phoebe in Corinth this must have happened right at the beginning before he had risen to prominence. Which explains why Paul says that the Corinthians are the "seal" of his apostleship; they are his very first success, the proof from God that he really is an apostle. However, his apostleship was not universally accepted in the church and he was repeatedly forced to defend himself. It is ironic that one who was doubted by so many in his own time should become the main authority for Christian doctrine. The loose cannon Paul became such an authority because of his evangelical role in developing the church among the Gentiles and his brilliance at writing letters. We hear from Paul but not from those who disagreed with him and the development of the church has been distorted ever since. From the evidence of his letters, Paul was un-spiritual in outlook despite his protestations to the contrary and his boasting of spiritual experiences. His obsession is with the world to come and with spreading the word in this world. We must remember that 1 Corinthians was written because Apollos is trying to correct Paul's teachings at Corinth. The Corinthians are confused and do not know who to believe. Paul is now desperately trying to impress them with a more spiritual gospel, to show that he, like Apollos, can talk wisdom among the perfect.

Paul clearly knows about the spiritual teachings; he claims that he has not passed them on because the Corinthians are not ready for them. But we may suspect that the real reason lies with Paul himself; that he has not fully internalised the teachings, and that perhaps ultimately he does not fully believe in them. Returning to 1 Corinthians 9 after outlining the issue of those who doubt him as an apostle he goes on to give his defence:

My defence to those that examine me is this,

Paul uses the legal terms for defence and examine as if he stood in a court of law. He is going to give the reasons why he is an apostle:

Have we not power to eat and to drink?
Have we not power to lead about a sister, a wife, as well as other apostles, and as the brethren of the Lord, and Cephas?
Or only I and Barnabas, do we not have the power not to work? (1 Corinthians 9:3-6)

The word here for power, *exousian*, is normally translated here as "right" but can mean either the authority to do a thing or the ability to do a thing. This is illustrated by two uses of the same word in Mark. In Mark 1:22 Jesus' audience are amazed because he teaches them as "*one that had authority (exousian).*" In Mark 3:15 Jesus gives his disciples "*power (exousian) to cast out demons.*" The two uses are not that different because the physical or spiritual ability to do a thing could be regarded as a type of authority that has come from God.

It is at first sight puzzling why Paul should claim the power to do these three things as his defence for being an apostle. It is even more puzzling that under the standard interpretation Paul then goes on to demonstrate that none of the three apply to himself! Instead of giving his defence he would seem to be convicting himself. There must be a meaning to Paul's words that has not been grasped by the standard interpretation.

We have seen that the second point gives an impressive list of authorities; the apostles, the brethren of the Lord, Cephas; a list that is in ascending order and ends with the highest human authority, Cephas. It is normally interpreted to mean that the apostle could take a wife around with him. However, Paul has told us elsewhere that he is not married so why does he include this point in his defence? There is a completely different interpretation possible of this line; that the wife and sister is a man's spirit. The power to lead about the wife and sister is a spiritual power. Although Paul is not married, he is claiming a spiritual wife so as to be included within his distinguished list alongside the other apostles.

Of course, Paul includes Cephas and we have argued that Cephas is a name used by Mary. As such she would not have a sister a wife but a brother and husband, namely Jesus. She has to be included in the list because she is the pre-eminent example of the phenomenon. The reasons why

Paul does not spell out that she has a husband are twofold. First Cephas is her male pseudonym and her true identity must be protected - there is no way that Paul can tell us that Cephas has a husband! Second Paul states only the male case but intends "a sister, a wife" to apply to women as well as men. This is clear from the fact that "apostles" as a group included some women and yet Paul does not specify "a brother, a husband" for them. He intended his listener to adjust his words to make them suitable to the female case where appropriate. It was not normal to specify the female case explicitly and until very recently this was also the practice in English. Victorian writers, both male and female, used "he" to include the female as well as the male. It is our culture that is odd in this respect for we are very conscious of the female reader or listener and will take care not to offend her. But this attitude did not exist before the twentieth century for it presupposes a culture where women have economic and political power equivalent to men.

The last point in Paul's list of three has a different form from the preceding two; "*or I only and Barnabas*". It is intended to contrast the two of them with the other apostles to make an ironic point. Paul then gives an elaborate explanation of why he does not have this right not to work. To understand Paul's argument we must grasp one fact that the reader is likely to miss; Paul is infringing the code of the Jesus movement by not being supported by the local church. He has broken a commandment and is defending himself by trying to turn this negative into a positive. He does this very successfully, showing his considerable skill in constructing an argument. First he sets out why he has a right to be supported. A soldier does not serve at his own expense nor does a man keep a vineyard and not drink the wine. A person serving at the temple can eat the things of the temple. However, although others have availed themselves of this right with the Corinthians (a dig at Apollos?) he and Barnabas do not. He requires no reward for preaching the gospel and indeed he has no choice but to preach the gospel.

Paul's argument is masterful and shows his genius in being able to frame an issue to suit his purpose. Paul does something very subtle; he portrays being supported by the flock as pay for services rendered. By waiving his pay, Paul casts himself in a magnanimous light and makes his opponents, who are supported by the flock, look like mercenaries. As he says "*that proclaiming the gospel without charge I shall make the gospel of the Christ, and not abuse my authority in the gospel*" (*1 Corinthians 9:18*). The implication is that those who have been supported have abused their authority. However, at one point of his argument Paul gives us a glimpse of the truth:

So also, the Lord has ordained that those who preach the gospel should live of the gospel. (1 Corinthians 9:14)

Jesus has commanded that preachers should be supported by their flock and should not pay their way! We can see this command being issued by Mary/Cephas. It fits in with everything we know about the early Jesus movement. In Thomas those who taught the gospel were to *"Become passers-by" (Thomas 42)* and were to be reliant on the hospitality of those who receive them.[255] In Mark, Jesus sends out his disciples to travel with nothing but a staff; no money and no spare cloths![256]The very early text, the Didache, shows a world of itinerant preachers and prophets who live in complete poverty and who are dependent upon more settled supporters for a meal and a bed for the night. From the very beginning, this commandment of total poverty and reliance on others has rarely been kept. Almost every Christian, from Paul onwards, has had to make their excuses.

The embrace of poverty freed the Christian from the power of the Seventy, but there were also practical benefits. Religions that make extreme demands on their converts are more successful than those that accept lukewarm adherents. And the instruction for poverty gave a powerful impetus to evangelism. There is nowhere for the itinerant preacher to rest or to hide. If they do not make converts they will starve. The support they receive from their fellow Christians is not pay. The preacher humbles him or herself to accept from those they teach and puts his or her trust completely in God to provide. But Paul does not do this. He has retained some means to pay his way.

Paul's three discourses

We can see that Paul is being defensive in relation to the third power, not to work. Because he fails this test, he immediately leaps into his own defence. But what about the other two powers? The power to eat and drink and the power to lead a sister, a wife? In the conventional interpretation, these are all bound up with the right not to work. Under this interpretation the right to eat and drink is the right to be given these essentials by the church, and the right to lead a sister, a wife is the right to have a spouse supported also. But why should Paul give these three criteria as his defence when he does not pass any of them? It would make more sense if Paul satisfied the first two but was deficient on the third, a deficiency he turns around brilliantly by claiming that he does better than if he exercised his right.

When Paul talks about the wife and sister does he mean a man's spirit? There is certainly no reference to a wife anywhere in Paul's defence of working and we know of no other source that suggests early preachers had a right to have a wife supported. However, if the wife and sister is spiritual then what is the meaning of the power to eat and drink?

Paul's defence of working does talk about food and drink as might be expected. He asks who plants a vineyard and does not eat of the fruit or who keeps a flock and does not drink of the milk. Does this mean that the first point is supposed to be ordinary food and drink, the right to be fed? If so the idea that the sister/wife is intended to be spiritual would be undermined for it is unlikely that the second point alone should be interpreted spiritually.

The resolution of this problem is that conventional interpreters have been looking at too short a section of 1 Corinthians. Under their interpretation, Paul expounds his three themes in the twenty-one verses from 9:7. Yet if we look at Paul's argument in the larger context of his letter we will see that Paul's discourse on the three proofs of an apostle is far longer than generally supposed. It actually runs for seventy verses all the way until section 11:16. After Paul states the three powers of an apostle he engages with the last one first, by claiming that he does have the power to be supported but chooses not to use it. He then goes back to the two other powers, eating and drinking, and male and female, and covers them in two sections. Each power in 1 Corinthians 9:4-6 corresponds to a section in the following passages in 1 Corinthians 9:7-11:16 as is shown below.

Paul's first discourse (1 Corinthians 9:7-27)

This addresses the third power - *"Or only I and Barnabas, do we not have the power not to work?"*

Paul first explains why he has the right to be supported and how the Lord has instructed that those who preach the gospel should receive their living from the gospel. He explains that he does not use this right for the sake of the Corinthians.

Paul then sets out his philosophy of being all things to all men for the sake of the gospel that he may "share in its blessings". Paul here is justifying his deviation from the Lord's instruction on the grounds of the greater good from bringing the Corinthians into the gospel. By doing this, Paul will share in the blessings spiritually rather than materially.

Paul makes a comparison with a runner winning a prize. It is necessary to train for a race and so he strikes a blow to his body to make it his slave. Paul lives lean, so he does not need to take advantage of the power of not working.

Paul's second discourse (1 Corinthians 10:1-33)

This addresses the first power *"Have we not power to eat and to drink?"*

Paul considers food and drink in the spiritual sense with reference to the Israelites in the desert and the blood and body of Christ.

He then develops the argument as to whether it is permissible to eat food sacrificed to idols.

Paul's third discourse (1 Corinthians 11:1-16)

This addresses the second power -- *"Have we not power to lead about a sister, a wife, as well as other apostles, and as the brethren of the Lord, and Cephas?"*

Paul considers the relationship of male and female in an abstruse passage with an underlying spiritual meaning. The head of the woman is the man, and a woman must be veiled for prophecy and prayer. A woman must have power over her head because of the angels. But also - *"Woman is not separate from man nor man from the woman in the Lord."*

The power to eat and drink

The passage on food and drink occupies the whole of chapter 10 of 1 Corinthians. Paul starts by telling of how the Israelites were baptised by Moses "under the cloud and under the sea" meaning the pillar of fire and cloud that accompanied the Israelites and the crossing of the Red Sea. These will symbolise the baptism of the spirit and the baptism of water. Paul continues:

They all ate the same spiritual food, and all drank the same spiritual drink. For they drank from the spiritual rock following them, and the rock was Christ. (1 Corinthians 10:3-4)

The word used for rock here, *petra*, is the base for Peter, the Greek form of Cephas. The Rock, Cephas and the Christ are one. The idea of the rock accompanying the Israelites is a Jewish legend. The rock struck by Moses to give water in the desert is supposed to have followed them around for forty years. Paul has applied it to the Christians; the Christ that is in Mary/Cephas is always with them. The water flowing from the rock is the spiritual baptism of Jesus, the water that cleanses the inside rather than the outside of the cup. The use of water is common imagery in early Christian sources. For example, in Thomas 13 Jesus says *"I am not your master, because you have drunk, you have become drunk from the bubbling spring that I have measured out."* And the Samaritan woman is offered living water. Drinking the water is the baptism of Jesus, the pouring in of the essence of Jesus into the person. Water is also a common image in the Old Testament:

For I will pour water upon the thirsty land and streams upon the dry ground. I will pour out my spirit on your seed and my blessing on your offspring. (Isaiah 44:3)

Paul warns the Corinthians not to be like the Israelites who although they had partaken of the spiritual water and bread yet fell away through lusting after evil things, such as idol worship and fornication. He continues:

The cup of blessing which we bless, is it not the communion of the blood of Christ? The bread which we break, is it not the communion of the body of Christ? (1 Corinthians 10:16)

This makes clear the meaning of the spiritual food and drink. Paul's power to eat and drink has come down to us as the Eucharist, not an empty ceremony as is practised in the churches today, but a filling of a person with the substance of Christ, a substance that has always been spiritual and not of the flesh. The spiritual food can probably also be found in the Lord's prayer: *"give us this day our epiousion bread"*. The word *epiousion* although normally translated "daily" is found nowhere else except here and was not in common use. It is a technical term invented by the Jesus movement and used specifically to describe the significance of the bread. St Jerome translated it two different ways; once as daily and once as *supersubstantial* bread. However, it cannot be daily that is meant because the phrase "give us this day our daily..." is redundant and because no one would use such an obscure word for such a simple everyday meaning. The word is a compound of *epi* which can be translated as "on" but which has a range of meanings depending upon the context and *ousia* meaning property or substance.

The only use of *ousia* in the New Testament is the story of the prodigal son in Luke 15:11-31. The younger son asks for his share of his father's property or estate and the word *ousia* is used to signify this property. This story shows some close affinities to the Hymn of the Pearl and can be interpreted with the younger son representing the human soul. The soul has journeyed from heaven to the distant country (the world) where it becomes corrupted by prostitutes (the demons) who consume its inheritance. The son eventually repents and returns to his father who greets him with joy and clothes him in a robe, his heavenly garment. The elder son, who is disgusted at this preference shown to his prodigal brother, represents the angels. The angels are portrayed as being older than mankind, of being in constant attendance on God just as the elder son is always with his father, as desiring mankind's punishment and of being jealous of God's redeeming love for mankind. If so then *ousia* represents the food and substance of heaven. This would be consistent with the Gospel of Thomas where property and riches represents the kingdom of heaven.

So our daily *epiousion* bread is the spiritual bread of heaven, and is the same as Paul's spiritual food. In Exodus 16 God sends down day by day the manna to the Israelites in the desert, the bread of heaven. In Psalm 78:25 this is called the "bread of angels". Later in 1 Corinthians Paul connects the food and drink to Jesus' death:

> For I received from the Lord that which also I delivered to you, that the Lord Jesus on the night he was delivered up (paredideto), took bread, and having given thanks, he broke it and said, "This is my body, which is for you; do this in remembrance of me." Likewise, after supper he took the cup saying, "This cup is the new covenant in my blood; do this as often as you drink it, in remembrance of me." (1 Corinthians 11:23-25)

Paul gives this as having been received from the Lord; that is as coming from Jesus himself. It can only be the resurrected Jesus that is intended here. Either Paul has received this through direct spiritual revelation from Jesus or he has heard it through the medium of the shaman Cephas/Mary. We can rule out direct revelation because Paul is not going to invent anything so fundamental as the Eucharist! The baptism of Jesus, the drinking and eating of his substance is intimately connected to the sacrifice of his death and with the resurrection. The idea that the flesh and blood of Jesus are bread and wine must go back to the founder.

This episode finds its way into the Gospel of Mark and becomes part of proto-orthodox belief. It is the only place in the letters of Paul where he seems to recount an actual incident from Jesus' life and ironically it is among the strongest evidence that Jesus was not a man who lived in the lifetime of the apostle. The reason is the source given by Paul for the information; Jesus himself. Had this been a real physical event then those present, the disciples including Cephas/Peter, would have told Paul about it directly, and he would have given them as the source. Instead, Paul tells us he received it from Jesus. There is no way that Paul could have got the information from the living Jesus before he died so his source can only be the resurrected Jesus. But we are talking about a supposedly real event in Jesus' life to which there had been eye witnesses, the same disciples who are now the leading apostles including Cephas. How can Paul possibly give his own spiritual revelations of such an event when these would be indignantly corrected by the leaders of the movement who were actually there? Paul would never have attempted this and if he had his version would have been immediately rejected by the movement. Paul must know that his account cannot be contradicted by those with higher authority; either it comes from Jesus through the medium of the leader; or it comes from his own direct revelations and takes place in heaven or a remote and mythical past.

Perhaps the best exposition of the bread and water of life comes in the Gospel of John. The previous day Jesus had performed the miracle of feeding the multitude with loaves and fishes. The people come searching for Jesus clearly expecting more miracles. He says to them:

Jesus answered them and said, "Truly, truly, I say to you, you seek me not because you saw signs, but because you ate of the loaves and were filled." (John 6:26)

The implication is that the bread he has given them is heavenly bread. The people press him for a sign that they might believe in him:

"Our fathers ate manna in the wilderness, as it is written: 'He gave them bread from heaven to eat.'"(John 6:31)

Not satisfied with the miracle of the loaves and fishes the people are asking him for a regular supply of bread as they imply Moses has given them. The author of John portrays his fellow Jews as being set only on material things, bread they can eat to fill their stomachs, unable to see Jesus for what he is. Jesus corrects their quotation of the manna from heaven:

Jesus said to them, "Truly, truly, I say to you, it is not Moses who has given you the bread from heaven, but my Father gives you the true bread from heaven." (John 6:32)

He continues:

For the bread of God is that which comes out of heaven and gives life to the world." Therefore they said to him, "Sir, always give to us this bread." Then Jesus declared, "I am the bread of life. Whoever comes to me will never hunger, whoever believes in me shall never thirst." (John 6:33-35)

Jesus is the bread and the water. He has come down from heaven and will fill his followers so that they will never hunger or thirst. Note how the author of John defines this as applying to those who believe in Jesus, which is typical of the Gospel of John. Of course at one level, it is only those who believe in Jesus, his followers, who will eat of the bread and drink of the water. But belief alone is not sufficient. The original followers of the way experienced the resurrected Jesus entering mystically into their very substance so that they became Jesus. This is what is meant by eating the bread and drinking the water. It is the baptism of Jesus, made possible only by his sacrifice.

The author of John, who thinks Jesus was a man, has to translate all this into his literalistic story. His problem is that Jesus offering his substance for the people to eat and drink makes Christianity resemble a cannibal feast. The substance of the real Jesus was spiritual and heavenly and by consuming his substance the believer shares in his life. Note the connections between the descriptions of the food and drink in Paul and John. Both Paul and John compare the spiritual bread to the manna in the desert. Earlier in 1 Corinthians Paul talks of the Jews as asking for a sign (1 Corinthians 1:22), which is exactly what they do in the John story.

We can see how important the power to eat and drink is and why it is a sign of the apostle. It is nothing less than the baptism of Jesus, so much greater than the original water baptism of the believer. The apostle brings this heavenly bread and drink to his flock as Paul does to the Corinthians.

After addressing the spiritual aspects of food and drink Paul moves on to the question of eating food sacrificed to idols. This was a significant issue to the early Jesus movement as much of the food that you could buy in public markets had been sacrificed to the Roman gods. Paul's argument here is contradictory. He starts by saying that the Corinthians should not participate in eating the sacrifices: "*You cannot drink the cup of the Lord and the cup of demons*" (1 Corinthians 10:21) but they also have freedom from the Jewish Law: "*all things are lawful but not all things are profitable*" (1 Corinthians 10:23). So they are able to eat anything bought at the market or the house of an unbeliever without raising questions of conscience. But he then makes an about turn by saying that if they know the food has been sacrificed to idols they should not eat out of conscience. This contradicts what he has just said about freedom from the law, and he quickly reverses again by saying this is not their own conscience but the conscience of the other person. He then gets defensive: "*For if I with thankfulness partake, why am I denounced for that for which I give thanks?*" (1 Corinthians 10:30). It seems some have been accusing Paul of eating food sacrificed to idols.

Paul's argument is confused because he oscillates between two positions; the Jewish position that it was never permitted to eat food sacrificed to idols; and the radical teachings of the Jesus movement that the Law no longer applied, so it was fine to eat such food so long as you did not believe that the idols were real gods. This reflects a fault line within the movement with those on the traditional side being very unhappy about the abolition of the Law. Paul is on the radical side of the divide but is attempting to compromise and not antagonise the traditionalists.

What we are seeing is resistance to the abolition of the Law, exactly as we would expect in response to such a radical new teaching. Paul's position is actually very similar to that in the Gospel of Thomas. Compare the instruction to eat food in the house of unbelievers with Thomas 14: "*And if you go into any land and walk in its regions, if they receive you eat what they set before you.*" However in Revelation we see a very different attitude. Some in the church of Pergamum are criticised: "*that hold the doctrine of Balaam, who taught Balak to cast a stumbling block before the sons of Israel, to eat things sacrificed to idols, and to commit sexual immorality*" (Revelation 2.14). The accusation is odd because Balaam was reputed to have devised a strategy in which the Israelite men were seduced by women of Moab and so turned to worship Baal-peor.[257] This cannot mean simply the taking of pagan wives or husbands because those of the church at Pergamum are accused of adopting the same philosophy as Balaam. This must mean that they are teaching those in the church to take a "wife" and that the taking of this wife then leads to eating food sacrificed to idols and sexual immorality. We find exactly this teaching in the belief that every man has a potential spiritual "wife" who brings freedom from the Law including the ability to eat food sacrificed to idols without sin. We know from the letters of Paul that some interpreted this freedom of the spirit to include sexual freedoms leading to the accusation from their traditionalist enemies that they were fornicators. This would also seem to be behind the criticism of the church in Thyatira:

"But I have this against you that you tolerate the woman Jezebel, the one calling herself a prophetess, and who is teaching and misleading my servants into sexual immorality and to eat things sacrificed to idols." (Revelation 2:20)

Who is this Jezebel? The Jesus of Revelation says that he will cast her on a bed of suffering along with those who commit adultery with her and will strike her children dead. The original Jezebel was the queen of King Ahab who, according to Kings, tried to bring in the worship of Baal and Asherah. With her husband, she ruled the northern kingdom of Israel from Samaria. Jezebel is clearly not the real name of the Christian prophetess. Neither does Jezebel represent a woman of the church of Thyatira, as such a woman would have only local significance. No, she must be the leader of a faction of the Jesus movement. The crimes alleged against her and her "children" are in fact the same as those made against the church in Pergamum, supposed crimes that arose from the freedom of the spirit; eating food sacrificed to idols and sexual immorality. Indeed in 1 Corinthians Paul is putting forward precisely the arguments on eating food sacrificed to idols that Revelation is condemning!

The author of Revelation is a Jewish minded traditionalist who rejects some of the innovations made by the early Jesus movement and has Jesus condemn those who follow these innovations through his message to the seven churches. And this brings us to the identity of Jezebel. The best fit for Jezebel is none other than Mary herself; she is the prophetess of the movement and the mother of the church; she has introduced the freedom under the spirit and the elimination of dietary rules; she was regarded by some as coming from Samaria like Jezebel. This is not to say that the author of Revelation was against Mary for she also appears in other very positive guises. This apparent contradiction is explained because the book of Revelation is written comparatively late in the 80s or 90s and is drawing upon earlier material both from the followers of Mary and from her enemies within the Christ movement. By the time of Revelation, things are so confused that people do not realise that the same woman is being spoken about in both positive and negative sources. The author of Revelation belongs to a group that has accepted the coming of Jesus through Mary but has rejected the abrogation of the law. So we have images of Mary both in her positive spiritual role (the woman in the heavens with a crown of twelve stars) and as the hated abrogator of the law (Jezebel).

Wife and sister

The second of Paul's list of powers, that of leading a sister, a wife, is addressed in the next section of Paul's letter (1 Corinthians 11:3-16) which ostensibly is about head covering. Paul begins with a statement about the relationship of man and woman:

But I would have you know, that the head of every man is Christ; and the head of the woman is the man; and the head of Christ is God.

Paul is saying that one of the attributes given to the male is authority. He establishes a hierarchy of God-Christ-Man-Woman. So does Paul mean that women are to be subservient to their husbands in things spiritual? There are two problems with this. First, Paul elsewhere recommends that those who are not married should stay as there are. Such advice contradicts the idea of a woman being spiritually dependent upon a man. The second problem is that of a female member of the movement married to an unbelieving husband, a very common occurrence at the time. Paul says that such a woman should remain married. But if her husband is her head then should she not follow her husband's religion? Is she not being disobedient by her very belief in Christ?

Even for women in a Christian marriage the sentiment expressed would seem to be at variance with everything we know about the movement. For if her husband is her head then is not her redemption conditional upon her husband? How can she be saved if her husband is not, since she is required to go through him to reach Christ? But nowhere else do we encounter this idea of one person being dependent spiritually on another.

Such considerations show that Paul is not talking about a physical wife or husband, but the spiritual wife or husband. A woman has a spiritual husband, and it is this spiritual husband who is her true "head". Of course, a woman should still obey her worldly husband if she has one, but only if this does not conflict with spiritual matters. In the case of a woman who is not married life becomes much simpler if she stays unmarried because she can then devote her existence to her spiritual husband and through him to Christ. A woman married in the flesh to an unbeliever is still married spiritually to her true angelic husband. So her obedience to her husband in the flesh will be limited to areas that do not conflict with her spirit. We know that a great deal of conflict arose in such cases because there are many areas in which Christian women did not obey their non-believing husbands.

Paul's hierarchy is probably his invention. The problem with the male-female spiritual model for males in the ancient world is that a man has to go through his spiritual wife to engage with the things of heaven. This means the male being subservient to the female spirit, something that is difficult for men like Paul to swallow. None of which applies to one who can see the spirit for his beloved has a beauty like no woman on earth. But it is difficult to believe that the spiritual wife was real in this sense to Paul; he claims his wife as he does not want to appear deficient, but she is nothing but an abstraction for him. His hierarchy has the advantage of bypassing the sister, the wife by putting Jesus directly as a man's head. In his letters, it is his direct spiritual revelations of Jesus that he continually stresses. There is little of the female spiritual in Paul's writings, and he is in perpetual conflict with someone or other, a sure sign that the female spiritual aspect is not ruling his behaviour.

It would seem that Paul was one of the small minority to whom the spiritual principle appears in the form of an angel of the same sex. For Paul, the spiritual partner is represented by Christ himself. There is nothing invalid about this; the male-female pairing of the person and spirit is ultimately a subjective way of experiencing something whose reality transcends categorisation. The spirit is the interface with God and for most people appears as a contra-sexual union, as represented by the prototype of Mary and Jesus. But there will always be those who see the spirit differently and their experiences are not less valid on that account.

Returning to Paul's argument concerning male and female he continues:

Every man praying or prophesying, having his head covered, dishonours his head. But every woman that prays or prophesies with her head uncovered dishonours her head: for it is as if she were shaven.

We must consider this in the light of the previous line where the head of a man is Christ, and that of a woman is man. Paul now uses head in its physical sense to consider whether the head should be covered or veiled. A man should not cover his physical head because this would dishonour his spiritual head, namely Christ; he is in the same image as Christ. A female, however, should have her physical head covered because otherwise this would dishonour her spiritual head. In Jewish culture, a woman would have her head covered in a public place just as Muslims do today. The reason is that her beauty, and particularly the beauty of her hair, should be reserved for her husband alone. By not being covered a woman would dishonour her husband.

Paul is quite specific about the times when a woman should be covered – in prayer and while prophesying. Invariably this is interpreted as meaning that she should be covered in church but this is not what Paul says. Church members ate a meal together and were involved in teaching and instruction. But Paul does not include any of these activities. Neither does he say that a woman only needs to be covered if she is praying or prophesying in church. Pray and prophecy would seem to be intended even if she is alone.

When reading these words of Paul, the standard interpretation is that a woman should be covered so as not to distract the male members of the congregation. But if her husband is a spiritual husband then the point is that she should not dishonour him. It is not a question of whom she is with; to pay him honour she should be dressed appropriately when invoking his presence even if alone. In the Shepherd of Hermas the woman who represents the church is at one point described as being covered as she comes from the bridal chamber:

> ... *a virgin arrayed as if she were going forth from a bridal-chamber all in white and with white sandals, veiled up to her forehead, and her head-covering consisted of a turban ... (Shepherd of Hermas 23:1)*[258]

So should a woman entering into the bridal chamber with her spiritual husband have her head covered? Paul continues:

> *For if the woman be not covered, let her also be shorn: but if it be a shame for a woman to be shorn or shaven, let her be covered.*

To be shorn is the sign of an adulteress or prostitute. What Paul is saying is that if a woman is not arrayed properly for the bridal chamber then she might as well be a whore. The Gospel of Philip talks in a similar way about the bride and the bridal chamber in a passage that is clearly intended to be spiritual:

If marriage is open to the public it has become prostitution and the bride plays the harlot not only if she is impregnated by another man but even if she slips out of her bedroom and is seen. (Gospel of Philip 82:10-14)[259]

Paul continues:

For a man indeed ought not to cover his head, for he is the image and glory of God: but the woman is the glory of the man. For the man is not of the woman; but the woman of the man. Neither was the man created for the woman; but the woman for the man.

Paul's argument is based on a very traditional view of a woman being subsidiary to the male. She was created for him, not the other way around. The woman is "*of the man*" because of the story of the creation in which woman was made from Adam. We might read "*woman is the glory of man*" as a reference to the beauty of the female so that she is man's ornament and chief pleasure, but we would be wrong. Note how man is "*the image and glory of God*" which is clearly not because of man's beauty. Instead what Paul is saying that that "glory" is passed down from the greater to the lesser. God has breathed his spirit into man, and so man has the glory of God because he is made spiritually out of the substance of God. The female spirit has been extracted from the male spirit, so a woman also has the glory emanating from God, which she has inherited through the male spiritual substance.

The point of this argument is that a woman should look to her spiritual husband and brother because she was made from his substance, whereas a man should look directly to God. Again the argument acts to eliminate the role of the female spirit of a man as an intermediary between him and God. If women feel aggrieved at Paul's argument, then they may reflect on Paul's considerable dilemma as a male in the macho first-century culture. Paul's first problem is that the standard male-female spiritual model should mean that while Mary has a direct spiritual relationship with Jesus, he, Paul, cannot because his spirit is supposed to be female. At a wider level, all men will have female spirits and so will be inferior spiritually to women who will have male spirits in the direct image of God. Paul's argument solves these problems by allowing men to have a direct relationship with God that sidesteps their female spirit. What never occurs to Paul is that the real problem is his assumption that what is female is inferior to what is male. The spirituality of the original Jesus movement originated from a philosophy in which God is hermaphrodite containing male and female aspects. Men and women are made in the image of God and are also hermaphrodite. Male and female are two equal aspects of humanity and God.

The traditionalist will, of course, reject the above argument and will say that Paul is not talking spiritually but simply about women covering their hair in church for the purpose of modesty. But Paul now says something that completely undermines this traditional interpretation:

For this reason the woman should have power on her head because of the angels.

The word for power, *exousian,* is the same that Paul uses to say that he has the power to lead a sister, a wife. Paul here tells us why a woman should have authority over her head, and that is because of the angels. The spirit would be called an angel.[260] A woman must have her head covered in circumstances where her angel is invoked so as to honour her angel.

The alternative explanation is that the angels are the fallen angels who, according to the Book of Enoch, descend to earth out of lust for women. The two explanations are two sides of the same coin. The Jesus movement believed that people were in danger of being seduced by demons such as Mary's seven demon husbands. The demons are the progeny of the fallen angels and are waiting to corrupt a person. As the Gospel of Philip tells us, these demons are male for a woman and female for a male. A person will be liable to be corrupted unless joined in marriage to their spiritual husband or wife. A woman in prayer or prophecy is entering a dangerous spiritual zone and is liable to be seduced, that is possessed, by the demons who inhabit that zone unless joined in a pure marriage with her spiritual husband. She has her hair covered as a sign that the authority of her husband is over her head, and so she guards against the lust of the demons by invoking the protection of her more powerful husband. If she does not have her head covered, she plays the whore and leaves herself open to demonic attack.

Up to now Paul's argument has been entirely one-sided relating only to the female case and the woman's relationship to her brother/husband. He has in fact devalued the role of the sister/wife, a sign of his sense of inferiority around this topic. Paul now seems to realise that his argument has been unbalanced, and he seeks to correct this:

Nevertheless neither is the man without the woman, neither the woman without the man, in the Lord.

If applied, as it commonly is, to marriage this makes absolutely no sense in the context of Paul's teachings. Elsewhere he advises those who are unmarried like himself to stay that way. If the woman is not without the man or the man without the woman in the Lord then why does he not push everyone to marry? Instead we find in this comment an echo of the Gospel of Thomas that to enter the kingdom of heaven *"you make the male and the female into a single one"*. The man and woman are the person and their spirit and it is their union that brings about the kingdom. Paul continues:

For as the woman is of the man, even so is the man also by the woman; but all things of God.

However way we look at it Paul is flatly contradicting his earlier statement that the male is not of the female. The likely reason is that Paul is rebalancing his remarks because he feels he strayed too far from the original doctrines of Mary to whom male and female aspects are equal. He is now reaffirming the central elements of the movement's doctrine even though it does contradict his earlier arguments. In the ancient world there were no word processors but only scribes. Paul will be thinking as he dictates and is developing his arguments to some extent on the fly.

The conventional view is that by saying the man is by the woman Paul is making a reference to worldly birth through the mother. Another possibility is that he is propounding an idea whereby what is of the flesh has been taken from what is spiritual in heaven, the remnant of the spirit. So a woman is made from the man because the female element of the original breath has been taken away from the male element; the male element remains in heaven as an angel whereas the female is encased in the body. But for a man it is the opposite way around. The male has been split off from the female half which remains in heaven. So a man is from a woman just as a woman is of a man. Paul ends with a straightforward appeal to custom and authority:

Judge in yourselves: is it becoming that a woman pray to God uncovered? Does not even nature itself teach you, that, if a man has long hair, it is a dishonour to him? But if a woman has long hair, it is a glory to her? For the long hair is given to her instead of a covering. If anyone is inclined to be contentious, we have no such practice, nor do the churches of God.

Paul's argument now descends from the spiritual and theoretical to the practical and directive. First, he suggests that it is natural for men to have their hair short and women their hair long, which he takes as implying that women should be covered. Then he tells his audience that if any should still dispute the point, it is simply not done any other way in the churches.

Paul's argument is difficult and contradictory because it operates at different levels; he is trying to enforce proper conduct within the Corinthian church and he is working against the background of the spiritual beliefs promulgated by Mary/Cephas. This is the wisdom spoken among the perfect with which he is trying to impress the Corinthians who have already been instructed in certain elements by Apollos. Against this background, he is propelled by his need to set out the arguments to support his own situation and establish a direct relationship between a man and the Christ. Given these conflicting demands it is not surprising that Paul is not completely coherent.

In the Odes of Solomon, there is an image that derives from the baptism of Jesus in the Gospel of Mark:

> *The dove fluttered over the head of our Lord Messiah because he was her head.*
> *(Odes Solomon 24:1)*[261]

We have seen how the dove was originally a title of Mary. The image of the dove over the head of Jesus comes from Mark but the idea that he is her head does not. Paul tells us that the head of a woman is the man, and we have interpreted this spiritually. Mary is the dove, and her man is Jesus the Messiah, so he is her head. The Odes frequently reveal the early imagery of the movement although here it also shows influence from the gospels. Either the Odist was familiar with 1 Corinthians or has a source that is dependent upon 1 Corinthians or, more likely, Paul is drawing on earlier imagery for his argument. Another example of the same imagery is found in the Wedding Hymn in the Acts of Thomas, which is dated to the early third century. We have seen how the female figure of the hymn represents Mary and about her it is said:

> *In the crown of her head the king is established,*
> *Feeding with his own ambrosia those who are set under him,*
> *Truth rests upon her head.*
> *(Wedding Hymn, the Acts of Thomas)*

A remarkable account of a woman prophesying, which dates from the second half of the second century, has come down to us from Irenaeus. In *Against Heresies*, he writes against the gnostic sects the foremost of which is that of Valentinus. There were many Valentinian teachers operating in the second century, and they can be divided into an Italian and an Oriental school. We have already seen that the Orientals believed that Jesus had come to earth spiritually through Mary. It would seem that the Valentinians preserved many features of the original movement although they were increasingly mixed with Hellenistic speculation and magical practices. The Valentinian whom Irenaeus most despised was his contemporary Marcus, who belonged to the Oriental school. Irenaeus paints him as a charlatan who uses magical tricks to delude wealthy women. Not only do these women support him financially, but he also seduces them. Such is the venom that Irenaeus directs at Marcus that it is difficult to get an impartial view of him. He must have been widely influential for Irenaeus to devote so much space to him, and this alone tends to dispel Irenaeus' depiction of him as a cheap confidence trickster. It would seem that Marcus was obsessed by the numerical speculations of Gematria, the translation of names into numbers. However, he preserved many Valentinian practices. As well as baptism there was a rite of Redemption, and those who were redeemed were the perfect. It would seem that prophecy was a speciality of Marcus. Interestingly, Irenaeus does not reject the validity of his prophecies but says that they did not come from God but from a demon who was his familiar spirit.[262] Marcus himself claimed that he received his revelations from a female spiritual visitor representing the Tetrad. In Irenaeus' account of the nefarious practices of Marcus we find what may be the best description of a woman in prophesy as practiced by the movement going back to Paul and beyond:

"I am eager to make you a partaker of my Grace since the Father of all does continually behold your angel before His face. Now the place of your angel is among us: it behoves us to become one. Receive first from me and by my Grace. Adorn thyself as a bride who is expecting her bridegroom, that you may be what I am, and I what you are. Establish the seed of light in your nuptial chamber. Receive from me a spouse, and become receptive of him, while you are received by him. Behold Grace has descended upon you; open your mouth and prophesy." (*Against Heresies* 1:13:3[263])

Irenaeus reports that the woman, after being excited to the required pitch of audacity *"utters some nonsense that happens to occur to her"*. He adds that henceforth she considers herself a prophetess. Irenaeus is unrelentingly negative, but he does not say why this is any different from the practice of the church in Paul's day. We know from Paul's letters that the first Christians would regularly prophesy in church and that this was not confined to a few but was widespread among both men and women. Doubtless in Paul's day a sceptic observer would have regarded these prophecies as some nonsense that happens to occur to the person uttering it. Note some illuminating features of this account:

The woman has an angel who the Father "beholds before his face". This links into what we have found with the spirit being regarded as still in heaven and with the Father.

The woman is to dress herself as a bride ready for the bridal chamber. Compare to Paul's having her head covered while prophesying.

The woman receives a spouse after which she can prophesy.

We can see that entering into the bridal chamber and receiving her husband, her angel who is before God's face, allows the woman to prophesy. In the Eucharist ceremony, Marcus tells a woman *"May that Grace who is before all things, and who transcends all knowledge and speech, fill your inner man ..."* (*Against Heresies* 1:13:2).[264] It is clear that Marcus had inherited a tradition that is very similar to what we have deduced from Paul and other sources, where a woman has a male angel as her spiritual counterpart.

Key points

1. In 1 Corinthians Paul is giving his defence against those who says that he is not an apostle. In this defence, Paul states that there are three "powers" that distinguish an apostle - the power to eat and drink, the power to lead a sister a wife and the power not to work.

2. The power to eat and drink is the power to absorb the substance of Christ, which is represented by bread, fruit, fish, wine and water. It is related to the Eucharist and the miracle of the loaves and fishes. One who can eat and drink can minister to others by sharing the substance of Jesus with them. For this reason, it is the first required power of an apostle.

3. The power to lead a sister, a wife, refers to the possession of the spirit (as always Paul only considers the male case). This is the second critical requirement of an apostle.

4. The power not to work refers to Jesus' command that apostles are not to work but are to be supported by those they convert and teach. The purpose is to give an impetus to conversion by making the apostle completely dependent on his or her converts. Paul's difficulty is that he fails this requirement. His argument brilliantly turns this around; he likens the support of an apostle to pay and then claims that he has done better by declining this pay.

5. Conventional commentators think that Paul is addressing one issue, the right to be supported by his flock, in an argument that ends at 1 Corinthians 9:7-27. However, the three issues are actually addressed in a much longer section of three discourses that ends at 1 Corinthians 11:16. Paul addresses the third power first because he is on the defensive. He then addresses the other two in order.

6. Paul's passage on food and drink is clearly spiritual. He compares the Corinthians to the Israelites who are fed by spiritual bread and water in the wilderness. The cup that they drink is the blood of Christ, and the bread is the body of Christ.

7. Paul defends the right to eat meat sacrificed to idols in a passage in which he comes over as very defensive. This shows that there was considerable opposition to the idea that it was ever permitted to defy the Jewish Law by eating such meat. The Jewish author of Revelation shares this view. Revelation singles out for condemnation a woman who it calls "Jezebel" whose "children" practice sexual immorality and eat food sacrificed to idols. Most likely Jezebel is a representation of Mary from her enemies. The author of Revelation has inherited sources both positive and negative about Mary and does not realise that they relate to the same woman.

8. Paul's discourse on male and female is one of the most difficult in his letters. Ostensibly it is about a woman covering her head in prophecy, but there is clearly a spiritual meaning intended. Paul talks about a hierarchy of God, Christ, man and woman in descending order. We can see this as a subversion of Mary's teachings in which an individual attains knowledge of Christ through their spirit. This is unacceptable for Paul because the spirit of a man is female, and he believes he has direct contact with Jesus.

9. Paul must realise that he has gone too far in his argument, for he then reaffirms Mary's doctrine that there is no man without the woman or woman without the man in the Lord. The meaning must be spiritual be-

cause Paul says elsewhere that those who are unmarried should remain unmarried.

10. Paul's instruction that a female should be veiled in prophecy must go back to the original practice of the movement. It is related to the bridal chamber, where a woman is veiled to receive her spiritual husband. The prophetic state is potentially dangerous as it opens a person to demonic possession. The covering of a woman's hair is symbolic of marriage and invokes the protection of her spiritual husband who will protect her from the demons, the "angels" that Paul warns about.

11. We have a remarkable account of a woman adorned as a bride and receiving her spiritual husband in prophecy in a story about the second-century gnostic, Marcus.

Conclusion

In Paul's three powers we get a glimpse of the beliefs of the Jesus movement. However, Paul the Pharisee is a poor guide to the original teachings of Mary because he continually attempts to intellectualise what has been taught. The context of 1 Corinthians is that Apollos has had to correct Paul's teachings to the Corinthians, and Paul is defending his right to be considered an apostle. In his discourse on the three powers, he misrepresents two of them. He casts the instruction not to work as pay for services rendered and changes the divine hierarchy to make it seem that men are not dependent upon their female spirit.

Chapter 35

Did Paul change his name from Saul?

According to Acts, Paul was called Saul when he persecuted the church and only later changed his name to Paul. This seems unlikely, as Paul never hints in his letters that he was called by another name. Can we trace the origins of this idea that Paul was called Saul? And if Paul was not a tent-maker, then how did he make a living?

The conversion of Saul

Paul never tells us what work he does in his letters. In Acts, we read that he is a tent maker but we have seen that this is a misunderstanding and that spreading the tent means spreading the church and the gospel. To understand how Paul can support himself if not by tent-making then we must understand some more of his background. Acts gives us a number of pieces of information about Paul that we find nowhere else – his original name was Saul, he came from the city of Tarsus in Cilicia, he was a Roman citizen and a disciple of the Pharisee Gamaliel. However, the author of Luke and Acts is an incorrigible fantasist and nothing she writes can be accepted without question. We can only really be sure of what Paul tells us in his letters. In Philippians, he does give us some of his background:

> *Circumcised the eighth day, of the nation of Israel, of the tribe of Benjamin, a Hebrew of the Hebrews; as touching the law, a Pharisee; concerning zeal, persecuting the church; touching the righteousness which is in the law, blameless. (Philippians 3:5-6)*

The most interesting piece of information here is that Paul claims to be a Pharisee. Acts tells us that he was a pupil of the great Pharisee teacher Gamaliel, but this is probably derived directly or indirectly from Philippians. Knowing that Paul was a Pharisee, the author of Luke leaps to the more impressive conclusion that he must have studied under the famous Gamaliel. The letters point to Paul having a Hellenistic background. He writes in Greek and when he quotes scripture he does so from the Greek translation of the Septuagint. There is no indication that he could even speak or read Hebrew yet attain to the learning we would expect of a pupil of Gamaliel.

We should treat the information that Paul came from Tarsus with caution because there is nothing in Paul's letters to collaborate it. Indeed, from the letters he appears to be connected to Jerusalem; he is a Pharisee, of the tribe of Benjamin and persecuting the Jesus movement all of which can be linked to Jerusalem. However, equally there is no reason the author of Luke should have invented this connection with Tarsus. In his letters, Paul comes over as a cosmopolitan who is very comfortable interacting with Gentiles and travelling throughout the Empire. We know that there was a Jewish community in Tarsus, and if this were his home, it would explain Paul's Hellenistic background. Perhaps Paul's family had emigrated from Jerusalem only a generation or two previously and kept close ties to their kin in their spiritual and ancestral home by sending their sons back to study. This would explain Paul's connections to that city. The idea that Paul was a Roman citizen is found only in Acts and is derived from his citizenship of Tarsus as the inhabitants had been granted Roman citizenship. However, even had Paul been born in Tarsus this may not have qualified him as a citizen because he was a Jew. In his letters, Paul talks about being beaten by rods which is not a punishment that would be meted out to a Roman citizen. However, at the end of Acts he is sent to Rome for trial which does suggest he was a citizen.

Was Paul named Saul before his conversion? The only evidence is again from Acts, and there is nothing in his letters to suggest he was ever named anything other than Paul. And in this case, we can be confident that the author of Acts has got it wrong. The starting point for understanding why the author of Luke thought that Paul had been called Saul is her fascinating account of his conversion:

Saul, still breathing out threats and murder against the disciples of the Lord, went to the high priest, and asked him for letters to the synagogues in Damascus, that if he found any of the Way, whether they were men or women, he might bring them bound to Jerusalem. And as he journeyed, he came near Damascus: and suddenly there shined round about him a light from heaven. He fell to the earth, and heard a voice saying to him "Saul, Saul, why do you persecute me?" And he said,

"Who are you Lord?" and he replied, "I am Jesus whom you are persecuting. Now arise, and go into the city, and it shall be told you what you must do." And the men travelling with him stood speechless, hearing a voice, but seeing no one. And Saul arose from the earth; and when his eyes were opened, he saw nothing. And leading him by the hand, they brought him to Damascus. And he was three days without sight, and neither did eat nor drink. (Acts 9:1-9)

Meanwhile, Jesus appears to a Christian at Damascus called Ananias in a vision:

And the Lord said to him, "Arise, and go into the street which is called Straight, and inquire in the house of Judas for one called Saul, of Tarsus, for he is praying. He has seen in a vision a man named Ananias coming in, and putting his hand on him, that he might see again." Then Ananias answered, "Lord, I have heard from many about this man, how much evil he has done to your saints at Je-rusalem. And here he has authority from the chief priests to bind all that call on your name." But the Lord said to him, "Go, for this man is my chosen instrument to take my name before the Gentiles, and kings, and the children of Israel. For I will show him how much he must suffer for my name." And Ananias went his way, and entered into the house; and putting his hands on him said, "Brother Saul, the Lord Jesus, who appeared to you on the road as you were coming, has sent me, that you might see again and be filled with the holy spirit." And immediately some-thing like scales fell from his eyes, and he regained his sight. Ho got up and was baptised. And when he had received food he was strengthened. (Acts 9:11-19)

Much of this is absurd. Quite apart from the supernatural elements it shows Paul seeking the authority of the high priest to bring Christians back to Jerusalem in chains. This is impossible because such authority did not belong to the Jews but the Romans. Paul's own description in Galatians is very different:

For you have heard of my former way of life in Judaism, how that beyond meas-ure I persecuted the church of God, and was destroying it. I was advancing in Ju-daism above many of my contemporaries in my own nation, being more exceeding-ly zealous of the traditions of my fathers. But when it pleased God, who set me apart from my mother's womb, and called me by his grace, to reveal his Son in me, that I might preach him among the Gentiles, immediately I did not consult with flesh and blood, nor did I go up to Jerusalem to those which were apostles before me, but I went into Arabia and again returned to Damascus. (Galatians 1:13-17)

There is enough in common with the Acts story to show that this passage in Galatians, either directly or indirectly, is one of the sources used by the author of Luke. Paul starts by saying how he persecuted the church and was an extremist in Judaism; in Acts, Paul is also persecuting the church. But the author of Luke/Acts exaggerates by making Paul breath out threats and murder and by adding the absurd detail of the letters from the high priest. The road to Damascus in the Acts account is clearly based on a misunderstanding of the Galatians passage. In Galatians, Paul returns to Damascus but only after he has travelled to Arabia, a detail that is left out in Acts. There is no suggestion from Paul that his experience took place on the road to Damascus, and neither does Paul mention any light or voice from heaven. And if he had really been struck blind would he not have mentioned that amazing fact?

Paul says that he consulted with no one but went straight to Arabia. Yet in Acts we have the story of Ananias restoring Paul's sight and then baptising him. Clearly Acts is drawing on other sources as well as Galatians. The idea of Paul being renamed on conversion is dubious. Most of the evidence for Christians being renamed in this way disappears on closer inspection (it is based, for example, on Simon being renamed Peter and the sons of Zebedee as Boanerges, but we have explained these in very different ways). The idea that Paul was called Saul in the period when he persecuted the church is suspicious because the name is symbolic of opposition to Christ. The meaning of Christ is the anointed one, the son of David who will inherit the throne of David. Saul was the king who ruled before David and who opposed David.

In fact, we can see close links between the road to Damascus account and the story of Saul and David. In 1 Samuel 26 it is recounted how Saul took an army to hunt down David. However, David slipped into his camp at night and stole his spear and a jug of water. David then calls out to Saul's camp and the sleepy Saul hears his voice although he does not see him. David asks him why he is being hunted:

He also said, "Why is my lord pursuing his servant? What have I done? Or what evil is in my hand?" (1 Samuel 26:18)

Compare this to the voice that Saul hears in the Acts passage:

He fell to the earth, and heard a voice saying to him "Saul, Saul, why do you persecute (diokeis) me?" And he said, "Who are you Lord?" and he replied "I am Jesus whom you are persecuting." (Acts 9:4-5)

The Greek word *dioko* means both to persecute and to pursue. It is used in both the Acts passage *"why do you persecute me?"* and in the Septuagint version of the 1 Samuel passage *"Why is my lord pursuing his servant?* Note the similarities between the two:

Both stories concern (i) Saul and (ii) David/Jesus, the son of David.

In one Saul is traveling with a group of men to apprehend David, in the other Saul is traveling with a group of men to apprehend the followers of Jesus.

In both cases, Saul hears the voice of David/Jesus but does not see him.

In both cases, David/Jesus asks Saul why he is pursuing him.

We can explain all this if the author of Luke has a source, either written by Paul or written about him, that compares Paul's pursuit of the church before his conversion with Saul pursuing David. This comparison draws upon 1 Samuel and has been misunderstood by the author of Luke. She interprets it as meaning that Paul was called Saul before his conversion and led an armed group in pursuit of Christians before hearing the voice of Jesus.

The second story of the conversion of Paul

We have seen that the principle of redundancy is vital to recover the earliest layer of material from the Jesus movement. We can apply this principle to the conversion of Paul because there is another form of the story in Acts. This other version is not one of the two conscious repetitions of the story in Acts 22:4-14 and Acts 26:4-18, but a passage that is not even recognisable as the same story. After the conversion of Saul in Acts, his name does not change to Paul immediately but only after an episode that occurs when Saul and Barnabas, accompanied by John Mark, visit Cyprus:

When they travelled through the whole island as far as Paphos, they found a certain magician, a Jewish false prophet whose name was Bar-Jesus, who was with the proconsul Sergius Paulus, an intelligent man. He summoned Barnabas and Saul because he wanted to hear the word of God. But Elymas the magician (for that is the meaning of his name) was opposing them, seeking to turn away the proconsul from the faith. And Saul, who was also called Paul, having been filled the Holy Spirit, looked intently upon him, and said, "O full of all deceit and all craft, son of the devil, enemy of all righteousness, will you not cease perverting the straight ways the of Lord? And now behold, the hand of the Lord is upon you, and you will be blind, not seeing the sun for a time." Immediately mist and darkness fell upon him, and he went about seeking someone to lead him by the hand. Then the proconsul, having seen that having happened, believed, being astonished at the teaching of the Lord. (Acts 13:6-12)

In this strange episode, the proconsul is called Sergius Paulus (the second name is identical to Paul) and the Jewish false prophet is called Bar-Jesus (son of Jesus). The false prophet is also called Elymas which the Acts says was a translation of *magus*, magician. The closest we can get to this is that Elymas is an Arabic name from *alim* meaning "wise". If so, then Sergius Paulus is described in similar terms as an "*intelligent man*". In fact, we can see that Sergius Paulus and Elymas are two representations of Paul himself. It is Paul who is the "son of Jesus" and who is called "wise" and "intelligent" and who was thought by some to be a magus, a magician. This idea of Paul as a magus is found in later literature where Simon Magus stands for Paul. Behind this story is another version of the conversion of Paul, a version that has elements contributed by Paul's enemies from within the movement. Certainly the accusations that Paul makes against Elymas including "*perverting the straight ways of the Lord*" are similar to the accusations that would be made against Paul by his opponents.

The author of Luke-Acts has not recognised this source as relating to Paul's conversion and drawing on her excellent knowledge of the Roman governance structure, she has confused Paul with the proconsul, Sergius Paulus. Hence the episode is set on Cyprus. The table below shows the similarities between the two stories in Acts.

Acts 13:6-12	Acts 9:1-19
Sergius Paulus (Paul) is converted	Paul is converted under the name Saul
Saul is renamed as Paul. Also shortly after there is a reference to Saul being replaced as king by David (Acts 13:21-22).	The story of the voice on the road to Damascus has been taken from the account of the pursuit of David by Saul in 1 Samuel 26.
Elymas is struck blind	Saul is struck blind
The blindness of Elymas is temporary lasting "for a time".	The blindness of Saul is temporary lasting three days.

Acts 13:6-12	Acts 9:1-19
About Elymas it is said *"he went about seeking someone to lead him by the hand."*	About Saul it is said *"but they led him by the hand."*
"... will you not cease to pervert the straight [eutheias] ways of the Lord?"	*"Arise, and go into the street which is called Straight [eutheian] ..."*

In both episodes, we can find references to Paul being compared to Saul. In the Sergius Paulus story this is present both in the statement that Saul was renamed Paul and also, perhaps, in a reference to Saul and David in a speech that Paul gives after he has left Cyprus:

And afterward they desired a king: and God gave to them Saul the son of Kish, a man of the tribe of Benjamin, for forty years. And when he had removed him, he raised up David to them as king. (Acts 13:21-22)

This is part of a brief history of the Jews, but it is significant that the focus of this speech is on Jesus as the son of David and the fact that David had replaced Saul.

The last point in the table is that Ananias is told to go to the house of Judas in the street called "straight". We can expect a very specific detail such as this to correspond to something in the author of Luke's source. In the story of Elymas we find a parallel in the accusation that he has perverted *"the straight ways of the Lord"*. This is linked to the quote we have already considered that occurs at the very start of Mark:

The voice of one crying in the wilderness, prepare you the way of the Lord, make his paths straight [eutheias]. (Mark 1:3)

This is a quote in turn from Isaiah 40:3 and was interpreted to mean that Jesus would come to enter into the new temple Mary and make straight the paths of the Lord, that is to bring in the kingdom of heaven. By opposing the church, Paul was perverting the "straight paths". But what does the house of Judas on the Straight street mean? It was common to refer to the temple as "the house" and Judas is the same as Judah, so perhaps it is a reference to the temple. And it is here that we see a clue as to the meaning of the episode with Ananias. The Acts account suffers from time compression. For example, it has missed out the visit to Arabia, although we can see a vestige of this visit in the Arabic name given to Paul, Elymas. The source used by the author of Acts must cover a period of a few years but in Acts these events have been compressed into a short episode. In Galatians, Paul says that he consulted no man but went to Arabia and then back to Damascus. Only after three years did he go to Jerusalem to visit Cephas (Galatians 1:18). It was a common Jewish practice to refer to years as days, and we find this repeatedly in the Jesus movement. In the Acts source the three years have been converted into three days; so Paul is blind for three days before the visit of Ananias and is unable to eat or drink. Behind this visit of Ananias we may have a genuine historical memory of a meeting that took place, not in Damascus, but Judah (Judas) in the temple (house) where the paths of the Lord have been made straight (the street called Straight). We have seen that when Paul visited Jerusalem after three years he was finally fully inducted into the movement, and given the spiritual baptism by Cephas/Mary. Before this meeting, he was like an abortion, born before time and not through the medium of the mother, Mary. After this meeting he is an apostle, able to eat and drink, that is to absorb the spiritual substance of Jesus, the bread and the wine. This completes the process that began with his initial conversion. Yet by the time Paul was writing Galatians this is all long in the past and he is at enmity with Mary over her appointment of James as leader, so he reduces her role by emphasising his initial conversion.

One detail that may not seem to fit is that it is Ananias and not Cephas who lifts the blindness of Paul and baptises him. A clue as to how Ananias became involved in the story is that this was the name of the High Priest with whom, according to Acts, Paul came into conflict.[265] It is also the same name as Annas who, according to Acts, was High Priest in the early days of the apostles.[266] The source used by the author of Luke must refer to "one named the high priest" which she has interpreted literally as a person with the same name as the high priest, hence Ananias. In reality, the "high priest" was a mystic title. We know that James was called the high priest and that he was living with Mary and was present at Paul's visit to Jerusalem. We have seen that this would not be the only time that James has been confused by the author of Luke with Ananias. It is probably this confusion that lies behind the story of Paul's trial by the Sanhedrin and the subsequent attempt to murder him, a melodramatic development of a source that records Paul's argument with James following the council in Jerusalem.

Having two very different versions of the conversion story enables us to identify the elements that lie behind both. The most striking common element is the temporary blindness that descends on Paul. In both cases, it is said that he has to be led by the hand. The blindness is clearly spiritual as it is lifted with his induction by Ananias. We can find a saying about the blind being led in both Thomas and the gospels:

Jesus said: "If a blind man leads a blind man, they both fall into a pit." (Thomas 34)

There are many representations in the gospels in which people are miraculously given sight and hearing. Beyond these stories are traditions of those who undergo the spiritual baptism being given new sight and new hearing. The resurrection is life and entry into spiritual life brings new senses. These are not physical but intuitive. It is not that the perfect see differently in a physical sense but that they perceive differently. They see the reality that lies behind the world and that the world that others perceive is no more than an illusion. Christians act differently because they are immersed in a different reality. The love of power, possessions and sexuality are revealed as false seed implanted into the heart of man by the fallen angels, the rulers of a fallen world. Those of the way turn from these things not because they are self-sacrificing but because with the new light of Christ what was previously desired is seen as ugly and false.

The saying about the blind leading the blind implies that the blind must be led by someone with sight. Thomas 24 refers to the light within the chosen: "*There is light within a man of light, and he becomes light to the whole world. If he does not become light, he is darkness.*" In Thomas 28 Jesus expresses sorrow for those who are spiritually blind: "*... and my soul was afflicted for the sons of men, for they are blind in their mind and do not see.*" And in Thomas 22, to enter the kingdom, you must gain new sight: "*... when you make eyes in the place of an eye..*". The blindness of Paul is spiritual and came from his persecution of the church. It left him when he was finally fully inducted into the movement by Mary.

We can see that there must be at least two sources behind the story of Paul's conversion in Acts. There is Paul's own account in Galatians, which was known either directly or indirectly to the author of Luke. Then there is a source, let us call it the Paul Conversion source (PC) which must have been available to the author of Luke in two forms; PC(a) which leads to the account of Paul's conversion and PC(b) which gives the story of the conversion of Sergius Paulus. The PC source covered the period from Paul's initial conversion to his induction in Jerusalem but was misunderstood by the author of Luke as spanning only a few days. In PC(b) Paul is also called by the name Elymas, the wise, which he may have acquired during his time in Arabia. The PC source also compared Paul to Saul when he was persecuting the church, which led the author of Luke to the false idea that Paul was called Saul before his conversion.

What was Paul's work?

Put it all together and we can conclude a few things about Paul's background:

He was probably a Hellenistic Jew from Tarsus.

He was a Pharisee.

He spent time as part of the establishment in Jerusalem involved in persecuting the Jesus movement.

He was well travelled.

He was well educated although not in the classical Greek sense.

We can tell he was well educated because of how well he writes. His language is Koine Greek, which played the same role as English does across the world now. A good proportion of those living within the Roman Empire spoke it, and it was the language of trade and commerce. Paul must have come from a family that was wealthy compared to most Jews of the time. Education was expensive in the ancient world. He would not have been able to afford to travel if he had been poor and he would not have been accepted into the Jewish establishment in Jerusalem if he had been of peasant stock. Most likely his family were merchants. This would explain his education, which would have been suitable for a merchant, and his familiarity with travel. Although living in a Greek-speaking city, they kept to their Jewish roots and sent their son to Jerusalem to study as a Pharisee where he was accepted enough into the establishment to have a role in persecuting the church.

We should note how different Paul's background would have been to that of Mary, James and others in the movement. He is cosmopolitan whereas they are from Palestine; he has been brought up as an establishment Jew whereas they are from an apocalyptic sect looking to Enoch; he is wealthy whereas they are poor; and most importantly he is well educated, able to express himself eloquently in Greek, and they are not. It is no surprise that with his background he came to play such a role in the movement particularly among Gentiles, and it is no coincidence that it is his letters that have come down to us. It is also no surprise that Paul never quite "gets" the movement and that his version of Christianity always is slightly off the mark. The Christianity that was to emerge from the first century was essentially a Greek and Gentile religion and the movement in Palestine quickly entered a decline. It is from this Greek world that the gospels were to emerge, and it is in this Greek world that the letters that Paul left behind were to have an enormous influence. We see the original light of Mary through the dark glass of Paul's interpretations.

With this background let us ask the question again; how did Paul support himself? We have discounted the idea that he was a tent maker. We can also eliminate the idea that he was doing some sort of manual work. Apart from the fact that it would have been very difficult for someone of Paul's upbringing to engage in such work without a loss of face, we must remember that the Roman Empire was a slave economy. Slaves were in plentiful supply and would have done most of the unskilled labour and much of the skilled labour also. A constant fear of the slave was to be released without his or her master's support. In such circumstances, they would most likely starve because there was not enough paid work available. Even had Paul been able to get manual work, the existence of slaves will have pushed wages down to subsistence level. He would have had to work all the time to support himself. Manual work in the ancient world was brutal and tiring and he would not have had enough energy left over to accomplish one-tenth of the things he did in the church. Indeed, he would have been at a crippling disadvantage to his rivals who were supported by the churches.

To support himself and his family, a free man would either have to own land or have some trade or business. A business requires a fixed abode to build up a clientele and Paul was continually on the move. Paul was certainly no farmer but it is possible that he did possess land that was rented out. It is most likely though that Paul was a merchant. His constant travelling would have been an advantage and if he came from a family of merchants he would have contacts. A background as a merchant would have been of great value in spreading the gospel because of his ability to travel and his connections in different places. Are there any clues in the New Testament that this may have been the case? In Acts 16 Paul meets and stays in the house of a woman called Lydia of the city of Thyatira who is described as a seller of purple fabric, a commodity in great demand. It is possible that this was originally a business connection.

More significantly when Paul tells in Galatians of how, with some trepidation, he submits the gospel he has been teaching for the approval of

James and the Jerusalem leadership they lay upon him only one requirement. Given the frequent discord and disagreements as revealed in Paul's
letters we may think that some important point of doctrine is at stake perhaps concerning circumcision or the Law. But what the leadership actually
urge upon him is *"that we should remember the poor"* which Paul adds is *"the
same which I was most ready to do"* (Galatians 2:10). Why should James stress
this one point? Most of the preachers of the gospel were poor themselves.
The fact they gave this instruction to Paul suggests that in James' eyes it
was a particular failing of his. They must have viewed him as being rich
and able to do more than he was doing to help the poor. If Paul were a
merchant, he would have required capital and others seeing his resources
may have asked why he did not give more away. The problem is that a
merchant needs capital to trade, and if he loses his capital he loses his in-
come also.

It is possible that there is a portrait of Paul as a rich man in the gospels.
In Mark 10:17-27 a young man runs after Jesus and kneels before him. Like
Paul it would seem that this young man is a Pharisee -- a short while before
this episode Jesus has been conversing with some Pharisees and this man
must be one of them for he believes in resurrection as the Pharisees did. He
addresses Jesus as *"Good master"* for which Jesus rebukes him saying *"there
is none good but the one God"*. This rebuke will strike most readers as surprising for the young man's words appear harmless. However, the significance
becomes plainer if the young man is intended to be Paul. The story is ultimately hostile to the young man and so must have come from the enemies
of Paul within the church. We know that Paul's bitterest enemies were the
group of Jewish Christians who believed in Law observance. They strongly
disagreed with Paul putting Jesus almost on the level with Yahweh. And
this is the purpose of Jesus' rebuke, to emphasise that there is only one God
and that Jesus is far below Yahweh and not a substitute. It is a denial of
Paul's doctrines. The young man asks Jesus how he could attain eternal life
and Jesus replies with the commandments: *"You know the commandments, do
not commit adultery, do not kill, do not steal, do not bear false witness, defraud
not, honour your father and mother"* (Mark 10:19). Again this is the doctrine of
the opponents of Paul who believed in the primacy of the Law. In contrast,
a major element of Paul's teaching is that the Law has been superseded,
and no longer applies. In answer to Jesus, the young man says about the
commandments *"Master, all these I have kept from my youth"* (Mark 10:20). It
may appear to us that this young man is overly full of himself yet Paul says
exactly the same thing in Philippians 3:6 that concerning the law he was
"blameless" -- that is completely law observant. After this Jesus looks upon

the young man "*and beholding him loved him*". Yet he lays one more command upon him; "*One thing you lack: go your way, sell whatsoever you have, and give to the poor*". Note the similarity with the instruction in Galatians from James that Paul is to remember the poor. In the Mark story, the young man turns sadly away for he is very rich. Jesus tells his disciples how hard it is for the rich to enter the kingdom of heaven and adds: "*It is easier for a camel to go through the eye of a needle, than for a rich man to enter into the kingdom of God*". The disciples are astonished saying among themselves "*Who then can be saved?*" Their astonishment is justified if the target of the story is Paul, for it is saying that he will not enter the kingdom of heaven as he refused to give up his belongings. If not even Paul will enter the kingdom who indeed will be saved?

The author of Mark would certainly not have made up a story like this about Paul nor would he have knowingly included such a story in his gospel. If it is about Paul, then it must be earlier than the Gospel of Mark and the author of Mark has not understood the identity of the rich young man. Normally we only read Paul's version of events, and we have to try to understand what the other side are saying by his responses to their arguments. But this time we may be hearing from the other side directly. Their chief criticism is a surprising one, but it does tie in with other fragments of evidence; that Paul had disobeyed the commands of Jesus to rid himself of his belongings and was "rich".

Who were these opponents? The Jesus movement was diverse and included both those who accepted the resurrection of Jesus through Mary/Cephas and the party of Christ who rejected this resurrection. The original movement was descended from Enochian Jews who did not cherish the Law but as it grew it would have attracted many from the mainstream. It was these mainstream Jews who formed Paul's most severe opponents. Paul did not invent the rejection of the law; it came directly from Mary/Cephas. But Paul was a more logical thinker than the spiritual Mary and took the idea much further. The original rejection seems to have been little more than a point of convenience to allow the Jewish disciples to operate more successfully among Gentiles. It was Paul who developed it into a philosophy. Ironically both Paul and his opponents had one thing in common; unlike Mary and the Jews who wrote the Animal Apocalypse they both took the Law seriously.

James was caught in the middle. He was operating in Jerusalem where the rejection of the Law would have caused him grave and potentially fatal difficulties. We can sense that he is back-pedalling furiously. His inherent nature seems to have been to appease and compromise. On the one side, he has the doctrine of Mary, his adoptive "mother", and its ultra development in Paul. On the other, he has the increasing numbers of Law observant Jews who are joining the movement. He tries to please both groups and fails miserably.

Even if his opponents thought that Paul was rich he surely made great sacrifices for the movement. In many ways, it would have been harder for Paul coming from a more privileged background than for those who had started out poor. He says nothing about his family but his espousal of the Jesus movement and his growing notoriety cannot have made him popular with his kin. And however he started out it is clear that he became progressively poorer in the service of the movement.

In 1 Corinthians, he is disclaiming his right not to work and proudly claiming that he does not need any pay for the work he does among the Corinthians. By the time he is writing 2 Corinthians (which is a composite of at least two letters) his attitude has subtly changed. He rails again against the false apostles and comparing himself as an equal to the "chief apostles" (2 Corinthians 11:5). And once again he is defending himself for preaching the gospel to the Corinthians without drawing upon them for support:

> Or did I commit a sin, humbling myself, so that you might be exalted, because I preached the gospel of God to you freely? (2 Corinthians 11:7)

His opponents are again accusing him of not relying upon the church's support. However his defence this time is very different. He claims that he has relied upon the financial support of others:

> I robbed other churches, by receiving support from them to serve you. And being present with you and having been in need, I did not burden anyone; for the brothers having come from Macedonia completely filled up my need, and in everything I kept and will keep myself from being a burden to you. (2 Corinthians 11:8-9)

The inconsistency with 1 Corinthians is striking. There he is claiming to work rather than live off those he teaches, whereas here he is being supported by other churches. It would seem that his financial position has deteriorated. Yet he still does not look to Corinthians for support perhaps because by now it has become a matter of pride for him. The support that has come from the Macedonians is mentioned in another letter, that to the church at Philippi in Macedonia. By this time Paul is certainly poor. He is in prison in Rome. He thanks the Philippians for a gift of money they have sent him, a gift which would have been sorely necessary. He then remembers that they had helped him before although they had stopped for a time:

Moreover, as you Philippians know, that in the beginning of the gospel, when I came out from Macedonia, not one church shared with me in the matter of giving and receiving, except you alone. For even in Thessalonica, you sent once and again for my needs. (Philippians 4:15-16)

The beginning of the gospel is when Paul first visited the Philippians. It seems that Paul relied upon their support for some time and that they were the only church that did support him.

Key points

1. The idea that Paul was originally called Saul appears only in Acts. The account of the conversion of Paul in Acts is based partly on the story of Saul pursuing David. The author of Acts has misunderstood a metaphor comparing Paul persecuting the church to Saul.

2. There is a second version of the conversion in Acts. This is when Saul and Barnabas visit Sergius Paulus and the magician Elymas. There are several links with the conversion story which show that the two have a common source. It is in this second story that Saul is called Paul for the first time.

3. The temporary blindness of Paul was originally spiritual but has become literal in Acts. The coming of Jesus was believed to give the disciple new senses, including spiritual sight.

4. The name Elymas, meaning "wise", may have come from Paul's stay in Arabia.

5. The story of the visit of Ananias goes back to Paul visiting Cephas/Mary in Jerusalem at which occasion he was inducted into the movement. The name Ananias would have arisen from the title of "high priest" given to James, which has been interpreted by the author of Acts as meaning the high priest Ananias/Annas. We know that James was present during Paul's first visit to Jerusalem and that James is confused with Ananias elsewhere in Acts.

6. Most likely Paul worked as a merchant and was believed by others in the movement to be rich. When Paul visits James and the other brethren in Jerusalem, the only instruction that James gives to him is to do more for the

poor. It is also likely that the rich young man in the Gospel of Mark was a portrait of Paul from his enemies in the movement. The main criticism made against Paul was that he did not give away his possessions like other Christians. However, Paul was to prove this criticism unfair for he would become poor in the service of the movement.

Conclusion

The idea that Paul was originally called Saul is a misunderstanding made by the author of Luke. The story of Paul's conversion is included twice in Acts, both explicitly and as the story of Sergius Paulus. The Acts story suffers from time compression, as it actually covers both Paul's initial spontaneous conversion and his induction with Cephas in Jerusalem three years later.

Chapter 36

Salome and Mary

The idea of the male-female pairing of a person and their spirit brings us to the Thomas saying concerning Salome, in which she shares the couch with Jesus. This saying has "two on a bed" and is linked to other sayings about "two on a bed, two in a field/road, two in a mill". Behind these sayings, we will see a spiritual meaning and the special role of Salome as the physical twin of the spiritual Jesus.

Salome

The Jesus movement believed that the spiritual spouse survives after death whereas the body does not. The survival of the person depends on the closeness of the link with the spiritual twin. If the two are linked in the divine marriage, then the person is preserved through the immortality of their spirit. In Thomas there is another saying about the two:

Jesus said: "Two shall rest upon a bed; one shall die, the other live." (Thomas 61a)

The two on a bed are a man and wife. The normal interpretation is that this is either about the arbitrariness of death taking one life and leaving another. Or more commonly, it is interpreted as about the apocalypse, that even among a married couple one will be saved and the other not. But with the background of the other sayings in Thomas concerning the heavenly twin, the husband/wife, we can see it as meaning the survival of one part of the body/spirit union after death whereas the other dies. The saying continues, although most commentators see this continuation as a separate saying:

Salome said: "Who are you man? While out of one, you have climbed onto my bed [couch], and ate from my table."

Jesus said to her: "I am he who is from that which is equal; to me was given of the things of my Father."

<... > "I am your disciple."

<... > "Therefore I say, when he should be equal[267] he will be filled with light, but when he should be divided he will be filled with darkness." (Thomas 61b)

Unfortunately, the saying is damaged with <...> indicating missing elements. The first missing part is often supplied to give: "*Salome says, I am your disciple*" and the second: "*Jesus says, therefore I say...*". But we cannot be sure that these are correct. The second part is linked to the first most obviously by the word "bed" that occurs in both. However, the context of the second saying with the table suggests that bed here is the couch on which people would recline for meals.

The situation is that an unknown man has shared Salome's couch and eaten from her table. She asks him who he is and Jesus answers by telling her that he is from that which is equal or undivided. He goes on to say that if one makes equal, he will be filled with light but if one divides he will be filled with darkness. We can see this as a reference to the marriage of the person and spirit. If the two are joined, made equal, then a person will be filled with light. If they are divided, the person is filled with darkness. The implication is that the light of God flows through the spirit. A person must be married to their spirit for the light to flow through them.

The phrase "*while out of one*" is translated literally here, but is seen by many commentators as a mistake. It has been rendered "*as if you are from someone*" or "*as a stranger*" or as an implied question "*whose son?*". However, we can note a link with Thomas 11: "*On the day when you were one, you were made two.*" This is about the spirit coming to a person making them both a unity and at the same time two (the physical person and the spirit). So "*out of one*" would mean that Jesus had come forth from Salome's unified (equal) nature.

Thomas 61 implies that Jesus is Salome's spiritual husband. He comes to her unexpectedly, yet he shares her couch if not her bed. But Jesus was seen as being Mary's spiritual husband. Who then is Salome?

The name is found in just one place in the New Testament, but that place is a critical one, the account of the crucifixion and resurrection in Mark. First Salome is present with Mary the Magdalene, and Mary the mother of James and Joses, looking at the crucifixion from afar. Then she is present with Mary the Magdalene, and Mary of James when they go and find the empty tomb and witness the angel. We have seen how Mary of James, Mary of Joses (Joseph), and Mary the Magdalene all refer to the same woman. There is only one odd name out, and that is Salome. And in the Thomas saying Salome occurs again when we would expect Mary.

The simplest explanation is that Salome is another name for Mary. It does seem to have been common in Palestine to carry two names, one in Aramaic, and the other in Greek. Was the Hellenised "Salome" the Greek name that Mary used? Certainly there is a tradition that Salome was also called Mary. In the gospels, only Mark has the name Salome; Matthew substitutes "the mother of the sons of Zebedee". We have seen how the story of the request for James and John to sit on the right and left side of Jesus has come down in two forms, a Z and S source. The first calls the woman making the request "the mother of the sons of Zebedee" and the second calls her Salome. Both "the mother of the sons of Zebedee" and Salome must be names for Mary.

Salome has a larger role in non-canonical sources than she has in the New Testament. The Gospel of the Egyptians only survives in the form of a few fragments quoted by Clement of Alexandria. The early writer Hippolytus said that this gospel was used by the Naassenes. It is normally dated to early second century or late first century and the fragments that survive show a strong link to the Gospel of Thomas. In these few fragments, Salome is mentioned more than once suggesting that she may have had a starring role in this gospel. The authors of the Gospel of the Egyptians were severe ascetics who disapproved of childbirth, as the following quotes from Clement make clear: [268]

Whence it is with reason that after the Word had told about the end, Salome said: "Until when shall men die?" (Now, the Scripture uses "man" in two senses, the visible form and the soul: and again, of him that is in a state of salvation, and him that is not: and sin is called the death of the soul.) Therefore the Lord answers advisedly "So long as women bear children." (Stromata 3:64)

And why do not they who walk by anything rather than the true rule of the Gospel go on to quote the rest of that which was said to Salome: for when she had said, "I have done well, then, in not bearing children?" (as if childbearing were not the right thing to accept) the Lord answers and says: Eat every plant, but that which has bitterness do not eat. (Stromata 3:66)

We can recreate the saying in the Gospel of the Egyptians as:

Salome asked, "Until when do men die? Jesus replied, "So long as women bear children". Salome said, "I have then done well in not bearing children?" Jesus said "Eat every plant, but that which has bitterness do not eat." (Gospel of Egyptians)

This saying shows that the authors of the Gospel of the Egyptians believed that Salome was a virgin. We have seen that this was also the case for Mary. Another saying is also repeated by Clement:

When Salome inquired when the things concerning which she asked should be known, the Lord said: "When you have trampled on the garment of shame, and when the two become one and the male with the female is neither male nor female." In the first place, then, we have not this saying in the four Gospels that have been delivered to us, but in that according to the Egyptians. (Stromata 3:92)

This is derived from two Gospel of Thomas sayings, Thomas 22 about making the two one, and Thomas 37:

His disciples said: "On what day will you appear to us, and on what day will we look upon you?" Jesus said: "When you strip naked and are not ashamed, and take your garments and put them beneath your feet like little children and trample them, then [you will see] the son of the Living One and you shall not fear." (Thomas 37)

The disciple should discard the garment of the body and put on the garment of the spirit. In the two sayings in Thomas, the disciples are unnamed but in the Gospel of the Egyptians, it is Salome who asks the question.

The pagan writer Celsus wrote a critique of Christianity around 175. His work is only known through the extensive quotes made from it by the church father Origen in his refutation *Against Celsus*. One of Celsus' accusations was that the Christians were divided into innumerable sects, and he lists the Helenians (after the sect of Simon Magus, see below) along with several others:

Celsus knows, moreover, certain Marcellians, so called from Marcellina, and Harpocratians from Salome, and others who derive their name from Mariamme, and others again from Martha. (Origen Contra Celsus 5:62)

It is striking that this list is all derived from female figures although Celsus also makes mention of the "*Marcionites, whose leader was Marcion*". It is possible that Celsus' intention is to ridicule Christianity by giving women as the authorities of the various sects. One of his themes is that Christianity appeals to the lower dregs of Roman society as well as women and children. Hippolytus tells us that the Naassenes claimed to have received their knowledge from James the brother of the Lord through Mariamme (Mary), and it may be the Naassenes who are intended by "those who derive their name from Mariamme".

As for the Harpocratians who look to Salome, they are to be identified with the notorious sect of the Carpocratians. From the description of Clement[269] they had an extremely radical philosophy akin to modern anarchism or communism whereby all things belonged to mankind in common and that it was human laws that broke this common ownership by establishing private property. Clement reports that this belief in holding things in common extended to their wives and that they had communal orgies after their feasts. However, it may be that Clement is exaggerating here and that the professed freedom from conventional morality was more theoretical than practical. Indeed, we can trace many of the beliefs of the Carpocratians back to the foundations of the Jesus movement. This lends credibility to the idea that they have remembered a genuine tradition if they did indeed hold Salome as a source of their teachings.

Salome is also found in the third-century Pistis Sophia. It is a long gnostic work containing revelations concerning the fallen Sophia in which a number of disciples ask the spiritual Jesus questions. One of the unusual features of the Pistis Sophia is the prominence it accords the female disciples including Salome, Martha and Mary the mother of Jesus. But the overwhelming majority of questions are asked by another woman; the Mary who is normally identified with Mary the Magdalene. Although Salome plays a role in the Pistis Sophia, she is only a minor character compared to this Mary. Salome is also linked to Martha in the first Apocalypse of James, which gives the names of four female disciples – Salome, Mary, Martha, and Arsinoe.

In these various sources, Salome is a prominent disciple, and she has an important role in the early Gospel of the Egyptians. This is all the more impressive because she only appears in the gospels once, in the minor role in Mark. Although Mark was the first to be written it was quickly supplanted by Matthew as the favourite gospel of the early Christians and she is not mentioned at all in Matthew. Also, it is never stated in any gospel that she saw the resurrected Christ; in Mark, she only sees the empty tomb and the angel. All this would make Salome an unlikely source of gnostic revelations unless there was some other tradition existing outside of the gospels. We can see evidence of such a tradition in the Gospel of Thomas.

In the above sources, Martha often appears alongside Salome. Celsus talks of a sect that takes its name from Martha although we know of no sect that was called after her or who looked to her teachings. In the gospels Martha is more prominent than Salome playing an important role in two stories; the story of Mary and Martha in Luke and of the raising of Lazarus in John. In both, she is represented as the sister of Mary and with her worldly temperament is contrasted unfavourably with Mary. In the famous story in Luke, Mary is sitting rapt at Jesus' feet while Martha is preparing the meal. Martha comes to complain about Mary to Jesus and to request her assistance. But she is rebuked by Jesus who says that Martha is concerned by many things whereas only one thing is needful: "*Mary has chosen the good part, which shall not be taken away from her*" (*Luke 10:42*). It is true that this is not supposed to be the same Mary as the Magdalene, but then the gospels are hopelessly muddled on such points and have taken the names from earlier traditions.

The occurrence of Martha as the sister of a Mary in Luke and John is a data point that suggests that Martha may have been a sister of the leader of the movement. This is supported by the fact that this Mary is portrayed as receiving teachings (or revelations?) from Jesus instead of undertaking her traditional female responsibilities, all of which is very apt if applied to the shaman. We should, however, be cautious because the earliest authority for this is the unreliable author of Luke. Martha does not appear in Mark, Matthew or Thomas, and the author of John has probably taken her from Luke. The other sources with Martha traditions are all quite late.

It is likely that Martha is, in fact, an imaginary creation of the author of Luke. The name Martha is a common woman's name of the time and is the feminine form of a word meaning master or lord. It would be a very apt title for Mary, as master of the movement. The house in which the story takes place is specifically identified as the house of Martha, which could mean the house of the master/mistress, that is Mary's house. In this house, Mary is in rapt communication with Jesus neglecting her domestic responsibilities.

The Martha of the gospels is inconsistent with the information that there was a sect that regarded her as their founder and with her portrayal in gnostic sources such as Pistis Sophia. In the gospels, she is the exact opposite of a gnostic, being concerned with the things of this world and neglecting the spiritual. So the gnostic sources which use Martha cannot be dependent upon the gospel accounts. Either they remember a Martha who was close to Mary, her sister, or there is confusion with "Martha" meaning "master". It seems more likely that Celsus has derived his information about a group looking towards Martha from a misunderstanding of "the master".

Returning to Salome, we can find a tradition where she is portrayed as a sister of a Mary and indeed of Jesus. In his *Panarion* (78.8.1 and 78.9.6), the fourth-century bishop Epiphanius says that Joseph had a previous marriage before Mary and had two daughters from this marriage called Salome and Mary. The idea of a previous marriage for Joseph is a common theory to account for the brothers and sisters of Jesus while preserving the perpetual virginity of Mary. But what is significant in Epiphanius' account is that Salome and Mary are both recorded as daughters of Joseph. We have seen how Mary was not the wife of Joseph, as the author of Matthew supposed, but his daughter, which is evidence that Epiphanius is reporting a genuine tradition. If so then the fact that Salome is also given as Joseph's daughter supports the idea that Mary and Salome are two names for the same woman.

Finally, there is a link between Salome and the two sacred names of Mary, the tower, and the rock. The Manichean Psalms of Thomas are preserved among the literature of the movement of the prophet Mani, an early offshoot from Christian gnosticism that became a world religion. The Psalms of Thomas are earlier than other Manichean Psalms. Psalm 16 starts with: "*Salome built a tower upon the rock of truth and mercy*". The righteous build it and the angels are the masons who hew stones for the tower. The link to the Shepherd of Hermas is striking. In the same Psalm, Salome calls to Jesus saying that she is not double minded and that there is no thought in her head that is split or divided. This is a clear echo of Thomas 61 where Jesus tells Salome that what is divided is full of darkness.

Overall, the connections between Mary and Salome are numerous and support the conclusion that Salome is another name used by Mary. It was common for Aramaic-speaking Palestinian Jews to use a Greek name and this practice could explain why Mary was called Salome. If so, then she probably only used Salome at the beginning of her ministry while in Palestine. The name soon fell into disuse because Greek-speaking Christians translated Mary's name directly into Greek as Maria. But it left a trace in sayings and traditions about Salome which exhibit a remarkable parallel to similar sayings and traditions about Mary.

It might be objected that when a Jew took a Greek name it usually had some reference to their Aramaic name. Both Mary and Salome were very common female names in first-century Judea, but there is no connection between the two. However, Salome would have been highly symbolic to Mary. The name comes from *salem* meaning peaceful and is the original name of Jerusalem. The word is used in Psalm 76 for Jerusalem as the place of the tabernacle which was to become the temple:

In Salem is his tabernacle, and his dwelling place in Zion. (Psalm 76:2)

In Genesis, the king of Salem is the mysterious Melchizedek:

And Melchizedek king of Salem brought forth bread and wine: and he was the priest of the most high God. (Genesis 14:18)

Melchizedek was equated by the movement with Jesus. So Salem stands for both the place of the temple and the dwelling place of Melchizedek/Jesus. It is therefore highly appropriate that Mary, the temple, and the new Jerusalem, should be called Salome. Indeed, it is possible that Salome was originally a title like the Magdalene. It would have been derived from Salem to identify her as the Jerusalem of Melchizedek, but then it became confused with the very common name Salome.

Two on a bed

Returning to Thomas 61 and the saying about the two on the bed, one who lives, and the other who dies, we find closely related sayings in the gospels in the context of the Apocalypse. In his account of the Apocalypse, the author of Matthew mostly follows Mark closely. But Matthew 24:37-41 is a section that does not appear in Mark comparing the days of Noah with the "*coming of the Son of Man*". The time before the Apocalypse is like the days before the flood in which men "*were eating and drinking, marrying and giving in marriage*". This is followed by a picture of two men and two women:

"Then two shall be in the field [agro]; one is taken, and one is left. Two women shall be grinding at the mill; one is taken, and one is left." (Matthew 24:40-41)

The Luke version also appears in a section about the coming of the Son of Man. The author of Luke repeats Matthew's story about Noah and adds to it the story of Lot. This is followed by the saying in expanded form:

"I tell you, in that night there shall be two in one bed; the one will be taken, and the other will be left. Two women shall be grinding together; the one will be taken, and the other will be left. [Two men shall be in the field; the one shall be taken, and the other left.]" (Luke 17:34-36)

A few copies add the "two in the field" saying as line 17:36 to make this conform to Matthew, but this was not in the original. So the author of Luke has changed Matthew's *"two in the field"* for *"two in one bed"*. Clearly the author of Luke has access to another version of this saying independent of Matthew. In fact, we can see the vestige of the *"two in the field"* saying in Luke. The gospel moves the saying at Matthew 24:18 about not returning from a field to collect your cloak to later in the narrative, just before the *"two in one bed"* saying. And it adds a comment about Lot's wife:

"And the one in the field let him not return back. Remember Lot's wife!" (Luke 17:31-32)

In the story of Lot, the patriarch is rescued along with his wife and two daughters by two angels from the destruction of Sodom. They are told to flee and not look back, but Lot's wife does look back and is turned into a pillar of salt.[270] The author of Luke has combined Matthew's two in a field saying and the saying about not returning from the field, and interpreted them in relation to the story of Lot; in this story one of a married couple turns back and is taken whereas another does not turn back and is left. This is typical of the author of Luke and demonstrates both her creativity and her tendency to change her sources to fit her own interpretation.

The same imagery is found in another work, The Apocalypse of Zephaniah. This is believed to be a Jewish work although it has survived only through the library of a Christian monastery. It was quoted by Clement of Alexandria and a dating between 100 BC to AD 175 is possible. Within it is a small section with clear affinities to the Jesus movement. Unfortunately, only about one-quarter of the text has survived.[271]

The fragment of interest starts with a mysterious funeral that is apparently going to happen in the future; mysterious because the context for the funeral, the beginning of the passage, is missing. It then continues with the narrator being taken up to heaven: [272]

Now I went with the angel of the Lord and he took me up over my city. There was nothing before my eyes. Then I saw two men walking together on one road. I watched them as they talked. And moreover I also saw two women grinding together at a mill. I watched them as they talked. And I saw two upon a bed each one of them acting for their mutual [...] upon a bed. (Apocalypse of Zephaniah 2:1-4)

The missing word [...] is unknown, but a word suggesting repose would fit and would be consistent with the Gospel of Thomas, which has resting on the bed. If walking together on a road is taken as the same as working together in a field then the same three pairs occur here as in the gospels:

Two men on a road/in a field
Two women in a mill
Two on a bed

If the two on a bed are man and wife, then we have all the possible combinations of two people (male/male, female/female and male/female) represented in everyday settings. But there are striking differences with the gospels. First, the context does not fit the apocalypse as depicted in the gospels. The seer is making a journey to heaven, but it is not the end of the world. This makes it unlikely that the Apocalypse of Zephaniah is copying from the gospels. The other major difference with both the gospels and Thomas is that we do not have one being taken, and one left. Instead, we are shown the pairs before they are split. In fact, the passage, at first sight, seems to serve no purpose in the Apocalypse of Zephaniah. To try and understand the meaning we must consider the continuation:

And I saw the whole inhabited world hanging like a drop of water which is hanging from a bucket when it comes up from a well.

This is related to Isaiah 40:15 where the nations are as a drop from a bucket. Isaiah 40:15 is the continuation of one of the key texts for the Jesus movement; the text quoted at the beginning of the first gospel Mark which leads to the female Zion going up a mountain to acclaim the good news and the good shepherd as the arm of Yahweh. This image of the drop of water coming from a key text and appearing as it does next to the three pairs increases the probability that the Apocalypse is linked to the early Jesus movement. The Apocalypse continues:

> I said to the angel of the Lord "Then does darkness or night not exist in this place?" He said to me "No because darkness does not exist in that place where the righteous and the saints are, but rather they always exist in the light.

The question about darkness or night seems to have no relationship to what has just gone before. However, it is linked to the earlier comment that when the narrator is taken above the city that: "*there was nothing before my eyes*". There must be something in the missing sections of the Apocalypse that explains this, and we can work out what that something must be; the journey must be made at night. This is why the narrator cannot see anything at first and is why after he is given sight he asks "*does ... night not exist in this place*".

This quite literally puts the three pairs in a new light. The narrator is not seeing a scene in daylight with his normal sight. He is observing a night scene through the light of heaven. It might be objected that two of the three (the road and the mill) concern activities that are more likely to take place in daylight. However, all three pairs have surely been taken from an earlier source. They are activities that would naturally take place at different times of day (with the bed being at night) and so were not originally intended to be happening all at once. The author of the Apocalypse makes them simultaneous so that they can all be observed by his narrator.

Understanding that the scene is viewed with heavenly light is the key to understanding its purpose in the apocalypse. With his new vision, the narrator can see the things of heaven that are normally invisible. Looking back towards the earth he sees men and women in pairs going about their business. These pairs are not two persons, but a person and their soul/spirit. The theme of the Apocalypse of Zephaniah is the punishment of the soul after death and this scene serves to link what happens on earth, the body/soul going about their daily business, with what will happen later. As the continuation says:

> And I saw all the souls of men as they existed in punishment.

Thus interpreted the saying gives in the three combinations the possibility that the soul is either of the same sex as a person or of the opposite sex. This ambiguity reflects the Jewish view where the soul of a man is sometimes addressed in the feminine but at other times is represented as a man.

The Gospel of Thomas picks up only the two on a bed, the male/female combination, and this is the principle way it is represented in the early Jesus movement.

The heavenly light in the apocalypse is another indication that this passage is related to the Jesus movement. It agrees with Thomas 11 which asks: *"When you come in the light, what will you do?"* The parallel to this question is the end of the saying which asks *"But when you have become two, what will you do?"* meaning the final dissolution of the body and spirit on death or at the end times. The light is the light of heaven as in the Apocalypse of Zephaniah. The soul will go to that place after it splits from the body after death.

At this one point, the Apocalypse of Zephaniah is most likely borrowing from literature that either was used as a source by the Jesus movement or was produced by the Jesus movement itself. Another possibility is that a copyist has inserted the section from another Christian document that is now lost. This is less likely because the passage is not overtly Christian, and it does not agree with the gospel depiction of the three pairs.

Turning to the gospels we can see that they cannot be dependent upon the Zephaniah passage because they have the "one taken, one left" theme. In Matthew, and hence Luke, this is interpreted in terms of the coming apocalypse when one person is taken up to heaven, and another left behind. But this is not the meaning in Zephaniah or Thomas. The author of Matthew has literalised the saying by making it apply to two people rather than a person and their spirit.

We can deduce that there must have been another source that shared the same combinations of the Zephaniah passage but which also had one being taken, and one left. The Thomas saying may have been extracted from this source, and it has also been used separately by Matthew. The author of Luke replaces the two in the field with the two on the bed; either she also has access to the original source or she has taken this from Thomas.

The Matthew saying uses the pairs in the context of the coming of the Son of Man. The Gospel of Thomas has the two on the bed in conjunction with the appearance to Salome at a meal where Jesus shares her couch. We have seen how this indicates the mysteries of the bridal chamber, the joining of Mary/Salome with Jesus in marriage. So the meal is the marriage feast of Salome and Jesus, which gives another potential link with Matthew. Immediately before the one taken, one left theme, the author of Matthew inserts the story about those in the time of Noah, a story which is not in Mark. He tells of how people *"were eating and drinking, marrying and giving in marriage"*. This can be explained if Matthew's source resembled

Thomas 61 but with the two on the bed elaborated to the three combinations. If so, then the author of Matthew has wrongly interpreted the marriage feast as negative, portraying it as people revelling up to the time of the apocalypse, whereas it was actually the celebration of the divine marriage.

We must now consider yet another occurrence of the pairs, and this is in the vital resurrection account in Mark. In the long ending after the appearance to Mary the Magdalene Jesus appears to the unnamed two disciples:

After that he appeared in another form to two of them, as they walked, and went into the country [agron]. (Mark 16:12)

This is part of what we have called the Gospel of the Long Ending, and it is this line that the author of Luke elaborates into her story of the road to Emmaus. The word *agron* meaning country or field is the same as used in the Gospel of Matthew for "two in a field". In fact, we can see that this line comes between the Apocalypse of Zephaniah, "two on a road", and Matthew "two in a field". The line does not have the one left, one taken theme but then neither does Zephaniah. We know from the other sayings that the two here must be a person and their spirit. These two see the risen Christ "*in another form*".

We have seen how the journey to heaven must be made by putting on the "garment" meaning the spirit. In Thomas 37 when Jesus is asked by his disciples when they shall see him, he replies that they must unclothe themselves and trample their garments beneath their feet. The garment here is the body that must be put off and the garment of the spirit put on if the disciples are to see Jesus. The ascent to heaven is made by the spirit alone and not by the body. And this gives a new meaning to "*one taken and one left*". The Matthew and Luke passages are in a context about the coming of the son of man and the Matthew lines are actually preceded by the words "*so shall also the coming of the Son of man be*". The link with the long ending of Mark where the two see the resurrected Jesus is clear. Both are about ascending to heaven and seeing Jesus. The "one taken" is the spirit and the "one left" behind is the body and there are three circumstances in which this split can occur:

During life, when by putting on the garment of the spirit and leaving temporarily behind the garment of the body the mystic ascends to heaven.

After death when the body dies, and the living spirit ascends to heaven.

At the end times when the body is left behind to be destroyed with the world, but the spirit is taken up to heaven.

We can find evidence in the early Jesus movement for all three. The third is found in Thomas 11 which talks about the one becoming two when coming into the light; the start of this saying makes it clear that it is about the end times. So although the author of Matthew has literalised the pairs as two people, one of which is taken and one left, he is not wrong to apply the saying to the apocalypse.

When we look at the account of the resurrection in Mark, we can see more links with the Salome saying in Thomas. They both concern the coming of Jesus, and both feature an appearance at a meal. In Thomas 61 Salome says that Jesus has come to share her couch (or bed) and eat from her table. In Mark when Jesus appears to all the disciples, he does so in a similar way: "*Afterward, he appeared to the eleven as they reclined at the table...*" (Mark 16:14).

Luke's account of the same has Jesus eating some food, again showing that Luke has copied the long ending (Luke 24:41-43). We can summarise the similarities between Mark and the Salome saying as follows:

They both concern the appearance of the risen Jesus.

They both involve Salome (in Mark she is among the women who go to the tomb).

They both involve a meal.

They both draw on the imagery of the pairs (the Thomas saying has two on a bed, Mark has two going into the country / field)

These indicate that the Mark resurrection account has used a source that is very similar to the Salome saying in Thomas. Apart from the name of Salome, all the above points of similarity concern features present in the Gospel of the Long Ending. Elements of the resurrection account in Mark that occur outside the long ending, such as the empty tomb, do not feature in the list. If Salome is the same as Mary, then she also is present in the Gospel of the Long Ending under the name Mary the Magdalene. We have argued that the Gospel of the Long Ending was an early form of the long ending that preceded the Gospel of Mark. We are now seeing the sources of the Gospel of the Long Ending. Behind the appearances of Jesus are two distinct forms of the resurrection appearance:

In the first is the two walking in the field – the emphasis is on the twin-ship of the individual, the person, and their soul/spirit. It is the spirit that perceives the Christ either during life or by ascending to heaven after death or at the end times.

In addition, there is a specific appearance to Mary/Salome whereby Je-sus shares her couch and her table.

The second is distinct from the first. It is not just that Mary is the first to see the risen Christ she also sees him differently. Others perceive him through their spirit, but she sees him directly. The reason for this is that Jesus is her spirit! She is the twin of Jesus and the female Christ. The shar-ing of the couch and table is the two on the bed.

We can, in fact, find Mary and the spirit of Jesus as "two on a bed" in a strange story in the Pistis Sophia. Mary, the mother of Jesus, is telling the story to the resurrected Jesus:

When you were little, before the spirit had come upon you, while you were in a vineyard with Joseph, the spirit came out of the height and came to me in my house, in your likeness; and I knew him not but thought he was you. And the spirit said to me: "Where is Jesus, my brother, that I meet with him?" And when he had said this to me, I was at a loss and thought it was a phantom to try me. So I seized him and bound him to the foot of the bed in my house, until I went forth to you, to you and Joseph in the field, and I found you on the vineyard, Joseph fencing the vineyard. Now it came to pass when you did hear me speak the word to Joseph, that you did understand the word, and were joyful and said: "Where is he, that I may see him; else I await him in this place." And it came to pass, when Joseph had heard you say these words, that he was startled. And we went down together, entered the house and found the spirit bound to the bed. And we looked on you and him and found you like unto him. And he who was bound to the bed was unloosed; he took you in his arms and kissed you, and you also did kiss him. You became one. (Pistis Sophia 61)[273]

The Pistis Sophia is third-century, so this story is quite late and is based on the gospels depiction of Jesus' life on earth. Note the circumstance of Jesus being in the vineyard which is being fenced by Joseph, linking to the parable of the vineyard in Isaiah. There is also evidence for the "two in a field" theme in that Mary finds Jesus and Joseph working in a field. If we take out the literalistic elements that the writer has taken from the gospels, such as the family setting of Mary, Joseph, and Jesus, there are two main features to this story:

(1) The spirit of Jesus descends to Mary. She binds this spirit to a bed.
(2) The spirit and Jesus are identical twins and merge into one.

Behind the first is the concept of "two on a bed" the two being Mary and the spirit of Jesus. The writer does not understand what is meant by the spirit of Jesus coming down to Mary on a bed, so he interprets this as Mary binding the spirit to a bed. The bed in question is described by Mary as "the bed in my house"; the spirit has come down to Mary's bed.

Behind the second is the idea that the spirit of Jesus is the twin that has come down and entered into the physical body. We have seen that the spirit of Jesus is "the twin" of Mary who has come down and occupied her body so that they "become one". But the writer has inherited the literalistic background of the gospels and thinks that Jesus was a physical man. So he portrays the spirit as the identical twin of Jesus, which then merges with him.

Key points

1. The name Salome occurs in a number of non-canonical sources, including the Gospel of the Egyptians. Celsus says that the Harpocratians, who are the same as the sect of the Carpocratians, derived from Salome.

2. The best explanation of Salome is that it is an alternative name for Mary. This is supported by a number of lines of evidence including her role in the resurrection account; the substitution of "the mother of the sons of Zebedee" for Salome; the information from Epiphanius that Mary and Salome were daughters of Joseph; links between Salome and the "tower" and "rock"; and the parallel nature of sayings about Salome and Mary.

3. Mary's use of Salome is likely to be connected to "Salem", meaning the temple, Jerusalem and the dwelling place of Melchizedek/Jesus. Salome may have been a name Mary used in Greek, or it could have been a title like the Magdalene, that then became confused with the name.

4. The name Martha is the feminine of "master". Traditions about Martha parallel those about Mary and are unlikely to be derived from the stories about Martha in the gospels. Most likely Martha was a title of Mary, "the master", which has become a name and a separate character through confusion.

5. There are a number of Christian sources that relate to "two in a bed, two in a field/road, two in a mill" with one taken and one left. The image of the pairs comes from a Jewish representation of a person and their soul, and the pairs could be male-female, male-male or female-female. In the Jesus movement, it became specifically a male-female pairing with only one of the two, the spirit, surviving after death or after the apocalypse. The gospels wrongly interpret it as meaning that only one person of a pair will be saved at the apocalypse.

6. The Salome saying in Thomas indicates her special role as the female component of Jesus so that he is her spirit. This only makes sense if Salome is Mary.

7. The resurrection story in Mark contains links to the Salome saying and the "two on a bed" theme, specifically the two on the road who witness the Christ, and the reclining at table. The belief was that, for anyone other than Mary, Jesus could only be perceived through the spiritual component of a person.

8. The Pistis Sophia has a strange story of the spirit of Jesus descending and being bound to Mary's bed. The author of this story has tried to combine the original spiritual imagery with the literalistic story of Jesus from the gospels.

Chapter 37

The beloved disciple

It is time to take a closer look at John Mark, the second adoptive son of Mary, and the person who was closest to her. We will find traditions linking Mark to Mary and to Peter, which is further evidence that the two were the same person. But we also find surprising traditions linking Mark to Barnabas, Paul's traveling companion, which parallel the links between Mark and Peter. The resolution of this mystery will help us understand other links between Barnabas and Cephas and will lead us to Antioch.

We will also look at the famous story of the beloved disciple reposing on the breast of Jesus at the last supper. The source of this tradition is a surprising one, a Thomas saying we have already considered.

John called Mark

The traditional view of Mark, who supposedly wrote the first gospel, comes from brief references to him in Acts, the letters of Paul and 1 Peter, and by Papias. In these sources he is a relatively obscure but well-connected person:

He is the nephew and close travelling companion of Paul's fellow apostle Barnabas.

He is called the "son" of Peter.

He is also called John and is the son of a woman called Mary who is a friend of Peter and who has a substantial house in Jerusalem.

He has a brother James who was put to death by Herod Agrippa.

He is the travelling companion and secretary to Peter.

He leaves Paul and Barnabas at Pamphylia.

Paul and Barnabas split after an argument about Mark in Antioch.

Mark does not come over as the type of person to name an otherwise anonymous gospel after. He is not prominent in his own right and is shown to be unreliable and a subject of contention. But more than this, the list shows some strange coincidences. Mark is the nephew of Barnabas and the "son" of Peter and also the son of Mary. He is the close traveling companion of Barnabas and yet he is also the close travelling companion of Peter. Paul has an argument with Barnabas about Mark in Antioch, and yet we know that Paul also had an argument with Cephas in Antioch. Mark is called John and is the brother of James, the son of Mary, and yet we know that a pair of brothers James and John the sons of Zebedee are prominent among the disciples of Jesus.

We have already seen explanations for some of these "coincidences". John Mark is really one of the two senior adopted sons of Mary, second only to his brother James. Mary and Peter are one and the same, and this is why John Mark is known as both the son of Mary and the son of Peter. With this understanding of Mark's role, it becomes clear why the first gospel should be named after him. But there is still one loose end, and that is the connection with Barnabas. Was Mark really the nephew of Barnabas? The only time we hear about Barnabas is as a companion of Paul. Barnabas belongs in Paul's circle, and it would be strange if he were also closely related to John and James and perhaps Mary herself.

Looking at the earliest evidence, the letters of Paul, there is one reference to a Mark that is certainly genuine:

Epaphras, my fellow prisoner in Christ Jesus, greets you, and so do Mark, Aristarchus, Demas, and Luke, my fellow workers. (Philemon 1:23-24)

This simply names Mark in a list of people whom Paul calls his "fellow workers". Although it is possible that this Mark has nothing to do with John called Mark there are a couple of pieces of information that suggest that this is the same person. One is the order of the greetings. Epaphras is mentioned first because he is in prison with Paul. Then comes Mark, suggesting that he is more important than the other named individuals. The other piece of evidence is circumstantial. Philemon is written from Rome, and we have strong reasons to believe that Mark was in Rome at this time. There is another apparent reference to Mark in a list of greetings at the end of Paul's letter to the Colossians:

Aristarchus my fellow prisoner greets you, and Mark, cousin of Barnabas (about whom you have received instructions: if he comes to you, receive him) and also Jesus called Justus, these being the only fellow workers for the kingdom of God among the circumcision, and they have been a comfort to me. (Colossians 4:10-11)

This time Mark is much more prominent. We learn that he is a cousin, that is a kinsman, to Barnabas and that he is Jewish. This might appear to settle the question; Barnabas had a relative called Mark, and this is the same person whose greetings are also sent in Philemon. But did Paul write this greeting or is Colossians one of the fake letters written later after his death? The letter to the Colossians certainly does not read like the genuine letters of Paul. In fact, it sets out the proto-orthodox position of the church as it stands towards the end of the first century. For example in Colossians 3:18-22 wives are told to submit to their husbands, children to obey their parents in everything and slaves to obey their masters. Contrast the instruction that children are to obey their parents with the genuine early sayings from the movement that Jesus' disciples are to hate (put aside) their parents.

When we look closely at the greetings in Colossians, we can see some remarkable similarities with the genuine greetings in Philemon suggesting that they are copied from that letter. For example the subject of Philemon, Onesimus, is mentioned in Colossians 4:9. Paul refers to Aristarchus as his fellow prisoner in Colossians just as he refers to Epaphras as his fellow prisoner in Philemon. Epaphras himself appears in Colossians 4:12 with no indication that he is a prisoner. In Philemon, Paul mentions four names in his list of fellow workers: *Marcus, Aristarchus, Demas, Luke.* Of these, the first two appear in Colossians 4:10-11 where they are also described as Paul's fellow workers. The other two come a few lines later: "*Salute you does Luke, the beloved physician, and Demas*" (Colossians 4:14). The forger has copied Paul's greetings in Philemon, altering them a little and adding some colour such as Luke being a physician and Mark being Barnabas's nephew. Colossians is a fake and the information that Mark was a cousin to Barnabas has been added by a forger late in the first century. There is nothing genuinely written by Paul to suggest any connection between Mark and Barnabas.

What about the idea that Mark was called John? The only time this connection is explicitly mentioned is in Acts:

And having considered this, he came to the house of Mary, the mother of John who is called Mark, where there were many gathered together and praying. (Acts 12:12)

This is part of the ascent to heaven passage with Peter escaping from prison and coming to the house of Mary. Although Acts is a dubious source of information, in this case we have considerable supporting evidence that John was called Mark. For example in the Gospel of John at the crucifixion Jesus asks the disciple he loves (John) to become his mother's son. So we have evidence that both Mark and John were regarded as sons of Mary.

Barnabas and Cephas

After Acts tells of the death of Herod Agrippa I it has John Mark accompany Barnabas and Paul as they leave Jerusalem:

And Barnabas and Saul returned from Jerusalem, when they had fulfilled their ministry, and took with them John, who was called Mark. (Acts 12:25)

Acts now jumps to the church in Antioch where there were "prophets and teachers" including Barnabas and Saul. Infused by the holy spirit the church select Paul and Barnabas for missionary work. They go on to Cyprus taking John Mark with them although he is not mentioned in the story of Sergius Paulus and Elymas, which we have seen has its source in another version of the conversion of Paul. Once they leave Cyprus John departs from them:

And those with Paul having set sail from Paphos, came to Perga in Pamphylia, and John left them and returned to Jerusalem. (Acts 13:13)

The significance of this only becomes apparent later in Antioch:

And some days after Paul said to Barnabas, "Let us go again and visit our brethren in every city where we have preached the word of the Lord and see how they do." And Barnabas determined to take with them John called Mark. But Paul thought fit not to take him along, because he had withdrawn from them at Pamphylia and not having gone with them to the work. Therefore a sharp disagreement

arose, so that they separated from each other. And Barnabas having taken Mark,
sailed to Cyprus. (Acts 15:36-39)

This argument between Paul and Barnabas that breaks their partnership
is the last we hear of Mark in Acts. We should note that the argument takes
place in Antioch. We know of another argument involving Paul that also
took place at Antioch and that is the argument with Peter/Cephas that
Paul himself tells us about in Galatians. In fact, the Acts narrative is parallel
to Galatians at this point. The argument with Barnabas is preceded by a
trip to Jerusalem in which Paul and Barnabas go to visit Peter, James and
the others to discuss the question of circumcision of gentile Christians. This
is clearly related to Paul's second visit to Jerusalem that he describes in Galatians. In both Acts and Galatians, the visit to Jerusalem is followed by an
argument in Antioch.

Has Barnabas somehow become confused in the Acts account with Pe-
ter/Cephas? The evidence that this confusion has indeed happened is
found in another episode that is recounted in both Galatians and Acts.
When Paul talks about his first visit to Jerusalem,[274] he says that he stayed
with Peter/ Cephas and saw only James out of the other apostles. But in
the brief account of this visit in Acts it is Barnabas who "takes up" Paul[275]
and introduces him to the other apostles. Peter/Cephas is not even mentioned. The timescale of this Acts account is also severely truncated. In Galatians, Paul goes to Arabia after his conversion and then returns to Damascus and only after three years does he go to Jerusalem. Yet in the Acts
account the trip to Arabia is not mentioned, and the impression is given
that Paul is only in Damascus for a short period before going to Jerusalem.

This is evidence that Acts is based not directly on Galatians but on another source that is dependent upon Galatians. This explains both the close
parallels between Acts and Galatians and also the wide divergences. The
Acts source does not include all the details that are in Galatians, and so the
author of Luke's version of events is distorted. But why should Barnabas
and Peter be confused? Barnabas was a genuine early apostle in Paul's circle and occupied a much less exalted position in the movement than either
Cephas or Peter.

There is one point of similarity between Peter and Barnabas and that is
that a Mark is a relative of each. Mark is called Peter's son in 1 Peter and
Mark is the cousin, meaning kinsman, of Barnabas in Colossians. But is this
another sign of confusion between the two rather than its cause? The only
evidence that Mark was related to Barnabas comes from Colossians, which

we have seen was not written by Paul. The "sons" of Mary/Cephas were probably her nephews or other younger relatives. If so then Mark would be related to Mary/Cephas as well as being her adopted "son". So the information that Barnabas had a relative called Mark could have come from a confusion between Cephas and Barnabas.

A further link is that Mark is portrayed as the travelling companion of Barnabas in Acts. We find a very similar relationship between Mark and Peter from the early writer Papias who describes Mark and Peter as living in Rome where Mark is the secretary of Peter writing down Jesus' sayings as remembered by Peter.

So we have multiple independent lines of evidence that point towards Cephas and Barnabas having been confused. How could such confusion arise? Acts tells us that Barnabas was from Cyprus, was originally called Joseph, that he was of the priestly Levite class, and that the name Barnabas was given by the apostles and means "*son of consolation/encouragement*" (Acts 4:36). The problem is that Acts is inherently unreliable. There is no need to suppose that he was given the name Barnabas on his conversion so we may doubt that he was ever called Joseph; certainly Paul always calls him Barnabas. The only reliable source is Paul's letters and in these Barnabas comes over as Paul's closest companion. There are four mentions of him in Paul's genuine letters. Of these four, one is in 1 Corinthians in the "power not to work" passage that has already been discussed, and the other three are all in Galatians. The answer to this mystery must be in Galatians.

It is in Galatians that Paul has used the two names, Cephas and Peter. We have seen how this gave rise to a great deal of confusion and that Peter has been changed to Cephas or vice versa in many manuscripts. The form of the name that won out was Peter, which became almost universal. Almost everyone except Paul translated the Aramaic Cephas into Greek as Peter. Probably Mary herself used Peter when communicating in Greek. Paul, however, keeps Cephas for the founder and uses Peter for Mary's "son" Simon Peter. Imagine an early Greek-speaking gentile Christian reading Paul's Galatians. He knows Peter well as the rock upon which the church is built. But he has never heard of Cephas, and if he does not speak Aramaic, he will not connect the name with Peter. He would wonder who this Cephas is. The conclusion that a naive reader of Galatians may come to is that Cephas is another name for Barnabas. To see how this could arise, consider the story in Galatians of Paul's two journeys to Jerusalem and the subsequent argument in Antioch. The table below shows the named individuals in these episodes in Galatians and the corresponding passages in Acts.

	Galatians	Acts
Paul's first visit to Jerusalem	1:18-19 Paul meets Cephas and James	9:27 Paul meets Barnabas and the apostles
Paul's second visit to Jerusalem	2:1-10 Paul, Barnabas, and Titus meet James, Peter and John	15:1-21 Paul and Barnabas meet James and Peter
Antioch	2:11-13 Paul and Barnabas travel to Antioch and later Cephas joins them. Paul argues with Cephas.	15:22-41 Paul and Barnabas travel to Antioch with Judas and Silas. Paul argues with Barnabas.

The important point is that the only time in Paul's letters that Barnabas and Cephas are together is the argument in Antioch. There is nothing in the two visits to Jerusalem that would contradict the idea that Barnabas and Cephas were the same person. The key lies in Paul's description of the Antioch meeting:

But when Cephas [or Peter] came to Antioch, I opposed him to his face because he stood condemned. For before certain ones came from James, he had been eating with the Gentiles. But when they came, he was drawing back and was separating himself, being afraid of those of the circumcision. And also the rest of the Jews acted hypocritically with him so that even Barnabas was carried away by their hypocrisy. But when I saw that they are not walking in line according to the truth of the gospel, I said to Cephas {or Peter} before them all, "If you being a Jew live like a Gentile, and not like a Jew, why do you compel the Gentiles to live like Jews? We are Jews by birth and not sinners of the Gentiles." (Galatians 2:11-15)

This might seem to disprove the idea that Barnabas could be confused with Cephas, for the two are both present. In fact, this very passage could have suggested the idea that Cephas was the same person as Barnabas. Paul tells us that he was with Cephas in Antioch when James sent some of his followers to persuade Cephas to separate from the Gentiles at meals. Cephas did as they said and other Jews followed Cephas' example including Paul's companion Barnabas. However, Paul's account could be misread. We should note that the passage has a parallel structure:

Those from James persuade Cephas not to eat with the Gentiles.

The other Jews dissemble and persuade Barnabas to dissemble.

This could be interpreted this as saying the same thing in two different ways. If so, then the other Jews would be the same as those who came from James, and Barnabas would be another name for Cephas. So Paul would be saying:

Those who came from James / other Jews
persuaded Cephas / Barnabas
to not eat with Gentiles / dissemble

This is not what Paul meant, but early Christians reading texts without the benefit of commentaries or the right background information came up with all sorts of misunderstandings.

If Cephas was confused for Barnabas, does this explain anything else? There is a strange episode in Acts that is sandwiched between the two other times that Barnabas is confused with Cephas. It starts with Paul curing a cripple at Lystra[276] after which the people worship Barnabas and Paul as gods:

And when the people saw what Paul had done, they lifted up their voices, saying in the speech of Lycaonia, "The gods are come down to us in the likeness of men." And they called Barnabas, Zeus, and Paul, Hermes, because he was the chief speaker. And the priest of Zeus, whose temple was just outside the city, having brought oxen and wreaths to the gates, was desiring to sacrifice with the crowds. (Acts 14:11-13)

Why is it Barnabas who is hailed as Zeus, the chief and father of the gods, whereas Paul is only Hermes, the messenger of Zeus? The author of Luke hero worships Paul and goes out of her way to make Paul preeminent in this episode. It is Paul's act of healing the cripple that precipitates the worship. And she offers the explanation that Paul is called Hermes, the messenger of the gods because he is the chief speaker. But it is the priest of Zeus who comes to make sacrifice, and it is clear that Barnabas as Zeus is the centre of this story. Moreover, in the continuation Barnabas is mentioned before Paul:

But the apostles Barnabas and Paul having heard tore their garments, and rushed out into the crowd, crying out ... (Acts 14:14)

The author of Acts thinks wrongly that the apostles were the same as the twelve disciples and so she limits the term to the twelve. This is the only exception, the only time in the whole of Acts the term is applied to others and the only time that Paul is called an apostle. The author of Luke must be drawing upon a source in which both Barnabas and Paul are called apostles with Barnabas compared to Zeus and Paul to Hermes. To compare Barnabas, the companion and follower of Paul, to Zeus makes no sense. There were, however, two apostles whom the early Gentile church venerated above all others; Peter and Paul. So if Paul is Hermes, then Peter must be Zeus. If Barnabas has been substituted for "Cephas", who is the founder of the religion, then everything becomes clear. Paul is being flatteringly compared to Hermes, the messenger of Zeus because he is the eloquent communicator of Cephas' new religion.

The argument in Antioch

The confusion of Barnabas and Cephas confirms that Colossians is fake. If the relationship between Barnabas and Mark has arisen from the Acts source, then Paul cannot have written that Mark was the cousin of Barnabas. This must come from a forger who was familiar, directly or indirectly, with the Acts source. It also confirms what we have deduced about where Paul wrote "Peter" and where he wrote "Cephas" in Galatians. When Paul first visits Jerusalem, he stays with Cephas and in Paul's second visit to James and the "pillars" it is Peter the apostle whom he meets.

But most significantly it demonstrates that it is Cephas whom Paul confronts in Antioch. When Paul is writing 1 Corinthians he looks upon Cephas as the undisputed leader of the movement, but by the time he writes Galatians he has become severely disillusioned. The reason is not hard to find. Mary/Cephas has appointed James to the position of leader and is deferring to him even as he attempts to move the early church in a backward direction. Paul is furious with her. This fury extends even to denying his dependence on Cephas:

Paul, an apostle, not from men, neither by man, but by Jesus Christ, and God the Father, who raised him from the dead ... (Galatians 1:1)

Many disputed that Paul was an apostle. Paul defies the doubters with a ringing declaration that he is an apostle, not by, or through, man but by the appointment of Jesus and God. In his account of his conversion in Galatians, he goes out of his way to stress his independence from the established leaders of the church. About his gospel, he says that he *"neither received it of man, neither was I taught it, but by the revelation of Jesus Christ" (Galatians 1:12).* This is flatly contradicted by what follows. By his own account, he sought out Cephas for instruction and fourteen years later submits his gospel to the approval of the brethren in his second visit to Jerusalem. The contradiction extends to his other letters from which it is clear that he was taught a great deal by the movement. In Galatians, he is giving a declaration of independence and already beginning to rewrite his personal history.

The Antioch episode also casts light on the relationship between Mary/Cephas and James. If it is Mary/Cephas and not Peter who was at Antioch then it confirms that Mary has appointed James as leader within her lifetime. As a woman, she was always handicapped as leader of the movement in Judea. She had to rule through her pseudonym Cephas and the movement needed a visible leader. We must also remember that she would have been old for the time, in her late fifties or sixties. So she decides to appoint James as the leader and withdraws from Jerusalem. James was to prove no mere figurehead but had ideas of his own. One innovation of Mary that he did not accept was her highly visible acceptance of uncircumcised Gentiles. As leader of the movement in Judea this would have caused him intense difficulties and danger. Accepting Gentiles into the movement on these terms would have been seen as a betrayal by most Jews. It would have stopped the flow of new Jewish recruits and enraged the Jewish establishment.

The evidence is that the rejection of the law came from Mary/Cephas and was not the huge step that it might seem because the apocalyptic movement from which Christianity evolved already devalued the law of Moses. However, at a practical level most Jews did look to the law and once the Jesus movement had expanded out of its original apocalyptic beginnings this would have become a burning issue. One of the signs of this conflict is Paul himself. For Paul, the Torah was vitally important. Once he had accepted Mary's law rejection he had to develop it into a philosophy; it is not unusual for a founder's followers to be more dogmatic than the founder would be. But Paul cannot have made the initial innovation. If Paul had taught rejection of the Torah in a movement that was law observant he would have known full well that he would be rejected. He would not have felt the bitterness that comes through in his letters, a bit-

terness born of a deep sense of betrayal. Paul tells us exactly why he feels
this bitterness towards James and the pillars:

*Those who wish to have a fair appearance in the flesh, these compel you to be
circumcised, only that they might not be persecuted for the cross of Christ. For not
even those being circumcised keep the Law, but they want you to be circumcised so
that they may boast in your flesh. (Galatians 6:12-13)*

Paul tells the Galatians bluntly that the reason for insisting on circumcision is to make a better impression among the Jews and so to avoid persecution. Significantly Paul accuses his opponents of not keeping the law
themselves showing that the rejection of the law is deep and long standing
in the movement. We may view James' difficulties more sympathetically
than Paul. He has to cope with the huge political problems that the acceptance of non-law observant Gentiles caused. It is a question of maintaining an outward show of Judaism even though the Jesus movement was not
law observant in private. Accepting non-circumcised Gentiles was too visible and too emotive for other Jews. It is this outward show that Paul calls
making a good appearance "in the flesh". But for James it is a matter of life
and death, and he will eventually pay the ultimate price at the hands of
Herod Agrippa II. His attempt at avoiding an outward split with Judaism
is futile because the Jesus movement is at heart deeply heretical.

Paul says that when Cephas first came to Antioch, he used to eat with
the Gentiles but then separated from them on the coming of "certain from
James". Eating with Gentiles and ignoring the purity laws in this way is
consistent with the Gospel of Thomas which says that the disciples while
travelling should accept hospitality and eat what is put before them. The
initial purpose may have been practical to enable missionaries to proselytise among Gentiles, but it was to have profound implications. But Paul accuses Cephas of something much wider than just eating with gentiles and
that is living like a Gentile and not like a Jew. This is all consistent with
Acts where it is Peter who decides that the purity laws no longer apply. It
is Mary/Cephas who alone was in a position to abandon the law, and she
lives what she preaches.

One senses that Mary must have been quite an embarrassment to James.
The evidence from the Barnabas-Cephas source used by Acts is that it is
Simon Peter the apostle and not Cephas that Paul met in Jerusalem. After
the Jerusalem meeting, Paul moves on to Antioch and waits for Cephas to
arrive. Neither this nor the subsequent arrival of those from James would
make sense if Cephas were present in Jerusalem. Mary/Cephas is arriving

from somewhere else, and Paul has arranged to meet her in Antioch. He accuses her of living as a Gentile and we may conclude that she has been living among Gentiles. In fact, all the evidence points to Mary having left Jerusalem at around the time she appointed James as leader and moved her base to Rome. At first the meeting between Mary and Paul goes well but then the delegation from James arrives. The "certain from James" have been sent to persuade Mary about not accepting uncircumcised Gentiles. To begin with, it looks like they have succeeded for she stops eating with Gentiles. The influence of Mary/Cephas is immediately apparent because all the other Jews, even Paul's closest companion Barnabas, follow her example. But we may suspect that this is a temporary concession on her part. While in the East and among Jews she will outwardly support James' leadership, but once back in Rome she will again live like a Gentile.

What is most fascinating in this episode is that Paul appears to accuse Cephas of being a sinner: *"If you being a Jew, live after the manner of gentiles, and not as the Jews, why compel the gentiles to live as do the Jews? We who are Jews by nature, and not sinners of the gentiles"* (*Galatians* 2:14-15). Paul and Cephas are "Jews by nature" that is by birth. The implication is that Cephas not only lives like a Gentile but is a sinner like the Gentiles. Paul cannot mean the purity laws here because he does not regard breaking these as a sin. It would seem that Cephas/Mary has taken advantage of the "freedom from the law" philosophy of the movement to act in ways that Paul considers sinful. The accusation in front of everyone that Cephas is a sinner is personal and would have been far more damaging to the relationship of Paul and Cephas than the disagreement about eating with Gentiles. Paul, despite all their differences, is careful in Galatians not even to hint at the nature of this sinful behaviour.

All of which brings us to John Mark. In Acts, the argument in Antioch is between Paul and Barnabas about taking John Mark with them on their journey. Paul objects because he *"departed from them at Pamphylia"*. We know that this comes from the Barnabas-Cephas source and that it must be Cephas whom Paul argues with in the original. The implication is that the argument was over Paul objecting to Cephas wanting to travel with John Mark! The author of Acts thinks that the reason Paul objects is that John left them at Pamphylia, but she is surely wrong. John Mark is Mary's constant companion, her "son" with whom she lives. It would have been unusual for the two to be separated, but we know they were separated at this time because Paul meets John in Jerusalem without Cephas being present. This parting was sufficiently unusual to have left its mark on the record. Acts recounts how John left Barnabas and Paul at *"Perga of Pamphylia"* to go to

Jerusalem, and this must again come from the Barnabas-Cephas source. So in the original source John parts from Cephas to go on to Jerusalem. The idea that Paul was with them is a mistake by the author of Luke arising from the confusion between Cephas and Paul's companion Barnabas. John Mark's real purpose would have been to visit his brother James whom he would not have seen for years, but in the Acts story it looks as though he has left for a lack of missionary zeal. If John Mark and Cephas had parted at Perga, it would have been perfectly logical for them to meet up again at Antioch.

It may have been that the long journey to Jerusalem was too much for Mary at her age, or it may have been that Jerusalem was too dangerous for her. Or perhaps she is deliberately avoiding James. Is it significant that Mary did not meet with James at any time on this visit? Whatever the reason, after a stay at Perga she would have travelled by boat along the coast to Antioch where she and John Mark could find a boat back to Rome. Paul would have learnt of her intentions from John Mark at Jerusalem and decided to go to Antioch to meet her. Acts says that John Mark went to Jerusalem and that later he was present at Antioch but does not tell us how he got from Jerusalem to Antioch. Logically he would have travelled with Paul and Barnabas. And this journey may have left its impression in Acts although it has been placed out of sequence:

And Barnabas and Saul returned from Jerusalem, when they had fulfilled their ministry, and took with them John, who was called Mark. (Acts 12:25)

In the narrative, the place that they come to is Antioch. In Acts, this is the return journey of a trip to deliver a collection from the church at Antioch to the saints in Jerusalem.[277] However, from the evidence of Galatians, Paul never made such a journey. He does mention a collection for the saints at Jerusalem in his letters, but not from Antioch. It would seem that the author of Luke heard of a collection and has wrongly inserted this extra visit from Antioch. One of her sources may be the recollection of the actual journey to Antioch by Barnabas, Paul and John at the conclusion of Paul's second visit to Jerusalem.

At Antioch, they wait until Mary joins them. At first all goes well. However, James either hears about how his "mother" is behaving or he is already alarmed at the prospect of this meeting between Mary and Paul. Either way he sends a delegation to persuade Mary to withdraw from eating with gentiles and she complies. It is then that Paul and Mary have their argument, and it is then that Paul may have raised accusations concerning her relationship with John. We should remember that this is probably the first time that Paul has spent any length of time with Mary since his first visit to Jerusalem and at that time John Mark would have been just a youth. His disillusionment with her may be due to more than just the appointment of James. He may have been shocked by her behaviour. Because of this argument Paul and Mary part in anger, with Mary and John Mark returning to Rome via Cyprus. The argument has left its trace both in Paul's letter to Galatians and in the Barnabas-Cephas source which has been used by Acts.

It is worth summarising the sequence of events in this journey by Mary and John:

1. Mary/Cephas and John travel to the eastern Mediterranean by boat from Rome. They split at either Cyprus or Perga, with John continuing to Jerusalem and Mary/Cephas going to or remaining at, Perga. They agree to meet again at Antioch.

2. Paul and Barnabas have travelled independently to Jerusalem where they find John together with James and Simon Peter.

3. Paul, Barnabas and John travel together back from Jerusalem to Antioch to meet with Mary/Cephas.

4. Mary/Cephas travels by boat along the coast to Antioch to make the planned rendezvous with John.

5. Initially, all goes well in this meeting in Antioch between Mary/Cephas and Paul.

6. However, James sends a delegation to Antioch to persuade Mary/Cephas to change her behaviour.

7. As a result, Paul and Mary/Cephas argue in Antioch.

8. Mary/Cephas and John get a boat back to Rome via Cyprus.

Salome and the beloved

Is there any evidence to support the idea that the argument in Antioch touched on Mary's relationship with John Mark? There is evidence that could be interpreted as implying that the relationship between the two was demonstratively affectionate. This relates to the Gospel of John which claims to be based on the testimony of the beloved disciple.[278] The Gospel of John describes how this beloved disciple shared a couch with Jesus:

There was reclining on Jesus' bosom one of his disciples, whom Jesus loved.
(John 13:23)

This disciple whom Jesus loved can be identified with John, who is traditionally the author of the Gospel of John. Of course, the Gospel of John
was not written by John Mark, but it does show that those who wrote the
gospel at around 100 had inherited a tradition that the disciple John was
especially loved. Under the shaman paradigm, there was no physical Jesus
to share a couch with. So this episode must either go back to the divine
marriage between Jesus and the shaman, or to the relationship between
John Mark and the shaman.

In fact, we can be sure that it is the divine marriage because we can
identify the source. The story is derived from a version of the Thomas 61
saying about Salome sharing a couch with Jesus. In the version used by
John, the disciple sharing the couch is unnamed, and the author of John has
wrongly assumed that it must be the beloved disciple, John. Salome was
another name for the founder, Mary, and Thomas 61 is about the divine
marriage, so it is not surprising that versions without the name "Salome"
were in circulation.

In the Gospel of John, the couch-sharing episode has become part of the
story of the betrayal by Judas Iscariot. The account of this betrayal is embellished as we go from gospel to gospel. In the first gospel, Mark, Judas plans
the betrayal in advance with the high priests for money[279] and at the last
supper Jesus predicts that one who dips bread into the bowl with him will
betray him.[280] Matthew is very similar to Mark except that the price is now
specifically thirty pieces of silver and Judas is identified as the betrayer at
the last supper.[281] The author of Luke adds the detail that Satan entered
Judas.[282] But the most developed account is in John, starting with the role
of Satan:

And supper having come, the devil had already put it into the heart of Judas of
Simon, Iscariot, that he may betray him. Jesus knew that the Father had given all
things into his hands, and that he was come from God, and was going to God;
(John 13:2-3)

Later it is told how Jesus predicts the identity of his betrayer and how
Satan enters into Judas:

Having said these things, Jesus was troubled in spirit, and testified, "Truly, truly, I say to you that one of you will betray me." The disciples began to look at one another, being uncertain of whom he is speaking. There was reclining on Jesus' bosom one of his disciples, whom Jesus loved. So Simon Peter motions to him, to ask who it is about whom he is speaking. Then he leaning on the breast of Jesus, says to him, "Lord, who is it?" Then Jesus answers, "It is he to whom I will give this morsel when I have dipped it." Then having dipped the morsel, he gives it to Judas, son of Simon Iscariot. And after the morsel, Satan entered into him. So Jesus says to him, "What you do, do quickly." Now none of those reclining knew why he said this to him. Since Judas had the money bag, some thought that Jesus was saying to him to buy the things needed for the feast, or that he should give something to the poor. Therefore having received the morsel, he went out immediately. And it was night. (John 13:21-30)

Why has the author of John involved the beloved disciple in this story of Judas? He does not appear in any of the other gospels. The answer lies in Thomas 61. The author of John has considered this saying and the contrast between the one who is equal and the one who is divided and concluded that it is all about the betrayal of Jesus (the one equal) by Judas (the one divided). We can see this from the similarities between Thomas 61 and the last supper in John in the table below:

Thomas 61	Correspondence in John 13:1-30
Jesus said: Two shall rest upon a bed [or couch]; one shall die, the other live.	The disciple whom Jesus loved is sharing a couch with Jesus. This is Jesus' last supper, and he will shortly die. Moreover, in John 21:22-23, Jesus says that the beloved disciple should live until he returns and there is a rumour that he will never die.
Salome said: Who are you man?	Simon Peter wishes to ask Jesus who will betray him, but instead of asking directly he goes through the disciple Jesus loved. This is evidence that the source had the question asked by this disciple. The question is very similar to Salome's: *Then he leaning on the breast of Jesus, says to him, "Lord, who is it?" (John 13:25)*

Thomas 61	Correspondence in John 13:1-30
While out of one,	This phrase can be interpreted as being the question - "Whose son?".[283] In reply, Jesus gives the morsel to "*Judas, son of Simon Iscariot*" (John 13:26). So we are told whose son Judas is - it is only the Gospel of John that gives a father to Judas, and he is called, unimaginatively, Simon Iscariot.
you have climbed onto my bed [couch], and ate from my table.	They are all eating around the table on couches - *Now there was reclining on Jesus' bosom one of his disciples, whom Jesus loved.* (John 13:23)
Jesus said to her: I am he who is from that which is equal;	This is interpreted as meaning that Jesus was part of God - ... *and that he was come from God, and was going to God;* (John 13:3)
to me was given of the things of my Father.	*Jesus knew that the Father had given all things into his hands ...* (John 13:3)
I am your disciple. (Probably said by Salome)	In John, the person reclining with Jesus is called "*one of his disciples, whom Jesus loved*" (John 13:23)
Therefore I say, when he should be equal he will be filled with light	There is a reference to Jesus and God being made equal and so "glorified". *When he was gone, Jesus said, "Now the Son of Man is glorified, and God is glorified in him. If God is glorified in him, God also will glorify him in himself, and will glorify him immediately."* (John 13:31-32)
but when he should be divided he will be filled with darkness.	Interpreted as meaning that Satan has entered into Judas so that he is divided, the darkness being represented as night; *And after the morsel, Satan entered into him.* (John 13:27). *Therefore having received the morsel, he went out immediately. And it was night.* (John 13:30)

One element obviously missing in John is any reference to Salome. The author of John's version could not have had this name but something like "the one whom Jesus loved". If we make this substitution then the agreement is very precise. We should note that everything in Thomas 61 is matched to something in John 13, which is linked to a passage concerning the betrayal of Judas. Also, all these matching elements are additions that the author of John makes to the basic Judas story from the other gospels. Moreover the two times a compound saying is split (*"I am he who is from that which is equal, to me was given of the things of my Father"* and *"therefore I say, when one makes equal they will be filled with light, but when one divides they will be filled with darkness"*) the matching elements in John are either two parts of the same line (John 13:3) or successive lines (John 13:30-32) although in both cases the order of the parts is reversed. We should also note the very particular agreement that Jesus is given the things of the Father in both Thomas 61 and John 13:3.

With the knowledge that the author of John has used Thomas 61 we can see something that we might otherwise miss; Jesus and Judas are presented as symmetrical opposites. The nature of Jesus is to be equal with God whereas the nature of Judas is to be divided by Satan. In Thomas 61 the one made equal is filled with light whereas, in John, Jesus and God are to be glorified (*doxazo*). But the "glory" (*doxa*) of God is equivalent to light in texts such as Isaiah 60:1: *"Arise, shine; for your light has come, and the glory of Yahweh is risen upon you."* Jesus is part of God and will return to God and so is made equal and glorified, that is filled with light. But Judas has been possessed by Satan, so his nature is divided, and he is cast into darkness (the night).

Of particular interest is the first element of Thomas 61, that two will lie on a "bed" (which can mean a couch at a table) and that one will die and the other live. The author of John must have interpreted this as being about Jesus and the beloved disciple; in the Gospel the two share a couch at the last supper before one of them, Jesus, dies. If so, then the beloved disciple must be the one who "lives" according to the saying. Is there any evidence for this interpretation? There is! In the final section of the Gospel is a story concerning the beloved disciple:

Peter turned and saw that the disciple whom Jesus loved following, the one who had leaned back against his breast at the supper and had said, "Lord, who is going to betray you?" When Peter saw him, he asked, "Lord, what about this man?" Jesus answered, "If I want him to remain until I return, what is that to you? You follow me." Because of this, the saying spread among the brothers that this disciple would not die. But Jesus did not say that he would not die, only "If I want him to remain until I return, what is that to you?" (John 21:20-23)

This fascinating episode tells us that there was a saying (*logos*) in existence that was interpreted as meaning that the beloved disciple will live forever. Moreover, it links back to the beloved disciple sharing Jesus' couch at the last supper. The saying must, in fact, be Thomas 61a! Since the beloved disciple is long dead at this point, the interpretation of this saying as meaning that he will live forever is an embarrassment. However, the original saying does not say he will live forever, but only that "*one shall die, the other live*". So an alternative explanation was developed that what Jesus meant was that although he would die, the disciple would survive to witness and share in Jesus' resurrection.

The author of the final section of John has inherited the understanding that (i) there is a saying existence predicting the beloved disciple will live and (ii) that it does not mean he will live forever but until Jesus returns. He literalises his understanding into a story in which Jesus predicts quite clearly that the beloved disciple will live until he returns. But this involves repositioning the prediction from the last supper, where it would make sense, to the resurrection appearances, where it makes absolutely no sense. Jesus is about to disappear until the apocalypse, so predicting that the disciple will live until he returns is equivalent to saying he will live forever! The person who had used Thomas 61 to evolve the story of the beloved disciple at Jesus' breast would never have addressed the issue in this way, so it supports the supposition that the author of this end section did not write the rest of the gospel.

It is clear that the couch story does not go back to a genuine recollection of an event concerning John. Yet it is still significant that the person who wrote the Gospel of John chose to identify John with the disciple portrayed on the couch with Jesus. There must have been some tradition that John was especially beloved by the founder of the movement. In fact, what has happened is that the author of John has created his "beloved disciple" from various scraps of sayings and traditions; some of these relate to Mary as the beloved of Jesus, and some to John Mark as the beloved of Mary. The author of John does not realise that his beloved disciple is actually two people. He attributes his gospel to the best possible authority; the founder and the person who was closest to her and who operated as her secretary. Both of these are described as beloved in his sources, and he does not distinguish between them.

After his story about the beloved disciple living forever, the author of the final section goes on to tell us something else:

This is the disciple who bears witness to these things and who wrote them down. We know that his witness is true. (John 21:24)

So the gospel is supposedly based on the testimony of the beloved disciple, who is actually a composite of the shaman Mary, and John Mark. We have seen how John draws on Thomas 61 for the story of the beloved disciple, and that the author of the last section had some knowledge of this fact. We have also seen that the Gospel of Thomas was originally called the Gospel of the Twin and that it records the sayings of the shaman Mary. We will see that John Mark also had an important role in compiling Thomas as a written document. So the beloved disciple is a composite of the two people who were both involved in the writing of Thomas. So when the author of the final section says that the Gospel of John is based upon the testimony of the beloved disciple, is he really saying that it was based on the Gospel of Thomas? In the next chapter, we will see that this is correct. The Gospel of John's use of Thomas 61 is not unique but part of a long section based, saying-by-saying, on Thomas.

John the beloved

To describe John as beloved is no more than we already know from the fact that he was Mary's constant companion. The only evidence that some may have thought the relationship was improper comes from Paul's accusation in Antioch that Cephas was a sinner and the hint from Acts 15:36-39 that the argument concerned the principle of John Mark accompanying Cephas (Barnabas). It also has to be said that Mary the Magdalene had the reputation of being a whore, although this can be explained by her possession by seven demon husbands before the coming of her true husband, the Christ. We do not need to invoke promiscuous behaviour on the part of Mary although equally such behaviour cannot be ruled out. Ultimately the evidence is ambiguous, and we cannot be sure of the exact nature of the relationship between Mary and her beloved "son".

After Antioch Mary/Cephas and John Mark sail off together leaving behind a fuming Paul. One must feel sorry for Paul for he is trying to apply principle to the chaotic philosophy of Mary and the movement yet he is always subtly wrong. It is clear from Galatians that he is in a minority of one and that even his close friend Barnabas followed Cephas. Was the argument between Mary and Paul ever mended? The Acts source records with a sense of finality that Barnabas and Paul *"were parted from one another"*

(Acts 15:39). This suggests a break-up between Cephas and Paul as is evident from Paul recasting his relationship with Jesus to avoid any dependence upon Cephas. But Paul does not split with the church and later when he writes Philemon from prison in Rome he is to name Mark prominently among those who send their greetings. Things have evidently been patched up. By this time external events and the active persecution of the movement by the Romans would have made internal disputes seem unimportant.

Key points

1. Mark is linked to both Peter and Mary as a "son" who lives with them. This is to be expected if Peter is the same as Mary. Although Mark comes over as a relatively obscure character from Acts, the fact that the first Gospel was named after him indicates his true importance in the early movement.

2. There are links between Mark and Barnabas that parallel those between Mark and Peter. These links suggest confusion between Barnabas and Peter/Cephas. In Colossians, Paul calls Mark a nephew of Barnabas. However the contents of Colossians, and the fact that the greetings have been forged using those in Philemon, show that Colossians was not written by Paul.

3. The evidence is best explained if Barnabas has been confused with Cephas in a source used by Acts. An early Christian has not recognised the unfamiliar name "Cephas" in Paul's letters as being the same as "Peter". Instead, he or she has equated Cephas with Barnabas due to a misreading of Paul's account in Galatians of the argument at Antioch.

4. The confusion explains why Acts has Paul stay with Barnabas on his first visit to Jerusalem whereas the evidence of Paul's own letters is that he stayed with Cephas.

5. The confusion also explains the story where Barnabas and Paul are worshipped as Zeus and Hermes. In the original source, Cephas must have been compared to Zeus and Paul with Hermes, the messenger of Zeus.

6. The confusion also explains the argument that Barnabas and Paul supposedly had about Mark at Antioch. This was really the argument between Paul and Cephas at Antioch.

7. With the realisation that Barnabas sometimes stands for Cephas in Acts, we can reconstruct the events that led to Antioch. John Mark travelled with Mary from Rome to Pamphylia where they parted. He continued on

to Jerusalem to meet with his brother James and was there when Paul also visited James. Meanwhile, Mary travelled the easier coastal route to Antioch. After the "council" in Jerusalem, Paul and Barnabas travel back with John Mark to meet Mary at Antioch. All went well until James, alarmed by this meeting between Paul and Mary, sent others to persuade Mary to alter her behaviour and not eat with Gentiles. This caused an argument between Paul and Mary in which he accused her of being a "sinner", possibly because of her relationship with John Mark. After the argument, Mary and John Mark leave for Rome.

8. The story of the beloved disciple John resting on the breast of Jesus in the Gospel of John shows that there was a tradition that John was especially beloved.

9. However, the story in John is based on a misunderstanding of Thomas 61 concerning Salome. The author of John must have a version of this saying that is not attached to the name Salome but to the beloved disciple.

10. In the Thomas saying, Salome is sharing a couch with Jesus. It is said that one who is united is full of light, which has been interpreted as Jesus being united with God, and so glorified. However, one who is divided is full of darkness, which is interpreted as Judas being possessed by the devil, and so divided.

11. If the version of Thomas 61 used by the author of John had the beloved disciple instead of Salome, this would explain John 21:20-23 where it is said that there is a saying circulating that the beloved disciple will not die. This saying is Thomas 61: *"Two shall rest upon a bed [or couch]; one shall die, the other live."*

Chapter 38

The Gospel of John's Last Supper

At the end of John, it is claimed that the Gospel is based on the testimony of the beloved disciple. In reality, the beloved disciple is a created character, a composite which draws on traditions of both Mary, as beloved of Jesus, and her favourite "son" John Mark, who was her constant companion and secretary. The one text which can be genuinely attributed to Mary and John Mark is the Gospel of Thomas, originally called the Gospel of the Twin. So is the "testimony" of the beloved disciple actually the Gospel of Thomas?

The last supper in John as an elaboration of Thomas

The Gospel of John is perhaps the most beautiful of all the books in the New Testament. As the most spiritual of all the gospels, it has fascinated readers for millennia. It has been seen as being "gnostic" which until recently was believed to imply that it was written long after the other gospels, perhaps even as late as the third century. We now know this idea of a late John is wrong, and most scholars would date it to around 100.

One of the parts of John that give the gospel its unique, spiritual, flavour is the account of the Last Supper, in which Jesus gives his followers a lengthy farewell discourse. There have been many theories to explain how it came to be written, including those who think in was the creation of more than one author. However, most would agree that it is a profound and poetic statement of Christian doctrine. It may have inspired many people, but what has probably never occurred to anyone that the discourse has been cobbled together from another source which has been completely misunderstood by the author of John. But this is exactly what has happened! We will trace how the Gospel's last supper account is based on the Gospel of Thomas.

The section dependent upon Thomas starts shortly before the Last Supper proper. Jesus has just entered triumphantly into Jerusalem with the people declaring "Hosanna!". At this point, the author of John begins using Thomas, starting with saying 24:

Thomas 24

His disciples said: "Show us the place where you are, for it is necessary for us to seek after it." He said to them: "He that has ears, let him hear. There is light within a man of light, and he becomes light to the whole world. If he does not become light, he is darkness." (Thomas 24)

The interpretation of this saying is split in the Gospel of John. For the first part, some "Greeks" seek after Jesus:

Now there were some Greeks among those coming up to worship at the feast. They came to Philip, who was from Bethsaida in Galilee, and they asked him, "Sir, we would like to see Jesus." (John 12:20-21)

The reason it has to be Greeks and not Jews will become clear a few sayings later. His disciples give the message to Jesus whose reply seems strange because it is derived from the Thomas saying in the next section. The second part of Thomas 24 is about light in the man of light, and how if there is not light, there is darkness. The corresponding John passage comes a little later:

So Jesus said to them, "You are going to have the light just a little while longer. Walk while you have the light, so that darkness does not overtake you." (John 12:35)

The Gospel of John interprets Jesus as being the light, with the state of darkness being the absence of Jesus. After Jesus finishes his speech he hides:

These things Jesus spoke, and having gone away was hidden from them. (John 12:36)

This matches the beginning of Thomas 24, which implies that Jesus is hidden so that it is necessary to seek after him.

Thomas 11

We must now go back to Jesus' answer when he is told that the Greeks want to see him. This is a development of Thomas 11:

Jesus said: "This heaven shall pass away, and that which above it shall pass away. And the dead are not alive and the living will not die. In the days you were eating that which is dead you were making it alive. When you come into the light, what will you do? On the day when you were one, you were made two. But when you have become two, what will you do?" (Thomas 11)

This is one of the most mystic sayings in Thomas, and is about a person and their spirit. We should not be surprised if the author of John misunderstands this saying, and he does! The part of John that uses this saying looks, at first sight, to be completely different from Thomas 11, so we shall take each part in turn to show the close similarity.

Thomas 11a
Jesus said: "This heaven shall pass away, and that which above it shall pass away."

This is matched to two passages, the first at the beginning of the Thomas 11 section and the other at the end:

Jesus replied, "The hour has now come for the Son of Man to be glorified. (John 12:23)

"Now is the time for judgment on this world; now the prince of this world will be cast out." (John 12:31)

The author of John interprets the crucifixion and resurrection as the beginning of the end of the world. The next section is taken out of sequence:

Thomas 11c
"In the days you were eating that which is dead you were making it alive."

This is interpreted as the necessity for Jesus dying:

"Truly, truly I tell you, unless a grain of wheat falls to the ground and dies, it remains alone. But if it dies, it bears much fruit." (John 12:24)

We can see the similarity between the two sayings; both are concerned with something that is eaten and in both cases, this thing dies to become alive. The author of John interprets Thomas 11c as being about the impending death of Jesus, and the necessity of his dying to give life to many. He thinks the "eating that what is dead" in Thomas 11 is a reference to the Eucharist.

Thomas 11b

"And the dead are not alive and the living will not die."

The author of John has interprets this in relation to a saying which is found in several versions in the synoptic gospels:[284]

"The one who loves his life will lose it, and the one who hates his life in this world will keep it for eternal life." (John 12:25)

As it is clear what the synoptic saying means, the author of John substitutes it for the puzzling Thomas saying. We can see the close link between the two; both sayings are organised as two contrasting but matching halves, both concern life and death, and both express themselves through paradox. The meaning of the two, though, is quite different.

Thomas 11d

"When you come into the light, what will you do? On the day when you were one, you were made two. But when you have become two, what will you do?"

This is interpreted in terms of the disciple becoming two through union with Jesus:

"If anyone serves me, let him follow me, and where I am, my servant will also be. If anyone serves me, the Father will honour him." (John 12:26)

The servant is one, but Jesus will be with him to make two. Jesus is the light, so when the servant is with Jesus he or she enters into the light. The

question "when you become two, what will you do?" is answered by the
servant of Jesus being honoured by the father.

Each successive part of the narrative John 12:23-26 corresponds to something in Thomas 11. It is vanishingly unlikely that this should arise by
chance.

Thomas 33

*Jesus said: "What you shall hear in your ear, proclaim to the other ear on your
housetops. For no man lights a lamp and puts it under a bushel, nor does he put it
in a hidden place; but he puts it upon the lamp-stand, that all who go in and come
out may see its light." (Thomas 33)*

The first part of this saying, about what is heard in the ear being proclaimed from the housetops, has been interpreted as a story about God
hearing Jesus, and then proclaiming what has heard as a great voice from
heaven:

*"Father, glorify your name!" Then a voice came from heaven, "I have glorified
it, and again will glorify it." The crowd standing there heard it and said there had
been thunder; others said an angel had spoken to him. (John 12:28-29)*

The correspondence of the second part of Thomas 33, involving the
theme of light, is more tentative because the concept of Jesus being light is
pervasive in this part of John. The idea of the light, which in John is Jesus,
being put on a high lamp stand is linked to something Jesus says:

And I, if I am lifted up from the earth, will draw all to myself. (John 12:32)

There could also be an influence in something that comes a little later:

*I have come into the world as a light, so that everyone who believes in me will
not abide in the darkness. (John 12:46)*

We then have the second half of Thomas 24 before the next saying.

Thomas 34

Jesus said: "If a blind man leads a blind man, they both fall into a pit." (Thomas 34)

The correspondence is straightforward:

"Whoever walks in the dark does not know where they are going." (John 12:35)

Thomas 31

Jesus said: "No prophet is acceptable in his village; a physician does not heal those who know him." (Thomas 31)

This has been interpreted as meaning that Jesus' own people, the Jews, have rejected him:

Even after Jesus had performed so many signs before them, they still would not believe in him. (John 12:37)

We see now why it is the Greeks who seek Jesus to become his disciples. This is all part of Jesus' rejection by the Jews. We now go back to the idea that the Jews have been blinded and so cannot see the light (Jesus).

Thomas 26

Jesus said: "The mote which is in your brother's eye, you see; the beam, however, in your eye, you do not see. When you cast out the beam from your own eye, then you will see to cast out the mote from your brother's eye." (Thomas 26)

The author John seems to have interpreted this (completely wrongly) as the Jews seeing the sin of the Gentiles (the mote) but not realising their own blindness (the large beam). They cannot do what Jesus tells them and remove the beam from their eyes because they have been blinded due to their rejection of God:

For this reason they could not believe, for again Isaiah says: "He has blinded their eyes and hardened their hearts, so that they should not see with their eyes, nor understand with their hearts, nor turn and I would heal them." (John 12:39-40)

Now that the author of John is getting warmed up on his favourite theme of the Jews, he skips ahead to deal with a saying about the Pharisees.

Thomas 39

Jesus said: "The Pharisees and the scribes have taken the keys of knowledge; they have hidden them. They did not go in, and those who wanted to go in they did not allow." (Thomas 39a)

The corresponding passage is:

Although indeed many even among the leaders believed in him. But because of the Pharisees they did not confess it so they would not be put out of the synagogue. (John 12:42)

Although some of the Jewish leaders believe in Jesus and want to "go in" to him, they are not allowed by the Pharisees.

Thomas 61

After Thomas 39 we get into the last supper, and we have seen how the Gospel of John draws on the Salome saying, Thomas 61, in the previous chapter. But that is not the only Thomas saying it uses.

Thomas 37

His disciples said: "On what day will you appear to us, and on what day will we look upon you?" Jesus said: "When you strip naked and are not ashamed, and take your garments and put them beneath your feet like little children and trample them, then [you will see] the son of the Living One and you shall not fear." (Thomas 37)

This is represented by the famous episode of Jesus washing the disciples feet:

So he got up from the meal, laid aside his garments, and taking a towel, girded himself. After that, he poured water into a basin and began to wash his disciples' feet, drying them with the towel with which he was girded. (John 13:4-5)

In this episode, Jesus strips and uses a towel as a garment, which he uses to wash the disciples' feet. We see that this is a literalisation of Thomas 37, which includes stripping off clothes and putting the garments beneath the feet. Jesus is very keen that his disciples should have their feet washed and when Peter objects, Jesus says that if he does not wash him *"you have no part with me"* (John 13:8). The reason for this insistence becomes clear. The washing of feet is equivalent to trampling the garments beneath the feet and is necessary, according to Thomas 37, to see Jesus as "the son of the Living One", meaning God. Shortly after the feet washing we have the conclusion of Thomas 37:

If you know me, you will know my Father as well. From now on, you do know him and have seen him. (John 14:7)

The disciples question how they can see the Father, and he explains that the Father is in him, so that by seeing Jesus they are seeing the Father. The author of John is grappling here with a problem; in Thomas 37 the disciples ask how they can see Jesus, even though, according to the literal view of Jesus, he is supposed to be right in front of them! So he takes the clue from "son of the Living One" to interpret this as the disciples asking to see the Father, the Living One, through the son.

When St Augustine was baptised in North Africa, the ceremony involved taking off clothes and trampling them beneath the feet just as in Thomas 37. The author of John has misunderstood the saying which is certainly not about the washing of feet. The garment that is taken off and trampled upon is the body, which is left behind either through martyrdom or spiritually, so that the person becomes spirit and can look upon Jesus.

We must next take the Thomas saying that comes immediately after Thomas 37.

Thomas 38

Jesus said: "Many times have you desired to hear these words which I speak to you, and you have none other from whom to hear them. Some days will come when you will seek after me, and you will not find me." (Thomas 38)

This saying has also been used earlier, split between John 6:68-69 and 7:33-34. The use of the first part is clearer in John 6:68-69 than here, but we can trace the idea that Jesus' words are especially respected by the disciples:

"You call me 'Teacher' and 'Lord,' and you say rightly, I am so indeed." (John 13:13)

This comes immediately after the foot washing from the previous saying Thomas 37. Also the first use of the saying in John 6:68-69 is followed by the line *"Then Jesus replied, 'Did I not choose you the Twelve? And one of you is a devil!'" (John 6:70).* A very similar line comes after the passage that begins with 13:13: *"I do not speak of all of you. I know whom I have chosen. But this is to fulfil the Scripture: 'One who has shared my bread has lifted up his heel against me.'" (John 13:18)* This similarity suggests that the author of John is connecting the two uses of the first part of Thomas 38.

After this comes the section which we have seen is based on Thomas 61. This includes the prediction of Judas' betrayal and the episode of the beloved disciple and ends at John 13:32. The immediate next line continues the second part of Thomas 38, that a time will come when the disciples will seek after Jesus and will not find him:

"My children, I will be with you only a little longer. You will look for me, and just as I told the Jews, so I now say to you: Where I am going, you cannot come." (John 13:33)

Thomas 25

Jesus said: "Love your brother as your soul; guard him as the apple of your eye."

Jesus gives the disciples (Christian brothers) the instruction to love each other:

"A new command I give you: Love one another. As I have loved you, so also you should love one another. By this all will know that you are my disciples, if you love one another." (John 13:34-35)

After this comes a section about finding Jesus, and seeing the Father through the Son, which develop the themes of Thomas 38 and 37.

Thomas 41

Jesus said: "He who has in his hand, to him shall be given; and he who has not, from him shall be taken even the little that he has." (Thomas 41)

This is given the meaning that those who love Jesus will be given much more, whereas those who do not love him, will lose what little they have. Jesus' followers are promised a number of things; they will have any wish granted, they will be able to see Jesus again, and most important of all, they will receive the gift of the Holy Spirit:

"If you ask me for anything in my name, I will do it. If you love me, keep my commands. And I will ask the Father, and he will give you another advocate to help you and be with you forever, the Spirit of truth." (John 14:14-17)

In contrast to those who love Jesus, those who do not love Jesus' teachings will be given nothing and will not be able to recognise the Spirit. However, the Thomas saying goes further and says that they will lose even what little they have. This has been interpreted as meaning that they will not be even able to see Jesus physically because he will soon depart from the world:

"Before long, the world will no longer see me, but you will see me. Because I live, you also will live. [...] The one who loves me will be loved by my Father, and I too will love them and show myself to them."
Then Judas, not the Iscariot, said, "But, Lord, what has then occurred that you intend to show yourself to us and not to the world?"
Jesus replied, "Anyone who loves me will keep my word. My Father will love them, and we will come to them and make our home with them. Anyone who does not love me will not keep my words." (John 14:19-24)

Thomas 42

Jesus said: "Become passers-by." (Thomas 42)

This is matched by one of the great puzzles of the Gospel of John:

"Get up, let us go from here." (John 14:41)

Why does Jesus interrupt his long discourse to say they should leave? Immediately after this, he continues his discourse for several more pages. One theory is that this is a discontinuity which shows that Jesus speech originally ended here and that what comes later was written by a different hand or by the same author at a different time. However there is no evidence that this is so, and what comes later appears to be one whole with what has come before. We will trace the links to Thomas across this supposed discontinuity, showing that it was all written at the same time by the same person.

The discovery that the author of John is copying Thomas solves this puzzle. Thomas 42, telling the disciples to become passers-by, follows on immediately from Thomas 41 which the author of John has just used. It is very short, and the author of John interprets it literally.

Thomas 40

Jesus said: "A vine was planted apart from the Father, and since it is not established it will be pulled up by its roots and destroyed." (Thomas 40)

This is matched by what comes immediately after Jesus telling the disciples that they should leave:

I am the true vine, and my Father is the gardener. Every branch in me that bears no fruit he takes away, and every one that does bear fruit he prunes so that it will bear even more fruit. (John 15:1-2)

The Father destroys the part of the vine that does not produce fruit, just as in Thomas the vine not planted in the Father is destroyed because it fails to become established. In the Gospel of John, it is a branch on the vine that is destroyed rather than a whole vine. This change is necessary because Jesus has been made into the vine.

Thomas 43 & 45

The metaphor of the vine in John has come from combining Thomas 40 with Thomas 43 and 45:

His disciples said to him: "Who are you, that you speak these things to us?"

"From what I say to you, you do not understand who I am, but you have be-come as the Jews; for they love the tree and hate its fruit, and they love the fruit and hate the tree." (Thomas 43)

Jesus said: "They do not harvest grapes from thorns, nor gather figs from this-tles; they do not yield fruit. A good man brings forth a good thing from his treas-ure; a bad man bring forth evil things from his evil treasure which is in his heart, and he says evil things; for out of the abundance of his heart he brings forth evil things." (Thomas 45)

The tree that bears good fruit is Jesus, who brings life, and the tree that bears bad fruit is the Jewish Law, which brings death. In the Deep Source, the tree that bears no fruit, meaning the Jewish Law and the establishment, is destroyed.

In Thomas 43 we have the concept of Jesus being the tree that yields the fruit of life, and this has been taken over in John where Jesus is the vine. The implication of Thomas 45 is that a good man will yield fruit such as grapes and figs whereas a bad man is like a thorn bush or thistle and will produce only bad things. The author of John has taken all these elements and framed a metaphor to combine them; Jesus is the tree or vine, the dis-ciples are the branches and the fruit comes from the branches. This enables the fruit to come both from the disciples (Thomas 45) and Jesus (Thomas 43). The disciples yield the fruit but only if they remain in the vine, Jesus:

"As no branch can bear fruit by itself unless it remain in the vine, neither can you bear fruit unless you remain in me. I am the vine; you are the branches. If you remain in me and I in you, you will bear much fruit; apart from me you can do nothing. If you do not remain in me, you are like a branch that is thrown away and withers; and the branches are gathered, thrown into the fire and burned." (John 15:4-6)

The branches that do not yield fruit are to be destroyed, which combines Thomas 40, Thomas 45 and the Deep Source version of Thomas 43. These withered branches are also "in" Jesus although they do not remain in him. So they are disciples who prove to be false followers. They are the disciples who in Thomas 43 question Jesus' authority, and whom Jesus rebukes by comparing them to "the Jews" whose tree does not yield good fruit.

Thomas 23

Jesus said: "I shall choose you, one out of a thousand, and two out of ten thousand, and they shall stand as a single one." (Thomas 23)

The author of John interprets this as meaning that the chosen are the disciples:

"You did not choose me, but I chose you and appointed you so that you might go and bear fruit ... " (John 15:16)

It should be noted that if we add "1 in 1000" and "2 in 10,000" we get "12 in 10,000". We cannot be sure if the author of John has realised this, although in John 6:70 he talks about the twelve as being chosen. In any case, he has interpreted the thousand and the ten thousand as the multitude, the world:

"As it is, you do not belong to the world, but I have chosen you out of the world." (John 15:19)

The second part of the saying comes a little later. Although the disciples are still physically in the world, they are not of the world and will become "one".

"I will be in the world no longer, but they are in the world, and I am coming to you. Holy Father, keep them in your name, that you have given me, so that they may be one as we are one." (John 17:11)

It is not just the Twelve who will become one, so will all the other true followers of Jesus:

"My prayer is not for them alone. I pray also for those who will believe in me through their word, that all of them may be one, Father, as you are in me and I am in you. May they also be in us so that the world may believe that you have sent me. I have given them the glory that you gave me, that they may be one as we are one, I in them and you in me, so that they may be perfected in one ..." (John 17:20-23)

Thomas 44

Jesus said: "Whoever blasphemes against the Father will be forgiven, and whoever blasphemes against the Son will be forgiven but whoever blasphemes against the holy spirit will not be forgiven, either on earth or in heaven." (Thomas 44)

This has been given the interpretation by the author of John that it is the world and the ruler of the world who blaspheme. Although they blaspheme the Son and the father they are not brought to judgement until after Jesus' resurrection when the Holy Spirit will convict them.

First we are told that the world hates the Son:

"If the world hates you, you know that it has hated me before you." (John 15:18)

The world also hates the Father:

Whoever hates me hates my Father as well. If I had not done among them the works no one else did, they would not be guilty of sin. As it is, they have seen, and hated both me and my Father. (John 15:23-24)

They would not have sin, meaning they would have been forgiven, if they had not seen the works that Jesus has done. But now the time for judgement approaches, so they have seen the works and have rejected both Jesus and the Father. So the Father will send the disciples the Holy Spirit, the Helper, the spirit of truth. It is the Holy Spirit that will convict both the world and its ruler, meaning that they will never be forgiven:

Unless I go away, the Helper will not come to you; but if I go, I will send him to you. When he comes, he will convict the world concerning sin and concerning righteousness and concerning judgment; concerning sin, because they do not believe in me; and concerning righteousness, because I am going to the Father, and you will see me no more; and about judgment, because the ruler [archon] of the world has now been judged. (John 16:7-11)

Note how the Holy Spirit will convict the world on three counts; sin concerning Jesus, the son; righteousness concerning the Father; and judgment. We have a series of three here, so that the last should logically concern the Holy Spirit who will bring judgement on the *archon* of the world.

Thomas 92

Jesus said: "Seek, and you shall find; but those things you asked me in those days, I did not tell you then. Now I wish to tell them, and you seek not after them." (Thomas 92)

This saying is used in John 16. There is a hint of it in the midst of the elaboration of Thomas 44 above:

"I have told you this, so that when their hour comes you will remember that I told you about them. I did not tell you this from the beginning because I was with you, but now I am going to him who sent me and none of you asks me, 'Where are you going?'" (John 16:4-5)

The main development of the saying, though, comes a little later. The first part is interpreted as the disciples seeking to know Jesus' meaning when he tells them he will go away from them:

At this, some of his disciples said to one another, "What is this that he says to us, 'In a little while you will see me no more, and then after a little while you will see me,' and 'Because I am going to the Father'?" They kept asking, "What is this that the says 'a little while'? We do not know what he is saying." Jesus saw that they desired to ask him, so he said to them, "Are you asking one another what I meant when I said, 'In a little while you will see me no more, and then after a little while you will see me'? (John 16:17-19)

This is followed by two verses which are linked to Thomas 79 which is considered below. We then have the continuation of Thomas 92, that a time will come when the disciples will not question Jesus:

"You therefore now have grief, but I will see you again and you will rejoice, and no one will take away your joy. In that day you will no longer ask me anything." (John 16:22-23)

Thomas 79

A woman in the crowd said to him: "Blessed is the womb which bore you, and the breasts which nourished you." He said to her: "Blessed are they who have heard the word of the Father and have truly kept it. For there shall be days when you will say: "Blessed is the womb which has not conceived, and the breasts which have not given suck." (Thomas 79)

The use of this saying is sandwiched between the two parts of Thomas 92. For the author of John, those who have heard the will of the Father and have kept it are the disciples. So the saying is interpreted as relating to the disciples:

"Truly, truly I tell you, you will weep and mourn while the world rejoices. You will grieve, but your grief will turn to joy. A woman giving birth to a child has pain because her time has come; but when she brings forth the child she forgets the anguish because of the joy that a child is born into the world." (John 16:20-21)

The disciples are compared to a woman who gives birth. They will have grief and sorrow because of the pain and danger of birth. At this time they would say: "*Blessed is the womb which has not conceived, and the breasts which have not give suck.*" However, the disciples' grief will change to joy, just as the labouring woman is joyful when her baby is born. This relates to the first part of the saying: "*Blessed is the womb which bore you, and the breasts which nourished you.*"

The account of the Last Supper ends with Jesus' prayer in John 17 which largely occupied with the conclusion of Thomas 23. After this, Jesus crosses the brook of Kidron where he is arrested.

The author of John's Gospel of Thomas

In total we have identified 20 Thomas sayings used in the Last Supper section of John. The list, in order of first occurrence, is:

24,11,33,34,31,26,39,61,37,38,25,41,42,40,43,45,23,44,92,79

If we put the same list in numeric order we see a pattern:

11,23,24,25,26,31,33,34,37,38,39,40,41,42,43,44,45,61,79,92

There are 114 numbered sayings in the Gospel of Thomas, but out of the 20 sayings used here, 16 come from between Thomas 23 and 45. Moreover, there is a sequence of 9 consecutive sayings between 37 and 45 that have all been used. In percentage terms, 80% of the sayings used in John's Last Supper come from a section that amounts to just 20% of the Gospel of Thomas.

Suppose the author of John did not really use Thomas and the observed level of similarity is just coincidence. Then we would expect the Thomas sayings to be scattered throughout the gospel. The probability that they would be concentrated in such small section is insignificant, with an order of magnitude of millions to one against.[285] So we conclude that the links between John and Thomas are not random.

We can also see a broad correlation in the order in which the sayings have been used. This correlation is by no means perfect, but then we would not expect it to be. The author of John is writing his own narrative, and if he has used Thomas, he would have moved things around to suit this narrative. We should note that he sometimes splits up a saying and moves the second part one or two sayings later, which shows that his method of composition is not to precisely follow the order of Thomas.

To verify that a correlation exists, we apply a robust statistical test, the Kendall tau rank correlation.[286] This measures pairwise correlations from two lists of the same items. We can apply it to the two lists above, one being the order of use in John and the other the order in our Coptic version of Thomas. A correlation of 1 would mean that the order was perfectly matched, whereas a correlation of 0 would mean that the order was random. The observed correlation is 0.54, and the probability of such a correlation arising by chance is less than 1 in 2000.[287]

If the order has arisen from the author of John's method of composing the gospel then we would not expect every saying to be in order. For a start, saying 61 is special because it is the foundation stone around which the whole story is constructed. We can also observe that the four sayings 23-26 are scattered around, suggesting that they were not added by the same process by which the other sayings were incorporated. Suppose we exclude these five sayings, we will then find an excellent match:

John order:
11,33,34,31,39,37,38,41,42,40,43,45,44,92,79
Thomas order:
11,31,33,34,37,38,39,40,41,42,43,44,45,79,92

Now no saying has moved more than one or two places. This is reflected in the correlation coefficient which is a very high at 0.85 for this sublist.

Although the two sayings at the end are in reverse order, we should note that 79 has actually been sandwiched between the two parts of 92.

We can deduce the following composition process:

1. The author of John starts with the synoptic account of the last supper and Thomas 61 which he interprets as also being about the last supper.

2. The author also has Thomas sayings 23-26 which he takes as major themes for his account.

3. As he composes his story, he goes through the Gospel of Thomas in order with particular emphasis on 31-45 but also including three other sayings.

4. He makes some very minor changes to the order of these sayings for the purpose of his narrative. He also sometimes splits a saying, in which case he will use the second part one or two sayings after the first part.

This leaves two questions. The first is why does the author of John use Thomas 23-26 in a different way to the other sayings? Perhaps this sequence of four sayings should be five with saying 27 also included: *Jesus said: If you fast not from the world, you will not find the kingdom; if you keep not the Sabbath as Sabbath, you will not see the Father. (Thomas 27)* The opposition of the disciples and the "world" is a major theme of the farewell discourse.

It might be that the author of John had considered these four or five sayings early in his composition process and so had a theory of their meaning before he started the detailed composition of his Last Supper account. For this reason, they do not fit neatly into sequence.

The second question concerns the concentrated use of Thomas 31-45. No less than 12 out of this sequence of 15 sayings has been used. Does this mean that the author of John's Gospel of Thomas was not our complete version but consisted of something like 23-45 and a few other sayings? We can answer this in the negative. Although the author of John used 31-45 intensively for the last supper account, he had access to a complete gospel that looked very much like ours. We can say this because the last supper is not the only place where John uses Thomas. We will see in the second book that the author of John has also used Thomas extensively for John 5-8, as well as dipping into Thomas in other places.

Key points

1. The Last Supper narrative from John 12:20 to John 16:33 has been based on twenty Gospel of Thomas sayings.

2. The sayings have been heavily interpreted and frequently misunderstood by the author of John.

3. Some sayings have been split into two parts with the second half used one or two sayings later than the first.

4. The Thomas sayings used are not a random selection from the Gospel; 16 come from between Thomas 23 and 45. This means that 80% of the Thomas sayings come from just 20% of the gospel. The probability of this being random is of the order of hundreds of millions to one against.

5. The order of the sayings as used in John is correlated to the order in Thomas. The Kendall Tau rank correlation is 0.54, and the chance of this being a random result is 2000 to 1 against.

6. If we omit the saying 61 which is the foundation of John's last supper account, and sayings 23-26 which have been scattered around, then the order of the remaining sayings shows a very high correlation of 0.85. None of the remaining 15 sayings have been moved by more than two places.

7. This is evidence for a composition process as follows. The author started with Thomas 61 which he regarded as being about the last supper. He then builds his last supper account around this, going through the Gospel of Thomas, but concentrating mainly on Thomas 31-45. He uses the sayings basically in order, although he will sometimes move a saying by one or two places for the sake of his narrative and he will sometimes split a saying up and use the two parts separated by a similar distance. As he works through, he interpolates the four sayings from Thomas 23-26 spreading these around.

8. The use of Thomas by the author of John resolves the mystery of why Jesus suggests that they should all leave in the midst of his discourse. The saying that the author of John has just used is Thomas 41 and the next saying, Thomas 42, just says *"Become passers-by."*

Conclusion

The testimony of the beloved disciple upon which the Gospel of John claims to be based is the Gospel of Thomas. The author of John had something very like our Gospel of Thomas and based his long Last Supper narrative upon it.

Chapter 39
Why did Mary move to Rome?

Mary has travelled with John Mark from Rome to Antioch and returns to Rome after her argument with Paul. We will now look at the evidence linking Mary/Peter with Rome. It is closely associated with John who in this context is known under his Greek name Mark. Why did Mary relocate to Rome from Jerusalem? One answer is that she went to Rome to confront the man who was regarded as both the anti-Christ and a dragon.

Rome and Babylon

The evidence linking Mary/Cephas with Rome is substantial. There is a long-standing tradition that the church in Rome was founded by Peter as its first bishop. However, some have rejected the idea that Peter was ever in Rome. Why should a Palestinian Jew choose to live in Rome? But if Peter/Cephas is really Mary then things become clearer. As the female leader of a religious movement, she is in a uniquely difficult position in Jerusalem. She is forced to hide her identity under a male pseudonym and even then she must have been in considerable danger. This cannot go on and for the sake of the movement she appoints James as leader. Rome must have beckoned with the promise of freedom from the suffocating restrictions imposed upon her by the conventions of her fellow Jews. While she is in Jerusalem, she has the undesirable choice of either obeying James at least in public or undermining his authority. By removing herself from Jerusalem she avoids this choice. Although she is no longer official leader, she is still the tower, the temple and the true centre of the movement.

If she did move to Rome, this challenges the idea of Christianity being originally a Jewish movement that miscarried when Paul recast it as a new

Gentile religion. If Mary is living as a Gentile in Rome and not obliging the Roman Gentiles to be circumcised, then it is Paul who is her loyal follower and James who is leading the movement astray from its foundations. Mary herself has spearheaded the movement's expansion among the nations and has relocated the heart of her church among Gentiles. She has appointed James to lead her church formally but it is clear that his influence declines with increasing distance from Jerusalem. The first piece of evidence linking Mary with Rome is found in the letter 1 Peter. The letter starts with a greeting from the supposed author:

> *Peter, an apostle of Jesus Christ, to the elect sojourners of the dispersion [diaspora] of Pontus, Galatia, Cappadocia, Asia, and Bithynia, ... (1 Peter 1:1)*

Whoever did write 1 Peter it was certainly neither Cephas nor Simon Peter, the apostle. It is a fake written in elegant Greek and advancing the proto-orthodox opinions of the late first or early second centuries. It is clearly written by someone who was familiar with the letters of Paul and the author's view of Paul's philosophy is similar to the fake Pauline epistles. We should note that the letter is addressed to a list of eastern locations rather than a church in a particular city. Paul never addresses his letters to such a list but always to a particular community or individual. Given the difficulties of transmitting letters in the ancient world, would anyone really write a letter addressed to such a list? Why not instead write separately to each community and customise each letter with messages of encouragement and greeting?

The letter form used by Christians has developed from Paul. He is writing real letters that address the burning issues and concerns faced by a particular community of the movement. In these letters Paul develops and sets out his philosophy; not a philosophy in the abstract but a philosophy that is aimed at addressing concrete concerns. The only exception to this general rule among Paul's letters is Romans and we shall come to the reasons for that shortly. It is part of the unique genius of Paul that he has developed this idea of the letter as a vehicle for disseminating his views. It was to turn out a far more successful strategy than he could have ever believed possible. His letters began to be copied and to circulate beyond their original audience. Others in the early movement saw the burgeoning success of Paul's letters and began to produce their own. However, unlike Paul's letters these were designed as literary creations intended for circulation rather than as part of a conversation with a specific audience of individuals at a particular time and place.

Those who contributed to this second wave of letter writing had a problem. Why would anyone want to read their letters? A letter gains its authority from its author. If the true author did not possess authority, then a simple and effective strategy was to pretend it was written by someone who did. Forged letters became common. A number of forgeries supposedly from Paul have made it into the New Testament. A forger would have to be clever to get his letter accepted because other similar fakes were in circulation and the audience were not uncritical. To make a letter convincing a forger would use various tricks. They would attempt to copy the style and vocabulary of the supposed letter writer and would incorporate names, phrases and tit-bits of information from other letters or sources. And sometimes they might copy whole fragments of genuine letters. For example 2 Thessalonians incorporates elements of 1 Thessalonians.

It is this last technique which makes 1 Peter really interesting. For at the very end, there are a few obscure lines that do not fit the main letter. The probability is that the forger has copied these lines from a genuine letter attributed to Peter. The main letter ends with an Amen at 5:11. This is followed by a postscript, perhaps written originally in the author's own hand, and added to the end of a letter that had been dictated to a scribe:

By Silvanus, the faithful brother as I regard him, I have written to you briefly, exhorting and testifying this to be the true grace of God, in which you stand. (1 Peter 5:12)

Unlike the rest of the letter, this line is not in elegant Greek but is confused. Silvanus is identified as the bearer or perhaps the scribe of the letter. Note the use of the concept of *"in which you stand"* which is genuine to the early movement and found in the letters of Paul and the Gospel of Thomas as well as a title applied to Simon Magus, the standing one. The writer of this postscript has written only briefly. In the context of 1 Peter this is a puzzle because the epistle, although certainly not long, can hardly be described as brief. It is a further sign that the postscript was originally attached to another letter and that this letter was very short.

Silvanus is mentioned in the letters of Paul as the companion of Paul and Timothy. In Acts he becomes Silas and is given a prominent role as the companion of Paul. It is possible that Cephas or Peter did ask Silvanus to write a letter. But the use of a person prominent from the letters of Paul, and who is clearly part of the circle of Paul, is suspicious. Paul gives Silvanus as one of the joint authors of 1 Thessalonians so the name would be a natural one for a forger to use. The key line is what comes next:

Greet you does she who is in Babylon, the co-elect woman, and Mark my son. (1 Peter 5:13)

Some translations of this line refer to the church that is in Babylon or even the church that is in Rome rather than "*she who is in Babylon*". But the word "church" does not appear in the original. From the start commentators and translators have puzzled over what this line means. The word for "co-elect" is *syneklekte* and is found only here. The conventional explanation links this to the start of the epistle which is addressed to the "*elect sojourners of the dispersion*". In this explanation, the woman is "co-elect" because she is elect along with those to whom she sends greetings. The "elect" are the chosen. The word is used several times in the New Testament and it is prominent in the book of Enoch. It goes back to beyond the Jesus movement to mean those redeemed in the end times. But it also has another meaning - it can refer to the Messiah, the Christ himself.

In the Book of Enoch, the most frequent use of elect to refer to the Christ is in the parables. This is believed to be later than the other writings that make up Enoch and is dated to around the first century, which makes it contemporary with the Jesus movement. In the parables the Son of Man, the Messiah, is frequently called the Elect/Chosen One. The use of "elect" can also be traced back to the Scriptures in a passage in Isaiah widely interpreted as being about the Messiah:

Behold my servant, whom I uphold; mine elect, in whom my soul delights; I have put my spirit upon him: he shall bring forth judgement to the Gentiles. (Isaiah 42:1)

This passage is quoted in Matthew 12:18 where it is applied to Jesus. Luke also describes Christ as the elect in two places (Luke 9:35; 23:35). So the elect or chosen one was sometimes used specifically as a title of Christ and this gives us an insight into the meaning of the "co-elect". The woman who is called *syneklekte* is the co-elect in the same way that Christ is called the elect. It is a title meaning that she was chosen along with Christ to fulfil God's purpose. It is Mary, the person through whom Christ was manifest, who is the co-elect woman.

Taking out the dubious reference to Silvanus we can reconstruct the postscript as it stood in the original letter:

By a faithful brother as I regard him, I have written to you briefly, exhorting and testifying this to be the true grace of God, in which you stand. Greet you does she who is in Babylon, the co-elect woman, and Mark my son.

The letter would have been quite brief and sent under the name of Cephas or Peter. But at the end Mary puts in a greeting that, to anyone who knows her true identity, effectively signs the letter. She describes herself as the co-elect and "*she who is in Babylon*" and specifically mentions her son, using the name Mark because she is writing in Greek. The letter was most likely sent by an anonymous brother whom, as she assures her readers, she credits or accounts as being faithful.

Instead of the literary creation of 1 Peter addressed grandly to five communities of Christians we get a picture of a brief letter, written quickly, and sent by means of a man who happened to be travelling to the destination, a man whom Mary hoped would be faithful. We do not know to whom this letter was sent but we can imagine that it was written to address some urgent problem or to give much-needed encouragement. Although brief, it was treasured by its recipients and was copied and preserved long enough to fall into the hands of the forger of 1 Peter. It probably did not survive longer because it addressed local issues and was not a polished statement of philosophy as people came to expect from writings attributed to the apostles. As fakes multiply they drive out the genuine article.

All of which brings us to the central mystery of the postscript to 1 Peter; what is meant by "*she who is in Babylon*". The conventional interpretation is that Babylon means Rome. The Book of Revelation uses Babylon as code for Rome as does the Sibylline Oracles (5.143). But both of these works are dated to after the destruction of the temple by the Romans. Following this destruction the link between Babylon and Rome would have been very obvious as both empires had sacked and destroyed the Jerusalem temple. But if it were this destruction of the temple that caused Rome to be equated to Babylon then this could not be the meaning of the words in 1 Peter if they were written before that destruction.

No one doubted that the Babylon of 1 Peter meant Rome until after the Reformation. Because the Roman Church claimed its authority by right of its descent from Peter the question of whether or not Peter was ever in Rome became a battleground between Catholics and Protestants. The sole evidence in the New Testament for Peter visiting Rome is this reference to Babylon at the end of 1 Peter. There is, of course, an alternative explanation that Peter was in the real Babylon. At the time, Babylon had a thriving Jewish community who were the descendants of the original exiles. But against this there is no tradition that Peter ever visited Babylon. Nor is there ever a hint of an early Christian church in Babylon whereas there was certainly an early church in Rome.

Knowing that "she who is in Babylon" is Mary gives another dimension to the problem. We have seen that a key text for deriving both the Magdalene and the title of James, Oblias, is this passage in Micah:

And you, O tower of the flock [Migdal-eder], the stronghold [ophel] of the daughter of Zion, unto you shall it come, even the first dominion; the kingdom shall come to the daughter of Jerusalem. Now why do you cry out aloud? Is there no king in you? Is your counsellor perished? For pangs have taken you like a woman in labour. Be in pain, and labour to bring forth, O daughter of Zion, like a woman in childbirth. For now shall you go forth out of the city, and you shall dwell in the field, and you shall go even to Babylon. There shall you be delivered. There Yahweh shall redeem you from the hand of your enemies. (Micah 4:8-10)

The passage contains a prophecy that "*she shall go forth out of the city [Jerusalem] and you shall dwell in the field and you shall go even to Babylon*". The original is all about the exile. But the prediction that the daughter of Jerusalem to whom the kingdom shall come will go to Babylon cannot be a coincidence. There are three ways to explain the "she who is in Babylon" description of Mary in the light of this passage:

1. Babylon is interpreted spiritually and means the whole world as a place of exile from heaven.
2. The Micah passage was taken literally and Mary moved from Jerusalem to Babylon to fulfil the prophecy.
3. Micah was interpreted as being metaphorical with Babylon standing for Rome and this influenced Mary to leave Jerusalem for Rome in the last years of her life.

If the first is true then "*she who is in Babylon*" is another title like the Magdalene and the co-elect that indicates Mary's status as the human part of the divine marriage. In this case, it tells us nothing about Mary's physical location and she could be writing from Jerusalem. If one of the other explanations is true, then the Micah prophecy has been interpreted as an instruction that Mary obeys by going physically to either Babylon or Rome. There is no other evidence connecting Mary or Peter with Babylon, but there is plenty of evidence connecting them with Rome. But this raises the question as to why Rome should stand for Babylon before the destruction of the second temple.

The answer lies in the apocalyptic idea that each of the nations was represented by an evil angel. Israel itself was ruled by a heavenly being, the Christ, who was secretly far more powerful than any of these angels. The most powerful of the angels who opposed Jesus was the one who had him put to death and who represented Babylon. He was also called the morning star and the adversary, he was represented as a great dragon, and we call him the devil. Mary and the early Jesus movement are living at the time of the resurrection of Jesus and the beginning of the end times. There is a powerful mythic requirement that if Jesus has returned then his greatest adversary should return also to confront and ultimately be defeated by Jesus. However, there was a problem. The empire of Babylon was no more and the new power that ruled the world was Rome. To satisfy the requirement that Jesus should face the king of Babylon it was necessary to equate Babylon and Rome. Although the two empires were physically distinct, they were mystically the same under one heavenly ruler. So in this spiritual sense, Rome was a continuation of Babylon. The angelic ruler of Babylon had returned through the Roman Empire to again subdue Israel and rule the world in the final run up to the end times.

Under this interpretation, it made no sense at all for Mary to go to the real Babylon as this was no longer the home of the empire of evil. It was Rome, the new Babylon, where the great dark angel, the dragon, had taken up residence and it was to Rome that Mary had to go. The angel did not just represent a nation in an abstract sense. The angel was also the nation's kings, not because the angel was seen as human, but because it possessed the kings until the kings became the angel. The person who was the "king" of Rome towards the end of Mary's life was the Emperor Nero. Mary had come to Rome to confront the dragon Nero spiritually, a confrontation that was to prove ultimately fatal.

Greet Mary

If the Babylon in 1 Peter is identified with Rome then we can locate Mary, the co-elect, in Rome together with Mark. Is there any evidence for this in our best early source, the letters of Paul? One of the arguments against Peter being in Rome is that he is never mentioned by Paul in connection with Rome, not even when Paul writes to the Romans. But this may be that people are looking for the wrong name! Cephas is the pseudonym of the leader, the name Paul uses when talking about her to others to protect her true identity. But if Mary is physically in Rome then those of the Rome church will know her under her real name and not under her male pseudonym. Her position in Rome would be just as dangerous as Jerusalem, but the danger would not come not from the Jewish people but the authorities. It would be critical not to be identified as the founder so her Cephas name would be a secret to be carefully guarded. Being a woman would be an advantage; who would expect an elderly lady as being the leader of a notorious sect?

So we would expect Paul to greet her as "Mary" and not connect her to Cephas. And this is what we find in Romans. In his letters Paul greets his intimate friends and fellow workers first and then greets others in order of status within the movement. In Romans Paul first greets Priscilla and Aquila with whom he is closely linked, and then greets Epenetus whom Paul calls his beloved. Are these Paul's three special intimates? If so then the highest status person in the Rome church is the person he greets next:

Greet Mary, who has worked so hard for us (or "for you"). (Romans 16:6)

Paul uses the Hebrew form of the name suggesting that this woman is Jewish and from Palestine where the name was common. By itself this by no means proves that it is our Mary. But there is a clue in Paul's form of words that this is indeed the founder. He says that she has "*worked hard for us*". Paul uses the same word for "worked" as he uses to describe his own missionary endeavours. It would seem that this Mary has worked hard at spreading the gospels and has worked "*for us*"; that is for all the members of the movement including Paul. Some early copies have "*for you*" instead of "*for us*" and this is often found in translations. However, the more difficult reading, in this case "*for us*", should be preferred. It is easy to see why copyists might want to change "*for us*" to "*for you*" but not the other way around. Under the traditional view "*for you*" is understandable if this Mary was a prominent member of the Rome church and one who had worked hard at spreading the gospel within Rome. But if Paul wrote "*for us*" then she would have had to work for Paul in some way. Those who favour "*for us*" typically interpret it as meaning that this Mary offered Paul some assistance such as lodgings. When Paul wrote Romans he had never visited the church at Rome, so this assistance would have had to be given in another location. Besides to act as a hostess is not the natural meaning of "work" in this context.

If Paul did write "*for us*" then the best interpretation is that this Mary was involved in spreading the gospel and that her evangelism has benefited many, including Paul himself. This makes perfect sense if this Mary is the founder of the movement. It might be objected that the greeting is buried within a list of others, is brief and not as effusive as would be expected in greeting the founder. But this is only to be expected if Paul is trying not to draw attention to her in a public letter. And if we look at the rest of Paul's letter to the Romans we find clues that it was written with Mary very much in mind as the intended recipient.

Romans is the anomaly among the letters of Paul. All the other letters are written to the churches with which Paul was heavily involved. (In the case of Philemon the letter is addressed to an individual and the church that met in his house.) Most are written in response to some pressing matter that Paul is keen to resolve. Although Paul takes the opportunity in his letters to set out his philosophy and teachings, they always function in the first place as real communications to real people that he knows well. And Paul's letters reveal the frequent conflicts between himself and other members of the movement, those who doubt that he is an apostle. Romans, however, is very different:

It is written to a church which he has not even visited.

There is no obvious purpose for the letter.

It is not concerned with any burning issue but is a statement of Paul's philosophy.

It is curiously impersonal; unlike his other letters Paul does not criticise or reveal conflict with others in the movement.

It is Paul's longest letter and his most logically coherent

These features mean that Romans reads very differently from the rest of Paul's letters. It resembles more closely the literary "letters" that others were to write later. Not real letters addressed to real people but attempts to set out the writer's teachings in the guise of the letter form. It reads, in fact, like a thesis prepared by a precocious student to impress his teacher. And perhaps that is what it is.

Why should Paul address his set piece to the church in Rome? If he wants to set out his philosophy, it would be more logical to do so to a church with which he is involved, such as Corinth, or to the movement's headquarters in Jerusalem. Although Rome is the capital of the Empire, it is a Gentile city far from the centre of the movement in the east. Why write his major work to what should be nothing more than a minor church on the fringes of the movement? The church in Rome must, in fact, be very important. If it is the new home of Mary then all becomes clear; she is the centre of the movement, and Paul writes to the Romans knowing that the letter will be read to her. The intellectual, cosmopolitan Paul is attempting to impress and influence Mary with the depth of his learning.

There is a subtle acknowledgement of Mary at the very start of Romans. Paul states that Jesus appeared *"of the seed of David according to the flesh"* (Romans 1:3). We have seen that this must refer to Mary. Paul is both acknowledging that Jesus has come through Mary and that she is of the house of David. Paul is being diplomatic here for he regarded his relationship with the heavenly Jesus as being as valid as Mary's. In the introductions of most of his other letters, Paul emphasises this direct relationship with Jesus and with God. In Galatians, which marks the low point of his relationship with James and Mary, he goes one further and denies that he relied upon any human agency for his gospel. The implication is that there is nothing special about Jesus' appearance to Mary and that the direct appearance of Jesus to Paul means that he is equally favoured. Romans is very different with Paul acknowledging both that Jesus has come through Mary and that she is of Davidic descent. He protects Mary's identity by not giving away her name while making this little bow to her at the beginning of his letter.

Papias and the unordered gospel

Further evidence that Cephas was in Rome comes from Papias who has left some of the earliest evidence concerning the origin of the gospels. None of his writings has survived intact, and they are known today only through a few fragments quoted in the works of later writers, most notably by the church historian Eusebius.[288] His dates are normally given as between 110 and 130 but the evidence for this is uncertain, and he could be writing somewhat later. Irenaeus calls him *"a hearer of John and a colleague of Polycarp"* meaning that he was a direct connection to the John who had followed Jesus. But this is contradicted by Papias' description of how he would love to learn from *"the presbyters"*:

If, then, any one came, who had been a follower of the presbyters, I questioned him in regard to the words of the presbyters, what Andrew or what Peter had said, or what by Philip, or by Thomas, or by James, or by John, or by Matthew, or by any other of the disciples of the Lord, and what things Aristion and the presbyter

John, the disciples of the Lord, say. For I did not think that what was to be gotten from the books would profit me as much as what came from the living and abiding voice." (Papias from Eusebius, Ecclesiastical History 3.39:4)

From this, it is clear that Irenaeus has confused "presbyter John" with the John mentioned alongside Matthew, James and the others. Papias is saying that his sources are Aristion and presbyter John, two obscure persons who are unknown outside the writings of Papias (unless 3 John and perhaps 2 John are by presbyter John). Even then he does not hear from them directly but only through travellers who had come from the presbyters. In other words Papias is presenting the teachings of obscure presbyters, heard through intermediaries, concerning what the disciples of the Lord were supposed to have said. As such he is a useful source of oral traditions circulating in the early second century but we must not assume that these traditions were a truthful reflection of what happened earlier in the mid first century. In fact, Papias lives in a church that is being increasingly shaped by the gospels which are already in free circulation. His list of the early disciples comes from the gospels, and the evidence of his writing shows that he did in fact make extensive use of written sources and that he is familiar with a number of gospels.

What is most interesting though is what Papias says about Peter, Mark and the origin of the gospels. He specifically locates Peter and Mark in Rome:

Clement in the eighth book of his Hypotyposes gives this account, and with him agrees the bishop of Hierapolis named Papias. And Peter makes mention of Mark in his first epistle which they say that he wrote in Rome itself, as is indicated by him, when he calls the city, by a figure, Babylon, as he does in the following words: "The church that is at Babylon, elected together with you, salutes you; and so doth Marcus my son." (Eusebius, Ecclesiastical History 2.15.2)

He then tells how Mark wrote down the teachings of Jesus from Peter:

"This also the presbyter said: Mark, having become the interpreter of Peter, wrote down accurately, though not in order, whatsoever he remembered of the things said or done by Christ. For he neither heard the Lord nor followed him, but afterward, as I said, he followed Peter, who would give the teachings in the form of chreiai,[289] but with no intention of giving an ordered arrangement of the logia of the Lord, so that Mark committed no error while he thus wrote some things as he

remembered them. For he was careful of one thing, not to omit any of the things which he had heard, and not to state any of them falsely."

And about Matthew:

"So then Matthew wrote the logia in an ordered arrangement[290] *in the Hebrew language, and every one interpreted them as he was able."*
(*Papias from Eusebius, Ecclesiastical History 3.39:15-16*)

We should be cautious about identifying Papias' gospels with our gospels of Mark and Matthew. If we examine Papias' description, we shall see that they do not fit the gospels that we know as Mark and Matthew. Starting with Matthew, Papias says that this was composed in Hebrew and that many interpretations or translations of it existed in his day. In fact, scholars know that Matthew was composed in Greek based on the Gospel of Mark. It is, however, believed to have been quickly translated into Aramaic in a version now lost. Papias has assumed that the Aramaic/Hebrew version was original and that the Greek is a translation. This is a very natural supposition as the Gospel of Matthew was clearly written by a Jewish author and was particularly treasured by Jewish Christians. It also fits in with the idea of Matthew being written by the disciple of Jesus of that name. But all of this is, in fact, wrong! Papias may have been early, but his knowledge of gospel origins is far from perfect. The truth is that even by Papias' day there was widespread confusion.

Papias also says about Matthew that "each interpreted them as he could" implying multiple versions in Greek. One of these interpretations would be our Gospel of Matthew. Another potential interpretation is what we now know as the Gospel of Mark. It is obvious to anyone who compares the two gospels that Mark and Matthew are intimately linked, and the early theory was that Mark was an abridgement of Matthew. However, Papias believed that Matthew was written originally in Hebrew. If so, then how could he explain the similarity between Mark and Matthew? He must have thought that Mark was an abridged translation of the Hebrew. So if Papias knew of an Aramaic version of Matthew, as well as our Matthew and Mark, then this would explain his description of Matthew. He thinks the Aramaic version is original and that there were multiple translations into Greek (our Matthew and Mark).

But if Papias included our Gospel of Mark as one of the interpretations of Matthew, then it cannot be the same as the first gospel he mentions.

And, in fact, Papias' description of this first gospel does not match our Gospel of Mark. The following discussion is indebted to Richard Bauckham's treatment of the subject in Jesus and the Eyewitnesses,[291] although as Bauckham is a believer in the gospels as eyewitness accounts the conclusions are very different. We can summarise a number of facts from Papias' account:

Mark had been Peter's interpreter (*hermeneutes*) which can mean either that he translated Peter's words or that he explained them.

Mark himself neither heard the Lord or followed him.

Peter would give the Lord's teachings in the form of *chreiai* that were unordered and that he did not intend to give an ordered arrangement of the logia or sayings of the Lord.

Mark reflected this unordered arrangement in his own writing, which was an accurate reflection of what Peter had said.

The word *chreia* is a technical rhetorical term meaning a concise account of something said or done attributed to a particular person. In other words, Peter gave the sayings and doings of the Lord in lots of short snippets and did not put them in any particular order. All of this is completely consistent with what we have deduced from the shaman paradigm. We know that John Mark was the closest person to Mary/Cephas and was called her "son". For him to operate as her secretary and translator would have been perfectly natural. We know that the original source of all the sayings and stories of Jesus was Mary/Cephas. And we also know that all these sayings and stories were given in a short form of anything between one and several lines. It would be accurate to call them *chreiai*; and, as Papias says, they were not put into a coherent structure until the narrative gospels were composed.

None of this matches the Gospel of Mark that has come down to us. If the shaman paradigm is correct, then that gospel with its literalistic viewpoint and complete misunderstanding of the sayings cannot possibly have been written by anyone close to Mary or the brethren. Even under the conventional view the Gospel of Mark does not match Papias' description. Papias says that Peter's reminiscences were "unordered" and that Mark was faithful in copying Peter. Being unordered can mean two things:

- The most natural interpretation is that the gospel was an unordered list of sayings and doings without a binding narrative structure.

- Alternatively the gospel did have a narrative structure but the order of events differed from that considered to be the true order.

The first possibility clearly does not fit our Gospel of Mark, which is a narrative gospel with a strong structure. The problem with the second possibility is that it presupposes that Papias has in mind an alternative, correct gospel, one with the doings and sayings in order. We know that the Gospel of Mark was the first to be written followed by Matthew, which quickly became dominant among Christians. Papias is evidently very familiar with Matthew. But Matthew copies exactly the same order of events as Mark. So anyone rejecting the order of Mark would also have to reject the order of Matthew and instead accept some third gospel as being more accurate. The Gospel of John has a very different order from Mark or Matthew; for example, Jesus confronts the sellers in the temple right at the beginning of his ministry. However, John was written later than the other gospels, and it is unlikely that an early figure such as Papias would have accepted it as being more accurate. Certainly we have no evidence that anyone else in the early church thought it was a more accurate portrayal of events than the synoptic gospels. Another possibility is the Gospel of Luke whose order differs in some respects from Mark and Matthew. The early movement of Marcion regarded it as being more correct than the other gospels. The Gospel of Luke, however, was also written late and had a natural appeal to Marcion because it was the most gentile and least Jewish of all the gospels. Marcion rejected both Yahweh and the Old Testament as scripture, but these motivations would not apply to Papias so there is no reason he should prefer the late written Luke to the earlier Mark or Matthew. Besides, when Papias talks about the Gospel of Matthew he does not say that it is not ordered. We must conclude that the gospel that Mark is supposed to have written down is not our Gospel of Mark, which Papias most likely regarded as a variant of Matthew.

Indeed, Papias must have regarded Matthew as being the correct order. He is defending the other gospel against being unordered in comparison to Matthew and Mark. Even though this other gospel is unstructured Papias still believes it to be original and based on sayings and stories spoken by Peter. We are, therefore, looking for a gospel that is:

Without narrative order
Consists of a number of *chreiai* being short sayings or doings of Jesus
Draws upon material originally spoken by Peter

We have a gospel that exactly fits the description given by Papias and that is the gospel attributed to the "twin" of Jesus; a "twin" whom we know was Mary/Cephas but whom became identified with an invented disciple under the name Thomas. We know that the Gospel of Thomas was still in popular circulation at the time of Papias although it was steadily losing out to the newly written narrative gospels. Papias gives us evidence of this process by feeling it necessary to defend Mark for having written down a gospel that is unordered and unstructured compared to the narrative gospels. Papias' gospel written down by Mark is what we know as the Gospel of Thomas!

The Gospel of Thomas was never known as the Gospel of Mark or John. But then Papias does not say that Mark composed the gospel! He says that he translated and wrote down *chreiai* originally spoken by Peter. This gospel would not have been regarded as coming from Mark but as coming from Peter; that is from the shaman we have identified as Mary/Cephas, the twin of Jesus. It is likely that the sayings in Thomas were purely verbal to begin with; they are short and memorable. Verbal transmission was more convenient than putting things in writing and left no incriminating evidence. Although quite a high proportion of people could read in the ancient world, not many could write. John Mark, according to Papias, was one of these few and functioned as Mary's scribe, secretary and translator. At some point, John Mark made a written transcription of the verbal sayings and for this purpose he interpreted them, meaning that he translated them. Although Mary would have been able to speak Greek, she was probably more comfortable composing in her native tongue, Aramaic. John Mark must have been proficient in Greek and performed the service of translation for Mary. This may have been done either in the lifetime of Mary or afterwards because Papias' account is ambiguous on this point.

The elect Lady

It is ironic that John Mark was involved with a single work, the Gospel of Thomas, that is not known under his name whereas he had nothing to do with the three major works in the New Testament, Mark, John and Revelation, that are attributed to him. The practice of pretending that your work was written by a famous early figure was universal within the church in the late first century and second centuries. If you were writing a big work, such as a gospel or Revelation, you would probably attribute it to a big figure, one who was known and trusted as a reliable source close to the origins of the movement. And it would seem that there was no one bigger in this sense than John Mark. This is understandable if John Mark were the constant companion, secretary and scribe to the founder of the movement.

In addition to the three major works, there are three letters supposedly being written by a John in the New Testament. It is probable that the longest, 1 John, is also attributed to John Mark. This letter is closely linked to, and written after, the Gospel of John. It is written supposedly by one of the original disciples:

That which was from the beginning, which we have heard, which we have seen with our eyes, which we have looked upon, and our hands have handled, of the word [logos] of life. (1 John 1:1)

The letter is against those within the church who believe that the coming of Jesus into the world was spiritual. It is intended to bolster the new literalist proto-orthodox position that has emerged from the popularity of the gospels. The literalists who believe that Jesus was really a man are now casting as heretics those who remember that Jesus, who appeared through Mary, was spiritual. So 1 John emphases the physical nature of Christ, the logos; the author, who is supposed to be an eyewitness, says "*we have seen with our eyes*" and "*our hands have handled*". This is all fakery as the letter was quite clearly written long after the supposed time of Jesus. It goes on to talk about how the antichrist is expected at the end and that many antichrists are now visible within the church so that this end must be close. The antichrists are those who have been members of the group but have now left: "*They went out from us, but they were not of us*" (1 John 2:19). Those whom the author of 1 John sees as having left the church would not have had the same view of things. They would believe that it was the author's party who had departed from the truth. Some of these antichrists are those who deny that Jesus was the Christ.[292] Most likely this is a reference to the descendants of Paul's party of Christ who belonged to the same apocalyptic group looking to the coming of the Christ as the Jesus movement but who denied the validity of the resurrection through Mary. However, the main targets of 1 John are the so-called Docetists who believed that Jesus was spiritual in nature:

Here is how you know the spirit of God: every spirit that confesses that Jesus Christ is come in the flesh is of God. And every spirit that confesses not that Jesus Christ is come in the flesh is not of God. And this is that spirit of antichrist, which you have heard that it should come and even now is already in the world. (1 John 4:2-3)

To the author of 1 John, it is not the resurrection that is an article of faith but acknowledging that Jesus had come in the flesh! Those who said that Jesus was spiritual and had not come in the flesh were clearly a sizeable group within the church at this time. They were seen by the author of 1 John as the main enemy from within.

The second letter, 2 John, is also aimed at the Docetists although this time the author is given simply as "the presbyter" meaning elder. The letter is related to 3 John also written by "the presbyter". The two letters are both very short and share the same vocabulary being believed to be by the same author. But there is another possibility; that one of the two is a forgery that has deliberately copied the style and language of the other. Such a fake would be very difficult to detect as both letters are very short. The epistle 3 John is undoubtedly genuine and has no theological axe to grind. However, it is suspicious that 2 John takes exactly the same position against the Docetists as the known forgery 1 John. So is it also a fake?

The obvious question is why anyone should want to forge a letter by the author of 3 John and indeed, why 3 John should be included in the New Testament. It is very short and with no obvious significance. It is a private letter written by the presbyter to one Gaius about the reprehensible conduct of Diotrephes who occupies a position of influence in Gaius' church. This Diotrephes has for some unknown reason refused to receive certain brethren. The letter cannot have been included in the New Testament for its content, so it must have been included because of its presumed author. The true author may be the same presbyter John who is mentioned by Papias although we cannot be sure of this. However, from an early date there was confusion concerning the Johns. For example, Irenaeus believed that Papias' presbyter John was the same as the disciple and apostle John. Such confusion would explain why 3 John is included in the New Testament if it were thought to be the work of the apostle John, the person we have traced back to John Mark. In reality, the letter was written much later than John Mark's time.

The letter 2 John is very different from 3 John. Unlike the genuine 3 John, its audience is vague. It is not written to address augments between individuals but to denounce a whole group of Christians, those who do not believe that Jesus came in the flesh:

For many deceivers are entered into the world, who confess not that Jesus Christ is come in the flesh. This is a deceiver and an antichrist. (2 John 1:7)

Both 1 John and 2 John attack the same group, those who said that Christ was spiritual and not physical, using the same vocabulary. Even if they are not by the same author, they are closely linked and must have been written at a similar time and place. The reader is intended to think that 1 John is written by the disciple and apostle John; it deliberately copies the style of the Gospel of John. In the case of 2 John, the author has copied the style of a letter, 3 John, that he believes (wrongly) to have also come from the apostle John. The real interest of 2 John lies in the opening:

The presbyter to the elect lady and her children, whom I love in the truth; and not I only, but also all they that have known the truth. For the truth's sake, which dwells within us, and shall be with us forever. (2 John 1:1-2)

There is no doubt that the author intends "*the elect lady*" to mean a church. This is clear from the ending – "*The children of your elect sister greet you*" *(2 John 1:13)* meaning that the letter is written from another (also un-named!) church. However, the phrase is clearly stylised and has been taken from somewhere else. The "*elect lady and her children*" describes Mary and the brethren. Here she is called "*elect*" compared to the "*co-elect woman*" in 1 Peter. The word for lady, Kuria, is the feminine of Kurios meaning Lord and commonly applied to God and the Christ. The Hebrew equivalent of Kuria is Martha, a title that may have belonged to Mary. The children of Mary represent both her sons and the church as a whole. Note how not just the author, but all who have known the truth love the elect lady. This means that the phrase could not originally have applied to an individual church. (Note also that the truth, which is Jesus, "dwells within us" mean-ing that Jesus is spiritual and internal.)

The date of composition of 2 John would be similar or slightly after that of the Shepherd of Hermas, which represents the lady who is the tower as the church. As the literalistic story of Jesus is developing the real woman who was the mother of all Christians is being abstracted to become the "church".

Key points

1. Although 1 Peter is a forgery, it is likely that the postscript has been taken from a genuine letter. The name Silvanus has been taken from Paul and would not be part of the original letter. The original source behind the postscript was a few words sent by an anonymous brother whom Mary thought she could trust.

2. The original letter attributed to Peter was signed as coming from the *"the co-elect woman, and Mark my son"*. The "co-elect woman" is a reference to Mary as co-elect with Christ.

3. The co-elect woman is also called *"she who is in Babylon"*. The reference is to Micah 4:8-10, which is linked to Mary's title "the Magdalene" and James' title "Oblias". This text was taken as an instruction that Mary was to go to "Babylon". The Jesus movement interpreted Babylon as meaning Rome, which they believed to be ruled by the same angel as the old kingdom of Babylon.

4. Further evidence that Mary was in Rome comes from Paul's letter to the Romans which includes a greeting to "Mary, who has worked so hard for us".

5. The presence of Mary at Rome explains why Paul wrote Romans. It is his most developed and coherent work and, unlike all his other letters, was sent to a church with which he had no connection. Romans is Paul's only letter which does not address some pressing problem; it is a statement of his philosophy intended to impress the leader of the movement.

6. The early church father Papias says that Mark was with Peter in Rome, as is indicated by 1 Peter.

7. Papias also said that Mark was Peter's interpreter/translator and wrote down the *chreiai* (sayings or very concise stories) of Jesus from Peter in a gospel that was unordered. Conventionally this gospel is regarded as the Gospel of Mark, even though our Mark is clearly not unordered and is a narrative rather than a saying gospel.

8. Papias also said that Matthew was written originally in Hebrew (which is incorrect) and existed in many versions/translations. Given the close similarity between Mark and Matthew, we can conclude that Papias would have regarded our Gospel of Mark as one of these translations.

9. The gospel that accurately fits Papias' description of the gospel that came from Peter as written down by Mark is the Gospel of Thomas.

10. The letters 1 and 2 John develop the idea that the "elect woman and her children", originally Mary and the brethren, meant the church. Both

letters are aimed against those who believed that Jesus was spiritual and not physical. We can see the letters as an attempt by the early proto-orthodox church to deal with early traditions that conflict with the gospel version of Jesus. Some of these traditions are absorbed (Mary becoming "the church") and others (Docetism) are rejected as heresy.

Conclusion

We can see evidence from 1 Peter, Romans and Papias that Mary lived in Rome with her son John Mark who acted as her secretary/translator. The evidence is closely connected with the name Peter showing that Mary used both identities in Rome. It was Mark who made the original collection of sayings from Mary that became known as the Gospel of Thomas. The religious reason why Mary relocated to Rome was to obey an instruction in Micah. She came to confront the dragon angel, the King of Babylon and Rome, in the form of his avatar, the Emperor Nero.

Chapter 40

Mary and the beast

The Book of Revelation was written at the same time as some of the gospels but does not reflect in any sense the gospel view of Jesus. At the heart of Revelation is an image of a great battle between a woman and a dragon. It is the conflict between Mary and the "king of Babylon" which lies behind this image, a conflict in which Mary appears to be utterly defeated, and yet will emerge eventually triumphant.

The number of the beast

We have seen how Mary has come to Rome to confront the "king of Babylon" in his lair and how this evil king was believed to have taken the form of Nero. And we find in Christian writings a deep and repeated connection between Nero, the devil and Babylon. Consider for example this Christian section of the Ascension of Isaiah that may be dated towards the end of the first century or the beginning of the second:

After it is consummated, Beliar the great ruler, the king of this world, will descend, who has ruled it since it came into being; yea, he will descend from his firmament in the likeness of a man, a lawless king, the murderer of his mother: who himself (even) this king. And will persecute the plant which the twelve apostles of the beloved have planted. Of the twelve one [or some] will be delivered into his hands. (Ascension of Isaiah 4:2-3) [293]

Beliar is another name for the devil. The "king of iniquity" and "murderer of his mother" is Nero, who had his own mother put to death. The Ascension states that one (or perhaps more than one) of the twelve has been killed by Nero. It is likely that Paul was put to death by Nero; such has always been the tradition and in his last letter he is in prison in Rome. But Paul cannot be intended here because he is not one of the twelve. The other person who traditionally was martyred in Rome at the orders of Nero is Peter. It is surely Peter who is meant here because he is included as one of the twelve from the Gospel of Mark onwards. And so if Cephas is a name used by Mary, we have an early tradition that Mary was put to death by Nero in Rome.

That the Ascension of Isaiah passage is drawing upon genuine traditions of the early movement is demonstrated by another feature; that the passage goes on to talk about the heavenly garment. It says how many will be corrupted by Beliar, even those of the church, until only a small remnant remain. Then the Lord will come accompanied by the saints:

But the saints will come with the Lord with their garments which are (now) stored up on high in the seventh heaven: (Ascension of Isaiah 4:16)[294]

The saints have their "robes" in the seventh heaven. We have seen how the spirit is called the garment and was a man's sister or wife; the half of the spirit which remained with God in heaven while the other half was breathed into Adam. The Ascension continues:

And afterwards they will turn themselves upward in their garments, and their body will be left in the world. (Ascension of Isaiah 4:17)[295]

The Ascension of Isaiah retains a memory of the early tradition that it is the "garment" only that can ascend to heaven although this tradition is being adjusted to the new orthodoxy.

The most famous depiction of the anti-Christ, although not called by that name, comes in the in the Book of Revelation:

And I stood upon the sand of the sea, and saw a beast rise up out of the sea, having seven heads and ten horns, and upon his horns ten crowns, and upon his heads the names of blasphemy. (Revelation 13:1)

The beast is obviously inspired by the book of Daniel. In Daniel 7 four beasts rise from the sea; the first, who was like a lion, was the image of Babylon and its king, and the second lion of the Thomas 7 saying. The traditional and best explanation of the beast in Revelation is that it represents the Roman Empire with the seven heads being seven Roman Emperors.

There were more than seven Emperors in the period but the number seven is symbolic, and the focus is on one Emperor in particular:

And I saw one of his heads as it were wounded to death, and his deadly wound was healed, and all the world wondered after the beast. (Revelation 13:3)

This has links to the Nero Redivivus legend that Nero did not die in 68 but had fled Rome to live among the Parthians. The idea that Nero was still alive and would return persisted for hundreds of years among Christians. The similarities to the resurrection of Christ are obvious and it is no surprise that he became a type for the emerging belief in the anti-Christ. It was not just Christians who believed that Nero was not dead; there were no less than three pretenders to the throne of Rome who claimed to be Nero and who led rebellions against the Emperor. The return of Nero is alluded to again in Revelation. It is Nero who is the eighth king who yet is one of the seven: "*And the beast that was, and is not, he is the eighth, and is of the seven, and he goes to destruction*" *(Revelation 17:11)*. Although the legend among the people was that Nero was still alive, Revelation goes further. The head is slain and yet comes alive. He who shall return as number eight has already been but "is not". Nero is returning not from Parthia but the dead.

After the beast rises from the sea, he obtains power from the dragon that represents the devil. None can resist the beast, not even the saints:

And it was given to him to make war with the saints, and to overcome them. And power was given him over all peoples, and tongues, and nations. (Revelation 13:7)

The beast, the Roman Empire, rules the earth. It makes war upon the saints, the early church, and it overcomes them. Revelation tells us that the number of the beast is 666 or in some early variants 616:

Let him that has understanding count the number of the beast, for it is the number of a man, and his number is six hundred and sixty-six [or six hundred and sixteen]. (Revelation 13:18)

Although "666" is more frequent among most surviving manuscripts some of the earliest sources have "616". The passage tells us that the number of the beast is the number of a man, meaning that it must spell out a name. The practice of converting words into numbers, Gematria, was common in the ancient world. The Latin title of Nero Caesar translated into

Hebrew would give 616 whereas the Greek spelling of the same would give 666. By itself this is hardly conclusive as there are other ways of accounting for the numbers. But combined with the other evidence in Revelation pointing to Nero it becomes persuasive, and most scholars accept that 616/666 refers to Nero.

Give to the beast what belongs to the beast

Revelation also says that those who belong to the beast (the great majority of the population) will be marked:

And he causes all, both small and great, rich and poor, free and slave, to receive a mark on their right hand, or on their foreheads. And that no man might buy or sell, save he that had the mark, either the name of the beast or the number of his name. (Revelation 13:16-17)

The mark of the beast on the forehead or hand is clearly metaphorical and is intended to reflect the practice of branding slaves. Those who belong to the beast bear his mark in an obvious way so that all can recognise them. The idea that no one can buy or sell without the mark, or the name of the beast, or his number is a way of saying that all commerce essentially belongs to the beast. The coins of the empire would carry the image of the Emperor and to the author of Revelation the use of coins to buy and sell constitutes a form of Emperor worship. In Mark following on from the important parable of the vineyard, some Jews ask Jesus whether it is lawful to pay taxes to Caesar. Jesus asks them to bring him a denarius:

So they brought it, and he says to them, "Whose likeness and inscription is this?" And they said to him, "Caesar's." Jesus said to them, "Give to Caesar the things of Caesar, and to God the things of God." (Mark 12:16-17)

A version of this saying appears as Thomas 100 but with a gold coin and without the image of Caesar. In this case the Mark version is to be preferred as being closer to the original than the surviving Thomas version; the idea of the coin bearing the image of Caesar, found in Mark but not Thomas, ties in naturally with the coin belonging to Caesar. Note the connection between Caesars "*image and superscription*" and the "*mark or the name of the beast*".

Commentators have offered up many explanations for this saying. The conventional interpretation is that people should be good citizens and cheerfully pay their taxes to the civil authorities. However, the early Jesus movement believed that evil forces were in control of the world and ruled all nations. The real interpretation is given by Revelation; the coins bear the mark of the beast, his "image and superscription" and so belong to the beast. All commerce takes place in the sphere of the beast and so is inherently corrupting. Caesar is evil, and his money is evil as well. We know that the early Christians had a philosophy of not owning anything but giving away their possessions and trusting to God to supply their needs. The same hostility to commerce is expressed in the Gospel of Thomas: "*The buyers and the merchants [will] not [enter] the places of my Father.*" (*Thomas 64*)

Caesar, the leader of the nations on earth, represents the leader of the demons in heaven. The deeper meaning is that the demons control the world and all things in it and that those who cherish material possessions have already submitted to their rule. Those of the way do not submit but neither do they rebel in a physical sense. Instead, they simply put themselves outside of the sphere of the demons and exist in the sphere of God. The demons are the rightful rulers of the world appointed by God, and a disciple should give to the demons what belongs to the demons. This includes money but also in extremis the disciple's body surrendered to the demons through martyrdom. Those who ask Jesus the question about taxes are so grounded in the material world that they cannot understand that both the money they begrudge paying and the authorities to whom they must pay it are equally evil.

The idea of the disciples giving to the demons what is theirs appears elsewhere. In Thomas, Mary asks Jesus a question:

Mary said to Jesus: "Whom are your disciples like?" He said: "They are like children dwelling in a field which is not theirs. When the Lords of the field come, they will say: 'Give our field back to us.' They strip naked in their presence to give it back to them, and they give their field to them." (Thomas 21a)

The field here is the world and the body. It is owned by the demons, the rulers of the world. When they ask for what belongs to them the disciples will become naked to give it back. This draws on the common image of the body as a robe or garment that must be given up for the disciple to put on the heavenly garment. The body is part of the world and belongs to the rulers of the world. The concept is the same as the coin belonging to Caesar and being paid to Caesar. The same image of being naked in the field occurs in Mark in a passage about the apocalypse: "*And let him that is in the field not turn back again to take up his garment*" *(Mark 13:16)*. The garment also appears in Matthew:

"*And if any man will sue you and take away your tunic, let him have your cloak also.*" *(Matthew 5:40)*

When a judgement was given against a man for a debt whereby they would lose their undergarment, their tunic, the more valuable over garment would also belong to the claimant. In the context in Matthew the meaning of this saying is that if someone takes one of your garments you should volunteer the other also. But this cannot have been the original meaning; the giving of the second garment is not a free choice but legally belongs to the person prosecuting in court. The garments are not being stolen, and the loser has no choice but to surrender them. The original meaning can be understood by the metaphor of the garment as the body/soul/spirit. The judge is God and the adversary to whom judgement is given, the devil. As a result of the judgement, a person's inner garment has been granted to the devil. This inner garment stands for both the physical body and the body's conscious nature, the soul that was breathed into Adam by God. The saying uses the analogy that if the inner garment has been given in judgement then the more valuable outer garment, meaning the spirit that is in heaven, belongs to the claimant, the devil, also. We should remember that Thomas 22 tells us that the inner and the outer must be made as one to enter the kingdom of heaven. The two garments saying is then very similar to the Jewish concept of the body and soul being judged and punished jointly. If this interpretation is correct, then the original saying must have been something like "if an evil one shall obtain judgement against you and take your shirt then he shall have your cloak also". The author of Matthew does not understand its metaphorical meaning and makes it literal in his sermon on the mount.

The depiction of the Roman Empire in Revelation is the type of all governments and authorities. Rome was the first modern state and its successors, whether monarchies, dictatorships, communistic or democracies, are built in its image. The culture of a modern democracy has benefited from two thousand years of Christianity; no one gets crucified anymore. But the very reasonableness of a democracy hides a subtle corruption, a corrupting of people from within. In a democracy, the cult of the material pervades across all classes and reaches heights never seen under more authoritarian regimes. The stench of the beast is never greater than among those who rule and in a democracy everyone is a ruler. Western democracies add to the appeal of affluence the allure of false sexuality. The image of the whore is seen on a thousand magazine covers and flickers on a billion television screens. It is not the act of sex itself that is offered. The women who become the whore and the men who are complicit in her presentation to the people sell an image; an illusion of sexuality divorced from reproduction, and divorced from the relationship of love.

The whore and the temple

The whore in another form enters into Revelation where she "*sits on many waters*" (Revelation 17:1) and is called Babylon.[296] The writer is conveyed by an angel to see the whore:

So he carried me away in the spirit into the wilderness: and I saw a woman sit upon a scarlet coloured beast, full of names of blasphemy, having seven heads and ten horns. And the woman was clothed in purple and scarlet, and decked with gold and precious stones and pearls, holding a golden cup in her hand full of abominations and filthiness of her fornication. And upon her forehead was a name written in mystery, Babylon the Great, the mother of harlots and abominations of the earth. And I saw the woman drunken with the blood of the saints, and with the blood of the witnesses of Jesus. (Revelation 17:3-6)

The name written "*in mystery*", indicating a symbolic meaning, is Babylon. The seven heads on which the whore sits are seven mountains as well as standing for seven kings. Rome was famously built on seven hills. The waters on which the whore sits are "*peoples, and multitudes, and nations, and tongues*" indicating that she represents a great empire. The whore is clearly Rome, the empire spread over the Mediterranean. To the author of Revelation Babylon and Rome are the same in "mystery", meaning the same in inner spiritual truth.

The great value of Revelation is that it is independent of the gospels. The author of Revelation does not seem to know of the gospels and so for once we get a wholly independent depiction of Christianity from towards the end of the first century. Revelation has a strong influence from the party of Christ talked about by Paul in 1 Corinthians;[297] those who remembered the apocalyptic origins of the movement, who believed that Christ had died and would return, but who did not accept the resurrection through Mary. The central image of Christ in Revelation is the lamb who has been sacrificed before the beginning of the world and who will return at the end of time. But scattered throughout Revelation are images that do relate to Mary and the coming of Jesus through her. Even by Paul's time the party of Christ seems to have been a minor element of the movement and the version of Christianity it passed down became increasingly mixed with imagery derived from the ever-swelling mainstream. In no place is the independence from the gospels more evident that the strange section that begins at 11:1:

And a reed like a staff was given to me, saying, "Rise and measure the temple of God, and the altar, and those worshiping in it. And leave out the courtyard outside the temple, and do not measure it, because it has been given up to the nations, and they will trample upon the holy city forty and two months." (Revelation 11:1-2)

The measuring of the temple is taken from Ezekiel where an angel with a reed measures out the temple.[298] The outer court where the Gentiles were allowed to go is not measured, reflecting the anti-Gentile bias of the author of Revelation. The holy city is given to the Gentiles, and they shall trample it down for forty-two months. The period of forty-two months is clearly symbolic and not literal. It is half of seven years and the same period is repeated throughout Revelation and is taken from the book of Daniel. The author of Revelation draws upon Daniel repeatedly; for example the image of the beast with seven heads and ten horns is derived from the fourth beast of Daniel, which also has ten horns.[299] In Daniel, the period before the final consummation is half a "week" of seven or a period of three and a half.

This image of the temple has puzzled commentators because the temple that is revealed later in Revelation is the heavenly temple yet here we seem to have the temple on earth. The obvious interpretation is that this is the temple in Jerusalem and that the trampling of the city for forty-two months by the Gentiles means the sacking of the city by the Romans. The problem with this is that although the outer court of the temple is in possession of the Gentiles Revelation represents the inner temple as continuing with worship within it. This does not fit the sacking of Jerusalem as the temple was destroyed, and the inner sanctum violated. So we must look for an alternative explanation.

We have seen that Mary was the temple, the Magdalene, was also called Jerusalem and Zion, and that she comes to represent the church. So does the temple here represent Mary? If so, then why are the gentiles in possession of the outer court and why do they trample on the "holy city"? This can only mean martyrdom. The outer court and the city have been taken by the gentiles, but the inner temple remains inviolate. The body of Mary has been killed but the spiritual woman, the real temple, is still living. She will return after the trampling at the end of the period of half seven years. This image of trampling is also found in Thomas 37 where the garment, meaning the body, is trampled underfoot.

When was Revelation written?

One clue as to the date of writing of Revelation comes from a description of the seven kings:

And there are seven kings; the five did fall, and the one is, the other is not yet come, and when he comes he must remain a little while. And the beast that was, and is not, he is the eighth, and is of the seven, and he goes to destruction. (Revelation 17:10-11)

Five of the kings have died; the sixth is ruling, and the seventh will only reign for a short time. After this the king who was, and is not, and yet who is to be, that is Nero, will return again as the eighth. It might be thought that this would reveal the date, but such is the nature of Revelation that nothing is that simple. The most likely list is Augustus, Tiberius, Caligula, Claudius, Nero and Vespasian. The sixth Emperor Vespasian is then followed by Titus and Domitian. This involves making certain judgements; the Emperors who ruled briefly in the short period of disorder between Nero and Vespasian have been omitted and the list has been started at the first Emperor Augustus rather than Julius Caesar. It is also possible that the seven heads are supposed to be angelic rulers. The ten horns of the beast are also spoken of as ten kings so perhaps these are the earthly Emperors. We shall see that the original calendar of the apocalypse had one angel ruler for each "day" so the last week would have seven rulers just as the beast has seven heads. The author of Revelation is combining multiple sources and it is not surprising that he is inconsistent.

If the seven heads do represent seven Emperors then there are two possibilities; either Revelation was written during the reign of the sixth king (Vespasian); or it is written during the reign of the eighth (Domitian) who the author of Revelation believes to be Nero returned in a different form. The rule of the seventh king is to be of short duration which suggests Revelation was written during the reign of Domitian, the eighth Emperor, whose reign was preceded by the short reign of Titus. If so, then Revelation has been deliberately set back in time so that the prediction of the short reign of the one *"who is not yet come"* would appear to have come true. Domitian used the title *"deus et dominus"*, Lord and God, a phrase that is used in Revelation to describe God and which may be a deliberate comment on the blasphemous pretensions of the Emperor. Domitian persecuted Christians just as Nero had done and would have been seen by them as a reincarnation of Nero.

Regardless as to when it was written, there are two glaring omissions from Revelation. At the centre of Revelation are the dragon and the beast that is the Roman Empire, the invincible opponent of the early Christians. Yet Revelation never accuses the beast of the greatest crime of all, one that the Roman Empire was supposedly responsible for, the crucifixion of Jesus. The lack of any confrontation between the beast and Christ on earth is inexplicable if the author of Revelation believed, as did the gospel writers, that Jesus had been put to death by the Romans. The figure of the Lamb, and the sacrifice of the Lamb are central to Revelation, but the nature and time of this sacrifice is left vague. Revelation describes him as the *"Lamb slain from the foundation of the world"* which locates his sacrifice in mythic time.[300] When the Lamb confronts the ten kings who are the horns he overcomes them and is not defeated by them.[301] It seems that the author of Revelation was unaware that the Romans were supposed to have crucified the Christ. This is not just an argument from silence; it is a failure to mention the great elephant in the room.

The crucifixion of Jesus is not the only thing missing in Revelation. There is also no destruction of the temple. In Revelation 11:1-2 the outer court of the temple is given to the gentiles and the holy city shall be trampled for forty-two months yet the temple itself is not destroyed. We have seen the explanation that the temple here is the spiritual temple Mary and that this spiritual temple cannot be destroyed even though the Romans might destroy her body.

The conventional academic view is that Christianity only gradually separated from Judaism and that under the leadership of James in Jerusalem it was effectively a Jewish sect at the time of the destruction of the temple. If so, then this destruction should be a seismic event for the movement. That this destruction was at the hand of the Romans would confirm Rome as the new Babylon and would give ample reason the author of Revelation should describe the Roman Empire as the whore and the beast. So on this view it is incredible that Revelation does not even bother to mention the Romans' desecration of the temple. But under the shaman paradigm, the Jesus movement did not accept the validity of the second temple in Jerusalem, so its destruction was of no importance.

Why is Jesus crucified in Rome?

After the section on the temple, Revelation describes two witnesses:

And I will give power to my two witnesses, and they shall prophesy a thousand two hundred and sixty days, clothed in sackcloth. (Revelation 11:3)

The two are given remarkable powers; for fire to come from their mouths, to shut up the heaven that it may not rain, to turn the waters into blood and to smite the land with plague. But despite these powers after the allotted time (which is equal to three and half years) the beast will rise and fight them and will overcome them and kill them.

And their dead body will be upon the broad street of the great city, which is called spiritually Sodom and Egypt, where also their Lord was crucified. (Revelation 11:8)

The "great city" would normally mean Babylon/Rome. The place that is spiritually Egypt is again Babylon since these were the two places of exile for the Jews. The reasons for Babylon and Rome being spiritually Sodom are obvious. Since Babylon/Rome is the plain meaning, it is surprising that many maintain that the city was Jerusalem. The reason is, of course, the last line: *"where also their Lord was crucified."* The fact that Revelation places the crucifixion of Jesus in Rome (or perhaps Babylon) and not in Jerusalem is a tremendous embarrassment for the literalist. The author of Revelation does not even know where Jesus was crucified! This is because the Jerusalem crucifixion is a detail invented by the author of Mark, and the author of Revelation is not familiar with the gospels. The letters of Paul never locate the crucifixion in space or time, and there is no other early source other than the gospels that give a Jerusalem location to the crucifixion.

If Babylon stood for Jerusalem and not Rome, then Revelation would be an anti-Jewish work rather than anti-Roman. The problem with this is the absurdity of making the place of exile (Babylon) stand for the very place from which the Jews have been exiled (Jerusalem). The whole imagery of the exile is about the contrast between Babylon and Jerusalem and the ultimate return home. If there is one place in the world that Babylon cannot be it is Jerusalem.

Revelation continues with the people celebrating over the deaths of the two witnesses:

And they of the peoples and tribes and tongues and nations shall see their dead bodies three and a half days, and they will not allow their bodies to be put into a tomb. And they that dwell upon the earth rejoice over them and make merry, and will send gifts to one another, because these two prophets have tormented those dwelling upon the earth. (Revelation 11:9-10)

After the same period of three and a half the resurrection occurs:

And after three days and a half, the spirit of life from God entered into them, and they stood upon their feet, and great fear fell upon those beholding them. And they heard a great voice from heaven saying to them, "Come up here." And they ascended up to heaven in a cloud, and their enemies beheld them. (Revelation 11:11-12)

This is followed by an earthquake and the time of judgement and the opening of the heavenly temple. The period of three and a half days must be the same as the three and a half years for the trampling of the temple. It was common for days to stand for years and the use of different units to describe the same period of time serves to indicate the symbolic nature of the period. The author of Revelation believes that events are in the last "week" a concept that comes from the book of Daniel. It divided the period from the exile into seventy weeks of years – a total of 490 years. The last week of seven years is crucial:

Know therefore and consider wisely, from the going forth of the word to restore and to build Jerusalem until the coming of an anointed one, a prince, shall be seven weeks, and sixty and two weeks (Daniel 9:25)

The Messiah, the anointed, will come after seven weeks and sixty-two weeks, that is after sixty-nine weeks, one week before the end.

And after the sixty and two weeks, an anointed one shall be cut off and shall have nothing, the people of the prince who has come do destroy the city and the sanctuary. And its end is with a flood, and till the end is war, and decreed are deso-lations. And he has made a covenant with many for one week, and in the middle of the week he causes sacrifice and offering to cease; and by the wing of abominations shall come he who makes desolate, even till the consummation, and that which is decreed is poured out on the desolate one. (Daniel 9:26-27)

The original is obscure and lends itself to being translated in a way that reflects the beliefs of the translator. Christians see the anointed one who is "cut-off" as Jesus the Messiah, to be followed by the people of the prince, the Romans under Titus, destroying the temple. Jews also tend to like the bit about the destruction of the temple being prophesied in advance in Daniel but naturally avoid the idea that the Messiah will be "cut-off" beforehand. Of course, Daniel predicts that all these events will take place within seven years whereas the destruction of the temple was some forty years after the supposed death of Jesus. To be cut-off does not imply death and the passage seems to suggest that it is the people of the anointed one who destroy the city and the temple presumably in revenge for being cut-off.

It is clear that this passage has profoundly influenced the author of Revelation. In the account of the resurrection in the Gospel of Mark, it is said that the resurrection appearance of Jesus to Mary the Magdalene occurs on the first day of the week. This does not mean that it took place on a Sunday but that the event marks the commencement of that last week, a week not of days but of a much larger period. In Daniel, the last week is intended to be a week of years but such a short timescale could not accommodate the events the first Christians saw taking place about them. So they expanded the first week to a longer period. There are a number of possibilities. One is that they expanded the time sevenfold, so that each of the "days" now became a week of seven years. This would expand the "week" to forty-nine years. Another possibility is a tenfold expansion so that each "day" becomes ten years and a "week" becomes the significant period of seventy years. A "week" would then cover the human lifespan or two generations.

Who are the servants in Revelation? If events take place in Rome then the only real options are Peter (Mary) and Paul both of whom were reputed to have been martyred in Rome under Nero. We have seen how Mary's life has been notionally divided into two generations, one generation before Christ and a second generation with the Christ living spiritually within her. This would fit in well with a tenfold expansion in Revelation as the week would cover two generations. The period of the second generation has been symbolically rounded up to forty years. We have dated the coming of Jesus to Mary very precisely from the actions of Pilate to the winter of AD 26. The Neronian persecution commenced and was at its peak in 64 after the great fire of Rome and ended with Nero's death in 68. If Mary died in 64, then this would give a mission of around 38 years, close to both the symbolic 40 years and to the 35 year period for half a "week" in Revelation. The best fit then is a tenfold increase. However, a conversion from symbolic time to real time is always approximate because real events never fit nicely into a regular temporal pattern.

The two servants prophesy for three and half days before being struck down by the beast. This is followed by another period of three and a half days after which they are resurrected. We can deduce that Revelation must have been written after the death of the two servants but before their resurrection at the expiry of the subsequent three and a half days. If the attack of the beast is the persecution of Nero, then Revelation must date from a period of 35 years starting at 64. We can go further and say that it must have been written not too long before the expiry of the period because the imminence of the end times is an imperative of the apocalyptic mindset. This suggests a date in the 90s or late 80s, consistent with Revelation being written in the reign of Domitian.

But can we be sure that the two servants are Peter and Paul? And if there are traditions about Peter's martyrdom in Rome and if Peter is the same as Mary then why do we not find similar traditions regarding Mary? We will return to the story of the two servants shortly and by applying to it the principle of redundancy find considerable evidence that it does relate to Mary. But first we must continue with Revelation.

The bodies lie in that same city *"where also our Lord was crucified"*. There are two explanations for this. The first is that this is a reference to the myth that Christ has been crucified in Babylon at the time of the destruction of the first temple. The idea that Christ had come to earth as a man and had died in the past was fundamental to the Jesus movement. The lion being the king of Babylon swallows the man being Christ. This death is coincident with the exile and must have either happened in Jerusalem at the destruction of the first temple or shortly later in Babylon. The second explanation is that this is a reference to Jesus being crucified in Rome through Mary/Cephas. The two explanations are not inconsistent. If there was a myth of Christ being crucified in Babylon then Mary suffering the same fate in Rome, the new Babylon, would have appeared a confirmation of the identity between Mary and Christ.

In the late second century romance the Acts of Peter there is a story of the second crucifixion of Jesus. Peter has angered Agrippa the prefect under Nero and the brethren in Rome persuade him to flee. But as he is leaving the city he has an encounter with Christ:

And as he went forth out of the city, he saw the Lord entering into. And when he saw him, he said: Lord, why go you here? And the Lord said to him: "I go into Rome to be crucified". And Peter said to him: "Lord, are you crucified again?" He said to him: "Yes, Peter, I am crucified again". (Acts of Peter 35)

After this Peter sees Jesus ascend to heaven and turns back to Rome to face his martyrdom, for the Lord had said: "*I am being crucified which was about to befall Peter*". We have in this story further evidence that Jesus was crucified in Rome under Nero combined with the idea that this crucifixion was through the physical form of Peter.

The woman and the dragon

Revelation repeats the same events in image after image. It is not a sequence in time but a range of perspectives on events. The next image is that of a woman who moves between heaven and earth and who gives birth to the Messiah. It is an image of Mary unlike any in the literalistic gospels:

And a great sign was seen in heaven: a woman clothed with the sun, and the moon under her feet, and on her head a crown of twelve stars. And she being with child cried, in birth pangs, and pained to be delivered. (Revelation 12:1-2)

The image of the sun, moon and twelve stars occurs in the story of Joseph who has a dream which annoys his eleven brothers and his father:

And he dreamed yet another dream, and told it his brethren, and said, Behold, I have dreamed a dream more; and, behold, the sun and the moon and the eleven stars made obeisance to me. (Genesis 37:9)

The eleven stars are implicitly made up to twelve by Joseph, the twelfth brother. His father Israel interprets this dream angrily as meaning that Joseph sees his father, mother and brothers all bowing down to him. But the story of the dream is surely older than the context in Genesis and is telling us about the powers of heaven. The sun is El, the moon his wife, and the twelve stars or constellations of the Zodiac represent the host of heaven, called elsewhere the seventy brothers. Joseph represents the younger brother who appears least but who is really the greatest. In the important work Joseph and Aseneth, Joseph is explicitly called the Messiah. The story of the dream of Joseph has become the source of a myth that the Christ will rule heaven on behalf of his father.

In Revelation, the woman is clothed by the light of the sun meaning that she has the power and light of God as her garment. She has beneath her feet the moon, the wife of El, the goddess Asherah, whose role is depreciated by the Jesus movement. Asherah is the mother who along with her sons is rejected by Jesus in favour of the mother, Mary, and brothers on earth. The woman's head is adorned with a crown of twelve stars representing her reign over Jesus' heavenly brothers and their replacement by the Twelve, those who hear the will of the Father and do it.

The pains of childbirth have been taken from the prophecies of Zion giving birth to the Messiah, not least the Micah passage from which migdal, the Magdalene, has been derived. We have seen how the contrary notion of there being no birth pangs, reflecting the spiritual nature of the birth, was prevalent in the early movement, but in Revelation it is reversed. A dragon awaits the birth of the child:

And there appeared another sign in heaven, and behold a great red dragon, having seven heads and ten horns, and seven crowns upon his heads. And his tail drags a third of the stars of heaven, and cast them to the earth. And the dragon stands before the woman who is about to bring forth, so that when she should bring forth, he might devour her child. (Revelation 12:3-4)

The stars of heaven represent the angels, the host of heaven. The stars who fall to earth are the fallen angels who serve the devil. The description of the dragon with seven heads and ten horns is identical to the beast. It is the heavenly representation of the beast for the nations are represented in heaven by angels, and the dragon is the chief of the evil angels, the one who represents Babylon and Rome. In Revelation, events are portrayed in multiple dimensions, in earthly and heavenly terms. The beast is symbolic of the earthly, the dragon symbolic of the heavenly.

And she brought forth a male child, who was to shepherd all nations with a rod of iron. And her child was caught up to God, and to his throne. (Revelation 12:5)

The man-child is clearly the Messiah, who was expected to rule the nations. We can see here the anti-Gentile bias of Revelation. The nations are to be ruled "with a rod of iron"; to the author of Revelation, Christ's kingdom is not one of love and forgiveness so far as Gentiles are concerned. The Christ child is taken straight up to heaven. There is no confrontation with the dragon, no crucifixion. This is consistent with what we have deduced, that Mary's "son" is the resurrected Jesus, who is spiritual and belongs in heaven. Revelation continues:

And the woman fled into the wilderness, where she had a place prepared of God, that they should feed her there one thousand two hundred and sixty days. (Revelation 12:6)

The wilderness may represent the world, or it could be a real desert. There is evidence that Mary did spend some time in the wilderness at the start of her ministry when her church was in competition with John the Baptist. The period given is three and a half years and is the same half a week as for the mission of the servants. We can see this as covering the period of 35 or 40 years allocated to her ministry after the coming of Jesus. What follows is a war in heaven as Michael and his angels confront the dragon and his angels.

And the great dragon was thrown out, that ancient serpent, called the Devil, and Satan, which deceives the whole world. He was thrown down to the earth, and his angels were thrown down with him. (Revelation 12:9)

The story of the descent of the fallen angels is given in the book of Enoch. In the original myth of the Jesus movement, they descend to rule the world from the beginning. However, authors repeatedly struggle with attempting to locate myth time into prophetic time. The descent takes place in myth time and is both at the beginning and the end, but it has to be placed in the time of the world. When the devil saw he had fallen into the world he chases after the woman who had given birth:

And when the dragon saw that he was cast to the earth, he persecuted the woman which brought forth the male child. And to the woman were given two wings of a great eagle, that she might fly into the wilderness, into her place, where she is nourished for a time, and times, and half a time, from the face of the serpent. And the serpent cast out of his mouth water as a flood after the woman, that he might cause her to be carried away by the flood. And the earth helped the woman, and the earth opened her mouth and swallowed up the flood which the dragon cast out of his mouth. And the dragon was angry with the woman and went to make war with the rest of her children, keeping the commandments of God, and holding the testimony of Jesus. (Revelation 12:13-17)

The woman has already encountered the dragon in heaven, but now the encounter is repeated on earth. The dragon persecutes the woman. She is already supposed to be in the wilderness, but is given wings to take her to the wilderness; again the logic of the story does not follow a linear path but double backs upon itself. Once again the confrontation is for three and a half periods: "*a time and times and half a time*". A river issues from the dragon's mouth to take her away. In the book of Daniel, the temple is destroyed by a flood. In the Odes of Solomon, there is a passage that either means that things were carried to the temple by a river or that a river carried away the temple:

> *For there went forth a stream and it became a river great and broad; indeed it carried away everything and it shattered and brought (it) to the temple [or it shattered and carried away the temple]. (Odes of Solomon 6:8)*[302]

The river here is the spirit, but behind both we seem to have the same image of a river carrying away the woman/temple. In Revelation, the flood is swallowed by the land, but elsewhere the temple is destroyed by the flood. Behind the Revelation version is the idea that the woman (Mary) was not really destroyed but taken away to another place to await the coming of Jesus. The flood is metaphorical, the flood of persecution that was unleashed by Nero. A tradition has it that Peter was simply caught up in the general persecution against the church in Rome. The Romans may never have understood whom they were killing in Mary; to them she would have been just one more Christian. Which may explain why her body could be recovered. Following the confrontation with the woman the dragon goes to make war with the "*rest of her seed*" that is her sons and daughters, the Church as a whole. These are "*keeping the commands of God*". In concept this is similar to Thomas 99 where the true mother and brothers of Jesus (Mary and the brethren under James) are those "*who do the will of my Father*". The conflict between the woman and the dragon is followed by the introduction of the beast who takes his power from the dragon.

The confrontation with the dragon is another version of the confrontation between the beast and the two servants. Just as the servants lay dead for three and a half periods, meaning a generation, so the woman flies away from the serpent for three and a half periods. The death of Mary must have caused great consternation in the movement. So they clung to the myth that she was not truly dead, but in some sense still alive and waiting for the generation to pass; a myth that we also ironically find repeated about Nero. In this myth, she had either been secreted in a remote place on earth or taken up in heaven.

The accounts in Revelation of the two servants and of the woman confronting the dragon are tantalising but also cloaked by the brilliance of the author's poetic genius. Is there some original source behind it all and if so how do we get back to that source? The answer lies in the principle of redundancy, for we will find the source reflected in at least nine different versions of the story including the two in Revelation. To understand the other versions we must follow up Peter's meeting with Jesus as he leaves Rome and consider a curious tradition about his martyrdom; that like Jesus he was crucified but upside down.

Key points

1. In the Ascension of Isaiah, the devil, Beliar, is represented as Nero who, it is said, has killed one of the Twelve. This is evidence of the tradition that Peter was put to death by Nero.

2. In Revelation, the number of the beast (given as both 666 and 616) indicates that the beast is Nero.

3. The temple in Revelation is derived from a tradition about Mary. The outer court is has been given to Gentiles, and they will trample the Holy City, meaning that Mary's body has been given into the hands of the Romans. However, those who wrote Revelation believed that Mary would return to life.

4. To the author of Revelation, all commerce belongs to the realm of the beast. This is backed up by the saying that the disciples should render unto Caesar what belongs to Caesar.

5. The author of Revelation believed that Jesus was crucified in Rome and not Jerusalem. The crucifixion is not blamed on the beast or the dragon.

6. The account of the two witnesses in Revelation is based on the martyrdom of Cephas/Mary and Paul. It reflects the belief that Mary will return after a generation.

7. The martyrdom is then repeated in the account of the conflict between the woman in the stars and the dragon. The woman is taken into the wilderness, which is a representation of her death combined with the belief that she would return.

8. The best dating of Revelation is that it was written in the reign of Domitian by someone who expected the imminent arrival of the end times.

Conclusion

Revelation gives us an insight into the early Jesus movement that is independent of the gospels. Although Revelation was written at around the
same time as the gospels, there is no overlap between Revelation and the
Gospel accounts of Jesus' life. There is a blatant contradiction in that the
author of Revelation believed that Christ was crucified in Rome and not
Jerusalem.

Chapter 41

The Martyrdom Source

Behind the stories of the two witnesses and the woman in the sky in Revelation lies a much earlier source. Using the principle of redundancy, we can show the existence of this "Martyrdom Source" both qualitatively and quantitatively. We will do this by identifying a number of other texts that have similarities with the two passages in Revelation and with each other. This source will enable us to reach back in time to the era of the martyrdom of Mary.

The upside-down crucifixion

The traditional story is that Paul as a Roman citizen was beheaded whereas Peter was crucified. The curious detail is that Peter requested to be crucified upside down because he was unworthy to suffer the identical death as Jesus. Where did this unusual story come from and does it preserve a memory of the fate of Peter?

In the earliest sources, there is no evidence for the martyrdom of either Paul or Peter. Writing towards the end of the first century, the author of Acts ends her account with Paul sent back to Rome in chains but omits a trial or martyrdom. A third part covering the trial of Paul must have been intended to follow on from Luke and Acts but was never written. We hear nothing in Acts of Peter's death, but this may also have been intended for the third part. The first indication of a martyrdom for Peter comes in the continuation to the Gospel of John. The original gospel ends with what is now chapter 20, but an additional episode has been added later by another author. This addition is a story about Jesus feeding his disciples fish by the sea of Tiberius. The dating of this episode is even more uncertain than the dating of the main gospel, and it may be quite late. The relevant section about Peter comes in this addition:

When they dined, Jesus said to Simon Peter, "Simon of Jonas, do you love me more than these?" he said to him, "Yes, Lord; you know that I love you." He said to him, "Feed my lambs." He said to him again, a second time, "Simon of Jonas, do you love me?" he said to him, "Yes, Lord; you know that I love you." He said to him, "Shepherd my sheep." He said to him the third time, "Simon of Jonas, do you love me?" Peter was grieved that he said to him the third time, "Do you love me?" and he said to him, "Lord, you know all things; you know that I love you." Jesus said to him, "Feed my sheep. Truly, truly I say to you, when you were younger, you girded yourself and walked where you would. But when you are old, you shall stretch forth your hands, and another will gird you, and shall bring you where you would not go". And this he said, signifying by what death he shall glorify God. And having said this, he said to him, "Follow me." (John 21:15-19)

The names given to Peter have been taken from the other gospels; Simon of Jonas from Mark and Simon Peter from Matthew. Simon is one of the "sons" of Mary, so the question is whether this remembers a tradition that goes back to Cephas/Mary or to Simon called Peter. Given the role of Peter in leading the church it is probably a Cephas tradition. The three-fold questioning of Peter, in which Peter maintains his love for Jesus, is a literary echo of Peter thrice denying Jesus in Mark and the other gospels. Unlike his earlier self before the crucifixion of Jesus, Peter shall now be loyal unto death. The author of the continuation of John clearly believes that Peter was martyred: *And this he said, signifying by what death he shall glorify God.* Notice how this is not spoken by Jesus but is a comment by the writer. If we take away the literary device of the three-fold affirmation by Peter and the added commentary we are left with a candidate for a pre-existing saying:

When you were younger, you girded (ezonnyes) yourself and walked where you would. But when you are old, you shall stretch forth your hands, and another will gird (zosei) you, and shall bring you where you would not go.

The word used here to mean to gird or dress is *zonnumi*. It refers to the belt or girdle that was tied around the waist to hold the flowing garments in place. It is derived from the word for belt or girdle, *zone,* and this is used in an intriguing story about Paul in Acts. Paul is in Caesarea on his way to Jerusalem when he is the subject of an ominous prophecy:

As we stayed there for some days, there came down from Judaea a certain prophet, named Agabus. And when he came to us, he took Paul's belt [zonen], and bound his own hands and feet, and said, "Thus says the holy spirit, 'so shall the Jews at Jerusalem bind the man that owns this belt [zone], and deliver him into the hands of the Gentiles'." (Acts 21:10-11)

We can see in this story the same features of the saying from John; we have the two uses of the belt used both to dress and bind, we have the feature that another does the girding or binding, and we have the prophecy of being led or carried away. The character of Agabus appears earlier in Acts[303] as a prophet who comes to Antioch and who predicts a coming famine. Most likely he is a fictional character invented by the author of Luke as a mouthpiece to express sayings as prophecy. We should note that the "*Jews at Jerusalem*" will "*deliver him into the hands of the Gentiles*". This is virtually identical to a prophecy made by Jesus in Mark about his own fate:

Saying, "Behold, we go up to Jerusalem; and the Son of man shall be delivered to the chief priests, and to the scribes; and they shall condemn him to death, and shall deliver him to the Gentiles." (Mark 10:33)

The situation of Paul, about to go to Jerusalem, is very similar. Has the author of Luke based the prophecy concerning Paul on Mark 10:33 or was this in the original source? If the later, then it is likely that the original saying did not apply to either Peter or Paul but was about Jesus. And if we look at the John version, being bound and taken somewhere is reminiscent of the exile. The people of Israel could go where they wish, but are given into the hands of Gentiles and taken where they would not go. In fact, there are prophecies of the exile that are very similar to the source that must have been used by the authors of John and Mark. In Isaiah, there is a prophecy against Judah and Jerusalem that blames the leaders for the exile. In a satire on the flirtatious habits of the women it talks about how they walk:

Because the daughters of Zion are haughty, and walk with stretched forth necks and seductive eyes, walking and mincing as they go, and making a tinkling with their feet. (Isaiah 3:16)

It goes on with a long list of the ornate way in which they dress[304] before coming to what will happen to the women when Jerusalem is taken:

And it shall come to pass, that instead of sweet smell there shall be stink; and instead of a belt, a rope; and instead of well set hair, baldness; and instead of a stomacher, sackcloth; and instead of beauty, branding. (Isaiah 3:24)

Note how their belt or girdle will be replaced by a rope; instead of being able to dress themselves in fancy clothes and walk around seductively their hands will be tied and they will be led away into captivity. This condemnation of the lascivious women of Jerusalem seems a world away from the prophecies in Mark and John, and yet it has several features in common with them. The explanation of how this ties in with the crucifixion of Jesus must come in the second book, but suffice to say here that the original prophecy had nothing to do with Peter or Paul. It is, however, significant that it was later applied to both Peter and Paul, for this suggests that it was taken, wrongly, as a prophecy of the persecution under Nero.

So far there has been nothing about an upside-down crucifixion. By the early fourth century, this was regarded as an established fact as cited by the first historian of the church, Eusebius. In his Ecclesiastical History written shortly after the conversion of the Emperor Constantine he says that both Paul and Peter died in the persecution of Nero; Paul beheaded and Peter crucified. He quotes as evidence the fact that there were cemeteries called after Paul and Peter and offers a quote from an early third-century churchman Gaius:[305]

"But I can show the trophies of the apostles. For if you will go to the Vatican or to the Ostian way, you will find the trophies of those who laid the foundations of this church." (Eusebius, Ecclesiastical History 2:25:7)

Eusebius continues with another quote from a letter written by Bishop Dionysius of Corinth (late second century) to the Romans:

"You have thus by such an admonition bound together the planting of Peter and of Paul at Rome and Corinth. For both of them planted and likewise taught us in our Corinth. And they taught together in like manner in Italy, and suffered martyrdom at the same time." (Eusebius Ecclesiastical History 2:25:8)

We have no other information that Peter taught at Corinth; it is likely that this is a misunderstanding of 1 Corinthians 1:12 where Paul talks of the parties of Paul, Apollos, Cephas and Christ among the Corinthians. It does show further evidence for the tradition that both Paul and Peter were martyred in Rome at the same time. Eusebius goes on to say of Peter:

And at last, having come to Rome, he was crucified head-downwards; for he had requested that he might suffer in this way. (Eusebius, Ecclesiastical History Book 3:1:2)

The earliest version of this story occurs in the Acts of Peter, written in the later half of the second century. Typical of the writings of this period it is full of amazing miracles performed by Peter and is mostly taken up with the magical contest in Rome between Peter and Simon Magus. After he defeats Simon, Peter falls foul of the Roman prefect Agrippa by converting the wives and concubines of the Romans to chastity. Agrippa is understandably upset by this development and has Peter arrested and executed. Before his crucifixion, Peter gives a fascinating speech on the meaning of the cross:

I will not keep the silence of the mystery of the cross which of old was closed and hidden from my soul. Let not the cross be to you, who hope in Christ, this which is visible: for my passion, as that of Christ, is different from that which is visible. [...] Separate your souls from everything that is of the senses, from everything that appears to be and does not exist in truth. Blind these eyes of yours, close these ears of yours, put away your doings that are seen; and you shall perceive the facts about Christ, and the whole mystery of your salvation. (Acts of Peter 37)

Works such as the Acts of Peter cannot be read as literal history but give a fascinating glimpse into the teachings and beliefs of early Christianity. Peter is here saying that the true crucifixion is a mystical and spiritual event and not visible. The true nature of reality and Christ is not to be perceived with the senses. Peter thanks Jesus with a voice "*which does not come through the organs of the body*" and "*which is not in the world or sounds upon the earth*". It is the voice of the spirit "*who loves you speaks with you and sees you*". Jesus is only to be perceived through this spirit.

It is in the Acts that Peter requests to be crucified upside down. He gives the reasons for this request in gnostic terms. The first man fell into the world from above, and so was born upside down, in a birth that was really death. He then established the cosmos in his fallen condition, in which opposites (left/right, up/down) were reversed so that the ugly became the beautiful, and the evil became good. To return to the heavenly condition, Christ taught his disciples to reverse the fallen state as Peter makes clear with a quote:

Concerning which the Lord said in a mystery, "Unless you make the right hand as the left and the left as the right, and the top as the bottom and the front as the back, you shall not have knowledge of the kingdom." (Acts of Peter 38)

We can find the source of this in the Gospel of Thomas:

[...] Jesus said to them: "When you make the two one, and when you make the inside as the outside, and the outside as the inside, and the upper side as the lower side; and when you make the male and the female into a single one, that the male be not male nor the female female; when you make eyes in the place of an eye, and a hand in place of a hand, and a foot in place of a foot, an image in place of an image, then you will enter into [the kingdom]." (Thomas 22)

Note how the Acts of Peter version has changed the words to support the upside-down crucifixion. Making the right left and the left right is not present in the Gospel of Thomas text, but it is easy to see how the saying could be interpreted as an 180 degree rotation of the human body; if a person is crucified upside down then upper becomes the lower, and the person's left side with its hand/foot/eye becomes the right side with its hand/foot/eye. We have hand in place of a hand, etc. just as in the Thomas saying. (The reading "eyes" instead of "eye" is probably a scribal error in the one copy of the saying that has come down to us.) Other aspects of the saying that do not support the upside down crucifixion (such as the male and female becoming a single one) have been omitted in the Acts of Peter.

The Thomas saying is very old, for it has been used in the composition of the Gospel of Mark, and it is more than a century earlier than the Acts of Peter. The same saying is quoted in 2 Clement which, like the Acts of Peter, dates from the second century. Again the saying is subtly changed to support a different meaning, this time strongly proto-orthodox, as is evident in the explanation of male/female:

And by "the male with the female neither male nor female" he means this, that when a brother sees a sister he should have no thought of her as female, nor she of him as male. (2 Clement 12:5[306]

What has happened is that Christians from the age of martyrdom have puzzled over the meaning of this obscure early gnostic saying. In the second century proto-orthodox Christians looked towards martyrdom as the supreme way of emulating Jesus and entering into the kingdom. So someone has come up with the theory of the upside down crucifixion to explain what Jesus meant by this saying. They have concluded that Jesus was predicting that some of his apostles/disciples were to be crucified upside down and by martyrdom would enter the kingdom.

As well as this false interpretation, the Acts of Peter preserves something like the correct interpretation. If you wish to enter the kingdom then the person and the spirit must be joined so that you have *"eye(s) in place of an eye"* that is new spiritual senses to replace the physical senses. It is just such spiritual senses that the Acts of Peter says are required to perceive and communicate with Christ.

We have traced the upside-down crucifixion of Peter to its ultimate source. The story has no basis in historical reality but is a misunderstanding of a deeply mystical saying in the Gospel of Thomas. But this story of the upside down crucifixion does not just appear in the Acts of Peter. Virtually the same story is found in the Acts of Philip, which dates from the fourth century. And it is this Acts of Philip version that will start to lead us to a deeper understanding of the account in Revelation.

The leopard and the snake

In the Acts of Philip, the upside down crucifixion is applied not to Peter but Philip. Although the Acts is quite late it gives evidence of being based on early traditions. The most interesting part is chapter 8 onwards, which is a separate work from the earlier chapters. At the start Philip is given a commission by Jesus to go to the Greeks. Philip despairs and cries at his fate until his "sister" Mariamne (Mary) goes to Jesus, who tells her to accompany Philip after putting on man's attire. We have seen how this is linked to Thomas 114 about Mary becoming male. Jesus also sends Bartholomew and John along with them, and they set out for the city of the snake. On the way they meet a talking leopard and kid; the leopard was hunting the kid, but the kid speaks to it and tells it that the apostles are coming and that it should put off the heart of a beast. At this the leopard begins to change, taking the heart of a man, and leaves the kid alone. The apostles cure the kid of its injuries and complete the transformation of both animals (translations of the Acts of Philip by M.R. James[307]): "*but that men's hearts may be given them, and they may follow us wherever we go, and eat what we eat, to thy glory, and speak after the manner of men, glorifying thy name*" (*Acts of Philip 99*). One influence for this bizarre story is clearly Isaiah 11:6: "*the leopard shall lie down with the kid*". But there is also a hint of Thomas 7: "*cursed is the man whom the lion will eat, and the lion become man.*" We have seen how the second lion of Thomas 7 represents the Babylonian empire of Nebuchadnezzar, which is represented as changing into a man in Daniel 7:4: "*and a man's heart was given to it*". The significance of this is that the dragon of Revelation is the great angel who represents Rome and Babylon. In the form of the King of Babylon, he has carried off Judah as prey in his mouth, before being turned into a man and being given a man's heart. In the Acts of Philip, the King of Babylon has become a leopard, and the prey is the talking kid. The leopard takes the kid and carries it off, before being given a man's heart.

The apostles journey on accompanied by the leopard and kid, and encounter a dragon in the desert with a following of many snakes. After Philip and the others pray, a flash of lightning descends from heaven and destroys the dragon. The continuation is missing so what happens between this dragon episode and the Martyrdom of Philip has been lost. The Martyrdom starts with Philip and his companions coming to the city Ophioryme or "snake street" which is also called Hierapolis in some surviving texts although not all. This city of Ophioryme is portrayed as the home of those who worship the snake. Was it the same as Hierapolis in the original source? Philip was associated with Hierapolis which preserved his supposed tomb, so it was the natural place for his martyrdom. But why should Hierapolis be associated with the worship of the snake? Some think it is because of the goddess Cybele, who was worshipped in Hierapolis, was associated with the snake in that city. However, Cybele is not generally linked to the snake and is portrayed as a protective and taming force over the powers of nature. So why should her worship be represented as snake worship? Rather, it is likely that the identification of Ophioryme and Hierapolis was made by the author of the Acts. He has an existing source referring to Ophioryme, and because he thinks the story relates to Philip he concludes that Ophioryme is another name for Hierapolis. But the original source was not about Philip or Hierapolis.

In Ophioryme, the apostles stay in the house of a Christian called Stachys. There Philip teaches them about the dragon "*who has no shape in creation*". They are then visited by the proconsul's wife Nicanora who has diseased eyes but who is cured by Mariamne (we should note Thomas 22: *"eye(s) in place of an eye"*). When her husband comes for her, she tells him to leave her and lead a chaste life. He is furious and drags her by the hair and has the apostles arrested and taken to the temple. There they are stripped and tortured although miraculously they feel no pain and there Philip is crucified upside down. John now appears (he has not been with them up to now) and warns the people about the serpent. The crowd become angry with him and threaten to mix his blood with wine and feed it to the *"Viper"*. At this point, Philip loses his temper and makes the ground open up and swallow up the men of the city, about seven thousand in total. We should note that Hierapolis was subject to earthquakes and was devastated by a particularly bad one in 60. Fortunately, Jesus appears and rebukes Philip for being wrathful. Although Philip will be martyred and will be taken by the angels to paradise, as a punishment he will remain outside it for forty days in fear of the flaming sword. Jesus adds that *"Bartholomew shall go to Lycaonia and be crucified there, and Mariamne's body shall be laid up in the river Jordan"* (*Acts of Philip 137*). Jesus then rescues those who have fallen into the earth with the exception of the proconsul and the Viper. Although some run to let Philip down from the cross he refuses to allow them to rescue him:

> *"Be not grieved that I hang thus, for I bear the form (type) of the first man, who was brought upon earth head downwards, and again by the tree of the cross made alive from the death of his transgression. And now do I fulfil the precept. For the Lord said to me: Unless you make that which is beneath to be above, and the left to be right (and the right left), you shall not enter into my kingdom. Be like me in this: for all the world is turned the wrong way, and every soul that is in it."* (*Acts of Philip 140*)

This is almost identical to the crucifixion of Peter in the Acts of Peter, and either has been taken from it or else both are derivative from an earlier unknown work. Philip goes on to tell them to build a church where he is buried (there was a church in Hierapolis dedicated to Philip) and makes the prophecy that a vine will grow where his blood falls. As in other versions of the ascent to heaven, Philip is stripped of one set of clothes which are replaced by a garment of light. He is physically stripped immediately before crucifixion and then on the cross he utters this prayer:

> *"Let not their dark air cover me, that I may pass the waters of fire and all the abyss. Clothe me in thy glorious robe and thy seal of light that ever shines, until I*

have passed by all the rulers of the world and the evil dragon that opposes us."
(Acts of Philip 144)

The gnostic garment of light, *"thy glorious robe"*, must replace the worldly clothes of the flesh for the ascent to be made past the *"rulers of the world"*
and the evil dragon.

Before we come to the connections between all this and Revelation, we
must consider another two sources. One of these we have already come
across, the account in Acts 14 of Paul and Barnabas being worshipped as
Hermes and Zeus. We have seen that it is derived from the Barnabas-
Cephas source and that originally it was Cephas who was Zeus and Paul
who was Hermes. After the attempted worship, Paul is stoned and lies as if
dead until he revives and goes back into the city.

The last source is the Apocalypse of Elijah (translations by O. S. Wintermute[308]), which is a work with both Jewish and Christian characteristics.
The academic view is that the work was Jewish but has received additions
and redactions from a Christian editor. This view is puzzling as the Christian elements are extensive, and it is better explained as coming from a
Jewish Christian group. There are no less than four extant early manuscripts and some of the Coptic manuscripts date to the early fourth century.
The work must have been popular and in existence by the mid-third century or earlier. The earliest date is constrained by dependencies on the New
Testament; there are influences from Revelation, the use of the name Tabitha seems to have come from Acts, and there is an apparent quote from 1
John. The relationship between the Apocalypse and Revelation is complex,
and it will be shown that the author of Apocalypse must have had access to
the source used by Revelation as well as Revelation itself. A dating of the
final work to between the mid second and mid third centuries is likely, but
the crucial question is the extent to which it uses earlier sources.

One such influence is the Gospel of Thomas. In 1:13-27 there is a section
that is a reaction towards the highly controversial saying Thomas 14a: *"If
you fast, you will beget a sin for yourselves; and if you pray, you will be condemned; and if you give alms, you will do evil to your spirits."* The apocalypse
starts by condemning those who set aside the Law of God saying: *"the fast
does not exist nor did God create it"*. This shows that the authors of the apocalypse were Law observant. But then, interestingly, it gets defensive. It explains that it is a *"pure fast"* that the Lord has created. One who fasts, but
not in a pure fast, has *"angered the Lord"* and has *"grieved his soul, gathering
up wrath for himself on the day of wrath"*. Compare to the Thomas saying *"you*

will be condemned" and *"you will do an evil to your spirits"*. The apocalypse then mentions sin and prayer: *"a release from sin by means of a pure prayer"*. It goes on to talk about being single minded rather than double minded: *"the one who is double minded in his prayer is darkness to himself"*.

The Apocalypse is trying to explain that if you fast while impure or pray while double minded you will draw upon yourself the evil consequences of Thomas 14a. The authors of the apocalypse are not rejecting Thomas 14a but are trying, with difficulty, to reconcile it with their belief in fasting and prayer. This is very similar to the approach that the author of Matthew takes in dealing with this troublesome Thomas saying. In Matthew 6:1-18 he also interprets it as meaning that the activities of prayer, fasting and giving alms should not be done in an incorrect way.

Another potential link with Thomas occurs in 2:35-39 where there is a prophecy concerning the mothers of Egypt. This prophecy involves a number of absurdities that must have come from a misunderstood source:

Nursing mothers are bound and forced to give suck to serpents.
Their blood is then used to poison arrows that are shot by children 12 or under.
The midwife grieves and those who have given birth regret that they sat upon the birth stool
The barren woman and the virgin rejoice
The Jews are taken from Egypt to Jerusalem

The source may be either Thomas 79 directly, or indirectly through the use of the saying made by the author of Luke.[309] Reconstruction B of Thomas 79 is given below:

A woman said to him: Blessed is the womb which bore you, and the breasts which nourished you. He said to her: Blessed are they who have heard the word of the Father and have truly kept it. Blessed is the womb which has not conceived, and the breasts which have not given suck. (Reconstruction B of Thomas 79)

As in Thomas 79 those who have not conceived and whose breasts have not given suck are "blessed". This is followed by the Jews of Egypt being taken to Jerusalem. Most likely these Jews are intended to reflect those in Thomas 79 who *"have heard the word of the father and have truly kept it"* and so are blessed. It would be natural for the Law observant authors to interpret those who keep the word of the father as meaning their fellow Jews as opposed to gentiles. One of the most intriguing features of this passage in the Apocalypse is what is said about the barren women:

The barren woman and the virgin will rejoice, saying, "It is our time to rejoice because we have no child upon the earth but our children are in heaven." (Apocalypse of Elijah 2:38)

We can see this going back to a genuine memory of Mary as the virgin who is mother to the movement and whose children are in heaven. The key part of the Apocalypse is the coming of the anti-Christ and a three-fold martyrdom at his hands. First is a confused account of wars between the Assyrians and Persians in which the wealth of the temple is carried off. Blood flows in Egypt until a king arises in the "city of the sun", presumably Heliopolis. This king is on the side of the Persians, and it seems that he shares in their triumph, killing the Assyrian king and then ruling in Egypt. There follows a period of three years and six months in which there is no royal decree and which is a time of abundance. In this period, the living appeal to the dead to rise up and join them.

Next is the coming of the anti-Christ, the *"son of lawlessness"*, who appears in the *"fourth year of the king"* and claims to be the Christ. The anti-Christ performs miracles that are surprisingly like those of Christ in the gospels. We then have the strange story of a virgin called Tabitha who follows the lawless one, scolding him, to Judea and Jerusalem. He chases her and sucks her blood throwing her body onto the temple where it is healing for the people. After this, she comes alive again and scolds him some more. Tabitha would seem to be named after the Tabitha, also called Dorcas, of Acts 9:36 who is resurrected by Peter.

This is followed by the martyrdom of Enoch and Elijah, which has many features in common both with the martyrdom and resurrection of Tabitha and with the martyrdom of the two witnesses in Revelation. In scripture, Enoch and Elijah are the only two humans to be taken up to heaven alive and in the Apocalypse they return to earth to battle with and rebuke the shameless one. He fights them "in the marketplace of the great city" for seven days. There he leaves them dead for three and a half days for the people to see. But after this they rise up again and scold him so that he fights with them again. This time he cannot harm them, and they shine so that all the people can see. The son of lawlessness turns instead to the saints and the priests and subjects them to horrific tortures. Those who are weak flee to the desert where their spirits are received by the Lord while their bodies are petrified until the final judgement. They will then find rest but in a second-class position to those who suffer martyrdom. This is very typical of Christianity in the second to third centuries when the cult of martyrdom developed. The question of what should happen to those Christians without the bravery to endure torture and death was a burning issue.

After this comes yet another martyrdom story, this time about sixty righteous ones who go to Jerusalem to fight the shameless one. It is a bit of an anti-climax following on from Tabitha, Enoch and Elijah since the shameless one kindles altars, lifts them up, and burns them. By the cruelty of this act, many realise that he is not the Christ. The three stories of martyrdom are followed by the end times when Christ sends his angels to take up to heaven those who bear his mark on their hand and forehead. After this many disasters and famine fall upon the earth and the anti-Christ realises that his time has come to an end. The Lord sends fire upon the earth. Enoch and Elijah return to kill the son of lawlessness by dissolving him into nothing. Those who follow him are cast into the abyss and thus starts the thousand year reign of Christ.

The relevant passages in Acts, Revelation, the Acts of Philip and the Apocalypse of Elijah are all very different, and yet we can discern that they all descend from the same original source. Indeed we can trace the same source at least twice in Revelation (A: the two witnesses and B: the woman in the sky) and no less than four times in the Apocalypse of Elijah (A: the Assyrian-Persian wars, B: Tabitha, C: Enoch and Elijah, and D: the sixty righteous ones). The source was ultimately about the events in Rome under the persecution of Nero, but it expressed these events in allegorical language. At its heart was the conflict between Mary and Nero the antichrist. Using the principle of redundancy, we can work out the major features that must have been present in the source by comparing the different versions. We will identify these as different "themes".

Ten themes

The following ten themes are found in the texts that are derived from the Martyrdom Source.

Theme 1 - the temple

One theme that is present in all versions, either explicitly or implicitly, is the "temple". In the original the temple was Mary, but as later authors did not realise that the temple was a person there is great confusion over the location of this temple. The following shows how the temple occurs in the different sources.

Revelation A - *"Rise and measure the temple of God, and the altar, and those worshiping in it. And leave out the courtyard outside the temple, and do not measure it, because it has been given up to the nations, and they will trample upon the holy city forty and two months."* (Revelation 11:1-2)

Revelation B - *"And the temple of God was opened in heaven, and there was seen in his temple the ark of his covenant: and there were lightnings, and voices, and thunderings, and an earthquake, and great hail. And a great sign was seen in heaven: a woman clothed with the sun, and the moon under her feet, and on her head a crown of twelve stars."* (Revelation 11:19-12:1)

Acts - *"And they called Barnabas, Zeus, and Paul, Hermes, because he was the chief speaker. And the priest of Zeus, whose temple was just outside the city, having brought oxen and wreaths to the gates, was desiring to sacrifice with the crowds."* (Acts 14:12-13). Note that Barnabas is substituted for Cephas in the Barnabas-Cephas source; so that in the original it is the temple of Cephas/Zeus that stands before the city.

Acts of Philip - *"And the apostles were arrested, and scourged and dragged to the temple, and shut up in it"* (Acts of Philip 120-122). The apostles are Philip, Mariamne (Mary) and Bartholomew. The subsequent description of their torture and the martyrdom of Philip must take place in this temple.

Elijah A - *"They will spend three years in that place until they carry off the wealth of the temple that is in that place."* (Apocalypse of Elijah 2:43)

Elijah B - About the shameless one and the virgin (Tabitha): *"He will suck her blood in the evening. And he will cast her upon the temple, and she shall become a healing for the people."* (Apocalypse of Elijah 4:4-5)

Elijah C - Following on from the story of Tabitha: *"Then when Elijah and Enoch hear that the shameless one has revealed himself in the holy place they will come down and fight with him..."* (Apocalypse of Elijah 4:7).

Elijah D - The sixty righteous ones go to Jerusalem where they are lifted up to be burned on kindled altars.

In these references we can see negative connotations of sacrifice and conflict with the temple being in control of evil or pagan forces.

Theme 2 - the supernatural powers of the witnesses

In Revelation A, the witnesses have special powers: *"And if anyone would harm them, fire comes out of their mouth and devours their enemies. And if anyone would harm them, he must be killed in this way. These have the power to shut the sky, so that no rain shall fall in the days of their prophecy; and they have power over the waters, to turn them into blood, and to strike the earth with every plague, as often as they wish." (Revelation 11:5-6)*

The issuing of fire from the mouth relates to Mary's title as "thunder". These powers are also found in some of the other sources.

In Revelation B when the temple is opened, and the woman appears this is accompanied by *"lightnings, and voices, and thunderings, and an earthquake, and great hail" (Revelation 11:19).*

In Acts there is an implicit link in that Cephas (Barnabas) is called Zeus who was closely associated with the lightning bolt and thunder. There is a second link in the speech of the apostles to the people about the living God who *"gave us rain from heaven, and fruitful seasons, filling our hearts with food and gladness" (Acts 14:17).* Compare this to Revelation A where the two witnesses have the power *"to shut heaven, that it rain not in the days of their prophecy".*

In the Acts of Philip, Mariamne is associated with fire and the other Apostles have the power to call down fire from heaven: *"But Mariamne on being stripped became like an ark of glass full of light and fire, and everyone ran away. And Philip and Bartholomew talked in Hebrew, and Philip said: Shall we call down fire from heaven?" (Acts of Philip 126-127).*[310] Eventually Philip summons another power to disastrous effect, the ability to open up the earth and swallow up the people.

In Elijah A there is a reference to water turning to blood: *"The river of Egypt will become blood and they will not be able to drink from it for three days" (Apocalypse of Elijah 2:44).*

Elsewhere in the Apocalypse, after the removal of the saints to heaven the waters dry up: *"The earth will be dry. The waters of the sea will dry up" (Apocalypse of Elijah 5:9).* The sinners lament that they have alienated the Christ and will die in the famine. In a confused passage the lawless one also laments about his fate: *"Seize the robbers and kill them. Bring up the saints. For because of them the earth yields fruit. For because of them the sun shines upon the earth. For because of them the dew will come upon the earth." (Apocalypse of Elijah 5:17-18)* Compare this to the power of the witnesses to cause the rain to cease in Revelation and the speech of the apostles about the kindness of God in Acts.

After this comes the bringing down of fire from heaven: "*It will come to pass on that day that the Lord will hear and command the heaven and the earth with great wrath. And they will send forth fire.*" (Apocalypse of Elijah 5:22) The ability to bring forth fire is later specifically associated with Elijah and Enoch, who confront the shameless one so that he dissolves like ice by fire (*Apocalypse of Elijah 5:33*).

Theme 3 - the dragon or serpent

The imagery of the confrontation with the dragon or serpent runs through many of the sources. The archetype is the dragon who confronts the woman from heaven in Revelation: "*And there appeared another sign in heaven, and behold a great red dragon, having seven heads and ten horns, and seven crowns upon his heads. And his tail drags a third of the stars of heaven, and cast them to the earth. And the dragon stands before the woman who is about to bring forth, so that when she should bring forth, he might devour her child.*" (*Revelation 12:3-4*) The dragon is also called a serpent and represents Satan: "*And the great dragon was thrown out, that ancient serpent, called the Devil, and Satan, which deceives the whole world.*" (Revelation 12:9)

In Revelation A, the beast who kills the two witnesses is associated with the dragon in Revelation 13:2: "*The dragon gave the beast his power and his throne and great authority.*"

In the Acts of Philip, the dragon or serpent is a major theme. Christ sends the apostles to the city where "*they worship the Viper, the mother of snakes*". On the way there they meet the leopard and the lamb and learn that the leopard was hunting on the mountain of the she-dragon, the mother of snakes. Not long afterwards they come across the dragon who, followed by its brood of serpents, confronts them. The apostles destroy the dragon and the snakes by bringing down a flash of lightning from heaven. They continue to the city called Ophioryme meaning "Snake street": "*for the men of the place worshipped the snake and had images of it.*" There they are arrested and taken to the temple where they are tortured and where Philip is crucified upside down. When Philip uses his powers to open the earth to swallow up the city and its people, Jesus comes to save them with his cross, bringing up all except "*the proconsul and the Viper*".

In Apocalypse of Elijah, the women of Egypt are made to suckle serpents. Later the lawless one pursues the saints in imagery reminiscent of the dragon pursuing the seed of the woman in Revelation: "*He will take his fiery wings and fly out after the saints. He will fight them again.*" *(Apocalypse of Elijah 5:20)* And finally when the lawless one is defeated by Elijah and Enoch he is explicitly called a serpent.

Theme 4 - the serpent drinks blood, but the blood of the martyr is a healing for the people

The drinking of blood is found in the Acts of Philip and the Apocalypse. In the Acts when John preaches to the people of Ophioryme they threaten to give his blood to the serpent: "*The priests are going to wring out your blood and mix it with wine and give it to the Viper.*" *(Acts of Philip 131)*

The same concept of blood mixed and wine occurs in a prophecy given by Philip on the cross: "*Where my blood is dropping a vine will grow, and you shall use the wine of it for the cup: and partake of it on the third day.*" *(Acts of Philip 143)*

In the Apocalypse it is said that the nursing mothers will be seized and bound: "*They will suckle serpents. And their blood will be drawn from their breasts and it will be applied as poison to the arrows.*" *(Apocalypse of Elijah 2:35)*

In Elijah B the shameless one will suck the blood of Tabitha and cast her upon the temple where she will become a healing for the people. When she is resurrected, she tells him "*my blood which you have cast upon the temple has become a healing for the people.*" *(Apocalypse of Elijah 2:35 4:6)*

Theme 5 - the flood from the serpent

In Revelation B when the dragon is cast down from heaven he pursues the woman and tries to drown her in a flood: "*And the serpent cast out of his mouth water as a flood after the woman, that he might cause her to be carried away of the flood. And the earth helped the woman, and the earth opened her mouth, and swallowed up the flood which the dragon cast out of his mouth.*" *(Revelation 12:15-16)* The earth swallowing up the water is hinted at in the Apocalypse of Elijah: "*We went to the deep places of the sea and we did not find water. We dug in the rivers and papyrus reeds and we did not find water.*" *(Apocalypse of Elijah 5:14)*

There is an echo of this in the Acts of Philip when it is said that *"Mari-amne's body shall be laid up in the river Jordan" (Acts of Philip 137)* suggesting that she would be martyred by being drowned in the river. The source for this flood imagery can be found in Daniel 9:26. To the Jesus movement Mary is both the temple and Jerusalem and her destruction by Nero is presented as a destruction by a flood so as to fulfil the Daniel prophecy.

Theme 6 - the dragon/serpent cast out of heaven

The dragon who is the devil is cast out of heaven in Revelation. His tail draws a third part of the stars from heaven and casts them to the earth.[311] After the confrontation with the woman, there is then a war in heaven between Michael and the dragon each with their army of angels. The dragon losses and is cast down to the earth along with his angels. The casting down of the stars and the angels are two representations of the same event, the descent of the fallen angels to earth that is found in the Book of Enoch.

In the Acts of Philip, John gives an explanation of the origin of the serpent: *"Then John addressed the people, warning them against the serpent. When all matter was wrought and spread out throughout the system of heaven, the works of God entreated God that they might see his glory: and when they saw it, their desire became gall and bitterness, and the earth became the storehouse of that which went astray, and the result and the superfluity of the creation was gathered together and became like an egg: and the serpent was born." (Acts of Philip 130)* This would seem to be a version of the myth of the angels, who were the first created beings by God, refusing to bow down to man and so being cast out of heaven.

In the Apocalypse there is also a reference to the falling out of heaven in the words spoken by Elijah and Enoch: *"You have acted against the angels, you are always a stranger, you have fallen from heaven like the morning stars." (Apocalypse of Elijah 4:10-11)*

Theme 7 - the earth swallows up

In Revelation A after the witnesses ascend to heaven there is an earthquake: *"And in that hour there was a great earthquake, and a tenth of the city fell, and seven thousand men were killed in the earthquake. And the rest were terrified and gave glory to the God of heaven." (Revelation 11:13)* In Revelation B the opening of the temple is also attended by earthquakes.

In the Acts, Philip asks the earth to open and swallow up the city: "*It opened and the whole place was swallowed, about seven thousand men, save where the apostles were.*" *(Acts of Philip 133)* The number agrees precisely with Revelation.

Theme 8 - the wilderness as a place of safety

In both Revelation and the Apocalypse of Elijah, the wilderness is represented as a place of safety. In Revelation, the woman flees to the wilderness and then is given wings to fly to the wilderness - in both times for a three and a half periods.

In the Apocalypse those who cannot endure tortures flee to the desert where they lie down as one who sleeps so that the Lord receives their souls and their bodies are preserved until the day of the last judgement.[312]

Theme 9 - Lycaonia

The same place is mentioned in two of the sources. The Acts episode is set in Lystra and Derbe in Lycaonia. In the Acts of Philip it is predicted that Bartholomew will go to Lycaonia and be crucified there *(Acts of Philip 137).*

Theme 10 - the resurrected witnesses

The most obvious theme is the resurrection of the witnesses. The account in Revelation A sets out the pattern:

The witnesses preach for three and a half years and are given supernatural powers.
They are then killed by the beast.
Their bodies lie and are mocked over by the people for three and a half years.
They are resurrected and ascend to heaven.

The story of the woman in the heavens does not explicitly say that she was killed and resurrected. However, there is the repeating pattern of her fleeing to the wilderness for three and a half years. In the Apocalypse of

Elijah, it is clear that those who are "protected" by fleeing to the wilderness actually die.

In Acts, the action follows a similar pattern to resurrection:

The two apostles Paul and Barnabas are viewed as Gods - compare to the powers given to the witnesses in Revelation.

They preach to the people.

The people then turn against them (persuaded by some "Jews" from Antioch and Iconium)

Paul is stoned until apparently dead.

His body is dragged and lies outside the city.

Paul then comes back alive and resumes his preaching.

In the Acts of Philip we again have a similar pattern:

The apostles preach to the people of Ophioryme.

The people are opposed to them - they are originally receptive to John before they decide he is not one of their own.

Philip is killed by the "serpent" in the form of the serpent's acolytes.

Philip is dead for forty days with his body wrapped in papyrus.

After forty days, he is "resurrected" and is received into heaven.

In Revelation, the time for which the witnesses lay dead is three and a half years which we have suggested should be multiplied by ten to give the period of 35 years, or half a generation. In other places, this period is rounded up to the significant forty years and often represented as forty days. In the Acts there is the curious detail that Philip's entry into paradise is delayed, supposedly as a punishment for his rashness. There must have been something in the source suggesting this delay and we can see that it follows the same pattern as Revelation and Acts. The period of Philip's death is forty days before he reappears: "*And at the end of forty days the Saviour appeared in the form of Philip and told Bartholomew and Mariamne that he had entered paradise, and bade them go their ways.*" (Acts of Philip 148)

There is a residual confused reference to the resurrection in Elijah A. The Assyrians seize the temple for three and a half years, and this is followed by much bloodshed in Egypt. Then comes a time of peace in which resurrection occurs: *Those who are alive will go to those who are dead saying "Rise up and be with us in this rest"* (Apocalypse of Elijah 2:53).

It is in Elijah B and C that the resurrection pattern is most prominent. The structure of the two is virtually identical:

Tabitha chides the shameless following him to Jerusalem
He sucks her blood and casts her down onto the temple in the evening
She rises up in the morning and resumes her scolding
Her blood becomes a healing for the people

Enoch and Elijah fight with the shameless one in the holy place
They fight in the marketplace of the great city for seven days
They lie dead for three days and a half
On the fourth day, they rise again and resume their scolding
The shameless one does not prevail over them, but they shine where all the people can see them

The only place the delayed resurrection is not found is Elijah D where the sixty righteous ones are sacrificed but do not resurrect.

The existence of the Martyrdom Source

Putting things in numbers can help verify that the level of agreement is non-random. In total there are some forty-one points of similarities between the texts as split out in the following table:

Text	No of themes
Revelation A	5
Revelation B	7
Acts	4
Acts of Philip	9
Elijah A	3
Elijah B	3
Elijah C	5
Elijah D	1
Elijah other	4
Elijah all	9

Text	No of themes
Total themes	41
Average (Elijah as four)	5.1
Average (Elijah as one)	6.8
Average from control group	0.3
Maximum from control group	2

In the Apocalypse of Elijah, some of the themes are present in the four sections influenced by the Martyrdom Source whereas other themes are spread throughout the work. If we regard the four sections as separate texts, then we have eight texts with an average of 5.1 themes per text. If we count Elijah as one, then we have five texts but a higher average of 6.8 themes per text.

To put these numbers in context, a control group of 75 passages chosen at random have been evaluated for the presence of the ten themes. This control group includes 50 passages from the Gospels/Acts and 25 passages from Apocryphal texts.[313] On average the control group have 0.33 themes present per passage. Mostly the themes occur as singletons but in two passages 2 themes were present. The most common themes in the control passages are a temple reference (0.11 per passage), a resurrection (0.09 per passage), supernatural powers like the witnesses (0.08 per passage), and a snake reference (0.04 per passage). Although some passages had one or more themes present, none of them was qualitatively similar to the Martyrdom Source passages. For example, there were several passages with a resurrection, but none had the specific form of the resurrection of the witnesses.

We can calculate the probability of the number of themes in each passage arising by chance. For 4 themes, such as the Acts passage, this is about 1/5,000. The improbability rises to 1/120,000 for 5 themes, and 1/216,000,000 for 7 themes. For more than 7 themes the probability of the combination arising by chance is negligible, less than 1/1,000,000,000.[314] Some of the Elijah texts have a lower number of themes present. However, these texts are found in close proximity to each other and share qualitative features. Also, the 9 themes in the Apocalypse of Elijah as a whole could not have arisen by chance.

Although the low probability of the themes arising by chance strongly supports the existence of the Martyrdom Source, there are two issues that need to be addressed. The first is that the themes have been deduced from the same texts to which the probabilities are being applied. If we had only one text then even if the number of themes were very high this would tell us absolutely nothing as the themes have been taken from that one text. What is significant is when we find one or more other texts that share a number of themes with the first. In this case, we have a large number of texts, between five and eight, which include the same themes. It is this clustering of themes over a number of different texts that shows the existence of a link.

The other issue is whether the link between the texts could have arisen through the later texts copying the earlier texts. There are six combinations of pairs between the four works. For one pair, the Apocalypse of Elijah and Revelation, there is certainly a link with the Apocalypse being influenced by Revelation. However, the similarities exist between all texts and it is difficult to see any obvious links between the other five pair combinations. And even with the Apocalypse, there are many points of similarity that have not been copied from Revelation. For example, the story of Elijah and Enoch shares many features with the story of the two witnesses in Revelation, and it is easy to see it may have been largely based on Revelation. However, the story of Tabitha, which has many similarities to the story of Elijah and Enoch, is very different from anything in Revelation.

Instead of direct copying, we must have an example of redundancy. Not only is the level of similarity clearly non-random, but there are also too many differences for it to be due to simple copying of the earlier texts. The only explanation that makes sense is an early Martyrdom Source.

The Martyrdom Source

The Martyrdom Source most likely started out as a verbal tradition transmitted through a range of different channels, some of which then gave rise to written sources which were available to later authors. The source can certainly not be any later than Acts or Revelation, which both probably date from the early 90s. We can push the date back further because the Acts section belongs to the Barnabas-Cephas source that must have been in existence before Acts. Also, the differences between the Revelation and Acts evocation of the Martyrdom Source mean that the tradition has had time to evolve down separate paths. All of which is consistent with a martyrdom date in the mid-60s which would allow two to three decades for the traditions to mutate into the stories we find in Acts and Revelation.

The Martyrdom Source enables us to reach back in time to events that happened decades before Revelation and Acts were written. So what does the Martyrdom Source tell us? It is the story of the martyrdoms of Mary/Cephas and Paul, presented as an allegory. The serpent or beast is the Emperor Nero, who was believed to be the avatar of Satan and the anti-Christ. Mary is represented in two ways; as one of the two witnesses and as a female figure linked to the temple.

In Revelation, the female figure is the woman in the sky, and in the Apocalypse she is Tabitha. Clearly the name "Mary" was not part of the source. The author of the Apocalypse has hit on the name "Tabitha" because, according to Acts, she was a female Christian who was resurrected. In reality, there was no person called Tabitha this being a confusion with *Talitha koum* or "little girl arise". The author of the Apocalypse may have borrowed the name Tabitha, but the sequence shows signs of being close to the original source; it has links to both the story of the woman in heaven and the temple in Revelation.

In the Tabitha sequence, she puts on her garment and confronts the lawless one. The garment is the spirit, which in Mary's case is Jesus himself. It is Mary/Jesus who initiates the confrontation by following the king of Babylon to Rome. There she meets apparent defeat at the hands of the Antichrist, being put to death, alongside Paul, by Nero. The death of Mary would have been a seismic event for the movement because she was believed to be the avatar of the Christ on earth. How could she die before the time had come in which Jesus would appear in the skies? This question was resolved by the myth that Mary was not really dead, but would return after a generation of thirty-five or forty years. This does not mean that the movement denied her physical death but that they believed that she survived spiritually. As the Apocalypse says about Tabitha: *and she will live and scold him saying "O shameless one, you have no power against my soul or my body because I live in the Lord always"* (*Apocalypse of Elijah 4:5*). In the confrontation between the woman and the dragon, the woman withdraws to the wilderness. But the story of Tabitha makes clear that she is killed, as does the information in Revelation that the outer court of the temple, the body, is trampled upon by the Gentiles for three years and a half.

The martyrdom is represented as the sucking out of blood by the serpent. But the blood is also healing for the people, meaning that the movement saw the redemption of the world through the sacrifice of Mary. The dragon unleashes a flood after the woman, signifying the persecution that followed the fire in Rome. In Revelation, the earth swallows the flood but in the Odes of Solomon a flood carries away the temple and in the Acts of Philip it is predicted that Mariamne's body will lie beneath the Jordan.

An alternative account of the martyrdom exists in the story of two witnesses. Given the wide variation in names and the fact that the two are not named in Revelation, the names must again have been missing in most versions of the Martyrdom Source. The ultimate source behind the Acts story, however, has them correctly as Cephas and Paul although Cephas then becomes confused with Barnabas. Both Cephas and Paul were believed to have made the journey to heaven, and the Jewish Christian author of the Apocalypse confuses them with the two who did the same in the Jewish scripture, Elijah and Enoch. In the Acts of Philip, there are three or four apostles; Philip, Mariamne and Bartholomew make the journey together, and John appears as an extra at the temple. We can understand this grouping if Mary (Mariamne) is included under her own name and also as one of the "two witnesses" who in the Acts become Philip and Bartholomew. The appearance of John may go back to a genuine memory that John Mark was also in Rome; we would expect him to have suffered martyrdom at around the same time. We can see that Mary's two identities were beginning to separate in the original source. As Mary, she was the female figure associated with the temple and as Cephas, she was one of the two witnesses. The stories share the same form which shows that the stories about the female figure and those about the two witnesses are two versions of the same original.

Key points

1. Although the ending of John contains a prediction of the martyrdom of Simon Peter, this is very similar to a prophecy in Acts about Paul. The ultimate source for both is a prophecy in Isaiah about the exile.

2. The tradition of the upside down crucifixion of Peter is found in the Acts of Peter and the Acts of Philip. The origins of the tradition lie in a literalisation of Thomas 22; if a person is crucified upside down, then the upper becomes the lower, and the left eye/hand/foot becomes the right eye/hand/foot.

3. The Acts of Philip and the sequences in Revelation have features in common that indicate a common influence. We can also identify other texts that share these features. In total we have eight such texts; the two Revelation passages about the two witnesses and the woman in the sky; the Acts

of Philip; the passage in Acts of the Apostles in which Paul and Barnabas are worshipped; and four separate sections of the Apocalypse of Elijah.

4. A total of ten themes linking these texts can be identified. There must be a common ultimate source, either written or oral, behind all eight texts. We call this the "Martyrdom Source".

5. The main theme is that the witness or witnesses preach to the people, they are killed, they are dead for a period, and then resurrected. Behind this theme we can see the belief that Mary, although put to death, will return.

6. The other themes are (i) the temple; (ii) the supernatural powers of the witnesses; (iii) the dragon or serpent; (iv) the serpent drinks blood, but the blood of the martyr heals the people; (v) the flood from the serpent; (vi) the dragon/serpent cast out of heaven; (vii) the earth swallows up; (viii) the wilderness as a place of refuge; (ix) Lycaonia.

7. The principal evidence for the existence of the Martyrdom Source is qualitative; the occurrence in different texts of a number of interlinked themes all relating to the confrontation between Mary and Nero, all of which share the same underlying form. However, we can also back this up with quantitative evidence by counting the number of themes in each text.

8. In total, we identify 41 points of similarity. The average text has 5.1 themes compared to an average of 0.3 themes per passage for a random control group. The control group enables us to calculate the probability of the number of themes arising by chance; it is a vanishingly small probability that the number of observed themes could be shared by several different texts.

9. There must be a link between the Martyrdom Source texts, but they are so different from each other that this link cannot, in most cases, be direct copying. So we must have an early Martyrdom Source, which has influenced each of the texts.

10. The Martyrdom Source would have been in existence decades before the 90s to give time for the variations we find in Acts and Revelation to emerge. We conclude that it goes back to traditions arising from a martyrdom under Nero in the 60s.

Conclusion

The Martyrdom Source enables us to penetrate back in time to beyond the literalisations of the Gospels and Acts. Behind the Martyrdom Source is a memory of the martyrdom of Mary/Cephas and Paul under Nero. Mary was represented in two different ways; as one of the two witnesses, and as a female figure associated with the temple. Nero is represented as a dragon/snake and the anti-Christ. Although it seemed that Mary had been defeated and killed by the dragon, it was believed that she would shortly return in triumph.

Chapter 42

Mary and the fire from heaven

We can collaborate the Martyrdom Source with external sources and search for other passages to which it may be linked. We will find one further text which is certainly derived from the Martyrdom Source and, most interesting of all, we will find links to the Gospels of Matthew and Mark. Does the story of Jesus' crucifixion owe much to the Martyrdom Source?

The Martyrdom Source will also give us a surprising insight into events in Rome. Nero's persecution of the Christians after the fire of Rome may not be as completely unjustified as it seems. Did some Christians claim that Mary had destroyed the city by summoning the fire from heaven?

Mary and Nero

The best external account of Nero's persecution of Christians comes from Tacitus, who was writing around 116. He tells of how Nero was accused of deliberately setting fire to Rome and that to counter this belief he blamed the Christians:

Consequently, to get rid of the report, Nero fastened the guilt and inflicted the most exquisite tortures on a class hated for their abominations, called Christians by the populace. Christus, from whom the name had its origin, suffered the extreme penalty during the reign of Tiberius at the hands of one of our procurators, Pontius Pilatus, and a most mischievous superstition, thus checked for the moment, again broke out not only in Judaea, the first source of the evil, but even in Rome, where all things hideous and shameful from every part of the world find their centre and become popular. Accordingly, an arrest was first made of all who pleaded guilty; then, upon their information, an immense multitude was convicted, not so much of the crime of firing the city, as of hatred against mankind. Mockery of every sort was added to their deaths. Covered with the skins of beasts, they were torn by dogs and perished, or were nailed to torture-stakes, or were doomed to the flames and burnt, to serve as a nightly illumination, when daylight had expired. Nero offered his gardens for the spectacle, and was exhibiting a show in the circus, while he mingled with the people in the dress of a charioteer or stood aloft on a car. Hence, even for criminals who deserved extreme and exemplary punishment, there arose a feeling of compassion; for it was not, as it seemed, for the public good, but to glut one man's cruelty, that they were being destroyed. (Tacitus Annals 15:44)[315]

This passage is often used as evidence for the historical Jesus, but we must remember that the passage was written some forty years after the Gospel of Mark. At this time, the literalistic gospels were in wide circulation. All the information contained in the passage about "Christus" being put to death under Pilate could have come from Mark or one of the other gospels. But there is another and better source for Tacitus' information about Jesus, a source to which Tacitus is known to have access and which shows similarities to his description. This source is the Testimonium Flavianum, the account concerning Jesus in Josephus' Jewish Antiquities.

The passage from Tacitus provides evidence both for the persecution of Christians by Nero and for Christians being sufficiently prominent in Nero's Rome to be used as scapegoats. Suetonius in his Life of Nero backs this up, although he does not go into detail: *"Punishment was inflicted on the Christians, a class of men given to a new and mischievous superstition."*

Can we find some trace of the tortures inflicted on Christians by Nero? The Apocalypse of Elijah contains some very graphic details of torture that follows on from the story of the two witnesses:

He will pursue all of the saints. They and the priests of the land will be brought back bound. He will kill them and destroy them [...] them. And their eyes will be removed with iron spikes. He will remove the skin from their heads. He will remove their nails one by one. He will command that vinegar and lime is put in their nose. (Apocalypse of Elijah 4:21-23)[316]

This has the brutal feel of realism. What comes after, the story of the righteous sixty, who are lifted up and burned, agrees precisely with what Tacitus tells us about those Christians who were set on fire to serve as torches. The sixty are not resurrected and their story does not follow the identical pattern to Tabitha or Elijah and Enoch. The reason for this becomes clear if they represent the many Christians who were executed at the same time; the extras in history whose names are unknown and yet who shared the same torments as Mary and Paul and made the same sacrifice. In the apocalypse, the sixty are kindled on altars, a remembrance of their role as sacrificial victims.

The murder of Mary, the temple, by Nero may have left its traces in another first-century source, the Sibylline Oracles 4 and 5. Most scholars think these were originally Jewish but they have survived only through Christian channels and so must have been cherished by Christians and subject to Christian editing. Nero plays a prominent part in the Sibylline oracles, and they form with Revelation and the Ascension of Isaiah the evidence for the prominence of Nero within the Christian movement in the late first century. The Oracles are concerned with prophecies of prominent historical events; we would expect the destruction of the temple in Jerusalem to be included, and it is. But there is something very odd about how it is described in these two Oracles. In Oracle 4, events around the reign of Nero are recounted culminating in him fleeing Italy "like a runaway slave" to go and live with the Parthians. This is the Nero Redivivus legend that was suggested by the mysterious circumstances of his death in a villa outside the city walls. After the disappearance of Nero the Oracle moves on to the destruction of the temple:

A leader of Rome will come to Syria who will burn the temple of Jerusalem with fire, at the same time slaughter many men and destroy the great land of the Jews with its broad roads. (Sibylline Oracles 4:125-7)[317]

The destruction of the temple is described as happening after the reign of Nero. But what is odd is that the destruction of the temple has already been mentioned out of place immediately before Nero flees Rome:

An evil storm of war will also come upon Jerusalem from Italy and it will sack the great temple of God, whenever they put their trust in folly and cast off piety and commit repulsive murders in front of the temple. (Sibylline Oracles 4:115-8)[318]

Why should the destruction of the temple be mentioned twice and why should it be put out of sequence in this the first mention? The "evil storm of war" that comes to Jerusalem may make sense because the Jewish war started under Nero but the sacking of the temple does not. The answer is that this first sacking of the temple must be a Christian interpolation into the Jewish original. Its purpose of making this insertion is to blame Nero for the destruction of the temple and is evidence of an early Christian tradition that Nero did destroy the temple. The author of the interpolation has inherited this tradition but does not understand that the temple that Nero has destroyed is Mary. So instead he makes it the literal temple in Jerusalem.

The fourth Sibylline oracle was written by someone who rejected the validity of the second temple and who objected to temple worship; views shared by the Jesus movement and its predecessors. Another sign that this passage has been influenced by Christians is that it blames the sacking on the Jews due to the committing of *"repulsive murders in front of the temple"*. This is also likely derived from the Martyrdom Source because the martyrdoms are associated with the temple. It could also be linked to the (mythical) story of the martyrdom of James at the temple. The accounts of the death of James have some features that suggest that they also may be descended from the Martyrdom Source. Most notably, in the version in the Pseudo-Clementine Recognitions, James is struck apparently dead in front of the temple but later revives.[319] James could have been associated with the witnesses due to his role as "the temple" in succession to Mary. According to Eusebius, Josephus wrote that the siege of Jerusalem and the destruction of the temple arose because of the murder of James the Just by the Jews.[320] We have seen that this is due to confusion with John the Baptist, but it is evidence for such a belief among the Christians. The Oracle expresses the same belief that murders in front of the temple caused the war.

The flight of Nero and the destruction of the temple are also covered by Sibylline Oracle 5 and again Nero is accused of the destruction. The passage starts by saying about Nero that "He will flee from Babylon" meaning Rome and go to the Medes and Persians. It is then said how he destroyed the temple:

"He seized the divinely built temple and burned the citizens and peoples who went into it, men whom I rightly praised" (Sibylline Oracles 5:150-1)[321]

Again we see that the author of the fifth Oracle is determined to blame the temple destruction on Nero and not the Emperor Vespasian or Titus who were responsible for the destruction. In Oracle 4 and 5 we have evidence for an earlier tradition that Nero destroyed the temple even though the authors of these statements may not have understood the meaning of this tradition. Although the second temple was destroyed by fire, that fire was started accidentally, and the statement that the citizens and peoples were burned does not fit the siege of Jerusalem. It does fit very well the persecution in Rome where the Christians were burnt alongside the temple, Mary. And note how similar it is to the story of the "sixty righteous" who enter the holy place and are burnt in the Apocalypse of Ezekiel.

Nero and the fire

Nero has had a bad press but is unlikely to have been guilty of the fire of Rome. According to Tacitus, he was not present in Rome when it started, and he did everything he could to help extinguish it and to provide for those who were affected. And he had Rome rebuilt out of stone leaving fire gaps between buildings to help stop anything like it happening again. Indeed, his role in dealing with the fire seems to have been one of efficient and exemplary leadership. Most likely the fire started the way most fires start, through a mundane accident or an act of petty arson. Yet the unfair rumour that Nero had started the fire persisted. And so, according to Tacitus, he fixed on the Christians as a cynical manoeuvre to deflect attention from his own suspected guilt. But is this charge also unfair? Did Nero punish the Christians to deflect attention from himself or did he punish them because he genuinely believed that they were guilty? A belief in their guilt would explain his cruelty towards them, lighting them as torches in revenge for the many Romans, noble and plebeian, men, women and children, who had burnt in the fire. But if so then how did Nero come to this belief? The Martyrdom Source provides a disturbing answer. Nero may have believed that the Christians were guilty because they said they were guilty, because they boasted about their role in the fire and how their leader, the mysterious person they called Cephas, had summoned the fire from heaven.

Mary had come to Rome in the belief that it was the spiritual continuation of Babylon under its angelic ruler Satan, the King of Babylon who had taken human form through his avatar, the Roman Emperor Nero. Mary was known for her ability to summon fire from heaven, a power symbolised in her title as Thunder, and originally meaning the spiritual fire of Thomas 82: *Jesus said: "He who is close to me is close to the fire, and he who is far from me is far from the kingdom."* But as ever some Christians interpreted the spiritual in literal terms, and when the great city caught fire they saw this as a punishment upon Rome from God and the miraculous confirmation of Mary's power to bring down fire. They exalted in her triumph over the dragon of Rome as the beginning of the end times, but their boasting reached the ears of Nero. The persecution started with the small minority who believed that Mary had started the fire; Tacitus records that those who were first arrested pleaded guilty; but it then spread to the vast majority of Christians who would have had no such thought. Tacitus does not believe that this majority were guilty of firing the city but only of "*hatred against mankind*" suggesting that they saw the fire as divine vengeance for the sins of the Romans. Mary herself was caught up in the persecution and was killed along with Paul, who was already in prison. Most likely the Romans never realised her true identity; she was simply an old woman who was rounded up with the others. The execution of Mary created a crisis of confidence for the movement as it appeared that she had been defeated by the dragon. The movement resolved this crisis by developing a myth. Mary had not been truly killed but only appeared dead for a time, having been taken up to heaven or to the wilderness inviolate, and she would return along with Paul at the end of the appointed generation.

The evidence for the belief that Mary had called down the fire lies in the source behind the two witnesses passages. In Revelation the two witnesses have the power to visit plagues and drought upon the earth but their most remarkable power is that fire can issue from their mouths. In the Acts of Philip, the apostles also have the power to summon fire from heaven, and Philip rashly calls down a similar power to destroy the city. Significantly Mary is depicted as having the same power of fire issuing from her mouth in "The Questions of Bartholomew", a work of uncertain date but which may be as early as the second century.[322] So great are Mary's powers in the Questions that the very existence of the world is put in danger. This happens when the apostles ask Mary how she conceived the incomprehensible and bore him who cannot be carried. She tries to warn them of the consequences if she attempts to answer this question: "*If I should begin to tell you, fire will issue forth out of my mouth and consume all the world*" (*Questions of Bartholomew 2:5*). Unwisely they press her, and she is unable to refuse them. They argue over priority with each wanting to defer to the other: "*In you did the Lord set his tabernacle, and it was his good pleasure that you should contain him...*" (*Questions of Bartholomew 2:8*) Peter tells her. When they start the four apostles press around her, with Peter on her right, Andrew on her left, John holding her bosom (note the intimate role assigned to the beloved disciple!) and Bartholomew behind her. She describes how she was living in the temple when she was visited by one like an angel whose face was incomprehensible: "*And straightway the robe (veil) of the temple was rent and there was a very great earthquake, and I fell upon the earth*" (*Questions of Bartholomew*

2:16). She falls down, but he raises her up, wipes her with his garment, and then smites his garment on the right hand and the left, producing a loaf of bread and a cup of wine which he gives her. He promises to return in three years when she will conceive his son after which he leaves, and the temple is restored. At this point the world comes close to disaster: "*And as she was saying this, fire issued out of her mouth; and the world was at the point to come to an end*" *(Questions of Bartholomew 2:22).*

There are several points of similarity between the Questions and the Martyrdom Source. This similarity becomes clearer in a strange episode where Bartholomew, on behalf of the apostles, requests to see the Adversary. Jesus warns them of the dire consequences, that they will fall down dead, but they persist and so he calls for Satan, who is also called Belair, to be summoned from the pit. Beliar is described as an enormous beast with wings and a face like lightning fire, and eyes full of darkness, and from his nostrils comes forth smoke. He is a "*dragon of the pit*".[323] When the apostles see him they do indeed fall down dead.[324] But Jesus raises them up and gives them a spirit of power so that Bartholomew can put his foot on Beliar's neck. This resurrection of the apostles brings out the similarities between the Questions and the Martyrdom Source. These similarities are shown in the following table.

Themes	Questions of Bartholomew
Theme 1 - the temple	Mary receives the visitation in the temple and the veil of the temple is rent before being restored. Mary is repeatedly called the tabernacle or temple.
Theme 2 - the supernatural powers of the witnesses	Mary has the power of fire that issues forth from her mouth. Jesus gives all the apostles a spirit of power
Theme 3 - the dragon or serpent	Beliar, the devil and antichrist, is represented as a dragon.
Theme 6: The dragon/serpent cast out of heaven	There is an account in *Questions of Bartholomew 4:52* of how Satan refused to bow down to man and so was cast out of heaven.
Theme 7: The earth swallows up	There is an earthquake with the temple veil rent in two, and later Beliar is brought out of the earth.

Themes	Questions of Bartholomew
Theme 10: The resurrected witnesses	When the apostles confront Beliar they fall down dead but are then resurrected and resume the confrontation.

There are six of the Martyrdom Source themes present and the probability of this being random is of the order of 1/4,000,000 so we can be confident of the link.[325] The main apostles in the Questions are Mary and Peter, but it is Bartholomew who asks the questions. Bartholomew also appears as an "extra" apostle in the Acts of Philip where he accompanies Philip and Mariam. We have been led to the Questions of Bartholomew by the fact that it has the power of fire issuing from Mary's mouth and have then found other connections with the Martyrdom Source texts. But the Questions of Bartholomew will in turn lead us to another extraordinary connection.

The crucifixion in Mark and Matthew

When Mary says, "*the veil of the temple was rent and there was a very great earthquake*" her words tie in with another more familiar source, although they have apparently been applied to a completely different context. This other source is the account of the crucifixion in Mark and most especially in Matthew:

And, behold, the veil of the temple was torn in two from the top to the bottom. And the earth did quake, and the rocks were split. And the tombs were opened, and many bodies of the saints having fallen asleep arose. And came out of the tombs after his resurrection, they entered into the holy city and appeared to many. (Matthew 27:51-53)

Here closely associated with Mary's words we find another example of the resurrection of the witnesses. Matthew's "zombie apocalypse" is extremely odd. It is not found in Mark or any of the other gospels, and it destroys the buildup to the resurrection of Jesus. Why of all places, put a general resurrection at the moment of the death of Jesus when Jesus himself will not be resurrected for two days? The text implies that the tombs are opened, and the saints resurrected at the same instant as the earthquake that marks Jesus' death. And yet it then adds that the saints arise after "his resurrection". Clearly the author of Matthew is troubled as to how the saints can be resurrected before Jesus and adds this qualification even though it is inconsistent with the order of events. Typically the author of Matthew is very faithful to his sources and Mark in particular. He tends only to change the earlier gospel to address some deficiency. So, for example, he has a guard placed on the tomb to address the obvious objection to the account in Mark that the body could have been stolen by the disciples. However the "zombie apocalypse" addresses no such issue with Mark. Not only does it interfere with the narrative but it involves the complete absurdity of dead bodies climbing from their graves and wandering into Jerusalem. Even the most fundamentalist reader is challenged to believe in the dead saints, although it is a tribute to the faith of some that they manage the extraordinary feat of summoning sufficient gullibility for the task. To have placed this story in his narrative, the author of Matthew must have believed it to be true because it was in one of his sources. And he must have recognised that this source had also been used by the Mark crucifixion narrative otherwise he would have placed it later after the resurrection. In Revelation, the resurrection of the two witnesses is followed immediately by the earthquake and the destruction of a tenth of the city. And in the parallel passage in Acts when Paul rises after having been thought dead he enters into the city[326] just as the risen saints do in Matthew. If the author of Matthew had a source that associated the rising of the saints with the earthquake, then this would explain why the author of Matthew places the episode where he does.

So has the Martyrdom Source also been used by the author of Mark in his crucifixion account? One clue that he may have lies in the references to the temple. When Jesus is on the cross he is mocked by passersby: "*Ah, the destroyer of the temple, and in three days the builder*" (Mark 15:29). In Revelation the outer court of the temple is in the hands of the gentiles for three and a half years (it being common to interchange days and years). This trampling by gentiles is a reference to the death of Mary whose body had come under the power of the angels who ruled the physical world. So it is fitting that the temple veil should be torn in two at the moment of Jesus' death.

In the narrative of the two witnesses, the two prophets preach to the people who reject them and who rejoice over their death. We find a similar dynamic in the crucifixion in Mark. When Jesus first entered Jerusalem, the people rejoice and lay down branches at his feet. But the Jews turn against him, and when Pilate offers to free one of two prisoners, Jesus and Barabbas, the crowd demand that Jesus is the one who dies. In the Acts passage derived from the Martyrdom Source, the crowd are also initially enthusiastic, wanting to offer worship and sacrifice to Paul and Barnabas. But then the Jews turn against them and select one of the two, Paul, for death. The one who "survives" is called Barabbas in one story and Barnabas in the other. The names are not identical, but they are close! It is easy to see how a Greek speaking Christian could have substituted Barabbas (son of the father) for the rare name Barnabas.

There is a further trace of the two witnesses in another odd episode in Mark. When Jesus is close to death, he calls out on the cross:

And at the ninth hour Jesus cried with a loud voice, saying, "Eloi, Eloi, lema sabachthani?" which is translated "My God, my God, why have you forsaken me?" And some of them that stood by, when they heard it, said, "Behold, he calls Elijah." And one ran and filled a sponge full of vinegar wine, and put it on a reed, and gave him to drink, saying, "Let alone; let us see whether Elijah will come to take him down." And Jesus cried with a loud voice and breathed his last. And the veil of the temple was rent in two from the top to the bottom. (Mark 15:34-38)

Jesus' words are from Psalm 22 but his listeners seem to think that instead of calling on God, *Eloi*, he is calling on Elijah to come and save him. The author of Mark must have some source for this odd notion, or he would not bring in Elijah here. Earlier in the gospel Elijah was present along with Moses and Jesus on the mountain,[327] and some of the people think Jesus is Elijah.[328] But why should Elijah come to save Jesus from the cross? The answer perhaps lies in the Martyrdom Source. In Revelation, after being dead for three and a half days the spirit of life enters into the witnesses, and they are called to ascend to heaven. In the Apocalypse of Elijah, the two are identified as Elijah and Enoch. When they come back to life they are surrounded by the people: "*On that day they will shout up to heaven as they shine while all the people and all the world see them*" (*Apocalypse of Elijah 4:19*).[329] There are elements in this in common with the crucifixion, such as shouting up to heaven and being observed by the people. If the author of Mark has a "two witnesses" source, he may have misunderstood the reference to Elijah and tried to explain it as a mistaken notion of the onlookers.

If the crucifixion accounts have followed the Martyrdom Source then that source must have been available, either directly or indirectly, to both the authors of Mark and Matthew. The author of Mark must have been influenced by the Barnabas-Cephas source which makes the mistake of confusing Barnabas for Cephas, and which we have hypothesised arose from a mistaken reading of Galatians. There are some twenty years between the most likely dates of composition for Galatians and Mark, which is long enough for the Barnabas-Cephas source to emerge and be used by Mark. The author of Mark must also have been influenced by another version of the Martyrdom Source in which Elijah is a witness as in the Apocalypse of Elijah. As for the author of Matthew he must have had a version that he recognised as being related to the crucifixion account in Mark otherwise he would not have placed his zombie apocalypse where he did. And this brings us to the most likely scenario, that the authors of Mark and Matthew were not using the Martyrdom Source directly; they are using an early proto-crucifixion story which depends upon multiple versions of the Martyrdom Source.

The Martyrdom Source texts

It is worth summarising all the texts that depend on the Martyrdom Source:

Revelation A: the two witnesses
Revelation B: the woman in the sky
Acts: Paul and Barnabas worshipped
Apocalypse of Elijah A: the Assyrian-Persian wars
Apocalypse of Elijah B: Tabitha
Apocalypse of Elijah C: Enoch and Elijah
Apocalypse of Elijah D: the sixty righteous ones
The Acts of Philip
The Questions of Bartholomew

Probable:
The crucifixion account in Mark
The "zombie apocalypse" in Matthew

The number of distinct versions of the Martyrdom Source that have survived is unusually high. This tells us that it must have been very important to the Jesus movement. It was widely circulated and was sufficiently early to allow several variations to emerge. These features are explained if the Martyrdom Source was an account of the martyrdom of the founder, Mary/Cephas along with Paul in Rome. This also explains why it should have been used as a source for the proto-crucifixion story. It would seem that the martyrdom of Mary, the shaman and twin of Christ, was an inspiration for the story of Christ's crucifixion.

One feature of the Martyrdom Source texts is the variation in location. The story is set either in Jerusalem, or Lycaonia, or Hierapolis, or Egypt or Rome. The Apocalypse of Elijah sites the conflict between the two prophets and the anti-Christ in the *"marketplace of the Great City"* (*Apocalypse of Elijah 4:13*) which would normally mean Rome, but in this case would seem to be Jerusalem. Revelation places the conflict in the *"broad street of the great city, which is called spiritually Sodom and Egypt, where also their Lord was crucified"* (*Revelation 11:8*). This can only mean Babylon or Rome and discounting Babylon it is clearly Rome that is intended. The *"broad street"* or *"broad place"* refers either to the circus of Nero, which is where Peter was reputedly martyred, or the Via Cornelia which passed by it. The reason for all the confusion is the central role of the temple in the Martyrdom Source. Most of the early authors understood this as the temple in Jerusalem, which is why texts like Revelation and the Apocalypse of Elijah are apparently inconsistent in having the action set in a place which seems to be both Rome and Jerusalem at the same time. Others took the view that the temple could not be the Jewish temple since the story was set in a pagan city; and so we have Lystra or Hierapolis as locations. As for the proto-crucifixion source, it had to situate the death of Jesus in Jerusalem both because of the temple and because it was known that Jesus was resurrected in Jerusalem after three days. But what all these early authors failed to understand is that the temple was not a building but a person. Mary was the temple, and she was martyred in Rome.

The martyrdom of Mary

We cannot be sure exactly how Mary was executed, although some form of crucifixion seems the most likely. Although Tacitus talks about the many who were burnt he also mentions some being nailed to torture stakes. There is evidence that burning was not the fate of Mary. First there is no source that mentions burning in relation to Peter or Mary or the two witnesses. The Apocalypse of Elijah records death by burning as the fate of sixty righteous ones but not of either Tabitha or the two witnesses. Similarly, the Sibylline Oracles says that the divinely built temple has been seized, and the people in it burnt. It does not say that the temple has been burnt.

Most significantly, there is positive evidence in the form of an early source that vehemently denies that Mary was burnt. Stories of the Dormition (sleeping or passing away) or assumption of the Virgin Mary became immensely popular among Christians. Many versions of the story survive dating from around the fourth century, and there are texts in Coptic, Greek, Latin and Syriac. There is no doubt that these stories show influence from the gospels, but there are intriguing features that suggest that they preserve some original kernel of truth that has been embellished from later sources. The Dormition is always set in Jerusalem (or Jerusalem and then Bethlehem), which we have seen is a common error of the two sources texts arising originally from confusion with the temple. Mary is typically shown as living with John and some virgin attendants but in some texts Peter is also living with her. We know that Mary/Cephas was living with John in Rome at the time of her martyrdom, so this household could go back to a genuine memory. In the Greek and Latin versions, the apostles are spread out across the world but are all miraculously brought to Mary instantly, although John is still singled out for special treatment. The story is absurd but interesting because it hints at a Thomas saying:

The disciples said to Jesus: "We know you will go from us. Who shall be great over us?" Jesus said to them: "In the place to which you come, you shall go to James the Just for whom the heaven and earth came into being." (Thomas 12)

The words "*In the place to which you come, you shall go to James...*" is a praise formula that appoints James as successor to Mary. But it would seem that there was also a version applying this to Mary which has been misunderstood by one of the authors of the Dormition and taken quite literally.

In the Dormition accounts, Mary is told about her approaching death either by Jesus or an angel. In each case garments play a key role. Mary is given new garments that she puts on or lays down upon, and sometimes these are said to be her burial garments. We can see in this a memory of replacing the worn garments of the body by the spiritual garment that will survive death. Fearing death Mary prays: "*she asked to be delivered from the terrors of the next world, the dragon and the river of fire*" (The Twentieth Discourse of Cyril of Jerusalem).[330] We should note the recurrence of the dragon motif which represents the evil forces that would capture the unwary spirit. In one text Jesus gives the reason she must die and not simply be translated to heaven: "*wicked men will think concerning you that you are a power which came down from heaven and that the dispensation took place in appearance*" (The discourse of Theodosius, Archbishop of Alexandria).[331] This is a clear reference to the belief in the spiritual rather than physical Christ, although here it is applied to Mary.

One feature that all the accounts have in common is the insistence that the body was not burned. Typically while Mary's body is being carried to the tomb, "the Jews" make an unsuccessful attempt to burn her. To give an example:

We carried the body out to the field of Jehoshaphat. The Jews saw it and took counsel to come and burn it. The apostles set down the bier and fled. Darkness came on the Jews and they were blinded and smitten by their own fire. They cried out for mercy and were healed and many were converted. (The discourse of Theodosius, Archbishop of Alexandria) [332]

Jews did not practise cremation and the idea that they wanted to burn Mary's body is odd. We can, however, understand it in relation to the Martyrdom Source; in some versions the hostile crowd (originally the Romans) have become "the Jews". If the same has happened in the Dormition accounts, then the "the Jews" are standing in for the Romans. So the idea that "the Jews" tried unsuccessfully to burn Mary's body can be traced back to the events in Rome where many of the Christians were burned but Mary was not. In several versions of the Dormition the body is attacked by a Jew who then has his hands struck off:

"And behold, as they carried her a certain Hebrew named Jephonias, mighty of body, ran forth and attacked the bed as the apostles carried it and lo an angel of the Lord with invisible power struck his two hands from off his shoulders with a sword of fire and left them hanging in the air beside the bed." (The discourse of St John the Divine) [333]

Then by a miracle his hands are reconnected by either Peter or Mary. We can see in this a reference to Thomas 22 *"when you make [...] a hand in place of a hand"* that has been misunderstood and made into a literalistic story. What is significant is that this is exactly the same Thomas saying that has given rise to the upside-down crucifixions of Philip and of Peter in Rome. It is one of several hints that the Dormition accounts are also closely related to the Martyrdom Source.

The new Jerusalem

For the Jesus movement the death of Mary was not the end. Although Mary appeared to have been defeated by Nero, the defeat was an illusion. Within a few years Nero would be dead and the movement that Mary founded would last far longer than the Roman Empire. The Book of Revelation does not end in defeat, but in triumph. Revelation, of course, never gives a straightforward account. The author of Revelation is more interested in the symbol than a rational account of events, and it is this obsession with the symbol that has fascinated his readers for thousands of years. So Revelation ends with the marriage of the Lamb. The beast is defeated, Babylon is no more, and Satan is bound for a thousand years:

"Let us be glad and rejoice, and give honour to him: for the marriage of the Lamb is come, and his bride has made herself ready. And to her was granted that she should be arrayed in fine linen, clean and white." For the fine linen is the righteousness of saints. And he said to me, "Write, Blessed are they which are called to the marriage supper of the Lamb." (Revelation 19:7-9)

The divine marriage is originally between Mary and Jesus, but becomes a marriage between the church and Jesus. The kingdom of the Lamb will be established with a new heaven and a new earth. The bride is the new Jerusalem:

And I John saw the holy city, new Jerusalem, coming down from God out of heaven, prepared as a bride adorned for her husband. And I heard a great voice out of heaven saying, "Behold, the tabernacle of God is with men, and he will dwell with them, and they shall be his people, and God himself shall be with them as their God. And God shall wipe away all tears from their eyes; and there shall be no more death, neither sorrow, nor crying, neither shall there be any more pain: for the former things are passed away." (Revelation 21:2-4)

There is no explicit mention of a temple in this new Jerusalem, but it is represented by the tabernacle, the predecessor of the temple, and by the holy city of Jerusalem itself. The tabernacle of God is Mary who is now with men and through her alchemy the presence of God will dwell with men. The new Jerusalem is Salome, also Mary, the bride of the lamb. The descent of the new Jerusalem is described a second time with repetition that is typical of Revelation:

And he carried me away in the spirit to a great and high mountain, and showed me that great city, the holy Jerusalem, descending out of heaven from God ... (Revelation 21:10)

We see here the idea of the vision coming on a "great and high mountain". Elsewhere the lamb stands on Mount Zion surrounded by the one hundred and forty-four thousand faithful. The images are of the holy mountain, the "rock" that is Cephas. Both the mountain and the new Jerusalem are Mary.

Key points

1. Tacitus records Nero's persecution of Christians following the fire of Rome. They were executed in the gardens of Nero, including many who were burnt.

2. The Sibylline Oracles says that Nero was responsible for the destruction of the Jerusalem temple and places this destruction out of sequence. We can see this as due to a Christian interpolation with the "temple" being Mary.

3. Mary has the power to summon fire from heaven in the Questions of Bartholomew. In the same work, she is called the tabernacle of God and almost brings the world to an end.

4. Nero blamed the fire of Rome on the Christians because some of them were claiming that Mary had brought about the destruction of the city by calling down the fire from heaven.

5. It is unlikely that the Romans ever identified Mary as the leader. She was simply caught up in the general destruction. This gives rise to the possibility that her body was recovered by the Christians after her execution.

6. Six out of ten Martyrdom Source themes are present in the Questions of Bartholomew. The probability of this being a random coincidence are 4 million to one against, so it must be another Martyrdom Source text.

7. The Martyrdom Source may also have influenced the Gospels. In particular, the "zombie apocalypse" in Matthew shows links to the Martyrdom Source.

8. The crucifixion in Mark also shows affinities to the Martyrdom Source. This suggests that the story of the crucifixion has been influenced by the martyrdom of Mary, which would explain why Revelation places the crucifixion in Rome.

9. Most likely the authors of Mark and Matthew both have access to an intermediary source that is itself dependent upon the Martyrdom Source. It is difficult to see why the author of Matthew would have included the "zombie apocalypse" unless it was present in a source which he identified as being behind the account of the crucifixion in Mark.

10. The Dormition accounts are adamant that the body of Mary was not burnt. The most likely method of death was some form of crucifixion.

Chapter 43

Mary, Peter and the tomb

The New Testament ends with the marriage of the Lamb and the coming of the new Jerusalem. This is also the real end of Mary's story just as it began that story. But there is a postscript. Mary's poor, elderly body was cruelly put to death by Nero. But the evidence points to her not being burned like many of the other Christians. The stories of her burial hint that the movement were able to retrieve her remains. In fact, it is a strong possibility that her grave has been found and that her bones now lay, unacknowledged, in the Vatican.

The discovery of the tomb

In one of the Coptic Dormition accounts, Jesus gives Mary a promise:

"I will hide your body in the earth. No man will find it until the day when I raise it incorruptible. A great church shall be built over it." (The Twentieth Discourse of Cyril of Jerusalem)[334]

Did this record a recent memory? Was a great church built over Mary's body? The greatest church in Christendom is St Peter's, which stands on the Vatican hill in Rome. Constantine built the original church in 323-333, around the time of the Dormition accounts. The first written mention of a possible link between the Vatican and Mary/Peter comes from the early churchman Gaius at around 200:

But I can show the trophies (tropaia) of the apostles. For if you will go to the Vatican or to the Ostian way, you will find the trophies of those who laid the foundations of this church. (Eusebius, Ecclesiastical History 2:25:7)

The word *tropaia* means a monument erected to mark the place of a victory. The early Christians considered martyrdom to be such a victory, and the *tropaia* were probably monuments that marked the graves of the apostles. The alternative is that the trophies mark the place of martyrdom, but this is unlikely. It is doubtful that the precise location of the martyrdom would have been known or considered important. Besides, Christians were in no position to erect monuments on public land in the second century. No, it was the remains of the apostles that connected the believer with those who had founded and suffered for the church.

The Vatican was the location of Nero's gardens at the foot of the Vatican hill. Indeed, St Peter's is centred on a point adjacent to the circus of Nero mentioned in Tacitus' account of the martyrdoms. It is just on the other side of the road passing by the circus, the Via Cornelia. All of which makes perfect sense. The terrified Christians probably had to bribe a soldier to release the body of the insignificant old lady and would want to bury her quickly, and at night, somewhere nearby. It is clear that a strong tradition linking the site to Peter persisted to Constantine's day. If Mary's body had been retrieved, then her grave would be a place of pilgrimage, treated with a reverence that would be passed down from generation to generation. The Christians would have kept track of the grave even through the difficult reign of Nero and the later persecutions of Domitian. And when Christians began to enjoy a degree of tolerance in the second century they could then have marked the grave with a more impressive monument. It is this monument that Gaius would be familiar with, and which located the grave for Constantine to build his church upon.

All of which would be nothing more than conjecture were it not for a series of remarkable discoveries that revealed the Roman necropolis that underlay St Peter's.[335] The site of the tomb had long since disappeared beneath later structures even before the original basilica of Constantine was rebuilt in the grand Renaissance style in the sixteenth and seventeenth centuries. Above ground, the basilica was completely remodelled but below ground, the old church was almost undisturbed. The new church had a higher floor, so the work did not interfere with what lay below the original floor except where new pillars were sunk to support the vast structure. The fantastic Baldacchino designed by Bernini now marked the tomb's position. This elaborate bronze monument stands 30 metres tall and is in the form of a pavilion with four fantastically curved pillars. Under its canopy the Eucharist is administered upon an altar set exactly over the centre of the tomb.

What lay below the floor of the original basilica remained hidden as it had since the time of Constantine but hints kept emerging. In 1574 men working on floor alterations accidentally broke through into a small tomb. They peered down through the roof at a body preserved on a marble slab covered in lime. On the walls were beautiful mosaics including a pair of prancing horses. The men withdrew and resealed the tomb to leave the body to its long sleep. On a later occasion, the elaborately carved lid of a large marble sarcophagus belonging to one Flavius Agricola was dug up. It bore a scandalous epigram of Epicurean philosophy: "*Mix the wine, drink deep, and do not refuse to pretty girls the sweets of love, for when death comes earth and fire devour everything.*" The shocked clerics had the pagan artefact broken up and thrown into the Tiber.

So it was well known that there was a pagan necropolis beneath St Peters. But the uncovering of the secrets of this necropolis started only accidentally with the internment of Pope Pius XI in the Grottoes in 1939. These Grottoes lay underneath the great central aisle and were a historic burial place of popes and monarchs. At the time of the internment it was decided to convert part of the Grottoes into an underground chapel, the problem being that the ceiling was low, and at its highest only 8 feet. The way to gain more headroom was to sink the floor and so excavations for a new lower floor began. Immediately a number of sarcophagi were uncovered; ancient burials lowered through the floor of the original church. The sarcophagi were removed, and the digging continued. The first significant find was the unearthing of an ancient brick wall, covered on one side with elaborately decorated plaster. This wall proved to be part of a small building measuring about six by seven metres. The building had no roof and only the top of the wall was visible, the building being filled with earth. Removing the earth revealed a pagan tomb. There were niches in the wall for cremation urns (which must be pagan because Christians were buried) and a painting of Venus rising from the sea. The tomb belonged to a rich family; the decorations were fine and elaborate, and the doorway was outlined by slabs of travertine. In this tomb was found the first trace of Christian activity. Set into the floor was a later burial, that of a woman of twenty-eight years, Aemelia Gorgonia. Her epitaph records she was beautiful and innocent and ends with the undeniably Christian "*dormit in pace*". Alongside the epitaph is a touching drawing showing a woman holding a bottle over a square column, perhaps a well. Above this sketch are the words "*anima dulcis Gorgonia*" meaning "sweet souled Gorgonia". Like the

Samaritan woman, Gorgonia is about to drink the living water from the well.

The inscriptions in the tomb showed that the original owners were the Caetennius family, descended from a freed slave. The tomb dated to around the year 150, which was very early, although not back to the time of Peter. However, cemeteries were used and developed over a long period and later more elaborate tombs would often be placed next to, or over, earlier plain graves. The Caetennius tomb showed that there was something of great archaeological interest under the floor of St Peters. It was not alone because already the wall of a second tomb had been uncovered. A formal excavation would be undertaken by four Vatican archaeologists under the nominal authority of the administrator of the Basilica, Ludwig Kaas.

As the excavations progressed, a narrow street of tombs was uncovered. This road of the dead ran straight towards the central point of St Peters with tombs on either side. Along from the Caetennius tomb, and separated from it by a smaller tomb, was the tomb of the Valerius family. This tomb had been decorated with amazing white stucco; portraits of the men and women whose remains lay in the tomb and dancing Bacchanalian figures. In the floor were two more Christian burials, including that of a man who "had a joke for everyone". Most significantly a link with Peter was found in the form of a crude drawing on a wall of this tomb. This shows two heads; the Christ, indicated by a Phoenix and the word for "living" and lower down a bald man possibly Peter. Around and besides the lower figure is an inscription - "Peter pray Christ Jesus for the holy ..". The remainder of the line is obscure although it was reconstructed rather hopefully by Margherita Guarducci as "Christian men buried near your body". Regardless of the reading it was the first clear evidence linking the area to Peter. As to the date, putting such a graffiti in a tomb was a desecration that was a serious crime in Roman times. So it was probably made by one of Constantine's workmen as the cemetery was being destroyed and filled in on imperial orders. As such it gives us little new information, as we know that Constantine believed he was building the church over the grave of St Peter.

Only one tomb could be shown to be Christian but it was remarkable. Originally missed because it was below the level of the street, it is located beneath the alleyway running between two other tombs and accessed by a hole in the ceiling. The decoration of this tomb is an amazing gold mosaic rich in Christian symbolism; Jonah being swallowed by a whale, a fisherman standing on a rock who had caught one fish while another swam away; the Good Shepherd carrying a sheep. But most significant of all is a depiction of Christ portrayed as the pagan sun god Helios in a chariot pulled by two horses. The tomb is believed to belong to a family who converted to Christianity and dated from around 250. There is no doubt that this was the tomb unearthed by the workmen in the seventeenth century although the body was gone.

The excavation of the necropolis had revealed that the engineers of Constantine had pulled off an amazing feat in the construction of St Peter's. Their problem was that the cemetery was on a quite steep hillside and to build the church they had to make a level base. They did this by cutting into one side of the slope and moving the earth to fill in the other side; one half of the cemetery had to be obliterated while the other half was buried to make the foundations of the new church. In dealing with the tombs, the builders sheared off the roofs and then filled the shell with earth that preserved what lay beneath. All of this to centre the church on a single tomb that would be at floor level in the new building. As you walk towards the central point, the height of the remaining tomb walls diminishes because you are walking up the original hill towards the level of this central tomb. The desecration of the cemetery must have been shocking to the people of Rome, the majority of whom were not Christians. The cemetery was still in use and graves either had to be moved or rendered inaccessible. Even for an Emperor as powerful as Constantine there must have been a powerful imperative to desecrate the cemetery when a perfectly good level site lay nearby.

Following the necropolis to the centre of the church, only the area under the Baldacchino remained to be investigated. This area, where the tomb of Peter was supposed to be found, had originally been forbidden to the excavators. But because of the discoveries it was decided to continue to Peter's tomb. And so the investigation entered its final phase breaching the walls around the tomb. The point about which the church was centred was revealed to be a section of wall covered in red plaster that became known as the "red wall". This wall formed one side of a small courtyard area the original dimensions of which were 7 metres by 4 metres, although Constantine's engineers had shortened the space. Two tombs formed two of the other sides and both had staircases that let into the courtyard. The suspicion must be that these neighbouring tombs belonged to Christian families. The street of the necropolis led past the fourth side that had once been partially closed by a wall that was demolished by the church builders. Behind the red wall was an alley bounded on the other side by the tomb of the girl chasing Flavius Agricola, his sarcophagus now missing its lid, and his pious wife who had pre-deceased him. Next to this tomb was a little antiroom with a cistern. This room may either have been part of the Agricola tomb or may have been used by the Christians. If you walked further along the alley and up some stairs you would come to a small enclosed grave-yard. This was almost certainly the resting place of the early bishops of Rome which was reputed to be next to the grave of Peter.

At the precise central point of the basilica was a simple monument standing ten feet tall and built into the red wall. The monument is comprised of two niches in the wall, one above the other, with a slab of travertine jutting between them like a table top supported by two elegant marble legs. The top of the monument had been destroyed; reconstructions show it as a pediment, although we cannot be sure that this was the design. The investigators called this monument the "aedicula" or little temple. Close beside the aedicula was a thick wall that stood at right angles to the red wall. It was built to shore up the red wall when it began to develop an alarmingly large crack. The building of this supporting wall had destroyed the symmetry of the monument; the right side of the table and the supporting leg had to be moved closer to the centre to make room for the new wall. The supporting wall was plastered and covered on the side away from the aedicula in an amazing web of graffiti, evidence for Christian veneration at the site. Set in the ground below the table-roof was a grave marked by a marble slab. The slab was not quite perpendicular to the wall but was curiously out of alignment, at an angle of about ten degrees. In Constantine's church, the whole of the aedicula including the graffiti wall and the remains of the red wall stood at floor level encased in marble.

It was with huge anticipation, but also with some trepidation, that the grave was penetrated. Even if this were Peter's grave the bones may have long since disappeared. There was an alternative tradition linking Peter and Paul with the Appian Way where at one time two arches had stood in memory of the apostles. Some maintained that Peter's bones had been removed from the original grave for safety and taken to the Appian Way in 258. Constantine built a church on this spot dedicated to Peter and Paul although it was later rededicated to St Sebastian. But there was a worse threat than the counter-tradition for the Appian Way, for St Peter's had briefly been occupied by forces hostile to Christianity. This had happened in 846 when Rome had fallen to an army of Saracens. They rampaged through the holy sites and pillaged St Peter's where according to one source they practised "unspeakable iniquities". The Saracens were soon evicted but no one knew for sure if they had penetrated the tomb itself and destroyed the bones.

The excavators breached the grave through the foundations of the graffiti wall. The first person to look into the grave was one of the archaeologists, Father Engelbert Kirschbaum. He shone his light around in the small enclosed space and saw that the grave was empty. Looking upwards he could see the reverse of the marble slab that formed the ceiling of the grave and could make out an inscription to one Aelius Isidorus. This slab had once marked another grave and had been reused to cover Peter's grave. It seemed that the original burial had been a very poor one with just a few tiles to cover it. The reused slab had a hole cut in it. We know from a sixth century account that the faithful would talk into the grave through this hole to petition Peter and would lower cloths through it to make relics. Along one side, the edge of the grave was defined by two low walls separated by some earth. Here the grave abutted onto yet another niche in the foundations of the red wall, this one roughly hewed and lying directly below the two above ground. Looking closely, Kirschbaum noticed a small gap below this niche. He reached his hand in and encountered a piece of bone. He realised that what he had thought a gap was actually a feature of the wall that came up in an inverted v leaving a space below it. And buried in this space were a number of bones.

Pope Pius XII was informed and came to witness the removal of the bones as one by one they were brought out and placed in a casket. It was clear that the skeleton was very partial with the major bones missing. There was no skull but then there was an existing tradition that the skull was in the church of St John Lateran. An initial examination by the Pope's physician came to the optimistic conclusion that the bones were those of a robust but elderly male. It seemed that the bones of St Peter had been found. There was, however, some disquiet about the location of the bones. Why were they not in the main grave? Perhaps they had been hidden under the wall at the back at the time of the Saracens and then simply left there.

The aedicula is surely the "trophy" of Gaius and was intended as a shrine to the founder. The red wall has been dated from some tiles found in a drainage trench to between 147 and 161. This must also be the date of the aedicula because the niches were built into the wall from the start and not hollowed out at a later date. The dating of the aedicula is significant because it shows that it was a site of veneration within a century of the martyrdom. The other tombs in the necropolis are also from around the middle of the second century; at this time the previously poor cemetery was colonised by the wealthy middle class. The families who built the tombs were largely descended from freed slaves, so they had little social status but had become well off through their trades.

The little courtyard, with its red wall, must have been established to protect the existing grave from the new development. The courtyard was always open to the sky and never roofed over until the building of Constantine's church. Originally it was unpaved, and the investigators found a large number of graves beneath its surface. Clearly Christians had been using this as a place of burial, wanting to get as close as possible to the grave beneath the aedicula without intruding upon it. The red wall and courtyard followed the alignment of the new tombs, but the grave was at an angle of about 10 degrees to the perpendicular in relation to the wall. This suggested that the orientation of the graveyard had changed over time. It was significant that a few other graves shared this earlier alignment. One of these, called gamma, was a child's grave that included a lead pipe leading down to it and a little temple built over it. The pipe was used in a pagan custom where a little wine would be poured down into the grave to honour the dead. This grave lay right next to the grave under the aedicula, and the little temple had been destroyed when the aedicula was built. Another grave called theta was a poor burial with the grave just covered in tiles. Crucially one of the tiles could be dated from its maker's stamp to the reign of Vespasian in 69-79. This is within fifteen years of the likely date of death of Mary/Cephas showing that the cemetery was in use at around that time.

Everything is consistent with this being the genuine grave. The two witnesses passage in Revelation says that *"their dead bodies shall lie in the broad street of the great city" (Revelation 11:8)*. It adds that the bodies will be displayed unburied to be gloated over by all the peoples of the world. The grave at the centre of St Peters would have been in an open cemetery a little way up from the side of a road on the opposite side of which was the Circus of Nero. It would have been in plain view from the Circus where Nero would show off his supposed skills with the chariot to the dutifully applauding people. This was the main circus in Rome at the time, and it would have attracted all those who visited the city. When there was an event the peoples of the Empire would have thronged the road below the grave. Their shouting and drunken laughter would have seemed to those in the Jesus movement a mockery of Mary in her miserable pauper's grave in full view from the road. The author of Revelation would have misunderstood something like this to mean that the body of the witnesses were unburied.

The monument

The aedicula is distinctly odd, even unique. For a start, it is very much a vertical monument with the two niches, one above the other and separated by the tabletop, with a third niche underground. The closest examples are in pagan tombs, but these were far smaller with a covered lower section with doors and a niche above used to hold a cremation urn. Although the builders of the aedicula may have been influenced by such pagan designs their monument could not have served the same purpose. The Christians did not cremate bodies, and they are not going to allow the tomb of the founder to be used to hold someone else's remains. Also, the tabletop like slab built into the aedicula is not found in the pagan examples. This tabletop looks very much like an altar except that it is six feet from the ground.

Then there is the fact that the foundations of the wall rise in the inverted V. One theory is that this is to avoid the wall intruding onto the grave. However, the grave was originally longer and extended over the other side of the wall. At some point, it has been shortened, and this most likely happened when the wall was being built otherwise they would have left some of the remains under the alley behind. At this time they would have gathered the bones together and would have rearranged them; such secondary burials, once the body had been reduced to bones, were normal. But if they were shortening the grave then why not extend the wall down to its full depth and place all the bones in the more than ample space in the main grave below the monument? The inverted V weakened the wall, and there must have been some purpose for it.

In fact, the inverted V explains why the aedicula could be built at all. At this time, Christianity was an illegal religion. Bouts of active persecution would periodically flare up and even in the times of relative tolerance being a Christian could still earn you a death sentence. And yet here are the Christians erecting a monument over the grave of the condemned criminal who they said was the founder of their religion in Rome. Would not the Roman authorities sooner or later open the grave and confiscate the bones either to destroy them or to bury them in secret? Why draw attention to a grave that had previously been anonymous? The answer must be that the grave was already drawing attention to itself as the most sacred place of pilgrimage for the ever-growing population of Christians in Rome. The bones while they rested in the earth were vulnerable. So a new monument was designed to formalise the pilgrimage and bring it under the control of the proto-orthodox church while also safeguarding the precious remains.

The inverted V was created as a secret hiding place for the bones. Within this protected space under the wall the bones would still be in the original grave yet when covered over by earth they would be invisible. Anyone who inspected the grave would never know that the inverted V was there. They would assume that the foundation walls extended down the whole way. It would have been the work of a few moments for Roman soldiers to lift the marble grave cap but all they would find is an empty grave.

The aedicula was in one sense deceptive because the grave beneath its table was always empty. But in another sense it proclaimed to the faithful the resting place of the bones. The most significant feature of the monument is the two niches, one above the other. They are located precisely where the grave intersects the red wall. A line running down the centre of the niches marks the axis of symmetry of the original aedicula. It is also marks the central point of the original grave. If you extend this line down into the ground, you come to the top of the inverted V and the place where the bones were kept. The niches are telling us that the bones are directly beneath them.

At some point, the wall was hacked out to make the niche below ground. If the bones rested in this newly opened niche, they would be in the same location as before but would now be visible to anyone who opened the grave. Presumably this was done at a time when the church felt more secure. Making the bones visible in this way would have helped counter the rumours that the grave was empty. The hiding place of the bones would have been a closely guarded secret and not known to most Christians. The grave was probably opened now and then, either by the church or by the Romans, and the fact that it appeared to be empty would have caused disquiet among the faithful. We find a hint of this in several versions of the Dormition accounts. After Mary is buried, her grave is found to be empty as her body has been translated to heaven.

What is the purpose of the large travertine shelf that divided the two niches? It looks like an altar, and probably that is what it was. The upper niche would have been the main focal point of the monument. It was made wider than the lower niche with a square frame and a curious window-like aperture in the wall in the middle of the niche. The space before this niche is where something important must have taken place. The standard objection to the altar theory is that it was almost six feet from the ground. In fact, it could still have been used at this height with the aid of a movable platform consisting of a couple of steps. No one would have chosen to set an altar that high but the builders of the monument faced certain constraints. The first constraint was that the table had to protrude out from the wall further than the grave otherwise anyone conducting a ceremony on it would be standing over the grave. Hence the width of about 1 metre. The second constraint was that it had to preserve access to the grave. The Christians of Rome would have been in the habit of visiting the grave, of kissing it, of leaving little devotions or placing charms upon it to be imbued with its holiness. If the altar had been at a convenient height as a table, then anyone accessing the grave would have to grope around banging their head beneath it. This would have been unacceptable. The altar had to be much higher than a normal table to give headroom to the grave below. The gap between the grave and the top shelf was 1.4 metres which is about the minimum for dignified access.

If it was an altar then what ceremony was it used for? We can be sure that it was not the Eucharist as this could be administered on any table; no one would have chosen an altar this high. No, it had to be something linked to the grave, something that could only be performed upon the grave. We have seen that the niches had significance in marking the place of the bones. But they were also spiritual conduits linking what was happening on the top shelf to the bones below.

We can find a clue as to the nature of the ceremony in the Martyrdom Source. In the Apocalypse of Elijah A, after the defeat of the evil forces there is the command "*to build the temples of the saints*" (*Apocalypse Elijah 2:48*). More significantly, in Apocalypse of Elijah B, when Dorcas is killed and her body thrown onto the temple she heals the people: "*my blood which you have cast upon the temple has become a healing for the people*" (*Apocalypse Elijah 4:4-5*).[336] In the Acts of Philip, when the apostle is upside down upon the cross he gives the instruction "*build a church in the place where I die*" (*Acts of Philip 142*). He adds "*Where my blood is dropping a vine will grow, and you shall use the wine of it for the cup: and partake of it on the third day*" (*Acts of Philip 143*).[337]

We can deduce from these sources that the early Christians were drinking the blood of Mary / Cephas. They were doing this by drinking wine that had been spiritually transformed into her blood in a ceremony that is very close to the Eucharist but centred on the remains of the founder. By absorbing the substance of the blessed martyr, they were "healed" that is given life. If this seems strange to us, we must remember that in the neighbouring grave pagan parents were pouring wine in a tube to feed their dead child. The drinking of the wine as Mary's "blood" merely reverses the process.

Without any written sources, any reconstruction of the details of the ceremony must be speculative. It is notable that the upper niche was very wide, wider than the niche below. A large shallow bowl of about one metre in diameter could have nestled snuggly in this niche and extended to the opposite side of the shelf. Wine could have been poured into it, perhaps after having been first consecrated by resting in the lower niche immediately above the bones. Alternatively the curious window-like aperture in the upper niche could have been designed to hold an "arm" extending out over the bowl. This arm would hold a container at the end from which wine dripped into the bowl. In this way, there would be a line of direct contact from the bones, up through the niches, and along the arm, and to the wine, which would mystically become the blood of the martyr. A person mounting a low step could drink the wine from the bowl either directly or using a spoon or other implement.

Any such ceremony must have originated long before the aedicula was built. The odd design of the little temple meets the need of building a permanent structure to give effect to a long-established ritual. The table top and the long slender legs of the aedicula suggest that what came before it was an altar-table that straddled the grave. Wine that had been brought into contact with the grave could be poured into a bowl upon the table to be drunk from there. The height of such a table would have been more convenient because it was a temporary structure that was removed afterwards to give access to the grave.

This drinking of the blood would have caused the developing proto-orthodox church some disquiet, and it is understandable why they would want to replace it by an orthodox Eucharist in which the wine was Jesus' blood. After the building of the church of Constantine the ceremony on the monument ceased. The shelf was occupied by a large cross made of solid gold and bearing the names of the Emperor and his mother, Helena. The faithful would have to make do with the Eucharist administered in side chapels although a degree of contact was still allowed with the tomb. This arrangement must have been unpopular because around 600 a new altar was built, raising the floor and covering the upper portion of the monument. The Eucharist was now administered on an altar table which incorporated the top of the aedicula, the very place where the original drinking of the wine/blood may have taken place.

The aedicula may be modest and open to the air but in one sense it is the first Christian church. One of the mysteries of early Christian history is how the church as a sacred space developed. Mary's philosophy was that the physical temple had been destroyed to be replaced by human temples. From now on God would dwell within the chosen and there were to be no more sacred spaces. Christians assembled in house churches where they performed the Eucharist and other rites. The building itself was irrelevant and was simply someone's house. And yet over time the Christians moved to purpose-built churches, places that were consecrated and sacred to God. They lavished enormous wealth in building and decorating these places of worship. This development took place gradually over several centuries and was a complete betrayal of Mary's teachings. Ironically, we can see it as starting with Mary's own grave. When the temple, the Magdalene, was dead her followers substituted a physical temple in her place. The grave and the aedicula that was built a century later were sacred because they were the resting place of her bones. The rituals that took place at the aedicula could not be replicated anywhere else because they depended on the holiness of the site and the remains. Christians had made the momentous retrograde step of beginning to worship at a new physical temple. The concept of place specific holiness spilled over to other sites. Other martyrs were venerated, their bones cherished, shrines built over their graves. The church that Constantine built over the aedicula became a model for the concept of a church; a sacred space in which the Christian rites could be performed and ideally boasting the grave or relic of a saint. All this was of course pagan, the continuation of temple and ancestor grave worship. Mary's decision to move the head of her church to Rome was brilliant and led to the development of that church into a world religion. And yet it also had drawbacks. The newly developing Catholic church based as it was on literalism and infected by paganism was a long way from the original spiritual Christianity.

Both Peter and Mary

We have suggested that the grave at the heart of St Peter's was originally that of Mary who was also called Cephas, or in Greek, Peter. But the church is named after Peter and not after Mary. If the early traditions linked the grave to the founder using both the names "Mary" and "Peter" we can expect the proto-orthodox church to prefer the later. They had absorbed Mary into orthodoxy under her identity as the mother of Jesus, although under her name "the Magdalene" she had been appropriated dangerously by gnostic groups. However, it was to Peter that they looked to their authority, and the growing patriarchal nature of the church made them want to avoid casting any female in a leadership role. Moreover, in the literalistic story that had developed, both Mary the Mother of God and the Magdalene were supposed to have remained in the Jerusalem area, so how could either be buried in Rome? But even if the church preferred Peter, the link to Mary must have remained for a long time in the minds of the people. So what evidence is there for a link to either Mary or Peter in the aedicula?

The first piece of negative evidence is the curious fact that there is not a dedication anywhere on the monument. We would expect the aedicula to have some sort of inscription recording the name of the person over whose grave it was erected. The normal explanation is security at a time when the religion was persecuted. However, the Christians were confident enough to build the conspicuous monument, and the site must have been a place of pilgrimage visited by thousands of people over the years. We know that a fair proportion of Christians gave up their faith under persecution, so the authorities could easily have found out who was buried in the Vatican grave. Besides if the Christians did not want to identify the gravesite in an obvious way they were adept at the use of symbols that outsiders would not recognise. Perhaps the real reason for a lack of official dedication is two separate traditions of who was buried at the site, both Mary and Peter.

For positive evidence, we must turn to the graffiti wall. This is believed to have been built about a century after the aedicula at around 250 to shore up the red wall that had developed a crack. The current remains of the wall are quite small; 0.87 metres in length, 0.45 metres thick and 0.47 metres high, although before the workers of Constantine cut it down it was higher.[338] When the excavators first examined the graffiti wall, they were disappointed that there was no mention of Peter. The wall itself was a bewildering maze of lines, graffiti carved into the plaster surface with a sharp point. They could, though, make out the chi-rho symbol for Christ, which shows that it was certainly a site for Christian devotion. The first explicit reference to Peter was discovered on some graffiti written on the red wall itself where the graffiti wall meets it. Within the graffiti wall there was a cavity, a marble-lined repository for bones 0.77 metres long and 0.3 metres square that had been made in the wall sometime after its construction. This niche butted on to the original plaster of the red wall and was empty apart from a few fragments of bones, metal, cloth and coins. A few years after the original excavation some of the plaster from the red wall fell into this cavity. It was found to be marked with a crudely written graffiti. The initial letters of the name Peter in Greek were clearly visible along with a second word below that might be "eni". The whole has been recreated as "Petros eni" which may stand for "Peter within".[339] Although this reading is uncertain, it is clear that there is a reference to Peter. The inscription must date between the construction of the red and the graffiti walls, that is around 160 to 250.

It is odd that Christians would write this graffiti so close to the grave itself on a wall that was part of the tomb and that here alone they should openly use the name Peter. The best explanation is that it was written by the builders who constructed the graffiti wall in the knowledge that their words would soon be covered up.

If there was an unwillingness to write on the red wall itself, there was no such unwillingness to write on the graffiti wall. The side facing away from the grave is covered with graffiti. This must have been produced sometime between the building of the wall around 250 and the church in 323-333 at which time the remains of the wall were encased in marble. But what was the meaning of the apparently indecipherable maze of lines? The solution to this puzzle came through the work of Margherita Guarducci, who was also to be central to the greatest controversy of the excavation. Dr Guarducci was a highly experienced professor of Greek epigraphy at the University of Rome. She was not a member of the original team and only became involved ten years after the first excavations. Her initial interest was an attempt to decipher the graffiti in the Valerius tomb, but she soon became interested in the challenge of the graffiti wall. She was eventually to spend five years studying this wall.

Tracing the outlines on the wall she began to decipher letters and words.[340] Mostly these were the names of individuals, some fifty in all, who would have lived in the third and fourth centuries. These were, in fact, the names of dead people, written on the wall by those who loved them so that they could share in the life of the person who lay in the grave. Many of the names were joined to symbols, most noticeably the Chi-Rho symbol representing Christ. One discovery came when Guarducci realised that five letters in two lines, HO and VIN represented IN HOC VINCE meaning "In this conquer". These were the words that Constantine heard in his supposed vision before the battle of Milvian Bridge in 312 in which he defeated Maxentius his rival for Emperor. For this battle, Constantine had the Chi-Rho symbol engraved on his soldiers' shields and he attributed his victory to Christ. The appearance of IN HOC VINCE on the wall meant that some at least of the graffiti could be dated to after this victory and only a few years before construction on the basilica commenced. The Chi-Rho symbol itself became very popular following the battle of Milvian Bridge, although it was in use before this date.

The real breakthrough was in realising that the writers of the graffiti used a system of cryptograms. The Chi-Rho symbol was an example of such a cryptogram combining the first two letters of Christ in Greek, the chi

(X) and rho (P). Another well-known example was the A and O represent-ing the alpha and omega, the beginning and end. The two letters had been found together frequently in Christian inscriptions, and Guarducci found them on the wall. However, she noticed something strange, that the letters were often reversed with a line leading from an O to an A. Also the two letters were sometimes written the wrong way round as O followed by A. After some research she found that this reverse representation had been found before on funeral inscriptions, and interpreted as the engraver's mis-take. But it was now clear that it was quite deliberate; instead of "beginning to end" it had "end to beginning". With her conventional Catholic faith Guarducci interpreted this as meaning that the end of life on earth (O) was the beginning of eternal life (A). But we can see it as expressing a different belief that goes right back to the origins of the religion. We shall see that the Jesus movement used an "apocalyptic calendar" that measured the whole age of the earth in seventy periods. The alpha was the beginning of time, the commencement of the first period, and the omega was the de-struction of the earth at the end of the last period. One of the secrets of the Jesus movement was that the calendar was chiastic, that is symmetrical about the midpoint, which meant that the alpha was the same as the ome-ga. The Jesus movement believed that the spiritual way of understanding the calendar was to read it backwards, from the end, the omega, back to the beginning, the alpha. We find these same beliefs in a Thomas saying:

The disciples said to Jesus: "Tell us how our end shall be." Jesus said: "Have you discovered then the beginning, that you seek after the end? For where the be-ginning is, the end will be also. Blessed is he who will stand in the beginning, and he will know the end and not taste of death." (Thomas 18)

The fact that A and O are found inverted on the graffiti wall is very sig-nificant because it shows that writers had retained a memory of the teach-ings of the original movement.

Guarducci next recognised a cryptogram representing Peter. The first two letters of his name, P and E, were combined to give a P with two or three arms extending from the downward stroke to the right. The resulting symbol looked a little like a key, a play on Peter being given the keys of heaven in the Gospel of Matthew. This symbol had been found in numer-ous places in Rome, from gaming boards to funeral monuments but had not been previously associated with the name Peter. On the wall, Peter was indicated most often by this symbol but also by the first two letters of his name. In two cases, the Chi-Rho symbol had been modified so that the

Greek Rho also represented the similar Latin P with an E added to the downward stroke. This combination of the Chi-Rho and the Peter symbols indicated the overlapping nature of Peter and Christ. Indeed, this was a theme of the wall, and the Peter symbol was often closely associated with the Christ symbol.

But what is most intriguing is another name found upon the wall. Mary was indicated by either the first letter of her name M or by MA. The M and A are the first two letters as well as the first and the last letters of Maria. The combination of M and A overlapping has been found elsewhere to indicate Mary. Guarducci shows a picture of a small piece of marble kept in the Lapidary in the Vatican Museums that shows the letter M in between a drawing of a vase or pitcher and a dove followed by the letters RA.[341] The vessel is an image of life which was also found on the grave of Gorgonia and which recalls the tale of the Samaritan woman, originally Mary. The dove we have seen is another title of Mary, which is confused in the gospels with the spirit. Finding M for Mary associated with these two images again shows that the Roman Christians did preserve early teachings. Guarducci explains the R and A as standing for the resurrection and life. So Mary, the dove, is linked to the resurrection with symbols for life at the start and end of the sequence.

On the wall, the name Maria is traced once by Guarducci and also found several times in the form M or MA. Like Peter, her symbols are also linked to Christ. Most interestingly, in two places we find a combination of Mary with Peter and Christ, all interlinked. Curiously, Guarducci never asks herself why Mary is found on the wall so closely associated with Christ and Peter. After all, Mary the Virgin is supposed to be in Jerusalem. But we can see the wall as preserving a secret; Mary, Peter and Christ are one single unified nature. The survival of the association of the grave with Mary is impressive considering that the graffiti date from between 200-250 years after her death, and bearing in mind the strong political reason for the church to favour the Peter association.

It has to be said that Guarducci's readings have an amazing tendency to reflect Catholic orthodoxy and seem fanciful at times; do three interlinked A's really represent the concept of the trinity? But there is no doubt that the early Christians did use simple cryptographs to represent the concepts of their religion. If Guarducci's work on the wall was controversial, she was soon to be engulfed in a much greater controversy.

The saga of the bones

The bones had been examined by the Pope's physician who concluded that they had belonged to an elderly but robust male. However, the physician was a medical doctor and Vatican insider who was not otherwise qualified for the task. This attracted criticism and in 1956 a specialist was brought in to re-examine the bones.[342] The man chosen was Venerando Correnti, a distinguished anthropologist and Professor at Palermo University. As he sorted through the bones he realised that the previous analysis was seriously deficient. A significant proportion of the bones, about a quarter, could be seen to belong to animals including cows, horses, sheep and goats. Even worse it was clear that the human bones came from more than one individual. The skeleton was very fragmentary and most of the major bones were missing. Correnti's task of making sense of the collection of bones was going to be a long and painstaking one. Each bone had to be carefully measured and fitted into the emerging picture. The bones could not be removed from the Vatican and Correnti had teaching and other commitments, so his work took several years to complete. Correnti eventually concluded that although the bones of three individuals were present the great majority of the bones came from a single person.

The two interlopers were men in their fifties, so neither of them was quite old enough to be Peter.[343] The presence of their bones could be explained by contamination from neighbouring graves. We should remember that the cemetery was chaotic. The sides of the original grave had not been demarcated by slabs or walls, and it was probably just separated from other graves by earth. In such circumstances contamination is to be expected and it is a piece of evidence supporting the genuineness of the remains. And as to the third individual to whom most of the bones belonged it was, unfortunately, clear that this was not Peter.

Finding that the tomb did not in fact contain the bones of St Peter was an enormous disappointment for those involved with the excavation and for the Catholic Church as a whole. That some of the bones were those of farmyard animals was a source of amusement for atheists and other opponents of the church. However, the presence of animal bones is entirely typical of the site and is found in the other burials. At one time, the ground must have been used to dispose of the remains of animals. It is a further demonstration of the poverty of the original grave that it was located in a cemetery built on such a site.

As for the incompleteness of the remains, perhaps this was due to the Saracens. Although they were anti-Christian, their activities seemed more like spontaneous vandalism than an organised attempt to destroy the shrine. They could have fired the whole church or destroyed the central monument, but they did neither of these things. If they breached the grave would they have bothered to remove all the scraps of bone? Most likely it is the major bones such as the skull that they were interested in removing and abusing. It is suspicious that a skull supposedly of St Peter appeared in the Lenten church at this time. The faithful would have been disturbed by the disappearance of Peter's skull, so perhaps the church decided they needed a miracle to find it.

The Catholic Church is never far from absurdity and what followed next verged upon the farcical. A few years after telling the world that the bones were not those of Peter the church announced that Peter's bones had been found after all! It was claimed that a near complete skeleton of a strong male aged between sixty and seventy had been retrieved from the monument in the original investigation but had been mislaid for twenty years. The person responsible for this revelation was none other than Margherita Guarducci. According to her story, the bones had been removed from the cavity in the graffiti wall in secret. When the graffiti wall was first uncovered by the excavators, the cavity was visible through a narrow strip of missing plaster. The archaeologists had taken a quick look in it but seeing nothing of interest had left it for later investigation. A day or two afterwards, Monsignor Kaas the church administrator was doing his rounds accompanied by one of the foremen of the Vatican workmen, Giovanni Segoni. Kaas was officially in charge of the investigation but had fallen out with the archaeologists whom he viewed as too casual in their treatment of the church and its burials. Looking into the slit-like entrance of the cavity he noticed some bones within. He instructed Segoni to extract them and to put them in a box to protect them from the archaeologists. The workman had to break some of the plaster away to gain access and lifted out bone after bone. After clearing the cavity, the workman wrote a label on the box and then moved it on Kaas' orders to an obscure storeroom. When the excavators returned to the cavity a few days later, they did not notice that the slit had been made bigger or that any of the contents was missing. All they found in the cavity was a few remaining fragments. The box would have remained unrecognised in the storeroom had not a chance conversation between Guarducci and Segoni revealed its story. Segoni showed her the box, and she read the label recording it as "bones graffiti urn" but did not realise the importance of its contents at this stage. Nonetheless, Guarducci caused the box to be transferred and kept with the other remains from the area of the tomb.

Only after the bones found in the tomb were found not to be those of Peter did a new theory occur to Guarducci. She remembered the graffiti on the red plaster at the end of the cavity that she had interpreted as meaning "Peter within". Everyone had assumed this graffiti was written before the construction of the graffiti wall but was it possible that it was written much later from inside the niche? It would have been awkward but just about feasible. If so, was it marking the place where the bones of Peter had been placed for safekeeping? Fortunately, the bones identified as coming from the depository had already been examined by Correnti as a control and proved to be a perfect match for St Peter. The skeleton had every part of the body represented apart from the feet. It was well known that Peter had been crucified upside down, and the Roman soldiers could have hacked the feet off from the cross when removing the body. Everything seemed to fit. Guarducci developed a theory that the bones had been placed in the cavity on the orders of Constantine just before the monument was encased in marble to protect them from the damp.

And so with the Pope's blessing Guarducci published a book some twenty-two years after the excavation of the aedicula announcing that the bones of St Peter had been found. Discussion among Catholics was inhibited by the papal support for the theory but among non-Catholics it was met by astonishment and ridicule. Even the faithful found it difficult to believe that the bones of St Peter would have been placed in the graffiti wall cavity and not in the main grave. After all, Constantine had gone to significant trouble to erect the great basilica precisely centred on the aedicula and its niches. Would he then have ordered the bones to be transferred out of the grave at the centre of the basilica to a rough cavity in a half-demolished wall to one side? And having built the finely decorated church as a monument to Peter would the presence of the precious bones be recorded only by a crude graffiti scribbled on a wall? As to the alternative that the bones were already in the cavity to hide them, Constantine had requested to know the location of the bones and one did not attempt to fool the Emperor.

In fact, we can understand the cavity in the graffiti wall as all one with the burials that crowd around the tomb. Early Christians wanted to be close to the grave without intruding into its space. The graffiti wall was a rough supporting wall, and the fact that the people covered it in writing shows that it was not considered sacred as such. There is no way they would have written all over the actual tomb of Peter. Because the wall was not part of the tomb it was considered acceptable for the bones of one or more individuals to rest within it to be as close as possible to Peter.

So even if the supposed bones of Peter were really retrieved from the cavity they would not have been in the place where the real bones of Peter should lie. But it is doubtful that these bones were ever in the wall. The whole fabulous story shows all the signs of being a pious fraud perpetrated by Giovanni Segoni and Margherita Guarducci. The story rests on the testimony of a single individual, the workman Segoni. The person who was supposed to have ordered the removal, Kaas, was long since dead and there were no other witnesses. Moreover, the story told by Segoni was contradicted by the four professional archaeologists who first uncovered the graffiti wall. They were insistent that they had examined the cavity before anyone could have tampered with it and that it had contained nothing more than a few fragments. This was embarrassing to the Vatican because it implied that Segoni and Guarducci were liars. Guarducci had the full support of the Pope, and considerable pressure would have been placed on the four, all Vatican insiders, to conform to the story. One of them did change his story and said it was possible that something had been missed. However, the other three maintained to the end that they had examined the cavity and it had been empty.[344] The bones that were alleged to have been in place in the cavity numbered 135 and represented all the major bones. The cavity was only two and a half feet by a foot square. Is it really possible that four experienced archaeologists could have missed so many bones in such a small place? And if they had missed the bones, then how had Kaas noticed them?

Another problem with the story is the strange behaviour and even stranger silence of Monsignor Kaas. Guarducci presents him as an irrational individual who was conducting a private war with the archaeologists. But if we see things from his point of view we can understand his frustration. His was the responsibility to protect the church and its contents. Reading accounts of the excavation today it is disturbing how ready the archaeologists were to break through walls and dispose of graves that were in their way. Kaas was acting responsibly in trying to restrain them and in tidying up behind them. But in the Guarducci story he is portrayed as doing the exact opposite. He supposedly removes the bones from an important grave damaging the precious graffiti wall in the process. He then translates those bones to an obscure storeroom. And he says nothing to anyone about it! Kaas was a learned man. He would have understood the potential significance of a bone depository so closely associated with Peter's tomb. He would realise that such a grave could hold the bones of someone very important, perhaps an early Pope, a saint or even another apostle. They may even have been the bones of Peter's younger relative Mark who was known to have been in Rome as his secretary and who was believed to be the author of the gospel that bears his name. And yet he shows no interest in the bones after their removal, leaves no written record, and tells no one about them in the several years before his death. How do we explain this strange behaviour? Is it because he never removed the bones in the first place?

And then we have the strange behaviour and strange silence of Margherita Guarducci herself. She also kept quiet about the bones until a very late stage. When she did mention her theory, she kept it to a tiny circle of a few close associates. It was only when an old friend of her family became Pope Paul VI in 1963 that she saw her chance. She arranged an audience with the new Pope, an audience that she was very concerned should be completely private. She won him over completely and only when she had the powerful backing of the new Pope did she expose her theory more widely. Is this how we would expect a responsible scientist to behave? She had supposedly learnt years before that the excavation had been compromised by the removal of the bones. Why did she never discuss this with the archaeologists responsible for the excavation?

If fraud were committed, then it could not have been the responsibility of Giovanni Segoni alone. As a mere workman he would not have been believed were it not for the supporting testimony of the distinguished Doctor Guarducci. She testified that she had discussed the bones with him at an early stage and seen the label on the box, a label that no one else appears to have seen. Most likely the two of them really believed that the bones had come from the graffiti wall and were those of Peter. Probably Guarducci's account of her inspiration, her sudden understanding of what "Peter within" meant was genuine. She must have been disconcerted and puzzled when the remains in the grave were found not to be those of Peter. It was she who had proposed the reading "Peter within" although many others disagreed with her. So her sudden inspiration that this marked the location of the bones vindicated her own reading as well as solving the mystery of the empty grave. We must remember that she was obsessed by the graffiti wall and had spent several years of her life working on it. To prove that it was the repository of Peter's bones would have been very dear to her. She would have heard from Correnti about a skeleton he was using as a control that fitted the traditional picture of Peter perfectly. Could this skeleton have somehow been in the cavity? It was at this point perhaps that she approached Segoni who had been present at the time of the original excavation. Was it possible, she may have asked him, that the cavity had not been empty? He would have recalled that the archaeologists had only taken a quick look into the cavity at the time and agreed that it was possible that they could have missed the bones. He would also have told her about Kaas' habit of going around without the archaeologists being present and tidying up behind them. If anyone had removed the bones it would be Kaas. And so the two of them may have come to the theory that Kaas had removed the skeleton of St Peter from the cavity. The bitter irony of the bones of St Peter having been found and then lost would have haunted Guarducci. She had worked so hard to prove that this was really the tomb of St Peter, and there was more than just historical interest at stake. The Catholic Church drew its authority from St Peter, and the Protestant churches were keen to deny the connection. If they could prove to the world that the tomb was really that of Peter and restore the bones to their rightful place then this might start to heal the great rift in the church. Were they to give up all this, to see the real bones of Peter consigned to an anonymous grave, when all that was required to supply the evidence was a slight adjustment to the story? Giovanni Segoni just had to say that he had been present when the bones were removed. Margherita Guarducci just had to testify that these were the same bones examined by Correnti. Two little white lies told in the greater service of God.

Perhaps it was like this, or perhaps the whole fantastic story was somehow true. It does not matter. The real bones were never in the cavity but where they had always been, directly under the niches in the monument, exactly where they were found. But there was a compelling reason the Catholic Church thought it was impossible for these remains to be those of Peter. The bones found in Peter's grave were those of an elderly woman of around seventy.[345]

Key points

1. The first basilica of St Peters at the Vatican was built over the supposed grave of Peter on the orders of Constantine the Great in 323-333.

2. The early churchman Gaius records that the "trophies" (monuments) of those who founded the church are to be found at the Vatican and the Ostian Way.

3. In the Dormition stories of the death of Mary, "the Jews" attempt to burn Mary's body after her death but do not succeed. One account says that

a great church will be built over her body. We can see these stories as going back to early traditions about the death and burial of Mary in Rome with "the Jews" replacing the Romans. They are evidence that Mary's body was recovered unburnt from Nero's gardens.

4. Excavation beneath the floor of St Peters uncovered an ancient Roman necropolis. The tombs dated from the mid-second century onwards and belonged to prosperous freedman class. Some Christian burials were found in the floors of the tombs and there was a graffiti of Christ and Peter which was probably made when the church was built.

5. The old necropolis was on the slope of a hill. Constantine's engineers had to dig out one side of the cemetery, destroying the tombs completely, and use the earth to infill the other side to make level foundations for the basilica. It was the remains of this infilled side that the excavators uncovered. The lane of tombs, with their roofs and upper walls sheared off, led up to the central altar.

6. Excavations under the altar have found a monument, the "aedicula", dating from 160 that is precisely aligned at the central point of the basilica. This must be the "trophy" described by Gaius.

7. The aedicula was built into the "red wall" which was one side of an open courtyard in which there were many Christian burials. It is an unusual vertical monument with two niches separated by a travertine slab resembling a tabletop. Below ground there is a third niche roughly hewn out of the wall foundation where it goes up in a strange V shape.

8. The monument was built over an earlier very poor grave. The three niches, one above the other, mark the centre of this grave. The grave can be dated to the first century; a neighbouring gave that shared the same alignment incorporated a tile from 69-79. The grave would have been just across the road from the gardens of Nero where the Christians were martyred.

9. The "graffiti wall" is covered by a mass of intricate lines written by early Christians wishing to link the memory of their dead loved ones to the tomb. The Chi-Rho symbol, signifying Christ, is found. Another symbol combining P and E represents Peter. Mary is also represented by her full name (Maria) as well as by M and A, and a symbol made from M and A overlapping. The names are interlinked, and in two places the symbols for Christ, Peter and Mary are all combined.

10. A very incomplete set of bones was found buried under the lower niche. These were originally identified as the remains of Peter but this was subsequently realised to be incorrect. It is possible that the grave had been desecrated in 846 when Rome and St Peters had briefly fallen to an army of Saracens.

11. Some twenty-two years after the original investigation, Margherita Guarducci claimed, based on the testimony of a Vatican workman, Segoni, that the true bones of Peter had been found in a cavity of the graffiti wall and hidden away by Monsignor Kaas, the church administrator. This account was contradicted by the four professional archaeologists who uncovered the aedicula and who insisted that the cavity had been empty. Kaas had been dead for several years and there were no independent witnesses to the hiding of the bones other than Guarducci and Segoni. The theory of Guarducci was not widely accepted but received papal backing.

12. Even if the bones found had really been in the graffiti wall as claimed, this is not where we would expected the bones of Peter to have been interred. The cavity was rough whereas enormous expense had been made to beautify the church and the monument had been covered in marble. Also the whole basilica had been precisely orientated on the original grave and not the graffiti wall.

13. The bones that were found in the niche beneath the aedicula mostly belonged to one person, but had been contaminated animal bones, and also included a few bones from two other individuals. The presence of animal bones and the mixing of different individuals is consistent with the bones coming from the original very poor cemetery, which was built on ground used to dispose of the remains of animals.

14. Most of the bones found in the grave belonged to one individual, an elderly woman of about 70.

Conclusion

Everything about the grave is consistent with this being the true burial place of Mary. The graffiti wall shows that symbols for "Mary" were associated with the grave along with "Peter". Most likely, the aedicula was used for a ceremony in which wine was transformed mystically into the blood of Mary that was then drunk. The aedicula and basilica was the start of the Christian tradition of venerating the remains of saints and building churches as sacred spaces rather than as simple meeting places. It is possible that the bones found in the tomb are those of Mary, although it also possible that the true bones were lost following the Saracens' desecration.

About the author

S.P. Laurie was born on the outskirts of London but has lived for many years in the beautiful countryside of the Welsh Marches. He attended Grammar schools at Upminster and Torquay and went on to study mathematics at Balliol College, Oxford. He is married with three children, a one-eyed cat, and a large telescope.

Following a career in finance, he now conducts independent research into Christian origins and the earliest Christianity. For up to date news on his work, follow his blog and website below.

www.splaurie.com

Notes

1. Thomas 13.

2. Mark 4:11.

3. Rev. James Ussher, The Annals of The World (London, 1658). PDF version retrieved from the Internet Archive, Aug. 2016. See 'The First Age of the World 1': "In the beginning God created the heaven and the earth (Ge 1:1). This beginning of time, according to our chronology, happened at the start of the evening preceding the 23rd day of October in the year of the Julian calendar, 710 [4004 BC]."

4. Joshua 10:12-13.

5. 2 Kings 20:9-11; Isaiah 38:8.

6. Josephus, Jewish War 6.326.

7. Timothy Freke and Peter Gandy, The Jesus Mysteries (London: Thorsons, 1999). The book resulted in a Yahoo group of the same name to discuss the book, although this group was not connected to the authors. The group rapidly outgrow the book and became a focus for discussion and research for a wide selection of people interested in the idea that Jesus was not a historical figure.

8. Translation by J. H. MacMahon from The Ante-Nicene Fathers, ed. Alexander Roberts and James Donaldson, American Edition ed. A.C. Coxe, (1885).

9. Hippolytus, Refutation of all Heresies 5:3.

10. Marvin W. Meyer, The Ancient Mysteries: A sourcebook of Sacred Texts (Pennsylvania: University of Pennsylvania Press, 1999), Ch. 4.

11. Meyer, p101.

12. Meyer, Ch. 6.

13. Meyer, Ch. 7.

14. 1 Corinthians 10:4.

15. Refutation of all Heresies, Book 5.

16. Refutation of all Heresies 5:4.

17. It is in this exposition of the beliefs of the Naassenes that Hippolytus gives his account of the ear of corn as the innermost mystery of the Eleusinian rites.

18. Freke and Gandy, p40.

19. Clement Stromata 1.21.145.

20. Thomas J. Talley, The Origins of the Liturgical Year, 2nd. Ed., (Minnesota: The Liturgical Press, 1991), p85.

21. See Talley, pp. 85-145.

22. For example, see Richard L. Bushman, Joseph Smith and the beginnings of Mormonism, (Urbana: University of Illinois Press, 1984).

23. This passage could involve a confusion with the "child of seven days" in Thomas 4.

24. Translation by J. H. MacMahon from The Ante-Nicene Fathers, ed. Alexander Roberts and James Donaldson, American Edition ed. A.C. Coxe, (1885).

25. Translation by Alexander Roberts and James Donaldson from The Ante-Nicene Fathers.

26. See, for example, G.A. Wells, *Did Jesus exist?* (London: Elek/Pemberton, 1975) and *The Historical Evidence for Jesus*, second edition (Amherst, NY: Prometheus Books, 1988).

27. Earl Doherty, *The Jesus Puzzle, Did Christianity begin with a mythical Christ?* (Ottawa: Age of Reason Publications, 2005), and *Jesus: Neither God Nor Man - The case for a mythical Jesus* (Ottawa: Age of Reason Publications, 2009). The website is <Jesuspuzzle.humanists.net>.

28. L. W. Hurtado, 'Christian Literary Texts in Manuscripts of Second & Third Centuries', from *The Earliest Christian Artefacts: Manuscripts and Christian Origins* (Grand Rapids: Eerdmans, 2006), Appendix 1, pp. 209-229. Latest update 31 January 2011.

29. Against Heresies 4:20:2.

30. Nicholas Perrin, *Thomas and Tatian: the relationship between the Gospel of Thomas and the Diatessaron*, (Leiden:Brill, 2002).

31. Stevan Davies, *The Gospel of Thomas and Christian Wisdom, Second Edition*, (California: Bardic Press, 2005).

32. Stevan Davies, 'Mark's use of the Gospel of Thomas' in *Neotestamentica* 30 (2)(1996), pp. 307-334. Stevan Davies and Kevin Johnson 'Mark's use of the Gospel of Thomas, Part 2' in *Neotestamentica* 31 (2) (1997), pp. 233-261.

33. Davies 2005, p. 3.

34. Stephen Patterson, *The Gospel of Thomas and Jesus*, (Sonoma CA: Polebridge Press, 1993), p. 120.

35. Elaine Pagels, *Beyond Belief*, (New York: Random House, 2005).

36. Ibid., p. 58.

37. April D. DeConick, *Recovering the Original Gospel of Thomas* (London: T&T Clark, 2005).

38. Ibid., p.92.

39. Mark Goodacre, *The Case Against Q: Studies in Markan Priority and the Synoptic Problem*, (Harrisburg, PA: Trinity Press international, 2002).

40. Acts 1:4-8.

41. Eusebius, To Marinus 1.

42. Translation by Alexander Roberts and James Donaldson from *The Ante-Nicene Fathers, American Ed.* edited by A.C. Coxe, (1885).

43. Ibid.

44. Bruce Terry, *The Style of the Long Ending of Mark*, (1996), <http://bible.ovu.edu/terry/articles/mkendsty.htm> [accessed 17 August 2016]

45. Matthew 3:7; 12:34; 23:32; see also Luke 3:7.

46. Acts 1:23-26.

47. Eusebius, Ecclesiastical History 3:39.

48. Acts 5:16.

49. Acts 16:18.

50. Mark 16:7.

51. John 20:14-18.

52. 1 Corinthians 15:4.

53. Mark 2:11.

54. Translation by Wesley W. Isenberg in *Nag Hammadi Library in English, Revised Edition*, Ed. James M. Robinson, (Leiden: Brill, 1988).

55. Translation by J.H. Charlesworth, in *The Old Testament Pseudepigrapha*, Vol2, ed. James H. Charlesworth (New York: Doubleday, 1985).

56. Ibid.
57. Ibid.
58. Revelation 1:10.
59. Acts 12:9.
60. 2 Corinthians 11:4.
61. 2 Corinthians 11:23.
62. 2 Corinthians 13:3.
63. 2 Corinthians 11:16.
64. The precise timing of Paul description of the third heaven is difficult because 2 Corinthians is a composite made up of at least two and possibly more individual letters. One of these letters is written with Paul in Macedonia, intending to visit Corinth on his way to Judea. This letter is light in tone and optimistic, being mainly concerned with a collection, to which end Paul is sending Titus and two other brothers to Corinth in preparation for his own visit. The second letter is very different, being an angry defence against the accusations of other apostles that Paul is not a real apostle. The first letter talks about a previous "letter of tears" but it seems unlikely that the second letter is this letter of tears. Instead the second letter is most likely written soon after the first, probably triggered by the visit of Titus and his colleagues (or colleague) on their collection mission, as one of the Corinthians complaints is that they are being exploited by Titus or another brother. We do not know how this argument resolves itself. Conventional Christian accounts belong to the "happy ending" school. But it may be that the disagreement between Paul and Corinthians was terminal and that the church at Corinth ultimately rejected Paul as an apostle.
65. Galatians 1:18-19.
66. Acts 8:1-24.
67. Acts 6:5.
68. John 1:44.
69. Acts 21:8-9.
70. Acts 8:26-40.
71. Acts 10.
72. 1 Corinthians 16:12.
73. Translation by William Whiston accessed from ccel.org.
74. Translation by William Whiston.
75. Translation by William Whiston.
76. Josephus, Jewish War 6.316.
77. Nowhere in Paul's letters does he tell us anyone's age.
78. Translation by Lancelot C. L. Brenton, (1851).
79. 2 Peter 3:10.
80. Galatians 4:9.
81. Galatians 4:19.
82. Paul writes about male and female in 1 Corinthians11. Paul is struggling with a philosophy of the spiritual wife/husband he has inherited from Mary and which is not entirely to his liking. He interprets this philosophy in such a way as leads some later gnostic Christians into thinking that a woman needs to become male to enter the kingdom whereas a man is already in the image of God: *"For a man indeed ought not to cover his head, for he is the image and glory of God: but the woman is the glory of the man." (1 Corin-*

thians 11:7). The fact that Paul says that the male is in the image of God could be taken as implying that the spiritual part of a person is male.
83. Luke 8:1-3.
84. Jerusalem Talmud, Sotah.
85. Mishnah, Sotah 3:4.
86. John 4:24.
87. John 11:16; 20:24; 21:2.
88. Mark 3:16-19; Matthew 10:2-4.
89. Mark 6:3.
90. Luke 6:16.
91. John 14:22.
92. John 11:16.
93. Jude 1:1.
94. The Acts of Thomas 11.
95. Translation by Han J.W. Drijvers from 'The Acts of Thomas' in *New Testament Apocrypha*, Vol. 2, ed. Wilhelm Schneemelcher, English translation ed. R. McL. Wilson, (Cambridge: James Clarke & Co: 1991).
96. Ibid.
97. Ibid.
98. Acts of Thomas 9-16.
99. Ibid.
100. Ibid.
101. Schneemelcher Vol2, Han J.W. Drijvers, The Acts of Thomas 3.
102. Revelation 17:18.
103. Translation by J. H. MacMahon, *The Ante-Nicene Fathers.*
104. Translation by Alexander Roberts, *The Ante-Nicene Fathers.*
105. Protoevangelium of James 10:1.
106. Translation by M.A. Knibb in *The Old Testament Pseudepigrapha*, Vol2., ed. James H. Charlesworth (New York: Doubleday, 1985).
107. Catholic Encyclopedia: Genealogy of Christ.
108. 1 Chronicles 22:9-10.
109. Luke 1:32.
110. Note: The details of the probability calculation are thus. We start with 39 names between Joseph and Nathan. The probability of a name on list (A) occurring in (B) is assessed by counting the first occurrence of the names in (B). That is if we have four occurrences of a name in sequence we count only the first and ignore the other three from both the numerator and denominator of the probability. We must also ignore the number of first occurrences from the denominator because the subsequent name (or the first name after the end of a sequence) does not have a chance of being a first occurrence. For the narrow definition we have 4 first occurrences; Levi, Joseph, Joseph and Levi; and 4 subsequent occurrences; Judas, Simon, Judas and Joseph. The probability of a first occurrence is $4/(39-8) = 0.13$. The longest sequence is 4 names.

For the wide definition we have 6 first occurrences; Matthat, Joseph, Matthathias, Joseph, Jose, Matthat; and 9 subsequent occurrences; Levi, Mattathias, Judas, Joanna, Levi, Simon, Judas, Joseph, Jonan. The probability of a first occurrence is $6/(39-15) = 0.29$. The longest sequence is 6.

The expected no of sequences of at least as many members as the longest sequence is then calculated as -

Number of first occurrences * (Probability of first occurrence) ^ (No in longest sequence - 1).

111. James D. Tabor, *The Jesus Dynasty*, (London: HarperElement, 2006) pp.44-45.

112. Translation by Charles Duke Yonge, (1854-5).

113. See for example James D. Tabor, *The Jesus Dynasty*, (London: HarperElement, 2006) pp.73.

114. The calculation uses Bayes' Theorem where H is the hypothesis that the names Alphaeus and Clopas are the same and E is the observed degree of linguistic evidence.

Let $P(H)$ = the a priori probability, that is the probability that Alphaeus is the same as Clopas from the evidence of the names in the gospel. This probability is not 100% because there are two men given as fathers for a James in Mark (Alphaeus and Zebedee) and because Mary of Clopas may not be the same as Mary of James. Taking a 50% factor for each uncertainty we get a probability of 25%.

Let $P(E \mid not\ H)$ = the probability that the degree of potential linguistic link observed between Alphaeus and Clopas could arise from two different names chosen at random. This is very hard to quantify precisely but will be small as most pairs of names will have no connection. For the sake of this example we will take it as 1% meaning that we would have to select 100 pairs of male names at random before we get two with as good a case for a link on linguistic grounds as Alphaeus and Clopas.

$P(E \mid H)$ = probability of a linguistic link if the two names are the same which we will take as 1.

So $P(E) = P(E \mid H) *P(H) + p(E \mid not\ H) * P(not\ H) = 1 * 0.25 + 0.01 * 0.75 = 0.2575$

From Bayes' Theorem $P(H \mid E) = P(E \mid H)*P(H)/P(E) = 1 * 0.25 / 0.2575 = 97.1\%$ which is equivalent to a 1 in 34 chance that the names are not connected.

This calculation is sensitive to $P(E \mid not\ H)$ which is an unknown. As a sensitivity if we were to take this as 4% (1in 25 chance of linguistic link from two random names) then $P(H \mid E)$ would fall to 89% which is equivalent to a 1 in 10 chance that the names are not the same.

115. Ecclesiastical History 3:11:2.

116. Ecclesiastical History 2:23.

117. Ecclesiastical History 2:23.

118. Ecclesiastical History 3:32:3.

119. For example, see Strong's Exhaustive Concordance and Thayer's Greek Lexicon entries for *Alphaeus*.

120. James D. Tabor, *The Jesus Dynasty*, (London: HarperElement, 2006) pp.73.

121. Mark 1:20.

122. Mark 10:41.

123. Mark 15:40.

124. See for example Acts 8:10, Hebrews 8:11, Revelation 11:18.

125. Mark 6:17-28.

126. Mark 6:22.
127. Josephus, Jewish Antiquities 18:5:2.
128. Josephus, Jewish Antiquities 18:5:1.
129. Josephus, Jewish Antiquities 18:5:4.
130. Eusebius, Church History 2:23.
131. Acts 12:21-23.
132. Josephus, Jewish Antiquities 20:7.
133. Acts 26:28.
134. Acts 26:32.
135. Translation by William Whiston.
136. Richard Carrier, *On the Historicity of Jesus*, (Sheffield: Sheffield Phoenix Press, 2014) pp.337-342.
137. Eusebius Ecclesiastical History Translation by A.C. McGiffert 1890.
138. Translation by William Whiston.
139. Translation by Arthur C. McGiffert, *The Church History of Eusebius*, (New York: Eerdmans,1890).
140. Ibid..
141. Translation by Charles W. Hedrick, ed. Douglas M. Parrott in the *Nag Hammadi Library in English*, Revised Edition, ed. James M. Robinson, (Leiden: Brill, 1988).
142. The name of James' father is given here as Theuda. There is no support from any other source for the father of James being called this, but the name is found as the claimed link between the gnostic teacher Valentinus and the apostle Paul:

> Likewise they allege that Valentinus was a hearer of Theudas. And he was the pupil of Paul. (Clement of Alexandria, Stromata 7:17)

The Stromata was written c200, so we have a record of a second-century belief that the source of the Valentinians' special knowledge was Theudas, who was a pupil of Paul. The second Apocalypse of James is gnostic although there is not enough information about the beliefs of the authors to specifically tie it to the Valentinians. However, the first apocalypse is certainly Valentinian - the formula that James is to recount to get past the powers is the same as Irenaeus attributes to the Marcosian Valentinians Irenaeus Against Heresies 121:5, See Schneemelcher Vol1 p318. Given the similarities between the two apocalypses, it is reasonable to conclude that they emerged from the same environment that had links to the Valentinians. So it is likely that the author of the second apocalypse has confused and conflated two separate traditions; (i) that special knowledge has been passed down through a male relative of James, possibly his father; (ii) that special knowledge has been passed down through Theudas. Because of this mistake Theudas becomes the father of James.
143. Hippolytus, Refutation of all Heresies 5:2.
144. Translations by William R. Schoedel, ed. Douglas M. Parrott in the *Nag Hammadi Library in English*, Revised Edition, ed. James M. Robinson, (Leiden: Brill, 1988).

145. Irenaeus, Against Heresies 3:1:1.

146. Translation by Alexander Roberts and James Donaldson from *The Ante-Nicene Fathers*.

147. Ibid.

148. Ibid.

149. All translations from Against Heresies in this chapter by Alexander Roberts and James Donaldson from *The Ante-Nicene Fathers*.

150. Eusebius, Ecclesiastical History 3:32.

151. Luke 2:36.

152. Catholic Encyclopedia entry for Pionius.

153. Ibid.

154. Eusebius, Ecclesiastical History 3:22; 36.

155. Eusebius Ecclesiastical History 3:36.

156. Translations of the Ignatius-Polycarp letters in this chapter are based on the Lightfoot translations with some minor alterations: J.B. Lightfoot (and J.R. Harmer), *The Apostolic Fathers: Revised Texts with Short Introductions and English Translation*, (1891).

157. Translations based on the Lightfoot translations with some minor alterations: J.B. Lightfoot (and J.R. Harmer), The Apostolic Fathers: Revised Texts with Short Introductions and English Translation, (1891).

158. Ignatius to Polycarp 5.

159. Irenaeus, Against Heresies 3:3.

160. Irenaeus, Against Heresies 4:26:2.

161. Irenaeus, Against Heresies 3:3.

162. 1 Clement 44.

163. Irenaeus, Against Heresies 1:14,3.12,3.18.

164. Ignatius, Smyrnaeans 2.

165. Ignatius, Trallians 10.

166. Ignatius, Ephesians 21, Magnesians 14, Trallians 13, Romans 9.

167. Acts 5.

168. 2 Corinthians 2:5-8.

169. Polycarp to Philippians 3.

170. Polycarp to Philippians 13.

171. Ignatius to Polycarp 8.

172. Matthew 16:17.

173. John 1:42.

174. Song of Songs 7:4.

175. Mark 3:17.

176. Luke 9:51-56.

177. I have used the counts in Strong's Hebrew concordance entries 7482 (6 occurrences) and 7481 (13 occurrences). I have used an estimate of 23,000 total verses for the Old Testament.

178. Based on Strong's Hebrew concordance entry 7264 (41 occurrences) and 23,000 total verses.

179. *The Nag Hammadi Library in English*, Revised Edition, ed. James M. Robinson, (Leiden: Brill, 1988).

180. Thomas 23.

181. Translation by Wesley W. Isenberg in *The Nag Hammadi Library in English*.

182. Translation by Wesley W. Isenberg in *The Nag Hammadi Library in English*.
183. Ibid.
184. Richard Bauckham, *Gospel Women: Studies of Named Women in the Gospels*, (Edinburgh: T&T Clark, 2002) pp. 227-229.
185. Translation by Bentley Layton in the *Nag Hammadi Library in English*.
186. Translation by Hans-Gebhard Bethge, Bentley Layton, Societas Coptica Hierosolymitana in the *Nag Hammadi Library in English*.
187. Translation by Charles W. Hedrick, ed. Douglas M. Parrott in the *Nag Hammadi Library in English*.
188. Origins of the World 116:8-117:28.
189. Translation by Alexander Roberts and James Donaldson from *The Ante-Nicene Fathers*.
190. Translation by Wesley W. Isenberg in the *Nag Hammadi Library in English*.
191. Translation by Wesley W. Isenberg in *The Nag Hammadi Library in English*.
192. Song of Songs 4:6.
193. Song of Songs 5:1.
194. Song of Songs 5:13.
195. Gospel of Philip 68.
196. Translation by Wesley W. Isenberg in *The Nag Hammadi Library in English*.
197. *Translation by Wesley W. Isenberg in The Nag Hammadi Library in English.*
198. Eugnostos the Blessed 82:5-6.
199. Eugnostos the Blessed 63:33-64:10.
200. Translation by Wesley W. Isenberg in *The Nag Hammadi Library in English*.
201. Translation by William C. Robinson, Jr. in *The Nag Hammadi Library in English*.
202. Exegesis of the Soul 132:27-133:3.
203. Translation by William C. Robinson, Jr. in *The Nag Hammadi Library in English*.
204. Joseph and Aseneth 18:11.
205. John 8:48.
206. John 8:49.
207. John 8:57.
208. Irenaeus, Against Heresies 2:22:3-6.
209. Mark 1:24; 10:47; 14:67; 16:6.
210. J.R. Mueller and S.E. Robinson, *Apocryphon of Ezekiel, A New Translation and Introduction* in *The Old Testament Pseudepigrapha*, Vol. 1, ed. James H. Charlesworth (New York: Doubleday).
211. Translation by M.A. Knibb in *The Old Testament Pseudepigrapha*, Vol 2.
212. Ibid.
213. Translation by George W. MacRae in *The Nag Hammadi Library in English*.
214. *The Old Testament Pseudepigrapha*, Vol2.
215. Luke 1:18.
216. 1 Samuel 2:1-10.

217. Stevan Davies and Kevin Johnson 'Mark's use of the Gospel of Thomas, Part 2' in *Neotestamentica* 31 (2) (1997), pp. 233-261.

218. Matthew 13:55.

219. See for example Thomas 51, 52, 104.

220. Translation by Wesley W. Isenberg in *The Nag Hammadi Library in English.*

221. Catholic Encyclopedia entry for 'Magdala'.

222. Josephus, Jewish War 3:10.

223. Josephus, Jewish War 3:10.

224. Mark S. Smith, *The Early History of God*, Second Edition, (Grand Rapids: Eerdmans, 2002) pp. 54-56.

225. Translation by R.H. Charles, *The Book of Enoch,* (London: Society for Promoting Christian Knowledge, 1917).

226. Translation by R.H. Charles, *The Book of Enoch,* (London: Society for Promoting Christian Knowledge, 1917).

227. Shepherd of Hermas 4:8.

228. Translation by Kirsopp Lake, *The Apostolic Fathers*, Vo. 2, (London: Heinemann, 1913).

229. Translation by George W. MacRae in The Nag Hammadi Library in English.

230. Translation by Kirsopp Lake, The Apostolic Fathers.

231. Ibid.

232. Ibid.

233. Ibid.

234. Ibid.

235. Ibid.

236. Ibid.

237. Ibid.

238. Translation by Arthur C. McGiffert, The Church History of Eusebius, (New York: Eerdmans,1890).

239. Richard Bauckham, *Jesus and the Eyewitnesses: The Gospels as Eyewitness Testimony*, (Grand Rapids: Eerdmans, 2006), pp. 445-452.

240. Epiphanius, Panarion 29:4; 78:13-14.

241. Eusebius, Ecclesiastical History 5:24.

242. Lawlor, H.J., *Eusebiana: Essays on the Ecclesiastical History of Eusebius Bishop of Caesarea* (Oxford: Clarendon Press, 1912).

243. Richard Bauckham 'For what offence was James put to death?' in *James the Just and Christian Origins,* Ed. Chilton & Evans, (Leiden: Brill, 1999) p209.

244. Mark 14:62.

245. Ezekiel 43:15-16.

246. Malachi 1:10.

247. Ruth 3:9.

248. *Translation by Wesley W. Isenberg in The Nag Hammadi Library in English.*

249. Stevan Davies, 'Mark's use of the Gospel of Thomas' in *Neotestamentica* 30 (2)(1996), pp. 307-334.

250. Translation by J.B. Lightfoot, *The Apostolic Fathers: Revised Texts with Short Introductions and English Translation*, (1891).

251. 1 Corinthians 15:12.

252. Corinthians 16:19.

253. 1 Corinthians 1:14-16.

254. 1 Corinthians 16:15.

255. Thomas 14.

256. Mark 6:8-9.

257. Numbers 25:1-3.

258. Translation by J.B. Lightfoot, *The Apostolic Fathers*.

259. Translation by Wesley W. Isenberg in *The Nag Hammadi Library in English*.

260. For example in Acts, when Peter escapes from prison and knocks on the door of Mary's house the people inside say it his angel (Acts 12:15) meaning it is his spirit.

261. Translation by J.H. Charlesworth, in *The Old Testament Pseudepigrapha, Vol2*.

262. Against Heresies 1:13:3.

263. Translation based on (with some minor changes) that of Alexander Roberts and James Donaldson from *The Ante-Nicene Fathers*.

264. *Ibid*.

265. Acts 23:2; 24:1.

266. Acts 4:6.

267. *The text has "destroyed" but this is probably a scribal error for the similar Coptic word meaning "equal"*.

268. Translation based on (with some minor alterations) that of Montague Rhode James in *The Apocryphal New Testament (Oxford: Clarendon Press 1924)*, pp. 10-12. From the Early Christian Writings website, <http://earlychristianwritings.com/text/gospelegyptians.html> accessed [31 August 2016].

269. Clement Stromata 3:5-10.

270. Genesis 19:26.

271. O.S. Wintermute, 'Apocalypse of Zephaniah: A New Translation and Introduction' in *The Old Testament Pseudepigrapha*, Vol2. (New York: Doubleday, 1985) pp497-506.

272. Translations by O.S. Wintermute in *The Old Testament Pseudepigrapha*, Vol. 2.

273. Based on the translation (with minor changes) by G.S.R. Mead, *Pistis Sophia* (London: J.M. Watkins, 1921).

274. Galatians 1:17-24.

275. Acts 9:27.

276. Acts 14:8-10.

277. Acts 11:27-30.

278. John 21:24.

279. Mark 14:10.

280. Mark 14:18-21.

281. Matthew 26:25.

282. Luke 22:3.

283. This phrase in Thomas 61 is translated "*Who are you man, whose son?*" by Beate Blatz in 'The Coptic Gospel of Thomas', *New Testament Apocrypha*, Vol. 1, ed. Wilhelm Schneemelcher, English translation ed. R. McL. Wilson, (Cambridge: James Clarke & Co: 1991).

284. Mark 8:35; Matthew 10:39;16:25; Luke 9:24;17:33.

285. The cumulative binomial distribution for 16 successful trials out of 20 with each having a probability of 20% is 1.25 billion to one. This overestimates the unlikeliness as the range in which the sayings are clustering has been fitted from the data. Making an order of magnitude adjustment for such fitting gives a probability of the order of 100 million to one.
286. Wessa, (2012), Kendall Tau Rank Correlation (v1.0.11) in Free Statistics Software (v1.1.23-r7), Office for Research Development and Education, <http://www.wessa.net/rwasp_kendall.wasp>.
287. The two-sided p-value is 0.00085, but we are only interested in the one-sided test that the positive correlation is as great as observed.
288. Translation based upon (with minor changes) Arthur C. McGiffert, *The Church History of Eusebius*, (New York: Eerdmans,1890).
289. See Richard Bauckham, *Jesus and the Eyewitnesses*, p. 203.
290. Ibid.
291. Richard Bauckham, *Jesus and the Eyewitnesses*, Chapter 9.
292. 1 John 2:22.
293. Based on (with minor changes) the translation by R.H. Charles, *The Ascension of Isaiah*, (London: A&C Black,1900).
294. Translation by R.H. Charles, *The Ascension of Isaiah*.
295. Ibid.
296. Revelation 14:8.
297. 1 Corinthians 1:12.
298. Ezekiel 40:3.
299. Daniel 7:7.
300. Revelation 13:8.
301. Revelation 17:14.
302. Translation by J.H. Charlesworth, in *The Old Testament Pseudepigrapha*, Vol2.
303. Acts 11:28.
304. Isaiah 3:18-23.
305. Translation by Arthur C. McGiffert, *The Church History of Eusebius*.
306. Translation by Kirsopp Lake, *The Apostolic Fathers*, Vo. 1, (London: Heinemann, 1912).
307. M.R. James, *The Apocryphal New Testament*, (Oxford: Clarendon Press, 1924).
308. Translations by O.S. Wintermute, in *The Old Testament Pseudepigrapha*, Vol. 1, ed. James H. Charlesworth (New York: Doubleday, 1985).
309. Luke 23:28-29.
310. M.R. James, *The Apocryphal New Testament*, (Oxford: Clarendon Press, 1924).
311. Revelation 12:4.
312. Apocalypse of Elijah 4:24-29.
313. For the gospels and Acts, the first episode from each of the following chapters has been taken; Matthew 2 to 16; Mark 2 to 11; John 2 to 11; Acts 2 to 17 excluding 14. This gives 50 separate passages. In addition 25 random passages have been chosen from three Apocryphal works that are similar in nature to the Acts of Philip; Acts of John (9), Acts of Paul (6), Pseudo-Clementines (10).

314. These probabilities are calculated using a binomial distribution and a probability of a theme being present of 0.033 which is derived from the control group.

315. Translation by Alfred John Church & William Jackson Brodribb, *The Complete Works of Tacitus*, (1864-77).

316. Translation by O.S. Wintermute, in *The Old Testament Pseudepigrapha*, Vol. 1, ed. James H. Charlesworth (New York: Doubleday, 1985).

317. Translation by J.J. Collins in in *The Old Testament Pseudepigrapha*, Vol. 1.

318. Ibid.

319. Pseudo-Clementine Recognitions 1:66-70.

320. Eusebius Ecclesiastical History 2:23:20.

321. Translation by J.J. Collins in in *The Old Testament Pseudepigrapha*, Vol. 1.

322. Translations of The Questions of Bartholomew by M.R. James, *The Apocryphal New Testament*, (Oxford: Clarendon Press, 1924).

323. Questions of Bartholomew 4:46.

324. Questions of Bartholomew 4:14.

325. It should, however, be noted that the Questions of Bartholomew is longer than the control group texts used as the basis of this probability calculation. This will tend to overstate the unlikeliness of a link.

326. Acts 14:20.

327. Mark 9:4.

328. Mark 6:15.

329. Translation by O.S. Wintermute, in *The Old Testament Pseudepigrapha*, Vol. 1.

330. J.K. Elliott, *The Apocryphal New Testament*, (Oxford: Oxford University Press, 1993), p. 698.

331. Ibid. p. 699.

332. Ibid. p. 699.

333. Ibid. p. 707.

334. J.K. Elliott, *The Apocryphal New Testament*, p. 698.

335. The factual evidence about the excavations under St. Peter's is largely based upon two books; John Evangelist Walsh, *The Bones of Saint Peter*, (Manchester, NH: Sophia Institute Press, 2011) and Margherita Guarducci (translated by Joseph McLellan), *The Tomb of St. Peter: The New Discoveries in the Sacred Grottoes of the Vatican*, (London: G.A. Harrap, 1960). However, Walsh does not doubt the authenticity of the testimony of Segoni and Guarducci concerning the supposed finding of St. Peter's bones (Guarducci's book was written before the controversy). The theory as to the purpose of the tabletop on the aedicula is my own.

336. Translations by O.S. Wintermute, in *The Old Testament Pseudepigrapha*, Vol. 1.

337. Translations by M.R. James, *The Apocryphal New Testament*.

338. Guarducci, Ch. V.

339. Ibid.

340. For her account of the inscriptions see Guarducci, Ch. 5.

341. Guarducci, Fig 30.

342. Walsh, Ch.9.

343. Walsh, p.103.

344. See Walsh p.117. Walsh believes Guarducci's version and his account here is one-sided; he reports that the three who continued to dissent fell *"into a morose silence"*.
345. Walsh, p.104.

Index

mother of John the Baptist, 431, 432, 445–49
Elymas, 579–82
Emmanuel, 426–29
Enoch, 46, 47, 274, 484, 490, 584, 700, 701, 702, 704, 705, 706, 709, 711, 713, 717, 725, 726, 767
1 Enoch, 8, 403, 418, 436, 490, 568, 652, 685
  1 Enoch 89.29-32, 495
  1 Enoch 89.50, 491
  Animal Apocalypse. see Animal Apocalypse
  Dream vision. see Animal Apocalypse
Ephesians, 66
Ephesus, 336–38
Epiphanius
  Panarion, 512, 597
    Pan. 30:30:3, 436
Epiphany, 433
Eucharist, 32, 40, 58, 364, 373, 406, 558, 559, 572, 633, 735, 743, 744, 745
Eugnostos the Blessed, 408
Eusebius, 292
  Ignatius, 347
  long ending of Mark, 112
  Ecc. Hist. 2: 1: 4, 330
  Ecc. Hist. 2:15: 2, 659
  Ecc. Hist. 2:23, 330, 510
  Ecc. Hist. 2:23:20, 328
  Ecc. Hist. 2:25: 7, 692, 733
  Ecc. Hist. 2:25: 8, 692
  Ecc. Hist. 3: 1: 2, 693
  Ecc. Hist. 3:11: 2, 293
  Ecc. Hist. 3:31: 3, 336
  Ecc. Hist. 3:39: 4, 659
  Ecc. Hist. 3:39:15-16, 660
  Ecc. Hist. 5:20, 346
Eve
  separation from Adam, 535–41
Exegesis of the Soul
  Exeg. Soul 128:14, 410
  Exeg. Soul 132:2-23, 411
  Exeg. Soul 133:31-134:4, 412
Ezekiel
  temple, 511–12, 516
  Ezek. 27:35, 386
  Ezek. 43: 4, 516
  Ezek. 44:17-21, 511
  Ezek. 8:14, 44
Ezekiel, Apocryphon of, 245, 434, 435–36

Freke, Timothy, 37

Gaius, 665
Galatians, 65, 67, 163, 173, 211, 611–16
  Cephas and Peter, 184–91
  Gal. 1:1, 616
  Gal. 1:12, 617
  Gal. 1:13-17, 577
  Gal. 1:15-19, 207
  Gal. 1:18, 189
  Gal. 1:18-19, 614
  Gal. 2:10, 586
  Gal. 2:1-10, 614
  Gal. 2:11-13, 614
  Gal. 2:11-14, 190
  Gal. 2:11-15, 188, 614
  Gal. 2:14-15, 619
  Gal. 2:20, 47
  Gal. 2:6-10, 186
  Gal. 2:7-8, 189
  Gal. 2:9, 190
  Gal. 3:13, 527
  Gal. 3:28, 250
  Gal. 4:1-5, 453
  Gal. 4:19, 213, 454
  Gal. 4:24-26, 455
  Gal. 4:27, 455
  Gal. 4:31, 456
  Gal. 4:3-5, 219, 222
  Gal. 4:5, 473
  Gal. 4:8, 220
  Gal. 6:12-13, 618
Galilee, 17, 18, 89, 101, 102, 103, 105, 115, 121, 126, 127, 132, 135, 136, 140, 143, 144, 148, 165, 202, 423, 424, 431, 477, 478, 497, 520, 631
Galileo, 21
Gamaliel, the Pharisee, 575, 576
Gandy, Peter, 37
garment as spirit or body, 46, 153, 155, 157, 241, 349, 380, 506, 534, 535, 539, 559, 594, 603, 637, 670, 673, 674, 677, 697, 712, 728
Genesis, 534, 536, 540
  Gen. 1:27, 535
  Gen. 11: 4, 480
  Gen. 14:18, 598
  Gen. 28:12, 415
  Gen. 28:17, 415
  Gen. 29:20, 415
  Gen. 29:31, 416
  Gen. 35:21, 481
  Gen. 37: 9, 683
Gethsemane, 18, 149
gnostics, 19, 229, 230, 260, 364, 369
Goodacre, Mark, 83

Printed in Great Britain
by Amazon